The Official
World Wildlife Fund Guide to
Endangered Species of North America

Volume 4

Species Listed
December 1991 to July 1994

BEACHAM PUBLISHING, INC.

W A S H I N G T O N ,   D . C .

The Official
World Wildlife Fund Guide to
Endangered Species of North America

Originating Editor
John R. Matthews

Editor
Walton Beacham

Photo Editor
Deborah Beacham

Book and Cover Design
Amanda Mott

Species Accounts
TESII

Library of Congress
  Cataloging-in-Publication Data
The Official World Wildlife Fund Guide to Endangered Species
  of North America, Volume 4 / editor. Walton Beacham
Includes bibliographical references.
  Includes index and appendices.
  Describes 223 endangered or threatened species, listed
between December 1991 and July 1994, including their
habitat, behavior, and recovery.
  1. Nature conservation—North America. 2. Endangered
  species—North America. 3. Rare animals—North America. 4.
  Rare plants—North America. I. Walton Beacham, 1943. II.
  World Wildlife Fund.
QL84.2.035 1990   574.5'29'097—dc20   89-29757
ISBN 0-933833-33-4

Printed in the United States of America
First Printing, August 1994

Contents
Volume 4

Editor's Introduction

At the time of publication of volume 3 of *The Official World Wildlife Guide to Endangered Species of North America* many controversies involving the Endangered Species Act were attracting wide national media attention. Efforts to protect the northern spotted owl had curtailed federal timber sales on almost 7 million acres of old-growth forest in the Pacific Northwest. The listing of the Snake River sockeye salmon and proposals to list Columbia and Snake River runs of chinook and coho salmon raised the possibility of changes in the operation of a number of hydroelectric dams, which would affect a large number of people and industries in Washington and Oregon. The reauthorization of the Endangered Species Act itself was uncertain and has still not been resolved.

Since March 1992 when volume 3 was published, much has changed and much has remained the same about the status of species and the legal instruments used to protect them. Vice President Albert Gore campaigned on environmental issues and has spent his first years in office championing their causes. Interior secretary Bruce Babbitt has successfully implemented the Clinton administration's policy of environmental compromise, whose premise is that it is more prudent to enlist the cooperation of the private sector by granting the rights to conduct commercial activities on protected lands in exchange for securing sufficient habitats for endangered populations.

The listing process has been heavily influenced by the legal process. A number of species, including the northern spotted owl and the silver rice rat, were listed as the result of court decisions. Other legal actions have produced settlements that have had an even greater effect on the number and types of species listed. In settling a lawsuit brought by the Sierra Club Legal Defense Fund on behalf of a Hawaii conservation group, the Fish and Wildlife Service (FWS) agreed to propose for listing all 186 Category 1 Hawaiian candidate plant species. Of the 169 new plant listings in this volume, 103 are Hawaiian species. The settlement of a similar lawsuit in California requires the proposed listing of over 100 Category 1 California plant species by the mid-1990s.

The organization of volume 4 is different, partly dictated by the mass listing process. So many species were listed at the same time from specific habitats that we decided to create some sections comprised of species related by geography. Some California plants are grouped according to their vernal pool habitats, as are central Florida plants, mussels from the Mobile River basin, snails from Idaho, Puerto Rican plants, and plants from each of the five main Hawaiian Islands.

As in the previous volumes the species accounts are arranged alphabetically by scientific name within their group, such as plants on Molokai, mammals, birds, etc. What was the Ready Reference Index in volumes 1-3, which indexes the species by common name, is now the Common to Scientific Name Index, beginning on page 2229. A state-by-state listing of the species in volume 4 supplements the lists in previous volumes. There is also a greatly expanded glossary and a metric conversion table. The index is cumulative for all four volumes and has entries for families, scientific names, and a variety of common name combinations.

The large number of newly listed Hawaiian plants has presented a challenging photo research task. Because many of these species are extremely rare (many are located in remote areas and some have not been seen in years), we have used line drawings to illustrate the accounts when a photo was not available, but in some cases even drawings were not available. Most of the drawings have been reproduced from the *Manual of the Flowering Plants of Hawai`i* by S. H. Sohmer, Derral Herbst, and Warren Wagner, published by the University of Hawaii Press and the Bishop Museum Press. We wish to thank the authors and their publishers for granting us permission to reproduce some of Yevonn Wilson-Ramsey's excellent illustrations.

We are most grateful to the cadre of Hawaiian botanists who have spearheaded the research that has led to the listing of many vulnerable Hawaiian species. Several of these botanists have been instrumental in providing or helping us locate photos of Hawaiian species. Our special appreciation goes to Robert J. Gustafson, David Lorence, Steve Perlman, Loyal Mehrhoff, Jack Jeffrey, and John Obata; to A. E. Spreitzer for his extensive collection of freshwater mussels; and to B. "Moose" Peterson for his splendid photos of California species.

At the end of many of the species accounts, recognition is given to the Threatened and Endangered Species Information Institute (TESII). We adapted this information from much longer articles TESII compiled for *Beacham's International Threatened, Endangered and Extinct Species* on CD ROM. The first release of this electronic database contains all of the listed U.S. species, several hundred international species protected under the Endangered Species Act, and 150 species that have become extinct in modern times. The program features full screen color photos of the species, habitat photos, locator maps, 20-60 page species accounts, all FWS *Technical Bulletins*, fully indexed since the first issue in 1976, the full CITES list, the full FWS Animal and Plant Notice of Review (3,700 species), a forum for scientific exchange, and much more data to facilitate research in the field. We are most appreciative of TESII's important contribution to the CD ROM, to this volume of the *WWF Guide*, and to species research in general.

We also wish to express appreciation to many of the FWS regional offices for their assistance in collecting photos. Without the generous help of so many biologists and botanists, these print and electronic databases could not have been compiled. We invite others to join us in our continuing effort to provide photos and accurate, current information on species and their habitats.

As he has from the beginning of this series in 1988, Rich Block of World Wildlife Fund provided the knowledge, inspiration, and guidance required to see a project of this magnitude to publication.

Walton Beacham
August 1994

Color Photo Credits — Volume 4

The Official World Wildlife Fund Guide to Endangered Species of North America

PLANTS

Sensitive Joint-vetch
Aeschynomene virginica

Southern Weed Science Society

Status	Threatened
Listed	May 20, 1992
Family	Fabaceae (Pea)
Description	Annual legume growing 3-6 feet in height with single stems, irregular legume-type yellow flowers streaked with red.
Habitat	Freshwater tidal marshes.
Threats	Habitat destruction due to impoundments, road construction, commercial and residential development.
Range	Maryland, New Jersey, North Carolina, Virginia

Description

Sensitive joint-vetch, is an annual legume of the pea family that attains a height of 3 to 6 feet in a single growing season. The stems are single, sometimes branching near the top. Leaves are even-pinnate, 0.8 to 4.8 inches long, with entire, gland-dotted leaflets. The irregular, legume-type flowers are about 0.4 inch across, yellow, streaked with red, and grow in racemes (elongated inflorescences with stalked flowers). The fruit is a loment with 6 to 10 segments, turning brown when ripe.

Flowering begins in late July and continues through September. Fruits are produced from July to the first frost. Some observations indicate that seedlings may germinate only in "flotsam" (plant material) that has been deposited on the riverbank.

Sensitive joint-vetch requires the unique growing conditions occurring along segments of the river system that are close enough to the coast to be influenced by tidal action, yet far enough upstream to consist of fresh or slightly brackish water.

The present distribution of sensitive joint-vetch includes New Jersey (two occurrences), Maryland (one occurrence), Virginia (six occurrences), and North Carolina (three marginal occurrences).

Habitat

A rare and specialized ecological community type occurs a short distance upstream of where certain rivers in the coastal plain of the eastern United States meet the sea. Referred to as freshwater tidal marshes, these communities are close enough to the coast to be influenced by tidal fluctuations, yet far enough upstream to consist of fresh or only slightly brackish water. Plants that grow in this environment are subjected to a cycle of twice-daily flooding that most plants cannot tolerate. Sensitive joint-vetch is a plant of such freshwater tidal communities.

Historic Range

The number of sensitive joint-vetch populations has declined significantly throughout the species' range, and this plant has been extirpated entirely from Pennsylvania and Delaware. At present there are two known populations in New Jersey, one in Maryland, six in Virginia, and three in North Carolina.

Whether due to causes mentioned above, or to other as yet unidentified threats, the range of sensitive joint-vetch along river systems in Virginia is contracting. On both the Rappahannock and the James Rivers, sensitive joint-vetch was collected historically some 10 miles further upstream and downstream than it is currently known to exist. It remains on only one section of the Chickahominy River, where it once had a much broader distribution.

Current Distribution

The currently known distribution of sensitive joint-vetch is as follows. New Jersey: one small occurrence (approximately 50 individuals) on the Wading River in Burlington County and one large occurrence (approximately 2,000 individuals) on the Manumuskin River in Cumberland County. Maryland: one occurrence of several hundred individuals on Manokin Creek, in Somerset County. North Carolina: sensitive joint-vetch was known to occur in two ditches in Hyde County and one ditch in Beaufort County. Virginia: it is believed that the total number of plants in the state is in the vicin-

ity of 5,000.

Observations in North Carolina have indicated severe predation of seeds by tobacco budworms and corn earworms. However, it is unlikely that these predators will prove to be a problem in other populations throughout the species' range, as they do not occur in typical wetland habitats.

It has been speculated that the existence of sensitive joint-vetch may be threatened over the long-term by sea level rise. This phenomenon could result in merely "pushing" the species' habitat upstream from its present position. However, the location of major cities and other developed area upstream from the fresh/brackish water interface in many locations may block the migration of natural freshwater marsh communities and their component species, including sensitive joint-vetch.

Conservation and Recovery

The extirpation of sensitive joint-vetch from Delaware and Pennsylvania and its elimination from many sites in other States can be directly attributed to habitat destruction. Many of the marshes where it occurred historically have been dredged and/or filled and the riverbanks bulkheaded or stabilized with riprap. This is most evident in historic locations around Philadelphia. Other sources of potential or actual habitat destruction include impoundments and water withdrawal projects, road construction, commercial and residential development, and resultant pollution and sedimentation.

The remaining stronghold of sensitive joint-vetch is in Virginia, along the relatively narrow band of freshwater tidal sections of several river systems on the coastal plain. These river sections are quite pristine, despite their proximity to the major metropolitan areas of Washington D.C. and Richmond, Virginia. As the suburbs associated with these cities expand, the impacts to these river sections from residential and commercial development, shoreline stabilization activities, point and non-point source discharges, recreational use, water development projects, and sedimentation from building and road construction are all expected to increase greatly.

Certain of these factors are known to be harmful to sensitive joint-vetch; others require further study to determine their effects. Shoreline stabilization, as in placement of riprap, can destroy the species' habitat directly. Increased motorboat traffic is known to be detrimental to freshwater tidal systems. In addition to direct toxic effects from fuel leaks, the wave action from boat wakes can rapidly erode the mudflats and banks where sensitive joint-vetch grows.

Sedimentation could effect sensitive joint-vetch by inhibiting germination, smothering seedlings, and/or promoting the invasion of weedy species. Establishment of Phragmites or other invasive species could be especially detrimental to sensitive joint-vetch, which has evolved to thrive in an environment with little competition from other plants.

Two specific projects could threaten New Jersey's large population of sensitive joint-vetch. One is the extension of a major highway, which is proposed to cross the Manumuskin River in the vicinity of the population. The plants and their habitat could be destroyed directly, during the construction process, or indirectly, through input of sediments, road salt or petrochemicals. The other project is a coal-fired electric generating facility, proposed to be upstream from the population. There is concern that the disposal of by-products from this facility could degrade the species' habitat.

Maryland's one known sensitive joint-vetch population is in an area heavily impacted by humans, adjacent to a major highway, a sewage treatment plant, and a residential development. The population is also flanked by invasive weeds, including Phragmites australis and multiflora rose. Fortunately, a larger segment of this population was discovered nearby in 1991, in a less heavily impacted setting.

Among the conservation benefits authorized for Threatened species under the Endangered Species Act are: protection from adverse effects of Federal activities; restrictions on take and trafficking; the requirement for the Service to develop and carry out recovery plans; the authorization to seek land purchases or exchanges for important habitat; and Federal aid to State and Commonwealth conservation departments that have approved cooperative agreements with the Service. Listing also lends greater recognition to a species' precarious status, which encourages other conservation efforts by State and local agencies, independent organizations, and concerned individuals.

Because sensitive joint-vetch occurs in wetland habitats, many projects potentially affecting it would be within the permitting authority of the U.S. Army Corps of Engineers.

Bibliography

U.S. Fish and Wildlife Service. "Endangered and Threatened Wildlife and Plants; Determination of Threatened Status for the Sensitive Joint-vetch (*Aeschynomene virginica*)." *Federal Register* Vol. 57 No. 98, May 20, 1992: 21569-21574.

Contacts

USFWS Regional Office
300 Westgate Center Drive
Hadley, MA 01035
Phone: 413-253-8659

Ecological Services Field Office
Bldg D, 927 North Main St.
Pleasantville, NJ 08232
Phone: 609-646-0620
FAX: 609-646-0352

Ecological Services Field Office
1825-B Virginia Street
Annapolis, MD 21401
Phone: 410-269-5448
FAX: 410-269-0832

Ecological Services Field Office
Mid-County Center, U.S. Route 17
P. O. Box 480
White Marsh, VA 23183
Phone: 804-693-6694
FAX: 804-693-9032

Adapted from data compiled by the Threatened
and Endangered Species Information Institute
(13950 W. 20th Ave., Golden, CO 80401) for
*Beacham's International Threatened, Endangered, and
Extinct Species* published on CD ROM, available
from Beacham Publishing.

Seabeach Amaranth

Amaranthus pumilus

USFWS

Status	Threatened
Listed	April 7, 1993
Family	Amaranthaceae (Amaranth)
Description	Annual herbaceous plant forming clumps with pink-red or reddish stems and small rounded leaves.
Habitat	Atlantic coastal plan on barrier island beaches.
Threats	Construction of beach stabilization structures, fencing and planting of beach-grasses.
Range	New York, North Carolina, South Carolina

Description

Seabeach amaranth is an annual herbaceous plant. Germination takes place over a relatively long period of time, generally from April to July. Upon germinating, this plant initially forms a small unbranched sprig, but soon begins to branch profusely into a clump, often reaching a foot in diameter and consisting of 5 to 20 branches. Occasionally a clump may get as large as a yard or more across, with a hundred or more branches. The stems are fleshy and pink-red or reddish, with small rounded leaves that are 1.3 to 2.5 cm in diameter. The leaves are clustered toward the tip of the stem, are normally a spinach-green color, and have a small notch at the rounded tip. Flowers and fruits are relatively inconspicuous, borne in clusters along the stems.

Flowering begins as soon as plants have reached sufficient size, sometimes as early as June, but more typically commencing in July and continuing until the death of the plant in late fall. Seed production begins in July or August and reaches a peak in most years in September but continues until the death of the plant.

Weather events, including rainfall, hurricanes, and temperature extremes, and predation by webworms have strong effects on the length of seabeach amaranth's reproductive season. As a result of one or more of these influences, the flowering and fruiting period can be terminated as early as June or July. Under favorable circumstances, however, the reproductive season may extend until January or later.

Habitat

Seabeach amaranth is an endemic species that is only found along the Atlantic coastal plain where it inhabits barrier island beaches. Overwash flats at the accreting ends of the islands and lower foredunes and upper strands of noneroding beaches support the largest percentage of this species' populations. Seabeach amaranth is, on occasion, found in other habitats including sound-side beaches, blowouts in foredunes, and sand and shell material placed as beach replenishment or dredge spoil. It is a pioneer species, preferring disturbed or unvegetated sites; well vegetated sites are not occupied. This plant's root system helps to stabilize the sand where it occurs. One large plant can create a dune up to 6 decimeters high that contains 2 to 3 cubic meters of sand; most clumps are smaller.

Historic Range

Historic records indicate that seabeach amaranth was found in 31 counties in 9 states including Massachusetts, Rhode Island, Connecticut, New York, New Jersey, Delaware, Virginia, North Carolina, and South Carolina.

Current Distribution

There are 13 known populations in New York, 34 populations in North Carolina, and 8 populations in South Carolina. Only one of New York's populations has over 100 plants and the largest population in South Carolina contains only 188 plants. The remaining small populations are highly vulnerable to extirpation from a variety of natural and manmade factors.

Of the 55 populations in New York, North Carolina, and South Carolina, 9 of these sites are on lands administered by the National Park Service, 1 on Department of Defense land, 1 is in a New York City park, 9 are on State park and reserve lands, 3 are in county parks, 2 and part of a 3rd are on municipal land, 1 is on U.S. Fish and Wildlife Service property, and the remaining 28 and part of another population are on private lands.

Conservation and Recovery

The 41 populations that have been extirpated were lost to beach stabilization structure construction, such as seawalls and riprap, storm-related erosion, heavy recreational beach use by off-road vehicles and possibly as a result of herbivory by webworms.

The remaining populations are threatened by these activities/events as well as beach grooming and some less invasive beach stabilization projects that involve fencing and planting of beach-grasses.

Hurricane Hugo (September, 1989), several severe Northeasters in the winter of 1989-1990, and Hurricane Bertha (late summer, 1990) together caused a great deal of flooding and beach erosion in many areas that support populations of seabeach amaranth. Surveys in 1990 indicate the impacts (positive and negative) to the species were substantial. Thirteen populations of seabeach amaranth on Long Island reappeared on sites that had been occupied for several years. These populations could have become established by the exposure of seedbanks in the areas, long-distance dispersal of seeds, or short-distance dispersal of seeds from unknown populations. Damage to South Carolina populations was extensive. Hurricane related damages and post hurricane dune reconstruction activities were responsible for a dramatic drop in this state's population of seabeach amaranth (1,800 plants in 1988 to 188 in 1990). Rangewide losses were about 76% of the population; this includes the addition of the new populations in New York.

Man-related activities far inland can impact this plant and its habitat. Damming of major rivers reduces the sediment load that is carried to the coast. This sediment helps to maintain barrier islands. Without it, many islands are eroding away and with them seabeach amaranth' habitat.

A recovery plan has not been completed for this species. Research concerning the propagation and reintroduction of this species is needed to insure the success of attempted transplants and to provide an herbarium population capable of providing stock for future transplants. Further research concerning the plant's life history and ecological requirements is also needed.

Bibliography

U.S. Fish and Wildlife Service. "Endangered and Threatened Wildlife and Plants; *Amaranthus pumilus* (Seabeach Amaranth) Determined to Be Threatened." *Federal Register* Vol. 58, No. 65. April 7, 1993: 18035-18041.

Contacts

USFWS Regional Office
300 Westgate Center Drive
Hadley, MA 01035
Phone: 413-253-8659

USFWS Regional Office
Suite 200, 1875 Century Blvd.
Atlanta, GA 30345
Phone: 404-679-4000

Ecological Services Field Office
330 Ridgefield Court
Asheville, NC 28806
Phone: 704-665-1195
FAX: 704-665-2782

Ecological Services Field Office
P. O. Box 12559
Charleston, SC 29422-2559
Phone: 803-727-4707
FAX: 803-727-4218

Adapted from data compiled by the Threatened and Endangered Species Information Institute (13950 W. 20th Ave., Golden, CO 80401) for *Beacham's International Threatened, Endangered, and Extinct Species* published on CD ROM, available from Beacham Publishing.

Marsh Sandwort

Arenaria paludicola

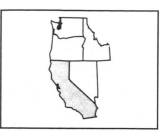

Malcolm McLeod, California Native Plant Society

Status	Endangered
Listed	August 3, 1993
Family	Caryophyllaceae (Pink)
Description	Herbaceous perennial with singular flowers, and angled and smooth stem.
Habitat	Small freshwater marsh with active to partially stabilized beach dunes.
Threats	Overpopulation of eucalyptus trees, alterations in hydrologic regime, erosion and sedimentation.
Range	California

Description

The marsh sandwort is an herbaceous perennial member of the pink family. This slender plant roots at the nodes of procumbent stems. The small, inconspicuous, singular flowers are located in the axils on the narrow, opposite leaves. The stem is angled and smooth. Flowering occurs from May through August.

Habitat

The marsh sandwort is classified as an obligate wetland plant. Obligate means that a plant almost always (greater than 99% of the time), under natural conditions, occurs in wetlands.

Historically, it was found in freshwater marshes and swamps along the California and Washington coasts. Marsh sandwort is now restricted to a small persistent emergent marsh complex near the Nipomo Dunes Mesa, San Luis Obispo County, California. Marsh sandwort is found in association with Gambel's watercress, another endangered plant, stream orchis, bur-reed, sedges, and rushes.

This marsh complex is characterized as a series of small freshwater marshes associated with active to partially stabilized beach dunes which extend a distance of 5 miles from Oceano south to the Oso Flaco Lakes area. Just inland from this "dune lakes" area lies the Nipomo Mesa, a broad mesa comprised of old Oceano sands deposited 40,000 years ago, and bisected by Black Lake Canyon. Pockets of freshwater marsh habitat in Black Lake Canyon and the dune lakes area

Black Lake Canyon and the dune lakes area harbor a unique flora that includes remnant populations of marsh sandwort and Gambel's watercress.

Historic Range and Current Distribution

The marsh sandwort has been reduced to one remnant population located in a wetland complex near the Nipomo Mesa in San Luis Obispo County, California. Marsh sandwort is restricted to one site, and recent surveys found only 3 individual plants.

Because of this species' limited population size and limited distribution, it is vulnerable to extinction. The small population size also means there is a limited gene pool. The lack of genetic diversity means the species may not have the capabilities to evolve to adjust to changes in its environment.

Conservation and Recovery

The wetland complex supporting the marsh sandwort population is threatened by alterations in hydrologic regime, natural succession, runoff from upstream developments, erosion and sedimentation, and filling for development.

The area's hydrologic regime may have been altered over an extended period of time by the planting of eucalyptus trees. This species was introduced in the late 1800's and has spread throughout the lower half of the canyon. The eucalyptus has an extensive root system that can draw out soil moisture; that, coupled with the large evaporative surface of its foliage, has probably resulted in a significant drawdown of the water table compared to that which the surrounding native vegetation would have accomplished. Agricultural and urban use of groundwater may also impact these wetlands but studies concerning groundwater hydrology have not fo-

cused on which portions of the canyon have been affected. Additional urban development and the associated increase in drilling of wells could potentially impact these wetlands.

Natural succession in the area from a wetland to a more mesic grass or shrub-dominated ecosystem has apparently been accelerated, possibly due, in part, to the above mentioned changes in hydrologic regime. Drops in water table levels will decrease the soil moisture levels in certain areas which could allow the invasion of upland plant species. Aerial photographs from 1949 show the lower portion of the canyon as one wetland with open water and freshwater marsh or bog vegetation along its margins. By 1956, however, aerial photographs showed that willows had encroached into the wetlands and 30% of the area was covered with trees.

Plans to develop a golf course with 515 residential units upstream of the wetland complex were recently approved; there are additional plans to subdivide other parcels in the area for further residential and commercial development.

Erosion in the canyon has been exacerbated by off-road vehicles, horses, hikers, and pipeline easement construction and maintenance. Eucalyptus trees may also contribute to increased sedimentation in bog and pond areas by inhibiting the decay of debris because of acid tannins contained in the tree's leaves. Large or old trees that fall tend to destabilize the sandy slopes of the canyon, exposing unconsolidated patches of loose soil.

The U.S. Army Corps of Engineers, under Section 404 of the Clean Water Act, regulates the discharge of fill into waters of the United States, including wetlands. However, no permit is required to fill less than 1 acre, and if the fill is between 1 and 10 acres in size, a Nationwide Permit Number 26 is issued by default within 20 days unless it is determined that an individual permit is required. Ongoing activities related to urban and agricultural use of the area that may result in the filling of wetlands in the Black Lake Canyon may, therefore, have little to no regulation by the Corps, since these areas are typically less than 10 acres in size.

Bibliography

U.S. Fish and Wildlife Service. "Endangered and threatened wildlife and plants; determination of Endangered status for *Arenaria paludicola* (Marsh Sandwort)." *Federal Register* Vol. 58, No. 147, August 3, 1993.

Contacts

USFWS Regional Office
Eastside Federal Complex
911 N.S. 11th Avenue
Portland, OR 97232-4181
Phone: 503-231-6118

Sacramento Ecological Services Field Office
Room E-1803/1823
2800 Cottage Way
Sacramento, CA 98525
Phone: 916-978-4866
FAX: 916-978-4613

Ventura Ecological Services Field Office
Suite 100, 2140 Eastman Avenue
Ventura, CA 93003
Phone: 805-644-1766
FAX: 818-904-6288

Adapted from data compiled by the Threatened and Endangered Species Information Institute (13950 W. 20th Ave., Golden, CO 80401) for *Beacham's International Threatened, Endangered, and Extinct Species* published on CD ROM, available from Beacham Publishing.

Applegate's Milk-vetch
Astragalus applegatei

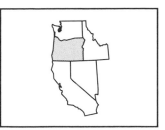

Status	Endangered
Listed	July 28, 1993
Family	Fabaceae (Pea)
Description	Perennial herb growing to 1 foot high with whitish petals, lilac keep tip, and green or faintly purple speckled pod valves.
Habitat	Flat, open moist areas of floodplain alkaline grasslands in the Klamath Basin, Oregon.
Threats	Conversion of native vegetation to agricultural use, road construction.
Range	Oregon

Kagan/Yamamoto, Oregon Natural Heritage

Description

Applegate's milk-vetch, *Astragalus applegatei*, is a perennial herb that grows to a height of about 1 foot and reproduces only by seed. The leaves are 3.5 to 7.0 centimeters long with 7 to 11 leaflets. The racemes are 8 to 20 millimeters long with 10 to 18 flowers. The flowers are early spreading and ultimately declined; the axis elongates to 3 to 7 centimeters in the fruit. The calyx is hairy. The petals are whitish, to 7 millimeters long, with a keel tip that is tinged a faint lilac. The pod is widely spreading or declined, stipitate, straight or nearly so, 8 to 11 millimeters long, with a diameter of 2.4 to 8 millimeters. The pod valves are green or faintly purple speckled or mottled; dehiscence (splitting) begins at the top of the pod and continues downward. There are 8 to 10 ovules.

Flowering and pod production occur in June and July.

Habitat

Applegate's milk-vetch occurs in flat, open, seasonally moist remnants of floodplain alkaline grasslands in the Klamath Basin, Oregon. The species is a member of the Poa nevadensis-Puccinellia lemmonii grassland community. This community is characterized as a bunchgrass flat, with about 10 to 20 percent exposed ground. The substrate is poorly drained, fine silt loam with an underlying hardpan about 20 to 40 inches below the surface. Periodic flooding was probably a natural feature of this habitat type. The adjacent community is alkaline open shrubland dominated by *Sarcobatus vermiculatus* and *Distichlis stricta*. *S. vermiculatus* periodically is found in the grassland community.

Historic Range

Applegate's milk-vetch historically occurred at 3 sites near Klamath Falls, Oregon. One extirpated site was last known to support the species in 1931. Further surveys near Keno, Oregon failed to locate the plants on this former site.

Current Distribution

The largest remaining population is near Klamath Falls. The other known site is about 6 miles from the previous population's location. It is located on the State's Klamath Management Area.

Conservation and Recovery

A recovery plan has not been completed for this species. Recovery activities should include surveys to locate new populations and/or sites suitable for reintroduction, studies to develop propagation and transplanting techniques, studies to determine the species' life history and ecological requirements, and plans to protect and enhance known populations.

Bibliography

U.S. Fish and Wildlife Service. "Endangered and Threatened Wildlife and Plants; Determination of Endangered Status for *Astragalus applegatei* (Applegate's milk-vetch)." *Federal Register* Vol. 58, No. 143. July 28, 1993: 40547-40551.

Contacts

U.S. Fish and Wildlife Service
Regional Office
Eastside Federal Complex
911 N.S. 11th Avenue
Portland, OR 97232-4181
Phone: 503-231-6118

Portland Ecological Services Field Office
2600 SE 98th Avenue
Portland, OR 97266
Phone: 503-231-6179
FAX: 503-231-6195

Adapted from data compiled by the Threatened and Endangered Species Information Institute (13950 W. 20th Ave., Golden, CO 80401) for *Beacham's International Threatened, Endangered, and Extinct Species* published on CD ROM, available from Beacham Publishing.

Howell's Spineflower
Chorizanthe howellii

Rich York, California Native Plant Society

Status	Endangered
Listed	June 22, 1992
Family	Polygonaceae (Buckwheat)
Description	Shaggy-haired, short annual herb with spatula-shaped long leaves.
Habitat	Coastal dunes.
Threats	Habitat destruction, competition from introduced plants, off-road vehicle damage.
Range	California

Description

Howell's spineflower (*Chorizanthe howellii*) is a shaggy-haired, short annual herb with spatula-shaped long, basal leaves and spreading to decumbent stems that branch from the base. Flowers of this buckwheat appear from May through July and are white to rose in color. The flowers measure from 3.5 to 4.5 millimeters. This species' flowers possess tepals, involucres and involucral teeth and awns which distinguish it from other *Chorizanthe.*

Habitat

Howell's spineflower is associated with the California Coastal Redwood Belt, Siskiyou-Trinity Area, Central California Coastal Valleys and Central California Coast Range.

Broadly, these regions have an elevation from sea level to 900 meters; average annual precipitation of 300 to 850 millimeters distributed throughout the year; perennial streams and lakes are distributed throughout the regions and glacial and alluvial deposits in the valley also yield large quantities of water; the dominant soils are Umbrepts, Xerults, Xerolls, Humults or Ochrepts, well drained and gently sloping to very steep soils with a mesic to xeric temperature regime and a mixed mineralogy. The erosion hazard is high in this area and is stabilized only by plant cover. Much of this land is federally owned and the remaining is used for lumbering, grazing, wildlife habitat and recreation.

This species is restricted to the coastal foredunes and coastal dune scrub communities and associated habitats occupied by coastal scrub or coastal terrace prairie. In the dune systems north of Monterey Bay, sand-stabilizing rhizomatous grasses, Ammophila arenaria and Elymus mollis generally dominate the vegetation of the foredunes. European beach grass (Ammophila arenaria) or marram grass, is an alien species that has largely replaced the native Elymus-dominated foredune community. Beach grass is believed to be a powerful geomorphic agent due to its ability to build continuous wall-like foredunes, which were not previously in this region. Although the Elymus-dominated foredune community exists around Monterey Bay, these foredunes typically consist of low hillocks and mounds that are sparsely populated with generally succulent, tap-rooted perennial herbs. *Abronia latifolia, Ambrosia chamissonis, Calystegia solandella, Camissonia spp., Carpobrotus aequilaterus, C. edulis* and *Fragaria chiloensis* are common associates. The stabilization of the dunes by Ammophila arenaria has permitted the colonization of formerly active backdune areas with a mixture of native and alien plants. These backdune areas consist of a soft, woody, dense plant community of short shrubs and sub-shrubs, and herbaceous plants.

Historic Range

Howell's spineflower is restricted to coastal foredunes and adjacent sandy habitats and is discontinuously distributed within the southern portion of the dunes south of Ten mile River. This area stretches continuously from the mouth of the Tenmile River to Laguna Point, with isolated dunes as far south as Pudding Creek on the north edge of the community of Fort Bragg. This species' past and present distribution are the same, although present distribution is much more disjunct. Howell's spineflower occurs on State-owned Mackerricher State Park.

Current Distribution

This taxon is currently threatened by competition, and habitat destruction. Stochastic events or extreme climatic changes could adversely affect this species due to the low number of extant individuals and its restricted distribution.

Conservation and Recovery

The native plant fauna of the California coast dune scrub communities is threatened by a number of factors including: invasion of alien plants, proposed commercial and residential development, military operational uses, off-road vehicle damage, and trampling by equestrians, hikers and livestock. Potential threats include sand mining, disposal of dredged material from adjacent bays and waterways and stochastic extinction due to depauperate numbers.

The introduction and invasion of California's ecosystems by alien plants has adversely affected this species. The invasion of Ammophila arenaria has resulted in the development of wall-like foredunes and colonization of native and alien plants. Other alien species include sea-rocket, ice plant or sea-fig (*Carpobrotus* spp), and several annual grasses and forbs generally restricted to wetland habitats within the dunes. In many cases, these aliens outcompete and largely supplant the native dune vegetation. Typically, annuals and monocarpic plants such as this species are vulnerable to random fluctuations or variation in annual weather patterns and other environmental factors.

This species has limited historical distributions and likely has been eliminated from all but a small fraction of its historical dune or associated habitats. Today, this species generally persists as small "island" populations surrounded by urban areas, roads, trails, agricultural lands, competing alien plants, and other lands made unsuitable for this species.

All known locations of Howell's spine-flower occur within Mackerricher State Park. Due to a lack of preservation or management strategy for this species on park land, the species has been variously affected by off-road vehicle use and trampling by hikers and equestrians.

Conservation measures provided to species listed as endangered or threatened pursuant to the Act include recognition, recovery actions, requirements for Federal protection, and prohibitions against certain practices. Recognition through listing encourages conservation measures by Federal, international, and private agencies, groups, and individuals.

Federal activities potentially impacting this species would likely involve restricting/managing navigation and port-related projects and perhaps grazing practices on Federal land.

Bibliography

U.S. Fish and Wildlife Service. "Endangered and Threatened Wildlife and Plants; Six Plants and Myrtle's Silverspot Butterfly From Coastal Dunes in Northern and Central California Determined to Be Endangered." *Federal Register* Vol. 57 No. 120, June 22, 1992: 27848-27858

Contacts

Carlsbad Ecological Services Field Office
2730 Loker Avenue, West
Carlsbad, CA 92008
Phone: 619-431-9440
FAX: 619-431-9624

USFWS Regional Office
Eastside Federal Complex
911 N.S. 11th Avenue
Portland, OR 97232-4181
Phone: 503-231-6118

Adapted from data compiled by the Threatened and Endangered Species Information Institute (13950 W. 20th Ave., Golden, CO 80401) for *Beacham's International Threatened, Endangered, and Extinct Species* published on CD ROM, available from Beacham Publishing.

Monterey Spineflower
Chorizanthe pungens var. *pungens*

Deborah S. Hillyard

Status	Threatened
Listed	February 4, 1994
Family	Polygonaceae (Buckwheat)
Description	Wiry, annual herb with white flowers growing in a dense cluster.
Habitat	Sandy soils within coastal dunes, scrub, grassland, maritime chaparral, and oak woodland communities.
Threats	Industrial and residential development, recreational use, and dune stabilization
Range	California

Description

The Monterey spineflower has small white (rarely pink) flowers growing in a dense cluster. The inner and outer petal-like sepals (green covering of the flower) are equal in length and are lobed rather than fringed. The flowers filaments are free, and there are 3 to 9 stamens. There are six bracts below the flowers: three are toothed with the alternating three shorter. It grows along the ground or slightly erect, which distinguishes it from the robust spineflower, an endangered species.

Habitat

The robust spineflower is endemic to sandy soils of coastal habitats in southern Santa Cruz and northern Monterey counties.

The inner rim of Monterey Bay is characterized by broad, sandy beaches backed by an extensive dune formation. Just inland from the immediate coast, maritime chaparral occupies areas with well-drained soils. Coastal dunes and coastal scrub communities exist along the inner rim of Monterey Bay.

The plant is found scattered on sandy soils within coastal dunes, scrub, grassland, maritime chaparral, and oak woodland communities along and adjacent to the coast of southern Santa Cruz and northern Monterey counties, and inland to the coastal plain of Salinas Valley.

Recent surveys at Fort Ord indicated that within grassland communities the plant occurs along roadsides, in firebreaks, and in other disturbed sites. In oakland woodland, chaparral and scrub communities, the plants occur in sandy openings between shrubs. In older stands with a high cover of shrubs, the plant is restricted to roadsides and fire-breaks. The highest densities are located in the firing range, where disturbance is most frequent. There seems to be a correlation between open conditions resulting from activities that disturb habitat.

Historic Range

Historically, the plant ranged along the coast from southern Santa Cruz County to northern San Luis Obispo County, and from Monterey inland to the Salinas Valley. The plant was probably extirpated from a number of historical locations due to the conversion of the original grasslands and valley oak woodlands to agricultural crops.

Current Distribution

Significant populations of Monterey spineflowers, representing upwards of 70 percent of the range of the plant, were recently documented by the Army Corps of Engineers (1992) from Fort Ord.

The Fish and Wildlife Service considers the specimens collected from certain populations of Chorizanthe in the vicinity of Sunset State Beach to be the Monterey spineflower, about 7,000 individuals in 1990.

Conservation and Recovery

The coastal dunes and coastal scrub habitat that support the Monterey spineflower were affected by industrial and residential development, recreational use, and dune stabilization. The introduction of non-native plants to the coastal dunes for the purpose of sand stabilization adversely affected the native dune flora. Such introduced species as European beach grass, seafig and iceplant invaded dune habitats and out-competed native flora.

Along the coast of the north side of the Monterey Peninsular, human and equestrian use threatened scattered populations, and a development is planned by the Pebble Beach Corporation. Other small scattered occurrences within maritime chaparral habitat may become affected by residential development and by realignment of highway 101.

The Fort Ord Army Bases probably supports the largest extant population of the Monterey spineflower. In recent years road development and construction of an ammunition depot on the base eliminated some of the habitat, and fragmented the remaining habitat.

The Department of Defense and the California Native Plant Society established a series of small preserves, ranging in size from 1 to 15 acres, for the purpose of protecting rare species. The small size of these preserves, however, is not likely to be sufficient to ensure long-term protection of the plant. Just prior to the listing of the species as threatened, the Department of Defense announced intentions to close the base at Fort Ord, and the impact of the base closing on the species will be determined by its alternative use.

Bibliography

U.S. Fish and Wildlife Service. "Endangered and Threatened Wildlife and Plants; Determination of Endangered Status for Three Plants and Threatened Status for One Plant from Sandy and Sedimentary Soils of Central Coastal California." *Federal Register*. Vol. 59, No. 24. February 4, 1994: 5499-55113.

Contacts

U.S. Fish and Wildlife Service
2140 Eastman Avenue, Suite 100
Ventura, CA 93003
805-644-1766

Ben Lomond Spineflower

Chorizanthe pungens var. *hartwegiana*

Deborah S. Hillyard   *Color Plate C-2*

Status	Endangered
Listed	February 4, 1994
Family	Polygonaceae (Buckwheat)
Description	Wiry, annual herb with medium-size dark pink to purple flowers growing in a dense cluster.
Habitat	Sandstone and mudstone deposits in the Santa Cruz Mountains
Threats	Golf course development, agricultural land conversion, sand mining and military activity.
Range	California

Description

Ben Lomond spineflower has medium-sized dark pink to purple flowers growing in a dense cluster. The inner and outer petal-like sepals (green covering of the flower) are equal in length and are lobed rather than fringed. The flowers filaments are free, and there are 3 to 9 stamens. There are six bracts below the flowers: three are toothed with the alternating three shorter. The shrubs can grow along the ground or erect, covered with short hairs.

Habitat

Ben Lomond spineflower is found on sandy soils that are the basis for the Ben Lomond sandhills communities in the Santa Cruz mountains, mostly on privately owned land. It is confined to outcrops of sandstone soils that support several unique plant communities, including the ponderosa pine.

Historic Range

It was not until 1969 that James Reveal and Clare Hardham distinguished Ben Lomond's spineflower from Ben Lomond's wallflower, another endangered species. Ben Lomond's wallflower was widely spread throughout the sandy soils of coastal habitats in southern Santa Cruz and northern Monterey counties.

Current Distribution

Fish and Wildlife Service has not released population data, except to say that because the numbers are so low, and the incidence of vandalism high, proposed documentation of their habitat would make them more vulnerable.

Conservation and Recovery

At least half of the habitat occupied by Ben Lomond spineflower is on land owned by sand and gravel companies. Populations located on land owned by the San Lorenzo Valley Water District were badly damaged by off-road vehicles despite efforts to fence off the area.

Sand quarrying resulted in the direct removal of the Ben Lomond spineflower, and a currently proposed expansion of operations of Quail Hollow Quarry may eliminate additional populations. Residential development on smaller parcels of privately owned lands have also contributed to the elimination of the species and the fragmentation of the remaining habitat.

Protective management for sandhill parkland communities will be developed for one parcel of the Ben Lomond spineflower's habitat recently acquired by the State of California. Quail Hollow Ranch, which supports the largest population, was recently acquire by Santa Cruz County and the State of California. Management plans for Quail Hollow Ranch are under development, and recreational facilities may adversely affect the populations.

Bibliography

U.S. Fish and Wildlife Service. "Endangered and Threatened Wildlife and Plants; Determination of Endangered Status for Three Plants and Threatened Status for One Plant from Sandy and Sedimentary Soils of Central Coastal California." *Federal Register*. Vol. 59, No. 24. February 4, 1994: 5499-55113.

Contacts

U.S. Fish and Wildlife Service
Ventura Field Office
2140 Eastman Avenue, Suite 100
Ventura, CA 93003
805-644-1766

Adapted from data compiled by Beacham Publishing for *Beacham's International Threatened, Endangered, and Extinct Species* published on CD ROM.

Robust Spineflower

Chorizanthe robusta var. *robusta* var. *hartwegii*

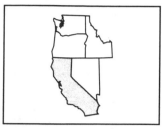

Deborah S. Hillyard

Status	Endangered
Listed	February 4, 1994
Family	Polygonaceae (Buckwheat)
Description	Wiry, annual herb with medium-size to large notched, pinkish flowers growing in a dense cluster.
Habitat	Sandy and gravelly soils in the southern Santa Cruz mountains.
Threats	Residential and golf course development, agricultural land conversion, sand mining and military activity.
Range	California

Description

The robust spineflower, *Chorizanthe robusta* var. *robusta,* is a wiry, annual herb with large notched, white to pinkish flowers growing in a dense cluster. The shrub grows in a variety of postures, from erect to spreading or growing flat along the ground.

The robust spineflower's closely related species is Scotts Valley spineflower (*Chorizanthe robusta* var. *hartwegii*), which has medium-sized pinkish flowers growing in a dense cluster. The inner and outer petal-like sepals (green covering of the flower) are equal in length and are lobed rather than fringed. The flowers filaments are free, and there are 3 to 9 stamens. There are six bracts below the flowers: three are toothed with the alternating three shorter. The shrubs can grow along the ground or erect, covered with short hairs.

Habitat

The robust spineflower is endemic to sandy soils of coastal habitats in southern Santa Cruz and northern Monterey counties. The inner rim of Monterey Bay is characterized by broad, sandy beaches backed by an extensive dune formation. Just inland from the immediate coast, maritime chaparral occupies areas with well-drained soils. Coastal dunes and coastal scrub communities exist along the inner rim of Monteray Bay.

Scotts Valley spineflower occurs on Purisima sandstone, with bedrock overlain with a thin soil layer that supports a meadow community comprised of herbs and low-growing grasses. The presence of certain associated species, such as toad rush (*Juncus bufonis*), sand pigmyweed (*Crassula erecta*), mosses, and lichens suggest a high seasonal moisture content.

Historic Range

The robust spineflower was first described by Charles Parry in 1889 from collections he made six years earlier north of Monterey Bay. The species was endemic to sandy soils of southern Santa Cruz and northern Monterey counties.

Current Distribution

The only known populations of Scotts Valley spineflower occur in Scotts Valley in the Santa Cruz Mountains north of the city of Santa Cruz. Virtually the entire population resides on three parcels, all privately owned.

The only known populations of the robust spineflower occurs northeast of the city of Santa Cruz on property recently acquired by the University of California.

Shortly after the species was rediscovered in 1989, the total number of individuals was estimated to be 6,000. Results of 1992 surveys were that two populations on developments named Glenwood Estates totaled between 30,000 and 100,000 individuals. The numbers of this annual plant are expected to fluctuate from year to year, depending on climate conditions.

The robust spineflower populations are known from Sunset State Beach. In 1988 the population was believed to be about 5,000. Smaller populations of a few hundred each are near Manresa State Beach and on property owned by the city of Santa Cruz.

Conservation and Recovery

Populations of the robust spineflower in coastal dune and coastal scrub habitats were affected by residential development, recreational use, and the introduction of non-native species.

The only known populations of Scotts Valley spineflower occur in Scotts Valley in the Santa Cruz Mountains north of the city of Santa Cruz. Virtually the entire population resides on three parcels, all privately owned. Two parcels are currently proposed for a residential development and golf course named Glenwood Estates Development. Although the developers plan to set aside a portion of the habitat, the reserves may be affected by the application of pesticides, herbicides and fertilizers on the adjacent golf course. The third parcel was scheduled for residential development but the ownership was transferred to a software development firm that intends to build its headquarters on the site.

The introduction of non-native plants to the coastal dunes for the purpose of sand stabilization adversely affected the native dune flora. Such introduced species as European beach grass, seafig and iceplant invaded dune habitats and out-competed native flora.

Management plans for the robust spineflower at Sunset State Beach have not yet been developed. Sunset State Beach has the largest known population, numbering 5,000 individuals in 1988. Smaller populations of a few hundred each near Manresa State Beach and on property owned by the city of Santa Cruz are not currently protected. The city will be developing a management plan to manage the property as a "low impact" park, and intends to protect habitat for the plant. A patch of 300 individuals located at Manresa State Beach could be relocated.

One of the three habitats for Scotts Valley spineflower was scheduled for residential development but the ownership was transferred to a software development firm that intends to build its headquarters on the site. The firm, Borland Corp., indicated that pending expansion, it intended to set aside the species habitat. It still may be threatened by secondary impacts.

As currently proposed, the Glenwood

Estates Development would destroy numerous small colonies of *C. robusta* var. *hartwegii*, but would set aside several reserves for the densest concentration of the plants. These reserves would be left as small islands within the golf course portion of the project.

Bibliography

U.S. Fish and Wildlife Service. "Endangered and Threatened Wildlife and Plants; Determination of Endangered Status for Three Plants and Threatened Status for One Plant from Sandy and Sedimentary Soils of Central Coastal California." *Federal Register*. Vol. 59, No. 24. February 4, 1994: 5499-55113.

Contacts

U.S. Fish and Wildlife Service
Ventura Field Office
2140 Eastman Avenue, Suite 100
Ventura, CA 93003
805-644-1766

Adapted from data compiled by Beacham Publishing for *Beacham's International Threatened, Endangered, and Extinct Species* published on CD ROM.

Sonoma Spineflower
Chorizanthe valida

J. Fraser Muirlead, California Native Plant Society

Status	Endangered
Listed	June 22, 1992
Family	Polygonaceae (Buckwheat)
Description	Erect shaggy-haired annual herb with white, lavender, or rose colored flowers.
Habitat	Coastal foredunes and coastal dune scrub communities.
Threats	Invasion of alien plants, proposed commercial and residential development, hikers, livestock trampling.
Range	California

Description

The Sonoma spineflower, an erect to spreading buckwheat that grows to 1 to 3 decimeters, is a shaggy-haired annual herb with 1 to 5 centimeters long, basal leaves that are typically wider near the tip. Flowers appear in June-August. These flowers are white, lavender, or rose colored; are 5 to 6 millimeters long; and occur in dense, ball-shaped, pink clusters with green bracts below. This species' flowers habit, petal-like sepals (tepals) and involucres as well as its involucral teeth and spike tips separate the Sonoma Spineflower from other taxa.

Habitat

The Sonoma Spineflower is associated with the California Coastal Redwood Belt, Siskiyou-Trinity Area, Central California Coastal Valleys and Central California Coast Range. Broadly, these regions have an elevation from sea level to 900 meters; average annual precipitation of 300 to 850 millimeters distributed throughout the year; perennial streams and lakes are distributed throughout the regions and glacial and alluvial deposits in the valley also yield large quantities of water; the terrain is well drained and gently sloping, and the erosion hazard is high in this area and is stabilized only by plant cover. Much of this land is federally owned and the remaining is used for lumbering, grazing, wildlife habitat and recreation.

The Sonoma Spineflower is restricted to the coastal foredunes and coastal dune scrub communities and associated habitats occupied by coastal scrub or coastal terrace prairie. In the dune systems north of Monterey

Bay, sand-stabilizing rhizomatous grasses, *Ammophila arenaria* and *Elymus mollis* generally dominate the vegetation of the foredunes. *Ammophila arenaria* (also called European beach grass or marram grass) is an alien species that has largely replaced the native *Elymus*-dominated foredune community. Beach grass is believed to be a powerful geomorphic agent due to its ability to build continuous wall-like foredunes, which were not previously in this region. Although the *Elymus*-dominated foredune community exists around Monterey Bay, these foredunes typically consist of low hillocks and mounds that are sparsely populated with generally succulent, tap-rooted perennial herbs. *Abronia latifolia, Ambrosia chamissonis, Calystegia solandella, Camissonia* spp., *Carpobrotus aequilaterus, C. edulis* and *Fragaria chiloensis* are common associates. The stabilization of the dunes by *Ammophila arenaria* has permitted the colonization of formerly active backdune areas with a mixture of native and alien plants. These areas consist of a soft, woody, dense plant community of short shrubs and subshrubs, and herbaceous plants.

Historic Range

The past and present distribution of the Sonoma Spineflower are the same excluding the wider distribution of the past.

Current Distribution

Today the Sonoma Spineflower is restricted to sandy places within coastal prairie near the south end of Abbotts Lagoon. This dune system ranges form south of Tomales Point to Point Reyes within Point Reyes National Seashore in Marin County.

Conservation and Recovery

The native plant fauna of the California coast dune scrub communities is threatened by a number of factors including: invasion of alien plants, proposed commercial and residential development, military operational uses, off-road vehicle damage, and trampling by equestrians, hikers and livestock. Potential threats include sand mining, disposal of dredged material from adjacent bays and waterways and stochastic extinction due to depauperate numbers.

The introduction and invasion of California's ecosystems by alien plants has adversely affected the Sonoma Spineflower. The invasion of Ammophila arenaria has resulted in the development of wall-like foredunes and colonization of native and alien plants. Other alien species include sea-rocket (*Cakile* spp), ice plant or sea-fig (*Carpobrotus* spp), and several annual grasses and forbs generally restricted to wetland habitats within the dunes. In many cases, these aliens outcompete and largely supplant the native dune vegetation. Typically, annuals and monocarpic plants such as the Sonoma Spineflower are vulnerable to random fluctuations or variation in annual weather patterns and other environmental factors.

The Sonoma Spineflower has limited historical distributions and likely has been eliminated from all but a small fraction of its historical dune or associated habitats. Today, this species generally persists as small "island" populations surrounded by urban areas, roads, trails, agricultural lands, competing alien plants, and other lands made unsuitable for the Sonoma Spineflower. The Sonoma Spineflower is restricted to the Point Reyes National Seashore. Other historical populations within the national seashore have been lost. Development is probably the primary contributor to this species status. Cattle ranching is an important secondary factor and the lone population occurs within an active cattle ranch, although, it has been enclosed.

Conservation measures provided to species listed as endangered or threatened pursuant to the Act include recognition, recovery actions, requirements for Federal protection, and prohibitions against certain practices. Recognition through listing encourages conservation measures by Federal, international, and private agencies, groups, and individuals.

Federal activities potentially impacting the Sonoma Spineflower would likely involve restricting/managing navigation and port-related projects and perhaps grazing practices on Federal land.

The population within Point Reyes National Seashore has been enclosed in a 360 acre pasture to protect the plants from grazing cattle.

Bibliography

U.S. Fish and Wildlife Service. "Endangered and Threatened Wildlife and Plants; Six Plants and Myrtle's Silverspot Butterfly From Coastal Dunes in Northern and Central California Determined to Be Endangered." *Federal Register* Vol. 57, No. 120, June 22, 1992: 27848-27858

Contacts

Sacramento Ecological Services Field Office
Room E-1803/1823
2800 Cottage Way
Sacramento, CA 98525
Phone: 916-978-4866
FAX: 916-978-4613

Adapted from data compiled by the Threatened and Endangered Species Information Institute (13950 W. 20th Ave., Golden, CO 80401) for *Beacham's International Threatened, Endangered, and Extinct Species* published on CD ROM, available from Beacham Publishing.

Morefield's Leather Flower

Clematis morefieldii

Milo Pyne

Status	Endangered
Listed	May 20, 1992
Family	Ranunculaceae (Buttercup)
Description	Perennial vine with urn-shaped flowers, white hairs on the shoot and pinkish flowers.
Habitat	Clay-loam soils in rocky limestone woods on the south and southwest facing slopes of mountains.
Threats	Residential development, illegal collecting, seed predation by insects, limited range.
Range	Alabama

Description

Morefield's leather flower is a perennial vine in the buttercup family and is a north Alabama endemic. The species is distinguished by urn-shaped flowers which occur singly or in few-flowered groups in leaf axils. Its primary flower stalks (peduncles) are subtended by leafy bracts. It has white hairs on the shoot, velvety lower leaf surfaces, and stouter, usually shorter (0.6 to 1.0 inch long) peduncles with sessile to nearly sessile bracts at the base. It attains heights up 16 feet and its compound leaves may attain lengths of 8 inches. Leaves have 9 to 11 leaflets form tendrils. The flowers are pinkish and grow from 0.8 to 1.0 inch long. Fruits are clusters of achenes. Flowering occurs from late May to early June.

Habitat

The species' vines are rooted in basic clay-loam soils in rocky limestone woods on the south and southwest facing slopes of mountains. Plants often sprawl over shrubs and boulders or climb understory shrubs. It occurs locally near seeps within a juniper-hardwoods community with Smoketree as the principal indicator species.

Historic Range

The species' known distribution in the past is limited to Alabama. When the species was first collected, there were eight reported populations. Three of these are believed to have been destroyed.

Current Distribution

Presently, the species occurs at only five sites in Madison County in Alabama. All of them occur on private or city-owned land. The species is limited by restricted ecological requirements. Plants are locally distributed and seem to require areas where shale seeps are moist for a good part of the year. Only five sites remain where this species is known to occur. Four of the five populations are within 0.2 to 1.1 miles of one another. A single vine represents one site. Two sites have approximately 20 plants. And the fourth site has several hundred. The fifth site is disjunct, approximately 6 miles from the other sites, and has an estimated 300 vines. On all sites, the plants are clustered within a small area (0.25 acre).

Conservation and Recovery

The species' range is currently recognized as limited to five sites in northern Alabama, all in Madison County. While surveying potential habitat for additional populations, it was noted that residential development had destroyed or adversely modified similar habitats. Residential development on mountains in the Huntsville area is increasing. Two of the existing populations are imminently threatened due to their precarious location on lots in a residential area. Clearing has already impacted habitat and individuals on these sites. Destruction of these two sites would result in approximately a 55% loss of total known individuals. At this time, only two of the five sites (22 of 300 plants, respectively) appear to be secure. Within the last few years, three populations have been destroyed by road building, clearing, and herbicide use associated with residential development.

The species is attractive and has horticultural potential. Publicity from its listing could generate an increased demand. Taking and vandalism pose threats because of its visibility when flowering and the accessibility of many of the sites. Overcollecting for any purposes could extirpate populations, especially at sites with only a few plants.

Seed predation by insects was noted in several populations and requires further investigation.

This species is extremely vulnerable because it has a limited range and low numbers of plants at many of the sites. One population has one plant, two have approximately 20 plants, and all sites occupy less than an acre in area. A single unnatural or natural disturbance could destroy a significant percentage of the known populations. In addition, the small number of individuals at three sites may indicate a limited gene pool and without infusion of gene flow, it is questionable if these smaller populations can survive.

The species seems to have restricted ecological requirements. Plants are locally distributed and seem to require areas where shale seeps are moist for a good part of the year. One population, located under a closed canopy, appeared to be stressed. Individuals were smaller and fewer flowers were observed, when compared to populations where the canopy was somewhat "open". This species may require habitat management to curtail succession.

Federal involvement in conservation is expected to include the Environmental Protection Agency in consideration of the Clean Water Act's provision for pesticides registration, and waste management actions. The Corps of Engineers will include this species in project planning and operation and during the permit review process. The Federal Highway Administration will consider impacts of bridge and road construction at points where known habitat is crossed. Urban development within the drainage basin may involve the Farmers Home Administration and their loan programs.

Bibliography

U.S. Fish and Wildlife Service. "Endangered and Threatened Wildlife and Plants; Endangered Status Determined for the Plan Clematis Morefieldii (Morefield's leather flower)." *Federal Register* Vol. 57, No. 98, May 20, 1993: 21562-27564.

Contacts

USFWS Regional Office
Suite 200, 1875 Century Blvd.
Atlanta, GA 30345
Phone: 404-679-4000

Ecological Services Field Office
P. O. Drawer 1190
Daphne, AL 36526
Phone: 205-441-5181
FAX: 205-441-6222

Alabama Natural Heritage Program
Department of Conservation and
    Natural Resources
Folsom Administration Building
Room 421, 64 N. Union St.
Montgomery, AL 36130
Phone: 205-242-3484
FAX: 205-242-0999

Adapted from data compiled by the Threatened and Endangered Species Information Institute (13950 W. 20th Ave., Golden, CO 80401) for *Beacham's International Threatened, Endangered, and Extinct Species* published on CD ROM, available from Beacham Publishing.

Short-Leaved Rosemary

Conradina brevifolia

K. R. Langdon, Florida Department of Agriculture

Status	Endangered
Listed	July 12, 1993
Family	Lamiaceae (Mint)
Description	Short-leaved perennial rosemary shrub.
Habitat	Sand pine scrub vegetation on Lake Wales Ridge, Florida.
Threats	Residential development and conversion of habitat to citrus groves and pastures.
Range	Florida

Description

Short-leaved rosemary is a perennial shrub with larger leaves on well-developed flowering branches that are 6.0 to 8.2 millimeters long, mostly shorter than the internodes. Short-leaved rosemary has 1 to 6 flowers per axil.

Habitat

Short-leaved rosemary inhabits sand pine scrub vegetation on the Lake Wales Ridge in Florida. Scrub vegetation on the ridge is generally dominated by evergreen scrub oaks and other shrubs, with sand pine and open areas with herbs and small shrubs. This vegetation type supports many endemic species including 13 plants Federally listed as endangered or threatened, the Federally threatened Florida scrub jay, and two threatened lizards (blue-tailed mole skink and sand skink).

Historic Range

The historic range is believed to be similar to the current range.

Current Distribution

This species distribution is restricted to less than 6,000 acres. This area supports about 30 individual short-leaved rosemary shrubs. It is one of the most narrowly distributed of the Lake Wales Ridge endemic plants.

Because of this species' limited population size and limited distribution, it is vulnerable to extinction. The small population size also means there is a limited gene pool. The lack of genetic diversity means the species may not have the capabilities to evolve to adjust to changes in its environment.

Conservation and Recovery

Short-leaved rosemary is found on the Lake Wales Ridge in Polk and Highlands Counties, Florida. This species occurs on the Lake Arbuckle State Forest and on land currently owned by The Nature Conservancy at Saddle Blanket Lakes. Further State, Federal, and private land purchases are planned in the area, including the proposed Lake Wales Ridge National Wildlife Refuge.

Except for two protected colonies, short-leaved rosemary is threatened by destruction of its central Florida scrub habitat for agricultural purposes (citrus groves and pastures) and for residential development.

Fire frequency in this species' primary habitat is variable but fire control could adversely impact the species by allowing succession to progress; short-leaved rosemary may not be able to compete with later succession species.

Protection of this species from collection may be difficult due to the presence of *C. canescens*, a widespread, secure species, that is morphologically variable, and some individuals belonging to this species may be indistinguishable from individuals belonging to *C. brevifolia*.

Short-leaved rosemary will benefit from the recovery plans already prepared for other Federally listed plants in the same area, from actions taken to protect the threatened Florida scrub jay, from planning that is underway to create a Lake Wales Ridge National Wildlife Refuge for endangered and threatened plants and animals, and from State and private land acquisition projects.

Research concerning the propagation and reintroduction of this species is needed to insure the success of attempted transplants and to provide an herbarium population capable of providing stock for future transplants. Further research concerning the plant's life history and ecological requirements is also needed.

Land acquisition within the range of short-leaved rosemary is planned by the State of Florida and the U.S. Fish and Wildlife Service.

Contacts

U.S. Fish and Wildlife Service. "Endangered and Threatened Wildlife and Plants; Endangered or Threatened Status for Five Florida Plants." *Federal Register* Vol. 58, No. 131. July 12, 1993: 37432-37443.

Bibliography

USFWS Regional Office
Suite 200, 1875 Century Blvd.
Atlanta, GA 30345
Phone: 404-679-4000

Ecological Services Field Office
Suite 310, 6620 Southpoint Drive, South
Jacksonville, FL 32216-0912
Phone: 904-232-2580
FAX: 904-232-2404

Adapted from data compiled by the Threatened and Endangered Species Information Institute (13950 W. 20th Ave., Golden, CO 80401) for *Beacham's International Threatened, Endangered, and Extinct Species* published on CD ROM, available from Beacham Publishing

Etonia Rosemary
Conradina etonia

Robert Kral

Status	Endangered
Listed	July 12, 1993
Family	Lamiaceae (Mint)
Description	Minty rosemary shrub with dense hairs matted under the surfaces of the leaves with sharply bent corolla tube.
Habitat	Scrub vegetation with sand pine and shrubby evergreen oaks.
Threats	Residential development, commercial trade, limited distribution.
Range	Florida

Description

Conradina (minty rosemary) is a genus of minty-aromatic shrubs belonging to the mint family that resemble the herb rosemary (Rosmarinus officinalis), native to the Mediterranean region. Conradina is characterized by dense hairs appressed or matted on the under surfaces of the leaves, and by the flower's corolla tube, which is sharply bent above the middle, rather than straight or gently curved. The genus consists of 6 allopatric species, i.e., the ranges of the species do not overlap.

Etonia rosemary has large flowers, broad leaves, and lateral veins that are clearly visible on the undersurface (a feature not seen in any other species in this genus).

Habitat

The species occurs in Florida scrub vegetation with sand pine and shrubby evergreen oaks. Scrub in this area is the northeastern range limit for several plant species of Florida scrub, including silk bay, sand holly, *Garberia heterophylla*, and the scrub palmetto, which is named for this area but does not occur in the immediate vicinity of *Etonia rosemary*. The threatened Florida scrub jay occurs in the same habitat as *Etonia rosemary*.

Historic Range

Since the species was discovered only in 1991, its past distribution is not known.

Current Distribution

Etonia rosemary is presently known from only two sites in Putnam County in northeastern Florida. These sites occur on privately owned land and are subdivided for residential development. The species is limited by low numbers which greatly reduce its gene pool.

Conservation and Recovery

The species is threatened by residential development of its two sites, one in a subdivision where houses are being built, and the other in an area where the landowner has obtained all necessary permits to create a residential development.

There is commercial trade in the genus *Conradina*, whose species have considerable horticultural potential. All the species of Conradina are easily propagated and are in cultivation. Commercial trade in the rarer species of Conradina should not adversely affect those species, provided that it is dependent upon plants propagated from plants in cultivation. Inappropriate collecting from plants in the wild is a threat to this species.

The threats listed above are exacerbated by a number of factors, including: the limited geographic distribution of this species; and the small size of the existing populations of this species. Limited gene pools may depress reproductive vigor, or single human-caused or natural environmental disturbances could destroy a significant percentage of the individuals of this species.

Bibliography

U.S. Fish and Wildlife Service. "Endangered and Threatened Wildlife and Plants; Endangered or Threatened Status for Five Florida Plants." *Federal Register* Vol. 58, No. 131, July 12, 1992: 37432-37443.

Contacts

USFWS Regional Office
Suite 200, 1875 Century Blvd.
Atlanta, GA 30345
Phone: 404-679-4000

Ecological Services Field Office
1612 June Avenue
Panama City, FL 32405-3721
Phone: 904-769-0552
FAX: 904-763-2177

Ecological Services Field Office
Suite 310, 6620 Southpoint Drive, South
Jacksonville, FL 32216-0912
Phone: 904-232-2580
FAX: 904-232-2404

Adapted from data compiled by the Threatened and Endangered Species Information Institute (13950 W. 20th Ave., Golden, CO 80401) for *Beacham's International Threatened, Endangered, and Extinct Species* published on CD ROM, available from Beacham Publishing.

Apalachicola Rosemary

Conradina glabra

K. R. Langdon, Florida Department of Agriculture

Status	Endangered
Listed	July 12, 1993
Family	Lamiaceae (Mint)
Description	Many-branched shrub with evergreen needle-like, hairless leaves and flowers in groups of 2 or 3.
Habitat	Apalachicola ravines, and barren soil next to pine trees, pine plantations, cleared edges of pine plantations.
Threats	Deforestation, herbicides, limited distribution.
Range	Florida

Description

The Apalachicola rosemary is a many-branched shrub that grows to a height of 2 meters. The shrubs often occur in clumped patterns but rhizomatal reproduction has not been confirmed. The branches of this species are spreading or upright. The leaves are evergreen, opposite, with additional leaves in short shoots in the axils giving the appearance of fascicles (small bundles). The leaves are needle-like and hairless on the upper surface. The flowers are generally in groups of 2 or 3. The corolla is 1.5 to 2.0 centimeters long, from its base to the tip of its longest lobe, with a slender corolla tube that is straight for about 5 millimeters long, then bends sharply downward to form a funnel-shaped throat 5 millimeters long, then widens out into upper and lower lips. The out-

side of the tube and throat are white, with the lobes and lips lavender blue at the tips. The lower lip of the corolla is three-lobed, with a band of purple dots extending along its inner side. The four stamens are paired. Many flowers are male sterile. In extreme cases, the stamens are malformed and petaloid in shape, texture and color. Male sterility may be the result of inbreeding and homozygosity.

Habitat

Apalachicola rosemary is located in an area of gently undulating upland habitat originally dominated by longleaf pine-wiregrass vegetation. The area is dissected by ravines of the Sweetwater Creek system, which drains westward to the Apalachicola River. Parts of the Apalachicola ravines are incorporated in public and private nature preserves that protect rich hardwood forests with the narrowly endemic Florida torreya and Florida yew. Heads of ravines, called steepheads, have slopes that are undermined by groundwater seeping into the ravine bottom causing the slopes to gradually slump, carrying the vegetation with it. The edges of ravines support mature shrubs which are sometimes carried into the ravines during slumping. Younger Apalachicola rosemary shrubs are found in the barren, exposed soil adjacent to the pines and often extend into the pine stand. This suggests that the species is able to compete effectively in open, newly exposed areas but is unable to compete in closed stands of mixed hardwoods or pines. This species is probably a component of the secondary successional plant community in the area; fires in the area are frequent.

Apalachicola rosemary is also found along roadsides, in planted pine plantations, and along the cleared edges of pine plantations.

This species apparently requires full sunlight or partial shade.

Historic Range and Current Distribution

This species is only found in Liberty County, Florida, west of Tallahassee near the Apalachicola River. There are 4 natural colonies on lands owned by a forest products company and on public road rights-of-way. Another artificial colony is being created a short distance from the plant's natural range, on similar ravine edges, in the Apalachicola Bluffs and Ravines Preserve, owned by The Nature Conservancy.

Conservation and Recovery

This species appears to require full sunlight or partial shade. Planted pine trees are likely, by the time they mature, to produce dense shade that could kill this species. Another possible problem in planted pines is that sand pine does not tolerate prescribed fire, which may help keep the habitat open for Apalachicola rosemary. Forestry practices may kill the species directly when areas are cut and site-prepared. These plants survived on areas where chopping had not occurred, and did not survive in areas where chopping did occur.

The herbicide hexazinone is sometimes used in timber regeneration areas and its use could affect Apalachicola rosemary.

The very limited distribution of this species and management of most of that range by a single landowner exacerbates the threat to this plant from forestry practices, because the same management practices are likely to be applied rangewide, at the same time.

Some areas formerly occupied by this species have been converted to improved pasturelands, destroying the plants in the process and leaving the area unsuitable for it.

Research concerning the propagation and reintroduction of this species is needed to insure the success of attempted transplants and to provide an herbarium population capable of providing stock for future transplants. Further research concerning the plant's life history and ecological requirements is also needed.

Bibliography

U.S. Fish and Wildlife Service. "Endangered and Threatened Wildlife and Plants; Endangered or Threatened Status for Five Florida Plants." *Federal Register* Vol. 58, No. 131. July 12, 1993: 37432-37443.

Contacts

U.S. Fish and Wildlife Service
Regional Office
Suite 200, 1875 Century Blvd.
Atlanta, GA 30345
Phone: 404-679-4000

Adapted from data compiled by the Threatened and Endangered Species Information Institute (13950 W. 20th Ave., Golden, CO 80401) for *Beacham's International Threatened, Endangered, and Extinct Species* published on CD ROM, available from Beacham Publishing.

Pima Pineapple Cactus

Coryphantha scheeri var. *robustispina*

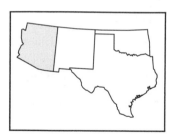

USFWS, Albuquerque

Status	Endangered
Listed	September 23, 1993
Family	Cactaceae (Cactus)
Description	Hemispherical cactus with strong, centralized hooked spines, short and light yellow, turning black with age, having yellow flowers.
Habitat	Slopes in semi-desert grassland in shallow to deep soil.
Threats	Alteration of habitat due to recreational activities, agriculture, road construction; illegal collecting.
Range	Arizona, Mexico

Description

The pima pineapple cactus is a hemispherical cactus measuring 10 to 46 centimeters tall and 7.5 to 18 centimeters in diameter. The spine clusters have one centralized spine that is especially strong and usually hooked. The spines are short and light yellow; with age the spines turn black. This plant may be single-stemmed, multi-headed, or in clusters. The clustered appearance is a result of the seeds germinating at the base of a mother plant or when a tubercle of the mother plant roots. The flowers are a silky yellow and appear in July through August. The green fruit is ellipsoidal, succulent and sweet.

Habitat

This cactus grows in alluvial basins or on slopes in semidesert grassland and Sonoran desert-scrub. Soils range from shallow to deep, and silty to rocky. It seems the pima pineapple cactus prefers silty to gravelly deep alluvial soils. This plant occurs most frequently in open areas on flat ridgetops or areas with very little slope at an elevation of 700 to 1,400 meters. Associated vegetation includes white-thorn acacia, creosotebush, velvet mesquite, triangle-leaf bursage, thread snakeweed, chain fruit cholla, *Isocoma tenuisecta*, Lehman's lovegrass, and other cacti species.

Historic Range

The pima pineapple cactus is known from Pima and Santa Cruz Counties, Arizona and northern Sonora, Mexico.

Current Distribution

The range of this cactus extends from the Baboquivari Mountains east to the western foothills of the Santa Rita Mountains. It is difficult to ascertain the hectares of potential habitat for this species due to its habitat requirements and the topographic complexity within its range.

The population density is difficult to attain as well because the pima pineapple cactus is difficult to find in the field. Minimum density estimates for areas near the Sierrita Mountains of Arizona range from a low of 0.12 plants/hectare to 0.54 plants/hectare.

This plant must compete for space, light and nutrients with exotic vegetation. Some plants seem to be damaged by the larval stage of lepidopteran.

Conservation and Recovery

The pima pineapple cactus is currently threatened by many factors including illegal collection, habitat degradation due to recreational activities, habitat destruction by livestock, and habitat loss due to mining, agriculture, road construction, and urbanization.

It is approximated that about 75% of the pima pineapple cactus's range is threatened by construction associated with growing human populations. Home building, commercial development, road construction and maintenance, and utility corridor construction are only a few of the activities destroying this species' habitat.

Mining activities have resulted in the loss of hundreds of pineapple cacti because they were not salvaged before expansion. Mineral extraction activities such as road access, tailing piles and settling or leaching ponds have also adversely affected this species.

Those areas that are currently undeveloped are utilized for livestock grazing. Overgrazing has most likely resulted in the current alteration of the ecosystem in this area. Erosion; changes in hydrology and microclimate; invasion of exotic vegetation; shifts in density, relative abundance, and vigor of native species; and increases in woody perennials have all been a result of this overgrazing.

This species is also faced with competition from aggressive exotics such as Lehman's lovegrass and Mediterranean grass.

Bibliography

U.S. Fish and Wildlife Service. "Endangered and Threatened Wildlife and Plants; Determination of Endangered Status for the Plant Pima Pineapple Cactus (*Coryphantha scheeri* var. *robustispina*)." *Federal Register* Vol. 58, No. 183, September 23, 1993: 49875-49879.

Contacts

USFWS Regional Office
P. O. Box 1306
Albuquerque, NM 87103
Phone: 505-766-2321
FAX: 505-766-8063

Albuquerque Ecological Services
Field Office
Suite D, 3530 Pan American Highway, NE
Albuquerque, NM 87107
Phone: 505-883-7877
FAX: 505-883-7876

Adapted from data compiled by the Threatened and Endangered Species Information Institute (13950 W. 20th Ave., Golden, CO 80401) for *Beacham's International Threatened, Endangered, and Extinct Species* published on CD ROM.

Okeechobee Gourd

Cucurbita okeechobeensis ssp. *okeechobeensis*

Jonathan Shaw, Bok Tower Gardens

Status	Endangered
Listed	July 12, 1993
Family	Cucurbitaceae (Gourd)
Description	Annual, fibrous-rooted, high-climbing vine with tendrils, heart-to-kidney shaped leaf blades and bell-shaped cream-colored flowers.
Habitat	Heavy, tangled canopy of the shores of Lake Okeechobee, Florida Everglades.
Threats	Lowering of the lake level, construction of water management facilities, intrusion of other plants.
Range	Florida

Description

The Okeechobee gourd is an annual, fibrous-rooted, high-climbing vine with tendrils, belonging to the gourd family. Its leaf blades are heart-to-kidney shaped, with 5 to 7 shallow, angular lobes and irregularly serrated margins. Young leaves are covered with soft hairs. The cream colored flowers are bell-shaped, with the corolla 2 to 3 inches long; they can be distinguished from flowers of the Martinez gourd (*C. o. martinezii*) by the presence of dense pubescence (hairs) on the hypanthium (the tube formed by the fused bases of the petals and sepals) of the male flower and on the ovary of the female flower. The gourd is globular or slightly oblong, light green with 10 indistinct stripes, and hard shelled with bitter flesh. The seeds are gray-green and flat.

Seeds of this species germinate readily on alligator nests, where water-dispersed gourds wash up on shores with warm soil, full sun, and no competition from other plants. Primary terrestrial seed dispersing agents are marsh rabbits. Rabbits have been observed gnawing on green gourds and gnawed and broken gourds have been found in the animal's nests.

Habitat

The Okeechobee gourd is endemic to the shores of Lake Okeechobee in the Florida Everglades. Historically, the species was found in the pond apple (Annona glabra) hammocks surrounding this lake. This species seems to prefer a heavy, tangled canopy. It appears to rely on the natural trellises of pond apple branches, although the pond apple persists at some sites where this species has not been seen. Germination requires exposed, bare, dry ground during the winter and early spring. Seedlings do not tolerate water-soaked soils for extended periods of time. By the rainy season, the vines have climbed shrubs, avoiding complete inundation as the lake rises. Individuals are found climbing on pond apple trees, and, more abundantly, on elderberries and other woody plants, including papaya. Individuals also sprawl across herbaceous plants.

Historic Range

This species is endemic to the southern shores and islands of Lake Okeechobee in the Florida Everglades. Historically, the species was locally common in the Okeechobee pond apple forests. The species was infrequently observed after 1930; in 1941, it was found on Observation Island in Lake Okeechobee, Glades County. It has not since been relocated on this island. A population was discovered in Broward County in 1978, and was destroyed by road construction the following year.

Current Distribution

The Okeechobee gourd has been observed in the pond apple hammocks of the Lake Okeechobee region throughout this century. How much the species has declined is not exactly known, though 95 percent of the pond apple hammock has been destroyed over the years. This species reached endangered numbers by the 1930s. Continued loss of habitat, flooding, and competition with exotic species continues to threaten the species. Due to few remaining individuals, genetic diversity is low, making the plant less adaptable to change.

Currently, approximately 11 populations exist with the largest containing 50 individuals. Populations have been found on the banks of Kreamer and Torry Islands, and have also been seen in an agricultural area of Dade County. The species was also sighted in near Fisheating Bay in Glades County. The species occurs on U.S. Department of Defense land and on South Florida Water Management District managed land where it receives some protection.

Conservation and Recovery

The Okeechobee gourd has suffered substantial decreases since the 1920s. This can be related to the loss of the pond apple forests during this time. Since 1930, natural vegetation that remained along the lake shores was further affected by lowering of the lake level from a maximum of about 20 feet above sea level. During the 1920s, attempts were made to keep the lake within 13.5 to 16.5 feet (with the lake staying below minimum for most of 3 years). The current preferred range is 15.5 to 17.5 feet. The lake level has fallen below the preferred range during dry periods in recent years, providing bare muck where the species' seeds can germinate. Any change in lake level management that would reduce the likelihood of low water would threaten this species. Construction of the Hoover Dike and other water management facilities, planting of exotic melaleuca trees, the spread of Australian pine (Casuarina), and the use of Torry and Kreamer Islands for pasture also affected the habitat of this plant. Use of herbicide for vegetation management purposes may have adversely affected this species. One population that was discovered on a disturbed roadside in Broward County, was destroyed by road construction the next year.

Due to the extremely small numbers of remaining individuals, the remaining populations of this species require careful management. This may include a program of habitat modification and enhancement, should such measures prove feasible. Control or extirpation of exotic pest plants such as melaleuca and Brazilian pepper and planting of pond apple may be necessary or desirable to protect existing populations or to restore former habitat. The Bok Tower Gardens, a botanical garden near the species' habitat, has begun a cultivation program for the species. Nine seeds were collected, and at this time 11 healthy gourds exist. It is hoped that these plants will yield the seeds to keep this species alive.

Bibliography

U.S. Fish and Wildlife Service. 1993. "Endangered and Threatened Wildlife and Plants: Endangered or Threatened Status for Five Florida Plants." *Federal Register* Vol. 58, July 12, 1993: 37432-37443.

Contacts

USFWS Regional Office
Suite 200, 1875 Century Blvd.
Atlanta, GA 30345
Phone: 404-679-4000

Ecological Services Field Office
Suite 310, 6620 Southpoint Drive, South
Jacksonville, FL 32216-0912
Phone: 904-232-2580
FAX: 904-232-2404

Adapted from data compiled by the Threatened and Endangered Species Information Institute (13950 W. 20th Ave., Golden, CO 80401) for *Beacham's International Threatened, Endangered, and Extinct Species* published on CD ROM, available from Beacham Publishing.

Smooth Coneflower
Echinacea laevigata

Milo Pyne

Status	Endangered
Listed	October 8, 1992
Family	Asteraceae (Aster)
Description	Perennial herb with glabrous stems and light pink to purplish flowers.
Habitat	Open woods, cedar barrens, roadsides, dry limestone bluffs.
Threats	Encroachment of woody vegetation, residential and industrial development.
Range	Georgia, North Carolina, South Carolina, Virginia

Description

The Smooth coneflower is a rhizomatous perennial herb. This plant grows up to 1.5 meters tall. The stems are glabrous and possess only a few leaves (up to 20 centimeters long, 7.5 centimeters wide). The smooth to slightly rough basil leaves are elliptical to lanceolate with long stems. The mid-stem leaves have shorter stems and are smaller in size than the basal leaves. The rays of the flowers are light pink to purplish and the flower heads are usually solitary. Flowering occurs May through July. The fruit is a gray-brown, oblong-prismatic achene, 4 to 4.5 millimeters long. The seeds are 0.5 cm long.

Habitat

The Smooth coneflower inhabits open woods, cedar barrens, roadsides, clearcuts, dry limestone bluffs, and power line rights-of-way. In Virginia the soils are magnesium and calcium rich associated with limestone. In North Carolina the magnesium and calcium rich soils are associated with gabbor; diabase in North and South Carolina; and marble in South Carolina and Georgia.

The Smooth coneflower favors sites characterized by an abundant amount of sunlight with little or no competition in the herbaceous layer. Natural fires and large herbivores are part of this species' habitat. Many associated herbs are cormophytic, sun-loving species that depend on periodic disturbances. These disturbances reduce shade and threats of competition by woody plants.

Historic Range

Historically, the Smooth coneflower was distributed in Pennsylvania, Maryland, Virginia, North Carolina, South Carolina, Georgia, Alabama, and Arkansas. This species is known extant only in Virginia, North Carolina, South Carolina, and Georgia. Sixty-four percent of this species' populations have been extirpated since 1888.

Current Distribution

The Smooth coneflower is currently located in Pulaski, Montgomery, Campbell, and Franklin Counties, Virginia; Durham and Granville Counties, North Carolina; Oconee and Anderson Counties, South Carolina; and Stephens County Georgia. Additionally this species occurs on lands managed by the U.S. Forest Service, U.S. Army Corps of Engineers, South Carolina Department of Highways and Public Transportation, Clemson University, North Carolina Department of Agriculture, the Nature Conservancy (private) and the South Carolina Heritage Trust Program (private). Of the 21 remaining populations, 13 are considered declining in numbers of plants, 7 are stable, and 1 is increasing.

Conservation and Recovery

The Smooth coneflower is endangered by collecting, encroachment of woody vegetation, residential and industrial development, and certain types of roadside and power line right-of-way maintenance.

The Smooth coneflower is and has been threatened by alteration of its habitat. Silvicultural and agricultural practices, and industrial and residential development have partially contributed to the alteration of habitat.

Highway construction, construction of a gas line, and conversion of a site to pine plantation have been known factors in extirpation of at least one population. Many populations are on the edges of highways' utility rights-of-way.

Many common native coneflowers are in demand for horticultural use and are a significant part of the commercial trade. Publicity may generate an increased demand for this species. Many species of the genus Echinacea have been harvested for pharmaceutical trade.

This species relies on some type of periodic disturbance to clear encroachment of woody vegetation and reduce shading. Fire, well-timed mowing or careful clearing is essential to maintaining the glade remnants occupied by this plant.

Although this species is given State protection in four states, state prohibitions against taking are difficult to enforce and do not cover adverse alterations of habitats, such as exclusion of fire.

In North Carolina the Smooth coneflower is given legal protection by North Carolina general statutes. This legislation provides for protection from intrastate trade, provides for monitoring and management of State-listed species and prohibits taking of plants without the written permission of landowners.

In Georgia this species is also given legal protection under the Wildflower Preservation Act of 1973. Georgia legislation prohibits taking of listed plants from public lands (without a permit) and regulates the sale and transport of plants within the State.

Bibliography

U.S. Fish and Wildlife Service. "Endangered and Threatened Wildlife and Plants; *Echinacea laevigata* (Smooth coneflower) Determined to be Endangered." *Federal Register* Vol. 57, No. 196, October 8, 1992: 46340-46344.

Contacts

USFWS Regional Office
Suite 200, 1875 Century Blvd.
Atlanta, GA 30345
Phone: 404-679-4000

Adapted from data compiled by the Threatened and Endangered Species Information Institute (13950 W. 20th Ave., Golden, CO 80401) for *Beacham's International Threatened, Endangered, and Extinct Species* published on CD ROM, available from Beacham Publishing.

Star [=Sea Urchin] Cactus
Astrophytum asterias

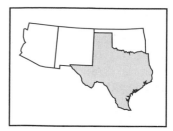

Jackie M. Poole   *Color Plate C-2*

Status	Endangered
Listed	October 18, 1993
Family	Cactaceae (Cactus)
Description	Small, spineless cactus, brownish or dull green and speckled with tiny white scales; flowers are yellow with orange centers.
Habitat	Sparse, open brushland.
Threats	Collecting; habitat loss due to agricultural development.
Range	Texas

Description

The star cactus is a small, spineless cactus. It is disk- or dome-like in shape, 2 to 15 centimeters across and up to 7 centimeters tall. This species is brownish or dull green and speckled with tiny white scales. Eight triangular sections are a result of vertical grooves dividing the main body. Each section is marked with a central line of circular indentations filled with straw-colored to whitish wooly hairs. The flowers are yellow with orange centers. These flowers are up to 5 centimeters in diameter. The fruits are green to grayish-red, about 1.25 centimeters long, oval, and fleshy.

Habitat

The star cactus is associated with low elevations in grasslands and shrublands. The area in which this cactus is found (Rio Grande Plains and Tamaulipan thorn shrub) was originally a subtropical grassland. Due to extensive suppression of fire and overgrazing, much of the area is now invaded with thorny shrub and tree species. The star cactus is found in sparse, open brushland, most commonly associated with partial shade of other plants or of rocks growing on gravelly saline clays of loams overlaying the Tertiary Cathoula and Frio formations.

Historic Range

Historically, the star cactus occurred in Cameron, Hidalgo, and Starr counties in Texas, and the adjacent states of Nuevo Leon and Tamaulipas in Mexico.

Current Distribution

The star cactus is presently known from one locality in Texas and one in Tamaulipas, Mexico. Only about 2,100 plants are known to exist in the wild. The Nuevo Leon site is believed extirpated due to collecting activities. The Tamaulipas site has been reduced to very few individuals.

Conservation and Recovery

Much of the native habitat of the star cactus has been converted to agriculture or improved pasture. In the areas where this plant presently occurs, pasture improvement is done through a process of shrub clearing and then planting buffelgrass, *Cenchhrus ciliaris*. Therefore a mosaic of buffelgrass pasture and shrub stands results. It is unlikely that the star cactus would be able to withstand this type of land management. In Mexico, much of the once suitable habitat has been converted to corn fields or orange groves.

This cactus has been a favorite collection among succulent dealers for many years. Despite the fact that this plant is easily propagated, wild specimens are found in the commercial market. In Texas, about 400 wild specimens were found at one nursery.

As the star cactus is easily grown from seed and has been for many years by the succulent trade, propagation techniques are currently under investigation. Plants have been grown from seed in a greenhouse environment. These plants seems to be consistently hardier and more disease resistant than plants taken from the wild.

Bibliography

U.S. Fish and Wildlife Service. "Endangered and Threatened Wildlife and Plants; Determination of Endangered Status for the Plant *Astrophytum Asterias* (Star Cactus)." *Federal Register* Vol. 58, No. 199, October 18, 1993: 53804-53807.

Contacts

USFWS Regional Office
P. O. Box 1306
Albuquerque, NM 87103
Phone: 505-766-2321
FAX: 505-766-8063

Austin Ecological Services Field Office
Suite 449, 611 East Sixth Street
Austin, TX 78701
Phone: 512-482-5436
FAX: 512-482-5442

Arlington Ecological Services Field Office
Suite 252, 711 Stadium Drive East
Arlington, TX 76011
Phone: 817-885-7830
FAX: 817-885-7835

Houston Ecological Services Field Office
Suite 211, 17629 El Camino Real
Houston, TX 77058
Phone: 713-286-8282
FAX: 713-488-5882

Adapted from data compiled by the Threatened and Endangered Species Information Institute (13950 W. 20th Ave., Golden, CO 80401) for *Beacham's International Threatened, Endangered, and Extinct Species* published on CD ROM, available from Beacham Publishing.

Ben Lomond Wallflower
Erysimum teretifolium

Deborah S. Hillyard

Status	Endangered
Listed	February 4, 1994
Family	Brassicaceae (Mustard)
Description	Biennial plant of the mustard family with deep yellow flowers and simple and narrowly linear leaves.
Habitat	Sandstone deposits in the Santa Cruz mountains.
Threats	Residential and golf course development; agricultural land conversion, recreational use, sand mining, dune stabilization projects, and military activities.
Range	California

Description

Ben Lomond wallflower is a biennial, or occasionally an annual, plant of the mustard family. Seedlings form a basal rosette of leaves, which wither as the main stem develops flowers clustered in a terminal raceme. The flowers are a deep yellow with petals of 1.9 to 2.5 centimeters (0.5 to 1 inch) long; the slender capsule reaches 10 centimeters (4 inches) in length and is covered with three-parted hairs. The leaves are simple and narrowly linear, a characteristic that separates this plant from other wallflowers.

Habitat

Ben Lomond wallflower is endemic to pockets of sandstone deposits in the Santa Cruz mountains and is presently known from only a dozen scattered occurrences. These sandstone deposits support the unique ponderosa pine sandhill community, and *E. teretifolium* seems to prefer sites with loose, uncompacted sand in openings between scattered chaparral shrubs. Another endangered plant, the robust spineflower (*Chorizanthe robusta* var. *robusta*) is found in close proximity at some locations.

Historic Range

Ben Lomond wallflower was first collected in Santa Cruz county by Horace Davis in 1914. It was spread throughout the sandstone deposits of the Santa Cruz mountains.

Current Distribution

Ben Lomond wallflower is endemic to pockets of sandstone deposits in the Santa Cruz mountains and is presently known from only a dozen scattered occurrences within the area generally bounded by the communities of Ben Lomond, Glenwood, Scotts Valley and Felton, with one outlying population occuring in the Bonny Doon area 5 miles west of Felton. One population occurs at Quail Hollow Ranch, which is jointly owned by Santa Cruz County, The Nature Conservancy, and the California Department of Fish and Game. All other populations are on privately owned lands.

The largest population of Ben Lomond wallflower, about 5,400 individuals (Bittman, 1986) is at the Quail Hollow Quarry. This represents 75 percent of the surviving individuals. Quail Hollow Ranch supports fewer than 300 individuals. Of the remaining populations, none comprise over 400 individuals and about half totaled less than 100 individuals each.

Conservation and Recovery

Three endangered species, Ben Lomond wallflower (*Erysimum teretifolium*), Ben Lomond spineflower (*C. pungens hartwegiana*), and robust spineflower (*C. robusta* var. *hartwegiia*) are restricted to sandstone and mudstone soils in the Santa Cruz mountains. These species and their associated habitats are threatened by one or more of the following: residential and golf course development; agricultural land conversion, recreational use, sand mining, dune stabilization projects, and military activities. Currently proposed expansion of operations of the Quail Hollow Quarry may eliminate additional populations. At least half of the habitat occupied by Ben Lomond spine-flower is on land owned by sand and gravel companies. Populations located on land owned by the San Lorenzo Valley Water District were badly damaged by off-road vehicles despite efforts to fence off the area.

Alteration of Ben Lomond wallflower habitat may also be occuring in the form of increased canopy density within the Ben Lomond sandhills as a result of fire suppression. The suppression of wildfires caused the density of woodland and the pine sandhill community to increase, which may reduce the availability of suitable habitat for the wallflower.

Small populations of Ben Lomond spineflower occur on the Bonny Doon Ecological Preserve, managed by The Nature Conservancy, and at Big Basin and Henry Cowell State Park, but no managerial plans have yet been developed to protect the species.

Bibliography

U.S. Fish and Wildlife Service. "Endangered and Threatened Wildlife and Plants; Determination of Endangered Status for Three Plants and Threatened Status for One Plant from Sandy and Sedimentary Soils of Central Coastal California." *Federal Register*. Vol. 59, No. 24. February 4, 1994: 5499-55113.

Contacts

U.S. Fish and Wildlife Service
Ventura Field Office
2140 Eastman Avenue, Suite 100
Ventura, CA 93003
805-644-1766

Adapted from data compiled by Beacham Publishing for *Beacham's International Threatened, Endangered, and Extinct Species* published on CD ROM.

Menzies' Wallflower
Erysimum menziesii

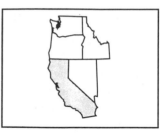

Ken Berg, California Native Plant Society

Status	Endangered
Listed	June 22, 1992
Family	Brassicaceae (Mustard)
Description	Perennial herb with dense clusters of bright yellow flowers, fleshy, spoon-shaped rosette leaves.
Habitat	Coastal foredunes and coastal dune scrub communities.
Threats	Invasion of alien plants, proposed commercial and residential development, off-road vehicle damage.
Range	California

Description

Menzies' wallflower is a low growing succulent, rosette-forming, biennial to short-lived perennial herb. This species usually produces dense clusters of bright yellow flowers in the winter and early spring. However, this species may flower in early summer. The characteristic fleshy, spoon-shaped, rosette leaves of this species are used to distinguish this taxa. The divergent fruits or siliques and smaller consistently yellow petals separate this species from other *Erysimum* species.

Habitat

Menzies' wallflower is associated with the California Coastal Redwood Belt, Siskiyou-Trinity Area, Central California Coastal Val-

leys and Central California Coast Range. Broadly, these regions have an elevation from sea level to 900 meters; average annual precipitation of 300 to 850 millimeters distributed throughout the year; perennial streams and lakes are distributed throughout the regions and glacial and alluvial deposits in the valley also yield large quantities of water; the soils are well drained on gently sloping to very steep slopes. The erosion hazard is high in this area and is stabilized only by plant cover. Much of this land is federally owned and the remaining is used for lumbering, grazing, wildlife habitat and recreation.

Menzies' wallflower is restricted to the coastal foredunes and coastal dune scrub communities and associated habitats occupied by coastal scrub or coastal terrace prairie. In the dune systems north of Monterey Bay, sand-stabilizing rhizomatous grasses, *Ammophila arenaria* and *Elymus mollis* generally dominate the vegetation of the foredunes. *Ammophila arenaria*, European beach grass or marram grass, is an alien species that has largely replaced the native Elymus-dominated foredune community. Beach grass is believed to be a powerful geomorphic agent due to its ability to build continuous wall-like foredunes, which were not previously in this region. Although the Elymus-dominated foredune community exists around Monterey Bay, these foredunes typically consist of low hillocks and mounds that are sparsely populated with generally succulent, tap-rooted perennial herbs. The stabilization of the dunes by *Ammophila arenaria* has permitted the colonization of formerly active backdune areas with a mixture of native and alien plants. These backdune areas consist of a soft, woody, dense plant community of short shrubs and subshrubs, and herbaceous plants.

Menzies' wallflower is restricted to isolated occurrences within wind-sheltered, sparsely vegetated areas and is associated with coastal dune scrub or Flandrian dune habitat.

Historic Range and Current Distribution

Menzies' wallflower is discontinuously distributed within the coastal foredune community of four dune systems within Humboldt Bay, Humboldt County, the Ten mile River dune system and Monterey Bay dune system in Mendocino County and the Monterey Peninsula dune system. This species occupies lands owned by The Nature Conservancy and the State of California.

Conservation and Recovery

The native plant fauna of the California coast dune scrub communities is threatened by a number of factors including: invasion of alien plants, proposed commercial and residential development, military operational uses, off-road vehicle damage, and trampling by equestrians, hikers and livestock. Potential threats include sand mining, disposal of dredged material from adjacent bays and waterways and stochastic extinction due to depauperate numbers.

The introduction and invasion of California's ecosystems by alien plants has adversely affected Menzies' wallflower. The invasion of *Ammophila arenaria* has resulted in the development of wall-like foredunes and colonization of native and alien plants. Other alien species include sea-rocket (*Cakile* spp), ice plant or sea-fig, and several annual grasses and forbs generally restricted to wetland habitats within the dunes. In many cases, these aliens outcompete and largely supplant the native dune vegetation. Typically, annuals and monocarpic plants such as Menzies' wallflower are vulnerable to random fluctuations or variation in annual weather patterns and other environmental factors.

Menzies' wallflower has limited historical distributions and likely has been eliminated from all but a small fraction of its historical dune or associated habitats. Today, Menzies' wallflower generally persists as small "island" populations surrounded by urban areas, roads, trails, agricultural lands, competing alien plants, and other lands made unsuitable for this species.

Menzies' wallflower is restricted to isolated sites within coastal dune scrub communities. The construction of a golf course in 1987 near Spanish Bay on the Monterey Peninsula eliminated a significant portion of a population. The developer attempted to mitigate for the project via the transplantation of this subspecies on an artificial dune, to no avail. Populations within Salinas River State Beach remain subject to off-road vehicle use, and trampling by hikers and equestrians. The population within Asilomar State Beach is on a steep bluff face, inaccessible to the public. Commercial and residential development threatens the remaining populations.

Bibliography

U.S. Fish and Wildlife Service. "'Endangered and Threatened Wildlife and Plants; Six Plants and Myrtle's Silverspot Butterfly From Coastal Dunes in Northern and Central California Determined to Be Endangered." *Federal Register* Vol. 57, No. 120, June 22, 1992: 27848-27858

Contacts

Sacramento Ecological Services
Field Office
Room E-1803/1823
2800 Cottage Way
Sacramento, CA 98525
Phone: 916-978-4866
FAX: 916-978-4613

Adapted from data compiled by the Threatened and Endangered Species Information Institute (13950 W. 20th Ave., Golden, CO 80401) for *Beacham's International Threatened, Endangered, and Extinct Species* published on CD ROM, available from Beacham Publishing.

Telephus Spurge
Euphorbia telephioides

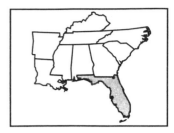

Loran C. Anderson

Status	Threatened
Listed	May 8, 1992
Family	Euphorbiaceae (Spurge)
Description	Bushy perennial herb with a stout storage root.
Habitat	Grassy vegetation on poorly drained sandy soils.
Threats	Habitat degradation due to lack of fire and forestry practices.
Range	Florida

Description

The telephus spurge is a bushy-looking perennial herb with a stout storage root. The stems are numerous and up to 30 centimeters tall. Both the stems and leaves are glabrous and possess latex. The largest leaves are 3 to 6 cm, long, elliptic or oblanceolate. The midrib and margins are usually maroon. The inflorescence is a cyathium. Flowering occurs from April through July.

Habitat

This species is restricted to the Gulf coastal lowlands near the mouth of the Apalachicola River. This species inhabits grassy vegetation on poorly drained, infertile sandy soils. The wettest sites are grassy seepage bogs on gentle slopes at the edges of forested or shrubby wetlands. This species also inhabits grass-sedge bogs (savannahs), which are nearly treeless and shrubless but have a rich flora of grasses, sedges and herbs. Telephus spurge also occurs in scrubby oak vegetation' near the shoreline of the Gulf of Mexico.

Grassy savannahs and bogs are maintained by periodic fires. Lightning fires usually occur during the growing season. Fire during the growing season can stimulate and/or synchronize flowering in many species. The Apalachicola region has many endemic plant species, most of them are native to savannahs.

Savannahs have a greater economic value when they are planted with pine trees or converted to pasture. Prior to planting pines, the site is prepared by bedding and using other mechanical methods which are destructive to the vegetation.

This species is associated with the Eastern Gulf Coast Flatwoods. The Kuchler system places this species' habitat within the longleaf-slash pine ecosystem, restricted to flat and irregular southern Gulf Coastal Plains. Local relief is less than 300 feet. Much of this area is forested. The elevation ranges from sea level to 75 feet. This nearly level low coastal plain is crossed by many large streams, lakes and ponds. The average annual precipitation is 1,325 to 1,625 millimeters. The abundant rainfall and the many perennial streams are important sources of water. The dominant soils are Aquults, Aquepts, and Aquods. These soils have a thermic temperature regime and an aquic moisture regime. They are, also, sandy and poorly drained or very poorly drained.

This area supports pine forest vegetation. Chalky bluestem, indian grass, and several panicum species make up the understory. Palmetto, gallberry, and waxmyrtle are the dominant woody shrubs. Longleaf and slash pine are the major trees. The fauna associated with longleaf-slash pine forest include the white-tailed deer, raccoon, the opossum, tree squirrels, rabbits, and numerous species of ground-dwelling rodents. The bobwhite and the wild turkey are the principal gallinaceous game birds. Resident and migratory nongame bird species are numerous, as are migratory waterfowl.

Historic Range and Current Distribution

Telephus spurge is known from only 22 sites, all within 4 miles of the Gulf of Mexico. This plant occurs in Bay, Gulf, and Franklin Counties from Panama City Beach to east of Apalachicola.

Conservation and Recovery

This species has fallen vulnerable to habitat degradation due to lack of prescribed fire and forestry practices.

Development of improved cattle pastures has probably destroyed habitat of this species. The forest products industry has modified habitat by planting and harvest slash pine and by the Forest Service planting of longleaf pine. Site preparation that precedes tree planting may destroy plants. Shading of this species by neighboring grasses and by pine trees after canopy closure most likely adversely affects the species.

Landowner liability for fire has discouraged prescribed burning of pineland in Florida which, also, may have adversely affected this species. The Forest Service conducts some prescribed burns during the growing season to reduce the incidence of Brown-spot infection of longleaf pine seed-lings.

Five of 22 known sites are on highway right-of-ways posing a threat if the roads were ever widened.

Conservation measures provided to species listed as endangered or threatened pursuant to the Act include recognition, recovery actions, requirements for Federal protection, and prohibitions against certain practices. Recognition through listing encourages conservation measures by Federal, international, and private agencies, groups, and individuals.

Bibliography

U.S. Fish and Wildlife Service. "Endangered and Threatened Wildlife and Plants; Threatened Status for Three Florida Plants." *Federal Register* Vol 57, No 90, May 8, 1992: 19813-19819.

Contacts

USFWS Regional Office
Suite 200, 1875 Century Blvd.
Atlanta, GA 30345
Phone: 404-679-4000

Ecological Services Field Office
1612 June Avenue
Panama City, FL 32405-3721
Phone: 904-769-0552
FAX: 904-763-2177

Adapted from data compiled by the Threatened and Endangered Species Information Institute (13950 W. 20th Ave., Golden, CO 80401) for *Beacham's International Threatened, Endangered, and Extinct Species* published on CD ROM, available from Beacham Publishing.

Penland Alpine Fen Mustard

Eutrema penlandii

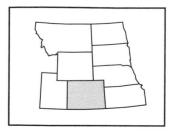

Jeff Dawson

Status	Threatened
Listed	July 28, 1993
Family	Brassicaceae (Mustard)
Description	Small, herbaceous shiny green peren-nial with heart-shaped basal leaves and small, white clustered flowers.
Habitat	Alpine marshes of Colorado.
Threats	Surface disturbances due to ditching; recreational sports, such as hiking.
Range	Colorado

Description

Members of the mustard family are characterized by erect, branching glabrous, glacous or pubescent stems. The flowers are in racemes; the sepals are erect; and the petals are large.

The penland alpine fen mustard, *Eutrema penlandii*, is a small herbaceous perennial. This plant grows 3 to 8 centimeters. This glabrous species is shiny-green with long-petioled, heart-shaped basal leaves. Penland alpine fen mustard possesses clusters of small, white flowers on top of the stems. The fruit is small, rounded and hollow.

Habitat

Penland alpine fen mustard grows in a harsh Colorado alpine environment. Alpine winters in Colorado may last 5 or more months and summer temperatures are usually below 16 degrees Celsius. Low plant productivity in the tundra is a result of soli-fluction, drying winds and windblown snow and ice crystals.

This plant is habitat-specific and grows only in alpine marshes lacking in plant nutrients. It grows in a climate of long, cold, wet winters and cool, windy summers. This species inhabits moss-covered peat fens, perennial subirrigation and high elevations (3,703 meters). Snowfields provide water required to sustain and develop peat mats. Conditions best for maintaining these persistent snowfields exist along the east-west trending portion of the Continental Divide. It is here that Penland alpine fen mustard can be found on slopes that vary from southerly to easterly.

Penland alpine fen mustard is found on

deep organic soils in moist areas that are generally adjacent to running water from snowmelt. It has been reported that plant emergence at a site is directly dependant on the availability and timing of sufficient water to moisten the peat mosses in which this taxon roots.

Historic Range

There are a few scenarios for the introduction of this taxon to its Arctic environment. Penland alpine fen mustard may be a glacial relict from the Pleistocene epoch that migrated south of the Arctic with glaciation and was left stranded as the glaciers retreated. Alternatively, populations of Penland alpine fen mustard may be a relict of a more widespread Tertiary flora.

Current Distribution

Five to fourteen small populations of Penland alpine fen mustard are distributed in a 40 kilometer stretch of the Continental Divide in central Colorado. The total number of individuals is estimated to be 10,000 to 16,400. This species is restricted to wetland habitats irrigated by melting snowfields. Penland alpine fen mustard is directly threatened by activities of man.

At present population levels, Penland alpine fen mustard is not likely to become extinct in the foreseeable future. However, threats concentrated towards this species indicate that it is likely to become endangered in the near future in all or most of its present range.

The largest populations of Penland alpine fen mustard occur on Federal lands administered by the Forest Service and Bureau of Land Management.

Conservation and Recovery

Penland alpine fen mustard is a restricted endemic species, whose fragile wetland habitat is being threatened by anthropogenic development.

Suitable habitat for Penland alpine fen mustard is rare; it appears that this species does not exist outside the Mosquito Range in Colorado. The most crucial aspect of this species' habitat is the continuous need for water to maintain the peat fens in which this species takes root. Because stands of this plant are so small, they are vulnerable to surface disturbances that reroute the needed water supply. This can occur from ditching, diking, or other watershed perturbations that alter surface water flow.

Old mines occur near all populations of this plant and most mines on public lands are active. These activities adversely affect Penland alpine fen mustard and if allowed to continue it will surely mean extirpation of population.

Recreation activities are increasing in alpine areas of the Mosquito Range and pose a potential threat to the success of this species' recovery. Hiking seems rather benign until faced with the bipedal tracks of four thousand visitors. Off-road vehicles are adversely impacting alpine areas of the Mosquito Range. Numerous roads associated with tracts of privately owned mining claims provide vehicular access to most alpine areas.

Conservation measures provided to species listed as endangered or threatened under the Endangered Species Act include recognition, recovery actions, requirements for Federal protection, and prohibitions against certain practices. Recognition through listing encourages conservation measures by Federal, international, and private agencies, groups, and individuals.

The Bureau of Land Management considers this plant a sensitive species for management planning purposes. However, the species is not necessarily given priority in multipleuse considerations. The area around Mosquito Pass has been nominated as an Area of Critical Environmental Concern. If designation is accepted, managers can take values into consideration when developing resource management plans. Populations of Penland alpine fen mustard are included within the nominated area.

Bibliography

U.S. Fish and Wildlife Service. "Endangered and Threatened Wildlife and Plants; The Plant *Eutrema penlandii* (Penland Alpine Fen Mustard) Determined to be a Threatened Species." *Federal Register*. Vol. 58, No. 143. July 28, 1993: 40539-40547.

Contacts

USFWS Regional Office
P. O. Box 25486
Denver, CO 80225
Phone: 303-236-7920

Adapted from data compiled by the Threatened and Endangered Species Information Institute (13950 W. 20th Ave., Golden, CO 80401) for *Beacham's International Threatened, Endangered, and Extinct Species* published on CD ROM, available from Beacham Publishing.

Monterey Gilia

Gilia tenuiflora ssp. *arenaria*

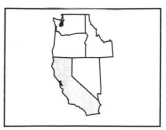

Status	Endangered
Listed	June 22, 1992
Family	Polemoniaceae (Phlox)
Description	Annual herb with rosettes, narrow petals and narrow purple throat.
Habitat	Coastal foredunes and coastal dune scrub communities.
Threats	Invasion of alien plants, proposed commercial and residential development, off-road vehicle damage.
Range	California

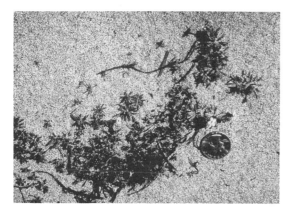

Susan Cochrane, California Native Plant Society

Description

The Monterey gilia is an erect short rosette-forming, annual herb, usually less than 1.7 decimeters tall. The narrow petals and narrow purple throat of the funnel-shaped flower, the open inflorescence, the short fruits or capsules measuring 3.5 to 5 millimeters and the slightly exerted stamens separate this subspecies from the other *gilia tenuiflora* subspecies.

Habitat

The Monterey gilia is associated with the California Coastal Redwood Belt, Siskiyou-Trinity Area, Central California Coastal Valleys and Central California Coast Range. Broadly, these regions have an elevation from sea level to 900 meters; average annual precipitation of 300 to 850 millimeters dis-

tributed throughout the year; perennial streams and lakes are distributed throughout the regions and glacial and alluvial deposits in the valley also yield large quantities of water; the soils are well drained on gently sloping to very steep slopes. The erosion hazard is high in this area and is stabilized only by plant cover. Much of this land is federally owned and the remaining is used for lumbering, grazing, wildlife habitat and recreation.

The Monterey gilia is restricted to the coastal foredunes and coastal dune scrub communities and associated habitats occupied by coastal scrub or coastal terrace prairie. In the dune systems north of Monterey Bay, sand-stabilizing rhizomatous grasses, *Ammophila arenaria* and *Elymus mollis* generally dominate the vegetation of the foredunes. *Ammophila arenaria*, European beach grass or marram grass, is an alien species that has largely replaced the native Elymus-dominated foredune community. Beach grass is believed to be a powerful geomorphic agent due to its ability to build continuous wall-like foredunes, which were not previously in this region. Although the Elymus-dominated foredune community exists around Monterey Bay, these foredunes typically consist of low hillocks and mounds that are sparsely populated with generally succulent, tap-rooted perennial herbs. The stabilization of the dunes by *Ammophila arenaria* has permitted the colonization of formerly active backdune areas with a mixture of native and alien plants. These backdune areas consist of a soft, woody, dense plant community of short shrubs and subshrubs, and herbaceous plants.

The Monterey gilia is restricted to isolated occurrences within wind-sheltered, sparsely vegetated areas and is associated with coastal dune scrub or Flandrian dune habitat.

Historic Range and Current Distribution

The past and present distribution of the Monterey gilia is essentially the same given the discontinuous isolated populations of present. This taxon is restricted to portions of the Monterey Bay and Monterey Peninsula in Monterey County, California. This species' range inhabits portions of Salinas River State Beach and private land.

Conservation and Recovery

The native plant fauna of the California coast dune scrub communities is threatened by a number of factors including: invasion of alien plants, proposed commercial and residential development, military operational uses, off-road vehicle damage, and trampling by equestrians, hikers and livestock. Poten-

tial threats include sand mining, disposal of dredged material from adjacent bays and waterways and stochastic extinction due to depauperate numbers.

The introduction and invasion of California's ecosystems by alien plants has adversely affected the Monterey gilia. The invasion of *Ammophila arenaria* has resulted in the development of wall-like foredunes and colonization of native and alien plants. Other alien species include sea-rocket (Cakile spp), ice plant or sea-fig, and several annual grasses and forbs generally restricted to wetland habitats within the dunes. In many cases, these aliens outcompete and largely supplant the native dune vegetation. Typically, annuals and monocarpic plants such as the Monterey gilia are vulnerable to random fluctuations or variation in annual weather patterns and other environmental factors.

The Monterey gilia has limited historical distributions and likely has been eliminated from all but a small fraction of its historical dune or associated habitats. Today, the Monterey gilia generally persists as small "island" populations surrounded by urban areas, roads, trails, agricultural lands, competing alien plants, and other lands made unsuitable for this species.

The Monterey gilia is restricted to isolated sites within coastal dune scrub communities. The construction of a golf course in 1987 near Spanish Bay on the Monterey Peninsula eliminated a significant portion of a population. The developer attempted to mitigate for the project via the transplantation of this subspecies on an artificial dune, to no avail. Populations within Salinas River State Beach remain subject to off-road vehicle use, and trampling by hikers and equestrians. The population within Asilomar State Beach is on a steep bluff face, inaccessible to the public. Commercial and residential development threatens the remaining populations.

Bibliography

U.S. Fish and Wildlife Service. "Endangered and Threatened Wildlife and Plants; Six Plants and Myrtle's Silverspot Butterfly From Coastal Dunes in Northern and Central California Determined to Be Endangered." *Federal Register* Vol. 57, No. 120, June 22, 1992: 27848-27858

Contacts

Sacramento Ecological Services
    Field Office
Room E-1803/1823
2800 Cottage Way
Sacramento, CA 98525
Phone: 916-978-4866
FAX: 916-978-4613

Adapted from data compiled by the Threatened and Endangered Species Information Institute (13950 W. 20th Ave., Golden, CO 80401) for *Beacham's International Threatened, Endangered, and Extinct Species* published on CD ROM, available from Beacham Publishing.

Holy Ghost Ipomopsis
Ipomopsis sancti-spiritus

Anne Cully, USFWS

Status	Endangered
Listed	March 23, 1994
Family	Polemoniaceae (Phlox)
Description	Erect plant with solitary stems, oval leaves, and tubular, pink flowers.
Habitat	Small openings or clearings on steep forested slopes.
Threats	Road maintenance, wildfire, fire management, and possible pesticide spraying.
Range	New Mexico

Description

The Holy Ghost ipomopsis is an erect, biennial to short lived perennial plant, 12 to 31 inches tall, with mostly solitary stems, and occasionally branched from the base. The leaves are oval, 1 to 2.4 inches long, with 9 to 15 linear divisions. The basal leaves form a loose to compact rosette that dies back at flowering. The leaves are gradually reduced in size up the length of the stem. The flowers are tubular, pink, and about 0.8 to 1 inch long. The stamens do not extend beyond the corolla tube. This species is distinguished from others in the genus by its shorter flower ovary and stigma.

Habitat

The single known population occurs at approximately 8,000 feet in a 2 mile segment of a canyon in the Sangre de Cristo mountains of New Mexico. The plants are restricted to steep, south- or southwest-facing slopes, primarily in openings under ponderous pine, Douglas fir, Gambel oak, and quaking aspen. The substrate is a sandy to pebbly limestone conglomerate derived from the Terrero and Spiritu Santo formations.

The plant grows in small openings or clearings on the forested slopes, and it is likely that fire may have played a role in the past in maintaining open habitat for this species. Plants have colonized the cut-and-fill slopes of a Forest Service road, indicating some preference for open, disturbed areas.

Historic Range

The historic range is not known but apparently occurs only in the Sangre de Cristo mountains.

Current Distribution

The entire population of the Holy Ghost ipomopsis consists of approximately 1,200 to 2,500 plants, located on Forest Service and private lands within boundaries of the Santa Fe National Forest. Approximately 80 percent of the population occupies the cut-and-fill slopes along a Forest Service road; the remaining 20 percent occurs on the natural dry and open habitat higher up on the canyon slope.

Surveys conducted in 1991 by Forest Service personnel and New Mexico Energy, Minerals and Natural Resources Department botanists within a 15 mile radius of the known population failed to locate any additional populations of the species.

Conservation and Recovery

Most of the occupied habitat is along a Forest Service road that provides access to summer homes and Forest Service campgrounds. In this location, the plants and their habitat are vulnerable to harm from road maintenance, wildfire, fire management, and possible pesticide spraying.

The species occurs in an area that has been heavily used for recreation for at least 50 years, which includes 36 cabins, a campground, and a nearby trout stream. Because of its recreational use, the forest has been protected from timber harvests, and as the forest has matured and natural openings become less numerous, Holy Ghost ipomopsis has become associated with man-made disturbances which created open land. The presence of people in these manmade areas creates a threat to the species. For example, a Forest Service road was graveled with crushed waste rock from an abandoned mine. The sulfides in this mine waste created highly acidic road runoff that killed the surrounding vegetation.

The biological pest control BT is commonly used for outbreaks of spruce budworm. Both the U.S. Forest Service and the State of New Mexico have used BT. Because of the anatomical characteristics of its flower, Holy Ghost ipomopsis is thought to be pollinated by various moths and butterflies, which are highly susceptible to BT. Elimination of these pollinators could reduce seed production and seedling recruitment, and contribute to the decline of the plant.

Propagation material was obtained by a commercial grower of native plants. Nursery propagation of this species could provide a commercial source and thus discourage the collection or digging of plants from wild populations. Propagation knowledge gained by the commercial grower may be of considerable value in establishing refugial populations in natural habitats within the species range.

Because of Holy Ghost ipomopsis's showy flowers, overcollection could present a serious threat. Horticulturists and rare plant enthusiasts are constantly looking for new plants for commercial use.

Bibliography

Sivinski, R. and K. Lightfoot. 1991. Status report on *Ipomopsis sancti-spiritus*. U.S. Fish and Wildlife Service. Albuquerque, NM. 17 pp.

U.S. Fish and Wildlife Service. "Endangered and Threatened Wildlife and Plants: Endangered Status for the Plant *Ipomopsis Sancti-Spiritus* (Holy Ghost Ipomopsis). *Federal Register* Vol. 59, No. 56. March 23, 1994: 13836-13840.

Contacts

USFWS New Mexico Ecological Services
    Field Office
3530 Pan American Highway, NE, Suite D
Albuquerque, NM 87107
505-883-7877

Adapted from data compiled by Beacham Publishing for *Beacham's International Threatened, Endangered, and Extinct Species* published on CD
ROM.

Louisiana Quillwort

Isoetes louisianensis

Julia Larke, Louisiana Department of Fisheries and Wildlife

Status	Endangered
Listed	October 28, 1992
Family	Isoetaceae (Quillwort)
Description	Small, grasslike aquatic herb with rounded, hollow numerous leaves.
Habitat	Small to medium-sized shallow, clear streams through riparian forests.
Threats	Clearcutting of streambank timber, canopy removal.
Range	Louisiana

Description

The Louisiana quillwort is a small, grass-like aquatic herb in the quillwort family. Louisiana quillwort is a seedless vascular plant which reproduces by spores and is closely related to ferns. The species' slender quill-like leaves arise from a short fleshy stem or corm that is shallowly rooted in the substrate. The leaves are rounded, hollow and swollen at their base. Leaves are numerous, varying in length from 6 to 16 inches depending on water depth. The sporangia, or spore-containing structures, are embedded in the broadened bases of the leaves. The species is heterosporous, producing both megasporangia and microsporangia. The species is characterized by its born-spotted sporangial walls and megaspores with high reticulate ridges producing a spiny effect. Louisiana quillwort has been reported to sporulate twice a year, producing megaspores in the spring and microspores in the fall.

Habitat

This semi-aquatic plant is known from 3 locations in Louisiana. The streams in which the species is found are typically small to medium sized, shallow and with clear, tannin-colored water, running through narrow riparian forest communities. Preferred substrates are stable mixtures of silt, sand, and gravel. Louisiana quillwort occurs predominately on sand and gravel bars on accreting sides of streams and in moist overflow channels. The species is found less commonly on low sloping banks near, and occasionally below, the low water level. Individuals are regularly inundated as much as 20 inches of water following rains, and may be inundated for long periods in wet seasons. Corm depth has been found as great as 1.2 inches, indicating a tolerance for some deposition of materials. The species may be found singly or in numbers of several hundred.

Historic Range and Current Distribution

Louisiana quillwort is known to exist in 3 locations in Washington and St. Tammany Parishes in Louisiana. The largest two populations contain several hundred individuals each; the smallest contains only 4 immature individuals. It is possible the species was once more widespread, but there is no concrete evidence to support this. The most extensive population occurs in portions of Thigpen and Clearwater Creeks. Four individuals are known from the Mill Creek area. A population in the Little Bogue Falaya Creek contains several hundred individuals.

Conservation and Recovery

The primary threats to Louisiana quillwort are activities that would affect the hydrology or stability of the streams in which it occurs. The species has been eliminated from one location by construction activities and canopy removal. It has been affected in another portion of this area by changes in vegetation composition due to clearcutting of streambank timber and flow diversion.

All known stream habitat supporting this species is associated with a well-developed stream canopy. Canopy removal alters the light regime under which the species is currently known to exist. Some streambank timber harvest have occurred at various locations along all streams supporting Louisiana quillwort. It is believed that these harvests have adversely affected the species. Streambank timber removal can also lead to an increase in surface runoff and contribute to stream erosion and/or siltation.

Sand and gravel mining along the species' range is affecting the hydrology, water quality, and substrate stability of that area. Portions of the area have been completely cleared, channelized or rerouted by sand and gravel mining activities. Headwaters into one area have been ditched to direct surface drainage away from the mining operation. Excessive algal growth and sediment pollution has occurred due to this alteration of the hydrologic regime. All of these factors threaten the existence of this species.

The recovery efforts of Louisiana quillwort include the following. Further searches for undiscovered individuals in similar habitats need to be conducted. Studies into the reproductive cycle and specific habitat requirements could lead to a better understanding of the species. This information could be used to develop a cultivation and seed bank program that could be used to reintroduce the species in appropriate habitat. Binding agreements with private landowners or possible land acquisition should be considered to protect the few remaining populations that occur on private land. Timber harvesting throughout the species' range should be carefully monitored to help keep the canopy intact. Further mining permits and water diversions throughout the species' range should be carefully considered so as not to further impact Louisiana quillwort.

Bibliography

U.S. Fish and Wildlife Service. "Endangered and Threatened Wildlife and Plants: Determination of Endangered Status for the Plant *Isoetes louisianensis* (Louisiana Quillwort)." *Federal Register* Vol. 57, October 28, 1992: 48741-48746.

Contacts

Ecological Services Field Office
Suite 102, Brandywine II
825 Kaliste Saloom Road
Lafayette, LA 70508
Phone: 318-262-6630
FAX: 318-262-6663

Louisiana Natural Heritage Program
Department of Wildlife and Fisheries
P. O. Box 98000
Baton Rouge, LA 70898-9000
Phone: 504-765-2821
FAX: 504-765-2607

Adapted from data compiled by the Threatened and Endangered Species Information Institute (13950 W. 20th Ave., Golden, CO 80401) for *Beacham's International Threatened, Endangered, and Extinct Species* published on CD ROM, available from Beacham Publishing.

Beach Jacquemontia

Jacquemontia reclinata

Roger L. Hammer

Status	Endangered
Listed	November 24, 1993
Family	Convolvulaceae (Morning-glory)
Description	Sprawling, perennial vine with fleshy oval leaves, with glabrous margins and flowers in the axils.
Habitat	Tropical maritime hammocks or the coastal strand vegetation.
Threats	Habitat loss due to creation of parking lots, pedestrian routes, and picnic areas.
Range	Florida

Description

The beach jacquemontia is a sprawling, perennial vine whose stems are 1 meter long. The elliptic to oval leaves are fleshy, with glabrous margins. Younger leaves and stems are hairy enough to appear white. The flowers are in the axils of the leaves and may be in groups or solitary. The outer sepals of the flower have tiny hairs along the margins.

Habitat

The beach jacquemontia inhabits disturbed or sunny areas in tropical maritime hammocks or the coastal strand vegetation. Associated species included sea grape shrubs, Madagascar periwinkle, sand spurs, and dwarfed trees. Occasionally, the beach jacquemontia is found in the beach dune community associated with sea oats.

Historic Range and Current Distribution

The beach jacquemontia is native to coastal barrier islands in southeast Florida and Miami northward to Palm Beach County. This plant is known from Palm Beach County, Broward County and Dade County, Florida.

Conservation and Recovery

Much of this plant's habitat has been destroyed by urban development. Its primary habitat (beach strand and maritime hammock vegetation) is being destroyed and modified for parking lots, pedestrian routes, picnic areas and other park uses.

Habitat degradation due to exotic plant invasion has adversely affected this plant. A site in northern Palm Beach County is being overgrown by Brazilian pepper. Mowing, possible herbicide use, and park maintenance activities also threaten the beach jacquemontia.

Conservation measures provided to species listed as endangered or threatened pursuant to the Act include recognition, recovery actions, requirements for Federal protection, and prohibitions against certain practices. Recognition through listing encourages conservation measures by Federal, international, and private agencies, groups, and individuals.

The beach jacquemontia has been propagated from seed at Fairchild Tropical Garden and is thriving in cultivation at the Garden despite Hurricane Andrew.

Bibliography

Humphrey, Stephen R. "How Species Become Vulnerable To Extinction and How We Can Meet the Crisis." *Animal Extinctions: What Everyone Should Know.* Washington, DC: Smithsonian Institution Press, 1985.

U.S. Fish and Wildlife Service. "Endangered and Threatened Wildlife and Plants: Determination of Endangered Status for the Plant *Jacquemontia reclinata* (Beach Jacquemontia)." *Federal Register.* November 24, 1993.

Contacts

U.S. Fish and Wildlife Service
Regional Office
Suite 200, 1875 Century Blvd.
Atlanta, GA 30345
Phone: 404-679-4000

Ecological Services Field Office
Suite 310, 6620 Southpoint Drive, South
Jacksonville, FL 32216-0912
Phone: 904-232-2580
FAX: 904-232-2404

Ecological Services Field Office
1612 June Avenue
Panama City, FL 32405-3721
Phone: 904-769-0552
FAX: 904-763-2177

Adapted from data compiled by the Threatened and Endangered Species Information Institute (13950 W. 20th Ave., Golden, CO 80401) for *Beacham's International Threatened, Endangered, and Extinct Species* published on CD ROM, available from Beacham Publishing.

Beach Layia
Layia carnosa

Ken Berg, California Native Plant Society

Status	Endangered
Listed	June 22, 1992
Family	Asteraceae (Aster)
Description	Low growing winter annual with white flowers and sticky fleshy leaves.
Habitat	Coastal foredunes and coastal dune scrub communities.
Threats	Invasion of alien plants, proposed commercial and residential development, hikers, livestock trampling.
Range	California

Description

The beach layia is a low growing (less than 15 centimeters), succulent, glandular winter annual. These highly branched individuals often disperse more than 4 decimeters in diameter. The sticky fleshy leaves are short (2 to 4 millimeters). The ray flowers are white, and the bristles about the summit of the achene differentiate this taxa from other species of Layia.

Habitat

The beach layia is associated with the California Coastal Redwood Belt, Siskiyou-Trinity Area, Central California Coastal Valleys, and Central California Coast Range. Broadly, these regions have an elevation from sea level to 900 meters; average annual precipitation of 300 to 850 millimeters distributed throughout the year; perennial streams and lakes are distributed throughout the regions and glacial and alluvial deposits in the valley also yield large quantities of water; the dominant soils are Umbrepts, Xerults, Xerolls, Humults or Ochrepts, well drained and gently sloping to very steep soils with a mesic to xeric temperature regime and a mixed mineralogy. The erosion hazard is high in this area and is stabilized only by plant cover. Much of this land is federally owned and the remaining is used for lumbering, grazing, wildlife habitat and recreation.

This species is restricted to the coastal foredunes and coastal dune scrub communities and associated habitats occupied by coastal scrub or coastal terrace prairie. In the dune systems north of Monterey Bay, sand-stabilizing rhizomatous grasses, *Ammophila arenaria* and *Elymus mollis* generally dominate the vegetation of the foredunes. *Ammophila arenaria,* European beach grass or marram grass, is an alien species that has largely replaced the native Elymus-dominated foredune community. Beach grass is believed to be a powerful geomorphic agent due to its ability to build continuous wall-like foredunes, which were not previously in this region. Although the Elymus-dominated foredune community exists around Monterey Bay, these foredunes typically consist of low hillocks and mounds that are sparsely populated with generally succulent, tap-rooted perennial herbs. *Abronia latifolia, Ambrosia chamissonis, Calystegia solandella, Camissonia* spp., *Carpobrotus aequilaterus, C. edulis* and *Fragaria chiloensis* are common associates. The stabilization of the dunes by European beach grass has permitted the colonization of formerly active backdune areas with a mixture of native and alien plants. These backdune areas consist of a soft, woody, dense plant community of short shrubs and subshrubs, and herbaceous plants.

Historic Range

Historically, Beach layia was restricted the coastal foredunes of eight dune systems of western California. It has been extirpated from Santa Barbara County.

Current Distribution

Presently, the species occurs from the Humboldt Bay dune system in Humboldt County, California, and within privately owned Lanphere-Christensen Dunes Preserve (The Nature Conservancy). The species also occurs on Samoa Peninsula which is managed by the Bureau of Land Management.

Conservation and Recovery

The native plant fauna of the California coast dune scrub communities is threatened by a number of factors including: invasion of alien plants, proposed commercial and residential development, military operational uses, off-road vehicle damage, trampling by equestrians, hikers and livestock. Potential threats include sand mining, disposal of dredged material from adjacent bays and waterways and stochastic extinction due to depauperate numbers.

The introduction and invasion of California's ecosystems by alien plants has adversely affected Beach layia. The invasion of European beach grass has resulted in the development of wall-like foredunes and colonization of native and alien plants. Other alien species include sea-rocket ice plant or sea-fig, and several annual grasses and forbs generally restricted to wetland habitats within the dunes. In many cases, these aliens outcompete and largely supplant the native dune vegetation. Typically, annuals and monocarpic plants such as Beach layia are vulnerable to random fluctuations or variation in annual weather patterns and other environmental factors.

Beach layia has limited historical distributions and likely has been eliminated from all but a small fraction of its historical dune or associated habitats. Today, this species generally persists as small "island" populations surrounded by urban areas, roads, trails, agricultural lands, competing alien plants, and other lands made unsuitable for Beach layia.

Exotic vegetation and highway construction reportedly eliminated Beach layia and other native plant community members from the Little River area. The development of the Golden Gate Park in 1904 (San Francisco County) and the urban growth of San Francisco eliminated this population and the dune system in which it occurred.

Conservation measures provided to species listed as endangered or threatened pursuant to the Act include recognition, recovery actions, requirements for Federal protection, and prohibitions against certain practices. Recognition through listing encourages conservation measures by Federal, international, and private agencies, groups, and individuals.

Federal activities potentially impacting Beach layia would likely involve restricting/managing navigation and port-related projects and perhaps grazing practices on Federal land.

Bibliography

U.S. Fish and Wildlife Service. "Endangered and Threatened Wildlife and Plants; Six Plants and Myrtle's Silverspot Butterfly From Coastal Dunes in Northern and Central California Determined to Be Endangered." *Federal Register* Vol. 57, No. 120. June 22, 1992: 27848-27858.

Contacts

U.S. Fish and Wildlife Service
   Regional Office
Eastside Federal Complex
911 N.S. 11th Avenue
Portland, OR 97232-4181
Phone: 503-231-6118

Sacramento Ecological Services Field Office
Room E-1803/1823
2800 Cottage Way
Sacramento, CA 98525
Phone: 916-978-4866
FAX: 916-978-4613

Adapted from data compiled by the Threatened and Endangered Species Information Institute (13950 W. 20th Ave., Golden, CO 80401) for *Beacham's International Threatened, Endangered, and Extinct Species* published on CD ROM, available from Beacham Publishing.

Kodachrome Bladderpod
Lesquerella tumulosa

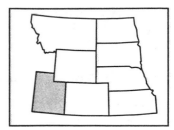

Ben Franklin   *Color Plate C-2*

Status	Endangered
Listed	October 6, 1993
Family	Brassiaceae (Mustard)
Description	Herbaceous perennial growing in dense, cushionlike clumps, with branches that have numerous withering leaves, and yellow flowers.
Habitat	Restricted to very dry shale outcrops.
Threats	Limited population; off-road vehicles, and mineral development.
Range	Utah

Description

The Kodachrome bladderpod is a herbaceous perennial. This species grows in dense, cushionlike clumps born from a many-branched caudex (thicked base of the stem). The caudex branches are clothed with numerous marcescent (withering) leaves and leaf bases. The stems are 1 to 4 centimeters long and have basal leaves. The leaves are 2 to 10 millimeters long and are not differentiated into a blade and petiole. The flowers have spatula-like, yellow petals 5 to 7 millimeters long. The fruit of this species is an ovoid silicle (pod) about 3 millimeters long, and containing 204 seeds.

Habitat

The Kodachrome bladderpod is endemic to lower elevations of the Paria River drainage in Kane County in southern Utah, were it grows on soils derived from the Carmel geological formation. This plant is restricted to very dry shale outcrops at about 1,740 meters elevation.

It is often associated with pinyon pine, Utah juniper, Betterbrush, *Purshia tridentata*, Yellow cryptantha, *Cryptantha flava*, Indian rice grass, *Stipa hymenoides*, Wild buckwheat, *Eriogonum corymbosum*, Pallid milkweed, *Asclepias cryptoceras*, Hyaline herb, *Hymenopappus filifolius*, and Morning-lily, *Oenothera caespitosa*.

Historic Range and Current Distribution

This species is restricted to one population of about 20,000 plants that have a total range of about 2.5 miles. It is found only in the Kodachrome flats near the Paria Ridge drainage on public lands in northern Kane County, in south-central Utah.

Conservation and Recovery

This plant is threatened by off-road vehicles and mineral development. A single small population remains and is additionally threatened by a limited range. The population is on State and Federal lands and is vulnerable to surface disturbance associated with industrial development within its habitat. An active gravel quarry is present on the habitat of this species, and the remainder is subject to leasing for oil and gas mining. Portions of the habitat have been destroyed by prospecting and excavating gravel and clay. A paved road which was recently constructed provides increased access to what is left of the population.

Sheep and cattle grazing may have affected this species in the past, but is not considered a certain threat.

Conservation measures provided to species listed as endangered or threatened pursuant to the Act include recognition, recovery actions, requirements for Federal protection, and prohibitions against certain practices. Recognition through listing encourages conservation measures by Federal, international, and private agencies, groups, and individuals.

The Utah State Land Board is authorized to provide conservation planning for federally listed endangered and threatened plant species; the listing of this species delegate new attention will be paid to its conservation in the future.

As this species also occurs on lands administered by the Bureau of Land Management, special consideration will be made to the Kodachrome bladderpod in issuing leases of minerals.

Bibliography

Soil Conservation Service. *Land Resource Regions and Major Land Resource Areas of The United States*. Soil Conservation Service, 1981. 156 pp.

U.S. Fish and Wildlife Service. "Endangered and Threatened Wildlife and Plants; Final Rule to Determine a Utah Plant, *Lesquerella tumulosa* (Kodachrome bladderpod), as an Endangered Species." *Federal Register*. Vol. 58, No. 192. October 6, 1993: 52027-52031.

Contacts

U.S. Fish and Wildlife Service
Regional Office
P. O. Box 25486
Denver, CO 80225
Phone: 303-236-7920

Ecological Services Field Office
Lincoln Plaza
145 East 1300 South, Suite 404
Salt Lake City, UT 84115

Adapted from data compiled by the Threatened and Endangered Species Information Institute (13950 W. 20th Ave., Golden, CO 80401) for *Beacham's International Threatened, Endangered, and Extinct Species* published on CD ROM, available from Beacham Publishing.

Butte County Meadowfoam
Limnanthes floccosa ssp. *californica*

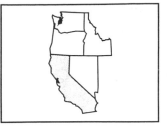

Jim Jokerst, California Native Plant Society

Status	Endangered
Listed	June 8, 1992
Family	Limnanthaceae (False Mermaid)
Description	Hairy winter annual herb with dark-yellow veined white flowers at the base of each of the five petals.
Habitat	Edges of deep vernal pools in undisturbed areas.
Threats	Urban and agricultural development.
Range	California

Description

The false mermaid family contains plants characterized by alternate leaves, and 3 to 5 flowers that are regular and perfect. The Butte County meadowfoam is a densely hairy winter annual herb. The stems, which grow along the ground, are 3 to 25 centimeters long. Appearing in late March through April, the flowers of this plant are white with dark yellow veins at the base of each of the five petals.

Habitat

Butte County meadowfoam is known to grow in seasonal wetlands, and has been reported to inhabit edges of deep vernal pools in undisturbed areas. It occurs in ephemeral drainages, vernal pool depressions in ephemeral drainages and occasionally around the edges of isolated vernal pools.

Vernal pools form in regions with Mediterranean climates where shallow depressions fill with water during fall and winter rains. Downward percolation is prevented by the presence of an impervious subsurface layer, such as a clay bed, hardpan, or volcanic stratum. Plant species occurring in vernal pools are uniquely adapted to this "amphibious ecosystem" seasonal alteration of very wet and very dry conditions. Upland plants cannot tolerate the temporarily saturated to flooded soils of winter and spring while the seasonal drying makes the pool basins unsuitable for marsh or aquatic species requiring a permanent source of water.

A unique flora is represented within the vernal pool system, with species and genera which occur nowhere else.

Historic Range and Current Distribution

The Butte County meadowfoam is restricted to a narrow strip along the eastern flank of the Sacramento Valley from central Butte County to the northern portion of Chico in Tehama County, California.

Conservation and Recovery

The Butte County meadowfoam is primarily threatened by urban development in and around Chico in Butte County, California. Nine of the 11 populations occurring either partially or totally on private lands in the Chico area are threatened by urbanization. These sites have been zoned by the City of Chico for various types of urban uses, like residential, neighborhood commercial, or manufacturing-industrial park. Twelve of the remaining populations are vulnerable to urban development as well as airport maintenance activities.

Ninety percent of the population at the type locality was destroyed due to agricultural development (ag-land conversion).

One population outside the Chico area is threatened by the proposed construction of housing funded by U.S. Department of Housing and Urban Development.

This species may have agronomic value and has already been the focus of potential for agricultural use.

Livestock grazing has eliminated the meadowfoam from suitable habitat in the Chico area. This species seems tolerant to light to moderate to periodic heavy grazing pressure.

In 1989 a conservation plan was developed for the City of Chico that details various actions designed to conserve the Butte County meadowfoam in the Chico area. The plan was adopted on October 17, 1989 with an addendum which instituted the City's mitigation procedure for projects affecting the subspecies. The addendum called for the establishment of two "core preserves" and four "secondary preserves." On paper this plan should be an applauded effort, however, it relies primarily on dedication by the developer.

Bibliography

U.S. Fish and Wildlife. "Endangered and Threatened Wildlife and Plants; Determination of Endangered Status for the Plant *Limnanthes floccosa* ssp. *californica* (Butte County Meadow foam)." *Federal Register* Vol. 57, No. 110, June 8, 1992: 24192-24199.

Contacts

Sacramento Ecological Services Field Office
Room E-1803/1823
2800 Cottage Way
Sacramento, CA 98525
Phone: 916-978-4866
FAX: 916-978-4613

Adapted from data compiled by the Threatened and Endangered Species Information Institute (13950 W. 20th Ave., Golden, CO 80401) for *Beacham's International Threatened, Endangered, and Extinct Species* published on CD ROM, available from Beacham Publishing.

Clover Lupine

Lupinus tidestromii

Ronilee Clark   *Color Plate C-1*

Status	Endangered
Listed	June 22, 1992
Family	Fabaceae (Pea)
Description	Silky, creeping perennial herb with blue to lavender-colored flowers.
Habitat	Coastal foredunes and coastal dune scrub communities.
Threats	Proposed residential and commercial development, off-road vehicle damage.
Range	California

Description

The Clover Lupine is a low growing (1 to 3 decimeters), silky, creeping, sand-binding perennial herb. This species produces whorls of blue to lavender-colored flowers from May to June. The generally prostrate habit, bright yellow root, small leaflets (1.3 to 2 centimeters) long, and densely pubescent foliage distinguish this species from other members of Lupinus.

Habitat

This species is associated with the California Coastal Redwood Belt, Siskiyou-Trinity Area, Central California Coastal Valleys and Central California Coast Range. Broadly, these regions have an elevation from sea level to 900 meters; average annual precipitation of 300 to 850 millimeters distributed throughout the year; perennial streams and lakes are distributed throughout the regions and glacial and alluvial deposits in the valley also yield large quantities of water; the dominant soils are Umbrepts, Xerults, Xerolls, Humults or Ochrepts, well drained and gently sloping to very steep soils with a mesic to xeric temperature regime and a mixed mineralogy. The erosion hazard is high in this area and is stabilized only by plant cover. Much of this land is federally owned and the remaining is used for lumbering, grazing, wildlife habitat and recreation.

This species is restricted to the coastal foredunes and coastal dune scrub communities and associated habitats occupied by coastal scrub or coastal terrace prairie. In the dune systems north of Monterey Bay, sand-stabilizing rhizomatous grasses, *Ammophila arenaria* and *Elymus mollis* generally dominate the vegetation of the foredunes. European beach grass, or marram grass, is an alien species that has largely replaced the native Elymus-dominated foredune community. Beach grass is believed to be a powerful geomorphic agent due to its ability to build continuous wall-like foredunes, which were not previously in this region. Although the Elymus-dominated foredune community exists around Monterey Bay, these foredunes typically consist of low hillocks and mounds that are sparsely populated with generally succulent, tap-rooted perennial herbs. *Abronia latifolia, Ambrosia chamissonis, Calystegia solandella, Camissonia spp., Carpobrotus aequilaterus, C. edulis* and *Fragaria chiloensis* are common associates. The stabilization of the dunes by European beach grass has permitted the colonization of formerly active backdune areas with a mixture of native and alien plants. These backdune areas consist of a soft, woody, dense plant community of short shrubs and subshrubs, and herbaceous plants.

Historic Range and Current Distribution

Clover lupine is restricted to coastal foredunes and is discontinuously distributed in three dune systems. One locality is an isolated population along the south bank of the Russian River in Sonoma County, California. This distribution is the same as historical records indicate, although the populations are much more scattered and sparse. This species occurs on private, state and federally owned lands including lands owned by the U.S. Coast Guard, Point Reyes National Seashore, and Asilomar State Beach.

Conservation and Recovery

The native plant fauna of the California coast dune scrub communities is threatened by a number of factors, including invasion of alien plants, proposed commercial and residential development, military operational uses, off-road vehicle damage, and trampling by equestrians, hikers and livestock. Potential threats include sand mining, disposal of dredged material from adjacent bays and waterways and stochastic extinction due to depauperate numbers.

The introduction and invasion of California's ecosystems by alien plants has adversely affected this species. The invasion of European beach grass has resulted in the development of wall-like foredunes and colonization of native and alien plants. Other alien species include sea-rocket (*Cakile* spp), ice plant or sea-fig (*Carpobrotus* spp), and several annual grasses and forbs generally restricted to wetland habitats within the dunes. In many cases, these aliens outcompete and largely supplant the native dune vegetation. Typically, annuals and monocarpic plants such as this species are vulnerable to random fluctuations or variation in annual weather patterns and other environmental factors.

This species has limited historical distributions and likely has been eliminated from all but a small fraction of its historical dune or associated habitats. Today, this species generally persists as small "island" populations surrounded by urban areas, roads, trails, agricultural lands, competing alien plants, and other lands made unsuitable for this species.

Clover lupine is a coastal foredunes species occurring near the mouth of the Russian River and is discontinuously distributed on the Point Reyes and Monterey Peninsulas. Golf course construction in 1987 near the Spanish Bay on the Monterey Peninsula eliminated a portion of this species' population. The developer attempted to propagate the species in a false dune, but to no avail.

Though *L. tidestromii* occurs on Federal lands (U.S. Coast Guard and Point Reyes National Seashore), it has continued to be threatened by trampling by hikers and livestock. Those populations occurring on private lands are zoned for residential use, giving rise to the potential of further habitat alteration/destruction.

Conservation measures provided to species listed as endangered or threatened pursuant to the Act include recognition, recovery actions, requirements for Federal protection, and prohibitions against certain practices. Recognition through listing encourages conservation measures by Federal, international, and private agencies, groups, and individuals.

Federal activities potentially impacting this species would likely involve restricting/managing navigation and port-related projects and perhaps grazing practices on Federal land.

Boardwalks at Asilomar State Beach have been used to direct visitors away from sensitive areas and populations of this species.

Bibliography

U.S. Fish and Wildlife Service. 1992. "Endangered and Threatened Wildlife and Plants; Six Plants and Myrtle's Silverspot Butterfly From Coastal Dunes in Northern and Central California Determined to Be Endangered." *Federal Register*. Vol. 57, No. 120. June 22, 1992: 27848-27858.

Contacts

U.S. Fish and Wildlife Service
Eastside Federal Complex
911 N.S. 11th Avenue
Portland, OR 97232-4181
Phone: 503-231-6118

Adapted from data compiled by the Threatened and Endangered Species Information Institute (13950 W. 20th Ave., Golden, CO 80401) for *Beacham's International Threatened, Endangered, and Extinct Species* published on CD ROM, available from Beacham Publishing.

White Birds-in-a-Nest

Macbridea alba

Loran C. Anderson   *Color Plate C-4*

Status	Threatened
Listed	May 8, 1992
Family	Lamiaceae (Mint)
Description	Upright, single-stemmed, odorless perennial with fleshy rhizomes.
Habitat	Grassy vegetation on poorly drained, infertile sandy soils.
Threats	Habitat degradation due to lack of fire and forestry practices.
Range	Florida

Description

White birds-in-a-nest is an upright, usually single-stemmed, odorless perennial herb with fleshy rhizomes. This mint is about 30 to 40 centimeters tall with opposite leaves up to 10 centimeters long, 1 to 2 centimeters broad, with winged petioles. All the plants at a site will be either glabrous or pubescent. The clustered flowers are in a short spike with bracts. Each flower has a green calyx about 1 centimeters long and a brilliant white corolla 3 centimeters long. The corolla is two-lipped, and the upper lip hooklike. In flower, white birds-in-a-nest is conspicuous and unmistakable.

Habitat

This species is restricted to the Gulf coastal lowlands near the mouth of the Apalachicola River. This species inhabits grassy vegetation on poorly drained, infertile sandy soils. The wettest sites are grassy seepage bogs on gently slopes at the edges of forested or shrubby wetlands. This species also inhabits grass-sedge bogs (savannahs), which are nearly treeless and shrubless but have a rich flora of grasses, sedges and herbs. white birds-in-a nest also occurs in scrubby oak vegetation near the shoreline of the Gulf of Mexico.

Grassy savannahs and bogs are maintained by periodic fires. Lightning fires usually occur during the growing season. Fire during the growing season can stimulate and/or synchronize flowering in many species. The Apalachicola region has many endemic plant species, most of them are native to savannahs.

Savannahs have a greater economic value

when they are planted with pine trees or converted to pasture. Prior to planting pines, the site is prepared by bedding and using other mechanical methods which are destructive to the vegetation.

This species is associated with the Eastern Gulf Coast Flatwoods. The Kuchler system places this species habitat within the longleaf-slash pine ecosystem, restricted to flat and irregular southern Gulf Coastal Plains. Local relief is less than 300 feet. Much of this area is forested. The elevation ranges from sea level to 75 feet. This nearly level low coastal plain is crossed by many large streams, lakes and ponds. The average annual precipitation is 1,325 to 1,625 millimeters. The abundant rainfall and the many perennial streams are important sources of water. The dominant soils are Aquults, Aquepts, and Aquods. These soils have a thermic temperature regime and an aquic moisture regime. They are, also, sandy and poorly drained or very poorly drained.

This area supports pine forest vegetation. Chalky bluestem, indian grass, and several panicum species make up the understory. Palmetto, gallberry, and waxmyrtle are the dominant woody shrubs. Longleaf and slash pine are the major trees. The fauna associated with longleaf-slash pine forest include the white-tailed deer, raccoon, the opossum, tree squirrels, rabbits, and numerous species of ground-dwelling rodents. The bobwhite and the wild turkey are the principal gallinaceous game birds. Resident and migratory nongame bird species are numerous, as are migratory waterfowl.

Historic Range and Current Distribution

White birds-in-a-nest occurs in Bay, Gulf, Franklin, and Liberty Counties, Florida. The Apalachicola National Forest has the most vigorous populations, with the largest num-
bers of individuals. Exact population numbers are not known, but a plant inventory conducted by the Florida Natural Areas Inventory listing "occurrences" recorded more occurrences than are now thought to be extant. Forty-one of 63 reported localities are in the Post Office Bay area of Apalachicola National Forest.

Conservation and Recovery

This species has fallen vulnerable to habitat degradation due to lack of prescribed fire and forestry practices.

Development of improved cattle pastures has probably destroyed habitat of this species. The forest products industry has modified habitat by planting and harvest of slash pine and by the Forest Service planting of longleaf pine. Site preparation that precedes tree planting may destroy plants. Shading of this species by neighboring grasses and by pine trees after canopy closure most likely adversely affects the species.

Landowner liability for fire has discouraged prescribed burning of pineland in Florida which, also, may have adversely affected this species. The Forest Service conducts some prescribed burns during the growing season to reduce the incidence of Brown-spot infection of longleaf pine seedlings.

Five of 22 known sites are on highway right-of-ways posing a threat if the roads were ever widened.

Conservation measures provided to species listed as endangered or threatened pursuant to the Act include recognition, recovery actions, requirements for Federal protection, and prohibitions against certain practices. Recognition through listing encourages conservation measures by Federal, international, and private agencies, groups, and individuals.

Bibliography

U.S. Fish and Wildlife Service. "Endangered and Threatened Wildlife and Plants; Threatened Status for Three Florida Plants." *Federal Register* Vol. 57, No. 90. May 8, 1992: 19813-19819.

Contacts

USFWS Regional Office
Suite 200, 1875 Century Blvd.
Atlanta, GA 30345
Phone: 404-679-4000

Ecological Services Field Office
1612 June Avenue
Panama City, FL 32405-3721
Phone: 904-769-0552
FAX: 904-763-2177

Adapted from data compiled by the Threatened and Endangered Species Information Institute (13950 W. 20th Ave., Golden, CO 80401) for *Beacham's International Threatened, Endangered, and Extinct Species* published on CD ROM, available from Beacham Publishing.

Godfrey's Butterwort

Pinguicula ionantha

Andy Robinson

Status	Threatened
Listed	July 12, 1993
Family	Lentibulariaceae (Bladderwort)
Description	Perennial, carnivorous plant with rosette of fleshy, oblong, green flowers, and flowers on leafless talks.
Habitat	Gentle slopes, deep quagmire bogs, ditches, and depressions in grassy pine flatwoods.
Threats	Roadside maintenance, fire control, land conversion to pine plantations, pasture, or agricultural use.
Range	Florida

Description

Godfrey's butterwort is a perennial, carnivorous plant and is closely related to the snapdragon family. It has a rosette of fleshy, oblong, bright green leaves that are rounded at their tips, with only the edges rolled upward. The rosette is about 6 inches across. The upper surfaces of the leaves are covered with short glandular hairs that capture insects. The flowers are on leafless stalks (scapes) about 4 to 6 inches tall. When a flower is fully open, its corolla is about 1 inch across. The five corolla lobes are pale violet to white. The throat of the corolla and the corolla tube are deeper violet with dark violet veins. The corolla has a spur 0.2 inches long that is yellow to olive in color.

Habitat

Godfrey's butterwort inhabits seepage bogs on gentle slopes, deep quagmire bogs, ditches, and depressions in grassy pine flatwoods and grassy savannahs. It often occurs in shallow standing water most often in full sunlight or partial shade. A similar species, *P. primulifolia*, occurs in the same geographic area, but it often occupies flowing water and shaded areas. Another endemic butterwort species, *P. planifolia*, occurs with Godfrey's butterwort at one site. In Franklin County, Godfrey's butterwort occurs at a savannah with a particularly rich flora, including white birds-in-a-nest and Florida skullcap, both Federally listed as threatened species.

Savannahs (e.g., grass-sedge bogs or wet prairies) are nearly treeless and shrubless and have a large diversity of grass, sedge, and herb species.

Godfrey's butterwort is one of three *Pinguicula* species in the southeastern United States whose leaves are usually submerged. It is a carnivorous plant species that traps insects on its leaves and then consumes them.

Historic Range

Historic records concerning the distribution of this species are rare. Records dating back to the 1950's indicate the species occurred in the Florida panhandle near the Gulf Coast between Tallahassee and Panama City. Four occurrences are in the Apalachicola National Forest in Liberty County. Other records exist for Bay, Franklin, Gulf, and Liberty Counties.

Current Distribution

Distribution records for Godfrey's butterwort prior to 1970 listed 8 occurrences; none have been relocated. There are 12 occurrences for the period 1980 to 1990.

Populations of Godfrey's butterwort fluctuate in size. A site at Carrabelle that supported an abundant population in 1990 contained few plants in 1991. Such changes mean that long-term changes in abundance of this plant are probably difficult to assess.

This species is locally abundant on the Apalachicola National Forest and was, until recently, locally abundant on unprotected sites.

Conservation and Recovery

Savannahs and related vegetation are commercially valueless unless they are converted to pine plantations, pasture, or agricultural lands. Methods used to prepare sites for these uses can be detrimental to native herbaceous vegetation. Godfrey's butterwort may initially do well in areas converted to pine plantations if pockets of standing water exist. As the pines mature shading increases and Godfrey's butterwort will, most likely, be shaded out. The species is unlikely to recolonize pine plantations following conversion.

Savannah herbs such as Godfrey's butterwort may exist in powerline or roadside right-of-ways. These sites are not necessarily permanent and maintenance activities could disturb or destroy the plants.

Fire control has allowed woody vegetation to invade savannahs and to eventually exclude Godfrey's butterwort and other endemic plants.

Godfrey's butterwort was a highly prized carnivorous plant to collectors in the 1970's. This consumptive practice has died down since that time but collecting still occurs. The species is sold by at least 3 nurseries in the United States.

Savannah vegetation, grassy seepage bogs, and the grassy understory of flatwoods (largely wiregrass, Aristida stricta) are maintained by frequent, low-intensity fires. Lightning fires tend to occur during the growing season. The frequency and season of fire is important to the plant species that make up the vegetation, but fire effects can be subtle and more research is needed if fire management is to be applied scientifically to conserve the native flora.

Bibliography

U.S. Fish and Wildlife Service. "Endangered and Threatened Wildlife and Plants; Endangered or Threatened Status for Five Florida Plants." *Federal Register* Vol. 58, No. 131. July 12, 1993: 37432-37443.

Contacts

USFWS Regional Office
Suite 200, 1875 Century Blvd.
Atlanta, GA 30345
Phone: 404-679-4000

Ecological Services Field Office
P. O. Box 2676
Vero Beach, FL 32961-2676
Phone: 407-562-3909
FAX: 407-562-4288

Ecological Services Field Office
1612 June Avenue
Panama City, FL 32405-3721
Phone: 904-769-0552
FAX: 904-763-2177

Adapted from data compiled by the Threatened and Endangered Species Information Institute (13950 W. 20th Ave., Golden, CO 80401) for *Beacham's International Threatened, Endangered, and Extinct Species* published on CD ROM, available from Beacham Publishing.

Barneby Reed-Mustard

Schoenocrambe barnebyi

Stanley L. Welsh

Status	Endangered
Listed	January 14, 1992
Family	Brassicaceae (Mustard)
Description	Perennial herbaceous plant with sparsely leafed stems, light purple petals with prominent darker purple veins.
Habitat	Red clay soils rich in selenium and gypsum in the lower elevations of the Unita Basin in northeastern Utah.
Threats	Low population, habitat destruction due to potential uranium development.
Range	Utah

Description

A perennial herbaceous plant, the Barneby reed-mustard, has sparsely leafed stems 22 to 35 centimeters tall arising from a woody root crown. The leaves have smooth margins, are entire, and grow between 1.5 to 5 centimeters long and about half as wide. The alternately arranged leaf blades are attached to the stem by a petioles. The flowers have light purple petals with prominent darker purple veins. The entire flower spans about 1 centimeter in diameter when in full anthesis and is displayed in unbranched flower clusters (racemes) of 2 to 8 flowers at the end of the plant's leafy stems.

Habitat

The Barneby reed-mustard is endemic to soils derived from specific geologic substrates in the lower elevations of the Unita Basin in northeastern Utah and in the lower elevations of the Fremont River and Muddy Creek drainages in Central Utah. These red clay soils are rich in selenium and gypsum, and are overlain by sandstone talus.

This species' range falls within the Central Desertic Basins, Mountains, and Plateaus. The region is characterized by alluvial fans, piedmont plains, and pediments sloping from the surrounding mountains to form broad intermountain basins. The average annual precipitation is 175 to 300 millimeters and the elevation ranges from 1,900 to 2,200 meters. The dominant soils are Orthents. These soils are shallow to very deep and medium textured to fine textured with a frigid temperature regime, an ardic moisture regime, and mixed or montmorillonitic mineralogy.

The Central Desertic Basins, Mountains, and Plateaus support a grass-shrub vegetation. Rhizomatous wheatgrasses, needle-and-thread, Indian ricegrass, and big sagebrush are the dominant species of this region. Other plant species associated with Barneby reed-mustard include *Ephedra torreyana, Atriplex confertifolia, Eriogonum corymbosum,* and *Stanleya pinnata.*

Historic Range and Current Distribution

Two populations of the species are currently known. One population site is in the southern portion of the San Rafael Swell, and the other is located in the Sulphur Creek drainage in Capitol Reef National Park.

Conservation and Recovery

Human overuse leading to loss of habitat is the primary culprit in the dwindling numbers of Barneby reed-mustard. Significant portions of two known populations of the species are vulnerable to potential uranium development or trampling by visitors of Capitol Reef National Park.

This species is threatened by habitat destruction due to uranium mining activities. The hillside where the species occurs in its San Rafael Swell population has an access road bulldozed across it with mining prospects near the species' limited distribution. Portions of the species' habitat lie within six mining claims at Sy's Butte, which require annual assessment work which could further degrade the species' habitat.

This species was listed as endangered in part because of the potential of mineral development actions adversely impacting it. A threat to the Barneby reed-mustard is habitat destruction associated with potential uranium mining activity. Assessment work re-lated to mining claims for uranium is a chronic threat to this mustard and its habitat. The BLM requires a mine plan be prepared for mining assessment areas within environmentally critical areas which must provide for the conservation of those environmental values.

Formal land management designations need to be established to provide habitat protection. Such designations may include the following: Research Natural Areas, Areas of Critical Environmental Concern, or designated Wilderness. Special protected areas similar to those mentioned above should ensure the long term protection of enough populations of this mustard to ensure its survival as a vigorous reproducing species. The Center for Plant Conservation should consider inclusion of individual living specimens of this mustard in the "National Collection of Endangered Plant Species" and subsequently, propagation. These collections are for the purpose of maintaining a refuge garden population for those species which are threatened in their natural habitat and for conducting research beneficial to the species' conservation and recovery, including techniques necessary for the establishment of additional populations in suitable habitat.

Introduction of new stands into or proximal to the species' current range may be conducted if suitable habitat is found and if such introduction is determined to be desirable or feasible. Because no reintroductions have previously been undertaken, the success of such reintroductions is uncertain. Reintroductions, however, should be considered for the biological information that would be obtained and for the possibility of successful establishment of viable stands of the species.

Bibliography

U.S. Fish and Wildlife Service. "Endangered and Threatened Wildlife and Plants; Final

Rule to determine the Plant *Schoenocrambe Argillacea* (Clay Reed-Mustard) To be a Threatened Species, and the Plant *Schoenocrambe Barnebyi* (Barneby Reed-Mustard) To be an Endangered Species." *Federal Register* Vol. 57, No. 9. January 14, 1992: 1398-1402.

U.S. Fish and Wildlife Service. "Utah Reed-Mustards: Clay Reed-Mustard (*Schoenocrambe Argillacea*), Barneby Reed-Mustard (*Schoenocrambe barnebyi*), Shrubby Reed-Mustard (*Schoenocrambe suffrutescens*) Recovery Plan." Denver, CO, 1993. 18 pp.

Contacts

U.S. Fish and Wildlife Service
Regional Office
P. O. Box 25486
Denver, CO 80225
Phone: 303-236-7920

Ecological Services Field Office
Lincoln Plaza
145 East 1300 South, Suite 404
Salt Lake City, UT 84115
Phone: 801-524-5001

Adapted from data compiled by the Threatened and Endangered Species Information Institute (13950 W. 20th Ave., Golden, CO 80401) for *Beacham's International Threatened, Endangered, and Extinct Species* published on CD ROM, available from Beacham Publishing.

Gambel's Watercress

Rorippa gambelli

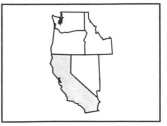

Malcolm McLeod, California Native Plant Society

Status	Endangered
Listed	August 3, 1993
Family	Brassicaceae (Mustard)
Description	Perennial herb with dense inflorescence of white flowers, having narrow fruits with seeds in one row with angular, sharply toothed leaflets.
Habitat	Freshwater or brackish marshes along lake margins.
Threats	Erosion and sedimentation, filling for development.
Range	Californla

Description

Gambel's watercress is a perennial herb that characteristically roots from the stem nodes of a horizontal rootstock. The species produces dense inflorescence of white flowers from April through June. The narrow fruits with seeds arranged in one row (rather than two) and the more angular and sharply toothed leaflets distinguish this species from the more common non-native *R. nasturtiumaquaticum*.

Habitat

Rorippa gambelli (listed as *Nasturtium gambelli*) is classified as an obligate wetland plant, which means that it almost always (greater than 99% of the time), under natural conditions, occurs in wetlands.

Gambel's watercress occurs in freshwater or brackish marshes along the margins of lakes or along slow-moving streams, from 20 to 60 feet in elevation. The species requires a permanent source of water. Gambel's watercress is found in association with cattails, bulrush, and *Arenaria paludicola*, an endangered species.

Gambel's watercress co-occurs with *A. paludicola* in a small persistent emergent marsh complex near the Nipomo Dunes Mesa, San Luis Obispo County, California. Other species found in this wetland complex include stream orchis, bur-reed, sedges, and rushes.

This marsh complex is characterized as a series of small freshwater marshes associated with active to partially stabilized beach dunes which extend a distance of 5 miles from Oceano south to the Oso Flaco Lakes area. Just inland from this "dune lakes" area lies the Nipomo Mesa, a broad mesa comprised of old Oceano sands deposited 40,000 years ago, and bisected by Black Lake Canyon. Pockets of freshwater marsh habitat in Black Lake Canyon and the dune lakes area harbor a unique flora that includes remnant populations of *Arenaria paludicola* and *Rorippa gambelli*.

Historic Range

Gambel's watercress was historically found at about a dozen sites in southern California, including interior wetland areas of San Diego, San Bernardino, and Los Angeles Counties, as well as coastal wetland areas of San Luis Obispo and Santa Barbara Counties, and from near Mexico City in the Valley of Mexico. The sites in San Bernardino and San Diego Counties have been extirpated due to habitat alteration. In 1980, 2 individual plants may have been observed in Barka Slough on Vandenberg Air Force Base, Santa Barbara County. Subsequent surveys of the same area in 1989 failed to find the species. The populations near Small Twin Lake and Oceano Beach in San Luis Obispo County have been extirpated.

Current Distribution

Gambel's watercress is currently found on 3 sites in San Luis Obispo County: Black Lake Canyon; Oso Flaco Lake; and Little Oso Flaco Lake. These 3 populations contain about 1,000 individual plants. The Oso Flaco Lake and Little Oso Flaco Lake sites are on lands owned by the California Department of Parks and Recreation (Pismo Beach State Vehicle Recreation Area). The portion of the Recreation Area containing the lakes is closed to recreational vehicles and is being managed by The Nature Conservancy.

Because of this species' limited population size and limited distribution, it is vulnerable to extinction. The small population size also means there is a limited gene pool. The lack of genetic diversity means the species may not have the capabilities to evolve to adjust to changes in its environment.

Conservation and Recovery

The wetland complex supporting the Gambel's watercress and *A. paludicola* populations is threatened by alterations in hydrologic regime, natural succession, runoff from upstream developments, erosion and sedimentation, and filling for development.

The area's hydrologic regime may have been altered over an extended period of time by the planting of eucalyptus trees. This species was introduced in the late 1800s and has spread throughout the lower half of the canyon. The eucalyptus has an extensive root system that can draw out soil moisture; that, coupled with the large evaporative surface of its foliage, has probably resulted in a significant drawdown of the water table compared to that which the surrounding native vegetation would have accomplished. Agricultural and urban use of groundwater may also impact these wetlands but studies concerning groundwater hydrology have not focused on which portions of the canyon have been affected. Additional urban development and the associated increase in drilling of wells could potentially impact these wetlands.

Natural succession in the area from a wetland to a more mesic grass or shrub-dominated ecosystem has apparently been accelerated, possibly due, in part, to the above mentioned changes in hydrologic regime. Drops in water table levels will decrease the soil moisture levels in certain areas which could allow the invasion of upland plant species. Aerial photographs from 1949 show the lower portion of the canyon as one wetland with open water and freshwater marsh or bog vegetation along its margins. By 1956, however, aerial photographs showed that willows had encroached into the wetlands and 30% of the area was covered with trees.

Bibliography

U.S. Fish and Wildlife Service. "Endangered and Threatened Wildlife and Plants; Determination of Endangered Status for Gambel's Watercress." *Federal Register*, August 3, 1993.

Contacts

USFWS Regional Office
Eastside Federal Complex
911 N.S. 11th Avenue
Portland, OR 97232-4181
Phone: 503-231-6118

Sacramento Ecological Services Field Office
Room E-1803/1823
2800 Cottage Way
Sacramento, CA 98525
Phone: 916-978-4866
FAX: 916-978-4613

Ventura Ecological Services Field Office
Suite 100, 2140 Eastman Avenue
Ventura, CA 93003
Phone: 805-644-1766
FAX: 818-904-6288

Adapted from data compiled by the Threatened and Endangered Species Information Institute (13950 W. 20th Ave., Golden, CO 80401) for *Beacham's International Threatened, Endangered, and Extinct Species* published on CD ROM, available from Beacham Publishing.

Clay Reed-Mustard

Schoenocrambe argillacea

Ben Franklin   *Color Plate C-2*

Status	Threatened
Listed	January 14, 1992
Family	Brassicaceae (Mustard)
Description	Perennial herb with sparsely leafed stems 6-12 inches tall from a woody root crown.
Habitat	Desert shrub on clay soils which are rich in gypsum and overlain with sandstone talus.
Threats	Surface disruption associated with oil and gas development.
Range	Utah

Description

The clay reed-mustard is a perennial herb with sparsely leafed stems 6 to 12 inches tall which rise from a woody root crown. The leaves are very narrow with smooth margins and grow to 0.4 to 1.4 inches in length and less than 0.1 inch in width. Leaves are alternately arranged on the stem and are attached directly without a petiole. Flowers range in color from pale lavender to whitish with purple veins. Petals measure from 0.3 to 0.4 inch in length and from 0.14 to 0.18 inch in width. The entire flowers are 0.4 inch across in full anthesis and are displayed in clusters of from 3 to 20 at the end of the leafy stems. Flowering occurs in May to early June.

Habitat

This species occurs in mixed desert shrub and shadscale communities between the elevations of 5,000 to 5,650 feet. It grows on clay soils which are rich in gypsum and overlain with sandstone talus. The soils are derived from a mixture of shales and sandstones from the zone of contact between the Uinta and Green River geologic formation. The species is associated with *Eriogonum carymbosum*, *Ephedra torreyana*, *Atriplex* spp., and *Artemisia* spp.

Historic Range and Current Distribution

Past distribution of this species is unknown. At present, the species occurs in only 2 populations in Uintah County, Utah. Both are Federally owned (Bureau of Land Management, Vernal District and Diamond Mountain Resource Area, and Utah Indian Tribal lands) and are subject to mineral leasing by the government. Clay reed-mustard may occur on Ute Indian Tribal lands.

Conservation and Recovery

The species is threatened by surface disruption associated with energy development within its habitat. All known populations occur on Federal lands that are leased for their oil and gas energy reserves. An increase in oil and gas exploratory activity could lead to further development. The entire habitat of the species is underlain by oil shale which may be mined when economic conditions favor it.

In the past, grazing has negatively impacted the species but no longer is a threat due to the management efforts of the Bureau of Land Management. Some sites do not support enough individuals to maintain genetic viability.

All populations of this species occur on lands administered by the Bureau of Land Management or the Ute Indian Tribal lands. The Bureau is responsible for leasing mineral rights under the jurisdiction of the United States. It may not lease any rights which may cause harm to this species without first consulting with the U.S. Fish and Wildlife Service. In the meantime, specific recovery goals are being drafted by the Fish and Wildlife Service.

This species was listed as endangered in part because of the potential of mineral development actions adversely impacting it. A threat to the clay reed-mustard is habitat destruction associated with potential uranium mining activity. Assessment work related to mining claims for uranium is a chronic threat to this mustard and its habitat. The BLM requires a mine plan be prepared for mining assessment areas within environmentally critical areas which must provide for the conservation of those environmental values.

Formal land management designations need to be established to provide habitat protection. Such designations may include the following: Research Natural Areas, Areas of Critical Environmental Concern, or designated Wilderness. Special protected areas similar to those mentioned above should ensure the long term protection of enough populations of this mustard to ensure its survival as a vigorous reproducing species. The Center for Plant Conservation should consider inclusion of individual living specimens of this mustard in the "National Collection of Endangered Plant Species" and subsequently, propagation. These collections are for the purpose of maintaining a refuge garden population for those species which are threatened in their natural habitat and for conducting research beneficial to the species' conservation and recovery, including techniques necessary for the establishment of additional populations in suitable habitat.

Introduction of new stands into or proximal to the species' current range may be conducted if suitable habitat is found and if such introduction is determined to be desirable or feasible. Because no reintroductions have previously been undertaken, the success of such reintroductions is uncertain. Reintroductions, however, should be considered for the biological information that would be obtained and for the possibility of successful establishment of viable stands of the species.

Bibliography

U.S. Fish and Wildlife Service. "Endangered and Threatened Wildlife and Plants; Final Rule to determine the Plant *Schoenocrambe Argillacea* (Clay Reed-Mustard) To be a Threatened Species, and the Plant *Schoenocrambe Barnebyi* (Barneby Reed-Mustard) To be an Endangered Species." *Federal Register* Vol. 57, No. 9. January 14, 1992: 1398-1402.

Contacts

U.S. Fish and Wildlife Service
Regional Office
P. O. Box 25486
Denver, CO 80225
Phone: 303-236-7920

Ecological Services Field Office
Lincoln Plaza
145 East 1300 South, Suite 404
Salt Lake City, UT 84115
Phone: 801-524-5001

Adapted from data compiled by the Threatened
and Endangered Species Information Institute (13950
W. 20th Ave., Golden, CO 80401) for *Beacham's
International Threatened, Endangered, and Extinct Species*
published on CD ROM, available from Beacham
Publishing.

Florida Skullcap

Scutellaria floridana

Loran C. Anderson

Status	Threatened
Listed	May 8, 1992
Family	Lamiaceae (Mint)
Description	Perennial herb with swollen storage roots with long, linear leaves and solitary flowers with bell-shaped calyx.
Habitat	Grassy vegetation on poorly drained, infertile sandy soils.
Threats	Habitat degradation due to cattle pasture development.
Range	Florida

Description

The Florida skullcap is a perennial herb with swollen storage roots. This species' stems are little branched, solitary or in small groups. The leaves are opposite, 2 to 4 centimeters long, linear, with the margins inrolled with a blunt, purplish tip. The solitary flowers are located in the axils of the short leafy bracts. The flower stalks are 5 millimeters long. The calyx is bell shaped with a scutellum on its upper side. The bright lavender-blue corolla is about 2.5 centimeters long. The corolla possesses a throat and upper and lower lip. The lower lip is centrally white. Flowering occurs in May and June.

Habitat

This species is restricted to the Gulf coastal lowlands near the mouth of the Apalachicola River. This species inhabits grassy vegetation on poorly drained, infertile sandy soils. The wettest sites are grassy seepage bogs on gently slopes at the edges of forested or shrubby wetlands. This species also inhabits grass-sedge bogs (savannahs), which are nearly treeless and shrubless but have a rich flora of grasses, sedges and herbs. The Florida skullcap is most commonly found in seepage bog communities or savannahs such a bay stringers.

Grassy savannahs and bogs are maintained by periodic fires. Lightning fires usually occur during the growing season. Fire during the growing season can stimulate and/or synchronize flowering in many species. The Apalachicola region has many endemic plant species, most of them are native to savannahs.

Savannahs have a greater economic value when they are planted with pine trees or converted to pasture. Prior to planting pines, the site is prepared by bedding and using other mechanical methods which are destructive to the vegetation.

This species is associated with the Eastern Gulf Coast Flatwoods. The Kuchler system places this species' habitat within the longleaf-slash pine ecosystem, restricted to flat and irregular southern Gulf Coastal Plains. Local relief is less than 300 feet. Much of this area is forested. The elevation ranges from sea level to 25 meters. This nearly level low coastal plain is crossed by many large streams, lakes and ponds. The average annual precipitation is 1,325 to 1,625 millimeters. The abundant rainfall and the many perennial streams are important sources of water. The dominant soils are Aquults, Aquepts, and Aquods. These soils have a thermic temperature regime and an aquic moisture regime. They are, also, sandy and poorly drained or very poorly drained.

This area supports pine forest vegetation. Chalky bluestem, Indian grass, and several panicum species make up the understory. Palmetto, gallberry, and waxmyrtle are the dominant woody shrubs. Longleaf and slash pine are the major trees. The fauna associated with longleaf-slash pine forest include the white-tailed deer, raccoon, the opossum, tree squirrels, rabbits, and numerous species of ground-dwelling rodents. The bobwhite and the wild turkey are the principal gallinaceous game birds. Resident and migratory nongame bird species are numerous, as are migratory waterfowl.

Historic Range

The historic range of the Florida skullcap is not known.

Current Distribution

The Florida skullcap is extant in Gulf, Franklin and Liberty Counties, Florida in the Apalachicola National Forest. The limited population numbers and restricted range of this species implies a serious potential for extinction from stochastic events. Limited gene pool may depress reproductive vigor, or a single man-caused or natural environmental disturbance could destroy a significant percentage of extant individuals.

Conservation and Recovery

This species has fallen vulnerable to habitat degradation due to lack of prescribed fire and forestry practices.

Development of improved cattle pastures has probably destroyed habitat of this species. The forest products industry has modified the habitat by planting and harvest of slash pine and by the Forest Service planting of longleaf pine. Site preparation that precedes tree planting may destroy plants. Shading of this species by neighboring grasses and by pine trees after canopy closure most likely adversely affects the species.

Landowner liability for fire has discouraged prescribed burning of pineland in Florida which, also, may have adversely affected this species. The Forest Service conducts some prescribed burns during the growing season to reduce the incidence of brown-spot infection of longleaf pine seedlings.

The Forest Service is currently protecting this plant and its habitat; however, the area in which this species is found on Forest Service land is suitable for timber management. The current acceptable management practice of the Forest Service, such as intense mechanical treatments and target stocking densities, most likely threatens the viability of the Florida skullcap.

Conservation measures provided to species listed as endangered or threatened pursuant to the Act include recognition, recovery actions, requirements for Federal protection, and prohibitions against certain practices. Recognition through listing encourages conservation measures by Federal, international, and private agencies, groups, and individuals.

This species is listed as endangered under the Preservation of Native Flora of Florida law, which regulates taking, transport, and sale of plants but does not provide for habitat protection.

This species will be provided protection for its population located on Forest Service lands. Landowners and involved parties can be notified of the location and importance of protecting this species and its habitat.

Bibliography

U.S. Fish and Wildlife Service. "Endangered and Threatened Wildlife and Plants; Threatened Status for Three Florida Plants." *Federal Register* Vol. 57, No. 90. May 8, 1992: 19813-19819.

Contacts

USFWS Regional Office
Suite 200, 1875 Century Blvd.
Atlanta, GA 30345
Phone: 404-679-4000

Ecological Services Field Office
P. O. Box 2676
Vero Beach, FL 32961-2676
Phone: 407-562-3909
FAX: 407-562-4288

Ecological Services Field Office
1612 June Avenue
Panama City, FL 32405-3721
Phone: 904-769-0552
FAX: 904-763-2177

Adapted from data compiled by the Threatened and Endangered Species Information Institute (13950 W. 20th Ave., Golden, CO 80401) for *Beacham's International Threatened, Endangered, and Extinct Species* published on CD ROM, available from Beacham Publishing.

American Chaffseed

Scwalbea americana

D. A. Sorrie

Status	Endangered
Listed	September 29, 1992
Family	Scrophulariaceae (Snapdragon)
Description	Perennnial herb with unbranched stems with large, purplish-yellow flowers.
Habitat	Pine flatwoods, savannas in moist to dry acidic sandy loams.
Threats	Residential and commercial development, forestry practices, encorachment of exotic vegetation.
Range	Alabama, Connecticut, Delaware, Florida, Georgia, Kentucky, Massachusetts, Maryland, Mississippi, North Carolina, New Jersey, New York, South Carolina, Tennessee, Virginia

Description

The American chaffseed is a perennial member of the snapdragon family. This plant is an erect herb with unbranched stems or branched only at the base and grows to a height of 3 to 8 decimeters. It is densely pubescent. The leaves are alternate, lanceolate to elliptic, stalkless, 2 to 5 centimeters long, and entire. The upper leaves are reduced to narrow bracts. The flowers are large, purplish-yellow and tubular. The flowers are borne singly on short stalks in the axils of the uppermost, reduced leaves form a many-flowered, spike-like raceme. The flowers have a high degree of bilateral symmetry elaborated for pollination by bees. The capsule is long and narrow and is enclosed in a loose-fitting sac-like structure that provides the basis for the common name.

Habitat

The American chaffseed inhabits open pine flatwoods, savannas, and other open areas, in moist to dry acidic sandy loams or sandy pest loams in Florida, Georgia, Mississippi, New Jersey, North Carolina, and South Carolina. This species is associated with areas described as open, moist pine flatwoods, fire-maintained savannas, ecotonal areas between peaty wetlands and xeric sandy soils, and other open grass-sedge systems. However, one population is known to occur in a heavy clay soil in a hayfield. This plant relies on fire, mowing, or fluctuating water tables to maintain the crucial open to partly-open conditions that it requires.

Historically, this plant occurred on savannas and pinelands throughout the coastal plain and on sandstone knobs and plains inland where frequent, natural fires maintained the communities. Fire-maintained areas which this species favors include plantations that are prescribed burned for management of quail and other game species, an army base impact zone that burns regularly due to live artillery shelling, forest management areas that are burned to maintain habitat for wildlife, including the red-cockaded woodpecker, and various other private lands that are burned to maintain open fields.

The American chaffseed occurs in species-rich plant communities where grasses, sedges, and savanna dicots are numerous.

Historic Range and Current Distribution

Historically, this species was known from Alabama, Connecticut, Delaware, Kentucky, Maryland, Massachusetts, New York, Tennessee, and Virginia.

Conservation and Recovery

This species is threatened by habitat destruction due to development and from fire suppression. Both of these factors favor the encroachment and invasion of exotic vegetation.

Sixty percent of known populations have been extirpated due to conversion of habitat to residential and commercial purposes, adverse agricultural and forestry practices, and encroachment of exotic vegetation. The sandy pineland where this plant is associated has been very vulnerable to development because the soils are level, deep, and suitable for building sites. Populations near the Atlantic Coast are particularly vulnerable to development pressures. In Florida four of seven historic sites are confirmed extirpated as a direct result of habitat destruction. A New Jersey population was extirpated in 1968 by the construction of a residential street.

This species remains threatened by habitat destruction resulting from development, forestry practices, agricultural practices, and encroachment of exotic vegetation.

Conservation measures provided to species listed as endangered or threatened pursuant to the Act include recognition, recovery actions, requirements for Federal protection, and prohibitions against certain practices. Recognition through listing encourages conservation measures by Federal, international, and private agencies, groups, and individuals.

Conservation and management of the American chaffseed will most likely involve a combination of site protection through land acquisition or cooperative agreements with land owners, and, also, habitat manipulation to maintain early successional habitats. This species will also be the focus of research on life history, population ecology, effects of fire, mowing and soil moisture variation on population establishment and maintenance.

Bibliography

U.S. Fish and Wildlife Service. "Endangered and Threatened Wildlife and Plants; Endangered Status for *Scwalbea Americana* (American Chaffseed)." *Federal Register.* Vol. 57, No. 189. September 29, 1992: 44703-44708.

Contacts

U.S. Fish and Wildlife Service
Regional Office
300 Westgate Center Drive
Hadley, MA 01035
Phone: 413-253-8659

Adapted from data compiled by the Threatened and Endangered Species Information Institute (13950 W. 20th Ave., Golden, CO 80401) for *Beacham's International Threatened, Endangered, and Extinct Species* published on CD ROM, available from Beacham Publishing.

Leedy's Roseroot

Sedum intergrifolium ssp. *leedyi*

Wayne Ostlie

Status	Threatened
Listed	April 22, 1992
Family	Crassulaceae (Stonecrop)
Description	Tall floral stems with blue-green oblong leaves.
Habitat	Crevices of rock cliffs where cold water drips into the soil.
Threats	Development, groundwater contamination, erosion, and grazing.
Range	Minnesota, New York

Description

Leedy's roseroot possesses tall floral stems with leaves glaucous, oblong, and blue-green. The leaves average 30 millimeters long with irregularly dentate to entire margins. The subspecies is dioecious and the flowers are small, arranged in corymobose cymes. Petals are dark red with varying shades of yellowish white at the base. Thick, scaly rhizome are conspicuous. This subspecies is more robust than most other Sedum species. The flower heads have been noted to have orange coloration.

Habitat

Leedy's roseroot grows in the crevices of rock cliffs where cold water drips into the soil. Soils are limestone with bands of bentonite.

The subspecies sometimes occurs on shale cliffs. Individuals are limited to areas on the cliffs where ground water seeps through cracks in the rock. The local environment is cool and wet throughout the summer which is similar to the climate of the last ice age.

This subspecies' ranges overlap the Northeastern forage and Forest Region. This cold, humid region consists of plateaus, plains, and mountains. The average annual precipitation ranges from 750 to 1,325 millimeters. In most of the region more than one-half of the precipitation falls during the freeze-free season. The average annual temperature is 3 to 11 degrees Celsius.

Most of the land in this region, especially the steeper areas, is forested. Significant amounts of lumber and pulpwood are produced. Locally, Christmas trees and maple syrup are important forest products. Forage and grains for dairy cattle are the principal crops. In places where markets, climate, and soils are favorable, fruits, tobacco, potatoes, and vegetables are important crops. Wildlife habitat and recreation are important land uses.

Historic Range

In the past, the subspecies is thought to have been distributed throughout North America. Although Leedy's Roseroot is rare, it has survived since the ice age, adapted to current conditions, and does not appear to have difficulty surviving. Current habitat loss and degradation is threatening this robust subspecies.

Current Distribution

Presently, the subspecies occurs at only six sites, five of which arc viable. Four occur in Fillmore County, Minnesota, and two occur near Seneca Lake in New York. In New York, the largest population occurs on land privately owned. A one-acre parcel of land containing the subspecies along 289 feet of Seneca Lake is legally protected by the Finger Lakes Land Trust with a conservation easement through the Nature Conservancy. In Minnesota, three sites are owned privately and occur in agricultural areas. The fourth site is state-owned and protected by the State of Minnesota.

Conservation and Recovery

Leedy's roseroot is threatened due to development, ground water contamination, erosion, and grazing. In Minnesota, ground water contamination occurs through filling or dumping in sink holes adjacent to cliffs where the subspecies occurs. Sink holes provide direct access to the ground water and are the main source of seepage on the cliffs.

In New York, many sites are threatened by residential development. Uplands adjacent to the cliff are wooded and homes are being built away from the cliff edge. Yet, many homeowners have built stairs down to the lake shore and have cleared vegetation from the cliff to enhance their view of the lake. In some areas, trees have been cut and dumped over the cliff edge where the subspecies grows.

In both states, the use of agricultural pesticides in farmland upland and adjacent to cliffs affect underground water quality. Erosion of the cliffs is another threat. Slopes are unstable. Rock slides often result in the loss of individual plants. In 1990, runoff from heavy rains dislodged many plants. At one site in Minnesota, grazing threatens the subspecies.

Protection through perpetual conservation easements will be enhanced by compensation or tax relief. Because much of the shoreline at the Glenora Cliff site is residential, acquisition and/or easements will probably cost several thousand dollars per 30 meters of shoreline. If the proximity of protected land is considered an amenity, tax rates on protected properties and adjoining properties might rise and make enrollment in easements too costly unless landowners are provided tax relief. Neither Minnesota nor New York has a mechanism which provides permanent funding for easements on protected species' habitat. The Federal government or State legislatures may act to establish such funding, or one or more permanent private conservation trusts may be endowed for this purpose.

Educational materials should be developed and opportunities to acquaint landowners and other members of the public with the taxon and its need for protection. A program of individual landowner contact and public education in the first year of recovery should be initiated, especially in New York, where such efforts can pave the way for conservation actions. Because the majority of populations occur on private lands, such efforts in New York may be most effective when they can involve landowners as educators or guides.

The cool microclimates in which Leedy's roseroot occurs may be affected by global warming or other unforeseen circumstances. Seeds and/or cuttings should be contributed to a genetic bank for preservation and possible reintroduction if needed in the future. Plants collected in Minnesota have been brought into cultivation at a Center for Plant Conservation garden.

Bibliography

U.S. Fish and Wildlife Service. "Endangered and Threatened Wildlife and Plants: Determination of Threatened Status for *Sedum Integrifollum* ssp. *leedyi* (Leedy's roseroot)." *Federal Register* Vol. 57, No. 78, April 22, 1992: 14649-14653.

Contacts

USFWS Regional Office
Federal Building
Fort Snelling
Twin Cities, MN 55111
Phone: 612-725-3500
FAX: 612-725-3526

USFWS Regional Office
300 Westgate Center Drive
Hadley, MA 01035
Phone: 413-253-8659

Ecological Services Field Office
500 Saint Marks Lane
P. O. Box 608
Islip, NY 11751
Phone: 516-581-2941
FAX: 516-581-2972

Adapted from data compiled by the Threatened and Endangered Species Information Institute (13950 W. 20th Ave., Golden, CO 80401) for *Beacham's International Threatened, Endangered, and Extinct Species* published on CD ROM, available from Beacham Publishing.

Nelson's Checker-Mallow
Sidalcea nelsoniana

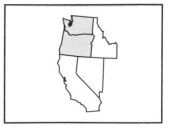

Andy Robinson

Status	Threatened
Listed	February 12, 1993
Family	Malvaceae (Mallow)
Description	Perennial herb with pinkish-lavender to pinkish-purple flowers in clusters.
Habitat	Gravelly, well-drained soils, clay loam, grassland areas, edges of plowed fields adjacent to wooded areas.
Threats	Conversion of habitat to agricultural use, stream channel alterations.
Range	Oregon, Washington

Description

Nelson's checker-mallow is a perennial herb with pinkish-lavender to pinkish-purple flowers borne in clusters at the end of 1 to 2.5 feet tall stems. Inflorescences of plants from the Willamette Valley are usually somewhat spikelike, usually elongate and somewhat open. Inflorescences of plants from the Coastal Range are shorter and not as open.

Nelson's checker-mallow is a gynodioecious species, which means that plants have either perfect flowers (male and female), or pistillate (female) flowers. The plant can reproduce vegetatively by rhizomes and produces seeds that drop near the parent plant.

The woody, rhizomatous (underground) stem of Nelson's checker-mallow enables the plant to persist in some disturbed situations, such as roadside ditches and mowed hayfields.

Flowering can occur as early as mid-May and extends into September in the Willamette Valley, depending on weather and site conditions. Fruits have been observed as early as mid-June and as late as mid-October.

Coastal Range populations generally flower later and produce seeds earlier, probably because of the shorter growing season.

Habitat

Nelson's checker-mallow was once very occasional in the Willamette Valley, Oregon, from Linn and Benton Counties north to near Portland and westward to eastern Tillamook County, but mainly occurred in Marion County, on more or less gravelly, well drained soils.

Other habitat descriptions have been offered. Some describe the plant's habitat as "moist, open ground and thickets." Others have described the plant as growing on moist to dry sites with poorly drained to well drained clay, clay loam, and gravelly loam soils, in meadow, and rarely, wooded habitats.

Nelson's checker-mallow is occasionally found in areas where prairie or grassland remnants persist, such as along fence rows, drainage swales, and at the edges of plowed fields adjacent to wooded areas.

Within the Willamette Valley, Nelson's checker-mallow most frequently occurs in Fraxinus (ash) swales and meadows with wet depressions, or along streams. The species also grows in wetlands within remnant prairie grasslands. Some sites occur along roadsides at stream crossings where exotics such as blackberry and Queen Anne's Lace are also present.

The woody, rhizomatous (underground) stem of Nelson's checker-mallow enables the plant to persist in some disturbed situations, such as roadside ditches and mowed hayfields.

Historic Range and Current Distribution

Nelson's checker-mallow occurs in two different physiographic provinces. The majority of sites occur in the Willamette Valley of Oregon; the plant is also found at several sites in the Coastal Range of Oregon, and at one site in Cowlitz County, in southwestern Washington.

A population center is a geographical area that, at least historically, was composed of interbreeding populations. Based on current and historic distribution, Nelson's checker-mallow occurred in at least six population centers in Oregon. Since the extirpation of one population center in the Willamette Valley, one population center currently remains in the Coastal Range in Oregon, and four remain in the Willamette Valley. The Cowlitz County population in Washington represents a separate population center. Thus, a total of six popula-

tion centers remain throughout the range of Nelson's checker-mallow.

The species occurs at 48 sites within the five populations centers in Oregon, and at one site in the populations center in Washington. Four additional sites with previously recorded occurrences apparently have been extirpated as a result of plowing, deposition of fill material or yard debris, or intense roadside management.

Counts have been made at 9 of the 52 population sites. Six populations had more than 1,000 plants each, 18 populations contained between 100 and 999 plants, 16 included between 10 and 99 plants, and 12 contained fewer than 10 plants.

An additional concern for the species is the small number of plants in many of the sites. Twenty-three sites (48 percent) contain 100 or fewer plants; 15 sites (31 percent) contain 25 or fewer plants. Within smaller populations, the sex ratios—number of plants with perfect plants to number of pistillate-flowered plants — may be the controlling factor in seed production. Thus, small, isolated Nelson's checker-mallow populations are more vulnerable to extirpation due to demographic effects. In addition, small populations are more vulnerable to extirpation from random events than are larger populations.

Conservation and Recovery

Since 1985, habitat loss, primarily through conversion to agricultural use (resulting in plant destruction or extirpation) has occurred at several Valley sites: Lewisberg, Philomath North, Mount Jefferson Farm, Dallas South, Starker Park, and the Salem Municipal Airport. In addition, habitat loss has been reported at Van Well Road, Dyck Road, McTimmonds Valley, Hess Road, Nelson's Golden Valley, and Finley National Wildlife Refuge.

Stream channel alterations have also adversely impacted the species. Projects such as stream straightening, construction of splash dams, and rip-rapping have resulted in an increase in instream flow, and reduced the amount of water that is diverted naturally into adjacent meadow land. This results in loss of habitat for the plant.

Mowing adversely impacts the plants if it takes place before the plants set seed. Mowing activities have adversely affected 11 sites in four population centers in the Willamette Valley.

Continued logging activities will eventually change the hydrologic regime at those areas where they occur. In the case of Nelson's checker-mallow, logging continues at the Nelson's Valley site in the Coastal Range. The extent to which these activities will impact the plant is not known; however, logging can directly destroy the plants, and a change in the hydrologic regime would likely adversely affect this species as well.

McMinnville Water and Light has planned to construct a reservoir on Walker Creek, a tributary of the Nestucca River in the Coast Range. The construction of this dam would inundate the entire Walker Flat population, the largest and one of the most hardy populations of Nelson's checker-mallow. Although the area is currently protected under the state Scenic Waterway System, there have been legislative efforts to remove Walker Creek from this protective designation; these efforts are likely to be renewed in the future.

Recreational motorcyclists use the area at Devil's Lake Fork site in the Coastal Range, and have disturbed the site to some degree.

The City of Hillsboro is proposing to raise the height of the Trask River Dam in Washington County, Oregon, by 50 feet to increase the storage capacity of Barney Reservoir from 4,000 to 20,000 acre-feet. The project is proposed in response to the increasing water needs of the City. If the project is approved, habitat in the immediate vicinity containing Nelson's checker-mallow will be inundated.

Although overutilization is not known to have occurred, some plant species have become vulnerable to collection for scientific or horticultural purposes, excessive visits by individuals interested in seeing rare plants, or vandalism following Federal listing. Several Nelson's checker-mallow sites in the Willamette Valley are readily accessible by road and could be vulnerable to vandalism or collection.

Although the extent to which this factor adversely affects the species is not known, instances of predation have been observed. A species of weevil utilizes Nelson's checker-mallow plants at several sites. The adult female insect bores a hole through the seed coat and deposits her eggs inside. When the larvae hatch, they feed on the developing seed. Damage to the seed reduces the reproductive potential of the species.

Encroachment of woody species is eliminating Nelson's checker-mallow habitat throughout the Willamette Valley. There is good evidence at Finley National Wildlife Refuge, Willow Creek and Wren Grassland Preserve, the Long Tom Area of Critical Environmental Concern, and the Fern Ridge Resource Natural Area, that secondary succession is occurring at grassland and meadow habitats in the Willamette Valley that adversely affects Nelson's checker-mallow.

In the past, occasional fires created openings facilitating the growth of the plant. Fires still regularly occur at the sites that currently have vigorous Nelson's checker-mallow populations. Fire management efforts to control invading Fraxinus, which competes with Nelson's checker-mallow at Finley National Wildlife Refuge, have also benefitted Nelson's checker-mallow.

An additional concern for the species is the small number of plants in many of the sites. Twenty-three sites (48 percent) contain 100 or fewer plants; 15 sites (31 percent) contain 25 or fewer plants. Within smaller populations, the sex ratios—number of plants with perfect plants to number of pistillate-flowered plants—

may be the controlling factor in seed production. Thus, small, isolated Nelson's checker-mallow populations are more vulnerable to extirpation due to demographic effects. In addition, small populations are more vulnerable to extirpation from random events than are larger populations.

In the past, occasional fires created openings facilitating the growth of the plant. Fires still regularly occur at the sites that currently have vigorous Nelson's checker-mallow populations. Fire management efforts to control invading Fraxinus, which competes with Nelson's checker-mallow at Finley National Wildlife Refuge, have also benefitted Nelson's checker-mallow. These efforts were designed to benefit geese.

Cutting has also been a management tool used to control encroaching vegetation. Nelson's checker-mallow appears robust at Refuge locations where management efforts have been employed, compared to those plants in another nearby location, the Fraxinus forest surrounding Muddy Creek. Since 1985, Nelson's checker-mallow has also increased in vigor at the University turkey farm site, in areas where Fraxinus has been controlled for several years to provide better habitat for turkeys.

Bibliography

U.S. Fish and Wildlife Service. "Endangered and Threatened Wildlife and Plants; Determination of Threatened Status for the Plant *Sidalcea nelsoniana* (Nelson's Checker-Mallow)." *Federal Register* Vol. 58, No. 28, February 12, 1993: 8235-8243.

Contacts

USFWS Regional Office
Eastside Federal Complex
911 N.S. 11th Avenue
Portland, OR 97232-4181
Phone: 503-231-6118

Adapted from data compiled by the Threatened and Endangered Species Information Institute (13950 W. 20th Ave., Golden, CO 80401) for *Beacham's International Threatened, Endangered, and Extinct Species* published on CD ROM, available from Beacham Publishing.

Ute Ladies' Tresses
Spiranthes diluvialis

USFWS, Salt Lake City

Status	Threatened
Listed	January 17, 1992
Family	Orchidaceae (Orchid)
Description	Perennial orchid 8 to 20 inches tall with white or ivory colored flowers clustered into spikes.
Habitat	Stream banks and flood plains.
Threats	Urbanization, stream channelization, construction projects.
Range	Colorado, Nevada, Utah

Description

Ute ladies' tresses is a perennial orchid that is 8 to 20 inches tall arising from tuberously thickened roots. The narrow leaves are about 11 inches long at the base of the stem and become reduced in size going up the stem. The flowers consist of 3 to 15 small white or ivory colored flowers clustered into a spike arrangement at the top of the stem. The species is characterized by whitish, stout, flowers gapping at the mouth. The sepals and petals, except for the lip, are rather straight, although the lateral sepals are variably oriented, with these often spreading abruptly from the base of the flower. Sepals are sometimes free to the base. The lip lacks a dense cushion of trichomes on the upper surface near the apex. The rachis is sparsely to densely pubescent with the longest trichomes 0.008 inches long or longer.

Ute ladies' tresses generally flowers from late July through August, occasionally into September and early October.

Habitat

This species is a riparian species endemic to moist soils in mesic or wet meadows adjacent to springs, lakes, or perennial streams between the elevations of about 5,500 to 6,850 feet. Within these habitat types Ute ladies' tresses can be found in the more open areas that have not been heavily grazed. The two eastern populations occur in mesic riparian meadows in relict tall grass prairie areas in Colorado. The central populations of Ute ladies' tresses are in wet or mesic riparian meadows or in understory meadows of riparian woodlands in eastern Utah. The western populations are found in riparian, lake and spring-fed wet or mesic meadows in western Utah and eastern Nevada.

Historic Range and Current Distribution

Ute ladies' tresses is found in three separate geographic areas of the interior western United States.

There are two populations in Colorado; one on property owned by the City of Boulder, Boulder County, and the other along Clear Creek in Jefferson County. Historic collections may have been made from either Weld or Morgan County along the South Platte River Valley in 1856 and in El Paso County in 1896.

The second area is along the Colorado River drainage in eastern Utah. Populations are found along: Green River, Daggett County; Dinosaur National Monument's Cub Creek drainage, Uintah County; Uinta and Whiterocks Rivers, Duchesne and Uintah Counties; Duchesne River, Duchesne County; Fremont River in Capitol Reef National Park, Wayne County; Deer Creek, Garfield County. All of the eastern Utah populations were discovered after 1977.

The third area is in western Utah and eastern Nevada including: Utah Lake, Utah County; Weber County, Utah; Jordan River drainage, Salt Lake County, Utah; Red Butte Canyon near Salt Lake City (plants in this population were last observed in 1966); Tooele County, Utah (plants in this population were last observed in 1956); and Lincoln County, Nevada (plants in this population were last observed in 1936. Most of the Utah populations are on Bureau of Land Management (Vernal and Cedar City Districts), National Park Service Dinosaur National Monument and Capitol Reef National Park), or U.S. Forest Service (possibly on Ashely, Dixie, Fishlake, Manti-Lasal, Uinta, and Wasatch-Cache National Forests) lands. One population is found on Ute Indian Tribal lands on the Uintah and Ouray Reservation. Two populations are found on private property.

Less than 6,000 individual plants of Ute ladies' tresses are known (as of 1992) in the 10 remaining populations. The Boulder County population is the largest of the known populations. In 1986 this site contained 5,500 plants.

Conservation and Recovery

Modifications to and losses of riparian habitat have adversely affected Ute ladies' tresses, especially along the Wasatch Mountains foothills in Utah. These areas have been affected by urbanization, stream channelization, and construction projects in and adjacent to the Jordan and Weber Rivers and their tributaries and in wetlands and wet meadows adjacent to Utah Lake and the Great Salt Lake. All but two populations in western Utah and Nevada are believed to be extinct due to the above mentioned activities. The Colorado populations are threatened by the potential conversion of open space areas to developed parks. Most of the populations are in areas where they could be impacted by livestock grazing and trampling. The actual impacts of these activities on Ute ladies' tresses are unknown. Intense grazing is thought to be detrimental but light to moderate grazing may actually be beneficial.

Localized catastrophic events could lead to the extinction of individual populations as could the indiscriminate use of herbicides or other chemicals.

All riparian plant species are vulnerable to alterations in stream flow and water table levels.

Recovery of Ute ladies' tresses will depend on the protection and restoration of the riparian habitats inhabited by this plant. Studies are needed to determine this species' specific life history and ecological requirements as well as how livestock grazing and other human related activities affect the plant. Propagation and transplant techniques should be developed and Ute ladies' tresses should be introduced or reintroduced into areas with suitable habitat to establish new populations.

Bibliography

U.S. Fish and Wildlife Service. "Endangered and Threatened Wildlife and Plants; Final Rule to List the Plant *Spiranthes Diluvialis* (Ute Ladies' Tresses) as a Threatened species." *Federal Register*. Vol. 57, No. 12, January 17, 1992: 2048-2053.

Contacts

USFWS Regional Office
P. O. Box 25486
Denver, CO 80225
Phone: 303-236-7920

Ecological Services Field Office
Lincoln Plaza
145 East 1300 South, Suite 404
Salt Lake City, UT 84115
Phone: 801-524-5001

Adapted from data compiled by the Threatened and Endangered Species Information Institute (13950 W. 20th Ave., Golden, CO 80401) for *Beacham's International Threatened, Endangered, and Extinct Species* published on CD ROM, available from Beacham Publishing.

Alabama Streak-Sorus Fern
Thelypteris pilosa var. *alabamensis*

A. M. Evans

Status	Threatened
Listed	July 8, 1992
Family	Thelypteridaceae (Marsh Fern)
Description	Small, evergreen fern with clustered fronds.
Habitat	Crevices or rough rock surfaces of Pottsville sandstone.
Threats	Road or dam construction, limited population.
Range	Alabama

Description

The Alabama streak-sorus fern is a small evergreen with linear-lanceolate fronds 4 to 8 inches long. The fronds appear clustered, arising from short, slender rhizomes covered with reddish-brown scales. The stipe portion of the frond (petiole) is slender, erect to ascending, 0.4 to 1 inch long, and covered with long hairs. The blade is typically 1 to 4 inches long, and divided once into many ovate to suborbicular leaf segments (pinnae). The sori (groups of spore-producing reproductive structures) occur on the underside of the blades and are linear in shape. This is the only southeastern species of *Thelypteris* which lacks indusia (a thin membrane covering the sori).

Habitat

The species takes root in crevices or on rough rock surfaces of Pottsville sandstone along the Black Warrior River in Alabama. Plants typically occur on "ceilings" of sandstone overhangs (rockhouses), on ledges beneath overhangs, and on exposed cliff faces. These bluffs and overhangs are usually directly above the stream; however, some are located a short distance away from the river. Locations vary in slope aspect and shade coverage, from completely shaded to partially sunny on exposed bluff faces. The sites are kept moist by natural water seepage over the sandstone from up-slope runoff. Water vapor from the stream increases the humidity for those sites directly above the water or nearby.

The species grows among various bryophytes and is often associated with climbing hydrangea (*Decumaria barbara*), *Thalictrum clavatum*, *Heuchera parviflora*, and the ferns *Osmunda cinnamonea*, *O. regailis*, and most notably, the Appalachian bristle fern (*Trichomanes boschianum*).

Historic Range

The species' known range is confined to an approximately 3.25 mile stretch along the Black Warrior River in Winston County, Alabama. Past distribution is thought to have been in this same general area.

Current Distribution

Presently in this area, 15 separate localities have been documented. All sites are within the boundaries of the Bankhead National Forest and the majority occur on U.S. Forest Service land. Several localities are on private inholdings.

Conservation and Recovery

The type locality, which is approximately five miles downstream of extant populations, was destroyed in 1960. The cliffs where the plants grew were leveled when a new bridge was constructed. The area was subsequently flooded with the completion of Lewis Smith Dam several miles downstream. The impoundment inundated suitable habitat, and perhaps plants, upstream and downstream of the type locality. Currently, plants are located on both sides of a highway bridge upstream of the reservoir's influence. Plants may have been destroyed by this bridge construction. Future road or dam construction along the upper reaches of the river poses a potential threat to extant populations.

Logging of woodlands above the occupied sites could adversely affect the micro-habitat needed by the species. The species is dependent on up-slope runoff and seepage to maintain the substrate moisture. Heavy timbering or clear-cutting could alter the area's hydrology by interrupting this natural seepage. Additionally, the loss of the canopy would increase ambient light and lower the humidity. Thus, timber removal would dehydrate the habitat and such could be detrimental to this species.

Overhangs or rockhouses are habitat for about 50% of the known populations. These areas are frequented by hikers, fishermen, and campers and are subject to vandalism. Two of the larger populations occur in rockhouses which are often used by humans, as evidenced by numerous footprints, abundant litter, and old campfires. Intentional or incidental damage caused by hikers and campers, in addition to the heat and smoke from campfires, threatens these populations.

Over-collecting for any purpose would adversely impact this species due to its rarity and the small number of individuals at several sites. The species' limited distribution makes it vulnerable to collectors and vandals.

No species specific diseases or predators have been identified. However, disease or predation could have a serious adverse impact on the small and fragmented populations.

The greatest threat to this species is its extreme vulnerability due to its limited range and small number of plants at many of the sites. A single natural or anthropogenic disturbance could seriously reduce the population size and affect the species' viability. Catastrophic flooding through the narrow gorge could possibly scour all the occupied sites to such a degree that the size of the population would be significantly reduced. Sites near the water have few individuals (one to three plants), probably because of scouring from seasonal (as opposed to catastrophic) flooding. Severe drought would decrease the substrate moisture and be detrimental to this species. A local drought in 1990 appeared to kill individual plants at several localities.

As a natural erosional process, sandstone overhangs and bluffs periodically erode small and large sections. A site could be completely eliminated (including one with a large number of plants) if one such incident occurred.

Conservation measures provided to species listed as endangered or threatened under the Endangered Species Act include recognition, recovery actions, requirements for Federal protection, and prohibitions against certain practices. Listing encourages and results in conservation actions by Federal, State, and private agencies, groups, and individuals. The Endangered Species Act provides for possible land acquisition and cooperation with the States and requires that recovery actions be carried out for all listed species.

Federal involvement is expected to include the Environmental Protection Agency in consideration of the Clean Water Act's provision for pesticides registration, and waste management actions. The Corps of Engineers will include this species in project planning and operation and during the permit review process. The Federal Highway Administration will consider impacts of bridge and road construction at points where known habitat is crossed. Urban development within the drainage basin may involve the Farmers Home Administration and their loan programs.

Bibliography

U.S. Fish and Wildlife Service. "Endangered and Threatened Wildlife and Plants; Threatened Status for the Plant *Thelypteris pilosa* var. *Alabamensis* (Alabama Streak- sorus fern)." *Federal Register*. Vol. 57, No. 131. July 8, 1992: 30164-30168.

Contacts

U.S. Fish and Wildlife Service
Regional Office
Suite 200, 1875 Century Blvd.
Atlanta, GA 30345
Phone: 404-679-4000

Ecological Services Field Office
P. O. Drawer 1190
Daphne, AL 36526
Phone: 205-441-5181
FAX: 205-441-6222

Adapted from data compiled by the Threatened and Endangered Species Information Institute (13950 W. 20th Ave., Golden, CO 80401) for *Beacham's International Threatened, Endangered, and Extinct Species* published on CD ROM, available from Beacham Publishing.

CALIFORNIA VERNAL POOL PLANTS

Vernal Pool Habitats
in San Diego County, California

On August 3, 1993, the U.S. Fish and Wildlife Service listed three vernal pool plants and the Riverside Fairy Shrimp as endangered. Vernal pool habitat conditions are described here rather than being repeated in each of the species accounts.

California Orcutt Grass
Otay Mesa Mint
Riverside Fairy Shrimp
San Diego Button Celery

The habitat and range of California vernal pools has been greatly reduced. Vernal pools, existing as slight depressions on flat mesas, are found in locations that are especially vulnerable to one or more of the following habitat disturbances: Urban and agricultural development, off-road vehicle use, cattle trampling, human trampling, road development, military activities, and water management activities. Many pool groups were entirely eliminated and replaced with urban or agricultural developments.

Otay Mesa has the most threats of habitat damage of all the sites where vulnerable species occur. The Service is aware of 37 separate proposed precise development plans and tentative maps that have been filed for this area, as required by the California Environmental Quality Act. These plans encompass approximately 80% of the undeveloped portion of the mesa within the jurisdiction of the City of San Diego and virtually all but four of the remaining vernal pool complexes. Of these four remaining pool complexes, three are adversely affected by other activities or development proposals.

Preliminary designs by the California Department of Transportation for a state route running near vulnerable species' habitat include alignments that sever the existing natural connection between two of the largest remaining vernal pool complexes on Otay Mesa. The construction of this new major highway access route into Otay Mesa would further facilitate its development.

An existing local airport is presently being evaluated as a potential site for an international airport servicing San Diego. This proposal includes alternative runway alignments that would destroy portions of one of the two largest remaining vernal pool complexes. A binational airport is also being considered for Otay Mesa, although these plans are too preliminary to allow assessment of potential impacts to vernal pools. An increase in the number of vehicle trips in this area would occur as a result of the airport, and this increased traffic would likely lead to a demand for more roads, which could directly impact the pools.

Habitat trampling, and in some cases trampling of the species itself, due to livestock grazing occurs on Otay Mesa in areas where several vernal pool complexes collectively contain all four of the proposed species. Organisms within the pools may be trampled and killed by livestock prior to reproduction. Soil may become compacted or eroded, and water may be impacted with sediment.

Otay Mesa is a common area for travel from Mexico to the United States; hence, habitat and plants are threatened with trampling by humans. Also, the Immigration and Naturalization Service has proposed several projects at the international border, including border lighting, that could result in direct adverse impacts to vernal pools on Otay Mesa, due to construction activities.

In 1979, vulnerable species occurred on Otay Mesa in seven pool groups containing 34 vernal pools. By 1986, agricultural plowing had destroyed 11 of these vernal pools. All of the remaining 10 pools supporting the species are grazed by livestock; hence, the habitat and plants are impacted by trampling. Five pools were adversely affected by trampling associated with immigrants attempting to cross the Mexico-United States border.

Vernal pool habitat in San Diego County has declined by 97%, and most of the remaining pools face one or more threats. Similar declines in habitat have occurred in Riverside and Ventura Counties, and to a lesser degree in Baja California, Mexico. Vernal pool habitat in Los Angeles County has been destroyed. In Orange County, 90 to 98% of the historical vernal pool habitat has been eliminated. Vernal pool flora in Orange County has not been well documented. Most of the remaining vernal pools face one or more threats in the rapidly growing southern California area.

The vernal pool habitat upon which vulnerable species depend is also vulnerable to destruction due to alteration of the watershed. In some cases, an increase in pool water volume due to urban run-off has led to more prolonged periods of inundation, and at the other extreme, some pools have been drained or blocked from their source of water.

Pools have also been degraded due to the use of off-road vehicles, which have impacted the habitats of vulnerable species. These vehicles compact soils, crush plants when water is in the pools, cause turbidity, and leave deep ruts. The damage may alter the microhydrology of the pools. Dirt roads that go through or adjacent to pools are widened as motorists try to avoid the inevitable mud puddles. Thus, pools are gradually destroyed by vehicles traveling on dirt roads. Vehicle access and damage has occurred on virtually all remaining vernal pool complexes.

Other factors have greatly impacted the existence of vulnerable species, including introduction of non-native plant species, competition with invading species, trash dumping, fire, fire suppression activities, and drought. The low numbers of vernal pool habitats remaining and their scattered distributions make vulnerable species vulnerable to extinction due to future events that are unpredictable, human, or naturally caused.

Trash dumping also degrades vernal pools. Chunks of concrete, tires, refrigerators, sofas, and other pieces of garbage or debris were found in pools containing vulnerable species. This trash crushes, or shades vernal pool plants, disrupts the hydrologic functions of the pool, and in some cases may release toxic substances.

Many vernal pools on Otay Mesa are dominated by non-native plants such as the common grass *Lolinm perenne*. Vulnerable species is tolerant of inundation and crowds out the native vernal pool species. Ranchers introduced non-native species into some areas to increase the amount of forage available to livestock.

The geographically restricted range and distribution of vulnerable species increase the possibility that agricultural activity, urban development, or other activities in or near remnant vernal pool ecosystems could destroy a significant portion of the species' remaining population and habitat. Unpredictable natural events, such as drought or fire, would be devastating to vulnerable species due to its fragmented and restricted range.

Three vernal pool groups in southwestern Riverside County also contain vulnerable species. One of these complexes is partially preserved within The Nature Conservancy's Santa Rosa Plateau Reserve. Another complex is often plowed and is within the general locality of a conditionally approved residential development. A proposed project in this area includes major improvements to roads and utility crossings that would directly impact 0.2 acres of this watershed. Proposed mitigation consists of experimental watershed creation. Soil sedimentation could still occur as well as impacts to hydrologic function. Several tract projects, already approved within the watershed, would alter the pool hydrology and adversely impact the species therein. The Service and California Department of Fish and Game are working to find a buyer for this site.

California Orcutt Grass
Orcuttia californica

Fred Roberts, USFWS

Status	Endangered
Listed	August 3, 1993
Family	Poaceae (Grass)
Description	Small annual reaching 4 inches in height, bright green colored and secretes sticky droplets.
Habitat	Vernal pools in areas with Mediterranean climates.
Threats	Urban and agricultural development, human and cattle trampling, road development.
Range	California

Description

California orcutt grass is a member of the grass family, associated with deep pools of water. It is a small annual that reaches 4 inches in height, is colored bright green, and secretes sticky droplets that taste bitter. Inflorescences, borne from May through June, consist of seven spikelets arranged in two ranks, with the upper spikelets overlapping on a somewhat twisted axis. The teeth of the lemma (bract enclosing the floret) extend 0.2 inches long or less. Its teeth are sharply pointed and its terminal bristles are 0.2 inches long or less. Stems usually are prostrate and the fruit grow from 0.06 to 0.07 inches long. Plants bear soft and straight spreading hairs and the spikelets are remote on the axis below, crowded toward the apex.

Habitat

The species occurs in vernal pools which form in areas with Mediterranean climates where slight depressions become seasonally wet or inundated following fall and winter rains. Water remains in these pools for a few months at a time, due to an impervious layer such as hard pan, clay, or basalt beneath the soil surface. Gradual drying occurs during the spring. The pools form on mesa tops or valley floors and are interspersed among very low hills usually referred to as mima mounds.

For a continued discussion of this habitat, see "The Vernal Pool Habitats of San Diego County," page 1761.

Historic Range and Current Distribution

The species once occurred in vernal pools from San Quintin, Baja California, Mexico, northward to Riverside, Los Angeles, and San Diego Counties in southern California. Historically, known populations from near Downey and Lakewood in Los Angeles County and near Murietta Hot Springs in Riverside County were extirpated. Presently, it occurs in vernal pools on The Nature Conservancy's Santa Rosa Plateau Preserve, and in Riverside County.

Conservation and Recovery

The habitat and range of this species have been greatly reduced. Vernal pools, existing as slight depressions on flat mesas, are found in locations that are especially vulnerable to one or more of the following habitat disturbances: urban and agricultural development, off-road vehicle use, cattle trampling, human trampling, road development, military activities, and water management activities. Many pool groups were entirely eliminated and replaced with urban or agricultural developments.

Three vernal pool groups in southwestern Riverside County also contain this species. One of these complexes is partially preserved within The Nature Conservancy's Santa Rosa Plateau Reserve. Another complex is often plowed and is within the general locality of a conditionally approved residential development. A proposed project in this area includes major improvements to roads and utility crossings that would directly impact 0.2 acres of this watershed. Proposed mitigation consists of experimental watershed creation. Soil sedimentation could still occur as well as impacts to hydrologic function. Several tract projects, already approved within the watershed, would alter the pool hydrology and adversely impact the species therein. The Service and California Department of Fish and Game are working to find a buyer for this site.

A third population exists on private unprotected land. One pool near a road in this area was disced. These pools are also potentially threatened by widening of an adjacent road.

Bibliography

U.S. Fish and Wildlife Service. "Endangered and Threatened Wildlife and Plants; Determination of Endangered Status for Three Vernal Pool Plants and the Riverside Fairy Shrimp." *Federal Register* Vol. 58, No. 147. August 3, 1993: 41384-41392.

Contacts

U.S. Fish and Wildlife Service
    Regional Office
Eastside Federal Complex
911 N.S. 11th Avenue
Portland, OR 97232-4181
Phone: 503-231-6118

Adapted from data compiled by the Threatened and Endangered Species Information Institute (13950 W. 20th Ave., Golden, CO 80401) for *Beacham's International Threatened, Endangered, and Extinct Species* published on CD ROM, available from Beacham Publishing.

Otay Mesa Mint

Pogogyne nudiuscula

Dave Bramlet, California Native Plant Society

Status	Endangered
Listed	August 3, 1993
Family	Lamiacese (Mint)
Description	Annual member of the mint family reaching 12 inches in height with bright green leaves, purple flowers and lack of hair on the calyx and bracts.
Habitat	Vernal pools in areas with Mediterranean climates.
Threats	Urban and agricultural development, human and cattle trampling, road development.
Range	California

Description

Otay Mesa mint typically blooms from May through June. This aromatic plant is an erect annual reaching 12 inches in height. The bright green, spatulate leaves have few hairs. Bright purple flowers occur in whorls on spikes. The lack of hairs on the calyx and bracts of this species differentiate it from *Pogogyne abramsii*.

Habitat

The species occurs in vernal pools which form in areas with Mediterranean climates where slight depressions become seasonally wet or inundated following fall and winter rains. Water remains in these pools for a few months at a time, due to an impervious layer such as hard pan, clay, or basalt beneath the soil surface. Gradual drying occurs during the spring. The pools form on Mesa tops or valley floors and are interspersed among very low hills usually referred to as mima mounds.

For a continued discussion of this habitat, see "The Vernal Pool Habitats of San Diego County," page 1761.

Historic Range

Otay Mesa mint once occurred from Otay Mesa of San Diego County to immediately south of the international border in Baja California, Mexico. The historic range may have extended to the Mesas east of Balboa Park and south of Mission Valley in San Diego where vernal pools contain P. abramsii, another endangered vernal pool plant. The sites in extreme northern Baja California,

Mexico, were very likely extirpated.

Current Distribution

The species is restricted to a few of the remaining vernal pools on Otay Mesa. Currently, the species' numbers are low and scattered across its range.

Conservation and Recovery

The habitat and range of Otay Mesa mint have been greatly reduced. Vernal pools, existing as slight depressions on flat mesas, are found in locations that are especially vulnerable to one or more of the following habitat disturbances: urban and agricultural development, off-road vehicle use, cattle trampling, human trampling, road development, military activities, and water management activities. Many pool groups were entirely eliminated and replaced with urban or agricultural developments.

Bibliography

U.S. Fish and Wildlife Service. "Endangered and Threatened Wildlife and Plants; Endangered Status for Three Vernal Pool Plants and the Riverside Fairy Shrimp." *Federal Register* Vol. 58, No. 147, August 3, 1993: 41384-41392.

Contacts

Sacramento Ecological Services Field Office
Room E-1803/1823
2800 Cottage Way
Sacramento, CA 98525
Phone: 916-978-4866
FAX: 916-978-4613

Ventura Ecological Services Field Office
Suite 100, 2140 Eastman Avenue
Ventura, CA 93003
Phone: 805-644-1766
FAX: 818-904-6288

Adapted from data compiled by the Threatened and Endangered Species Information Institute (13950 W. 20th Ave., Golden, CO 80401) for *Beacham's International Threatened, Endangered, and Extinct Species* published on CD ROM, available from Beacham Publishing.

San Diego Button-Celery

Eryngium aristulatum var. *parishii*

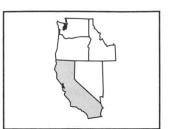

Status	Endangered
Listed	August 3, 1993
Family	Apiaceae (Parsley)
Description	Mostly annual parsley reaching 16 inches in height with gray green stems and leaves and spinose lobes.
Habitat	Vernal pools in areas with Mediterranean climates.
Threats	Urban and agricultural development, human and cattle trampling.
Range	California

Fred Roberts, USFWS

Description

San Diego button-celery is a member of the parsley family. It blooms from May through June and is usually an annual. However, under favorable conditions it facultatively becomes a perennial herb with a perennial tap root. The plant has spreading or ascending shape and reaches a height of 16 inches. The stems and lanceolate leaves are gray green with spinose lobes giving the plant a prickly appearance. Inflorescences form on short stalks with few-flowered greenish heads on the ends of branches. Its greenish heads, fruits with unequal scales, and bractlets without calloused margins separate it from other varieties.

Habitat

The species occurs in vernal pools which form in areas with Mediterranean climates where slight depressions become seasonally wet or inundated following fall and winter rains. Water remains in these pools for a few months at a time, due to an impervious layer such as hard pan, clay, or basalt beneath the soil surface. Gradual drying occurs during the spring. The pools form on mesa tops or valley floors and are interspersed among very low hills usually referred to as mima mounds.

For a continued discussion of this habitat, see "The Vernal Pool Habitats of San Diego County," page 1761.

Historic Range

The species once occurred from Riverside County, California, south to northern Baja California, Mexico.

Current Distribution

San Diego Button-celery currently occurs on the Santa Rosa Plateau in Riverside County; on Otay Mesa, Kearny Mesa, Del Mar Mesa, Miramar Naval Station, and Camp Pendleton in San Diego County; and in northern Baja California, Mexico.

Conservation and Recovery

The habitat and range of this species have been greatly reduced. Vernal pools, existing as slight depressions on flat mesas, are found in locations that are especially vulnerable to one or more of the following habitat disturbances: Urban and agricultural development, off-road vehicle use, cattle trampling, human trampling, road development, military activities, and water management activities. Many pool groups were entirely eliminated and replaced with urban or agricultural developments.

Bibliography

U.S. Fish and Wildlife Service. "Endangered and Threatened Wildlife and Plants; Endangered Status for Three Vernal Pool Plants and the Riverside Fairy Shrimp." *Federal Register* Vol. 58, No. 147, August 3, 1993: 41384-41392.

Contacts

USFWS Regional Office
Eastside Federal Complex
911 N.S. 11th Avenue
Portland, OR 97232-4181
Phone: 503-231-6118

Sacramento Ecological Services Field Office
Room E-1803/1823
2800 Cottage Way
Sacramento, CA 98525
Phone: 916-978-4866
FAX: 916-978-4613

Ventura Ecological Services Field Office
Suite 100, 2140 Eastman Avenue
Ventura, CA 93003
Phone: 805-644-1766
FAX: 818-904-6288

Adapted from data compiled by the Threatened and Endangered Species Information Institute (13950 W. 20th Ave., Golden, CO 80401) for *Beacham's International Threatened, Endangered, and Extinct Species* published on CD ROM, available from Beacham Publishing.

CENTRAL FLORIDA PLANTS

Central Florida's
High Pine and Scrub Communities

On April 7, 1993, the U.S. Fish and Wildlife Service listed seven central Florida plants as endangered. Because all of these species occur in the region, general habitat conditions are explained here rather than being repeated in each of the species accounts.

Avon Park Harebells
Scrub Buckwheat
Britton's Beargrass
Florida Perforate Cladoni.
Pigeon Wings
Lewton's Polygala
Sandlace

Habitat

The scrub community is xeromorphic and is dominated by a layer of evergreens (or nearly evergreen oaks) and/or Florida rosemary (*Ceratiola ericoides*). There may or may not be a pine overstory, generally sand pine (*Pinus clausa*), and the soils are sandy, well drained, and infertile. The Florida scrub jay, a threatened species, also inhabits this community type. Scrub occurs on dune ridges along Florida's Gulf and Atlantic coasts and on older inland sand ridges. Endemic plant species (species with limited geographic distributions) occur in scrub in various parts of Florida, with the largest concentration of endemics on the southernmost high interior ridge, the Lake Wales Ridge, northwest of Lake Okeechobee. Plants endemic to the Lake Wales Ridge are concentrated in scrub dominated by Florida rosemary on sites where the sand is apparently particularly devoid of nutrients; sites with slightly better nutrient status usually have dense stands of oaks, hickory, and sand pines. The scrub ecosystem is maintained by infrequent high intensity fires, with fires occurring as often as once a decade to less than once a century in sparsely-vegetated rosemary scrub.

The scrub community is able to withstand drought and is dominated by a layer of evergreens (or nearly evergreen oaks) and/or Florida rosemary. There may or may not be a pine overstory, generally sand pine, and the soils are sandy, well drained, and infertile. The Florida scrub jay, a threatened species, also inhabits this community type. Scrub occurs on dune ridges along Florida's Gulf and Atlantic coasts and on older inland sand ridges. Endemic plant species (species with limited geographic distributions) occur in scrub in various parts of Florida, with the largest concentration of endemics on the southernmost high interior ridge, the Lake Wales Ridge, northwest of Lake Okeechobee. Plants endemic to the Lake Wales Ridge are concentrated in scrub dominated by Ceratiola ericoides on sites where the sand is apparently particularly devoid of nutrients; sites with slightly better nutrient status usually have dense stands of oaks, hickory, and sand pines. The scrub ecosystem is maintained by infrequent high intensity fires, with fires occurring as often as once a decade to less than once a century in sparsely-vegetated rosemary scrub.

The high pine community (or sandhills vegetation) was once widespread in the southeastern United States from Virginia to Texas. The high pine community is a longleaf pine forest with an open, grassy understory of wiregrass (*Aristida stricta*) and other grasses, numerous herbs, and deciduous turkey oaks (*Quercus laevis*) or bluejack oaks (*Quercus incana*) that tolerate being burned to the ground. Frequent low-intensity fires maintained the grassy understory and prevented hardwoods from becoming established. In central Florida, high pine is intermingled with scrub; and "turkey oak barrens", intermediate between the two types of vegetation, exist in Polk and Highlands Counties. Most of the "barrens" that are in evidence today may represent the results of logging of longleaf pine, followed by fire suppression, which allowed turkey oaks to reach tree size, and allowed evergreen oaks to invade.

Thirteen plants, two lizards, and the Florida scrub jay, all endemic to the scrub or high pine communities, have been listed as threatened/endangered. Three other endemic plants, scrub bluestem (*Schizachyrium niveum*), Ashe's savory (*Calamintha ashei*), and cutthroat grass (*Panicum abscissum*), are candidate species.

Conservation and Recovery

Large sections of the high pine and scrub communities along Florida's Lake Wales Ridge have been and still are being converted to citrus groves, pasture and urban developments. Up to 85% of the estimated 546,800 acres of xeric upland vegetation originally found in Polk and Highlands Counties have been lost or altered.

Citrus groves are being expanded rapidly on the southern Lake Wales Ridge because the area escaped the worst effects of severe freezes during the 1980's.

Property taxation in most Florida counties favors agricultural land use and penalizes leaving land idle in native vegetation. These policies may be changing; Polk County has already passed a law for "preservation" zoning for the protection of natural vegetation.

Human activities, including off road vehicle use, trash dumping, and inadvertent tramping during outdoor recreational activities, threaten most of the endangered/ threatened species endemic to these ecosystems.

The limited geographic distribution of this species, the fragmentation of remaining habitat into small segments isolated from each other, and the relatively small size of the population have added to the threats faced by this species.

Efforts to preserve these endangered central Florida upland communities have been initiated. Activities include:

1. The State of Florida's Conservation and Recreation Lands program is buying land in Highlands and Polk Counties. A completed acquisition, the Arbuckle State Forest and Park (13,700 acres), includes a good representation of the scrub community.

2. The Nature Conservancy purchased property at Tiger Creek and Lake Apthorpe.

3. The U.S. Fish and Wildlife Service proposed the creation of a Lake Wales Ridge National Wildlife Refuge (10,000 acres) to protect/manage the endangered species inhabiting these ecosystems. The 12 sites that might be acquired overlap with those in State projects. A large tract at Carter Creek in Highlands County, is tentatively a high priority for acquisition, if funds become available.

Efforts by the U.S. Fish and Wildlife Service to protect the threatened Florida scrub jay may benefit all the plants and animals found in the scrub ecosystem.

Avon Park Harebells

Crotalaria avonensis

Steve Shirah   *Color Plate C-3*

Status	Endangered
Listed	April 27, 1993
Family	Fabaceae (Pea)
Description	Perennial herb with yellow, flowering racemes, and long, rounded, somewhat succulent, leaves coated with white or yellowish-white hairs.
Habitat	Dry, scrub, high pine communities.
Threats	Agricultural and urban development.
Range	Florida

Description

The Avon Park harebells is a perennial herb with a vertical tap root that produces flowering stems that originate as much as 4 inches below the surface. These stems grow upright for only a few centimeters above the surface and terminate in flowering racemes. The leaves are roughly 0.5 to 1.0 inch long, rounded, somewhat succulent, and coated with white or yellowish-white hairs. The racemes are both terminal and on short secondary branches opposite the leaves. The flower, shaped like a typical pea flower, has a yellow corolla about 0.3 to 0.4 inches long. The keel petal (at the bottom of the corolla) is shorter than the wing petals. The seed pods are inflated, tan to gray to maroon, nearly hairless, .56 to 1.0 inches long, and contain up to 18 seeds per pod. The pods can be nearly as long as the upright flower stalks that hold them in place. Flowering occurs between mid-March and June. After flowering, the plants enter a vegetative phase, forming clusters of stems that give a clumped or rosette appearance. The plants are dormant from late fall or early winter until March.

Habitat

Avon Park harebells occurs in dry upland communities in central Florida including scrub, high pine, or intermediate "turkey oak barrens," and in the coastal scrub community in the northwestern part of the state.

Avon Park Harebells typically grows in full sun on bare white sand or in association with clumps of reindeer lichens of the genus *Cladonia*, but many individuals are found in the partial shade of other plants.

For a continued habitat discussion of this species, see "Central Florida's High Pine and Scrub Communities," page 1773.

Historic Range and Current Distribution

Avon Park Harebells is one of the most narrowly distributed of the Lake Wales Ridge endemics. It is currently known from three sites in Polk County. The Saddle Blanket Lakes sites may fall within the areas purchased (or to be purchased) by the State of Florida's Conservation and Recreation Lands program.

Conservation and Recovery

This species is being displaced by the conversion of high pine and scrub communities to agriculture. It is also coming under pressure from property taxation that favors agriculture; human activities; and a limited geographic distribution.

For a continued discussion of the threats to this species, see "Central Florida's High Pine and Scrub Communities," page 1773.

Bibliography

U.S. Fish and Wildlife Service. "Endangered and Threatened Wildlife and Plants; Endangered or Threatened Status for Seven Central Florida Plants." *Federal Register* Vol. 58. No. 79. April 27, 1993: 25746-25755.

Contacts

U.S. Fish and Wildlife Service
Regional Office
Suite 200, 1875 Century Blvd.
Atlanta, GA 30345
Phone: 404-679-4000

Ecological Services Field Office
Suite 310, 6620 Southpoint Drive, South
Jacksonville, FL 32216-0912
Phone: 904-232-2580
FAX: 904-232-2404

Adapted from data compiled by the Threatened and Endangered Species Information Institute (13950 W. 20th Ave., Golden, CO 80401) for *Beacham's International Threatened, Endangered, and Extinct Species* published on CD ROM, available from Beacham Publishing.

Scrub Buckwheat

Eriogonum longifolium var. *gnaphalifolium*

Jim Yoakum

Status	Threatened
Listed	April 27, 1993
Family	Polygonaceae (Buckwheat)
Description	Perennial herb with long, narrow green or bronze-green leaves above and densely white-woolly beneath; and silvery, silky-pubescent flowers.
Habitat	High pine, scrub communities.
Threats	Agricultural and urban development.
Range	Florida

Description

Scrub Buckwheat is a perennial herb with a single stem that grows from a stout, woody root. Most of the leaves are at the base of the stem. The leaves are 6 to 8 inches long, narrowly oblanceolate, entire, and green or bronze-green above, densely white-woolly beneath. The leaves on the stem are smaller and arranged alternately. The stem is erect, up to 3 feet tall, and terminates in an open panicle. Each branch of the panicle ends in a cup-shaped involucre, with 5 to 8 teeth about 0.2 inch long. Within each involucre, 15 to 20 flowers form a cluster, with the stalk of each flower starting out erect, then reflexing so the flower hangs down below the involucre. Each flower is 0.2 to 0.3 inch long, with 6 linear sepals. The involucre and flowers are silvery, silky-pubescent.

Habitat

Scrub Buckwheat occurs in dry upland communities in central Florida including scrub, high pine, or intermediate "turkey oak barrens" and in the coastal scrub community in the northwestern part of the state.

Scrub Buckwheat occurs in habitats intermediate between scrub and sandhills (high pine), and in turkey oak barrens.

For a continued habitat discussion of this species, see "Central Florida's High Pine and Scrub Communities," page 1773.

Historic Range

Historic records exist for this species occurring in Lake County near Eustis; it still is found near Clermont in remnants of high pine.

Current Distribution

Scrub Buckwheat is found from Marion County to Highlands County. The northern range limit for this subspecies is in Ocala National Forest and areas of mixed scrub and high pine south of Ocala in Marion County. The plant may occur as far south as Sumter County. Other scattered localities include sites in Lake, southwest Orange, and northwest Osceola Counties as well as along the Lake Wales Ridge in Polk and Highlands County.

This species occurs on the following protected areas: Ocala National Forest, Lake Arbuckle State Forest and State Park, and The Nature Conservancy preserves at Tiger Creek and Lake Apthorpe. It also occurs on several sites that may be purchased by the State of Florida or the U.S. Fish and Wildlife Service.

Conservation and Recovery

This species is being displaced by the conversion of high pine and scrub communities to agriculture. It is also coming under pressure from property taxation that favors agriculture; human activities; and a limited geographic distribution.

For a continued discussion of the threats to this species, see "Central Florida's High Pine and Scrub Communities," page 1773.

Bibliography

U.S. Fish and Wildlife Service. "Endangered and Threatened Wildlife and Plants; Endangered or Threatened Status for Seven Central Florida Plants." *Federal Register* Vol. 58. No. 79. April 27, 1993: 25746-25755.

Contacts

U.S. Fish and Wildlife Service
Regional Office
Suite 200, 1875 Century Blvd.
Atlanta, GA 30345
Phone: 404-679-4000

Ecological Services Field Office
Suite 310, 6620 Southpoint Drive, South
Jacksonville, FL 32216-0912
Phone: 904-232-2580
FAX: 904-232-2404

Adapted from data compiled by the Threatened and Endangered Species Information Institute (13950 W. 20th Ave., Golden, CO 80401) for *Beacham's International Threatened, Endangered, and Extinct Species* published on CD ROM, available from Beacham Publishing.

Britton's Beargrass

Nolina brittoniana

K. R. Langdon

Status	Endangered
Listed	April 27, 1993
Family	Agavaceae (Agave)
Description	Perennial that grows from a bulblike root with flowering stem, symmetrical fruits bearing abundant seed.
Habitat	Dry upland communities in central Florida, and in coastal scrub community in northwestern Florida.
Threats	Conversion to citrus groves, pasture, and urban developments.
Range	Florida

Description

Britton's beargrass is a perennial that grows from a short, thick, fleshy, bulblike rootstock. The leaves are 3 to 6 feet long and 0.2 to 0.5 inches wide, forming a rosette with the youngest leaves upright and the oldest lying nearly flat on the ground. The flowering stem, usually solitary, grows at least 6 feet high from the rosette in April. The inflorescence is a panicle with about 6 branches; when in bloom, the branches are covered with small white six-parted flowers, making the plant very conspicuous. Individual plants appear to usually have all male or all female flowers. The fruits are symmetrical; triangular in cross-section. The plants bear abundant seed, which is easily germinated, and the plant is not difficult to propagate. In the natural setting, this species occurs as scattered specimens, and rarely if ever forms large colonies.

Habitat

Britton's beargrass occurs in dry upland communities in central Florida including scrub, high pine, or intermediate "turkey oak barrens" and in the coastal scrub community in the northwestern part of the state.

For a continued habitat discussion of this species, see "Central Florida's High Pine and Scrub Communities," page 1773.

Historic Range and Current Distribution

Britton's Beargrass is found from the south end of the Lake Wales Ridge in Highlands County north to Orange County near

Orlando and northern Lake County. An apparently isolated locality was reported from Hernando County, north of Tampa. On the Lake Wales Ridge, *N. brittoniana* occurs in most of the tracts that are targeted for acquisition by the State of Florida or the U.S. Fish and Wildlife Service.

Historical records indicate this plant also occurred in the northwest corner of Osceola County.

Conservation and Recovery

This species is being displaced by the conversion of high pine and scrub communities to agriculture. It is also coming under pressure from property taxation that favors agriculture; human activities; and a limited geo-graphic distribution.

For a continued discussion of the threats to this species, see "Central Florida's High Pine and Scrub Communities," page 1773.

Bibliography

U.S. Fish and Wildlife Service. "Endangered and Threatened Wildlife and Plants; Endangered or Threatened Status for Seven Central Florida Plants." *Federal Register* Vol. 58, No. 79. April 27, 1993: 25746-25755.

Contacts

U.S. Fish and Wildlife Service
Regional Office
Suite 200, 1875 Century Blvd.
Atlanta, GA 30345
Phone: 404-679-4000

Ecological Services Field Office
Suite 310, 6620 Southpoint Drive, South
Jacksonville, FL 32216-0912
Phone: 904-232-2580
FAX: 904-232-2404

Adapted from data compiled by the Threatened and Endangered Species Information Institute (13950 W. 20th Ave., Golden, CO 80401) for *Beacham's International Threatened, Endangered, and Extinct Species* published on CD ROM, available from Beacham Publishing.

Florida Perforate Cladonia
Cladonia perforata

Eric S. Menges, Archbold Biological Station

Status	Endangered
Listed	April 27, 1993
Family	Cladoniaceae (Reindeer Moss)
Description	Lichen with dense groupings with spore-producing branches.
Habitat	Scrub, high pine, dry upland communities in central Florida and in the coastal scrub of the northwestern part of the state.
Threats	Habitat conversion to citrus groves, pasture, and urban developments.
Range	Florida

Description

The Florida perforate cladonia is a conspicuous lichen that forms dense groupings 0.8 to 2.5 inches tall. The branches of Cladonia lichens differ from those of other branched lichens in that the Cladonia branches are developed from spore-producing structures, rather than from the vegetative body of the fungus that makes up the basic structure of a typical lichen. For the Florida perforate cladonia, the vegetative body is not in evidence, and the podetia, which grow in intricate tufts, are pale yellowish grey, and the surface appears more or less glossy. Individual podetia are mostly 1 to 1.5 inches tall and their larger axes measure 3 to 6 millimeters in diameter. The branches are either forked, or they form whorls, splitting into 3 or more branches. The surfaces of the branches are uniform.

The interior surface of the branches facing the central canal consist of loosely woven fungal strands. The Florida perforate cladonia produces para-depside squamatic acid. Although no medicinal or other uses for squamatic acid are currently known, this natural product has not been studied enough to be ruled unusable.

Habitat

The Florida perforate cladonia occurs in dry upland communities in central Florida including scrub, high pine, or intermediate "turkey oak barrens" and in the coastal scrub community in the northwestern part of the state.

For a continued habitat discussion of this species, see "Central Florida's High Pine and Scrub Communities," page 1773.

Historic Range

Historic specimen collections and data suggest that this species' historic range was extremely limited. No additional sites were noted.

Current Distribution

The Florida perforate cladonia is found on one of the Gulf barrier islands, Santa Rosa Island, which is found on Eglin Air Force Base.

The 1991 population was estimated at a minimum of 26,000 plants: 17,000 on one privately owned site; 4,400 on Archbold Biological Station; and 1,300 on Santa Rosa Island.

Conservation and Recovery

This species is being displaced by the conversion of high pine and scrub communities to agriculture. It is also coming under pressure from property taxation that favors agriculture; human activities; and a limited geographic distribution.

For a continued discussion of the threats to this species, see "Central Florida's High Pine and Scrub Communities," page 1773.

Bibliography

U.S. Fish and Wildlife Service. "Endangered and Threatened Wildlife and Plants; Endangered or Threatened Status for Seven Central Florida Plants." *Federal Register* Vol. 58. No. 79. April 27, 1993: 25746-25755.

Contacts

U.S. Fish and Wildlife Service
Regional Office
Suite 200, 1875 Century Blvd.
Atlanta, GA 30345
Phone: 404-679-4000

Ecological Services Field Office
Suite 310, 6620 Southpoint Drive, South
Jacksonville, FL 32216-0912
Phone: 904-232-2580
FAX: 904-232-2404

Adapted from data compiled by the Threatened and Endangered Species Information Institute (13950 W. 20th Ave., Golden, CO 80401) for *Beacham's International Threatened, Endangered, and Extinct Species* published on CD ROM, available from Beacham Publishing.

Pigeon Wings

Clitoria fragrans

John Fitzpatrick,
Archbold Biological Station

Color Plate C-1

Status	Threatened
Listed	April 27, 1993
Family	Fabaceae (Pea)
Description	Erect, perennial herb with one or a few stems growing from a thick horizontal root.
Habitat	Dry upland communities in central Florida, and in coastal scrub community in northwestern Florida.
Threats	Conversion to citrus groves, pasture, and urban developments.
Range	Florida

Description

Pigeon Wings is an erect, perennial herb, 6 to 20 inches tall, with one or a few stems growing from a thick horizontal root that may be more than 6 feet long. The stems are wiry 0.04 to 0.08 inch thick and somewhat zigzag in form. The leaves have 3 rather leathery leaflets. The leaflets of the upper leaves are linear (lower leaves somewhat wider) and are blunt at the tip.

Pigeon Wings has two types of flowers: those that are showy insect-pollinated, and those that are small, lacking petals, and self-pollinating. These flowers are usually borne in pairs. The flowers are inverted so that the anthers and stigma touch the backs of visiting insects. The corolla has one large petal, the standard petal, 1.5 to 2 inches long. This petal is lilac in color. The keel is small and white. The common name, pigeon wings, refers to the appearance of the flower. Flowers with petals appear from May to June, with a few petalless flowers borne as late as September. The seed pod is borne on a stalk that projects from the dried calyx.

Habitat

Piegon Wings occurs in dry upland communities in central Florida including scrub, high pine, or intermediate "turkey oak barrens" and in the coastal scrub community in the northwestern part of the state.

For a continued habitat discussion of this species, see "Central Florida's High Pine and Scrub Communities," page 1773.

Historic Range

There are historic records for specimens collected in Lake County in 1910 and in Osceola County in 1964.

Current Distribution

Pigeon Wings occurs primarily on the Lake Wales Ridge in Highlands and Polk Counties. It is found in Arbuckle State Forest and Park, on the Archbold Biological Station, on Lake Apthorpe and Tiber Creek properties owned by The Nature Conservancy, and at the State-owned Saddle Blanket Lakes area. Pigeon Wings is also found on several sites that may be purchased by the State or by the U.S. Fish and Wildlife Service. This plant may occur on the Avon Park Air Force Range (on the Bombing Range Ridge, a separate landform from the Lake Wales Ridge).

Conservation and Recovery

Large sections of the high pine and scrub communities along Florida's Lake Wales Ridge have been and still are being converted to citrus groves, pasture and urban developments. Up to 85% of the estimated 546,800 acres of xeric upland vegetation originally found in Polk and Highlands Counties have been lost or altered.

Citrus groves are being expanded rapidly on the southern Lake Wales Ridge because the area escaped the worst effects of severe freezes during the 1980's.

This species is being displaced by the conversion of high pine and scrub communities to agriculture. It is also coming under pressure from property taxation that favors agriculture; human activities; and a limited geographic distribution.

For a continued discussion of the threats to this species, see "Central Florida's High Pine and Scrub Communities," page 1773.

Bibliography

U.S. Fish and Wildlife Service. "Endangered and Threatened Wildlife and Plants; Endangered or Threatened Status for Seven Central Florida Plants." *Federal Register* Vol. 58. No. 79. April 27, 1993: 25746-25755.

Contacts

U.S. Fish and Wildlife Service
Regional Office
Suite 200, 1875 Century Blvd.
Atlanta, GA 30345
Phone: 404-679-4000

Ecological Services Field Office
Suite 310, 6620 Southpoint Drive, South
Jacksonville, FL 32216-0912
Phone: 904-232-2580
FAX: 904-232-2404

Adapted from data compiled by the Threatened and Endangered Species Information Institute (13950 W. 20th Ave., Golden, CO 80401) for *Beacham's International Threatened, Endangered, and Extinct Species* published on CD ROM, available from Beacham Publishing.

Lewton's Polygala

Polygala lewtonii

Jonathan Shaw, Bok Tower Gardens

Status	Endangered
Listed	April 27, 1993
Family	Polygalaceae (Milkwort)
Description	Perennial with upward-curving stems, often branched, and small leaves overlapping the stems like shingles.
Habitat	Dry upland communities in central Florida, and in coastal scrub community in northwestern Florida.
Threats	Conversion to citrus groves, pasture, and urban developments.
Range	Florida

Description

Lewton's polygala is a perennial with a taproot that produces one to several annual stems, which are spreading, upward-curving, or erect, and are often branched. The leaves are small, sessile, rather succulent, broader toward the tip, and are borne upright, tending to overlap along the stem, like shingles. The normally opening flowers are in erect, loosely flowered racemes up to 0.6 inches long. The racemes are about 0.5 centimeters long and are bright pink or purplish-red. Each flower is about 0.14 inches long. Two of the 5 sepals are enlarged and wing-like, between which the largest of the 3 petals forms a keel that ends in a tuft of finger-like projections.

Habitat

Lewton's polygala occurs in dry upland communities in central Florida including scrub, high pine, or intermediate "turkey oak barrens" and in the coastal scrub community in the northwestern part of the state.

Lewton's polygala is most often found in the habitats intermediate between high pine and scrub (turkey oak barrens) but does occur in both habitats.

For a continued habitat discussion of this species, see "Central Florida's High Pine and Scrub Communities," page 1773.

Historic Range and Current Distribution

Lewton's polygala has been collected in Highlands, Polk, Osceola, Lake, and Marion Counties.

The plant is currently found in Polk County on the Arbuckle State Forest and Park, the State's Catfish creek land acquisition project, The Nature Conservancy's Tiger Creek Preserve, and in the Poinciana residential development.

This species also occurs on Ocala National Forest in Marion County.

Conservation and Recovery

Large sections of the high pine and scrub communities along Florida's Lake Wales Ridge have been and still are being converted to citrus groves, pasture and urban developments. Up to 85% of the estimated 546,800 acres of xeric upland vegetation originally found in Polk and Highlands Counties have been lost or altered.

Citrus groves are being expanded rapidly on the southern Lake Wales Ridge because the area escaped the worst effects of severe freezes during the 1980's.

This species is being displaced by the conversion of high pine and scrub communities to agriculture. It is also coming under pressure from property taxation that favors agriculture; human activities; and a limited geographic distribution.

For a continued discussion of the threats to this species, see "Central Florida's High Pine and Scrub Communities," page 1773.

Bibliography

U.S. Fish and Wildlife Service. "Endangered and Threatened Wildlife and Plants; Endangered or Threatened Status for Seven Central Florida Plants." *Federal Register* Vol. 58, No. 79. April 27, 1993: 25746-25755.

Contacts

U.S. Fish and Wildlife Service
Regional Office
Suite 200, 1875 Century Blvd.
Atlanta, GA 30345
Phone: 404-679-4000

Ecological Services Field Office
Suite 310, 6620 Southpoint Drive, South
Jacksonville, FL 32216-0912
Phone: 904-232-2580
FAX: 904-232-2404

Adapted from data compiled by the Threatened and Endangered Species Information Institute (13950 W. 20th Ave., Golden, CO 80401) for *Beacham's International Threatened, Endangered, and Extinct Species* published on CD ROM, available from Beacham Publishing.

Sandlace
Polygonella myriophylla

Jonathan Shaw, Bok Tower Gardens

Status	Endangered
Listed	April 27, 1993
Family	Polygonaceae (Buckwheat)
Description	Sprawling shrub with reddish-brown bark and short lateral branches with white, pink, or yellow flowers.
Habitat	Dry upland communities in central Florida, and in coastal scrub community in northwestern Florida.
Threats	Conversion to citrus groves, pasture, and urban developments.
Range	Florida

Description

Sandlace is a sprawling shrub that is similar in habit to creeping juniper, a popular landscape shrub. The shrub's many branches zigzag along the ground and root at the nodes, forming low mats. The lower parts of the creeping branches have reddish-brown bark that cracks and partly separates in long, flat, interlacing strips. The short lateral branches are upright, leafy, and end in flowering racemes. Sandlace has the distinctive sheathing stipules typical of the buckwheat family. The leaves are needle-like, fleshy, and 0.1 to 0.4 inches long. The small flowers have white (or pink or yellow) petal-like sepals up to 0.1 inch long.

Habitat

Sandlace occurs in dry upland communi-

ties in central Florida including scrub, high pine, or intermediate "turkey oak barrens" and in the coastal scrub community in the northwestern part of the state.

For a continued habitat discussion of this species, see "Central Florida's High Pine and Scrub Communities," page 1773.

Historic Range and Current Distribution

Sandlace is absent from the southern tip of the Lake Wales Ridge. Its range extends from the Archbold Biological Station northward along the Lake Wales Ridge to the Davenport-Poinciana area in northern Polk County. Further northeast, it occurs on one site in Osceola County and three in western Orange County.

It occurs on the following protected areas:

Archbold Biological Stations; Saddle Blanket Lakes and Catfish Creek (State-owned); and Lake Apthorpe (owned by The Nature Conservancy). The species is abundant on several tracts proposed for acquisition by the State and the U.S. Fish and Wildlife Service.

Conservation and Recovery

Sandlace is propagated and sold commercially on a limited scale. Commercial trade in this species should not adversely affect it, providing that nursery operators abide by State law and the Florida Native Plant Society's policy on transplanting native plants from the wild.

Large sections of the high pine and scrub communities along Florida's Lake Wales Ridge have been and still are being converted to citrus groves, pasture and urban developments. Up to 85% of the estimated 546,800 acres of dry upland vegetation originally found in Polk and Highlands Counties have been lost or altered.

Citrus groves are being expanded rapidly on the southern Lake Wales Ridge because the area escaped the worst effects of severe freezes during the 1980's.

This species is being displaced by the conversion of high pine and scrub communities to agriculture. It is also coming under pressure from property taxation that favors agriculture; human activities; and a limited geographic distribution.

For a continued discussion of the threats to this species, see "Central Florida's High Pine and Scrub Communities," page 1773.

Bibliography

U.S. Fish and Wildlife Service. "Endangered and Threatened Wildlife and Plants; Endangered or Threatened Status for Seven Central Florida Plants." *Federal Register* Vol. 58 No. 79, April 27, 1993: 25746-25755.

Contacts

USFWS Regional Office
Suite 200, 1875 Century Blvd.
Atlanta, GA 30345
Phone: 404-679-4000

Ecological Services Field Office
Suite 310, 6620 Southpoint Drive, South
Jacksonville, FL 32216-0912
Phone: 904-232-2580
FAX: 904-232-2404

Adapted from data compiled by the Threatened and Endangered Species Information Institute (13950 W. 20th Ave., Golden, CO 80401) for *Beacham's International Threatened, Endangered, and Extinct Species* published on CD ROM, available from Beacham Publishing.

PUERTO RICAN PLANTS

Puerto Rican Palo Colorado Forest Habitat

The palo colorado forest is dominated by the palo colorado tree and occurs at elevations between 600 and 700 meters in valleys and on low gradient slopes with poorly drained soils. The palo colorado tree grows to about 16 meters in height with a broad spreading growth form; the trunk and branches are often twisted and hollow. Ferns and bromeliads (primarily Marcgravia) cover the trees. Associated tree species include: Miconia, Sierra palms, and *Clusia krugiana*. The dense ground vegetative cover is dominated by grasses, mats of common spikemosses, climbing bamboo, creeping treeferns, and sedges. Plant species diversity in the palo colorado zone (53 arborescent species) is much lower than that of the tabonuco zone (below 700 meters elevation, which contains 168 arborescent species).

The dwarf or elfin forest is located above 900 meters along high ridges and on isolated peaks. This forest association has an annual rainfall of over 380 centimeters Plant species diversity is fairly low and there is a high percentage of endemism in this community. Insect and bird species diversity is also low. The species that are present are subjected to: low light levels resulting from the low clouds that often envelope the peaks; frequent high velocity winds (often above 90 kilometers/hour); lower temperatures; humidity readings that average 98.5%; soil saturation; and excessive soil leaching. These factors have affected the native plants' growth habits and tolerance levels. The area is covered by a fairly dense stand of stunted trees and treeferns; these plants are often intertwined making movement through the area difficult. *Tabebuia rigida* and *Ocotea spathulata* are the dominant tree species. They make up about 70% of the crown canopy cover. The lower canopies are dominated by dense growths of bromeliads, ferns, epiphytic mosses, leafy liverworts, and lianas.

Adiantum vivesii

No Common Name

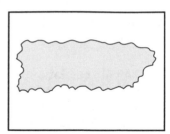

Status	Endangered
Listed	June 9, 1993
Family	Adiantaceae (Maidenhair Fern)
Description	Colonial fern with creeping rhizomes, erect-spreading fronds, and lustrous purple-black stalks.
Habitat	Deeply shaded hollow at the base of north-facing limestone cliffs at a low to middle elevation of about 250 ters.
Threats	Limited range
Range	Puerto Rico

No Photo Available for This Species

Description

Adiantum vivesii is a gregarious colonial (growing in colonies) fern with creeping rhizomes. The fronds are distichous (on opposite sides) and erect-spreading, approximately 0.5 centimeters apart, and 45 to 71 centimeters long. The stipes or stalks are lustrous purple-black, 25 to 46 centimeters long, irregularly branched, and have hairlike scales. The frond's blades are broad and irregular, 20 to 28 centimeters long, and 23 to 35 centimeters wide. The flower bearing stalks are more densely covered with hairlike scales than the main stem. The blades have 2 or 3 alternative or sometimes subopposite pinnae, with a larger terminal one that is oblong. The outer sterile margins of the pinnae are irregularly notched and the tissue is dull green on both sides.

Habitat

The one known population is locate deeply shaded hollow at the base of no. facing limestone cliffs at a lower to middle elevation of about 250 meters.

Historic Range and Current Distribution

The only known population of *A. vivesii* is located at Barrio San Antonio in the municipality of Quebradillas. This is where the type specimen was collected.

A. vivesii is found on private land. The only known population contains an estimated 1,000 individual plants or growing apices.

Conservation and Recovery

Because *A. vivesii* occurs on privately owned land, and is known from only a single locality, clearing or development of this area would result in the elimination of the only known population.

Research is needed to determine this species' life history and ecological requirements and to develop and refine propagation and transplant techniques. Surveys are needed to determine if other populations exist and to locate potential transplant sites.

Bibliography

U.S. Fish and Wildlife Service. "Endangered and Threatened Wildlife and Plants; Determination of Endangered Status for Four Endemic Puerto Rican Ferns." *Federal Register* Vol. 58, No. 109. June 9, 1993: 32308-32311.

Mickel, J. T. *How to Know the Ferns and Fern Allies*. Dubuque, IA: William C. Brown Publishing, 1979. 229 pp.

Contacts

U.S. Fish and Wildlife Service
Regional Office
Suite 200, 1875 Century Blvd.
Atlanta, GA 30345
Phone: 404-679-4000

Caribbean Field Office
Ecological Services Field Office
P. O. Box 491
Boqueron, PR 00622
Phone: 809-851-7297
FAX: 809-851-7440

Adapted from data compiled by the Threatened and Endangered Species Information Institute (13950 W. 20th Ave., Golden, CO 80401) for *Beacham's International Threatened, Endangered, and Extinct Species* published on CD ROM, available from Beacham Publishing.

Aristida chaseae

No Common Name

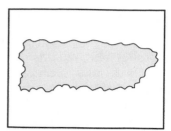

Status	Endangered
Listed	April 27, 1993
Family	Poaceae (Grass)
Description	A perennial grass with dense, spreading stems that may reach 50-60 centimeters.
Habitat	Rocky, exposed slopes of the oldest geologic formation in Puerto Rico.
Threats	Intense agricultural, rural and tourist development.
Range	Puerto Rico

Paul McKenzie

Description

Aristida chaseae is a perennial grass with dense, spreading culms (jointed stems) which may grow 50 to 60 centimeters long. The involute leaf blades are 2 to 3 millimeters wide and 10 to 15 millimeters long. The narrow panicles (inflouresences) are 10 to 15 centimeters long. The glumes (bracts) are equal, 10 to 13 millimeters long and are tapering. *A. chaseae's* lemma (bract enclosing the flower) is narrow at the summit and only somewhat beaked and rough on the upper half. The awns (tips) are equal, divergent, flat at the base, noncontorted and about 2 centimeters long.

Habitat

This species grows on rocky, exposed slopes of the oldest geologic formation in Puerto Rico. It is known from elevations of 150 to 300 meters.

The topography of this area is semi-arid mountains of near-vertical slopes. The average annual temperature is 26 degrees Celsius and the average annual precipitation is 1,150 millimeters. Most of the soils are Troperts which are shallow and moderately deep and medium textured. These soils have an isohyperthermic temperature regime and mixed mineralogy. The natural vegetation of this area is dominated by semideciduous broadleaf evergreen and broadleaf deciduous trees.

Historic Range and Current Distribution

The type (original) locality of this species was near Boqueron in 1913. In 1987 a second population was discovered on Cabo Rojo National Wildlife Refuge. A third population is located in the Sierra Bermeja mountain range near Cabo Rojo. Other localities have been identified in the Sierra Bermeja mountain range.

Conservation and Recovery

This species is currently being threatened by intense agricultural, rural and tourist development. The land on which this species occurs is being cleared for grazing by cattle and goats. Adjacent land is being subdivided for sale in small farms, and tourist/urban developments. *A. chaseae* also occurs within and along a roadway on Cabo Rojo National Wildlife Refuge.

This species receives special protection in that it is located on Cabo Rojo National Wildlife Refuge.

Conservation measures provided to species listed as endangered or threatened pursuant to the Act include recognition, recovery actions, requirements for Federal protection, and prohibitions against certain practices. Recognition through listing encourages conservation measures by Federal, international, and private agencies, groups, and individuals.

Bibliography

U.S. Fish and Wildlife Service. "Endangered and Threatened Wildlife and Plants; Determination of Endangered Status for Three Puerto Rican Plants." *Federal Register* Vol. 58 No. 79. April 27, 1993: 75755-75758.

Contacts

U.S. Fish and Wildlife Service
Regional Office
Suite 200, 1875 Century Blvd.
Atlanta, GA 30345
Phone: 404-679-4000

Caribbean Field Office
Ecological Services
P. O. Box 491
Boqueron, PR 00622
Phone: 809-851-7297
FAX: 809-851-7440

Adapted from data compiled by the Threatened and Endangered Species Information Institute (13950 W. 20th Ave., Golden, CO 80401) for *Beacham's International Threatened, Endangered, and Extinct Species* published on CD ROM, available from Beacham Publishing.

Auerodendron pauciflorum

No Common Name

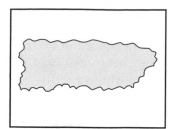

Status	Endangered
Listed	March 2, 1994
Family	Rhamnaceae (Buckthorn)
Description	Evergreen shrub or small tree with smooth oval to elliptical leaves that have minute black glandular dots; flower stalks bear 2-3 flowers.
Habitat	Semi-evergreen subtropical forests in limestone hills.
Threats	Resort development
Range	Puerto Rico

No Photo Available for This Species

Description

A. pauciflorum is an evergreen shrub or small tree which may grow as tall as 15 feet The oval to elliptical leaves are opposite or subopposite, and are 2.4 to 5.9 inches long and 1.4 to 2.4 inches wide. The smooth leaves have minute black glandular dots. There are oval to triangular-shaped stipules (leaflike appendages) on the leaf stalk. The flower stalks vary from .2 to .3 inches in length, and bear 2 to 3 flowers. The outer protective cover (calyx) is bell shaped. Nothing is known about the fruit at the present time.

Habitat

This species is restricted to the semi-evergreen forests (subtropical moist forest life zone) of the limestone hills of Isabela in northwestern Puerto Rico at elevations of less than 390 feet.

Historic Range

A. pauciflorum was not discovered until 1976, and its historic range is not known.

Current Distribution

The only known ten individuals are restricted to the semi-evergreen forests (subtropical moist forest life zone) of the limestone hills of Isabela in northwestern Puerto Rico at elevations of less than 390 feet.

Conservation and Recovery

Hills in the area of the known populations were destroyed for the construction of Highway 2. The area is privately owned and presently under intense development pressure. The construction of a resort development, including seven hotels, five golf courses, 36 tennis courts and 1,300 housing units is proposed for this area. Limestone hills are continuously being leveled for the production of construction material. These factors, as well as random cutting and the harvesting of yams, have apparently contributed to the decline of the species and continue to threaten the remaining individuals.

One of the most important factors affecting the continued survival of this species is its limited distributed. Because so few individuals are known to occur in a limited area, the risk of extinction is extremely high. The fruit has not been described and seedlings have not been observed in the field.

The Fish and Wildlife Service believes that to designate critical habitat, with habitat descriptions and maps, would increase the possibility of vandalism or theft. All involved parties and landowners have been notified of the location and importance of protecting this species' habitat.

Bibliography

U.S. Fish and Wildlife Service. "Endangered and Threatened Wildlife and Plants; Determination of Endangered Status for the Plant *Auerodedron Pauciflorum*." *Federal Register*. Vol. 58, No. 51, March 2, 1994: 9935-9936.

Contacts

U.S. Fish and Wildlife Service
Caribbean Field Office
P.O. Box 491
Boqueron, PR 00622
(809) 851-7297

Adapted from data compiled by Beacham Publishing for *Beacham's International Threatened, Endangered, and Extinct Species* published on CD ROM.

Capa Rosa
Callicarpa ampla

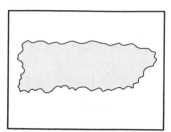

Luquillo Mountains Habitat   Bernice DeSantos

Status	Endangered
Listed	April 22, 1992
Family	Verbenaceae (Verbena)
Description	Evergreen tree growing to 50 feet high with green leaf surfaces and white below with whitish flowers and white fruit that matures purple.
Habitat	Palo colorado forests in the Luquillo Mountains.
Threats	Establishment of plantations, selective cutting, trail and road construction.
Range	Puerto Rico

Description

Capa rosa, *Callicarpa ampla*, is an evergreen tree that can grow to a height of 50 feet. The young twigs are 4-sided and whitish. Leaves are opposite, entire, broadest at the middle and taper to both ends. They are 4 to 10 inches long, 1.5 to 3 inches wide, green on the upper surface, densely white scurfy below, and borne on a petiole about 1 inch in length. The inflorescence is branched and has numerous, small, whitish flowers each with a four-lobed corolla about 1/8 inch long. Fruits are white when young but become purplish upon maturity, and are .25 inch in diameter, with the calyx attached at the base.

Habitat

Capa rosa is currently only found in the palo colorado forest association in the Luquillo Mountains, eastern Puerto Rico. This forest is dominated by the palo colorado tree (*Cyrilla racemiflora*) and occurs above 600 to 700 meters in valleys and on low gradient slopes with poorly drained soils.

For a continued discussion of this habitat, see "The Puerto Rican Palo Colorado Forest Habitat," page 1791.

Historic Range and Current Distribution

Since the original specimen was collected in 1827, Capa rosa has only been collected seven times. Six sites are located in Puerto Rico and one on St. Thomas, U.S. Virgin Islands. The validity of the collection on St. Thomas has been questioned. The Puerto Rican collections were located in Barranquitas, Adjuntas, Utuado, Cayey, and the Luquillo Mountains.

Capa rosa is currently restricted to sites in the palo colorado forest association in the Luquillo Mountains. These sites are found on the Caribbean National Forest.

Conservation and Recovery

Various forest management practices on the Caribbean National Forest could potentially impact this species, including establishment and maintenance of plantations, selective cutting, trail and road construction and maintenance, and shelter construction.

A proposed expansion of the U.S. Navy facilities on Pico del Este is being considered. Individuals are found along one road proposed for reconstruction and reopening. Federal Highway Administration funds will be used to complete this project.

This species' limited distribution and small population size leave it vulnerable to catastrophic events such as Hurricane Hugo. This hurricane was responsible for an immense amount of damage in the Caribbean National Forest. Many trees, including several endangered species, were defoliated and had several branches broken off.

Recovery activities should include surveys to locate new populations and/or sites suitable for reintroduction, studies to develop propagation and transplanting techniques, studies to determine the species' life history and ecological requirements, and plans to protect and enhance known populations.

Bibliography

U.S. Fish and Wildlife Service. "Endangered and Threatened Wildlife and Plants; Determination of Endangered Status for Five Puerto Rican Trees." *Federal Register* Vol. 57, No. 78, April 22, 1992: 14782-14785.

Contacts

Caribbean Field Office
Ecological Services Field Office
P. O. Box 491
Boqueron, PR 00622
Phone: 809-851-7297
FAX: 809-851-7440

Adapted from data compiled by the Threatened and Endangered Species Information Institute (13950 W. 20th Ave., Golden, CO 80401) for *Beacham's International Threatened, Endangered, and Extinct Species* published on CD ROM, available from Beacham Publishing.

Calyptranthes thomasiana
No Common Name

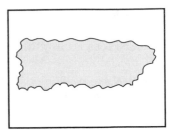

Susan Silander

Status	Endangered
Listed	February 18, 1994
Family	Myrtaceae (Myrtle)
Description	Evergreen shrub or tree with shiny, leathery leaves.
Habitat	Upland, moist forests of volcanic origin.
Threats	Stochastic extinction; land development.
Range	Puerto Rico, St. John, British Virgin Islands

Description

C. *thomasiana* is an evergreen shrub or small tree that may reach 30 feet in height and 5 inches in diameter. Leaves are opposite, obovate to oblong, .75 to 1.75 inches long, blunt at the apex, and short pointed at the base. The leaves are coriaceous (leathery), with gland dots, shiny of the upper surface, and dull on the lower surface. Flowers and fruit have not been described.

Habitat

C. *thomasiana* has been reported from Vieques Island in Puerto Rico and from St. John in the U.S. Virgin Islands. This small tree is located at elevations of approximately 350 meters in upland moist forest. Soils are volcanic in origin, shallow and well-drained. Rainfall on St. John varies from 89 to 140 centimeters, most of which falls between May and November.

Historic Range

C. *thomasiana* was first collected from St. Thomas, Virgin Islands but has not been reported on that island in recent years. It was previously thought to be endemic to Puerto Rico and the U.S. Virgin Islands, but was recently reported from Virgin Gorda, British Virgin Islands.

Current Distribution

The species is currently known from three locations: Monte Pirata on the island of Vieques, Puerto Rico; Bordeaux Mountain on the island of St. John; and Gorda Peak in Virgin Gorda. Ten to 12 individuals occur at Monte Pirata. This site is located on U.S.

Navy property and is in close proximity to naval communications facilities. It is not known if any individuals were eliminated during the construction of the facility.

On St. John, as many as 100 mature individuals are known in a small area on Bordeaux Mountain, which is within the Virgin Islands National Park. On Virgin Gorda, the species is found within a national park, but because the species is rare and localized, it may be impacted by park management practices.

Conservation and Recovery

The area occupied by *C. thomasiana* was severely damaged during Hurricane Hugo in 1989. The Navy has designated this area as an ecological conservation zone for all vulnerable species that occur there. However, should the communications facility require expansion, the species could be impacted. The St. John population is affected by park management practices and by the presence of feral pigs and goats.

One of the most important factors affecting this species is its limited distribution. Because so few individuals are known to occur in a limited area, the risk of extinction is extremely high.

Bibliography

U.S. Fish and Wildlife Service. "Endangered and Threatened Wildlife and Plants; Determination of Endangered Status for *Myrcia paganii* and *Calyptranthes thomasiana*." *Federal Register* Vol. 59, No. 34. February 18, 1994: 8138-8141.

Contacts

U.S. Fish and Wildlife Service
P. O. Box 491
Boquerón, PR 00622
Phone: 809-851-7297
FAX: 809-851-7440

U.S. Fish and Wildlife Service
Southeast Regional Office
75 Spring Street, SW, Suite 1282
Atlanta, GA 30303
404-331-3583

Adapted from data compiled by Beacham Publishing for *Beacham's International Threatened, Endangered, and Extinct Species* published on CD ROM.

Elaphoglossum serpens

No Common Name

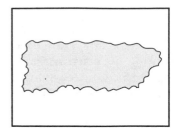

Status	Endangered
Listed	June 9, 1993
Family	Lomariopsidaceae (Vine Fern)
Description	Fern with a wide-creeping thick rhizome; apex and nodes have lustrous reddish-brown scales.
Habitat	Mossy trunks of trees found in a patch of a montane dwarf forest.
Threats	Construction of a communication facility; collecting; hurricanes.
Range	Puerto Rico

No Photo Available for This Species

Description

Elaphoglossum serpens is an epiphytic (growing on another plant for support) fern with a wide-creeping, 1.5 to 2.0 millimeter thick rhizome. The apex and nodes bear lustrous reddish-brown scales with ciliate (notched) margins which are lanceolate to attenuate and 3 to 4 millimeters long. This species has only a few, distant, and erect fronds. Sterile fronds are 7 to 19 centimeters long and the stipes, from 3.5 to 11.0 centimeters in length, are usually as long or longer than the blades. The blades are ovate, 3.5 to 8.0 centimeters long and 2.0 to 3.5 centimeters wide, obtuse at the apex, and cuneate at the base. The veins are free, reaching the margins of the blades. The coriaceous (leathery) tissue is opaque with only scattered scales on the abaxial side. The fertile fronds are 8.5 to 18.0 centimeters long, and in contrast to the sterile fronds the stipes are about three times longer than the blades. The blades are lanceolate to elliptic-oblong with a rounded or blunt apex, 2.5 to 4.5 centimeters long and 1.0 to 1.5 centimeters wide.

Habitat

The only known population of *E. serpens* (22 plants) is found on the mossy trunks of six trees. These trees are found in a patch of a montane dwarf forest at an elevation of about 1,300 meters.

Historic Range

The original specimen for *E. serpens* was collected from tree trunks at Monte Jayuya, Puerto Rico. This site was destroyed during the construction of a communication facility. Another population was later found by Roy O. Woodbury and others on the summit of Cerro Punta in Puerto Rico.

Current Distribution

The one known population contains 22 plants on the mossy trunks of 6 trees on the summit of Cerro Punta in Puerto Rico.

Because of this species' fairly limited population size and limited distribution, it is vulnerable to extinction. The small population size also means there is a limited gene pool. The lack of genetic diversity means the species may not have the capabilities to evolve to adjust to changes in it's environment.

Conservation and Recovery

The type specimen's site locality was destroyed during the construction of a communication facility. A second population was found at a later date; most of the plants at this site have been destroyed by the construction of telecommunications towers. Future maintenance activities or expansion of the facility will jeopardize the rest of this population. The remainder of this population (22 plants) was badly damaged in 1989 by Hurricane Hugo.

Collecting for private collections could present a problem, especially after the publicity generated following this species' listing.

Research is needed to determine this species' life history and ecological requirements and to develop and refine propagation and transplant techniques. Surveys are needed to determine if other populations exist and to locate potential transplant sites.

Bibliography

U.S. Fish and Wildlife Service. "Endangered and Threatened Wildlife and Plants; Determination of Endangered Status for Four Endemic Puerto Rican Ferns." *Federal Register* Vol. 58, No. 109, June 9, 1993: 32308-32311.

Contacts

Caribbean Field Office
Ecological Services Field Office
P. O. Box 491
Boquerón, PR 00622
Phone: 809-851-7297
FAX: 809-851-7440

Adapted from data compiled by the Threatened and Endangered Species Information Institute (13950 W. 20th Ave., Golden, CO 80401) for *Beacham's International Threatened, Endangered, and Extinct Species* published on CD ROM, available from Beacham Publishing.

Leptocereus grantianus
No Common Name

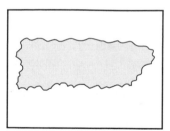

Susan Silander, USFWS

Status	Endangered
Listed	February 26, 1993
Family	Cactaceae (Cactus)
Description	Sprawling, nearly spineless cactus growing to 2 meters in height, with elongated stems having from three to five prominent ribs with broadly scalloped edges.
Habitat	Steep, rocky banks.
Threats	Low numbers; potential habitat destruction.
Range	Puerto Rico (Culebra Island)

Description

Leptocereus grantianus is a sprawling or suberect, nearly spineless cactus which may reach up to 2 meters in height and from .3 to 0.5 meters in diameter. The elongated stems have from three to five prominent ribs with broadly scalloped edges. The nocturnal flowers are solitary at terminal areoles, from 0.3 to 0.6 meters long. The outer perianth segments are linear, green, and tipped by an areola like those of the tube and ovary. The inner perianth segments are numerous, cream-colored, oblong-obovate, obtuse and about 8 millimeters long. The fruit is sub-globose to ellipsoid and about 4 centimeters in diameter.

Habitat

This endemic species is located close to shoreline on the steep rocky banks of Culebra Island.

Historic Range and Current Distribution

L. grantianus is an endemic species located just off the northeastern corner of Puerto Rico on the island of Culebra and along the rocky coast near Punta Melones.

Conservation and Recovery

This species is threatened by existing and potential habitat destruction and/or alteration due to rural and urban development. Due to its low numbers and distribution, stochastic events pose a high risk of extinction.

A recovery plan for this species has not yet been initiated.

Bibliography

U.S. Fish and Wildlife Service. ``Endangered and Threatened Wildlife and Plants; Final Rule to Determine the Plant *Leptocereus grantianus* to Be an Endangered Species.`` *Federal Register* Vol. 58, No. 37. February 26, 1993: 11550-11552.

Contacts

U.S. Fish and Wildlife Service
Regional Office
Suite 200, 1875 Century Blvd.
Atlanta, GA 30345
Phone: 404-679-4000

Caribbean Field Office
Ecological Services Field Office
P. O. Box 491
Boqueron, PR 00622
Phone: 809-851-7297
FAX: 809-851-7440

Adapted from data compiled by the Threatened and Endangered Species Information Institute (13950 W. 20th Ave., Golden, CO 80401) for *Beacham's International Threatened, Endangered, and Extinct Species* published on CD ROM, available from Beacham Publishing.

Lyonia truncata var. proctorii
No Common Name

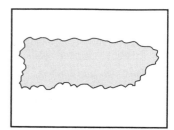

Status	Endangered
Listed	April 27, 1993
Family	Ericaceae (Heath)
Description	Evergreen shrub growing with small, white, urn-shaped flowers.
Habitat	Semi-arid mountains of near-vertical slopes with the area dominated by broadleaf trees.
Threats	Agricultural, rural and tourist development.
Range	Puerto Rico

No Photo Available for This Species

Description

Lyonia truncata var. *proctorii* is an ever-green shrub. This species may reach up to 2 meters in height. The leaves are alternate, elliptic to ovate, coriaceous, 0.9 to 4.5 centimeters long and 0.4 to 2.3 centimeters wide. The leaf margins may be toothed and the lower surface is sparsely to moderately lepidote and moderately to densely pubescent. The inflorescences are fasciculate with from 2 to 15 flowers. The pedicels are pubescent and from 2 to 5 millimeters in length. The flowers are small, white and urn-shaped. The fruit is a dry capsule, 3 to 4.5 millimeters in length and 2.5 to 4 millimeters in width, pubescent and contains seeds.

Habitat

The topography of this species' habitat is semi-arid mountains of near-vertical slopes. The average annual temperature is 26 degrees Celsius and the average annual precipitation is 1,150 millimeters. Most of the soils are are shallow and moderately deep and medium textured. These soils have an isohyperthermic temperature regime and mixed mineralogy. The natural vegetation of this area is dominated by semideciduous broadleaf evergreen and broadleaf deciduous trees.

Historic Range and Current Distribution

This species is only known from the Cerro Mariquita mountain range in Puerto Rico. There are two populations consisting of a total of 65 individuals.

Conservation and Recovery

This species is currently being threatened by intense agricultural, rural and tourist development. The land on which this species occurs is being cleared for grazing by cattle and goats. Adjacent land is being subdivided for sale in small farms, and tourist/urban developments.

Bibliography

U.S. Fish and Wildlife Service. "Endangered and Threatened Wildlife and Plants; Determination of Endangered Status for Three Puerto Rican Plants." *Federal Register* Vol. 58, No. 79, April 27, 1993: 75755-25758.

Contacts

Caribbean Field Office
Ecological Services Field Office
P. O. Box 491
Boqueron, PR 00622
Phone: 809-851-7297
FAX: 809-851-7440

Adapted from data compiled by the Threatened and Endangered Species Information Institute (13950 W. 20th Ave., Golden, CO 80401) for *Beacham's International Threatened, Endangered, and Extinct Species* published on CD ROM, available from Beacham Publishing.

Myrcia paganii

No Common Name

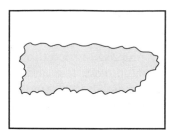

Status	Endangered
Listed	February 18, 1994
Family	Myrtaceae (Myrtle)
Description	Evergreen tree with mottled and flaky bark, and orange-brown inner bark.
Habitat	Limestone hills in northwestern Puerto Rico.
Threats	Stochastic extinction.
Range	Puerto Rico

No Photo Available for This Species

Description

M. paganii is an evergreen tree that may reach a height of 30 feet and 5 inches in diameter. The bark is mottled and flaky, and the inner bark is orange-brown. Young twigs are flattened and have numerous soft brownish hairs. The leaves are opposite, simple, entire, leathery, aromatic, and glandular punctate (spotted) below. The leaf blade is elliptic to elliptic-oblong, villous when young, then glabrescent, 4 to 6.5 inches wide. The leaf base is acute, the apex obtuse, and the midvein is clearly impressed above. Petioles are 4 to 4.5 millimeters long. The flowers and fruit have not been described.

Habitat

M. paganii grows in limestone hills or "mogotes" of the northwest coast of Puerto Rico. Soils in these hills are shallow, well-drained, alkaline, and interspersed between outcrops of hard limestone, which may cover up to 75 percent of the surface. Mean annual precipitation ranges from 150 to 200 centimeters; the heaviest rainfall is in the western portion of the area. Vegetation has been described as a semi-evergreen or evergreen seasonal forest type.

Historic Range

M. paganii was first collected during the last part of the nineteenth century but the type specimen was destroyed during World War II. It was not collected again until rediscovered in 1959 near the city of Arecibo, Puerto Rico.

Current Distribution

Six individuals are known from the privately owned site at Arcebio. Two other locations, with one individual each, were reported from the Quebradillas area of northwestern Puerto Rico.

Conservation and Recovery

The two populations of *M. paganii* found on privately owned land are currently subject to intense pressure for agricultural, rural, and tourist development. Adjacent land is being cleared for grazing cattle and goats. At another site, Guajataca Commonwealth Forest, one individual may be affected by forest management practices.

One of the most important factors affecting this species is its limited distribution. Because so few individuals are known to occur in a limited area, the risk of extinction is extremely high.

Bibliography

U.S. Fish and Wildlife Service. "Endangered and Threatened Wildlife and Plants; Determination of Endangered Status for *Myrcia Paganii* and *Calyptranthes Thomasiana*." *Federal Register* Vol. 59, No. 34. February 18, 1994: 8138-8141.

Contacts

U.S. Fish and Wildlife Service
P. O. Box 491
Boquerón, PR 00622
Phone: 809-851-7297
FAX: 809-851-7440

U.S. Fish and Wildlife Service
Southeast Regional Office
75 Spring Street, SW, Suite 1282
Atlanta, GA 30303
404-331-3583

Adapted from data compiled by Beacham Publishing for *Beacham's International Threatened, Endangered, and Extinct Species* published on CD ROM.

Polystichum calderonense
No Common Name

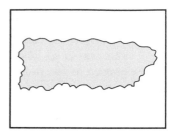

Eugenio Santiago

Status	Endangered
Listed	June 9, 1993
Family	Dryopteridaceae (Wood Fern)
Description	Evergreen terrestrial fern with a curved-ascending, rhizome; shining black scales; and erect, spreading fronds.
Habitat	Moist, shaded, non-calcareous ledges on mountain tops.
Threats	Indiscriminate cutting or fires; collecting.
Range	Puerto Rico

Description

Polystichum calderonense is an evergreen terrestrial fern. It has a curved-ascending, 7 millimeter thick rhizome which is clothed at the apex with lanceolate to oblong, curved, shining black, marginate scales up to 10 millimeters long. It's fronds are erect to spreading and may reach 60 centimeters in length. The pinnate blades are lanceshaped, 25 to 40 centimeters long, and narrowed and truncate at the top. Blades terminate in a scaly proliferous (producing offspring) bud which is somewhat narrowed toward the base. This species has 30 to 36 pairs of oblique, short-stalked pinnae (leaflets). It has a characteristic middle pinnae, with 8 to 19 pairs of free pinnae. The tissue is dark green, rigid, and opaque. From 1 to 5 sori are found dorsally on the veins of each pinnule, but are not clearly arranged in rows. The covering of the sori is light brown and deciduous.

Habitat

P. calderonense grows on moist, shaded, non-calcareous ledges on mountain tops at elevations of 1,000 to 1,150 meters.

Historic Range

The original specimen was collected from the summit of La Silla de Calderon, Monte Guilarte Commonwealth Forest, in the municipality of Adjuntas, Puerto Rico. A second population was found in 1987 on Cerrote de Penuelas, in the municipality of Penuelas. The Penuelas site is on private land.

Current Distribution

The two known populations contain a total of 57 individual plants, 45 (including juveniles) on La Silla de Calderon and 12 on Cerrote Penuelas.

Because of this species' fairly limited population size and limited distribution, it is vulnerable to extinction. The small population size also means there is a limited gene pool. The lack of genetic diversity means the species may not have the capabilities to evolve to adjust to changes in it's environment.

Conservation and Recovery

Both known populations of *P. calderonense* are vulnerable to indiscriminate cutting or fires. In Penuelas, the plants are on private lands which may be affected by industrial or residential development. Although *P. calderonense* occurs within the Guilarte Commonwealth Forest, this population may be affected by forest management practices.

Habitat modification, including indirect effects that alter the microclimatic conditions, may dramatically affect this species. These populations are vulnerable to damage caused by hurricanes.

Collecting for private collections could present a problem, especially after the publicity generated following this species' listing.

Research is needed to determine this species' life history and ecological requirements and to develop and refine propagation and transplant techniques. Surveys are needed to determine if other populations exist and to locate potential transplant sites.

Bibliography

U.S. Fish and Wildlife Service. "Endangered and Threatened Wildlife and Plants; Determination of Endangered Status for Four Endemic Puerto Rican Ferns." *Federal Register* Vol. 58, No. 109, June 9, 1993: 32308-32311.

Contacts

Caribbean Field Office
Ecological Services Field Office
P. O. Box 491
Boqueron, PR 00622
Phone: 809-851-7297
FAX: 809-851-7440

Adapted from data compiled by the Threatened and Endangered Species Information Institute (13950 W. 20th Ave., Golden, CO 80401) for *Beacham's International Threatened, Endangered, and Extinct Species* published on CD ROM, available from Beacham Publishing.

Palo de Jazmin
Styrax portoricensis

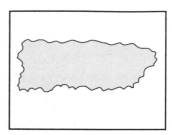

Carlos Laboy/Victor M. Cuevas, U.S. Department of Agriculture

Status	Endangered
Listed	April 22, 1992
Family	Styracaceae (Styrax)
Description	Evergreen tree growing to 66 feet with tapered shiny green leaves on upper surface, and pale green on lower surfaces.
Habitat	Palo colorado forests of Puerto Rico.
Threats	Establishment of plantations, selective cutting, trail and road construction.
Range	Puerto Rico

Description

The Palo de Jazmin is an evergreen tree that can grown up to 66 feet in height. The leaves are alternate, lack stipules, and have entire margins that are slightly turned under. The leaves are 2.5 to 4.0 inches long and are tapered at both ends; they are widest in the middle with a shiny green upper surface, a pale green lower surface, no hairs, and scattered star-shaped scales. The inflorescence is a 3 to 6 flowered raceme, each flower being borne on a curved pedicel. The fruits are a one to seeded elongated drupe, about .5 inch in diameter, densely covered with scales and maintaining the cup-shaped calyx at the base.

Habitat

The one remaining Palo de Jazmin tree is located in the palo colorado forest association.

For a continued discussion of this habitat, see "The Puerto Rican Colorado Forest Habitat," page 1791.

Historic Range and Current Distribution

Palo de Jazmin is currently restricted to one site in the palo colorado forest association in the Luquillo Mountains in the Caribbean National Forest. It has only been collected twice since its discovery in 1885, once in 1935 and again in 1954. There is currently only 1 known tree, which is immature.

Conservation and Recovery

Various forest management practices on the Caribbean National Forest could potentially impact this species. These practices include: establishment and maintenance of plantations, selective cutting, trail and road construction and maintenance, and shelter construction.

Any expansion or maintenance activities associated with the U.S. Navy and private entity communication facilities could potentially impact this species.

This species' limited distribution and small population size leave it vulnerable to catastrophic events such as Hurricane Hugo. This hurricane was responsible for an immense amount of damage in the Caribbean National Forest. Many trees, including several endangered species, were defoliated and had several branches broken off. The one remaining Palo de Jazmin tree was slightly damaged by the hurricane. The damage was caused by wind-thrown trees.

Recovery activities should include surveys to locate new populations and/or sites suitable for reintroduction, studies to develop propagation and transplanting techniques, studies to determine the species' life history and ecological requirements, and plans to protect and enhance known populations.

The U.S. Forest Service removed the wind-thrown trees that had fallen on the last remaining Palo de Jazmin tree during Hurricane Hugo. This endangered tree sustained only minor damage.

Bibliography

U.S. Fish and Wildlife Service. "Endangered and threatened wildlife and plants; determination of Endangered status for five Puerto Rican trees." *Federal Register* Vol. 57, No. 78, April 22, 1992: 14782-14785.

Contacts

Caribbean Field Office
Ecological Services Field Office
P. O. Box 491
Boqueron, PR 00622
Phone: 809-851-7297
FAX: 809-851-7440

Adapted from data compiled by the Threatened and Endangered Species Information Institute (13950 W. 20th Ave., Golden, CO 80401) for *Beacham's International Threatened, Endangered, and Extinct Species* published on CD ROM, available from Beacham Publishing.

Tectaria estremerana

No Common Name

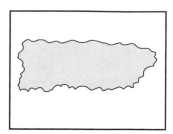

Susan Silander, USFWS

Status	Endangered
Listed	June 9, 1993
Family	Dryopteridaceae (Wood Fern)
Description	Fern with a woody, erect rhizome that bears a dense tuft of erect, brown, glabrous, narrow scales and orange-brown stipes covered with pale jointed hairs.
Habitat	Moist shaded humus on and among limestone boulders on a wooded rocky hillside.
Threats	Limited population size and limited distribution.
Range	Puerto Rico

Description

Tectaria estremerana has a woody, erect, 10 to 15 millimeter thick rhizome. The rhizome's apex bears a dense tuft of erect, brown, glabrous, narrowly tapering scales about 15 millimeters long. This fern has several loosely clustering long fronds. The light orange-brown stipes (stalks) are shorter or nearly as long as the blades and are covered with pale jointed hairs. Scales up to 12 millimeters long clothe the base. The blades are oblong-ovate, 35 to 41 centimeters long, 20 to 25 centimeters wide below the middle, and taper at the top. The sori are located nearer to the midvein than the margin of the pinna-lobes.

Habitat

T. estremerana is found in moist shaded humus on and among limestone boulders on a wooded rocky hillside at an elevation of 250-300 meters.

Historic Range

The original specimens were collected at Barrio Esperanza, Arecibo, in the vicinity of the Arecibo Tadiio Telescope in Puerto Rico. This is the only known site for this species.

Current Distribution

T. estremerana is known from only one site, at Barrio Esperanza, Arecibo, where a total of 23 individual plants are found.

Because of this species' fairly limited population size and limited distribution, it is vulnerable to extinction. The small population size also means there is a limited gene pool. The lack of genetic diversity means the species may not have the capabilities to adjust to changes in its environment.

Conservation and Recovery

The one known population of *T. estremerana* is located about 200 meters south of the Arecibo Radio Telescope, and any expansion or development of the facilities may adversely affect the habitat of this endemic fern.

Habitat modification, including indirect effects that alter the microclimatic conditions, may dramatically affect this species. These populations are vulnerable to damage caused by hurricanes.

Collecting for private collections could present a problem, especially after the publicity generated following this species' listing.

Research is needed to determine this species' life history and ecological requirements and to develop and refine propagation and transplant techniques. Surveys are needed to determine if other populations exist and to locate potential transplant sites.

Bibliography

U.S. Fish and Wildlife Service. "Endangered and Threatened Wildlife and Plants; Determination of Endangered Status for Four Endemic Puerto Rican Ferns." *Federal Register* Vol. 58, No. 109, June 9, 1993: 32308-32311.

Contacts

Caribbean Field Office
Ecological Services Field Office
P. O. Box 491
Boqueron, PR 00622
Phone: 809-851-7297
FAX: 809-851-7440

Adapted from data compiled by the Threatened and Endangered Species Information Institute (13950 W. 20th Ave., Golden, CO 80401) for *Beacham's International Threatened, Endangered, and Extinct Species* published on CD ROM, available from Beacham Publishing.

Palo Colorado
Ternstroemia luquillensis

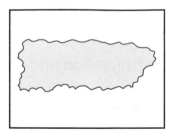

Luquillo Mountains Habitat   Bernice DeSantos

Status	Endangered
Listed	April 12, 1992
Family	Theaceae (Tea)
Description	Evergreen tree growing to 60 feet high with leathery leaves up to 4 inches long, and green leaf surfaces with undersides black, white or cream colored concave flowers.
Habitat	Dwarf forests in the Luquillo Mountains.
Threats	Establishment of plantations, selective cutting, trail and road construction.
Range	Puerto Rico

Description

Palo Colorado is an evergreen tree that grows to a height of 60 feet. The leaves are alternate, thick and leathery, and widest in the middle but acute at both ends. They are up to 4 inches long and about 3 times longer than wide. Both leaf surfaces are green and the underside is black punctate. The flowers are showy, about 1 inch in diameter and the 5 petals are white or cream colored and concave. The fruits are ovoid capsules which are terminated by the persistent style. The seeds are red and about 3 millimeters in length.

Habitat

Palo colorado is found in the palo colorado and dwarf or elfin forest associations in the Luquillo Mountains. It is now restricted to the palo colorado and dwarf or elfin forests in the Luquillo Mountains of eastern Puerto Rico.

For a continued discussion of this habitat, see "The Puerto Rican Colorado Forest Habitat," page 1791.

Historic Range and Current Distribution

Palo colorado is currently restricted to three or four sites in the palo colorado and dwarf/elfin forest associations in the Luquillo Mountains in the Caribbean National Forest. The four known populations contain a total of six individuals; three in the palo colorado association and one in the dwarf/elfin forest association. The population located adjacent to Road #191 has not been relocated in recent years and may have originally been misidentified.

Conservation and Recovery

Various forest management practices on the Caribbean National Forest could potentially impact this species. These practices include: establishment and maintenance of plantations, selective cutting, trail and road construction and maintenance, and shelter construction.

Two populations of palo colorado have been destroyed; one during the construction of the communication towers for the U.S. Navy and private entities communication facilities on El Yunque and the other by a hurricane.

This species' limited distribution and small population size leave it vulnerable to catastrophic events such as Hurricane Hugo. This hurricane was responsible for an immense amount of damage in the Caribbean National Forest. Many trees, including several endangered species, were defoliated and had several branches broken off.

Recovery activities should include surveys to locate new populations and/or sites suitable for reintroduction, studies to develop propagation and transplanting techniques, studies to determine the species' life history and ecological requirements, and plans to protect and enhance known populations.

Bibliography

U.S. Fish and Wildlife Service. "Endangered and Threatened Wildlife and Plants; Determination of Endangered Status for Five Puerto Rican Trees." *Federal Register* Vol. 57, No. 78, April 22, 1992: 14782-14785.

Contacts

Caribbean Field Office
Ecological Services Field Office
P. O. Box 491
Boqueron, PR 00622
Phone: 809-851-7297
FAX: 809-851-7440

Adapted from data compiled by the Threatened and Endangered Species Information Institute (13950 W. 20th Ave., Golden, CO 80401) for *Beacham's International Threatened, Endangered, and Extinct Species* published on CD ROM, available from Beacham Publishing.

Ternstroemia subsessilis
No Common Name

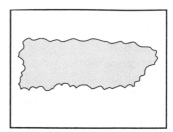

Luquillo Mountains Habitat   Bernice DeSantos

Status	Endangered
Listed	April 22, 1992
Family	Theaceae (Tea)
Description	Perennial herb with swollen storage roots with long, linear leaves and solitary flowers with bell-shaped calyx.
Habitat	Dwarf forests in the Luquillo Mountains.
Threats	Habitat loss due to trail and road construction, and establishment of plantations.
Range	Puerto Rico

Description

Ternstroemia subsessilis is an evergreen shrub or small tree up to 17 feet in height. The leaves are alternate, entire, stiffly coriaceous, obovate or oblanceolate, 1.25 to 3.0 inches long and .5 to 1.0 inches wide. Both leaf surfaces are dull green but the lower surface is black punctate. The flowers are solitary, white, .5 inch in diameter, sessile, and axillary at the ends of the branches. The fruit is an ovoid-conical capsule about 10 milli-meters long and tapering to a sharp point. Ripe fruits have been observed in May.

Habitat

T. subsessilis is now restricted to the palo colorado and dwarf or elfin forests in the Luquillo Mountains of eastern Puerto Rico.

For a continued habitat discussion of this species, see "The Puerto Rican Colorado Forest Habitat," page 1791.

Historic Range

Past distribution included Maricao Forest, where *T. subsessilis* was collected in 1960.

Current Distribution

T. subsessilis is currently restricted to sites in the palo colorado forest association and the dwarf or elfin forest association in the Luquillo Mountains. These sites are found on the Caribbean National Forest.

Three populations with 24 individual plants were known to exist in 1991. Four populations were known in 1992; three are in the palo colorado association and one is in the dwarf/elfin forest association. There were 37 individual plants in the four populations.

Because of this species' limited population size and limited distribution, it is vulnerable to extinction. The small population size also means there is a limited gene pool. The lack of genetic diversity means the species may not have the capabilities to adjust to changes in it's environment.

Conservation and Recovery

Various forest management practices on the Caribbean National Forest could potentially impact this species. These practices include: establishment and maintenance of plantations, selective cutting, trail and road construction and maintenance, and shelter construction.

A population of *T. subsessilis* was destroyed during the construction of a communication facility for the U.S. Navy and private entities on El Yunque, a peak in the Luquillo Mountains. The further expansion of this and other facilities will further endanger this species.

This species' limited distribution and small population size leave it vulnerable to catastrophic events such as Hurricane Hugo. This hurricane was responsible for an immense amount of damage on the Caribbean National Forest. Many trees, including several endangered species, were defoliated and had several branches broken off.

Recovery activities should include surveys to locate new populations and/or sites suitable for reintroduction, studies to develop propagation and transplanting techniques, studies to determine the species' life history and ecological requirements, and plans to protect and enhance known populations.

Bibliography

U.S. Fish and Wildlife Service. "Endangered and Threatened Wildlife and Plants; Determination of Endangered Status for Five Puerto Rican Trees." *Federal Register* Vol. 57, No. 78, April 22, 1992: 14782-14785.

Contacts

Caribbean Field Office
Ecological Services Field Office
P. O. Box 491
Boqueron, PR 00622
Phone: 809-851-7297
FAX: 809-851-7440

Adapted from data compiled by the Threatened and Endangered Species Information Institute (13950 W. 20th Ave., Golden, CO 80401) for *Beacham's International Threatened, Endangered, and Extinct Species* published on CD ROM, available from Beacham Publishing.

Thelypteris inabonensis
No Common Name

George Proctor

Status	Endangered
Listed	July 2, 1993
Family	Thelypteridaceae (Wood Fern)
Description	Terrestrial fern with an erect and slender rhizome that is clothed at the apex with numerous dark lustrous brown, scales.
Habitat	Deeply shaded humus near the summit in a montane mossy forest with sierra palms of Puerto Rico.
Threats	Hurricanes; collecting; limited population size.
Range	Puerto Rico

Description

Thelypteris inabonensis is a terrestrial fern with an erect and slender (about 0.5 centimeters diameter) rhizome that is clothed at the apex with numerous dark lustrous brown, and dense scales. The fronds are erect and arching, up to 60 centimeters long. The stipes (stalks) are 5-10 centimeters long and clothed with grayish pointed hairs, and they have numerous spreading scales similar to those of the rhizome. This species differs from all other Puerto Rican *thelypterid* ferns due to the presence of scales and pointed hairs on the rachis. The blades are narrowly elliptic, and up to 55 centimeters long. The species has 25-30 pairs of sessile pinnae, rounded at the apex, and with up to 7 pairs of simple veins. The tissue has numerous short, erect, pointed hairs and lacks glands.

The small sori, which have a densely long-ciliate indusium, are located dorsally on veins.

Habitat

The Toro Negro Commonwealth Forest population grows along a streambank in a sierra palm (Prestoea montana) forest, on the east bank of the Rio Inabon. The Cerro Rosa population is found in deeply shaded humus near the summit in a montane mossy forest with sierra palms.

Historic Range

The original specimens for *T. inabonensis* were collected from the headwaters of the Rio Inabon, Toro Negro Commonwealth

Forest, in the municipality of Ponce, Puerto Rico. A second population was found in 1988 near the summit of Cerro Rosa in the municipality of Ciales.

Current Distribution

There are two known populations of *T. inabonensis*; the Toro Negro Commonwealth Forest population contains 34 plants and the Cerro Rosa locality contains about 12 plants.

Because of this species' fairly limited population size and limited distribution, it is vulnerable to extinction. The small population size also means there is a limited gene pool. The lack of genetic diversity means the species may not have the capabilities to evolve to adjust to changes in it's environment.

Conservation and Recovery

Habitat modification, including indirect effects that alter the microclimatic conditions, may dramatically affect this species. These populations are vulnerable to damage caused by hurricanes. Hurricane Hugo caused a moderate amount of damage to the site where this species is found.

Collecting for private collections could present a problem, especially after the publicity generated following this species' listing. The size and beauty of this fern makes it especially vulnerable to collecting. Although *T. inabonensis* occurs within the Toro Negro Commonwealth Forest where collecting is not permitted, the areas are difficult to monitor. Forest management practices could also adversely affect this species.

Research is needed to determine this species' life history and ecological requirements and to develop and refine propagation and transplant techniques. Surveys are needed to determine if other populations exist and to locate potential transplant sites.

Bibliography

U.S. Fish and Wildlife Service. "Endangered and Threatened Wildlife and Plants; Determination of Endangered Status for Three Endemic Puerto Rican Ferns." *Federal Register* Vol. 58, No. 126, July 2, 1993: 35887-35891.

Contacts

Caribbean Field Office
Ecological Services Field Office
P. O. Box 491
Boqueron, PR 00622
Phone: 809-851-7297
FAX: 809-851-7440

Adapted from data compiled by the Threatened and Endangered Species Information Institute (13950 W. 20th Ave., Golden, CO 80401) for *Beacham's International Threatened, Endangered, and Extinct Species* published on CD ROM, available from Beacham Publishing.

Thelypteris verecunda
No Common Name

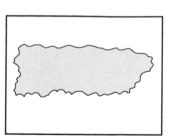

George Proctor

Status	Endangered
Listed	July 2, 1993
Family	Thelypteridaceae (Marsh Fern)
Description	Terrestrial fern with creeping rhizomes; and apex that bears brown scales; and fronds with star-shaped hairs.
Habitat	Unknown
Threats	Clearing or development of the privately owned lands where this species is found; hurricanes; collecting.
Range	Puerto Rico

Description

Thelypteris verecunda is a terrestrial fern with creeping, 2 to 3 millimeter thick rhizomes. The apex bears brown scales, 1 millimeters long and 0.5 millimeters wide. The species has dimorphic (having two distinct forms) fronds which are clothed throughout with star-shaped hairs, and numerous, much longer simple hairs. The stipes or stalks are 1 to 1.5 centimeters long. The sterile blades are oblongate, 2.5 to 4 centimeters long, with simple veins, while the fertile blades are linear to attenuate, 13 to 15 centimeters long, and truncated at the base. The flower-bearing stalk bears a minute reproductive bud below the apex. These blades have 15 to 20 pairs of mostly rounded-oblong to oval, 0.3 to 0.4 centimeters wide, short-stalked, undivided pinnae. The small and erect sori, which have a minute indusium (membrane), are located in an inframedial position, and bear a tuft of long, white, and simple hair.

Habitat

The sites where *T. verecunda* is found have not been described. Similar species, *T. inabonensis* and *T. yaucoensis* (both endangered as well) are found at higher elevations in shaded humus on ledges or along rocky streambanks.

Historic Range

The type (first) specimens for *T. verecunda* were collected from Barrio Charcas in the municipality of Quebradillas, Puerto Rico. This species is also found on two other sites, Barrio Bayaney, Hatillo, and Barrio Cidral in the municipality of San Sebastian. All three sites are on private lands.

Current Distribution

There are three known populations of *T. verecunda*. Two sites support only one individual plant each and the third site, Barrio Bayaney, contains about 20 plants.

Because of this species' fairly limited population size and limited distribution, it is vulnerable to extinction. The small population size also means there is a limited gene pool. The lack of genetic diversity means the species may not have the capabilities to evolve to adjust to changes in it's environment.

Conservation and Recovery

Habitat modification, including indirect effects that alter the microclimatic conditions, may dramatically affect this species. These populations are vulnerable to damage caused by hurricanes.

Clearing or development of the privately owned lands where *T. verecunda* is found would result in the elimination of the species.

Collecting for private collections could present a problem, especially after the publicity generated following this species' listing.

Disease and predation have not been documented as factors in the decline of this species.

Research is needed to determine this species' life history and ecological requirements and to develop and refine propagation and transplant techniques. Surveys are needed to determine if other populations exist and to locate potential transplant sites.

Bibliography

U.S. Fish and Wildlife Service. "Endangered and Threatened Wildlife and Plants; Determination of Endangered Status for Three Endemic Puerto Rican Ferns." *Federal Register* Vol. 58, No. 126, July 2, 1993: 35887-35891.

Contacts

Caribbean Field Office
Ecological Services Field Office
P. O. Box 491
Boqueron, PR 00622
Phone: 809-851-7297
FAX: 809-851-7440

Adapted from data compiled by the Threatened and Endangered Species Information Institute (13950 W. 20th Ave., Golden, CO 80401) for *Beacham's International Threatened, Endangered, and Extinct Species* published on CD ROM, available from Beacham Publishing.

Thelypteris yaucoensis
No Common Name

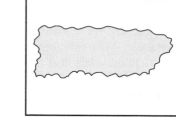

Eugenio Santiago

Status	Endangered
Listed	July 2, 1993
Family	Thelypteridaceae (Wood Fern)
Description	Terrestrial fern with an erect, thick rhizome, which is bearded at the apex with a tuft of brown scales. The few fronds have lustrous light brown, glabrous stipes.
Habitat	Humus on steep, shaded rocky banks and ledges at high elevations.
Threats	Collecting; habitat alteration; limited distribution.
Range	Puerto Rico

Description

Thelypteris yaucoensis is a terrestrial fern with an erect, 0.5 millimeter thick rhizome, which is bearded at the apex with a tuft of brown, narrowly to broadly lance-attenuate, 5 to 8 millimeters long scales. The few fronds are 44 to 52 centimeters long and have lustrous light brown, glabrous, 18 to 22 centimeters long stipes. The blades are narrowly deltate to oblong, 25 to 31 centimeters long, 10 to 14 centimeters wide, tapering at the apex, and truncated at the base. This fern has 13 to 15 pairs of alternate, irregularly linear-oblong pinnae. The pinnae are mostly simple, with 5 to 6 pairs of veins and are all free, except for the lowest pairs which are more or less joined.

Habitat

T. yaucoensis is found in humus on steep, shaded rocky banks and ledges at high elevations (850 to 1,200 meters).

Historic Range

The original specimens for *T. yaucoensis* were collected at Barrio Rubias in the municipality of Yauco, Puerto Rico. This species is also known from two other localities: Los Tres Picachos, Barrio Toro Negro in Ciales; and the summit area of Pico Rodadero, Barrio Sierra Alta in the municipality of Yauco. All sites are on private land.

Current Distribution

This species is known from three localities. Together, these sites support 65 individual plants.

Because of this species' fairly limited population size and limited distribution, it is vulnerable to extinction. The small population size also means there is a limited gene pool. The lack of genetic diversity means the species may not have the capabilities to evolve to adjust to changes in it's environment.

Conservation and Recovery

T. yaucoensis is located on privately owned land. Clearing or development of the areas would result in the elimination of the species. This species would be very attractive for collectors. The extreme rarity of this fern makes the species very vulnerable to the loss of any individual.

Habitat modification, including indirect effects that alter the microclimatic conditions, may dramatically affect this species. These populations are vulnerable to damage caused by hurricanes. Hurricane Hugo caused a moderate amount of damage to the site where this species is found.

Collecting for private collections could present a problem, especially after the publicity generated following this species' listing. The size and beauty of this fern makes it especially vulnerable to collecting.

Research is needed to determine this species life history and ecological requirements and to develop and refine propagation and transplant techniques. Surveys are needed to determine if other populations exist and to locate potential transplant sites.

Bibliography

U.S. Fish and Wildlife Service. "Endangered and Threatened Wildlife and Plants; Determination of Endangered Status for Three Endemic Puerto Rican Ferns." *Federal Register* Vol. 58, No. 126, July 2, 1993: 35887-35891.

Contacts

Caribbean Field Office
Ecological Services Field Office
P. O. Box 491
Boqueron, PR 00622
Phone: 809-851-7297
FAX: 809-851-7440

Adapted from data compiled by the Threatened and Endangered Species Information Institute (13950 W. 20th Ave., Golden, CO 80401) for *Beacham's International Threatened, Endangered, and Extinct Species* published on CD ROM, available from Beacham Publishing.

Vernonia proctorii

No Common Name

Susan Silander, USFWS   *Color Plate C-2*

Status	Endangered
Listed	April 27, 1993
Family	Asteraceae (Aster)
Description	Erect, small-sized shrub with knobby stems and trunk; olive-green to grayish-green leaves, and bright purple flowers.
Habitat	Semi-arid mountains of near-vertical slopes in areas of scrub woodland at elevations ranging 270-300 meters.
Threats	Habitat loss due to agricultural, rural and tourist development.
Range	Puerto Rico

Description

Vernonia proctorii is an erect, small-sized shrub which reaches heights of up to 1.5 meters. The stems and trunk appear knobby due to persistent petiole bases. Both the stems and trunk are pubescent, densely covered with silvery uniseriate hairs. The leaves are alternate, ovate to orbicular, subsessile or with the petioles appressed to the stem. The leaves are 1.5 to 3.5 centimeters long and 1.0 to 2.6 centimeters wide. A green to olive-green color is observed on the upper blade surface as well as scattered round trichomes. The undersurface appears gray-ish-green and is conspicuously sericeous. Silvery hairs cover the leaf margins. The flowers are found in terminal clusters of 2 to 5, each 3 millimeters long and displaying a bright purple color. The achene is 2 to 3 millimeters long and sericeous with silver-colored hairs.

Habitat

The topography within this species' range is that of semi-arid mountains of near-vertical slopes. The average annual temperature is 26 degrees Celsius and the average annual precipitation is 1,150 millimeters. Most of the soils are Troperts which are shallow and moderately deep and medium textured. These soils have an isohyperthermic temperature regime and mixed mineralogy. The natural vegetation of this area is dominated by semideciduous broadleaf evergreen and broadleaf deciduous trees. *V. proctorii* is found to inhabit areas of scrub woodland at elevations ranging 270-300 meters.

Historic Range and Current Distribution

V. proctorii is known only from the summit of Cerro Mariquita in the Sierra Bermeja of southwestern Puerto Rico. The one population consists of approximately 950 individuals.

Conservation and Recovery

This species is currently being threatened by intense agricultural, rural and tourist development. The land on which this species occurs is being cleared for grazing by cattle and goats. Adjacent land is being subdivided for sale in small farms, and tourist/urban developments.

Bibliography

U.S. Fish and Wildlife Service. "Endangered and Threatened Wildlife and Plants; Determination of Endangered Status for Three Puerto Rican Plants." *Federal Register* Vol. 58, No. 79, April 27, 1993: 75755-25758.

Contacts

Caribbean Field Office
Ecological Services Field Office
P. O. Box 491
Boqueron, PR 00622
Phone: 809-851-7297
FAX: 809-851-7440

Adapted from data compiled by the Threatened and Endangered Species Information Institute (13950 W. 20th Ave., Golden, CO 80401) for *Beacham's International Threatened, Endangered, and Extinct Species* published on CD ROM, available from Beacham Publishing.

HAWAIIAN PLANTS: HAWAII

Threats to Hawaiian Plants

The plant fauna of Hawaii has fallen vulnerable to habitat degradation and/or predation by wild, feral, or domestic animals (axis deer, goats, pigs, sheep, and cattle); competition for space, light, water, and nutrients by naturalized, exotic species; habitat loss due to fires; predation by rats; human recreational activities; and military exercises. Overgrazing by axis deer, and goats has irreparably damaged much native vegetation of Molokai and Hawaii. These feral animals overgraze and expose the soil to erosion. Eight Axis deer were introduced to Molokai in 1868 and flourished to thousands by 1960. Goats were also introduced to the island in the 1800s and despite the goatskin trade these goats invaded the high elevation dry forests and are now invading the wetter regions along the northern coast of East Molokai. Feral pigs inhabit the wetter forested regions of Molokai in the Molokai Forest Reserve. These pigs root, trample and degrade native vegetation and habitat.

With the introduction of cattle, goats, and deer much of the native forests of the State of Hawaii were converted to vast pastures of alien grasses. Molasses grass is probably the most disruptive to native dry forests. This alien species quickly spreads to dry and mesic forests previously disturbed by ungulates. Molasses grass produces a dense mat capable of smothering surrounding plants. As a fuel for fire molasses grass intensifies its heat and carries fire into areas with woody plants. It is then able to spread prolifically after a fire and effectively compete with less fire-adapted native plant species.

Goats have been on the islands for the past 170 years and despite the goatskin trade these goats invaded and flourished on the island. Their agility enables them to reach more remote areas. Feral goats now occupy a wide variety of habitats including: dry lowland forests and alpine grasslands. These goats consume the native vegetation, trample roots and seedlings, accelerate erosion and promote the invasion of alien plants.

Feral pigs have been on the islands for about 150 years. Like feral goats, these pigs root, trample and degrade native vegetation and habitat; these pigs are one of the major contributors to forest modification. Feral pigs encourage the expansion of alien plants and also disseminate alien species through their feces and on their bodies.

Cattle ranching on the islands has played a significant role over most of the past 150 years in reducing areas of native vegetation to vast pastures of alien grasses. Additionally, cattlemen failed to install adequate fencing and relied primarily on natural barriers of the Waianae Mountains. Cattle degrade the habitat by trampling and feeding on vegetation, eventually exposing the ground cover, increasing soil vulnerability to erosion. Red erosional scars resulting from decades of cattle disturbance, exacerbated by other feral ungulate activities, are still evident. Cattle facilitate the spread of alien grasses and other plants. Cattle ranching has been eliminated from the islands since 1990, but the long-term effects still persist. Alteration of vegetation limits natural areas. With the introduction of cattle, goats, and pigs much of the native forests of the Islands of Hawaii were converted to vast pastures of alien grasses.

Molasses grass is probably the most disruptive to native dry forests. This alien species quickly spreads to dry and mesic forests previously disturbed by ungulates. *M. minutiflora* produces a dense mat capable of smothering surrounding plants. As a fuel for fire, *M. minutiflora* intensifies its heat and carries fire into areas with woody plants. It is then able to spread prolifically after a fire and effectively compete with less fire-adapted native plant species. Christmas berry, Strawberry guava, koa haole, and firetree are popular alien species.

Christmas berry was introduced before 1911 and is a fast growing ornamental tree, able to form dense thickets. These thickets displace native species, competing for nutrients, space and light.

Koa haole is an alien tree in the southern Waianae Mountains of Oahu and the wet forests of Maui. Like Christmas berry, this species is capable of forming dense stands that exclude other plant species and is distributed mainly by feral pigs and fruit-eating birds.

Firetree was introduced sometime before 1900 as an ornamental tree or for firewood. This plant occupies dry to mesic habitats on most of the Hawaiian Islands. It was introduced to the Waianae Mountains as part of a reforestation project and now comprises a dense stand in the Honouliuli Forest Reserve and has spread approximately 2 miles to the north. Like Firetree, Koa haole is an alien tree which is an aggressive competitor that produces its own nitrogen.

Other threatening alien species include: Koster's curse, a noxious shrub rapidly displacing native vegetation by forming a dense understory, shading other plants and hindering plant regeneration; blackberry, a noxious weed which forms impenetrable thickets in disturbed areas; huehue haole, a smothering vine; and daisy fleabane, a low-growing smothering plant particular to cliffs.

Currently, Hawaii's economy is driven by the tourist industry. Hotels, paths and roads will inevitably affect the native vegetation. A water diversion plan currently under discussion proposes the extension of a tunnel from Waikolu Stream, now being tapped, to other potential watershed sources. Construction of the tunnel would likely favor the spread of alien species.

Recovery

The recovery of this and most other Hawaiian species depends on how well management practices can be implemented. The habitat of this and other Hawaiian species has undergone extreme alteration because of past and present land management practices, including deliberately introducing alien animals and plants, and agricultural and recreational development. To understand the recovery problems facing this species, it is necessary to understand the long-term causes of habitat destruction.

When Polynesian immigrants settled the islands, they brought with them water control and slash-and-burn systems of agriculture. Their use of the land resulted in erosion, changes in the composition of native communities, and a reduction of biodiversity. Many forested slopes were denuded by the mid-1800s to supply firewood to whaling ships, plantations, and Honolulu residents. Sandalwood and tree fern harvesting occurred in many areas, changing forest composition.

The 1848 provision for land sales to individuals allowed large-scale agricultural and ranching ventures to begin. So much land was cleared for these enterprises that climatic conditions began to change and the distribution of rainfall altered. Plantation owners supported reforestation programs that resulted in many alien trees being introduced. Beginning in the 1920s, water collection and diversion systems were constructed in upland areas to irrigate lowland fields, which opened new routes for the invasion of alien plants and animals into native forests.

Past and present activities of introduced alien animals are the primary cause of altering and degrading vegetation. A feral goat (*Capra hircus*), originally native to the Middle East, was successfully introduced to the islands in 1792. A pig (*Sus scrofa*) was introduced by Captain James Cook in 1778. Feral goats and pigs are managed in Hawaii as a game animal, but many herds populate inaccessible areas where hunting has little effect on their numbers. Goat and pig hunting is allowed year round, or during certain months, depending on the area. These animals eat native vegetation, trample roots and seedlings, cause erosion, and promote the invasion of alien plants. They are able to forage in extremely rugged terrain and have a high reproductive capacity.

Cattle native to Europe, North Africa and southwestern Asia, were introduced to the islands in 1793. Large feral herds developed as a result of restrictions on cattle killing. Cattle eat native vegetation, trample roots and seedlings, cause erosion, create disturbed areas which alien plants invade, and spread the seeds of alien plants in their feces. The forest, in areas grazed by cattle, becomes degraded to grassland pasture. Plant cover is reduced for many years following the removal of cattle from the area. Several alien grasses and legumes purposely introduced for cattle forage have become noxious weeds. Feral cattle have been able to multiply freely when the hunting of them was prohibited.

Feral mule deer and axis deer cause the same problems as feral cattle, and feral red jungle fowl (Gallus), which are ground-nesting chickens native to India and Asia, disturb the ground cover while foraging for seeds, fruits and small invertebrates.

Black twig borer is a small beetle that burrows into branches, introduces a pathogenic fungus as food for its larvae, and lays its eggs. Twigs, branches, and even the entire plant can be killed from such an infestation. The black twig borer has many hosts, disperses easily, and is especially prevalent in Melicope species.

Because Hawaiian plants were subjected to fire during their evolution only in areas of volcanic activity, and from occasional lightning strikes, they are not adapted to recurring fires and are unable to recover well from them. Alien plants are often better adapted to fire, and some fire-adapted grasses have become widespread. The presence of such vegetation increases the intensity, extent, and frequency of fire, and fire-adapted alien plants can reestablish a burned area, choking out the native plants.

Fire is an immediate threat along the Na Pali Coast, especially during drier months. Most of the fires there are caused by people pursuing recreational activities; prevailing winds spread fires to inland areas.

Illegal cultivation of marijuana occurs in isolated portions of public and private land. This agricultural practice opens areas in native forests which alien plants invade after marijuana is harvested.

At the present time recovery efforts related to these problems are restricted to legal instruments already in force. The Endangered Species Act requires Federal agencies to evaluate their actions with respect to any listed species. The act also prohibits any imports or exports of listed species, or to offer them for sale. Laws also prohibit any malicious damage or removal of species from their habitat.

Habitat Conditions on
the Island of Hawaii (the Big Island)

On March 4, 1994, the U.S. Fish and Wildlife Service listed as endangered or threatened twenty-one plants from the Island of Hawaii. The Service had listed the Ka'u Silversword (*Argyroxiphium kauense*) on April 7, 1993. Habitat conditions on the Big Island are described here rather than being repeated in each of the species accounts.

Argyroxiphium kauense
Clermontia peleana
Clermontia pyrularia
Clermontia lindseyana
Colubrina oppositifolia
Cyanea shipmanii
Cyanea stictophylla
Cyanea hamatiflora ssp. *carlsonii*
Cyanea copelandii ssp. *copelandii*
Cyrtandra tintinnabula
Cyrtandra giffardii
Ischaemum byrone
Isodendrion pyrifolium
Mariscus fauriei
Nothocestrum breviflorum
Ochrosia kilaueaensis
Plantago hawaiensis
Portulaca sclerocarpa
Pritchardi affinis
Silene hawaiiensis
Tetramolopium arenarium
Zanthoxylum hawaiiense

The island of Hawaii is the southernmost, farthest east, and the youngest of the eight major Hawaiian Islands. This largest island of the Hawaiian archipelago comprises 4,038 square miles, giving rise to its common name, the "Big Island."

The Hawaiian Islands are volcanic islands formed over a "hot spot," a fixed area of pressurized molten rock deep within the Earth. As the Pacific Plate, a section of the Earth's surface many miles thick, has moved to the northwest, the islands of the chain have separated. Currently, this hot spot is centered under the southeast part of the island of Hawaii, which is one of the most active volcanic areas on Earth.

Five large shield volcanoes make up the island of Hawaii: Mauna Kea at 13,796 feet and Kohala at 5,480 feet, both extinct; Hualalai at 8,271 feet, which is dormant and will probably erupt again; Mauna Loa at 13,677 feet and Kilauea at 4,093, both of which are currently active and adding land area to the island. Compared to Kauai, which is the oldest of the main islands and was formed about 5.6 million years ago, Hawaii is very young, with fresh lava and land up to 0.5 million years old.

Because of the large size and ranges of elevation of the island, Hawaii has a great diversity of climates. Windward (northeastern) slopes of Mauna Loa have rainfall up to 300 inches per year. The leeward coast, shielded by the mountains from rain brought by trade winds, has areas classified as desert and receiving as little as 8 inches of rain annually. The summits of Mauna Loa and Mauna Kea experience snowfall each year, and Mauna Kea was glaciated during the last Ice Age.

Plant communities on Hawaii include those in various stages of primary succession (initiated on newly produced bare areas) on the slopes of active and dormant volcanoes, some in stages of secondary succession (initiated by the disruption of a previously existing community by some major environmental disturbance), and relatively stable climax communities (one that has reached a state of equilibrium). On Hawaii, vegetation is found in all classifications of habitat: coastal; dryland; montane; subalpine and alpine; dry, mesic and wet; herblands, grasslands, shrublands, forests, and mixed communities.

The vegetation and land of the island of Hawaii have undergone much change throughout the island's history. Since it is an area of frequent volcanic activity, vegetated areas are periodically replaced with bare lava. Polynesian immigrants, first settling on Hawaii by 750 A.D., made extensive alterations in lowland areas for agriculture and habitation. European contact with the island brought intentional and inadvertent introductions of alien plants and animal species. By 1960, 65 percent of the total land area of the island of Hawaii was used for grazing, and much land has also been converted to modern cropland.

Ka'u Silversword

Argyroxiphium kauense

Derral Herbst

Status	Endangered
Listed	April 7, 1993
Family	Asteraceae (Aster)
Description	Rosette shrub with gray sword-like leaves and a tall stalk bearing many flowering heads.
Habitat	Moist mountain forests and bogs.
Threats	Feral pigs and goats, low reproduction.
Range	Hawaii (Hawaii)

Description

Ka'u silversword is an erect rosette shrub consisting of a woody vegetative stem, 1 to 27 inches high, and a flowering stem that grows to a height of 2 to 8.5 feet. The vegetative stem bears narrow, sword-shaped leaves, 7 to 16 inches long, which are nearly covered with dense, silky, silver-gray hairs and appear dull when dry. The flowering stem is branched, with each branch bearing a flower head producing 3 to 11 ray flowers that are 0.4 inches long and 50 to 200 smaller, disk flowers. Individual plants produce about 100 to 350 flower heads. The white or yellow to wine flowers bloom in August and September. Following its period of bloom, the plant dies.

The species has also been known as *Argyroxiphium sandwicense* var. *kauense*. It is closely related to the endangered Mauna Kea silversword (*A. sandwicense* ssp. *sandwicense*) which occurs on bare volcanic cinder on nearby Mauna Kea. Ka'u silversword has fewer ray flowers per head than ahinahina and its leaves are less completely covered by hairs.

Habitat

Ka'u silversword is found at elevations between 5,300 and 7,600 feet on the south slope of Mauna Loa on the island of Hawaii, mostly in moist forest openings and bogs. It grows on both flat and sloping ground in pahoehoe lava, sometimes mixed with wet humus. Associated vegetation is scrub and scrub forest, dominated by ohia trees (*Metrosideros polymorpha*). At the bog sites the surrounding vegetation consists primarily of sedges.

For a continued habitat description of Hawaii, see "Habitat Conditions on the Island of Hawaii (the Big Island), Hawaii," page 1834.

Historic Range

Ka'u silversword was first collected on the south slope of Mauna Loa in 1911 and has been found nowhere else. It may have once occurred in a band across the south, southeast, and northeast flanks of Mauna Loa at an elevation of about 6,000 feet.

Current Distribution

Populations of Ka'u silversword exist in three areas: Upper Waiakea Forest Reserve (South Hilo District), the Ainapo Trail in the Kapapala Forest Reserve and the Kahuku Ranch (Kau District), and at Ke a Pohina on the same ranch. The total species population is estimated at less than 400 plants. In the Upper Waiakea Forest Reserve about 80 plants are found at the Upper Waiakea Bog Plant Sanctuary off Powerline Road where one-third of an acre is fenced. Near the Ainapo Trail, a sparse population of a few dozen plants was scattered over 15 miles of habitat and, although not documented since 1984, presumably still exists. The only large population is on private land at Ke a Pohina where five acres of Ka'u silversword habitat, supporting less than 300 plants, are fenced.

Conservation and Recovery

The overwhelming threat to the Ka'u silversword is destruction of plants and habitat by feral herbivores, including mouflon (wild Mediterranean sheep), pigs, and goats. All graze on the plants and, in addition, rooting pigs inhibit the establishment of seedlings and uproot existing plants. Plants that have been grazed often resprout with branched stems and exhibit reduced vigor. The only large remaining population, at Ke a Pohina, has been greatly reduced by a herd of mouflon. In 1974 when the animals were released the Ka'u silversword population consisted of thousands of plants, many of them fully mature with rosettes 3.3 feet in diameter. Two years later only about 2,000 plants were over 3 inches wide. The decline has continued and today less than 300 plants remain. Before part of the plant's habitat at the Upper Waiakea Forest Reserve was fenced, that population fell from about 1,000 plants to 20 immature individuals.

As numbers decrease the species' reproductive habit adds to recovery problems. Besides flowering only once in its lifetime, the Ka'u silversword bears flowers that must be cross-pollinated from another plant in order to set seed. A low number of widely separated plants makes such cross-pollination less likely.

A small total population also puts the species in danger from natural catastrophes such as lava flows and wildfires. The only large population is only half a mile from a 1950 lava flow from the active southwest rift of Mauna Loa, and in 1984 a flow came near plants at the Upper Waiakea Forest.

For a continued discussion of the threats to Hawaiian plants, see page 1831.

Bibliography

Carr, G. D., ed. "*Argyroxiphium.*" In *Manual of the Flowering Plants of Hawai`i*, by W. L. Wagner, D. R. Herbst, and S. H. Sohmer. Honolulu: University of Hawaii Press and Bishop Museum Press, 1990.

Loope, L. L., A. C. Medeiros, and B. H. Gagne. "Recovery of Vegetation of a Montane Bog in Haleakala National Park Following Protection from Feral Pig Rooting." Honolulu: University of Hawaii, 1990.

Stone, C. P. "Alien Animals in Hawai`i's Native Ecosystems: Toward Controlling the Adverse Effects of Introduced Vertebrates." In *Hawai`i's Terrestrial Ecosystems: Preservation and Management.* Honolulu: University of Hawaii, 1985.

Contacts

Regional Office of Endangered Species
U.S. Fish and Wildlife Service
Eastside Federal Complex
911 N.S. 11th Avenue
Portland, Oregon 97232-4181
(503) 231-6118

U.S. Fish and Wildlife Service
300 Ala Moana Boulevard, Room 6307
P.O. Box 50167
Honolulu, Hawaii 96850
(808) 541-2749

Adapted from data compiled by the Threatened and Endangered Species Information Institute (13950 W. 20th Ave., Golden, CO 80401) for *Beacham's International Threatened, Endangered, and Extinct Species* published on CD ROM, available from Beacham Publishing.

'Oha wai

Clermontia lindseyana

Jack Jeffrey   *Color Plate C-1*

Status	Endangered
Listed	March 4, 1994
Family	Campanulaceae (Bellflower)
Description	Branched shrub or tree with alternate, stalked, toothed leaves and two whitish to purplish flowers, and orange berries.
Habitat	Koa and 'ohi'a dominated montane mesic forests, often not rooted in soil, at high elevations.
Threats	Competition from alien plants; habitat destruction by cattle, goats and pigs; limited numbers.
Range	Hawaii (Hawaii, Maui)

Description

This 'Oha wai, *Clermontia lindseyana*, is a terrestrial or epiphytic (not rooted in the soil) branched shrub or tree 8.2 to 20 feet tall. The alternate, stalked, toothed leaves are 5 to 9 inches long and 1.5 to 2.6 inches wide. Two flowers, each with a stalk 0.4 to 1 inch long, are positioned at the end of a main flower stalk 1 to 1.6 inches long. The calyx (fused sepals) and corolla (fused petals) are similar in size and appearance, and each form a slightly curved, five-lobed tube (2.2 to 2.6 inches) long and 0.4 to 0.7 inches wide, which is greenish white or purplish on the outside and white or cream-colored on the inside. The berries are orange and 1 to 1.6 inches in diameter. This species is distinguished from others in this endemic Hawaiian genus by larger leaves and flowers, similar sepals and petals, and spreading floral lobes.

Habitat

This species typically grows in koa and 'ohi'a dominated montane mesic forests, often epiphytically (on other plants) at elevations between 4,000 and 7,050 feet. Associated species include pilo, kawa'u, and kolea.

For a continued habitat description, see "Habitat Conditions on the Island of Hawaii (the Big Island), Hawaii," page 1834. and "Habitat Conditions on the Island of Maui," page 1951.

Historic Range

Historically, 'Oha wai was known from the island of Maui on the southern slope of

Haleakala, and from the island of Hawaii on the eastern slope of Mauna Kea and the eastern, southeastern, and southwestern slopes of Mauna Loa.

Current Distribution

One population of the species is known to be extant on state-owned land on Maui. This population extends from Wailaulau Gulch to Manawainui Gulch and contains between 100 and 150 plants. The 14 known populations on the island of Hawaii extend over a distance of about 53 by 13 miles. Populations are found near Laupahoehoe; in Piha; in Makahanaloe; near Puaakala; near Puu Oo; near Kulani Correctional Facility; near Kapapala; in Waiea Tract; near Kaapuna Lava Flow; and near Kahuku on private and state land. Approximately 125 to 175 individuals exist.

Conservation and Recovery

The major threats to 'Oha wai are competition from alien plants such as banana poka and Kikuyu grass, grazing and trampling by cattle and goats, and habitat disturbance by feral pigs.

The recovery of this and most other Hawaiian species depends on how well management practices can be implemented. The habitat of this and other Hawaiian species has undergone extreme alteration because of past and present land management practices, including deliberately introducing alien animals and plants, and agricultural and recreational development. To understand the recovery problems facing this species, it is necessary to understand the long-term causes of habitat destruction.

For a continued discussion of the threats to Hawaiian plants, see page 1831.

Bibliography

U.S. Fish and Wildlife Service. "Endangered and Threatened Wildlife and Plant; Determination of Endangered or Threatened Status for 21 Plants from the Island of Hawaii, State of Hawaii." *Federal Register* Vol 59, No. 43. March 4, 1994: 10305-10325.

Contacts

U.S. Fish and Wildlife Service
300 Ala Moana Boulevard, Room 6307
P.O. Box 50167
Honolulu, HI 96850
(808) 541-2749

Adapted from data compiled by Beacham Publishing for *Beacham's International Threatened, Endangered, and Extinct Species* published on CD ROM.

'Oha wai

Clermontia peleana

Robert J. Gustafson   *Color Plate C-3*

Status	Endangered
Listed	March 4, 1994
Family	Campanulaceae (Bellflower)
Description	Tall shrub with alternate, stalked, oblong toothed leaves; and blackish-purple or greenish-white petals.
Habitat	Montane wet forests dominated by koa, 'ohi'a and/or tree ferns.
Threats	Habitat disturbance caused by feral pigs and illegal cultivation of marijuana; roof or black rat damage; flooding, and stochastic extinction.
Range	Hawaii (Hawaii)

Description

This 'oha wai, *Clermontia peleana*, of which there are two subspecies, is a shrub or tree 5 to 20 feet tall, which does not root in soil and grows on the plants 'ohi'a, koa, and ama'u's. The alternate, stalked, oblong or oval toothed leaves reach a length of 3 to 8 inches and a width of 1.2 to 2 inches. Flowers are single or paired, each on a stalk 1.2 to 1.8 inches long with a main stalk 0.3 to 0.7 inches long. Five small green calyx lobes top the hypanthium. The blackish-purple (ssp. *peleana*) or greenish-white (ssp. *singuliflora*) petals 2 to 2.8 inches long and 0.3 to 0.5 inches wide, are fused into a one-lipped, arching tube with five down-curved lobes. Berries of spp. *peleana* are orange and 1 to 1.2 inches in diameter; berries of spp. *singuliflora* are unknown. This species is distinguished from others of the genus by its epiphytic growth habit; its small, green calyx lobes; and its one-lipped, blackish-purple or greenish-white corolla.

Habitat

This species typically grows epiphytically in montane wet forests dominated by koa, 'ohi'a and/or tree ferns at elevations between 1,740 and 3,800 feet. Associated species include 'olapa, kolokolo mokihana, and naupaka kuahiwi.

For a continued habitat description of Hawaii, see "Habitat Conditions on the Island of Hawaii (the Big Island), Hawaii," page 1834.

Historic Range

Historically, *C. peleana ssp. peleana* has been found on the island of Hawaii on the eastern slope of Mauna Loa and the north-eastern and southeastern slopes of Mauna Kea.

C. peleana spp. *singuliflora* was formerly found on the island of Hawaii on the northern slope of Mauna Kea and on East Maui on the northwestern slope of Haleakala, but the subspecies has not been seen in either place since the early part of the twentieth century and is believed to be extinct.

Current Distribution

Today, this species is known near Waiakaumalo Stream; by the Wailuku River; near Saddle Road; and between the towns of Glenwood and Volcano. The six known populations, which extend over a distance of about 12 by 5 miles, are located on state and Federally-owned land, and contain a total of approximately eight known individuals.

Conservation and Recovery

The major threats to this 'Oha wai are habitat disturbance caused by feral pigs and illegal cultivation of marijuana; roof or black rat damage; flooding, and stochastic extinction and reduced reproductive vigor due to the small number of existing individuals.

The recovery of this and most other Hawaiian species depends on how well management practices can be implemented. The habitat of this and other Hawaiian species has undergone extreme alteration because of past and present land management practices, including deliberately introducing alien animals and plants, and agricultural and recreational development. To understand the recovery problems facing this species, it is necessary to understand the long-term causes of habitat destruction.

For a continued discussion of the threats to Hawaiian plants, see page 1831.

Bibliography

U.S. Fish and Wildlife Service. "Endangered and Threatened Wildlife and Plant; Determination of Endangered or Threatened Status for 21 Plants from the Island of Hawaii, State of Hawaii." *Federal Register* Vol 59, No. 43. March 4, 1994: 10305-10325.

Contacts

U.S. Fish and Wildlife Service
300 Ala Moana Boulevard, Room 6307
P.O. Box 50167
Honolulu, HI 96850
(808) 541-2749

Adapted from data compiled by Beacham Publishing for *Beacham's International Threatened, Endangered, and Extinct Species* published on CD ROM.

'Oha wai
Clermontia pyrularia

Status	Endangered
Listed	March 4, 1994
Family	Campanulaceae (Bellflower)
Description	Terrestrial tree with alternate, toothed leaves, a cluster of up to five white or greenish-white flowers, five small green calyx lobes covered with fine hairs, and ovoid or pear-shaped orange berries.
Habitat	Koa- and/or 'ohi'a-dominated montane wet forests and subalpine dry forests.
Threats	Competition from alien plants; limited numbers.
Range	Hawaii (Hawaii)

Jack Jeffrey

Description

This 'Oha wai, *Clermontia pyrularia*, is a terrestrial tree 10 to 13 feet tall, has alternate, toothed leaves 5.9 to 11 inches long and 1 to 2 inches wide, with winged petioles. A cluster of up to 5 flowers has a main stalk 1.1 to 2.4 inches long; each flower has a stalk 0.3 to 0.8 inches long. Five small green calyx lobes top the hypanthium. The white or greenish-white petals are covered with fine hairs, measure 1.6 to 1.8 inches long, and are fused into a curved two-lipped tube 0.2 to 0.3 inches wide with five spreading lobes. The orange berry is inversely ovoid or pear-shaped. This species is distinguished from others of the genus by its winged petioles; its small, green calyx lobes; its two-lipped flowers with white or greenish-white petals; and the shape of the berry.

Habitat

This species typically grows in koa- and/or 'ohi'a-dominated montane wet forests and subalpine dry forests at elevations between 3,000 and 7,000 feet. Associated species include pilo, pukamole, and 'akala.

For a continued habitat description of Hawaii, see "Habitat Conditions on the Island of Hawaii (the Big Island), Hawaii," page 1834.

Historic Range

Historically, 'Oha wai has been found only on the island of Hawaii on the northeastern slope of Mauna Kea, the western slope of Mauna Loa, and the saddle area between the two mountains.

Current Distribution

Today, 'Oha wai is found near the Humu-ula-Laupahoehoe boundary, near Hakalau Gulch, near Kealakekua, and near Kaawaloa. The five extant populations, which extend over a distance of about 47 by 6 miles, are located on private, state, and Federal land. Although the number of individuals is not known, it is likely that not more than five individuals exist.

Conservation and Recovery

The major threat to *C. pyrularia* is competition from alien grasses and shrubs in the forest understory, from banana poka, and from stochastic extinction and reduced reproductive vigor due to the small number of existing populations.

The recovery of this and most other Hawaiian species depends on how well management practices can be implemented. The habitat of this and other Hawaiian species has undergone extreme alteration because of past and present land management practices, including deliberately introducing alien animals and plants, and agricultural and recreational development. To understand the recovery problems facing this species, it is necessary to understand the long-term causes of habitat destruction.

For a continued discussion of the threats to Hawaiian plants, see page 1831.

Bibliography

U.S. Fish and Wildlife Service. "Endangered and Threatened Wildlife and Plant; Determination of Endangered or Threatened Status for 21 Plants from the Island of Hawaii, State of Hawaii." *Federal Register* Vol 59, No. 43. March 4, 1994: 10305-10325.

Contacts

U.S. Fish and Wildlife Service
300 Ala Moana Boulevard, Room 6307
P.O. Box 50167
Honolulu, HI 96850
(808) 541-2749

Adapted from data compiled by Beacham Publishing for *Beacham's International Threatened, Endangered, and Extinct Species* published on CD ROM.

Kauila

Colubrina oppositifolia

Status:	Endangered
Listed:	March 4, 1994
Family:	Rhamnaceae (Buckthorn)
Description:	Tree with opposite stalked, oval, thin pinnately veined toothless leaves and 10 to 12 greenish-yellow or white bisexual flowers.
Habitat:	Lama-dominated lowland dry and mesic forests, often on lava.
Threats:	Competition from alien plants; habitat destruction by feral pigs; fire; insects; military exercises, and limited regeneration.
Range:	Hawaii (Oahu, Hawaii)

Robert J. Gustafson

Description

Kauila is a tree 16 to 43 feet tall, has opposite stalked, oval, thin pinnately veined toothless leaves with glands on the lower surface. Leaves measure 2.4 to 4.7 inches long and 1.2 to 2.8 inches wide in mature plants and are larger in seedlings. Ten to 12 bisexual flowers are clustered at the end of a main stalk 0.1 to 0.3 inches long; each flower has a stalk about 0.07 to 0.1 inch long which elongates in fruit. The five triangular sepals measure about 0.06 to 0.08 inches long, and the five greenish-yellow or white petals are about 0.06 inches long. The somewhat spherical fruit, 0.3 to 0.4 inches long is similar to a capsule and opens explosively when mature. This species can be distinguished from the one other species in the genus in Hawaii by its growth habit and the arrangement, texture, venation, and margins of its leaves.

Habitat

This species typically grows in lama-dominated lowland dry and mesic forests, often on lava, at elevations between 800 and 3,000 feet. Associated species include alahe'e and 'ohe.

Historic Range

Historically, *C. oppositifolia* was found on the island of Oahu in the central and southern Waianae Mountains and on the island of Hawaii in the following areas: The Kohala Mountains; the northern slope of Hualalai; and the western, southwestern, and southern slopes of Mauna Loa.

For a continued habitat description, see "Habitat Conditions on the Island of Oahu," page 2025; and "Habitat Conditions on the Island of Hawaii (the Big Island)," page 1834.

Current Distribution

Today, the species is known on Oahu in eastern Makaleha Valley, Mokuleia Forest Reserve, and Makua Valley; on Mt. Kaala; and near Honoulluli Contour Trail on private, state, and federally managed land. On the island of Hawaii the species occurs along the Mamalahoa Highway on the northern slope of Hualalai, as well as in Kapua and Puueo in the southernmost portion of the island.

The six extant populations on Oahu which extend over a distance of about 9 by 4 miles, contain approximately 94 individuals. On the island of Hawaii there are 7 extant populations which extend over a distance of about 16 by 4 miles, which are located on private and state land. These populations contain about 185 to 205 known individuals.

Conservation and Recovery

The major threats to Kauila are competition from alien plants such as lantana, fountain grass, and Christmas berry; habitat destruction by feral pigs; plant damage and death from black twig borer; fire; damage and disturbance from military exercises; and limited regeneration.

The recovery of this and most other Hawaiian species depends on how well management practices can be implemented. The habitat of this and other Hawaiian species has undergone extreme alteration because of past and present land management practices, including deliberately introducing alien animals and plants, and agricul-tural and recreational development. To understand the recovery problems facing this species, it is necessary to understand the long-term causes of habitat destruction.

For a continued discussion of the threats to Hawaiian plants, see page 1831.

Bibliography

U.S. Fish and Wildlife Service. "Endangered and Threatened Wildlife and Plant; Determination of Endangered or Threatened Status for 21 Plants from the Island of Hawaii, State of Hawaii." *Federal Register* Vol 59, No. 43. March 4, 1994: 10305-10325.

Contacts

U.S. Fish and Wildlife Service
300 Ala Moana Boulevard, Room 6307
P.O. Box 50167
Honolulu, HI 96850
(808) 541-2749

Adapted from data compiled by Beacham Publishing for *Beacham's International Threatened, Endangered, and Extinct Species* published on CD ROM.

Haha

Cyanea copelandii ssp. *copelandii*

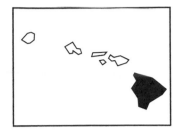

Joseph F. Rock

Status	Endangered
Listed	March 4, 1994
Family	Campanulaceae (Bellflower)
Description	Shrub with alternate, stalked, toothed leaves, clusters of 5 to 12 rose-colored flowers, and dark orange berries.
Habitat	Montane wet forests.
Threats	Limited numbers.
Range	Hawaii (Hawaii)

Description

This haha, *Cyanea copelandii*, is a shrub with a growth habit similar to that of a woody vine. The alternate, stalked, toothed leaves are 7.9 to 10.6 inches long and 1.4 to 3.3 inches wide, and have fine hairs on the lower surface. Five to 12 flowers are clustered on the end of the main stalk 0.8 to 1.8 inches long; each flower has a stalk of 0.2 to 0.6 inches long. The slightly hairy hypanthium (basal portion of the flower) is topped by five small, triangular calyx tubes. Petals, which are yellowish but appear rose-colored because of a covering of dark red hairs, are fused into a curved tube with five spreading lobes; the corolla is 1.5 to 1.7 inches long and about 0.2 inches wide. Berries are dark orange and measure 0.3 to 0.6 inches long. This subspecies is distinguished from ssp. *haleakalaensis*, the only other subspecies of *C. copelandii*, by its narrower leaves. The species differs from others in this endemic Hawaiian genus by its growth habit and the size, shape, and dark red pubescence of its corolla.

Habitat

This species often grows not rooted in soil and is typically found in montane wet forests at elevations between 2,200 and 2,900 feet. Associated species include tree ferns.

For a continued habitat description of Hawaii, see "Habitat Conditions on the Island of Hawaii (the Big Island), Hawaii," page 1834.

Historic Range

This species, which has been collected only twice on the southeastern slope of Mauna Loa near Glenwood, was last seen in 1957. It is difficult to adequately survey the area because of vegetation density and the terrain.

Current Distribution

The only known population, located on state land, was sighted recently enough that it is still considered extant, although it contains an unknown number of individuals.

Conservation and Recovery

The major known threat is stochastic extinction and reduced population vigor within the single population.

The recovery of this and most other Hawaiian species depends on how well management practices can be implemented. The habitat of this and other Hawaiian species has undergone extreme alteration because of past and present land management practices, including deliberately introducing alien animals and plants, and agricultural and recreational development. To understand the recovery problems facing this species, it is necessary to understand the long-term causes of habitat destruction.

For a continued discussion of the threats to Hawaiian plants, see page 1831.

Bibliography

U.S. Fish and Wildlife Service. "Endangered and Threatened Wildlife and Plant; Determination of Endangered or Threatened Status for 21 Plants from the Island of Hawaii, State of Hawaii." *Federal Register* Vol 59, No. 43. March 4, 1994: 10305-10325.

Contacts

U.S. Fish and Wildlife Service
300 Ala Moana Boulevard, Room 6307
P.O. Box 50167
Honolulu, HI 96850
(808) 541-2749

Adapted from data compiled by Beacham Publishing for *Beacham's International Threatened, Endangered, and Extinct Species* published on CD ROM.

Haha

Cyanea hamatiflora ssp. *carlsonii*

National Tropical Botanical Garden

Status	Endangered
Listed	March 4, 1994
Family	Campanulaceae (Bellflower)
Description	Palm-like tree with alternate, stalkless leaves, clusters of 5 to 10 magenta flowers, and purplish-red berries.
Habitat	'Ohi'a-dominated montane wet forests at elevations between 4,000 and 5,700 feet.
Threats	Competition from alien plants; habitat destruction by cattle; limited numbers.
Range	Hawaii (Hawaii)

Description

This haha, *Cyanea hamatiflora* ssp. *carlsonii*, a palm-like tree, grows 9.8 to 26 feet tall and has alternate, stalkless leaves 20 to 31 inches long and 3 to 5.5 inches wide. Clusters of 5 to 10 flowers have a main stalk 0.6 to 1.2 inches long; each flower has a stalk 0.2 to 0.5 inches long. The hypanthium is topped with five small, narrow calyx lobes. The magenta petals are fused into a one-lipped tube 2.3 to 3.1 inches long and 0.2 to 0.4 inches wide, with five down-curved lobes. The purplish-red berries are topped by the persistent calyx lobes. This subspecies is distinguished from ssp. *hamatiflora*, the only other subspecies, by its long flower stalks and larger calyx lobes. The species differs from others in the genus by its growth habit, its stalkless leaves, the number of flowers in each cluster, and the size and shape of the corolla and calyx.

Habitat

This species typically grows in 'ohi'a-dominated montane wet forests at elevations between 4,000 and 5,700 feet. Associated species include kawa'u, pilo, and naio.

For a continued habitat description of Hawaii, see "Habitat Conditions on the Island of Hawaii (the Big Island), Hawaii," page 1834.

Historic Range

This subspecies is known only to have occurred at two sites on the island of Hawaii, on the western slope of Hualalai and the southwestern slope of Mauna Loa.

Current Distribution

The two extant populations, located on private and state land at Honuaulu Forest Reserve and Keokea, are about 28 miles apart and contain approximately 19 individuals.

Conservation and Recovery

The major threats to this species are competition from alien plants such as banana poka; grazing and trampling by cattle; and stochastic extinction and reduced reproductive vigor due to the small number of existing populations and individuals.

The recovery of this and most other Hawaiian species depends on how well management practices can be implemented. The habitat of this and other Hawaiian species has undergone extreme alteration because of past and present land management practices, including deliberately introducing alien animals and plants, and agricultural and recreational development. To understand the recovery problems facing this species, it is necessary to understand the long-term causes of habitat destruction.

For a continued discussion of the threats to Hawaiian plants, see page 1831.

Bibliography

U.S. Fish and Wildlife Service. "Endangered and Threatened Wildlife and Plant; Determination of Endangered or Threatened Status for 21 Plants from the Island of Hawaii, State of Hawaii." *Federal Register* Vol 59, No. 43. March 4, 1994: 10305-10325.

Contacts

U.S. Fish and Wildlife Service
300 Ala Moana Boulevard, Room 6307
P.O. Box 50167
Honolulu, HI 96850
(808) 541-2749

Adapted from data compiled by Beacham Publishing for *Beacham's International Threatened, Endangered, and Extinct Species* published on CD ROM.

Haha

Cyanea shipmanii

Jack Jeffrey

Status	Endangered
Listed	March 4, 1994
Family	Campanulaceae (Bellflower)
Description	Unbranched shrub with small, sharp projections; wide, deeply cut, stalked leaves; and greenish-white flowers covered with fine hairs clustered in groups of 10 to 15.
Habitat	Koa- and 'ohi'a-dominated montane mesic forests at elevations between 5,400 and 6,200 feet.
Threats	Limited numbers.
Range	Hawaii (Hawaii)

Description

This haha, *Cyanea shipmanii*, is an un-branched or few-branched shrub 8 to 13 feet tall with small, sharp projections, especially in young plants. The alternate, stalked leaves are 6.7 to 12 inches long, 2.8 to 5.5 inches wide, and deeply cut into 20 to 30 lobes per leaf. Flowers are covered with fine hairs and are clustered in groups of 10 to 15, the main stalk 0.4 to 1.2 inches long, and each flower stalk 0.4 to 0.6 inches long. The hypanthium is topped with five small calyx lobes. The pale greenish-white petals, 1.2 to 1.4 inches long, are fused into a curved five-lobed tube 0.1 to 0.2 inches wide. The fruit is an ellipsoid berry. This species differs from others in the genus by its slender stems; stalked, pinnately lobed leaves; and smaller flowers.

Habitat

This species typically grows in koa- and 'ohi'a-dominated montane mesic forests at elevations between 5,400 and 6,200 feet. Associated species include kawa'u and kolea.

For a complete habitat description of Hawaii, see "Habitat Conditions on the Island of Hawaii (the Big Island), Hawaii," page 1834.

Historic Range

This species has been known from only one population, located on the island of Hawaii on the eastern slope of Mauna Kea on private land.

Current Distribution

When originally discovered, only one

mature plant was found. The current population is believed to be fewer than 50 individuals.

Conservation and Recovery

The major threat to this species is stochastic extinction and reduced reproductive vigor due to the single existing population and the small number of known individuals.

The recovery of this and most other Hawaiian species depends on how well management practices can be implemented. The habitat of this and other Hawaiian species has undergone extreme alteration because of past and present land management practices, including deliberately introducing alien animals and plants, and agricultural and recreational development. To understand the recovery problems facing this species, it is necessary to understand the long-term causes of habitat destruction.

For a continued discussion of the threats to Hawaiian plants, see page 1831.

Bibliography

U.S. Fish and Wildlife Service. "Endangered and Threatened Wildlife and Plant; Determination of Endangered or Threatened Status for 21 Plants from the Island of Hawaii, State of Hawaii." *Federal Register* Vol 59, No. 43. March 4, 1994: 10305-10325.

Contacts

U.S. Fish and Wildlife Service
300 Ala Moana Boulevard, Room 6307
P.O. Box 50167
Honolulu, HI 96850
(808) 541-2749

Adapted from data compiled by Beacham Publishing for *Beacham's International Threatened, Endangered, and Extinct Species* published on CD ROM.

Haha
Cyanea stictophylla

John Giffin

Status	Endangered
Listed	March 4, 1994
Family	Campanulaceae (Bellflower)
Description	Shrub or tree, sometimes covered with small, sharp projections, and yellowish-white or purple flowers.
Habitat	Koa- and 'ohi'a-dominated lowland mesic and wet forests.
Threats	Grazing and trampling by feral cattle; limited numbers.
Range	Hawaii (Hawaii)

Description

This haha, *Cyanea stictophylla,* is a shrub or tree 2 to 20 feet tall, sometimes covered with small, sharp projections. The alternate, stalked, oblong, shallowly lobed, toothed leaves are 7.8 to 15 centimeters long, and 1.6 to 3.1 inches wide. Clusters of 5 or 6 flowers have main flowering stalks of 0.4 to 1.6 inches long; each flower has a stalk of 0.3 to 0.9 inches long. The hypanthium is topped with 5 calyx lobes 0.1 to 0.2 inches long and 0.04 to 0.1 wide. The yellowish-white or purple petals, 1.4 to 2 inches long, are fused into an arched, five-lobed tube about 0.2 inches wide. The spherical berries are orange. This species differs from others in the genus by its lobed, toothed leaves, and its larger flowers with small calyx lobes and deeply lobed corollas.

Habitat

This species, sometimes growing epiphytically (not rooted in soil), is found in koa- and 'ohi'a-dominated lowland mesic and wet forests at elevations between 3,500 and 6,400 feet. Associated species include tree ferns, alani, and opuhe.

For a continued habitat description of Hawaii, see "Habitat Conditions on the Island of Hawaii (the Big Island), Hawaii," page 1831

Historic Range

Historically, this species was known only from the island of Hawaii on the western, southern, southeastern, and eastern slopes of Mauna Loa.

Current Distribution

Today, the species is known to be extant near Keauhou and in South Kona on private land. The 3 known populations, which extend over a distance of about 38 by 10 miles, contain a total of approximately 15 individuals.

Conservation and Recovery

The major threat to *Cyanea stictophylla* is grazing and trampling by feral cattle, as well as stochastic extinction and reduced reproductive vigor due to the small number of existing populations and individuals.

The recovery of this and most other Hawaiian species depends on how well management practices can be implemented. The habitat of this and other Hawaiian species has undergone extreme alteration because of past and present land management practices, including deliberately introducing alien animals and plants, and agricultural and recreational development. To understand the recovery problems facing this species, it is necessary to understand the long-term causes of habitat destruction.

For a continued discussion of the threats to Hawaiian plants, see page 1831.

Bibliography

U.S. Fish and Wildlife Service. "Endangered and Threatened Wildlife and Plant; Determination of Endangered or Threatened Status for 21 Plants from the Island of Hawaii, State of Hawaii." *Federal Register* Vol 59, No. 43. March 4, 1994: 10305-10325.

Contacts

U.S. Fish and Wildlife Service
300 Ala Moana Boulevard, Room 6307
P.O. Box 50167
Honolulu, HI 96850
(808) 541-2749

Adapted from data compiled by Beacham Publishing for *Beacham's International Threatened, Endangered, and Extinct Species* published on CD ROM.

Ha'iwale

Cyrtandra giffardii

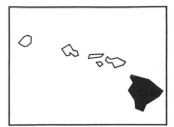

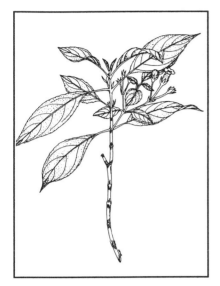

Yevonn Wilson-Ramsey

Status	Endangered
Listed	March 4, 1994
Family	Gesneriaceae (African Violet)
Description	Shrubby tree with opposite, stalked, papery-textured, toothed leaves having a few tiny, coarse hairs on the upper surface; and clusters of 3 to 5 white flowers.
Habitat	Shady koa- 'ohi'a- and tree fern-dominated montane wet forests.
Threats	Habitat destruction by feral pigs; limited numbers.
Range	Hawaii (Hawaii)

Description

This ha'iwale, *Cyrtandra giffardii*, is a shrubby tree usually 10 to 20 feet tall. The opposite, stalked, papery-textured, toothed leaves are usually 2.4 to 4.7 inches long and 1 to 1.8 inches wide and have a few tiny, coarse hairs on the upper surface. Clusters of 3 to 5 flowers have a moderate amount of short brown hairs throughout the cluster, a main stalk 1 to 1.4 inches long, two linear bracts about 0.25 inches long, and individual flower stalks 0.6 to 1.2 inches long. The calyx, 0.1 to 0.4 inches long, has an outer covering of short brown hairs and is divided into 5 narrowly triangular lobes. The corolla consists of 5 fused white petals about 0.5 inches long, with lobes about 0.08 to 0.1 inches long. Only immature berries have been observed, and they were white and about 0.4 inches long. Both this species and *C. tintinnabula* are distinguished from others of the genus and others on the island of Hawaii by a combination of the following characteristics: the opposite, more or less elliptic, papery leaves; the presence of some hairs on the leaves and more on the inflorescence; the presence of three to six flowers per inflorescence; and the size and shape of the flowers and flower parts.

Habitat

This species typically grows in shady koa- 'ohi'a- and tree fern-dominated montane wet forests at elevations between 2,400 and 4,900 feet. Associated species include other taxa of *Cyrtandra* (ha'iwale), *Hedyotis* spp., and *olomea.*

For a continued habitat description of Hawaii, see "Habitat Conditions on the Island of Hawaii (the Big Island)," page 1834.

Historic Range

Historically, *C. giffardii* was found on the island of Hawaii on the northeastern slope of Mauna Kea near Kilau Stream and south to the eastern slope of Mauna Loa near Kilauea Crater.

Current Distribution

The 3 extant populations on state land are located near Kilau Stream, Stainback Highway, and Puu Makaala, extending over a distance of approximately 31 by 3 miles and containing a total of about 14 to 20 plants.

Conservation and Recovery

The major threat to this species are habitat disturbance and plant damage by feral pigs, as well as stochastic extinction and reduced reproductive vigor due to the small number of existing populations.

The recovery of this and most other Hawaiian species depends on how well management practices can be implemented. The habitat of this and other Hawaiian species has undergone extreme alteration because of past and present land management practices, including deliberately introducing alien animals and plants, and agricultural and recreational development. To understand the recovery problems facing this species, it is necessary to understand the long-term causes of habitat destruction.

For a continued discussion of the threats to Hawaiian plants, see page 1831.

Bibliography

U.S. Fish and Wildlife Service. "Endangered and Threatened Wildlife and Plant; Determination of Endangered or Threatened Status for 21 Plants from the Island of Hawaii, State of Hawaii." *Federal Register* Vol 59, No. 43. March 4, 1994: 10305-10325.

Contacts

U.S. Fish and Wildlife Service
300 Ala Moana Boulevard, Room 6307
P.O. Box 50167
Honolulu, HI 96850
(808) 541-2749

Adapted from data compiled by Beacham Publishing for *Beacham's International Threatened, Endangered, and Extinct Species* published on CD ROM.

Ha'iwale

Cyrtandra tintinnabula

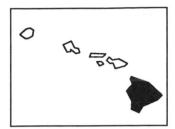

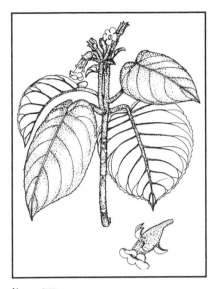

Yevonn Wilson-Ramsey

Status	Endangered
Listed	March 4, 1994
Family	Gesneriaceae (African Violet)
Description	Shrub with opposite, stalked, elliptical or oval, papery-textured yellow-brown leaves; and 3 to 6 flower clusters.
Habitat	Dense koa, 'ohi'a, and tree fern-dominated lowland wet forests at elevations between 2,100 and 3,400 feet.
Threats	Habitat destruction by feral pigs; limited numbers.
Range	Hawaii (Hawaii)

Description

This ha'iwale, *Cyrtandra tintinnabula*, is a shrub 3.3 to 6.6 feet tall, with opposite, stalked, elliptical or oval, papery-textured leaves 5 to 10 inches long and 2 to 4.8 inches wide. Leaves, especially the lower surfaces, have yellowish-brown hairs. Flower clusters, densely covered with long soft hairs, comprise 3 to 6 flowers, a main stalk 0.4 to 0.7 inches long, individual flower stalks 0.2 to 0.6 inches long, and leaflike bracts. The green, bell-shaped calyx is about 0.4 inches long and has triangular lobes. The hairy white corolla, about 0.5 inches long and about 0.2 inches in diameter, is divided into 5 lobes, each about 0.1 inches long. Fruit and seeds have not been observed. This species differs from *C. giffardii* by its growth habit, its larger leaves, and its shorter flower stalks.

Habitat

This species typically grows in dense koa, 'ohi'a, and tree fern-dominated lowland wet forests at elevations between 2,100 and 3,400 feet. Associated species include other kinds of ha'iwale and *Hedyotis* sp.

For a continued habitat description of Hawaii, see "Habitat Conditions on the Island of Hawaii (the Big Island)," page 1834.

Historic Range

Historically, *C. tintinnabula* was found only on the island of Hawaii on the northern to eastern slopes of Mauna Kea.

Current Distribution

Three populations are known to occur on

state land of the island of Hawaii, extending over approximately 6 by 1 mile from Kilau Stream to Honohina Gulch, and containing 18 known individuals.

Conservation and Recovery

The major threats to this species are habitat disturbance and destruction by feral pigs, and stochastic extinction and reduced reproduction vigor due to the small numbers of existing populations and individuals.

The recovery of this and most other Hawaiian species depends on how well management practices can be implemented. The habitat of this and other Hawaiian species has undergone extreme alteration because of past and present land management practices, including deliberately introducing alien animals and plants, and agricultural and recreational development. To understand the recovery problems facing this species, it is necessary to understand the long-term causes of habitat destruction.

For a continued discussion of the threats to Hawaiian plants, see page 1831.

Bibliography

U.S. Fish and Wildlife Service. "Endangered and Threatened Wildlife and Plant; Determination of Endangered or Threatened Status for 21 Plants from the Island of Hawaii, State of Hawaii." *Federal Register* Vol 59, No. 43. March 4, 1994: 10305-10325.

Contacts

U.S. Fish and Wildlife Service
300 Ala Moana Boulevard, Room 6307
P.O. Box 50167
Honolulu, HI 96850
(808) 541-2749

Adapted from data compiled by Beacham Publishing for *Beacham's International Threatened, Endangered, and Extinct Species* published on CD ROM.

Hilo Ischaemum

Ischaemum byrone

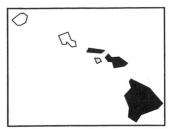

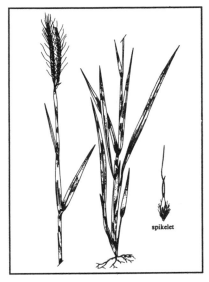

Yevonn Wilson-Ramsey

Status:	Endangered
Listed:	March 4, 1994
Family:	Poaceae (Grass)
Description:	Perennial plant with creeping stems and erect stems with inflated sheaths enclosing yellow to yellow-brown flowering clusters of 2 to 3.
Habitat:	Coastal dry shrubland among rocks or on basalt cliffs.
Threats:	Competition from alien plants; volcanic activity.
Range:	Hawaii (Molokai, Maui, Hawaii)

Description

Hilo Ischaemum is a perennial plant with creeping stems and erect stems 16 to 31 inches tall. The uppermost sheaths are often inflated and sometimes partially enclose the yellow to yellow-brown racemes. The hairless leaf blade is 2.8 to 7.9 inches long and 1.2 to 2 inches wide; the uppermost blades are much smaller in size. Flowers arranged in 2 and sometimes 3 digitate, elongate racemes 1.6 to 3.9 inches long, consist of two types of two-flowered awed spikelets. The fruit is a grain about 0.1 inches long. The only species of the genus found in Hawaii, Hilo Ischaemum differs from other grasses by its photosynthetic pathway; and its two-flowered awned spikelets.

Habitat

This species typically grows in coastal dry shrubland among rocks or on basalt cliffs at elevations between sea level and 250 feet. Associated species include ko'oko'olau and naupaka kahakai.

For a continued habitat description, see "Habitat Conditions on the Island of Molokai" page 1987; "Habitat Conditions on the Island of Maui" page 1951; "Habitat Conditions on the Island of Hawaii (the Big Island)" page 1834.

Historic Range

Historically, this species was found on Oahu at an unspecified location; on the northeastern coast of Molokai; on east Maui;

and along the central portion of the eastern coast of the island of Hawaii.

Current Distribution

Today, populations still occur on Molokai, Maui, and Hawaii. Two populations on east Molokai are located about 2 miles apart at the head of Wailau Valley and on Kikipua Point on private land. Six populations on east Maui are found along approximately 16 miles of coast on private, state, and Federal land on Pauwalu Point; on Kalahu Point; near Hana; on Kauiki Head; and on the following offshore islets: Keopuka, Mokuhuki, and Puukii. On the island of Hawaii, the species is still found in two populations at Auwae and Kamoamoa on private and Federal land. The total distribution of this species includes 10 populations on 3 islands with approximately 1,200 to 2,200 individuals, though the total number may be in the range of 5,000 individuals.

Conservation and Recovery

Because this species occupies lowland habitat, it is at risk from development, alien weeds, and in the past, feral animals. The major threats are competition from alien plants such as Henry's crabgrass, and habitat change from volcanic activity.

The recovery of this and most other Hawaiian species depends on how well management practices can be implemented. The habitat of this and other Hawaiian species has undergone extreme alteration because of past and present land management practices, including deliberately introducing alien animals and plants, and agricultural and recreational development. To understand the recovery problems facing this species, it is necessary to understand the long-term causes of habitat destruction.

For a continued discussion of the threats to Hawaiian plants, see page 1831.

Bibliography

U.S. Fish and Wildlife Service. "Endangered and Threatened Wildlife and Plant; Determination of Endangered or Threatened Status for 21 Plants from the Island of Hawaii, State of Hawaii." *Federal Register* Vol 59, No. 43. March 4, 1994: 10305-10325.

Contacts

U.S. Fish and Wildlife Service
300 Ala Moana Boulevard, Room 6307
P.O. Box 50167
Honolulu, HI 96850
(808) 541-2749

Adapted from data compiled by Beacham Publishing for *Beacham's International Threatened, Endangered, and Extinct Species* published on CD ROM.

Wahine Noho Kula

Isodendrion pyrifolium

Loyal A. Mehrhoff

Status	Endangered
Listed	March 4, 1994
Family	Violaceae (Violet)
Description	Shrub with lance-shaped, papery leaves; and fragrant greenish-yellow flowers.
Habitat	Dry sites in lowland dry to mesic forests at low elevations.
Threats	Competition from alien plants; habitat alteration by residential development; limited numbers.
Range	Hawaii (Hawaii)

Description

Wahine Noho Kula is a shrub about 2.6 to 6.6 feet tall, has persistent stipules and alternate, stalked, elliptic or sometimes lance-shaped, papery leaves that measure 1 to 2.6 inches long and 0.3 to 1.3 inches wide. The solitary or bilaterally symmetrical, fragrant flowers have five lance-shaped sepals 0.1 to 0.2 inches long with membranous edges fringed with white hairs and three types of clawed greenish-yellow petals 0.4 to 0.6 inches long with lobes about 0.2 inches long. The three-lobed, 0.5 inch long capsule opens to release olive-green seeds about 0.1 inch long and about 0.08 inch in diameter. This species differs from others in the genus by its slightly smaller, greenish-yellow flowers and by the presence of hairs on the stipule midribs and leaf veins.

Habitat

This species typically grows on dry sites in lowland dry to mesic forests at low elevations. Associated species include 'iliaki, mamane, and 'uhaloa.

For a continued habitat description of Hawaii, see "Habitat Conditions on the Island of Hawaii (the Big Island), Hawaii," page 1834.

Historic Range

Historically, this species was found at unspecified locations on Niihau, Molokai, and Lanai, as well as on Oahu in the central portion of the Waianae Mountains; on Maui in the northeastern to southwestern regions of the West Maui Mountains; and on the island of Hawaii at the western base of

Hualalai.

Current Distribution

The species had not been collected since 1870 and was presumed extinct until 1991 when four plants were found on Hawaii at Kealakehe near Kona on state land being developed for residential housing and a golf course. In late 1992 and early 1993, 50 to 60 additional plants were found at this site.

Conservation and Recovery

The major threats to this species are habitat conversion associated with residential and recreational development; competition from alien plants such as fountain grass; fire; stochastic extinction and reduced reproductive vigor due to the single known population and the small number of existing individuals.

The recovery of this and most other Hawaiian species depends on how well management practices can be implemented. The habitat of this and other Hawaiian species has undergone extreme alteration because of past and present land management practices, including deliberately introducing alien animals and plants, and agricultural and recreational development. To understand the recovery problems facing this species, it is necessary to understand the long-term causes of habitat destruction.

For a continued discussion of the threats to Hawaiian plants, see page 1831.

Bibliography

U.S. Fish and Wildlife Service. "Endangered and Threatened Wildlife and Plant; Determination of Endangered or Threatened Status for 21 Plants from the Island of Hawaii, State of Hawaii." *Federal Register* Vol 59, No. 43. March 4, 1994: 10305-10325.

Contacts

U.S. Fish and Wildlife Service
300 Ala Moana Boulevard, Room 6307
P.O. Box 50167
Honolulu, HI 96850
(808) 541-2749

Adapted from data compiled by Beacham Publishing for *Beacham's International Threatened, Endangered, and Extinct Species* published on CD ROM.

Mariscus fauriei
No Common Name

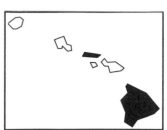

Yevonn Wilson-Ramsey

Status	Endangered
Listed	March 4, 1994
Family	Campanulaceae (Bellflower)
Description	Perennial plant with somewhat enlarged underground stems, three-angled, single or grouped aerial stems; and 3 to 10 unbranched clusters of unstalked flowers.
Habitat	Lama-dominated lowland dry forests, often on a substrate, at elevations between 880 and 6,000 feet.
Threats	Competition from alien plants; habitat destruction by feral goats; limited numbers.
Range	Hawaii (Hawaii, Molokai)

Description

Mariscus fauriei is a perennial plant with somewhat enlarged underground stems and three-angled, single or grouped aerial stems 4 to 20 inches tall, has leaves shorter than or the same length as the stems and 0.04 to 0.1 inches wide. Three to 5 bracts, the lowest one 2.4 to 7.9 inches long, are located under each flower cluster, which measures 0.8 to 1.8 inches long and 1.2 to 3.9 inches wide and is made up of 3 to 10 spikes. Each spike measures 0.3 to 1.2 inches long and 0.3 to 0.4 inches wide, and is made up of compressed spreading spikelets, each comprising seven to nine flowers. Fruits are three-angled achenes about 0.05 inches long and about 0.03 inches wide. This species differs from others in the genus in Hawaii by its smaller size and more spreading spikelets.

Habitat

This species typically grows in lama-dominated lowland dry forests, often on a substrate, at elevations between 880 and 6,000 feet. Associated species include alahe's, 'ala'ala wai nui, and hao.

For a continued habitat description, see "Habitat Conditions on the Island of Hawaii (the Big Island)," page 1834; and "Habitat Conditions on the Island of Molokai," page 1987.

Historic Range

Historically, this species was found on east Molokai, in the northwestern and southwestern portions of Lanai, and on the island of Hawaii on the northern slope of Hualalai on the northwestern and southernmost slopes of Mauna Loa.

Current Distribution

A total of 3 extant populations and about 33 to 43 known individuals are found on Molokai and Hawaii; the species is almost certainly extinct on Lanai. One population of about 20 to 30 plants occurs on Molokai on state land. Two populations located about 45 miles apart are known on Hawaii on the Hualalai side of Mauna Loa and in the South Point area. The land is privately owned, and there are a total of about 13 known individuals on the island.

Conservation and Recovery

The major threat on Molokai is grazing and trampling by feral goats and axis deer; and on Hawaii, competition from alien plants such as Christmas berry and basketgrass. On both islands the species is faced with stochastic extinction and reduced reproductive vigor due to the small number of populations and individuals.

The recovery of this and most other Hawaiian species depends on how well management practices can be implemented. The habitat of this and other Hawaiian species has undergone extreme alteration because of past and present land management practices, including deliberately introducing alien animals and plants, and agricultural and recreational development. To understand the recovery problems facing this species, it is necessary to understand the long-term causes of habitat destruction.

For a continued discussion of the threats to Hawaiian plants, see page 1831.

Bibliography

U.S. Fish and Wildlife Service. "Endangered and Threatened Wildlife and Plant; Determination of Endangered or Threatened Status for 21 Plants from the Island of Hawaii, State of Hawaii." *Federal Register* Vol 59, No. 43. March 4, 1994: 10305-10325.

Contacts

U.S. Fish and Wildlife Service
300 Ala Moana Boulevard, Room 6307
P.O. Box 50167
Honolulu, HI 96850
(808) 541-2749

Adapted from data compiled by Beacham Publishing for *Beacham's International Threatened, Endangered, and Extinct Species* published on CD ROM.

'Aiea

Nothocestrum breviflorum

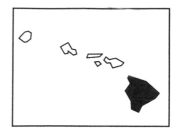

Loyal A. Mehrhoff

Status	Endangered
Listed	March 4, 1994
Family	Solanaceae (Nightshade)
Description	Stout tree with papery-textured toothless leaves, and greenish-yellow flowers.
Habitat	Lowland dry forests, and montane dry or mesic forests, often on substrate.
Threats	Residential development; competition from alien plants; browsing by cattle; fire; limited numbers.
Range	Hawaii (Hawaii)

Description

This 'Aiea is a stout tree 33 to 39 feet tall, with a trunk up to 18 inches in diameter, has deciduous, alternate, stalked, oblong or elliptic-oblong, thick and papery-textured toothless leaves which are 2 to 4.7 inches long and 1.2 to 2.4 inches wide. Numerous bisexual radically symmetrical flowers are clustered at the ends of the short spurs (branches with much shortened internodes) on individual stalks 0.2 to 0.4 inches long. Each flower consists of a 0.2 to 0.4 inch long, four-lobed tubular calyx split on one side and a greenish-yellow four-lobed corolla which barely projects beyond the calyx. The fruit, a somewhat spherical or oblong, orange-red berry about 0.2 to 0.3 inches in diameter, is enclosed by the calyx. Seeds have not been observed. This species can be distinguished from others of this endemic Hawaiian genus by the leaf shape; the clusters of more than three flowers arranged on the ends of short branches; and the broad fruit enclosed by the calyx.

Habitat

This species typically grows in koa- and 'ohi'a- or lama-dominated lowland dry forests, and montane dry or mesic forests, often on substrate, at elevations between 590 and

6,000 feet, Associated species include 'iliahi, uhiuhi, and wiliwili.

For a continued habitat description of Hawaii, see "Habitat Conditions on the Island of Hawaii (the Big Island), Hawaii," page 1834.

Historic Range and Current Distribution

Historically, this species was found only on the island of Hawaii from the southern portion of the Kohala Mountains; the northern slope of Hualali; and the eastern, southern and western slopes of Mauna Loa. Today, extant populations have been found in much of the species' historic range, from near Waimea; near Kiholo; in Puu Waawaa; in Hawaii Volcanoes National Park; in Kipuka Ki; near Holei Pali; and in the South Point area.

Conservation and Recovery

The major threats to this species are habitat conversion associated with residential and recreational development; competition from alien species such as Christmas berry, fountain grass, lantana, and koa haole; browsing by cattle; fire; and stochastic extinction and reduce reproductive vigor due to the small numbers of existing individuals.

The recovery of this and most other Hawaiian species depends on how well management practices can be implemented. The habitat of this and other Hawaiian species has undergone extreme alteration because of past and present land management practices, including deliberately introducing alien animals and plants, and agricultural and recreational development. To understand the recovery problems facing this species, it is necessary to understand the long-term causes of habitat destruction.

For a continued discussion of the threats to Hawaiian plants, see page 1831.

Bibliography

U.S. Fish and Wildlife Service. "Endangered and Threatened Wildlife and Plant; Determination of Endangered or Threatened Status for 21 Plants from the Island of Hawaii, State of Hawaii." *Federal Register* Vol 59, No. 43. March 4, 1994: 10305-10325.

Contacts

U.S. Fish and Wildlife Service
300 Ala Moana Boulevard, Room 6307
P.O. Box 50167
Honolulu, HI 96850
(808) 541-2749

Adapted from data compiled by Beacham Publishing for *Beacham's International Threatened, Endangered, and Extinct Species* published on CD ROM.

Hoiei
Ochrosia kilaueaensis

Status	Endangered
Listed	March 4, 1994
Family	Apocynaceae (Dogbane)
Description	Hairless tree with milky sap; lance- or ellipse-shaped toothless leaves arranged three or four per node; and open clusters of numerous, trumpet-shaped, greenish-white flowers.
Habitat	Koa- and 'ohi'a- or lama-dominated montane mesic forests.
Threats	Competition from alien plants; browsing by feral goats; fire; limited numbers.
Range	Hawaii (Hawaii)

No Photo Available for This Species

Description

Hoiei, *Ochrosia kilaueaensis*, is a hairless tree 49 to 59 feet tall, with milky sap. The lance- or ellipse-shaped toothless leaves are arranged three or four per node, are 2.4 to 7.5 inches wide, and have veins arising at nearly right angles to the midrib. Open clusters of numerous flowers have main stalks 1.8 to 2.5 inches long. Each flower has a five-lobed calyx about 0.4 inches long and a trumpet-shaped greenish-white corolla with a tube 0.3 to 0.4 inches long and lobes 0.5 to 0.6 inches long. The fruit is a drupe thought to be yellowish-brown at maturity, 1.8 to 1.9 inches long, and 0.9 to 1.1 inches wide. The species is distinguished from other Hawaiian species of the genus by the greater height of mature trees; the open flower clusters; the long flower stalks; and the larger calyx and lobes of the corolla.

Habitat

This species typically grows in koa- and 'ohi'a- or lama-dominated montane mesic forests at elevations between 2,200 and 4,000 feet. Associated species include 'aiea, kauila, and kopiko.

For a continued habitat description of Hawaii, see "Habitat Conditions on the Island of Hawaii (the Big Island), Hawaii," page 1834.

Historic Range

Historically, this species has been collected on the northern slope of Hualalai and on the eastern slope of Mauna Loa. There is one known extant population located at Puu Waawaa on state land.

Current Distribution

The one extant population on Puu Waawaa consists of an unknown number of individuals.

Conservation and Recovery

The major threats to Hoiei are competition from alien species such as fountain grass; browsing by feral goats; fire; and stochastic extinction and reduced reproductive vigor due to the single existing known population.

The recovery of this and most other Hawaiian species depends on how well management practices can be implemented. The habitat of this and other Hawaiian species has undergone extreme alteration because of past and present land management practices, including deliberately introducing alien animals and plants, and agricultural and recreational development. To understand the recovery problems facing this species, it is necessary to understand the long-term causes of habitat destruction.

For a continued discussion of the threats to Hawaiian plants, see page 1831.

Bibliography

U.S. Fish and Wildlife Service. "Endangered and Threatened Wildlife and Plant; Determination of Endangered or Threatened Status for 21 Plants from the Island of Hawaii, State of Hawaii." *Federal Register* Vol 59, No. 43. March 4, 1994: 10305-10325.

Contacts

U.S. Fish and Wildlife Service
300 Ala Moana Boulevard, Room 6307
P.O. Box 50167
Honolulu, HI 96850
(808) 541-2749

Adapted from data compiled by Beacham Publishing for *Beacham's International Threatened, Endangered, and Extinct Species* published on CD ROM.

Laukahi Kuahiwi

Plantago hawaiensis

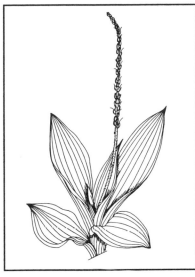

P. pachyphylla
(closely related species)

Yevonn Wilson-Ramsey

Status	Endangered
Listed	March 4, 1994
Family	Plantaginaceae (Plantain)
Description	Perennial herb with thick, leathery, narrowly oval and upward pointing, trumpet-shaped flowers
Habitat	Boggy conditions in montane wet herblands or in montane dry shrublands
Threats	Competition from alien plants; habitat destruction by cattle, goats and pigs; limited numbers.
Range	Hawaii (Hawaii)

Description

Laukahi kuahiwi is a perennial herb which grows from a stout, short stem; has thick, leathery, narrowly oval or oblong leaves located at the base of the plant, which measure 3 to 8.7 inches long and usually 0.6 to 1.3 inches wide. The flowering stalk is 7.9 to 35 inches long and is topped by a spike usually 5.9 to 9 inches long. Each upward pointing flower, subtended by a single bract 0.08 to 0.1 inches long, has a four-lobed calyx 0.06 to 0.09 inches long, and a trumpet-shaped corolla about 0.04 inches long. The capsule, 0.1 to 0.2 inches long and projecting from the calyx, opens to release four to six dull-black seeds about 0.04 inches long and winged on one end. This species is distin-guished from other endemic and naturalized species of the genus in Hawaii by its perennial herbaceous habit; its thick leathery leaves; its upward pointing flowers; and its capsules which project from the calyx.

Habitat

This species typically grows in boggy conditions in montane wet herblands or in montane dry shrublands dominated by koa or 'ohi'a trees of short stature; or sometimes in lava cracks at elevations between 5,900 and 6,400 feet.

For a continued habitat description of Hawaii, see "Habitat Conditions on the Island of Hawaii (the Big Island), Hawaii," page 1834.

Historic Range

Historically, this species was found only on the island of Hawaii on the southern slope of Mauna Kea; the northeastern, southeastern, and southern slopes of Mauna Loa; and the western slope of Hualalai.

Current Distribution

Today, the species is known to occur on the Humuula Saddle; in the Upper Waiakea Forest Reserve; and near the Keapohina Upland on private and state land. The four extant populations extend over a distance of approximately 14 by 4 miles. There are no more than ten known individuals.

Conservation and Recovery

The major threat is stochastic extinction and reduced reproductive vigor due to the small number of existing individuals.

The recovery of this and most other Hawaiian species depends on how well management practices can be implemented. The habitat of this and other Hawaiian species has undergone extreme alteration because of past and present land management practices, including deliberately introducing alien animals and plants, and agricultural and recreational development. To understand the recovery problems facing this species, it is necessary to understand the long-term causes of habitat destruction.

For a continued discussion of the threats to Hawaiian plants, see page 1831.

Bibliography

U.S. Fish and Wildlife Service. "Endangered and Threatened Wildlife and Plant; Determination of Endangered or Threatened Status for 21 Plants from the Island of Hawaii, State of Hawaii." *Federal Register* Vol 59, No. 43. March 4, 1994: 10305-10325.

Contacts

U.S. Fish and Wildlife Service
300 Ala Moana Boulevard, Room 6307
P.O. Box 50167
Honolulu, HI 96850
(808) 541-2749

Adapted from data compiled by Beacham Publishing for *Beacham's International Threatened, Endangered, and Extinct Species* published on CD ROM.

Po'e

Portulaca sclerocarpa

Robert J. Gustafson

Status	Endangered
Listed	March 4, 1994
Family	Portulacaceae (Purslane)
Description	Perennial herb with stalkless, succulent, grayish-green leaves; and tight clusters of 3 to 6 stalkless white or pink flowers.
Habitat	Montane dry shrublands, often on bare cinder.
Threats	Competition from alien grasses; habitat disturbance by feral animals and military exercises; fire.
Range	Hawaii (Hawaii, Lanai)

Description

Po'e, *Portulaca sclerocarpa*, is a perennial herb with a fleshy, tuberous taproot which becomes woody, has stems up to about 7.9 inches long. The stalkless, succulent, grayish-green leaves are almost circular in cross-section, 0.3 to 0.8 inches long, and about 0.06 to 0.1 inches wide. Dense tufts of hairs are located in each leaf axil and underneath the tight clusters of 3 to 6 stalkless flowers grouped at the ends of stems. Sepals are about 0.2 inches long and have membranous edges. Petals are white, pink, or pink with a white base, about 0.4 long, and surround about 30 stamens in an 8-branched style. The hardened capsules are about 0.2 inches long, have walls thick, open very late or not at all, and contain glossy, dark reddish-brown seeds about 0.02 inches long. This species differs from other native and naturalized species of the genus in Hawaii by its woody taproot, its narrow leaves, and the color of its petals and seeds. Its closest relative, *P. villosa*, differs mainly in its thinner-walled opening capsule.

Habitat

This species typically grows in montane dry shrublands, often on bare cinder, and even near steam vents, at elevations between 3,380 and 5,340 feet. Associated species include mamane and 'ohi'a.

For a continued habitat description of Hawaii, see "Habitat Conditions on the Island of Hawaii (the Big Island), Hawaii," page 1834.

Historic Range

Historically, this species was found on and islet off the south coast of Lanai, and on the island of Hawaii in the Kohala Mountains; on the northern slope of Haualalai; the northwestern slope of Mauna Loa; and near Kilauea Crater.

Current Distribution

There is one extant population on Poopoo Islet of the coast of Lanai that contains about 10 individuals. The eleven populations on island of Hawaii contain a total of approximately 72 to 122 individuals.

Conservation and Recovery

The major threats are competition from alien grasses, such as fountain grass and broomsedge; trampling and habitat disturbance by feral goats, pigs and sheep; habitat disturbance and damage to plants as a result of military exercises; and fire.

The recovery of this and most other Hawaiian species depends on how well management practices can be implemented. The habitat of this and other Hawaiian species has undergone extreme alteration because of past and present land management practices, including deliberately introducing alien animals and plants, and agricultural and recreational development. To understand the recovery problems facing this species, it is necessary to understand the long-term causes of habitat destruction.

For a continued discussion of the threats to Hawaiian plants, see page 1831.

Bibliography

U.S. Fish and Wildlife Service. "Endangered and Threatened Wildlife and Plant; Determination of Endangered or Threatened Status for 21 Plants from the Island of Hawaii, State of Hawaii." *Federal Register* Vol 59, No. 43. March 4, 1994: 10305-10325.

Contacts

U.S. Fish and Wildlife Service
300 Ala Moana Boulevard, Room 6307
P.O. Box 50167
Honolulu, HI 96850
(808) 541-2749

Adapted from data compiled by Beacham Publishing for *Beacham's International Threatened, Endangered, and Extinct Species* published on CD ROM.

Loulu

Pritchardia affinis

Waimea Arboretum and Botanical Gardens

Status	Endangered
Listed	March 4, 1994
Family	Arecaceae (Palm)
Description	Fan-leaved palm tree with pale or pinkish soft wool covering and scattered yellowish scales.
Habitat	Coastal mesic forests at coastal sites or in gulches further inland.
Threats	Predation on seeds by roof rats; development of land where individuals grow; limited numbers.
Range	Hawaii (Hawaii)

Description

Loulou is a fan-leaved palm tree 33 to 82 feet tall, with pale or pinkish soft wool covering the underside of the petiole and extending on the leaf blade. The wedge-shaped leaf has a green and smooth upper surface and a pale green lower surface with scattered yellowish scales. The branched, hairless flower clusters are located among the leaves. Each flower comprises a cup-shaped, three-lobed, calyx; three petals; six stamens; and a three-lobed stigma. The spherical fruit is about 0.9 inches in diameter. The species is distinguished from other species of *Pritchardia* by the long, tangled, wooly hairs on the underside of the petiole and the base of the lower leaf blade; the stout hairless flower clusters which do not extend beyond the wedge-shaped leaves;

and the smaller, spherical fruit.

Habitat

This species typically grows in coastal mesic forests at coastal sites or in gulches further inland, at elevations between sea level and 2,000 feet, possibly associated with brackish water. Native associated species are unknown since all trees are found in cultivated zones, which have long been cleared of their native cover.

For a continued habitat description of Hawaii, see "Habitat Conditions on the Island of Hawaii (the Big Island), Hawaii," page 1834.

Historic Range

Historically, this species was found only

on the island of Hawaii in the Kohala Mountains and along the western and southeastern coasts.

Current Distribution

Scattered individuals of the species can be found throughout much of the historically known coastal range at Kiholo; at Kukio; near Palani Road; on Alii Drive in Kukio; in Captain Cook; at Hookena; at Milolif; and at Punaluu. Most plants grow within areas of human habitation or development, and these trees may have been cultivated rather than having occurred in these areas naturally. There are an estimated 50 to 65 known individuals at 8 or more localities which extend about 110 miles along the coast on private and state land.

Conservation and Recovery

The major threats are predation on seeds by roof rats; development of land where individuals grow; and stochastic extinction and reduced reproductive vigor due to the small number of existing individuals. In the past, the species' natural habitat was cleared for agriculture and housing, and feral pigs destroyed seedlings, preventing regeneration.

Loulou is known to be susceptible to lethal yellows, which is a bacteria-like organism producing disease in many palms. This disease is not yet in Hawaii, but if it ever is accidentally introduced on plant material brought into the state, it is a potential threat to this species.

The recovery of this and most other Hawaiian species depends on how well management practices can be implemented. The habitat of this and other Hawaiian species has undergone extreme alteration because of past and present land management practices, including deliberately intro-

ducing alien animals and plants, and agricultural and recreational development. To understand the recovery problems facing this species, it is necessary to understand the long-term causes of habitat destruction.

For a continued discussion of the threats to Hawaiian plants, see page 1831.

Bibliography

U.S. Fish and Wildlife Service. "Endangered and Threatened Wildlife and Plant; Determination of Endangered or Threatened Status for 21 Plants from the Island of Hawaii, State of Hawaii." *Federal Register* Vol 59, No. 43. March 4, 1994: 10305-10325.

Contacts

U.S. Fish and Wildlife Service
300 Ala Moana Boulevard, Room 6307
P.O. Box 50167
Honolulu, HI 96850
(808) 541-2749

Adapted from data compiled by Beacham Publishing for *Beacham's International Threatened, Endangered, and Extinct Species* published on CD ROM.

Silene hawaiiensis
No Common Name

Status	Threatened
Listed	March 4, 1994
Family	Caryophyllaceae (Pink)
Description	Sprawling shrub with slanting or climbing stems, and stalkless, narrow; and purplish flowers.
Habitat	Montane or subalpine dry shrublands in decomposed lava and ash.
Threats	Competition from alien plants; browsing and habitat destruction by cattle, goats and pigs; military exercises; fire; volcanic activity.
Range	Hawaii (Hawaii)

Robert J. Gustafson

Description

Silene hawaiiensis is a sprawling shrub with slanting or climbing stems 6 to 16 inches long originating from an enlarged root; and is covered with short, often sticky hairs. The stalkless, narrow leaves are 0.2 to 0.6 inches long and 0.02 to 0.03 inches wide. Flowers are arranged in elongate clusters. Each flower has a stalk 0.1 to 0.2 inches long; a five-toothed purple or purple-tinged calyx 0.4 to 0.6 inches long; and five petals greenish-white above and maroon below, with a stalk-like base and a flat, two-lobed expanded portion about 0.2 inches long. The fruit is a capsule about 0.3 inches long which releases pale brown seeds 0.02 to 0.03 inches long. This species differs from others of *silene* in Hawaii by its growth habit; its covering of short, often sticky hairs; the shape of its leaves; the arrangement of its flower clusters; and the color of its petals.

Habitat

This species typically grows in montane or subalpine dry shrublands in decomposed lava and ash, but can be found on all ages of lava and cinder substrates at elevations between 3,000 and 4,300 feet and sometimes up to 8,500 feet. Associated species include 'a'ali'i, pukiawe, and 'ohelo.

For a continued habitat description of Hawaii, see "Habitat Conditions on the Island of Hawaii (the Big Island), Hawaii," page 1834.

Historic Range

Historically, this species was found only on the island of Hawaii from the western slope of Mauna Kea; the summit of Hualalai;

Humuula Saddle; the northern, western and northwestern slopes of Mauna Loa; and near Kilauea Crater.

Current Distribution

Today, over 50 populations are found in Hamakua District; on Humuula Saddle; at PTA; north of Puu Keanui; and in HVNP on private, state and Federal land. They extend over a distance of approximately 12 by 7 miles and contain over 3,000 individuals.

Conservation and Recovery

Many of the 50 populations are threatened by competition with alien plant species, particularly fountain grass; grazing, browsing, and trampling by feral goats, pigs and sheep; habitat disturbance and damage to plants as a result of military exercises; fire; and volcanic activity.

The recovery of this and most other Hawaiian species depends on how well management practices can be implemented. The habitat of this and other Hawaiian species has undergone extreme alteration because of past and present land management practices, including deliberately introducing alien animals and plants, and agricultural and recreational development. To understand the recovery problems facing this species, it is necessary to understand the long-term causes of habitat destruction.

For a continued discussion of the threats to Hawaiian plants, see page 1831.

Bibliography

U.S. Fish and Wildlife Service. "Endangered and Threatened Wildlife and Plant; Determination of Endangered or Threatened Status for 21 Plants from the Island of Hawaii, State of Hawaii." *Federal Register* Vol 59, No. 43. March 4, 1994: 10305-10325.

Contacts

U.S. Fish and Wildlife Service
300 Ala Moana Boulevard, Room 6307
P.O. Box 50167
Honolulu, HI 96850
(808) 541-2749

Adapted from data compiled by Beacham Publishing for *Beacham's International Threatened, Endangered, and Extinct Species* published on CD ROM.

Tetramolopium arenarium
No Common Name

Robert J. Gustafson

Status	Endangered
Listed	March 4, 1994
Family	Asteraceae (Aster)
Description	Tufted shrub covered with tiny glands and straight hairs; lance-shaped leaves; and 5 to 11 maroon flower heads.
Habitat	Open a'ali'i-dominated lowlands or montane dry forests.
Threats	Competition from alien plants; browsing and habitat destruction by cattle, goats and pigs; military exercises; fire; volcanic activity.
Range	Hawaii (Hawaii)

Description

Tetramolopium arenarium, an erect, tufted shrub 2.6 to 4.3 feet tall, is covered with tiny glans and straight hairs. The alternate, toothless or shallowly toothed leaves are more or less lance-shaped, 0.6 to 1.5 inches long. Five to 11 heads (dense flower clusters) are grouped at the end of each stem. Each head comprises a bell-shaped structure of 20 to 34 bracts 0.1 to 0.2 inches high and 0.2 to 0.4 inches in diameter beneath the flowers; a single series of 22 to 45 white, male ray florets 0.05 to 0.09 inches long; and 4 to 9 bisexual disk florets with maroon petals 0.12 to 0.17 inches long. Fruits are compressed achenes 0.06 to 0.1 inches long and 0.02 to 0.03 inches wide. This species is distinguished from others of the genus by its erect habit; the presence and types of glands and hairs on the plant; the fewer heads per flower cluster; the larger, male ray florets; the fewer, bisexual, maroon-petaled disk florets; and the wider achenes.

Habitat

This species typically grows in open a'ali'i-dominated lowlands or montane dry forests at elevations between 2,600 and 4,900 feet. Associated species include 'a'ali'a, puki-awe, 'akoko, and na'ena'a.

For a continued habitat description of Hawaii, see "Habitat Conditions on the Island of Hawaii (the Big Island), Hawaii," page 1834.

Historic Range

Historically, this species was found only on the island of Maui on the western slope of Halakeala; and on the island of Hawaii from the Kohala Mountains; the northwestern slopes of Mauna Kea and Mauna Loa; and the slopes of Hualalai.

Current Distribution

Only one population is known today, on the island of Hawaii in Kipuka Kalawamauna at PTA on Federal land. The one known population contained, at last count (January 1993), 29 reproductive and 79 juvenile plants in a 660 by 200 foot area.

Conservation and Recovery

The major threats are competition from alien plant species, particularly fountain grass; grazing, browsing, and trampling by feral goats, pigs and sheep; habitat disturbance and damage to plants as a result of military exercises; fire; and volcanic activity.

T. arenarium occurs in Kipuka Kalawamauna, and to protect this area from fires, the U.S. Army has installed firebreaks and now redirects ordance firing away from that kipuka.

The recovery of this and most other Hawaiian species depends on how well management practices can be implemented. The habitat of this and other Hawaiian species has undergone extreme alteration because of past and present land management practices, including deliberately introducing alien animals and plants, and agricultural and recreational development. To understand the recovery problems facing this species, it is necessary to understand the long-term causes of habitat destruction.

For a continued discussion of the threats to Hawaiian plants, see page 1831.

Bibliography

U.S. Fish and Wildlife Service. "Endangered and Threatened Wildlife and Plant; Determination of Endangered or Threatened Status for 21 Plants from the Island of Hawaii, State of Hawaii." *Federal Register* Vol 59, No. 43. March 4, 1994: 10305-10325.

Contacts

U.S. Fish and Wildlife Service
300 Ala Moana Boulevard, Room 6307
P.O. Box 50167
Honolulu, HI 96850
(808) 541-2749

Adapted from data compiled by Beacham Publishing for *Beacham's International Threatened, Endangered, and Extinct Species* published on CD ROM.

A'e

Zanthoxylum hawaiiense

Robert J. Gustafson

Status	Endangered
Listed	March 4, 1994
Family	Rutaceae (Citrus)
Description	Small to medium thornless tree with lemon-scented, toothed leaflets; and clusters of 15 to 20 flowers.
Habitat	'Ohi'a-dominated lowland dry or mesic forests, often on lava.
Threats	Competition from alien plants; habitat destruction by cattle, goats and sheep; limited numbers.
Range	Hawaii (Maui, Lanai, Kauai, Molokai, Hawaii)

Description

A'e, a thornless tree usually 10 to 26 feet tall with a trunk up to 10 inches in diameter, has alternate leaves comprising three leathery, triangular-oval or lance-shaped, gland-dotted, lemon-scented, toothed leaflets usually 1.3 to 3.9 inches long and 0.6 to 2 inches. The stalk of each of the two side leaflets has one joint, and the stalk of the terminal leaflets has two joints. Flowers are usually male or female, and usually only one sex is found on a single tree. Clusters of 15 to 20 flowers 1.6 to 3.1 inches long have a main flower stalk 0.8 to 2 inches long and individual flower stalks 0.08 to 0.2 inches long. Each flower has four narrowly triangular sepals about 0.04 inches long and four hairless petals (possibly absent in male flowers) of an unknown color. The fruit is a sickle-shaped follicle (dry fruit that opens along one side) 0.3 to 0.4 inches long, containing one black seed about 0.3 inches in diameter. This species is distinguished from other Hawaiian species of the genus by its leaves, which are always made up of three leaflets of similar size; the presence of only one joint on some of the leaf stalks; and the shorter follicle with a rounded tip.

Habitat

A'e typically grows in 'ohi'a-dominated lowland dry or mesic forests, often on lava, at elevations between 1,800 and 5,710 feet. Associated species include hame, on Kauai; hala pepe, on Molokai; a'ia'i on Maui; and mamane and naio on the island of Hawaii.

For a continued habitat description, see "Habitat Conditions on the Island of Molokai," page 1987; "Habitat Conditions on the Island of Hawaii (the Big Island)," page 1834; and "Habitat Conditions on the Island of Maui," page 1951.

Historic Range and Current Distribution

Historically, this species was known to occur in the central portion of the island of Kauai; on east Molokai; in the central part of the island of Lanai; on east Maui on the southern and southwestern slopes of Haleakala; and on the island of Hawaii in the Kohala Mountains; on the northern slope of Hualalai; and on the northwestern slope of Mauna Loa. On Molokai, three extant populations occur on private, state and Federal land in Kalaupapa National Historical Park; in Pelekunu Valley; and near Puu Kolekole. On Lanai, one population with an unknown number of individuals has been reported on private property in Kaiholena Gulch. On east Maui, extant populations have been found in Kahikinui, above Lualailua; above Kanaio; and in Auwahi. On the island of Hawaii, individuals are found at Puu Waawaa and at PTA on state and Federal land.

Conservation and Recovery

A threat to this species on Kauai is competition from alien plants such as lantana and Chinaberry. On Molokai the threats are competition with alien plant species, grazing, browsing, trampling and habitat destruction by feral goats. On Maui the threats are competition with Kikuyu grass, which forms a continuous mat in many areas, and grazing, browsing, trampling and habitat destruction by feral cattle and goats. The major threats on the island of Hawaii are competition from alien plants such as fountain grass; grazing, browsing, trampling and habitat destruction by feral sheep and goats; habitat

disturbance and damage to plants as a result of military exercises; and fire.

In all its populations the species is threatened by stochastic extinction and reduced reproductive vigor due to the small number of existing individuals.

The recovery of this and most other Hawaiian species depends on how well land management practices can be implemented. The habitat of this and other Hawaiian species has undergone extreme alteration because of past and present land management practices, including deliberately introducing alien animals and plants, and agricultural and recreational development. To understand the recovery problems facing this species, it is necessary to understand the long-term causes of habitat destruction.

For a continued discussion of the threats to Hawaiian plants, see page 1831.

Bibliography

U.S. Fish and Wildlife Service. "Endangered and Threatened Wildlife and Plant; Determination of Endangered or Threatened Status for 21 Plants from the Island of Hawaii, State of Hawaii." *Federal Register* Vol 59, No. 43. March 4, 1994: 10305-10325.

Contacts

U.S. Fish and Wildlife Service
300 Ala Moana Boulevard, Room 6307
P.O. Box 50167
Honolulu, HI 96850
(808) 541-2749

Adapted from data compiled by Beacham Publishing for *Beacham's International Threatened, Endangered, and Extinct Species* published on CD ROM.

HAWAIIAN PLANTS: KAUAI

Habitat Conditions on the Island of Kauai, Hawaii

On May 13, 1992 the U.S. Fish and Wildlife Service listed six plants from Kauai as endangered or threatened, one more on June 22, 1992, and on February 25 1994, listed another twenty-four plants from Kauai. Habitat conditions on Kauai are described here rather than being repeated in each of the species accounts.

Brighamia insignis
Chamaesyce halemanui
Cyanea asarifolia
Cyrtandra limahuliensis
Delissea rhytidosperma
Diellia pallida
Dubautia latifolia
Exocarpos luteolus
Hedyotis cookiana
Hibiscus clayi
Lipochaeta fauriei
Lipochaeta waimeaensis
Lipochaeta micrantha
Lysimachia filifolia
Melicope knudsenii
Melicope pallida
Melicope haupuensis
Melicope quadrangularis
Munroidendron racemosum
Nothocestrum peltatum
Peucedanum sandwicense
Phyllostegia waimeae
Poa sandvicensis
Poa siphonoglossa
Pteralyxia kauaiensis
Schiedea spergulina var. *leiopoda*
Schiedea spergulina var. *spergulina*
Solanum sandwicense
Stenogyne campanulata

Wilkesia hobdyi
Xylosma crenatum

The island of Kauai is the northernmost and oldest of the eight major Hawaiian Islands. This highly eroded island, characterized by deeply dissected canyons and steep ridges, is 553 square miles. It was formed about six million years ago by a single shield volcano. Its caldera, once the largest in the Hawaiian Islands, now extends about ten miles in diameter and comprises the extremely wet, elevated tableland of Alakai Swamp. Because the highest point of Kauai, at Kawaikini Peak, is on 5,243 feet in elevation, it lacks the contrasting leeward montane rainfall patterns found on the other islands that have higher mountain systems. Rainfall is, therefore, distributed throughout the upper elevations, especially at Mount Waialeale, Kauai's second highest point at 5,148 feet. Mount Waialeale is one of the wettest spots on Earth, where annual rainfall averages 450 inches.

To the west of Alakai Swamp is the deeply dissected Waimea Canyon, extending 10 miles in length and up to a mile in width. Later volcanic activity on the southeastern flank of the volcano formed the smaller Haupu caldera. Subsequent erosion and collapse of its flank formed Haupu Ridge.

Kokee State Park lies just north of Waimea Canyon, and has the Alakai Swamp to the east, the steep cliffs of the Na Pali coast to the north, and drier leeward ridges to the west. The park is surrounded by forest reserves, another state park, and a natural area reserve. In the Kokee region, the annual rainfall ranges from 45 to 80 inches; the average temperature is about 62 degrees F.

One of the island's most famous features is the Na Pali Coast, where streams and wave action have cut deep valleys and eroded the northern coast to form precipitous cliffs as high as 3,000 feet.

Because of its age and relative isolation, levels of floristic diversity and endemism are higher on Kauai than on any of the other Hawaiian Islands. However, the vegetation of Kauai has undergone extreme alterations because of past and present land use. Land with rich soils was altered by early Hawaiians, and more recently converted to agricultural use and pastures. Intentional and inadvertent introduction of alien plant and animal taxa has also contributed to the reduction of native vegetation. Native forests are now limited to the upper elevation mesic and wet regions within Kauai's conservation district.

The lowland dry forests, which extend into mesic forests, are characterized by annual rainfall of 20 to 80 inches, which falls between November and March, and a well-drained, highly weathered substrate rich in aluminum. Lowland mesic forest communities lie between 100 and 3,000 feet in elevation, and are characterized by a 6.5 to 65 foot tall canopy and a diverse understory of shrubs, herbs, and ferns. The annual rainfall of 45 to 150 inches falls predominantly between October and March. The mesic community often grades into lowland wet forests, which are typically found on the windward side of the island or in sheltered leeward situations between 330 and 3,940 feet in elevation. The rainfall in this lowland wet community may exceed 200 inches per year. These forests were once predominant vegetation on Kauai but now exist only on steep rocky terrain or cliff faces. The substrate is generally of well-drained soils that may support tree canopies up to 130 feet in height. The montane forest communities typically occur above 3,000 feet in elevation, where the annual rainfall may exceed 280 inches.

'Olulu

Brighamia insignis

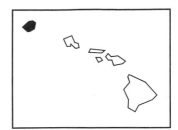

Jack Jeffrey   *Color Plate C-4*

Status	Endangered
Listed	February 25, 1994
Family	Campanulaceae (Bellflower)
Description	Unbranched plant growing to 16 feet, with fleshy leaves and fragrant yellow flowers clustering in groups of 3 to 8.
Habitat	Lowland dry grassland and shrublands communities in the Na Pali Coast region.
Threats	Goats, insects, alien plants, fire, human impact, limited numbers.
Range	Hawaii (Kauai)

Description

'Olulu, *Brighamia insignis*, is an unbranched plant 3 to 16 feet tall with a succulent stern that is bulbous at the bottom and tapers toward the top. The fleshy leaves, which measure 5 to 8 inches long and 2.5 to 4.5 inches wide, are arranged in a compact rosette at the top of the stem. Fragrant yellow flowers cluster in groups of 3 to 8 in the leaf axils (the point between the leaf and the stem), with each flower on a stalk 0.4 to 1.2 inches long. The hypanthium (basal portion of the flower) has 10 ribs and is topped with 5 oval or loosely triangular calyx lobes (partially fused sepals). The yellow petals are fused into a tube 2.8 to 5.5 inches long, which flares into 5 elliptical lobes. The fruit is a capsule about a half inch long, containing numerous seeds.

Habitat

Stream and wave action along the Na Pali Coast have cut deep valleys and eroded the northern coast to form precipitous cliffs as high as 3,000 feet. This species grows predominantly on the rocky ledges with little soil or steep sea cliffs in lowland dry grasslands and shrubland from sea level to 1,300 feet elevation.

For a continued habitat description of Kauai, see "Habitat Conditions on the Island of Kauai, Hawaii," page 1883.

Historic Range

Historically, *B. insignis* was known from the headland between Hoolulu and Waiabuakua valleys along the Na Pali coast on the island of Kauai, and from Kaali Springs on the island of Niihau. The Na Pali coast populations are still extant and additional populations are known from the same general area.

Current Distribution

The two Na Pali coast populations within or on the boundary of the Na Pali Natural Area Reserve are within 0.4 miles of each other. There are two populations in the Haupu range within 2.7 miles of each other. In 1992 Hurricane Iniki destroyed approximately half of the individuals in the Na Pali coast populations and 7 of the 12 individuals in the Haupu area. The 5 populations grow on state and private land and total fewer than 40 plants. The status of the small population on privately owned Niihau is not known, although there are reports that it was destroyed when the supporting cliff fell away.

Conservation and Recovery

Feral goats pose the major threat to *B. insignis* by causing defoliation and stem damage, restricting populations to inaccessible cliffs, and probably causing rock slides that degrade the plant's habitat. Alien plants pose another threat, especially introduced grasses such as molasses grass, yellow foxtail, and smutgrass, which prevent the establishment of seedlings. Other alien plants that potentially pose a threat are lantana, strawberry guava, common guava and Java plum.

Hikers transport weed seeds, which dislodge rocks and damage plants, to areas where *B. insignis* grows. Wildfire also poses a serious threat. Another problem is that some plants flower but fail to set seed, which may be due to a lack of pollinators or a reduction of genetic viability due to such few individuals. The carmine spider mite, an introduced insect, has been observed to cause leaf loss in both cultivated and wild individuals.

The recovery of this and most other Hawaiian species depends on how well management practices can be implemented. The habitat of this and other Hawaiian species has undergone extreme alteration because of past and present land management practices, including deliberately introducing alien animals and plants, and agricultural and recreational development. To understand the recovery problems facing this species, it is necessary to understand the long-term causes of habitat destruction.

For a continued discussion of the threats to Hawaiian plants, see page 1831.

Bibliography

U.S. Fish and Wildlife Service. "Endangered and Threatened Wildlife and Plant; Determination of Endangered or Threatened Status for 24 Plants from the Island of Kauai, HI." *Federal Register* Vol. 59, No. 38. February 25, 1994: 9304-9329.

Contacts

U.S. Fish and Wildlife Service
300 Ala Moana Boulevard, Room 6307
P.O. Box 50167
Honolulu, HI 96850
(808) 541-2749

Adapted from data compiled by Beacham Publishing for *Beacham's International Threatened, Endangered, and Extinct Species* published on CD ROM.

Chamaesyce halemanui

No Common Name

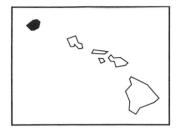

Loyal A. Mehrhoff

Status	Endangered
Listed	May 13, 1992
Family	Euphorbiaceae (Spurge)
Description	Climbing shrub with paired, inversely lanceolate leaves and clusters of flowers in the leaf axils.
Habitat	Steep slopes of gulches in mesic koa forests.
Threats	Invasive alien plants, feral pigs.
Range	Hawaii (Kauai)

Description

Chamaesyce halemanui is a climbing shrub of the spurge family that grows to a height of 3.3 to 13 ft. The elliptical to oblanceolate leaves, 4 to 13 centimeters (1.5 to 5 inches) long, are arranged in pairs along the stem with each succeeding pair at right angles to the previous one (decussate). Dense flower clusters (occasionally solitary flowers) are borne on short stems arising from the leaf axils. The fruits are green capsules that enclose gray to brown seeds. In the past this species has also been known as *Eurphorbia remyi* var. *wilkesii, E. remyi* var. *leptopoda,* and *E. remyi* var. *molesta.*

Habitat

Chamaesyce halemanui is one of a large number of species endemic to the Kokee area, roughly encompassed by the 8-square-mile Kokee State Park, located in the north-western part of the Hawaiian island of Kauai. This island was formed by a single shield volcano, the crater of which eventually formed the Alakai Swamp. Faulting and erosion on the western end of the swamp created the deeply cut Waimea Canyon, which runs north to south. The canyon is 10 miles long and a mile wide, with steep vertical cliffs more than 600 meters (2,000 feet) high. Kokee State Park lies just north of Waimea Canyon, and has the Alakai Swamp to the east, the steep cliffs of the Na Pali coast to the north, and the drier leeward ridges to the west. *Chamaesyce halemanui* is found on the steep slopes of gulches in the moist koa (*Acacia koa*) forests of Kokee at elevations between 660 to 1,100 meters (2,160 to 3,600 feet).

Five other plant species endemic to the Kokee region are federally listed as Endangered: *Dubautia latifolia,* Hawaiian bluegrass (*Poa sandvicensis*), *Poa siphonoglossa, Stenogyne campanulata,* and *Xylosma crenatum.*

For a continued habitat description of Kauai, see "Habitat Conditions on the Island of Kauai, Hawaii," page 1883.

Historic Range

Chamaesyce halemanui was first collected on Kauai in 1840. Since then it has been found at seven areas on the island: Kauhao and Makaha valleys in the Na Pali-Kona Forest Reserve; Mahanaloa Valley in Kuia Natural Area Reserve; the Halemanu drainage, near Waipoo Falls, and near Kokee Ranger Station in Kokee State Park; and Olokele Canyon on privately owned land.

Current Distribution

Populations of *Chamaesyce halemanui* are known today from the Kauhao, Makaha, and Halemanu sites, all on state land. These three populations, occurring in an area of about 3 miles, contain fewer than 25 plants, divided in roughly equal numbers. Two of the populations include seedlings.

Conservation and Recovery

The most immediate threat to *Chamaesyce halemanui* is vegetative competition from alien plant species. The Halemanu population in Kokee State Park is threatened by St. Augustine grass, which prevents the establishment of seedlings; the two populations in the Na Pali-Kona Forest Reserve are threatened by lantana and strawberry guava. In the Kuia Natural Area Reserve, illegal marijuana cultivation is a threat to native species, including *Chamaesyce halemanui.* Not only is native flora destroyed in clearing land for cultivation, but alien species are introduced into the area from soil and other material brought to the site.

In addition, feral pigs threaten to degrade native plant habitat in the forest reserve. Pigs have inhabited the forests of Kauai for over a century, and have proven extremely destructive to native plant species. Their rooting destroys vegetative cover, allowing the invasion of alien species. In addition, the pigs' feces add nutrients to poor soils which would otherwise favor native species.

Various human activities have promoted the spread of feral pigs on Kauai. In forested areas the pigs use paths made by other animals or humans to move into new areas. The logging of the Kokee area in the nineteenth century created a multitude of small trails that led to the southern coast; in the 1920s construction of the Kokee/Kekaha ditch and water diversion system, designed to irrigate lowland sugar cane fields, cut more roads into the area. In the 1930s plum trees were planted in Kokee State Park, providing a food source that attracted feral pigs.

In addition to these known threats, the low number of existing *Chamaesyce halemanui* plants puts the species at risk of extinction through unpredictible human or natural events.

For a continued discussion of the threats to Hawaiian plants, see page 1831.

Bibliography

Cuddihy, L. W., and C. P. Stone. 1990. *Alteration of Native Hawaiian Vegetation: Effects of Humans, Their Activities and Introductions.* Cooperative National Park Resources Study Unit, University of Hawaii Press, Honolulu.

Macdonald, G. A., A. T. Abbott, and F. L. Peterson. 1983. *Volcanoes in the Sea*. 2d ed. University of Hawaii Press, Honolulu.

Stone, C. P., and J. M. Scott, eds. 1985. *Hawai`i's Terrestrial Ecosystems: Preservation and Management*. Cooperative National Park Resources Study Unit, University of Hawaii Press, Honolulu.

U.S. Fish and Wildlife Service. "Endangered and Threatened Wildlife and Plants; Determination of Endangered Status for Six Plants from the Kokee Region, Island of Kauai, Hawaii." *Federal Register* Vol. 57, No. 93. May 13, 1992: 20580-20587.

Wagner, W. L., D. R. Herbst, and S. H. Sohmer. 1990. *Manual of the Flowering Plants of Hawai'i*. University of Hawaii Press and Bishop Museum Press, Honolulu.

Contacts

Regional Office of Endangered Species
U.S. Fish and Wildlife Service
Eastside Federal Complex
911 N.S. 11th Avenue
Portland, Oregon 97232-4181
(503) 231-6118

U.S. Fish and Wildlife Service
300 Ala Moana Boulevard, Room 6307
P.O. Box 50167
Honolulu, Hawaii 96850
(808) 541-2749

Adapted from data compiled by Beacham Publishing for *Beacham's International Threatened, Endangered, and Extinct Species* published on CD ROM.

Haha

Cyanea asarifolia

National Tropical Botanical Garden

Status	Endangered
Listed	February 25, 1994
Family	Campanulaceae (Bellflower)
Description	Sparingly branched shrub with heart-shaped leaves and 30-40 slightly curved white flowers with purple stripes.
Habitat	Pockets of soil on sheer rock cliffs in lowland wet forests.
Threats	Pigs, rats, natural disaster, over-collecting, limited numbers.
Range	Hawaii (Kauai)

Description

This haha, *Cyanea asarifolia*, is a sparingly branched shrub 1 to 3.3 feet tall. The heart-shaped leaves are 3.3 to 4.1 inches long and 2.8 to 3.1 inches wide, with leaf stalks 4.7 to 5.9 inches long. Thirty to forty flowers are clustered on a stalk about an inch long, each having an individual stalk about 0.3 inches in length. The slightly curved flowers are white with purple stripes, with wide spreading lobes. The five anthers have tufts of white hairs at the tips. The nearly spherical fruit is a dark purple berry. This species is distinguished from others of the genus that grow on Kauai by the shape of the leaf base, the leaf width in proportion to the length, and the presence of a leaf stalk.

Habitat

This species grows in pockets of soil on sheer rock cliffs in lowland wet forests at an elevation of approximately 1,080 feet.

Associated plant taxa include ferns, manono, `ohi`a, alona, and opuhe.

For a continued habitat description of Kauai, see "Habitat Conditions on the Island of Kauai, Hawaii," page 1883.

Historic Range

For over 20 years this species was known only from a population of five or six plants above the bed of Anahola stream on Kauai. Because recent attempts to locate this population have been unsuccessful, this population is thought to be extirpated.

Current Distribution

In 1991 Steve Perlman and Ken Marr discovered a population of 14 mature plants and 5 seedlings at the headwaters of the Wailua river in central Kauai on state owned land.

Conservation and Recovery

This species is threatened by stochastic extinction and/or reduced reproductive vigor due to the small number of existing individuals. Plants in the area in which the only currently known population occurs are vulnerable to occasional hurricanes, natural rock slides, and over-collecting for scientific purposes. In 1992 Hurricane Iniki heavily damaged the population, either directly or indirectly destroying all but four or five juvenile plants. Plants observed after Hurricane Iniki were frequently damaged by introduced slugs or rodents.

For a continued discussion of the threats to Hawaiian plants, see page 1831.

Bibliography

U.S. Fish and Wildlife Service. "Endangered and Threatened Wildlife and Plant; Determination of Endangered or Threatened Status for 24 Plants from the Island of Kauai, HI." *Federal Register* Vol. 59, No. 38. February 25, 1994: 9304-9329.

Contacts

U.S. Fish and Wildlife Service
300 Ala Moana Boulevard, Room 6307
P.O. Box 50167
Honolulu, HI 96850
(808) 541-2749

Adapted from data compiled by Beacham Publishing for *Beacham's International Threatened, Endangered, and Extinct Species* published on CD ROM.

Ha'iwale

Cyrtandra limahuliensis

Warren I. Wagner

Status	Threatened
Listed	February 25, 1994
Family	Gesneriaceae (African Violet)
Description	Shrub with opposite, toothed elliptic leaves that are moderately hairy on the upper surface; single downy flowers are borne in the leaf axils.
Habitat	Streams in lowland wet forests.
Threats	Pigs, alien plants.
Range	Hawaii (Kauai)

Description

Ha'iwale, *C. limahuliensis*, is an un-branched or few-branched shrub up to 5 feet tall. The opposite, elliptic leaves are usually 6 to 12 inches long and 2 to 4.7 inches wide. The upper surface of the toothed leaves is moderately hairy and the lower surface, with deep veins, is moderately or densely covered with yellowish brown hairs. Single downy flowers are borne in the leaf axils. The slightly curved corolla tube (fused petals) barely extends beyond the calyx. The calyx encloses long berries at maturity. This species is distinguished from others of the genus by hairy leaves, especially on the lower surfaces; the usually symmetrical calyx is tubular or funnel-shaped and encloses the fruit at maturity, and the flowers are borne singly.

Habitat

This species typically grows along streams in lowland wet forests at elevations between 800 and 2,850 feet.

Associated plant taxa include hame, ho'i'o, olomea, uluhe, 'ape'ape and kopiko.

For a continued habitat description of Kauai, see "Habitat Conditions on the Island of Kauai, Hawaii," page 1883.

Historic Range

Historically, this Haha was known from three areas on Kauai: Wainiha Valley, Lumahal Valley, and near Kilauea River. One population remains in Wainiha Valley and 11 others exist in Limahuli Valley, Waipa Valley, on Mount Kahili, the north fork of

Waioli Valley and near Powerline Trail on private and state land.

Current Distribution

The 12 known populations, distributed over a 13 by 18 miles area, range in size from solitary shrubs to large populations of over 1,000 plants. The largest populations occur in the upper Waioli Valley, where 3 populations total at least 2,100 individuals. Another location with hundreds or perhaps thousands of plants is limited to the 0.25 square mile area along the north fork of the Wailua River. Other botanists familiar with this population believe it to number no more than 500 individuals. A total of 2,800 to 3,000 plants are known from these 12 populations.

Conservation and Recovery

The major threat to this species is competition from invasive alien plants, especially strawberry guava. Each population has additional threats. Competition with introduced Hilo grass and *Melastoma candidum* at the Mount Kahili population; competition with common guava and habitat degradation by feral pigs at the Anahola stream population; and competition with yellow ginger at the Wainiha Valley population. Individuals of the Wailua stream population are situated at the base of a steep cliff and are vulnerable to natural landslides. The Waiolo Valley populations are threatened by several alien weeds, thimbleberry, Oriental hawksbeard and fireweed. Hurricanes are also a potential threat, but most of the plants have grown back vigorously since Hurricane Iniki.

The recovery of this and most other Hawaiian species depends on how well management practices can be implemented. The habitat of this and other Hawaiian species has undergone extreme alteration because of past and present land management practices, including deliberately introducing alien animals and plants, and agricultural and recreational development. To understand the recovery problems facing this species, it is necessary to understand the long-term causes of habitat destruction.

For a continued discussion of the threats to Hawaiian plants, see page 1831.

Bibliography

U.S. Fish and Wildlife Service. "Endangered and Threatened Wildlife and Plant; Determination of Endangered or Threatened Status for 24 Plants from the Island of Kauai, HI." *Federal Register* Vol. 59, No. 38. February 25, 1994: 9304-9329.

Contacts

U.S. Fish and Wildlife Service
300 Ala Moana Boulevard, Room 6307
P.O. Box 50167
Honolulu, HI 96850
(808) 541-2749

Adapted from data compiled by Beacham Publishing for *Beacham's International Threatened, Endangered, and Extinct Species* published on CD ROM.

Delissea rhytidosperma

No Common Name

Tom Lammers

Status	Endangered
Listed	February 25, 1994
Family	Campanulaceae (Bellflower)
Description	Branched shrub 1.6 to 8.2 feet tall, with lance-shaped or elliptic toothed leaves and clusters of 5 to 12 greenish-white or pale purple flowers.
Habitat	Lowland dry forests.
Threats	Deer, goats, pigs, rats, alien plants, fire, natural disaster, human impact, low populations.
Range	Hawaii (Kauai)

Description

Delissea rhytidosperma is a branched shrub 1.6 to 8.2 feet tall. The lance-shaped or elliptic leaves are 3.1 to 7.5 inches long and 0.8 to 2.2 inches wide, and have toothed margins. Clusters of 5 to 12 flowers are borne on stalks 0.4 to 0.8 inches long. Each flower has a stalk 0.3 to 0.5 inches long. The greenish white corolla is 0.6 to 0.8 inches long. The stamens are hairless, except for a small patch of hair at the base of the anthers. The nearly spherical dark purple fruits are 0.3 to 0.5 inches long and contain numerous white seeds. This species differs from other taxa of the genus by the shape, length and margins of the leaves and by having hairs at the base of the anthers.

Habitat

This species generally grows in diverse lowland mesic forests or Acacia koa-dominated lowland dry forests, characterized by an annual rainfall of 20 to 80 inches which falls between November and March. The terrain is a well-drained, highly weathered substrate with a fine textured subsoil rich in aluminum.

For a continued habitat description of Kauai, see "Habitat Conditions on the Island of Kauai, Hawaii," page 1883.

Historic Range

Historically, *D. rhytidosperma* was known from scattered locations throughout the island of Kauai. Populations ranged as far north as Wainiha and Limahuli valleys, as far east as Kapaa and Kealia, and as far south as Haupu range between the elevations of 1,000 and 3,000 feet.

Current Distribution

Only one population with six individuals exists. They are located on state owned Kuria NAR. The only other populations seen in recent years were a single plants in Limahuli valley, which is now dead, and 20 plants in the Haupu range. This population was destroyed by Hurricane Iniki in 1992.

Conservation and Recovery

Habitat degradation by mule deer or black-tailed deer, feral goats and feral pigs is the major threat. Other threats are predation by rats, fire, over-collecting for scientific or horticultural purposes, landslides, and competition with alien plants such as lantana, sweet granadillal and banana poka. With a single extant population of only six individuals, this species is threatened by stochastic extinction or reduced reproductive vigor. Hurricanes pose an additional threat.

The recovery of this and most other Hawaiian species depends on how well management practices can be implemented. The habitat of this and other Hawaiian species has undergone extreme alteration because of past and present land management practices, including deliberately introducing alien animals and plants, and agricultural and recreational development. To understand the recovery problems facing this species, it is necessary to understand the long-term causes of habitat destruction.

For a continued discussion of the threats to Hawaiian plants, see page 1831.

Bibliography

U.S. Fish and Wildlife Service. "Endangered and Threatened Wildlife and Plant; Determination of Endangered or Threatened Status for 24 Plants from the Island of Kauai, HI." *Federal Register* Vol. 59, No. 38. February 25, 1994: 9304-9329.

Contacts

U.S. Fish and Wildlife Service
300 Ala Moana Boulevard, Room 6307
P.O. Box 50167
Honolulu, HI 96850
(808) 541-2749

Adapted from data compiled by Beacham Publishing for *Beacham's International Threatened, Endangered, and Extinct Species* published on CD ROM.

Diellia pallida

No Common Name

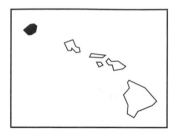

David Lorence, National Tropical Botanical Garden

Status	Endangered
Listed	February 25, 1994
Family	Aspleniaceae (Spleenwort)
Description	Tufts of three to four light green, lance-shaped dark purple to brownish grey fronds with short black hairs on the underside.
Habitat	Bare soil on steep, rocky dry slopes of lowland mesic forests.
Threats	Goats, pigs, deer, alien plants, fire, limited numbers.
Range	Hawaii (Kauai)

Description

This species grows in tufts of three to four light green, lance-shaped fronds along with a few persistent dead ones. The midrib of the frond ranges from dark purple to brownish grey in color and has a dull sheen. Scales on the midrib are brown, grey or black, about 0.1 inch long, and rather inconspicuous. The fronds measure 12 to 22 inches in length and 2 to 5 inches in width, and have short black hairs on the underside. Each frond has approximately 20 to 40 pinnae (divisions or leaflets). The largest pinnae are in the middle section of the frond, while the lower section has triangular, somewhat reduced pinnae, with the lowermost pair of pinnae raised above the plane of the others. The sori (groups of spore-producing bodies), which are frequently fused along an extended line, are encircled by a prominent vein. This species differs from others of this endemic Hawaiian genus by the color and sheen of the midrib, the presence and color of scales on the midrib, and the frequent fusion of sori.

Habitat

This species grows in bare soil on steep, rocky dry slopes of lowland mesic forests, 1,700 to 2,300 feet in elevation.

For a continued habitat description of Kauai, see "Habitat Conditions on the Island of Kauai, Hawaii," page 1883.

Historic Range

D. pallida was known historically from Halemanu on Kauai. This species has not been seen since 1949, when a collection was made in Kuia NAR.

Current Distribution

This species is currently known from two populations on state land within Kuia NAR and Koaie Canyon. The recently discovered population on the west side of Waimea Canyon within Puu Ka Pele Forest Reserve is apparently extirpated. The two known populations extend over a 7 by 3 mile area. In 1987 Joel Lau of The Nature Conservancy discovered the Koaie Canyon population of three or four individuals. Botanists discovered two plants in Puu Ka Pele Forest Reserve, but the plants have since disappeared and were likely destroyed by goats. Recent visits to the Kuia NAR and Koaie populations have found a total of less than 10 extant individuals.

Conservation and Recovery

Competition with alien plants, especially lantana and Chinaberry, constitutes the major threat. Introduced grasses, such as St. Augustine and basketgrass, degrade the species' habitat. Feral goats cause erosion near the plants, and trample them. Other threats include habitat degradation by mules and deer, fire, over-collecting for scientific purposes, and reduced reproductive vigor.

The recovery of this and most other Hawaiian species depends on how well management practices can be implemented. The habitat of this and other Hawaiian species has undergone extreme alteration because of past and present land management practices, including deliberately introducing alien animals and plants, and agricultural and recreational development. To understand the recovery problems facing this species, it is necessary to understand the long-term causes of habitat destruction.

For a continued discussion of the threats to Hawaiian plants, see page 1831.

Bibliography

U.S. Fish and Wildlife Service. "Endangered and Threatened Wildlife and Plant; Determination of Endangered or Threatened Status for 24 Plants from the Island of Kauai, HI." *Federal Register* Vol. 59, No. 38. February 25, 1994: 9304-9329.

Contacts

U.S. Fish and Wildlife Service
300 Ala Moana Boulevard, Room 6307
P.O. Box 50167
Honolulu, HI 96850
(808) 541-2749

Adapted from data compiled by Beacham Publishing for *Beacham's International Threatened, Endangered, and Extinct Species* published on CD ROM.

Dubautia latifolia

No Common Name

Robert J. Gustafson

Status	Endangered
Listed	May 13, 1992
Family	Asteraceae (Aster)
Description	Woody vine with opposite, untoothed leaves and clusters of yellow flower heads.
Habitat	Well-drained slopes in moist mountain forests.
Threats	Invasive alien plant species, low re-production.
Range	Hawaii (Kauai)

Description

Dubautia latifolia is a branched, woody vine of the aster family that grows to a height of 26 feet. The opposite, elliptical to oblong-elliptical leaves are 3 to 6.6 inches long and 1 to 3 inches wide. They have distinct leaf stems (petioles), untoothed margins, and are conspicuously net-veined. Small, yellow flower heads occur in dense clusters at the ends of the branches; the fruits are small dry seeds. *Dubautia latifolia* is distinguished from similar species in this endemic genus by its vining growth habit, and the distinct petioles and net-veins of the leaves. *Dubautia latifolia* has also been known by the names *Railliardia latifolia* and *Railliardia latifolia* var. *helleri*.

Habitat

Dubautia latifolia is one of a large number of species endemic to the Kokee area in the northwestern part of the Hawaiian island of Kauai, roughly encompassed by the 8-square-mile Kokee State Park. Kauai was formed by a single shield volcano, the crater of which eventually formed the Alakai Swamp. Faulting and erosion on the western end of the swamp created the deeply cut Waimea Canyon, running north to south. The canyon is 10 miles long and a mile wide, with steep vertical cliffs more than 2,000 feet high. Kokee State Park lies just north of Waimea Canyon, and has the Alakai Swamp to the east, the steep cliffs of the Na Pali coast to the north, and drier leeward ridges to the west. The park is surrounded by forest reserves, another state park, and a natural area reserve. *Dubautia latifolia* is found on well-drained, semi-open slopes in the moist koa (*Acacia koa*) forests of Kokee at elevations between 3,200 to 3,900 feet. To a lesser extent it grows in closed ohia (*Metrosideros polymorpha*) forests, and conifer plantations.

Five other plant species endemic to the Kokee region are federally listed as Endangered: *Chamaesyce halemanui*, Hawaiian bluegrass (*Poa sandvicensis*), *Poa siphonoglossa*, *Stenogyne campanulata*, and *Xylosma crenatum*.

For a continued habitat description of Kauai, see "Habitat Conditions on the Island of Kauai, Hawaii," page 1883.

Historic Range

Dubautia latifolia was first collected in 1840. Since then it has only been known from six areas of northwestern Kauai: Mukaha and Awaawapuhi valleys in Na Pali-Kona Forest Reserve, Nualolo Trail and valley in Kuia Natural Area Reserve, Halemanu in Kokee State Park, along Mohihi Road in Kokee State Park and Na Pali-Kona Forest Reserve, along the Mohihi-Waialae Trail on Mohihi and Kohua ridges in Na Pali-Kona Forest Reserve and Alakai Wilderness Preserve, and Kaholuamanu on privately owned land.

Current Distribution

At present, *Dubautia latifolia* is known to survive at all historic sites except Halemanu in the state park and the privately owned Kaholuamanu. Each of the surviving populations covers an area of from 25 to 1,600 square feet and consists of less than six individual plants. The total population of *Dubautia latifolia* is believed to be about 40 plants, all on state land.

Conservation and Recovery

The main threat to the survival of *Dubautia latifolia* is competition from alien plant species, most notably banana poka, which is invading the habitat of almost all known populations. Banana poka is an aggressive vine with an ecological niche similar to that of *Dubautia latifolia*. However, it kills trees by completely covering their canopies with heavy vines. The resulting forest openings promote the growth of other alien plant species at the expense of native plants. Blackberry, strawberry guava, black wattle, Australian blackwood, ginger, and Japanese honeysuckle threaten to displace *Dubautia latifolia* and other endemic native species.

In the Kuia Natural Area Reserve, illegal marijuana cultivation is a threat to native species, including *Dubautia latifolia*. Not only is native flora destroyed in clearing land for cultivation, but alien species are introduced into the area from material brought to the site.

In addition, feral pigs and goats degrade native plant habitat in the forest reserve, opening up ground for invasion by alien plant species. Feral pigs, which have inhabited the forests of Kauai for over a century, have proven extremely destructive to native species. In addition to the destructive rooting, pig feces add nutrients to poor soils which would otherwise favor native species.

Various human activities have promoted the spread of feral pigs on Kauai. In forested areas pigs use paths made by other animals or humans to move into new areas. The logging of the Kokee area in the nineteenth century created a multitude of small trails that led to the southern coast; in the 1920s construction of the Kokee/Kekaha ditch and water diversion system, designed to irrigate lowland sugar cane fields, cut more roads into the area. In the 1930s plum trees were planted in Kokee State Park, providing a food source that attracted pigs.

Besides this external threat, the low number of existing *Dubautia latifolia* and their wide separation has affected the species' reproductive success to the extent that establishment of seedlings is rare. Such low numbers also puts the species at risk of extinction through unpredictable natural or human events.

For a continued discussion of the threats to Hawaiian plants, see page 1831.

Bibliography

Cuddihy, L. W., and C. P. Stone. 1990. *Alteration of Native Hawaiian Vegetation: Effects of Humans, Their Activities and Introductions.* Cooperative National Park Resources Study Unit, University of Hawaii Press, Honolulu.

Macdonald, G. A., A. T. Abbott, and F. L. Peterson. 1983. *Volcanoes in the Sea.* 2d ed. University of Hawaii Press, Honolulu.

Stone, C. P., and J. M. Scott, eds. 1985. *Hawai`i's Terrestrial Ecosystems: Preservation and Management.* Cooperative National Park Resources Study Unit, University of Hawaii Press, Honolulu.

U.S. Fish and Wildlife Service. "Endangered and Threatened Wildlife and Plants; Determination of Endangered Status for Six Plants from the Kokee Region, Island of Kauai, Hawaii." *Federal Register* Vol. 57, No. 93. May 13, 1992: 20580-20587.

Wagner, W. L., D. R. Herbst, and S. H. Sohmer. 1990. *Manual of the Flowering Plants of Hawai'i.* University of Hawaii Press and Bishop Museum Press, Honolulu.

Contacts

Regional Office of Endangered Species
U.S. Fish and Wildlife Service
Eastside Federal Complex
911 N.S. 11th Avenue
Portland, Oregon 97232-4181
(503) 231-6118

U.S. Fish and Wildlife Service
300 Ala Moana Boulevard, Room 6307
P.O. Box 50167
Honolulu, Hawaii 96850
(808) 541-2749

Adapted from data compiled by Beacham Publishing for *Beacham's International Threatened, Endangered, and Extinct Species* published on CD ROM.

Heau

Exocarpos luteolus

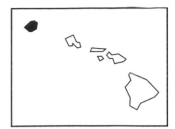

Derral Herbst

Status	Endangered
Listed	February 25, 1994
Family	Santalaceae (Sandalwood)
Description	Moderately branched shrub with knobby branches, green flowers that have 5 or 6 petals, and pale yellow fruit.
Habitat	Montane wet forests.
Threats	Goats, pigs, rats, alien plants, fire, natural disaster, limited numbers.
Range	Hawaii (Kauai)

Description

Heau, *Exocarpos luteolus*, is a moderately or densely branched shrub 1.6 to 6.6 feet tall with knobby branches. The leaves are of two kinds, minute scales and more typical leaves. The latter, which are usually present, are elliptical, lace-shaped or oval, usually 2 to 3.2 inches long and 1 to 1.4 inches wide, and lack a leaf stalk. The green flowers have 5 or 6 petals about 0.04 inch long. The pale yellow fruit is a drupe usually 0.4 to 0.7 inch long, with four distinct indentations at the apex. About 0.2 to 0.4 inch of the drupe is exposed above the fleshy, golden-yellow receptacle. This species is distinguished from others of the genus by its generally larger fruit and four indentations, and by the color of the receptacle and fruit.

Habitat

E. luteolus is found at elevations between 2,000 and 3,600 feet in a variety of habitats: wet places bordering swamps; on open, dry ridges; and lowland to montane 'ohi'a-dominated wet forest communities. Associated vegetation includes koa, pukiawe, and uluhe.

For a continued habitat description of Kauai, see "Habitat Conditions on the Island of Kauai, Hawaii," page 1883.

Historic Range

Historically, *E. leteolus* was known from three locations: Wahiawa Swamp, Naholuamanu, and Kumuwela Ridge.

Current Distribution

The species is now known to grow on Kumuwela Ridge as well as in Kauaikinana Valley, near Honopu Trail, Waialai, and on the rim of Kalalau Valley within the boundary of Kokee State Park in a 3 square mile area, and on Kamali Ridge in Kealia Forest Reserve, roughly 16 miles away. There are reliable but unconfirmed reports that this species was collected on the slopes of Anahola Mountain about 1970. All known populations are on state land and are estimated at 250 individuals.

Conservation and Recovery

Destruction of habitat by feral goats and pigs and competition with daisy fleabane are the major threats. Aggressive alien plants degrading this plant's habitat include black wattle, karakanut, firetree, and prickly Florida blackberry, all woody plants that displace native Hawaiian species. Other threats to this species include rats that eat the fruits; goats that browse the plants; and fire, erosion and over-collecting for scientific purposes.

The recovery of this and most other Hawaiian species depends on how well management practices can be implemented. The habitat of this and other Hawaiian species has undergone extreme alteration because of past and present land management practices, including deliberately introducing alien animals and plants, and agricultural and recreational development. To understand the recovery problems facing this species, it is necessary to understand the long-term causes of habitat destruction.

For a continued discussion of the threats to Hawaiian plants, see page 1831.

Bibliography

U.S. Fish and Wildlife Service. "Endangered and Threatened Wildlife and Plant; Determination of Endangered or Threatened Status for 24 Plants from the Island of Kauai, HI." *Federal Register* Vol. 59, No. 38. February 25, 1994: 9304-9329.

Contacts

U.S. Fish and Wildlife Service
300 Ala Moana Boulevard, Room 6307
P.O. Box 50167
Honolulu, HI 96850
(808) 541-2749

Adapted from data compiled by Beacham Publishing for *Beacham's International Threatened, Endangered, and Extinct Species* published on CD ROM.

'Awiwi

Hedyotis cookiana

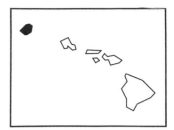

David Lorence, National Tropical Botanical Garden

Status	Endangered
Listed	February 25, 1994
Family	Rubiaceae (Coffee)
Description	Small shrub with many branches; long, narrow, papery-textured leaves; and fleshy-white flowers.
Habitat	Stream beds or on steep cliffs close to water sources in lowland wet forests.
Threats	Flooding, limited numbers (perhaps extinct).
Range	Hawaii (Kauai)

Description

'Awiwi, *Hedyotis cookiana*, is a small shrub with many branches 4 to 8 inches long. The papery-textured leaves are long and narrow, 1.5 to 3 inches long and about 0.2 to 0.5 inches wide, and fused at the base to form a sheath around the stem. The bisexual or female flowers are arranged in clusters of three on flower stalks about 0.3 to 0.6 inches long, with the central flower on the longest stalk. Beneath the flower clusters are sharp-pointed bracts. The fleshy white corolla is trumpet shaped and about 0.3 to 0.4 inches long, with lobes about 0.08 inches long. Fruits are top-shaped or spherical capsules about 0.1 inches long and 0.1 to 0.2 inches wide that open at maturity to release wedge-shaped reddish brown seeds. This plant is distinguished from other species in the genus that grow on Kauai by being entirely hairless.

Habitat

'Awiwi generally grows in stream beds or on steep cliffs close to water sources in lowland wet forest communities at elevations between 560 and 1,200 feet.

For a continued habitat description of Kauai, see "Habitat Conditions on the Island of Kauai, Hawaii," page 1883.

Historic Range

Historically, 'Awiwi was known from only three collections: Kealakekua on the island of Hawaii; Halawa and Kalawao on Molokai; and at the foot of the Koolau mountains on Oahu. There is no evidence that it still exists on any of those islands. It is believed to have been much more widespread on several of the main Hawaiian islands.

Current Distribution

Between 50 and 100 plants are scattered along a 0.25 mile distance in the streambedd of the lower waterfall in the Waiahuakua Valley on Kauai. Although this population has not been observed since its discovery in 1976, it is believed to be extant.

Conservation and Recovery

The major threat to *H. cookiana*, with only one known population, is stochastic extinction and/or reduced population vigor. Potential threats include competition with alien plants, and habitat modification by feral pigs and goats which have been observed in the area. *H. cookiana* grows in stream beds and on the side of a waterfall, which are areas vulnerable to flooding and other natural disturbances.

The recovery of this and most other Hawaiian species depends on how well management practices can be implemented. The habitat of this and other Hawaiian species has undergone extreme alteration because of past and present land management practices, including deliberately introducing alien animals and plants, and agricultural and recreational development. To understand the recovery problems facing this species, it is necessary to understand the long-term causes of habitat destruction.

For a continued discussion of the threats to Hawaiian plants, see page 1831.

Bibliography

U.S. Fish and Wildlife Service. "Endangered and Threatened Wildlife and Plant; Determination of Endangered or Threatened Status for 24 Plants from the Island of Kauai, HI." *Federal Register* Vol. 59, No. 38. February 25, 1994: 9304-9329.

Contacts

U.S. Fish and Wildlife Service
300 Ala Moana Boulevard, Room 6307
P.O. Box 50167
Honolulu, HI 96850
(808) 541-2749

Adapted from data compiled by Beacham Publishing for *Beacham's International Threatened, Endangered, and Extinct Species* published on CD ROM.

Clay's Hibiscus

Hibiscus clayi

Status	Endangered
Listed	February 25, 1994
Family	Malvaceae (Mallow)
Description	Shrub or tree with oval or elliptical leaves, and flaring, dark red petaled flowers.
Habitat	Lowland dry forests.
Threats	Alien plants, human impact, low populations.
Range	Hawaii (Kauai)

Loyal A. Mehrhoff   *Color Plate C-4*

Description

Clay's hibiscus is a shrub or tree 13 to 26 feet tall with stems bearing sparse hairs at the branch tips. The oval or elliptical leaves are usually 1 to 3 inches long and 0.6 to 1.4 inches wide and have a hairless upper surface and slightly hairy lower surface. The leaf margins are entire or toothed toward the apex. The flowers are borne singly near the ends of the branches. The flaring petals are dark red, 1.8 to 2.4 inches long, and 0.4 to 0.7 inches wide. The green tubular or urn-shaped calyx is usually 0.6 to 1 inch long with 5 or 6 shorter bracts beneath. The fruits are pale brown capsules, 0.5 to 0.6 inches long, containing about 10 oval, brownish-black seeds about 0.16 inches long. This species is distinguished from other native Hawaiian members of the genus by the lengths of the calyx, calyx lobes and capsule,

and by the margins of the leaves.

Habitat

This species is found lowland dry forests at elevations of 750 to 1,150 feet. The forest is characterized by an annual rainfall of 20 to 80 inches which falls between November and March. The terrain is a well-drained, highly weathered substrate rich in aluminum. Associated vegetation include Java plum, koa, kukui, and ti.

For a continued habitat description of Kauai, see "Habitat Conditions on the Island of Kauai, Hawaii," page 1883.

Historic Range

Clay's hibiscus is known from scattered locations on private and state land: the Kokee region on the western side of Kauai;

Moloaa Valley to the north; Nounou Mountain in Wailua to the east; and as far south as Haiku near Halii stream. It is unclear whether the one tree at the Kokee location was a cultivated plant.

Current Distribution

The only population known to exist in the Nounou mountains is comprised of four trees.

Conservation and Recovery

Before cattle were removed from the area, they greatly damaged the habitat of Clay's hibiscus. Competition with alien plants currently threatens this species. Strawberry guava is the greatest threat, but common guava, Hilo grass, Java plum, kukui, lantana, ti and Christmas berry are also present. The area of the Nounou mountain population has been planted with columnar araucaria, which is reseeding itself and may prevent regeneration of native plants. The close proximity of most of the plants to a hiking trail makes them prone to disturbance. Pigs pose a potential threat to the species. The small total number of existing individuals poses a threat of stochastic extinction and reduced reproductive vigor.

The recovery of this and most other Hawaiian species depends on how well management practices can be implemented. The habitat of this and other Hawaiian species has undergone extreme alteration because of past and present land management practices, including deliberately introducing alien animals and plants, and agricultural and recreational development. To understand the recovery problems facing this species, it is necessary to understand the long-term causes of habitat destruction.

For a continued discussion of the threats to Hawaiian plants, see page 1831.

Bibliography

U.S. Fish and Wildlife Service. "Endangered and Threatened Wildlife and Plant; Determination of Endangered or Threatened Status for 24 Plants from the Island of Kauai, HI." *Federal Register* Vol. 59, No. 38. February 25, 1994: 9304-9329.

Contacts

U.S. Fish and Wildlife Service
300 Ala Moana Boulevard, Room 6307
P.O. Box 50167
Honolulu, HI 96850
(808) 541-2749

Adapted from data compiled by Beacham Publishing for *Beacham's International Threatened, Endangered, and Extinct Species* published on CD ROM.

Nehe

Lipochaeta fauriei

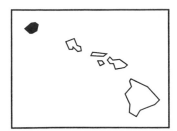

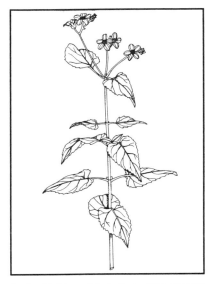

L. subcordata (close relative) Yevonn Wilson-Ramsey

Status	Endangered
Listed	February 25, 1994
Family	Asteraceae (Aster)
Description	Perennial herb with woody, erect or climbing stems up to 16 feet; narrowly triangular, slightly hairy, toothed leaves; and flower heads occurring in clusters of 2 to 3.
Habitat	Sides of steep gulches in diverse lowland mesic forests.
Threats	Goats, alien plants, fire, limited numbers.
Range	Hawaii (Kauai)

Description

This nehe, *Lipochaeta fauriei*, is a perennial herb with somewhat woody, erect or climbing stems up to 16 feet long. The toothed leaves are narrowly triangular, slightly hairy, 3 to 5 inches long, and about 1.2 inches wide. Flower heads occur in clusters of 2 to 3, each comprising 6 to 8 ray florets, 0.2 to 0.5 inches long and about 0.1 inches wide, and 30 to 35 disk florets 0.1 to 0.2 inches long. The bracts beneath the flower heads are purple near the base. Fruits are knobby-textured achenes about 0.1 inches long and 0.07 inches wide. The achenes of the disk florets are sometimes thinner and shorter than those of the ray florets. This species belongs to a genus endemic to the Hawaiian Islands and is one of three species found only on the island of Kauai. This species differs from others on Kauai by having a greater number of disk and ray flowers per flower head, typically longer leaves and leaf stalks, and longer ray flowers.

Habitat

This species most often grows in moderate shade to full sun, and is usually found on the sides of steep gulches in diverse lowland mesic forests at an elevation of about 1,570 to 2,950 feet. Associated vegetation includes basketgrass, kukui, lama, and *Hibiscus waimeae*. The major alien plant is lantana.

For a continued habitat description of Kauai, see "Habitat Conditions on the Island of Kauai, Hawaii," page 1883.

Historic Range

Historically, *L. fauriei* was known from Olokele Canyon on the island of Kauai.

Current Distribution

The species is now known from four other areas: Koaie Canyon; Poopooiki; Haeleele; and lower Hikimoe valleys. All five populations, totaling fewer than 70 individuals, are found on state land encompassing a 6 by 7 mile area.

Conservation and Recovery

The major threats are degradation of habitat by feral goats and competitive with invasive alien plants, especially lantana. Feral pigs pose a potential threat, and fire is a significant threat. The small total number of individuals comprises a threat of stochastic extinction and reduced reproductive vigor.

The recovery of this and most other Hawaiian species depends on how well management practices can be implemented. The habitat of this and other Hawaiian species has undergone extreme alteration because of past and present land management practices, including deliberately introducing alien animals and plants, and agricultural and recreational development. To understand the recovery problems facing this species, it is necessary to understand the long-term causes of habitat destruction.

For a continued discussion of the threats to Hawaiian plants, see page 1831.

Bibliography

U.S. Fish and Wildlife Service. "Endangered and Threatened Wildlife and Plant; Determination of Endangered or Threatened Status for 24 Plants from the Island of Kauai, HI." *Federal Register* Vol. 59, No. 38. February 25, 1994: 9304-9329.

Contacts

U.S. Fish and Wildlife Service
300 Ala Moana Boulevard, Room 6307
P.O. Box 50167
Honolulu, HI 96850
(808) 541-2749

Adapted from data compiled by Beacham Publishing for *Beacham's International Threatened, Endangered, and Extinct Species* published on CD ROM.

Nehe

Lipochaeta micrantha

Status	Endangered
Listed	February 25, 1994
Family	Asteraceae (Aster)
Description	Woody perennial herb that grows along the ground, with triangular leaves and flower heads that cluster in groups of 2 to 3.
Habitat	Exposed rocky slopes in diverse lowland mesic forests or on grassy ridges.
Threats	Goats, pigs, alien plants, limited numbers.
Range	Hawaii (Kauai)

Robert J. Gustafson

Description

This nehe, *Lipochaeta micrantha*, is a somewhat woody perennial herb. The 1.6 to 6.5 foot long stems grow along the ground and root at the nodes, with the tip of the stem growing upward. The roughly triangular leaves measure 0.8 to 3.8 inches long and 0.5 to 3.1 inches wide. They are sparsely hairy, with margins smooth or variously lobed. Flower heads are in clusters of two or three. Each head contains 4 to 5 ray florets, 0.1 to 0.2 inches long and 0.06 to 0.14 inches wide, and 5 to 9 disk florets, about 0.1 inches long. The two recognized varieties of this species, *exigua* and *micrantha*, are distinguished by different leaf length and width, degree of leaf dissection, and the length of the ray florets. The smaller number of disk florets separates this species from the other members of the genus on Kauai.

Habitat

Both varieties of this Nehe grow on exposed rocky slopes in diverse lowland mesic forests and sometimes on grassy ridges at elevations of 1,000 to 1,300 feet. Associated vegetation includes alahe's, lama, 'ohi'a and *Neraudia kauaiensis*.

For a continued habitat description of Kauai, see "Habitat Conditions on the Island of Kauai, Hawaii," page 1883.

Historic Range

Historically, *L. micrantha* var. *micrantha* appears to have been more widely distributed on Kauai in Olokele Canyon, Hanapepe Valley, and in the Koloa District.

Current Distribution

Only two populations of *L. micrantha* var. *exigua* are known from the vicinity of the Haupu Range on Kauai, which are distributed over a 1.5 mile distance on privately owned portions of Haupu Range and number between 100 and 500 individuals. *L. micrantha* var. *micrantha* is known only from 2 to 4 populations located on state land in Koaie Canyon, totaling 150 to 570 individuals.

Conservation and Recovery

The major threats to this nehe are habitat degradation by feral goats and pigs, and competition with alien plants, especially lantana. Daisy fleabane and *Stachytarpheta* spp. are also competitors. Both varieties are threatened by stochastic extinction and reduced reproductive vigor.

The recovery of this and most other Hawaiian species depends on how well management practices can be implemented. The habitat of this and other Hawaiian species has undergone extreme alteration because of past and present land management practices, including deliberately introducing alien animals and plants, and agricultural and recreational development. To understand the recovery problems facing this species, it is necessary to understand the long-term causes of habitat destruction.

For a continued discussion of the threats to Hawaiian plants, see page 1831.

Bibliography

U.S. Fish and Wildlife Service. "Endangered and Threatened Wildlife and Plant; Determination of Endangered or Threatened Status for 24 Plants from the Island of Kauai, HI." *Federal Register* Vol. 59, No. 38. February 25, 1994: 9304-9329.

Contacts

U.S. Fish and Wildlife Service
300 Ala Moana Boulevard, Room 6307
P.O. Box 50167
Honolulu, HI 96850
(808) 541-2749

Adapted from data compiled by Beacham Publishing for *Beacham's International Threatened, Endangered, and Extinct Species* published on CD ROM.

Nehe

Lipochaeta waimeaensis

Loyal A. Mehrhoff

Status	Endangered
Listed	February 25, 1994
Family	Asteraceae (Aster)
Description	Low growing, somewhat woody perennial herb with stems 3 to 6.5 feet; linear, hairy leaves; and flower heads borne singly or in clusters of 2 to 3.
Habitat	Eroded soil on a precipitous, shrub-covered gulch in a diverse lowland mesic forest.
Threats	Goats, alien plants, over-collecting, limited numbers.
Range	Hawaii (Kauai)

Description

This nehe, *Lipochaeta waimeaensis*, is a low growing, somewhat woody perennial herb with stems 3 to 6.5 feet long that root at the nodes. The linear or narrowly elliptical leaves are 1.9 to 2 inches long, 0.2 to 0.3 inches wide, hairy along the upper veins on the upper surface, and evenly hairy on the lower surface. Flower heads are borne singly or in clusters of two or three. The outer head bracts are lance-shaped and measure 0.1 to 0.2 inches long and 0.06 to 0.08 inches wide. The oval ray florets number 4 or 5 per head and are about 0.13 inches long and about 0.1 wide. The disk florets number 20 to 25 per head. The fruits are knobby, winged achenes 0.1 inch long and about 0.08 wide. The ray achenes are slightly wider and have longer wings than those of the disk. This species differs from the other taxa of the genus in having a different leaf shape and shorter leaf stalks and ray florets.

Habitat

L. waimeaensis grows on eroded soil on a precipitous, shrub-covered gulch in a diverse lowland mesic forest at an elevation between 1,150 and 1,300 feet. The vegetation at the site is primarily alien, consisting of silk oak, koa haole, and Natal redtop. Native plants include *Dodonaea viscosa* and *Lipochaeta connata*.

For a continued habitat description of Kauai, see "Habitat Conditions on the Island of Kauai, Hawaii," page 1883.

Historic Range

This species is known only from its place of original discovery, along the rim of Kauai's Waimea Canyon on state land.

Current Distribution

Fewer than 10 plants are scattered over a 2.5 acre area in Waimea Canyon.

Conservation and Recovery

Alien plants competing with and threatening this Nehe include koa haole, Natal redtop, silk oak, and prickly pear. The existing soil erosion problem is exacerbated by the presence of feral goats. The single population, and thus the entire species, is threatened by stochastic extinction and reduced reproductive vigor due to the small numbers. Over-collecting for scientific purposes also poses a threat.

The recovery of this and most other Hawaiian species depends on how well management practices can be implemented. The habitat of this and other Hawaiian species has undergone extreme alteration because of past and present land management practices, including deliberately introducing alien animals and plants, and agricultural and recreational development. To understand the recovery problems facing this species, it is necessary to understand the long-term causes of habitat destruction.

For a continued discussion of the threats to Hawaiian plants, see page 1831.

Bibliography

U.S. Fish and Wildlife Service. "Endangered and Threatened Wildlife and Plant; Determination of Endangered or Threatened Status for 24 Plants from the Island of Kauai, HI." *Federal Register* Vol. 59, No. 38. February 25, 1994: 9304-9329.

Contacts

U.S. Fish and Wildlife Service
300 Ala Moana Boulevard, Room 6307
P.O. Box 50167
Honolulu, HI 96850
(808) 541-2749

Adapted from data compiled by Beacham Publishing for *Beacham's International Threatened, Endangered, and Extinct Species* published on CD ROM.

Lysimachia filifolia
No Common Name

John Obata

Status	Endangered
Listed	February 25, 1994
Family	Primulaceae (Primrose)
Description	Small shrub with alternately arranged, single-veined, sparsely hairy or hairless linear leaves; and bell-shaped reddish-purple flowers.
Habitat	Mossy banks at the base of cliff faces within the spray zone of waterfalls or along streams in lowland wet forests.
Threats	Competition from alien plants, natural disaster, limited numbers.
Range	Hawaii (Kauai, Oahu)

Description

Lysimachia filifolia is a small shrub 0.5 to 1.6 feet tall. The linear leaves measure 0.6 to 2.1 inches long and 0.01 to 0.07 inches wide, and are usually alternately arranged. They are single-veined and sparsely hairy or hairless. The bell-shaped flowers are reddish purple, 0.2 to 0.4 inches long, and borne singly on flower stalks about 0.7 to 1.2 inches long that elongate upon fruiting. Fruits are thick, hard capsules about 0.2 inches long that contain numerous minute, nearly black, irregularly shaped seeds. This species is distinguished from other taxa of the genus by its leaf shape and width, calyx lobe shape, and corolla length.

Habitat

This species typically grows on mossy banks at the base of cliff faces within the spray zone of waterfalls or along streams in lowland wet forests at an elevation of 800 to 2,200 feet. Associated plants include mosses, ferns, liverworts, pili grass, *Culphea carthagenensis* and *Pilea peploides*.

For a continued habitat description of Kauai, see "Habitat Conditions on the Island of Kauai," page 1883; and "Habitat Conditions on the Island of Oahu," page 2031.

Historic Range

Historically, the species was known only from the upper portion of Olokele Valley on Kauai. The species is now known from two other areas: the headwaters of the Wailua River on Kauai; and the slopes of Waiahole Valley in the Koolau Mountains of Oahu. Both populations are located on state land.

Current Distribution

The populations on Kauai are located within a 0.5 square mile area and total 76 individuals. The Oahu population contains about 150 to 200 individuals.

Conservation and Recovery

The major threat to *Lysimachia filifolia* is competition with alien plants. Individuals of this species on Kauai are damaged and destroyed by natural rock slides in their habitat, which is near the bottom of a steep cliff. March pennywort, tarweed, and thumbleberry, although not invasive weeds, are present in this near-pristine area of Wailua Stream and may degrade the native ecosystem. At least one feral pig has made its way into this area, indicating that this disruptive animal is a potential threat.

Individuals on Oahu are vulnerable to rock slides and compete for space with alien plants, such as marsh pennywort, tarweed, Hamakua pamakani, and octopus tree.

Because only one population occurs on each of only two islands, the species is threatened by stochastic extinction. Hurricane Iniki caused at least some damage to the Wailua River population.

The recovery of this and most other Hawaiian species depends on how well management practices can be implemented. The habitat of this and other Hawaiian species has undergone extreme alteration because of past and present land management practices, including deliberately introducing alien animals and plants, and agricultural and recreational development. To understand the recovery problems facing this species, it is necessary to understand the long-term causes of habitat destruction.

For a continued discussion of the threats to Hawaiian plants, see page 1831.

Bibliography

U.S. Fish and Wildlife Service. "Endangered and Threatened Wildlife and Plant; Determination of Endangered or Threatened Status for 24 Plants from the Island of Kauai, HI." *Federal Register* Vol. 59, No. 38. February 25, 1994: 9304-9329.

Contacts

U.S. Fish and Wildlife Service
300 Ala Moana Boulevard, Room 6307
P.O. Box 50167
Honolulu, HI 96850
(808) 541-2749

Adapted from data compiled by Beacham Publishing for *Beacham's International Threatened, Endangered, and Extinct Species* published on CD ROM.

Alani

Melicope haupuensis

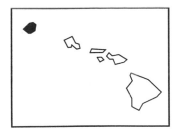

Status	Endangered
Listed	February 25, 1994
Family	Rutaceae (Citrus)
Description	Tree with oval leaves oppositely arranged and flowers growing in clusters of 5 to 7.
Habitat	Moist talus slopes in 'ohi'a-dominated lowland mesic forests.
Threats	Insects, limited numbers.
Range	Hawaii (Kauai)

No Photo Available for This Species

Description

This alani, *Melicope haupuensis*, is a tree about 26 feet tall. The oval leaves, 2 to 5.1 inches long and 1.1 to 2.2 inches wide, are oppositely arranged. Flowers grow in clusters of 5 to 7 on stalks usually 0.1 to 2.8 inches long, each flower on a stalk 0.04 to 0.12 inches long. Only female flowers are known. The flowers are about 0.14 inches long, dotted with oil glands, and covered with a dense mat of hairs. Fruits are distinct follicles (a dry fruit that splits open lengthwise), 0.35 to 0.43 inches long, with a hairless exocarp and endocarp (outermost and innermost layers of the fruit wall). Unlike other taxa of this genus on Kauai, the exocarp and endocarp are hairless and the sepals are covered with dense hairs.

Habitat

The two known plants grow on moist talus slopes in 'ohi'a-dominated lowland mesic forests. Associated vegetation include a'ali'a and hame, which grow at elevations between 1,230 and 2,690 feet.

For a continued habitat description of Kauai, see "Habitat Conditions on the Island of Kauai, Hawaii," page 1883.

Historic Range and Current Distribution

For 62 years, this alani was known only from the type locality on the north side of Haupu Ridge on Kauai. In 1989 two plants were discovered within 1 mile of each other along the banks of Koaie Stream on state owned land in Waimea Canyon.

Conservation and Recovery

Habitat degradation by feral goats and competition with invasive alien plant taxa such as lantana and yellow foxtail threatens *M. haupuensis*. A potential threat to members of this genus is their known susceptibility to black twig borer, a burrowing beetle ubiquitous in Hawaii at elevations below 2,500 feet. The existence of only two known trees of this species constitutes a threat of stochastic extinction and reduced reproductivity.

The recovery of this and most other Hawaiian species depends on how well management practices can be implemented. The habitat of this and other Hawaiian species has undergone extreme alteration because of past and present land management practices, including deliberately introducing alien animals and plants, and agricultural and recreational development. To understand the recovery problems facing this species, it is necessary to understand the long-term causes of habitat destruction.

For a continued discussion of the threats to Hawaiian plants, see page 1831.

Bibliography

U.S. Fish and Wildlife Service. "Endangered and Threatened Wildlife and Plant; Determination of Endangered or Threatened Status for 24 Plants from the Island of Kauai, HI." *Federal Register* Vol. 59, No. 38. February 25, 1994: 9304-9329.

Contacts

U.S. Fish and Wildlife Service
300 Ala Moana Boulevard, Room 6307
P.O. Box 50167
Honolulu, HI 96850
(808) 541-2749

Adapted from data compiled by Beacham Publishing for *Beacham's International Threatened, Endangered, and Extinct Species* published on CD ROM.

Alani

Melicope knudsenii

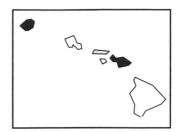

Yevonn Wilson-Ramsey

Status	Endangered
Listed	February 25, 1994
Family	Rutaceae (Citrus)
Description	Medium-size tree with smooth grey bark, yellowish brown to olive brown hairs on the tips of the branches, and densely hairy flowers that cluster in the leaf axils.
Habitat	Lowland dry forests.
Threats	Cattle, goats, pigs, alien plants, low populations.
Range	Hawaii (Kauai, Maui)

Description

This alani, *Melicope knudsenii*, is a tree usually 10 to 33 feet tall with smooth grey bark and yellowish brown to olive brown hairs on the tips of the branches. Leaves are variable, ranging from oblong to elliptic, 3.5 to 9.8 inches long and 1.8 to 3.9 inches wide. The lower surface of the leaves is uniformly covered with olive-brown hairs, but the upper surface is only sparsely hairy along the midrib. The densely hairy flowers are bisexual or may be unisexual. There are usually 20 to 200 flowers per cluster in the leaf axils. The sepals and petals are covered with silky grey hairs and the sepals persist in the fruit. The fruits are 0.7 to 1.2 inches wide and are comprised of distinct follicles, 0.3 to 0.6 inches long. The hairless exocarp is dotted with minute glands. The endocarp also lacks hairs. Seeds number 1 or 2 per carpel (ovule-bearing structure) and are about 0.2 inches long. The distinct carpels of the fruit, the hairless endocarp, the larger number of flowers per cluster, and the distribution of hairs on the underside of the leaves distinguish this species from others in the genus.

Habitat

This alani grows on forested flats or talus slopes in lowland dry to mesic forests at an elevation of about 1,500 to 3,300 feet. The lowland dry forests where this species is found is characterized by an annual rainfall of 20 to 80 inches which falls between November and March. The terrain is a well-drained, highly weathered substrate rich in aluminum. The Auwahi population on Maui grows on a substrate of 'a'a lava in a remnant native forest dominated by a continuous mat of Kikuyu grass. Plants associated with the Kauai populations include 'a'ali'i, hame, 'ohi'a, and Xylosma.

For a continued habitat description, see "Habitat Conditions on the Island of Kauai," page 1883; and "Habitat Conditions on the Island of Maui," page 1955.

Historic Range and Current Distribution

Historically, this species was known only from the southeast slope of Haleakala on Maui and from Olokele Canyon on Kauai. It remains in the Auwahi and Kanaio areas of Maui on privately owned land, but its numbers have decreased from being "very common" in 1920, to between 20 and 30 plants when it was last observed in 1983.

On Kauai, three populations, each consisting of one individual, remain on state land in the Koaie drainage area of Waimea Canyon, and are distributed across a distance of 1.6 miles.

Conservation and Recovery

Competition with alien plant taxa and habitat degradation by feral and domestic animals are the major threats affecting *M. knudsenii*. On Kauai, this species competes with lantana and is affected by feral goats and pigs. On Maui, the species grows in an area currently grazed by domestic cattle, where a continuous mat of kikuyu grass prevents seedlings from becoming established.

The recovery of this and most other Hawaiian species depends on how well management practices can be implemented. The habitat of this and other Hawaiian species has undergone extreme alteration because of past and present management practices, including deliberately introducing alien animals and plants, and agricultural and recreational development. To understand the recovery problems facing this species, it is necessary to understand the long-term causes of habitat destruction.

For a continued discussion of the threats to Hawaiian plants, see page 1831.

Bibliography

U.S. Fish and Wildlife Service. "Endangered and Threatened Wildlife and Plant; Determination of Endangered or Threatened Status for 24 Plants from the Island of Kauai, HI." *Federal Register* Vol. 59, No. 38. February 25, 1994: 9304-9329.

Contacts

U.S. Fish and Wildlife Service
300 Ala Moana Boulevard, Room 6307
P.O. Box 50167
Honolulu, HI 96850
(808) 541-2749

Adapted from data compiled by Beacham Publishing for *Beacham's International Threatened, Endangered, and Extinct Species* published on CD ROM.

Alani

Melicope pallida

Yevonn Wilson-Ramsey

Status	Endangered
Listed	February 25, 1994
Family	Rutaceae (Citrus)
Description	Medium-size tree with grayish white hairs and black, resinous new growth; and pale yellowish-green flowers clustered in groups of 3.
Habitat	Steep rock faces in drier regions of lowland mesic forests.
Threats	Feral animals, competition from alien plants, insects, fire, limited numbers.
Range	Hawaii (Kauai, Oahu)

Description

This alani, *Melicope pallida*, is a 20 to 33 foot tree with grayish white hairs and black, resinous new growth. The leaves, 2.4 to 8.3 inches long and 1 to 3.1 inches wide, are grouped in threes, with each leaf loosely folded. Fifteen to 35 pale yellowish-green flowers are clustered in groups of 3 along a fuzzy white stalk up to 2.4 inches long. The petals are usually lance-shaped and measure 0.1 to 0.2 inches long. Fruits contain two shiny black seeds about 0.1 inches long in each of the usually four distinct carpels. This specimen differs from other members of the genus by the following combination of characteristics: resinous new growth; leaves folded and in clusters of three; and fruits with separate carpels.

Habitat

This alani usually grows on steep rock faces in drier regions of lowland mesic forests at an elevation of 1,600 to over 3,000 feet. Associated plants include *Abutilon sandwicense*, *Alyxia oliviformis* (maile), *Dryopteris* sp., 'ohi'a, mamaki, lonomea, 'ohe, and mana.

For a continued habitat description, see "Habitat Conditions on the Island of Kauai" page 1883; and "Habitat Conditions on the Island of Oahu" page 2031.

Historic Range and Current Distribution

Historically, this species was known from various locations in the Waianae Mountains on Oahu and from Hanapepe on Kauai. The species is now known from two locations at the base of Mount Kaala and near Palikea, within The Nature Conservancy's privately owned reserve in the Waianae Mountains on Oahu, and from four state owned locations on Kauai in Kalalau Valley, Koaie Stream in Waimea Canyon, and Hanakapiai Valley.

Conservation and Recovery

The major threats to *M. pallida* are habitat destruction by feral animals and competition with alien plant taxa. On Kauai, feral goats and pigs destroy habitats, and weeds, such as daisy fleabane and prickly Florida blackberry, compete with the species. The Oahu populations of *M. pallida* face strong competition from introduced plants, especially Koster's curse and Australian red cedar. A potential threat is the black twig borer, which is known to occur in areas where this species grows and to feed on members of the genus *Melicope*. Additional threats are fire and stochastic extinction, and/or reduced reproductive vigor due to the small number of existing individuals.

The recovery of this and most other Hawaiian species depends on how well management practices can be implemented. The habitat of this and other Hawaiian species has undergone extreme alteration because of past and present land management practices, including deliberately introducing alien animals and plants, and agricultural and recreational development. To understand the recovery problems facing this species, it is necessary to understand the long-term causes of habitat destruction.

For a continued discussion of the threats to Hawaiian plants, see page 1831.

Bibliography

U.S. Fish and Wildlife Service. "Endangered and Threatened Wildlife and Plant; Determination of Endangered or Threatened Status for 24 Plants from the Island of Kauai, HI." *Federal Register* Vol. 59, No. 38. February 25, 1994: 9304-9329.

Contacts

U.S. Fish and Wildlife Service
300 Ala Moana Boulevard, Room 6307
P.O. Box 50167
Honolulu, HI 96850
(808) 541-2749

Adapted from data compiled by Beacham Publishing for *Beacham's International Threatened, Endangered, and Extinct Species* published on CD ROM.

Alani

Melicope quadrangularis

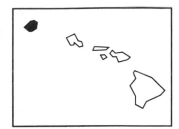

Status	Endangered
Listed	February 25, 1994
Family	Rutaceae (Citrus)
Description	Shrub or small tree with hairless branches; thin, leathery, elliptical leaves; and solitary flowers in clusters of two.
Habitat	Diverse lowland forest that ranges from mesic to wet conditions.
Threats	Over-collecting, limited numbers.
Range	Hawaii (Kauai)

No Photo Available for This Species

Description

This alani, *Melicope quadrangularis*, is a shrub or small tree. Young branches are generally covered with fine yellow fuzz but become hairless with age. The thin, leathery, elliptical leaves, 3.5 to 6 inches long and 2 to 3 inches wide, are oppositely arranged. The upper leaf surface is hairless and the lower surface is sparsely hairy, especially along the veins. Flowers are solitary or in clusters of two. The specific floral details are not known. The fruits are somewhat cube-shaped, flattened capsules about 0.5 inches long and about 0.8 inches wide with a conspicuous central depression at the top of the fruit. The capsules are four-lobed and completely fused. The exocarp is sparsely hairy and the endocarp is hairless. This species differs from others in the genus in having the following combination of characteristics: Oppositely arranged leaves; only one or two flowers per cluster; cube-shaped capsules with fused lobes; and a deep central depression at the top of the fruit.

Habitat

The 13 known plants grow in a diverse lowland forest that ranges from mesic to wet conditions. Associated vegetation includes 'ohi'a, opuhe, uluhe, kanawao, ha'iwale, other *Melicope* species, ferns and mosses.

For a continued habitat description of Kauai, see "Habitat Conditions on the Island of Kauai, Hawaii," page 1883.

Historic Range and Current Distribution

This species is known from the type locality in the Wahiawa Bog region of Kauai. One adult plant and two seedlings were discovered in this area in 1991 on an east-facing slope of Wahiawa Ridge at 2,800 feet elevation on privately owned land. Subsequent exploration has resulted in discovering the location of 13 individuals.

Conservation and Recovery

The existence of only 13 known plants of this species causes it to be threatened by over-collecting for scientific purposes, stochastic extinction, and reduced reproductive vigor. The alien strawberry guava grows in the area and is a potential threat.

The recovery of this and most other Hawaiian species depends on how well management practices can be implemented. The habitat of this and other Hawaiian species has undergone extreme alteration because of past and present land management practices, including deliberately introducing alien animals and plants, and agricultural and recreational development. To understand the recovery problems facing this species, it is necessary to understand the long-term causes of habitat destruction.

For a continued discussion of the threats to Hawaiian plants, see page 1831.

Bibliography

U.S. Fish and Wildlife Service. "Endangered and Threatened Wildlife and Plant; Determination of Endangered or Threatened Status for 24 Plants from the Island of Kauai, HI." *Federal Register* Vol. 59, No. 38. February 25, 1994: 9304-9329.

Contacts

U.S. Fish and Wildlife Service
300 Ala Moana Boulevard, Room 6307
P.O. Box 50167
Honolulu, HI 96850
(808) 541-2749

Adapted from data compiled by Beacham Publishing for *Beacham's International Threatened, Endangered, and Extinct Species* published on CD ROM.

Munroidendron racemosum

No Common Name

Robert J. Gustafson   *Color Plate C-3*

Status	Endangered
Listed	February 25, 1994
Family	Araliaceae (Ginseng)
Description	Medium-size tree with a straight, gray trunk and spreading branches; elliptical leaves; and pale yellow flowers.
Habitat	Steep exposed cliffs or on ridge slopes in coastal to lowland mesic forests.
Threats	Competition from alien plants, feral goats, insects, over-collecting, limited numbers.
Range	Hawaii (Kauai)

Description

Munroidendron racemosum is a tree that grows to about 23 feet, with a straight gray trunk crowned with spreading branches. The leaves are 6 to 12 inches long and comprise five to nine oval or elliptical leaflets with clasping leaf stalks. Each leaflet is 3.1 to 6.7 inches long and usually 1.6 to 3.9 inches wide. About 250 pale yellow flowers are borne along a stout hanging stalk 10 to 24 inches long. Each flower has 5 or 6 lance-shaped petals 0.3 to 0.4 inches long, emerging from a cup-shaped or ellipsoid calyx tube. Both the lower surface of the petals and the calyx tube are covered with whitish scaly hairs. The fruit is an egg-shaped drupe 0.3 to 0.5 inches long and nearly as wide, situated atop a flat, dark red disk (stylopod-ium). This species is the only member of a genus endemic to Hawaii, differing from other closely related Hawaiian genres of the family primarily in its distinct flower clusters and corolla.

Habitat

Most populations are found on steep exposed cliffs or on ridge slopes in coastal to lowland mesic forests, but a few populations are in mesic hala forests, lantana-dominated shrubland, or *Eragrotis* grasslands. Associated plants include common guava, kopiko, kukui and lama.

For a continued habitat description of Kauai, see "Habitat Conditions on the Island of Kauai, Hawaii," page 1883.

Historic Range

Historically, this species was known from scattered locations throughout the island of Kauai. Fifteen populations are now found at elevations of 390 to 1,310 feet on private and state land in the following areas: along the Na Pali Coast within the Na Pali Coast State Park and Hono O Na Pali NAR; in the Poomau and Koaie branches of Waimea Canyon; in the Haupu Range area; and on Nounou Mountain.

Current Distribution

Although widely distributed, the largest population contains fewer than 50 individuals with most populations numbering only one or two individuals. Estimates of the total number of individuals range from 57 to 100.

Conservation and Recovery

Competition with introduced plants is the major threat. Kukui and ti plants introduced by Polynesian immigrants to the Hawaiian Islands, compete with this species for space in the forests of Kauai. Other introduced plants threatening this species' habitat include Chinaberry, common guava, firetree, koa, haole, lantana and Sacramento burr. Feral goats degrade the habitat, and cattle were formerly present in areas where the trees grow. Fire is a threat to the habitat, and predation of the fruit by rats is probable. An introduced insect of the longhorned beetle family that killed a mature cultivated tree has the potential of affecting wild trees. Because each population of this species contains only one or a few trees, the total number of individuals is small, threatening the species through over-collecting for scientific or horticultural purposes, stochastic extinction, and reduced reproductive rigor.

The recovery of this and most other Hawaiian species depends on how well management practices can be implemented. The habitat of this and other Hawaiian species has undergone extreme alteration because of past and present land management practices, including deliberately introducing alien animals and plants, and agricultural and recreational development. To understand the recovery problems facing this species, it is necessary to understand the long-term causes of habitat destruction.

For a continued discussion of the threats to Hawaiian plants, see page 1831.

Bibliography

U.S. Fish and Wildlife Service. "Endangered and Threatened Wildlife and Plant; Determination of Endangered or Threatened Status for 24 Plants from the Island of Kauai, HI." *Federal Register* Vol. 59, No. 38. February 25, 1994: 9304-9329.

Contacts

U.S. Fish and Wildlife Service
300 Ala Moana Boulevard, Room 6307
P.O. Box 50167
Honolulu, HI 96850
(808) 541-2749

Adapted from data compiled by Beacham Publishing for *Beacham's International Threatened, Endangered, and Extinct Species* published on CD ROM.

'Aiea

Nothocestrum peltatum

Robert J. Gustafson

Status	Endangered
Listed	February 25, 1994
Family	Solanaceae (Nightshade)
Description	Small tree growing with ash-brown bark and woolly stems; leathery leaves, and densely hairy, yellowish flowers.
Habitat:	Rich soil on steep slopes in wet montane or mesic forests.
Threats	Deer, goats, pigs, alien plants, over-collecting, limited numbers.
Range	Hawaii (Kauai)

Description

'Aiea is a small tree growing as tall as 26 feet with ash-brown bark and woolly stems. The leathery leaves are usually peltate, measuring 2.4 to 9.1 inches long and 1.4 to 3 inches wide. They vary in shape from oval or elliptical to oblong. The densely hairy flowers number up to 10 per cluster. The corolla, 0.5 to 0.6 inches long, is greenish yellow fading to yellow orange. The orange berries are 0.5 to 0.6 inches long and contain numerous irregularly shaped seeds about 0.1 inches in diameter. The usually peltate leaves and shorter leaf stalks separate this species from others in the genus.

Habitat

This species generally grows in rich soil on steep slopes in montane or mesic forests dominated by koa or a mixture of 'ohi'a and koa, at elevations of 3,000 to 4,000 feet. Associated plants include hame, uluhe, kalia and more common *Melicope* species.

For a continued habitat description of Kauai, see "Habitat Conditions on the Island of Kauai, Hawaii," page 1883.

Historic Range

Historically, this species was known from Kauai at Kumuwela, Kaholuamanu, and the region of Nualolo.

Current Distribution

The species is now known from five populations on Kauai located near the Kalalau lookout area, in Awaawapuhi and Makaha Valleys, and in Waimea Canyon, scattered over a 5.5 by 2.5 mile area. These populations, totaling about 15 individuals, are on state owned land between 3,000 and 4,000 feet elevation.

Conservation and Recovery

Competition with alien plants and habitat degradation by introduced animals constitute the major threats to *N. peltatum*. Introduced plants competing with the species include banana poka, daisy fleabane, lantana, prickly Florida blackberry, and passion fruit. Animals disturbing the habitat include feral goats and pigs, mule deer, and red jungle fowl. Although plants of this species flower, they rarely set fruit, which could be the result of a loss of pollinators, reduced genetic variability, or self incompatibility. The species is threatened by fire, over-collecting for scientific and horticultural purposes, reduced reproductive vigor, and stochastic extinction.

The recovery of this and most other Hawaiian species depends on how well management practices can be implemented. The habitat of this and other Hawaiian species has undergone extreme alteration because of past and present land management practices, including deliberately introducing alien animals and plants, and agricultural and recreational development. To understand the recovery problems facing this species, it is necessary to understand the long-term causes of habitat destruction.

For a continued discussion of the threats to Hawaiian plants, see page 1831.

Bibliography

U.S. Fish and Wildlife Service. "Endangered and Threatened Wildlife and Plant; Determination of Endangered or Threatened Status for 24 Plants from the Island of Kauai, HI." *Federal Register* Vol. 59, No. 38. February 25, 1994: 9304-9329.

Contacts

U.S. Fish and Wildlife Service
300 Ala Moana Boulevard, Room 6307
P.O. Box 50167
Honolulu, HI 96850
(808) 541-2749

Adapted from data compiled by Beacham Publishing for *Beacham's International Threatened, Endangered, and Extinct Species* published on CD ROM.

Makou

Peucedanum sandwicense

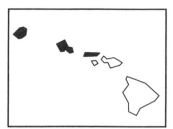

Robert J. Gustafson   *Color Plate C-1*

Status	Threatened
Listed	February 25, 1994
Family	Apiaceae (Parsley)
Description	Parsley-scented, sprawling herb with 10-20 white flowers bent inward at the tips.
Habitat	Cliff habitats from sea level to above 3,000 feet located in coastal to lowland dry to mesic shrublands and forests.
Threats	Goats, alien plants, fire, natural disaster, human impact, limited numbers.
Range	Hawaii (Kauai, Oahu, Molokai)

Description

Makou, *Peucedanum sandwicense*, is a parsley-scented, sprawling herb usually 20 to 40 inches tall. Hollow stems arise from a short, vertical, perennial stem with several fleshy roots. The compound leaves are generally three-parted with stalkless leaflets, each egg-shaped or lance-shaped and toothed. The larger terminal leaflet is usually one- to three-lobed and 2.8 to 5.1 inches long. The other leaflets have leaf stalks 4 to 20 inches long or are stalkless. Flowers are clustered in a compound umbel of 10 to 20 flowers. The round petals are white and bent inward at the tips. The flat, dry, oval fruits are 0.4 to 0.5 inches long and 0.2 to 0.3 inches wide, splitting in half to release a single flat seed. This species is the only member of the genus in the Hawaiian Islands. This species differs from the other Kauai members of the parsley family in having larger fruit and pinnately compound leaves with broad leaflets.

Habitat

This species is found within a variety of vegetation communities, ranging from coastal to lowland dry to mesic shrubland and forests to cliff habitats at elevations of 3,000 feet. Associated plants include 'akoko, kawelu, lama, 'ohi'a, 'ahinahina, and alien species such as common guava and lantana.

For a continued habitat description of Kauai, see "Habitat Conditions on the Island of Kauai," page 1883; "Habitat Conditions on the Island of Oahu," page 2031; and "Habitat Conditions on the Island of Molokai, Hawaii," page 1993.

Historic Range

Historically, this species was known from three islands: Kalaupapa, Pauonuakea Kui, Waikolu, and Wailau Valley on Molokai; Wailuku and Waiehu on Maui; and various locations in the Waimea Canyon and Olokele regions of Kauai.

Current Distribution

Discoveries in 1990 extended the known distribution of this species to the island of Oahu, where two populations totalling about 85 individuals exist in the Waianae Mountains on county and state land. One population of 20 to 30 individuals is known from state owned Keopuka Rock, an islet off the coast of Maui. On Molokai, three populations totalling fewer than 30 individuals are found on private and state owned land in Pelekunu Preserve, Kalaupapa National Historical Park, and Huelo, an islet off the coast of Molokai. The ten Kauai populations of 130 to 190 individuals are distributed in Waimea Canyon along the Na Pali Coast within 1.5 miles of the ocean. These populations are found within a seven by eight mile area on private and state land. The total number of plants in the known populations of this species is estimated to exceed 1,000 and possibly 5,000 individuals.

Conservation and Recovery

Competition with introduced plants and habitat degradation and browsing by feral goats are the major threats to Makou. Kauai populations are affected by alien plant species such as air plant, banana poka, common guava, daisy fleabane, firetree, introduced grasses, Java plum, and lantana, as well as by feral goats. The Hanakapiai population on Kauai is close enough to the trail that it is potentially affected by hikers and trail clearing. Oahu populations are threatened by alien plants such as Christmas berry, common guava, daisy fleabane, Hamakua pamakani, silk oak and Stachytarpheta; feral goats, fire and landslides. The Kalaupapa, Molokai population competes with Christmas berry, common guava and molasses grass. The Pelekunu, Molokai population is threatened by common guava, Hamakua pamakani, Maui pamakani, and potentially by axis deer. Plants on Huelo are vulnerable to natural rock slides. The population on Keopuka Rock is threatened by alien grasses, lantana and sourbush.

Makou is not in immediate danger of extinction, but if these threats are not curtailed, this species will become endangered.

The recovery of this and most other Hawaiian species depends on how well management practices can be implemented. The habitat of this and other Hawaiian species has undergone extreme alteration because of past and present land management practices, including deliberately introducing alien animals and plants, and agricultural and recreational development. To understand the recovery problems facing this species, it is necessary to understand the long-term causes of habitat destruction.

For a continued discussion of the threats to Hawaiian plants, see page 1831.

Bibliography

U.S. Fish and Wildlife Service. "Endangered and Threatened Wildlife and Plant; Determination of Endangered or Threatened Status for 24 Plants from the Island of Kauai, HI." *Federal Register* Vol. 59, No. 38. February 25, 1994: 9304-9329.

Contacts

U.S. Fish and Wildlife Service
P.O. Box 50167
Honolulu, HI 96850

Phyllostegia waimeae

No Common Name

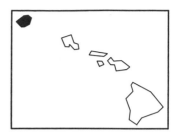

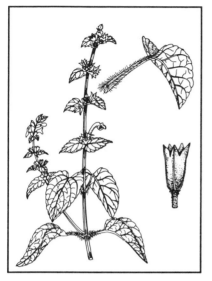

P. lantanoides (relative)   Yevonn Wilson-Ramsey

Status	Endangered
Listed	February 25, 1994
Family	Lamiaceae (Mint)
Description	Climbing perennial plant with hairy four-angled stems that are woody at the base, and flowers that grow in groups of 6 along an unbranched leafy stalk.
Habitat	Shallow to deep, well-drained soils in clearings or along the banks of streams of diverse montane mesic to wet forests.
Threats	Goats, alien plants, limited numbers.
Range	Hawaii (Kauai)

Description

Phyllostegia waimeae, a nonaromatic mint, is a climbing perennial plant with hairy four-angled stems that are woody at the base. The oval leaves are 2 to 5 inches long, 1 to 2.4 inches wide, and have rounded, toothed margins. They are wrinkled and sparsely dotted with oil glands. Flowers grow in groups of six along an unbranched leafy stalk usually 3.9 to 5.9 inches long. The bracts below each flower stalk are broad and partially overlap the flowers. The calyx resembles an inverted cone with broad lobes. The corolla, 0.3 to 0.5 inches long, is pinkish or may be white. The fruits, probably nutlets, have not been observed. Characteristics that distinguish this species from others in the genus are the nearly stalkless bracts that partially overlap and cover the flowers and

relatively fewer oil glands on the leaves.

Habitat

This species typically grows on shallow to deep, well-drained soils in clearings or along the banks of streams of diverse montane mesic to wet forests at elevations from 3,000 feet to 3,600 feet. Associated plant taxa include 'ohi'a and loulou.

For a continued habitat description of Kauai, see "Habitat Conditions on the Island of Kauai, Hawaii," page 1883.

Historic Range

Historically, *P. waimeae* was known from Kaholuamanu and Kaaha on Kauai. In recent years it is known from state land on Kauai in the Halemanu and Waimea Canyon areas.

Current Distribution

Because the Halemanu population has not been seen for almost 40 years, the number of extant individuals is not known. The Waimea Canyon population consists of a single plant which has not been observed recently.

Conservation and Recovery

Habitat destruction by feral goats, erosion, and competition with introduced grasses are the major threats. The species is also threatened by stochastic extinction and reduced reproductive vigor because of limited numbers.

The recovery of this and most other Hawaiian species depends on how well management practices can be implemented. The habitat of this and other Hawaiian species has undergone extreme alteration because of past and present land management practices, including deliberately introducing alien animals and plants, and agricultural and recreational development. To understand the recovery problems facing this species, it is necessary to understand the long-term causes of habitat destruction.

For a continued discussion of the threats to Hawaiian plants, see page 1831.

Bibliography

U.S. Fish and Wildlife Service. "Endangered and Threatened Wildlife and Plant; Determination of Endangered or Threatened Status for 24 Plants from the Island of Kauai, HI." *Federal Register* Vol. 59, No. 38. February 25, 1994: 9304-9329.

Contacts

U.S. Fish and Wildlife Service
300 Ala Moana Boulevard, Room 6307
P.O. Box 50167
Honolulu, HI 96850
(808) 541-2749

Adapted from data compiled by Beacham Publishing for *Beacham's International Threatened, Endangered, and Extinct Species* published on CD ROM.

Hawaiian Bluegrass
Poa sandvicensis

Loyal A. Mehrhoff

Status	Endangered
Listed	May 13, 1992
Family	Poaceae (Grass)
Description	Perennial grass growing to 3 feet with leaf sheaths surrounding the stem.
Habitat	Shaded slopes and ridges in moist to wet mountain forests.
Threats	Invasive alien plant species, low numbers.
Range	Hawaii (Kauai)

Description

Hawaiian bluegrass is a perennial grass with mostly erect stems growing 1 to 3 feet high. Short underground stems (rhizomes) form a hard base for the solid, slightly compressed stems. The leaf blades are 4 to 8 inches long and up to 0.2 inch wide; the leaf sheaths completely surround the stem. The flowers occur in a complex cluster; fruits are brown, oval grains. Hawaiian bluegrass is distinguished from similar species by, among other things, its shorter stems, closed leaf sheaths, and longer panicle branches. The species has also been known by the names *Festuca sandvicensis* and *Poa longeradiata*.

Habitat

Hawaiian bluegrass is one of a large number of species endemic to the Kokee area in the northwestern part of the Hawaiian island of Kauai. This area is roughly encompassed by the 8-square-mile Kokee State Park. Kauai was formed by a single shield volcano, the crater of which eventually formed the Alakai Swamp. Faulting and erosion on the western end of the swamp created the deeply cut Waimea Canyon, which runs north to south. The canyon is 10 miles long and a mile wide, with steep vertical cliffs more than 2,000 feet high. Kokee State Park lies just north of Waimea Canyon, and has the Alakai Swamp to the east, the steep cliffs of the Na Pali coast to the north, and the drier leeward ridges to the west. Hawaiian bluegrass is found on shaded, wet slopes, ridges, and rock ledges in moist to wet mountain forest dominated by ohia at elevations between 3,400 to 4,100 ft.

Five other plant species endemic to the Kokee region are listed as Endangered: *Chamaesyce halemanui, Dubautia latifola, Poa siphonoglossa, Stenogyne campanulata,* and *Xylosma crenatum.*

For a continued habitat description of Kauai, see "Habitat Conditions on the Island of Kauai, Hawaii," page 1883.

Historic Range

Hawaiian bluegrass was first collected in 1864 or 1865 from a location north of Waimea Canyon. Since then it has been found in six areas: the rim of Kalalau Valley in Na Pali Coast State Park, Halemanu and Kumuwela Ridge/Kauaikinana drainage in Kokee State Park, Awaawapuhi Trail in Na Pali-Kona Forest Reserve, Kohua Ridge/Mohihi drainage in the forest reserve and Alakai Wilderness Preserve, and Kaholuamanu on privately owned land.

Current Distribution

Hawaiian bluegrass is no longer known from two of its historic sites: Halemanu in Kokee State Park and the privately owned Kaholuamanu. The four surviving populations are spread over a 10-square-mile area. There are about 40 plants remaining in the species population, 80 percent of them at a single major site.

Conservation and Recovery

The major threat to the survival of Hawaiian bluegrass is competition from alien plant species. Daisy fleabane is the primary threat to the Kalalau population. Other alien spe-

cies, including blackberry, banana poka, and ginger threaten population habitats.

In addition, feral pigs threaten to degrade native plant habitat in Na Pali-Kona Forest Reserve and Na Pali Coast State Park. Pigs, which have inhabited the forests of Kauai for over a century, have proven extremely destructive to native Hawaiian plant species. Their rooting destroys vegetative cover, allowing the invasion of alien species. In addition, their feces add nutrients to poor soils which would otherwise favor native species.

Various human activities have promoted the spread of feral pigs on Kauai. In forested areas pigs use paths made by other animals or humans to move into new areas. The logging of the Kokee area in the nineteenth century created a multitude of small trails that led to the southern coast; in the 1920s construction of the Kokee/Kekaha ditch and water diversion system, designed to irrigate lowland sugar cane fields, cut more roads into the area. In the 1930s plum trees were planted in Kokee State Park, providing a food source that attracted the pigs.

In addition to this predictable threat, the low number of existing Hawaiian bluegrass plants and the fact that one population holds 80 percent of surviving plants puts the species at risk of extinction through unpredictible natural or human events.

For a continued discussion of the threats to Hawaiian plants, see page 1831.

Bibliography

Cuddihy, L. W., and C. P. Stone. 1990. *Alteration of Native Hawaiian Vegetation: Effects of Humans, Their Activities and Introductions.* Cooperative National Park Resources Study Unit, University of Hawaii Press, Honolulu.

Macdonald, G. A., A. T. Abbott, and F. L. Peterson. 1983. *Volcanoes in the Sea.* 2d ed. University of Hawaii Press, Honolulu.

Stone, C. P., and J. M. Scott, eds. 1985. *Hawaii's Terrestrial Ecosystems: Preservation and Management.* Cooperative National Park Resources Study Unit, University of Hawaii Press, Honolulu.

U.S. Fish and Wildlife Service. "Endangered and Threatened Wildlife and Plants; Determination of Endangered Status for Six Plants from the Kokee Region, Island of Kauai, Hawaii." *Federal Register* Vol. 57, No. 93. May 13, 1992: 20580-20587.

Wagner, W. L., D. R. Herbst, and S. H. Sohmer. 1990. *Manual of the Flowering Plants of Hawai'i.* University of Hawaii Press and Bishop Museum Press, Honolulu.

Contacts

Regional Office of Endangered Species
U.S. Fish and Wildlife Service
Eastside Federal Complex
911 N.S. 11th Avenue
Portland, Oregon 97232-4181
(503) 231-6118

U.S. Fish and Wildlife Service
300 Ala Moana Boulevard, Room 6307
P.O. Box 50167
Honolulu, Hawaii 96850
(808) 541-2749

Adapted from data compiled by Beacham Publishing for *Beacham's International Threatened, Endangered, and Extinct Species* published on CD ROM.

Poa siphonoglossa
No Common Name

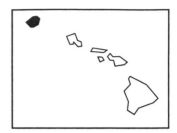

Loyal A. Mehrhoff

Status	Endangered
Listed	May 13, 1992
Family	Poaceae (Grass)
Description	Perennial grass with masses of long, tufted stems.
Habitat	Shaded slopes in moist mountain forest.
Threats	Feral pigs and goats, invasive alien plant species.
Range	Hawaii (Kauai)

Description

Poa siphonoglossa is a perennial grass that grows in masses to a height of 13 feet. The short underground stems (rhizomes) form a hard base for the stems, which are flattened and heavily tufted. The thin leaf blades are less than 4 inches long. The older stems are rushlike, with bladeless sheaths. *Poa siphonoglossa* can be distinguished from Hawaiian bluegrass by its longer stems and shorter panicles.

In 1988 a specimen was collected from Kaulaula Valley in Puu Ka Pele Forest Reserve that shared characteristics of *P. siphonoglossa* and the closely related *P. manii*. Some botanists believe that these two species are actually different growth stages of a single species. Even if this is so, the species would remain extremely rare; *P. manii* was last collected in 1916, and is presumed to be extinct.

Habitat

Poa siphonoglossa is one of a large number of species endemic to the Kokee area in the northwestern part of the Hawaiian island of Kauai. This area is roughly encompassed by the 8-square-mile Kokee State Park. Kauai was formed by a single shield volcano, the crater of which eventually formed the Alakai Swamp. Faulting and erosion on the western end of the swamp created the deeply cut Waimea Canyon, which runs north to south. The canyon is 10 miles long and a mile wide, with steep vertical cliffs more than 2,000 feet high. Kokee State Park lies just on shaded slopes near ridge crests in moist ohia (*Metrosideros polymorpha*) forests at elevations between 3,300 and 3,900 feet.

For a continued habitat description of Kauai, see "Habitat Conditions on the Island of Kauai, Hawaii," page 1883.

Historic Range

This grass was first collected in 1910 at an elevation of about 3,300 feet above Waimea town. It has since been found at only two locations: Kohua Ridge in Na Pali-Kona Forest Reserve and near Kohaluamanu on privately owned land. Specimens collected in 1988 from Kaulaula Valley in Puu Ka Pele Forest Reserve show characteristics of both *Poa siphonoglossa* and *P. manii*.

Current Distribution

Poa siphonoglossa is currently found only at the Kohua Ridge site and the recent Kaulaula Valley site, both on state land. These two locations support a total population of less than 30 plants.

Conservation and Recovery

The main threat to *Poa siphonoglossa* is habitat degradation by feral pigs and goats. This leads to the loss of plants through uprooting, erosion, and the invasion of alien plant species. At the Kohua Ridge site, pig activity has caused extensive erosion of the lower ridge. Disturbed areas are moving up the slope and approaching the *Poa siphonoglossa* population, as well as the site of the Endangered *P. sandvicensis*. The area is also heavily invaded by blackberry (*Rubus argutus*).

Feral pigs, which have inhabited the forests of Kauai for over a century, have proven extremely destructive to native Hawaiian plant species. Their rooting destroys vegetative cover, allowing the invasion of alien species. In addition, the pigs' feces add nutrients to poor soils which would otherwise favor native species.

Various human activities have promoted the spread of feral pigs on Kauai. In forested areas pigs use paths made by other animals or humans to move into new areas. The logging of the Kokee area in the nineteenth century created a multitude of small trails that led to the southern coast; in the 1920s construction of the Kokee/Kekaha ditch and water diversion system, designed to irrigate lowland sugar cane fields, cut more roads into the area. In the 1930s plum trees were planted in Kokee State Park, providing a food source that attracted the pigs.

In addition to this predictible threat, the low number of existing plants puts the species at risk of extinction through unpredictible natural or human events.

For a continued discussion of the threats to Hawaiian plants, see page 1831.

Bibliography

Cuddihy, L. W., and C. P. Stone. 1990. *Alteration of Native Hawaiian Vegetation: Effects of Humans, Their Activities and Introductions.* Cooperative National Park Resources Study Unit, University of Hawaii Press, Honolulu.

Macdonald, G. A., et al. 1983. *Volcanoes in the Sea.* 2d ed. University of Hawaii Press, Honolulu.

Stone, C. P., and J. M. Scott, eds. 1985. *Hawai`i's Terrestrial Ecosystems: Preservation and Management.* Cooperative National Park Resources Study Unit, University of Hawaii Press, Honolulu.

U.S. Fish and Wildlife Service. "Endangered and Threatened Wildlife and Plants;

Determination of Endangered Status for Six Plants from the Kokee Region, Island of Kauai, Hawaii." *Federal Register* Vol. 57, No. 93. May 13, 1992: 20580-20587.

Wagner, W. L., D. R. Herbst, and S. H. Sohmer. 1990. *Manual of the Flowering Plants of Hawai'i*. University of Hawaii Press and Bishop Museum Press, Honolulu.

Contacts

U.S. Fish and Wildlife Service
300 Ala Moana Boulevard, Room 6307
P.O. Box 50167
Honolulu, Hawaii 96850
(808) 541-2749

Adapted from data compiled by Beacham Publishing for *Beacham's International Threatened, Endangered, and Extinct Species* published on CD ROM.

Kaulu

Pteralyxia kauaiensis

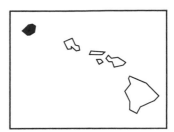

Robert J. Gustafson

Status	Endangered
Listed	February 25, 1994
Family	Apocynaceae (Dogbane)
Description	Small tree with dark green, egg-shaped leaves and pale-yellow, trumpet-shaped flowers.
Habitat	Sides of gulches in diverse lowland mesic forests and in lowland wet forests.
Threats	Habitat destruction by feral goats, pigs, and possibly rats; competition with introduced plants.
Range	Hawaii (Kauai)

Description

Kaulu, *Pteralyxia kauaiensis*, is a small tree growing 10 to 26 feet tall. The leaves are dark green and shiny on the upper surfaces but pale and dull on the lower surfaces. They are generally egg-shaped and usually 4.3 to 8.7 inches long and 1.6 to 2.6 inches wide. The pale yellow flowers are trumpet-shaped, 0.3 to 0.5 inches long, with each of the five lobes 0.1 to 0.2 inches long. The paired fruits, of which usually only one matures, are drupe-like, bright red, and fleshy. The woody endocarp that encloses the single seed has two prominent central wings and two reduced lateral wings. This species differs from the only other taxa in this endemic Hawaiian genus in having reduced lateral wings on the seed.

Habitat

Kaulu typically grows on the sides of gulches in diverse lowland mesic forests and sometimes in lowland wet forests at elevations between 820 and 2,000 feet. Associated vegetation includes hame, lama, lantana, 'oki'a and 'ala'a.

For a continued habitat description of Kauai, see "Habitat Conditions on the Island of Kauai, Hawaii," page 1883.

Historic Range

Historically, kaulu was known from the Wahiawa Mountains in the southern portion of Kauai.

Current Distribution

This species is now known from the

following scattered locations on private and state land on Kauai at elevations between 820 and 2,00 feet: Mahanaloa-Kuia Valley in Kuia NAR; Haeleele Valley; Na Pali Coast State Park; Limahuli Valley; the Koaie branch of Waimea Canyon; Haupu Range; Wailua River; and Moloaa Forest Reserve. There is an undocumented sighting of one individual at Makaleha, above the town of Kapaa.

Conservation and Recovery

The major threats to Kaulu are habitat destruction by feral animals and competition with introduced plants. Animals affecting the survival of this species include feral goats, pigs, and possibly rats, which may eat the fruits. Fire and over-collecting for scientific purposes could threaten some populations. Introduced plants competing with this species include common guava, daisy fleabane, kukui, lantana, strawberry guava, and ti.

The recovery of this and most other Hawaiian species depends on how well management practices can be implemented. The habitat of this and other Hawaiian species has undergone extreme alteration because of past and present land management practices, including deliberately introducing alien animals and plants, and agricultural and recreational development. To understand the recovery problems facing this species, it is necessary to understand the long-term causes of habitat destruction.

For a continued discussion of the threats to Hawaiian plants, see page 1831.

Bibliography

U.S. Fish and Wildlife Service. "Endangered and Threatened Wildlife and Plant; Determination of Endangered or Threatened Status for 24 Plants from the Island of Kauai, HI." *Federal Register* Vol. 59, No. 38. February 25, 1994: 9304-9329.

Contacts

U.S. Fish and Wildlife Service
300 Ala Moana Boulevard, Room 6307
P.O. Box 50167
Honolulu, HI 96850
(808) 541-2749

Adapted from data compiled by Beacham Publishing for *Beacham's International Threatened, Endangered, and Extinct Species* published on CD ROM.

Schiedea spergulina var. leiopoda
No Common Name

Robert J. Gustafson

Status	Endangered
Listed	February 25, 1994
Family	Caryophyllaceae (Pink)
Description	Tall subshrub with wide, one-veined, narrow, opposite leaves and clusters of three green and purple tinged flowers.
Habitat	Bare rock outcrops or sparsely vegetated portions of rocky cliffs or cliff bases in diverse lowland mesic forests.
Threats	Feral goats, competition from alien plants, limited numbers.
Range	Hawaii (Kauai)

Description

Schiedea spergulina var. *leiopoda* is a tall subshrub that grows 1 to 2 feet. The opposite leaves are very narrow, usually 1.2 to 2.6 inches long and about 0.04 inches wide, one-veined, and attached directly to the stem. The flowers are unisexual, with male and female flowers on different plants. Flowers occur in compact clusters of three. There are usually five green-and-purple tinged sepals. The capsular fruits are about 0.08 to 0.12 inches long and contain nearly smooth, kidney-shaped seeds. Of the 22 species in this endemic genus, only 2 other species have smooth seeds. This species differs from those two in having very compact flower clusters. The two weakly defined varieties differ primarily in the degree of hairiness.

Habitat

This species is usually found on bare rock outcrops or sparsely vegetated portions of rocky cliffs or cliff bases in diverse lowland mesic forests at elevations between 590 and 3,000 feet. Associated vegetation includes ko'oko'olau, kumuniu, and 'ala'ala wainui.

For a continued habitat description of Kauai, see "Habitat Conditions on the Island of Kauai, Hawaii," page 1883.

Historic Range

Historically, this species was found on a ridge on the east side of Hanapepe on Kauai.

Current Distribution

One population of 50 to 100 individuals of this variety is now known to grow in

Lawai Valley on Kauai on privately owned land.

Conservation and Recovery

Threats to this species are habitat destruction by feral goats and competition with introduced plants. Variety *leiopoda* competes with koa haole, lantana, and Mauritius hemp. Individuals are also damaged and destroyed by rock slides. This variety is potentially threatened by pesticide use in nearby sugarcane fields; and by stochastic extinction and reduced reproductive vigor as a result of limited numbers.

The recovery of this and most other Hawaiian species depends on how well management practices can be implemented. The habitat of this and other Hawaiian species has undergone extreme alteration because of past and present land management practices, including deliberately introducing alien animals and plants, and agricultural and recreational development. To understand the recovery problems facing this species, it is necessary to understand the long-term causes of habitat destruction.

For a continued discussion of the threats to Hawaiian plants, see page 1831.

Bibliography

U.S. Fish and Wildlife Service. "Endangered and Threatened Wildlife and Plant; Determination of Endangered or Threatened Status for 24 Plants from the Island of Kauai, HI." *Federal Register* Vol. 59, No. 38. February 25, 1994: 9304-9329.

Contacts

U.S. Fish and Wildlife Service
300 Ala Moana Boulevard, Room 6307
P.O. Box 50167
Honolulu, HI 96850
(808) 541-2749

Adapted from data compiled by Beacham Publishing for *Beacham's International Threatened, Endangered, and Extinct Species* published on CD ROM.

Schiedea spergulina var. spergulina

No Common Name

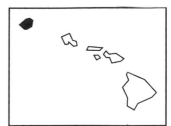

Loyal A. Mehrhoff

Status	Threatened
Listed	February 25, 1994
Family	Caryophyllaceae (Pink)
Description	Tall subshrub with wide, one-veined, narrow, opposite leaves and clusters of three green and purple tinged flowers.
Habitat	Bare rock outcrops or sparsely vegetated portions of rocky cliffs or cliff bases in diverse lowland mesic forests.
Threats	Feral goats, competition from alien plants, limited numbers.
Range	Hawaii (Kauai)

Description

Schiedea spergulina var. *spergulina* is a tall subshrub that grows 1 to 2 feet. The opposite leaves are very narrow, usually 1.2 to 2.6 inches long and about 0.04 inches wide, one-veined, and attached directly to the stem. The flowers are unisexual, with male and female flowers on different plants. Flowers occur in compact clusters of three. There are usually five green-and-purple tinged sepals. The capsular fruits are about 0.08 to 0.12 inches long and contain nearly smooth, kidney-shaped seeds. Of the 22 species in this endemic genus, only 2 other species have smooth seeds. This species differs from those two in having very compact flower clusters. The two weakly defined varieties differ primarily in the degree of hairiness.

Habitat

This species is usually found on bare rock outcrops or sparsely vegetated portions of rocky cliffs or cliff bases in diverse lowland mesic forests at elevations between 590 and 3,000 feet. Associated vegetation includes 'ahinahina, Chinaberry, lantana, Sacramento burr, and kulu'i.

For a continued habitat description of Kauai, see "Habitat Conditions on the Island of Kauai, Hawaii," page 1883.

Historic Range

This variety, more numerous than *Schiedea spergulina* var. *leiopoda*, was once found in

Olokele Canyon but is now known from Kalalau Rim and four locations in Waimea Canyon on state land.

Current Distribution

One population contains only five plants, whereas others number in the thousands. However, these populations are estimated to total no more than 5,000 individuals.

Conservation and Recovery

Threats to this species are habitat destruction by feral goats and competition with introduced plants. Variety *spergulina* competes with daisy fleabane and lantana. The area in which this variety grows is used heavily by feral goats, and there is evidence that plants are being browsed and trampled.

The intensity of threats and the small number of populations known for variety leiopoda indicate that this species is in serious danger of extinction.

The recovery of this and most other Hawaiian species depends on how well management practices can be implemented. The habitat of this and other Hawaiian species has undergone extreme alteration because of past and present land management practices, including deliberately introducing alien animals and plants, and agricultural and recreational development. To understand the recovery problems facing this species, it is necessary to understand the long-term causes of habitat destruction.

For a continued discussion of the threats to Hawaiian plants, see page 1831.

Bibliography

U.S. Fish and Wildlife Service. "Endangered and Threatened Wildlife and Plant; Determination of Endangered or Threatened Status for 24 Plants from the Island of Kauai, HI." *Federal Register* Vol. 59, No. 38. February 25, 1994: 9304-9329.

Contacts

U.S. Fish and Wildlife Service
300 Ala Moana Boulevard, Room 6307
P.O. Box 50167
Honolulu, HI 96850
(808) 541-2749

Adapted from data compiled by Beacham Publishing for *Beacham's International Threatened, Endangered, and Extinct Species* published on CD ROM.

Popolo 'aiakeakua

Solanum sandwicense

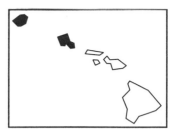

Robert J. Gustafson

Status	Endangered
Listed	February 25, 1994
Family	Solanaceae (Nightshade)
Description	Large sprawling shrub with oval leaves, and up to 40 white flowers, grouped in threes, with a purplish stripe.
Habitat	Open, sunny areas at higher elevations in diverse lowland and drier portions of montane mesic forests.
Threats	Pigs, alien plants, human impact, natural disaster, low populations.
Range	Hawaii (Oahu, Kauai)

Description

Popolo 'aiakeakua, *Solanum sandwicense*, is a large sprawling shrub that grows up to 13 feet tall. The younger branches are more densely hairy than older branches. The oval leaves are usually 4 to 6 inches long and 2 to 5.5 inches wide and have up to four lobes along the margins. Leaf stalks are 0.8 to 1.6 inches long. On the flowering stem, a few to as many as 40 flowers are grouped in threes, with each flower on a stalk about 0.6 inches long bent at the end so that the flower faces downward. The corolla is white with a faint purplish stripe, each lobe is curved somewhat backward. Stamens are attached low on the corolla tube, with anthers curved inward. The fruit is a berry 0.5 to 0.6 inches in diameter, black when ripe. This species differs from others in the genus in having dense hairs on young plant parts, a greater height, and its lack of prickles.

Habitat

This species is typically found in open, sunny areas at elevations between 2,500 and 4,000 feet in diverse lowland to montane mesic forests, and occasionally in wet forests. Associated vegetation includes koa, 'ohi'a, uluhe, and wet forest plants such as kopiko, ho'i'o, and more common *Melicope* species (alani).

For a continued habitat description, see "Habitat Conditions on the Island of Kauai," page 1883; and "Habitat Conditions on the Island of Oahu," page 2031.

Historic Range

Historically, *S. sandwicensis* was known from widely scattered populations throughout the Waianae Mountains and southern portions of the Koolau Mountains on Oahu. On Kauai, this species was known from locations in the Kokee regions bounded by Kalalau Valley to the north, Milolii Ridge to the west, and Kawaikoi to the east, extending southward to the Hanapepe River.

Current Distribution

On Oahu, this species is known from a single population on privately owned land in what is now Honouliuli Preserve. One other population was destroyed by a landslide in 1986.

The Kauai populations are on private and state land and most are from Kokee and Na Pali Coast State Park. Of the 12 known populations, only four are currently extant, and number about 20 plants.

Conservation and Recovery

The major threats to populations on Kauai are habitat degradation by feral pigs and competition with alien plants, especially banana poka, prickly Florida blackberry, strawberry guava, kahili ginger and Japanese honeysuckle. The species is also threatened by fire, over-collecting for scientific purposes, and stochastic extinction and reduced reproductive vigor as a result of limited numbers.

All Oahu populations except one are now apparently extinct, the result of habitat being destroyed by urbanization, landslides, feral pigs, and alien weeds.

The recovery of this and most other Hawaiian species depends on how well management practices can be implemented. The habitat of this and other Hawaiian species has undergone extreme alteration because of past and present land management practices, including deliberately introducing alien animals and plants, and agricultural and recreational development. To understand the recovery problems facing this species, it is necessary to understand the long-term causes of habitat destruction.

For a continued discussion of the threats to Hawaiian plants, see page 1831.

Bibliography

U.S. Fish and Wildlife Service. "Endangered and Threatened Wildlife and Plant; Determination of Endangered or Threatened Status for 24 Plants from the Island of Kauai, HI." *Federal Register* Vol. 59, No. 38. February 25, 1994: 9304-9329.

Contacts

U.S. Fish and Wildlife Service
300 Ala Moana Boulevard, Room 6307
P.O. Box 50167
Honolulu, HI 96850
(808) 541-2749

Adapted from data compiled by Beacham Publishing for *Beacham's International Threatened, Endangered, and Extinct Species* published on CD ROM.

Stenogyne campanulata
No Common Name

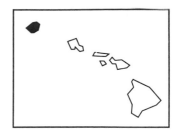

Ken Wood, National Tropical Botanical Garden

Status	Endangered
Listed	May 13, 1992
Family	Lamiaceae (Mint)
Description	Hairy vine with serrated, ovate leaves and clusters of tubular, white flowers with purple lobes.
Habitat	North-facing cliffs.
Threats	Feral goats and pigs, invasive alien plant species.
Range	Hawaii (Kauai)

Description

Stenogyne campanulata is a vine in the mint family with square, hairy stems. The hairy, serrated leaves are broadly ovate, about 2 inches long, and 1 inch wide. The white tubular flowers, about 0.5 inch long, have short purple lobes and occur in clusters of six at the leaf axils. Although the fruits have never been described, those of all other members of the genus are fleshy nutlets. It is distinguished by its large, broadly bell-shaped calyces that nearly enclose the relatively small, straight corollas, and by small calyx teeth that are half as long as wide.

Habitat

Stenogyne campanulata is one of large number of species endemic to the Kokee area in the northwestern part of the Hawaiian island of Kauai. This area is roughly encompassed by the 8-square-mile Kokee State Park. Kauai was formed by a single shield volcano, the crater of which eventually formed the Alakai Swamp. Faulting and erosion on the western end of the swamp created the deeply cut Waimea Canyon, which runs north to south. The canyon is ten miles long and a mile wide, with steep vertical cliffs more than 2,000 feet high. Kokee State Park lies just north of Waimea Canyon, and has the Alakai Swamp to the east, the steep cliffs of the Na Pali coast to the north, and the drier leeward ridges to the west. *Stenogyne campanulata* is found only on the nearly vertical rock face of north-facing cliff below the rim of Kalalau Valley, just north of Kokee State Park, at an elevation of about 3,700 feet.

Five other plant species endemic to the Kokee region are listed as Endangered: *Chamaesyce halemanui*, *Dubautia latifola*, *Poa siphonoglossa*, *Poa sandvicensis*, and *Xylosma crenatum.*

For a continued habitat description of Kauai, see "Habitat Conditions on the Island of Kauai, Hawaii," page 1883.

Historic Range

The species was discovered in 1986 at the Kalalau Valley cliff site in Na Pali Coast State Park. It has not been found at any other location.

Current Distribution

Known only from a single location on state land, the species' population is estimated at about 50 plants, restricted to an area of about 500 square feet.

Conservation and Recovery

The primary threat to the survival of *Stenogyne campanulata* is habitat disturbance by feral goats and pigs. Goats consume plants and eliminate native vegetation, allowing the expansion of alien plant species. The fact that *Stenogyne campanulata* now occurs only on a virtually inaccessible cliff site suggests that it may have been eliminated from more accessible sites by browsing goats.

Feral pigs, which have inhabited the forests of Kauai for over a century, have proven extremely destructive to native Hawaiian plant species. Their rooting destroys vegetative cover, allowing the invasion of alien species. In addition, their feces adds nutrients to poor soils which would otherwise favor native species. At its only known site *Stenogyne campanulata* is threatened by competition from daisy fleabane (*Erigeron karvinskianus*).

Various human activities have promoted the spread of feral pigs on Kauai. In forested areas pigs use paths made by other animals or humans to move into new areas. The logging of the Kokee area in the nineteenth century created a multitude of small trails that led to the southern coast; in the 1920s construction of the Kokee/Kekaha ditch and water diversion system, designed to irrigate lowland sugarcane fields, cut more roads into the area. In the 1930s plum trees were planted in Kokee State Park, providing a food source that attracted feral pigs.

In addition to these predictable threats, the low number of existing *Stenogyne campanulata* plants and the fact that they are concentrated in a single population puts the species at risk of extinction through unpredictable events.

For a continued discussion of the threats to Hawaiian plants, see page 1831.

Bibliography

Cuddihy, L. W., and C. P. Stone. 1990. *Alteration of Native Hawaiian Vegetation: Effects of Humans, Their Activities and Introductions.* Cooperative National Park Resources Study Unit, University of Hawaii Press, Honolulu.

Macdonald, G. A., A. T. Abbott, and F. L. Peterson. 1983. *Volcanoes in the Sea.* 2d ed. University of Hawaii Press, Honolulu.

Stone, C. P., and J. M. Scott, eds. 1985. *Hawai'i's Terrestrial Ecosystems: Preservation and Management.* Cooperative National Park Resources Study Unit, University of Hawaii Press, Honolulu.

U.S. Fish and Wildlife Service. "Endangered and Threatened Wildlife and Plants; Determination of Endangered Status for Six Plants from the Kokee Region, Island of Kauai, Hawaii." *Federal Register* Vol. 57, No. 93. May 13, 1992: 20580-20587.

Wagner, W. L., D. R. Herbst, and S. H. Sohmer. 1990. *Manual of the Flowering Plants of Hawai'i*. University of Hawaii Press and Bishop Museum Press, Honolulu.

Contacts

Regional Office of Endangered Species
U.S. Fish and Wildlife Service
Eastside Federal Complex
911 N.S. 11th Avenue
Portland, Oregon 97232-4181
(503) 231-6118

U.S. Fish and Wildlife Service
300 Ala Moana Boulevard, Room 6307
P.O. Box 50167
Honolulu, Hawaii 96850
(808) 541-2749

Adapted from data compiled by Beacham Publishing for *Beacham's International Threatened, Endangered, and Extinct Species* published on CD ROM.

Dwarf Iliau

Wilkesia hobdyi

Derral Herbst

Status	Endangered
Listed	June 22, 1992
Family	Asteraceae (Aster)
Description	Shrub that branches from the base with narrow leaves at the tip of each branch.
Habitat	Cliff faces and north-facing vertical rock outcrops on Kauai.
Threats	Habitat degradation and predation by feral goats.
Range	Hawaii (Kauai)

Description

Dwarf iliau is a shrub about 60 centimeters tall that branches from the base. The tip of each branch possesses a tuft of narrow leaves which are about 1.3 centimeters wide and 7.5 to 15 centimeters long. The whorls leaves are joined together in a short sheathing section at their bases. The flower heads are in clusters of about 25 to 45 centimeters long. Each head is cream colored and about 2 centimeters in diameter.

Habitat

Dwarf illiau grows on cliff faces and north-facing nearly vertical rock outcrops on Kauai, Hawaii. This island is the fourth largest island in the State. It is 33 miles long and 25 miles wide. The island rises to its highest point, 5,170 feet, at Kawaikini Peak, which is near the center of the island. The Kauai volcano is believed to have formed late in the Tertiary period. After the completion of the Kauai shield cone, there was a long period of erosion during which no volcanic activity occurred. The Koloa volcanics occurred later and covered many of the eroded areas. Waves cut high cliffs around the island and streams cut deep canyons.

For a continued habitat description of Kauai, see "Habitat Conditions on the Island of Kauai, Hawaii," page 1883.

Historic Range and Current Distribution

Dwarf illiau is known to occur on Polihale Ridge and adjacent Kaawaiki ridge, Kauai. A third poulation was discovered on a cliff face in Waiahuakua Valley in 1988. All populations occur on state-owned lands. Two populations are on Puu Ka Pele Forest Reserve and others are known from Hono O Na Pali Natural Area Reserve and the Na Pali Coast State Park. The three populations contain 360-450 individuals.

Conservation and Recovery

Like all of the Islands of Hawaii, the plant fauna of Oahu has currently fallen vulnerable to habitat degradation and/or predation by wild, feral, or domestic animals (goats, pigs, and cattle); competition for space, light, water, and nutrients by naturalized, exotic species; habitat loss due to fires; human recreational activities; and military exercises.

For a continued discussion of the threats to Hawaiian plants, see page 1831.

Bibliography

U.S. Fish and Wildlife Service. "Endangered and Threatened Wildlife and Plants; Determination of Endangered for *Wilkesia hobdyi* (Dwarf iliau), a Hawaiian Plant." *Federal Register* Vol. 57, No. 120, June 22, 1992: 27859-27862.

Contacts

Pacific Islands Ecological Services
Field Office
Room 6307, 300 Ala Moana Blvd.
Honolulu, HI 96850
Phone: 808-541-2749
FAX: 808-541-2756

Regional Office
Eastside Federal Complex
911 N.S. 11th Avenue
Portland, OR 97232-4181
Phone: 503-231-6118

The Nature Conservancy of Hawaii
Suite 201, 1116 Smith Street
Honolulu, HI 96817
Phone: 808-537-4508
FAX: 808-545-2019

Adapted from data compiled by the Threatened and Endangered Species Information Institute (13950 W. 20th Ave., Golden, CO 80401) for *Beacham's International Threatened, Endangered, and Extinct Species* published on CD ROM, available from Beacham Publishing.

Xylosma crenatum
No Common Name

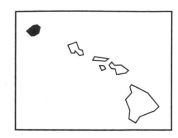

Marie Bruegmann

Status	Endangered
Listed	May 13, 1992
Family	Flacourtiaceae (Flacourtia)
Description	Tree with oval, leathery, roundly toothed leaves.
Habitat	Moist mountain forest.
Threats	Low numbers.
Range	Hawaii (Kauai)

Description

Xylosma crenatum is a tree with dark grey bark that grows to a height of 40 feet. The oval to elliptical-oval leaves, 4 to 8 inches long and 2.5 to 4 inches wide, are somewhat leathery, roundly toothed, and moderately hairy underneath. The species is dioeceous, with individual trees producing either male or female flowers. The male flowers have not been described. Female flowers occur in clusters of 3 to 11 per leaf axils. They consist of four short oval sepals; petals are absent. More coarsely toothed leaf edges and hairy undersides of the leaves distinguish *X. crenatum* from the other Hawaiian members of this genus. The species has also been known by the name *Antidesma crenatum*.

Habitat

Xylosma crenatum is one of a large number of species endemic to the Kokee area in the northwestern part of the Hawaiian island of Kauai. This area is roughly encompassed by the 8-square-mile Kokee State Park. Kauai was formed by a single shield volcano, the crater of which eventually formed the Alakai Swamp. Faulting and erosion on the western end of the swamp created the deeply cut Waimea Canyon, which runs north to south. The canyon is 10 miles long and a mile wide, with steep vertical cliffs more than 2,000 feet high. Kokee State Park lies just north of Waimea Canyon, and has the Alakai Swamp to the east, the steep cliffs of the Na Pali coast to the north, and the drier leeward ridges to the west. *Xylosma crenatum* is found in moist mountain forest dominated by ohia (*Metrosideros polymorpha*) and koa (*Acacia koa*) at elevations between 3,200 to 3,500 feet.

Five other plant species endemic to the Kokee region are federally listed as endangered: *Chamaesyce halemanui, Dubautia latifola,* Hawaiian bluegrass (*Poa sandvicensis*), *Poa siphonoglossa,* and *Stenogyne campanulata.*

For a continued habitat description of Kauai, see "Habitat Conditions on the Island of Kauai, Hawaii," page 1883.

Historic Range

Xylosma crenatum was first collected (but misidentified) in 1917 on the west side of the Waimea drainage basin. In 1968 it was again collected along the Mohihi Stream near the Alakai Swamp. Its only other known location was along the upper Nualolo Trail in Kuia Natural Area Reserve, just west of Kokee State Park.

Current Distribution

Only one *Xylosma crenatum* tree is known to exist; it is found along Mohihi Road between Waiakoali and Mohihi drainages in Na Pali-Kona Forest Reserve.

Conservation and Recovery

In 1982 Hurricane Iwa caused extensive damage to vegetation in the Kokee region of Kauai. It is believed that the two trees at the Nualolo Trail site were destroyed by the storm. Since only one male *Xylosma crenatum* is now known to exist, regeneration of the species cannot occur unless at least one female tree is discovered.

A single human or natural event could render the species extinct. In 1989 freshly bulldozed earth from road maintenance was found next to the tree.

The recovery of this and most other Hawaiian species depends on how well management practices can be implemented. The habitat of this and other Hawaiian species has undergone extreme alteration because of past and present land management practices, including deliberately introducing alien animals and plants, and agricultural and recreational development. To understand the recovery problems facing this species, it is necessary to understand the long-term causes of habitat destruction.

For a continued discussion of the threats to Hawaiian plants, see page 1831.

Bibliography

U.S. Fish and Wildlife Service. "Endangered and Threatened Wildlife and Plants; Determination of Endangered Status for Six Plants from the Kokee Region, Island of Kauai, Hawaii." *Federal Register* Vol. 57, No. 93. May 13, 1992: 20580-20587.

Wagner, W. L., D. R. Herbst, and S. H. Sohmer. 1990. *Manual of the Flowering Plants of Hawai'i.* University of Hawaii Press and Bishop Museum Press, Honolulu.

Contacts

U.S. Fish and Wildlife Service
300 Ala Moana Boulevard, Room 6307
P.O. Box 50167
Honolulu, Hawaii 96850
(808) 541-2749

Adapted from data compiled by Beacham Publishing for *Beacham's International Threatened, Endangered, and Extinct Species* published on CD ROM.

HAWAIIAN PLANTS: MAUI

Habitat Conditions on the Island of Maui, Hawaii

On May 15, 1992, the U.S. Fish and Wildlife Service listed as endangered or threatened fifteen plants from the island of Maui, Hawaii. Habitat conditions on Maui are described here rather than being repeated in each of the species accounts.

Acaena exigua
Alectryon macrococcus
Argyroxiphium sandwicense ssp. *macrocephalum*
Bidens micrantha ssp. *kalealaha*
Clermontia oblongifolia ssp. *mauiensis*
Cyanea lobata
Cyanea mceldowneyi
Cyrtandra munroi
Geranium multiflorum
Hedyotis coriacea
Huperzia mannii
Lipochaeta kamolensis
Lysimachia lydgatei
Melicope mucronulata
Schiedea haleakalensis

The islands of Hawaii are of volcanic origin and consist of coastal plains, upland slopes and mountain ranges and summits. Maui, the second largest island in the State, is 48 miles long and 26 miles wide. The land area is 465,920 acres. This island was formed from the remnants of two large shield volcanoes: the older West Maui volcano on the west and the larger but much younger Haleakala volcano on the east. These two volcanoes and the connecting isthmus formed by lava flows make up the three main areas: West Maui, East Maui, and Central Maui. Steam erosion has cut deep valleys and ridges into the originally shield-shaped West Maui volcano, and created a deeply dissected volcano that rises to 5,788 feet at Puu Kukui. With an average annual rainfall of 400 inches, Puu Kukui is the second wettest spot in Hawaii.

Having erupted just 200 years ago, East Maui's Haleakala (10,023 feet in elevation) has retained its classic shield shape and lacks the diverse vegetation typical of the older and more eroded West Maui mountain. Annual rainfall on Haleakala is about 350 inches, with its windward slope receiving the most precipitation. However, Haleakala's crater is dry cinder desert because it is below the level at which the precipitation develops and is sheltered from moisture-laden winds.

The central part of West Maui consists of canyons and steep ridges and is not easily accessible. It is surrounded by a moderately sloping, smooth narrow belt.

Central Maui is the isthmus that connects West and East Maui. This area is smooth and nearly level. It is used mainly for sugarcane. Much of the isthmus is covered with alluvium. Most of the soils are Andepts, Ustolls, and Humults. Andepts formed in regoliths consisting of volcanic ash or pumice. The soils have a low bulk density and therefore are light and fluffy. Most are acid, and some are strongly acid. Although not all these soils are well drained, none of them is hydric. Humults are the freely drained Ultisols that have a high content of organic matter. Ustolls are well drained and moderately well drained Mollisols of subhumid and semiarid regions. The moisture regime is predominantly ustic.

Along with this area's large mass is its

vast number of resource areas and subsequent land uses. Eight total, these resource areas comprised a variety of activities including urban development, military installation, crops, tourism, heavily vegetated native rain forests, wildlife, and pasture.

Maui supports a wide range of vegetation communities (shrublands, forests and bogs), elevation zones (lowland to alpine), and moisture regimes (dry to wet).

The *lowland dry vegetation* type occurs on the leeward side of the main Hawaiian Islands at an elevation of 15 to 2,000 feet. The climate of this vegetation is distinctly seasonal, with hot, dry summers and winter rainfall, usually less than 40 inches but sometimes ranging up to 80 inches annually. The soils range from weathered silty loam to stony clay; rocky ledges with very shallow soil and recent, little-weathered lava are present.

The *lowland mesic shrubland* and forest habitats on West Maui and other Hawaiian islands occur mainly at elevations between 100 and 5,300 feet in areas topographically unsuitable for agriculture. Annual precipitation ranges from less than 40 to 150 inches, falling mostly in the winter months. This community occurs on diverse, well-weathered and well-drained substrates, ranging from rocky, shallow, organic muck soils to steep, rocky talus slopes, shallow rocky soils on steep slopes, to deep soil over soft weathered rock and gravelly alluvium in gulches and erosional plains.

The *lowland wet forest* habitat is composed primarily of native vegetation with canopies from 10 to 130 feet high in sheltered, well-drained, leeward slopes at elevations between 300 and 3,900 feet. Annual rainfall ranges from 60 to 200 inches. The substrate ranges from clay or organic muck over 'a'a lava to volcanic ash beds or young lava flows.

The windward slopes contain the *montane wet communities*, which include bogs characterized by thick peat overlaying an impervious clay substrate with hummocks of sedges and grasses, stunted trees, and shrubs. The montane wet forests occur on Molokai, Maui, and Hawaii (the Big Island) at elevations between 3,900 and 7,200 feet, mainly on steep windward valley walls. The vegetation type is characterized by rich soil development, high rainfall of 100 inches annually, high diversity, and a rich understory.

The *subalpine dry vegetation* type occurs on East Maui (and the Big Island) between 5,600 and 9,800 feet. The substrate is of cinder or weathered volcanic ash or bare lava with little or no soil development, partly due to the low annual precipitation of 15 to 40 inches. Periodic frost and occasional snow cover occur on the upper limits.

The *alpine dry shrubland* community occurs above 9,800 feet. The precipitation is only 30 to 50 inches annually. The community is subjected to frequent frosts and arid extremes, limiting vegetation (grasses, mosses, and alpine-adapted shrubs) to near the lower boundary of the community on bare gravel, debris, and cinders.

Liliwai
Acaena exigua

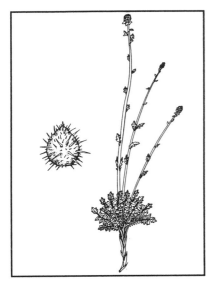

Yevonn Wilson-Ramsey

Status	Endangered
Listed	May 15, 1992
Family	Rosaceae (Rose)
Description	Perennial herb with flowering leafy stems and leaves that are glossy above and whitish below; the cone-shaped fruit is pale brown.
Habitat	Bogs with thick peat, grasses, stunted trees, and shrubs.
Threats	Habitat degradation by feral animals; competing species.
Range	Hawaii (Maui)

Description

Liliwai, *Acaena exigua*, is a perennial herb with leafy stems 0.4 to 1.6 inches long. The flowering stems of this plant are 2 to 6 inches long. The leaves are about 0.4 to 1 inch long, comprising 6 to 17 oval leaflets, which are glossy above and whitish beneath. The petalless flowers are in short, dense spikes 0.2 to 0.4 inches long. The receptacle is urn-shaped and encloses the fruit, which is a pale brown, cone-shaped achene.

Habitat

Liliwai grows in the Metrosideros ('ohi'a) Montane Bog Community, characterized by thick peat overlaying an impervious clay substrate with hummocks of sedges and grasses, stunted trees, and shrubs. The vegetation type is characterized by rich soil development, high rainfall of 100 inches annually, high diversity, and a rich understory. Associated species include: *Deschampsia nubigena, Dichanthelium* spp. *Oreobolus furcatus, Medtrosideros polymorpha* and *Vaccinium.*

For a continued habitat description of Maui, see "Habitat Conditions on the Island of Maui, Hawaii," page 1955.

Historic Range

Historically, Liliwai was known from Puu Kukui on West Maui and from Mount Waialeale on Kauai.

Current Distribution

In 1973 only a single individual was

extant. The species has not been seen since. Given the low population numbers, this species is immediately threatened by low genetic variation and gene pool. Stochastic events or severe climatic changes would surely mean the extirpation of the species.

Conservation and Recovery

The plant fauna of Maui has currently fallen vulnerable to habitat degradation and/or predation by wild, feral, or domestic animals (goats, pigs, sheep, and cattle); competition for space, light, water, and nutrients by naturalized, exotic species; habitat loss due to fires; human recreational activities; and military exercises.

The recovery of this and most other Hawaiian species depends on how well management practices can be implemented. The habitat of this and other Hawaiian species has undergone extreme alteration because of past and present land management practices, including deliberately introducing alien animals and plants, and agricultural and recreational development. To understand the recovery problems facing this species, it is necessary to understand the long-term causes of habitat destruction.

For a continued discussion of the threats to Hawaiian plants, see page 1831.

Bibliography

U.S. Fish and Wildlife Service. "Endangered and Threatened Wildlife and Plants; Determination of Endangered or Threatened Status for 15 Plants from the Island of Maui, Hawaii." *Federal Register.* Vol. 57, No. 95, May 15, 1992: 20772-20787.

Contacts

Pacific Islands Ecological Services Field Office
Room 6307, 300 Ala Moana Blvd.
Honolulu, HI 96850
Phone: 808-541-2749
FAX: 808-541-2756

Adapted from data compiled by the Threatened and Endangered Species Information Institute (13950 W. 20th Ave., Golden, CO 80401) for *Beacham's International Threatened, Endangered, and Extinct Species* published on CD ROM, available from Beacham Publishing.

Mahoe
Alectryon macrococcus

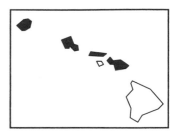

John Obata

Status	Endangered
Listed	May 15, 1992
Family	Sapindaceae (Soapwort)
Description	Tall tree with reddish brown branches and oval, glossy, smooth leaves with netted veins; the fruit is hard and spherical, enclosing a single glossy brown seed.
Habitat	Dry slopes or in gulches in north-facing, dry to mesic lowland forests
Threats	Habitat destruction by feral animals; insects and rodents.
Range	Hawaii (Maui, Molokai, Kauai, Oahu)

Description

Mahoe, *Alectryon macrococcus*, is a tall tree that grows to 36 feet. There are currently two varieties of this species, *A. macrococcus* var. *macrococcus* and *A. macrococcus* var. *auwahiensis*. *A. macrococcus* has reddish brown branches and its leaves are usually 20 to 55 centimeters long. The leaves have five pairs of egg-shaped, slightly asymmetrical leaflets, each 10 to 28 cm long. The leaves are glossy and smooth above and have a conspicuous netted pattern of veins. The lower surfaces of mature leaves possess a dense covering of rust-colored hairs. The flowers may be either bisexual or male. The petalless flowers occur in branched clusters 30 cm long. The single fruit is hard and spherical, enclosing a single glossy brown seed with a red aril. The primary difference between *A. m.* var *auwahiensis* and *A. m.* var.

macrococcus is that *A. m.* var. *macrococcus'* mature leaves are glabrous.

Habitat

This species typically grows on dry slopes or in gulches in north-facing, dry to mesic lowland forests at an elevation of 1,200 to 3,500 feet. The lowland dry vegetation type includes several plant communities and occurs on the leeward side of Maui. The climate of this vegetation type is distinctly seasonal with hot dry summers and winter rainfall, usually less than 100 cm.

For a continued habitat description, see "Habitat Conditions on the Island of Maui," page 1955; "Habitat Conditions on the Island of Oahu," page 2031; "Habitat Conditions on the Island of Molokai," page 1987; and "Habitat Conditions on the Island of Kauai" page 1883.

Historic Range

This variety still occurs on all four islands, but with restricted range. *A. m.* var. *macrococcus* is located on private, State land (Na Pali Coast State Park) and Federal land (Scholfield Barracks, Lualualei Naval Reservation and Makua Military Reservation). *A. m.* var. *auwahiensis* is comprised of a single population of nine individuals on East Maui.

Current Distribution

Historically and presently, *A. m.* var. *auwahiensis* occurs from Auwahi on East Maui on privately owned land, where a single population of nine individuals remains within a 72 acre area on privately owned land. *A. m.* var. *macrococcus* was found historically on Maui, Molokai, Kauai and Oahu, and has a much wider distribution.

The three existing populations on West Maui are along the Honokowai Ditch Trail and in Launiupoko Valley on privately owned land, and total just a few plants. The five extant populations on Molokai are restricted to Puu Kolekole jeep road, Kaunakaki Gulch, and Kamakou Preserve, with a total of six plants. The six populations on Kauai occur in Waimea Canyon and in Na Pali Coast State Park. The distribution of plants of Oahu is spotty, with the most recent sighting in the Waianae Mountains. Most of the 28 populations number only one or two individuals, but two populations number between 50 and 200 individuals. The total number of individuals on Oahu is estimated to be about 400. The entire species currently numbers about 500 individuals.

Conservation and Recovery

This species is vulnerable to infestations by the black twig borer; habitat degradation and/or predation by feral pigs; competition for space, light, water, and nutrients with alien plants, especially molasses grass, kikuyu grass, strawberry guava, and Christmasberry; fire; and the predation of fruits and flowers by rodents. Predation and habitat degradation by cattle and the smaller number of remaining individuals are specific threats to *A. m.* var. *auwahiensis*; whereas goat activity threaten *A. M.* var. *macrococcus*.

Two populations of *A. macrococcus* are located of Federal property (Scholfield Barracks and Lualualei Naval Reservation) and eight populations are on State land leased to Makua Military Reservation. The Army has constructed firebreaks on the Makua Military Reservation to minimize damage from unintentional fires that occasionally result from stray bullets.

The recovery of this and most other Hawaiian species depends on how well management practices can be implemented. The habitat of this and other Hawaiian species has undergone extreme alteration because of past and present land management practices, including deliberately introducing alien animals and plants, and agricultural and recreational development. To understand the recovery problems facing this species, it is necessary to understand the long-term causes of habitat destruction.

For a continued discussion of the threats to Hawaiian plants, see page 1831.

Bibliography

U.S. Fish and Wildlife Service. "Endangered and Threatened Wildlife and Plants; Determination of Endangered or Threatened Status for 15 Plants from the Island of Maui, Hawaii." *Federal Register*. Vol. 57, No. 95, May 15, 1992: 20772-20787.

Contacts

Pacific Islands Ecological Services
Field Office
Room 6307, 300 Ala Moana Blvd.
Honolulu, HI 96850
Phone: 808-541-2749
FAX: 808-541-2756

Adapted from data compiled by the Threatened and Endangered Species Information Institute (13950 W. 20th Ave., Golden, CO 80401) for *Beacham's International Threatened, Endangered, and Extinct Species* published on CD ROM, available from Beacham Publishing.

'Ahinahina
[=Haleakala Silversword]
Argyroxiphium sandwicense ssp. *macrocephalum*

Robert J. Shallenberger   *Color Plate C-3*

Status	Threatened
Listed	May 15, 1992
Family	Asteraceae (Aster)
Description	Perennial with a rosette of daggerlike leaves and a slender stalk bearing pinkish flowers.
Habitat	Barren alpine scrub on volcanic slopes.
Threats	Restricted range; predation by Argentine ants and yellow jackets.
Range	Hawaii (Maui)

Description

The Haleakala silversword is a single stemmed aster. This shrub with a rosette of narrowly sword-shaped leaves possesses a dense mat of silky, silvery hairs which cover the leaves. The narrow, branched flowering stalk is elliptic to lanceolate in outline, 9 to 31 inches wide and 2.3 to 4.9 feet long. This species can be branched or unbranched. The flowering heads are about 1 inch in diameter and have 11 to 42 pink petal-like ray florets. Central disk florets, pink to wine-red at the tip and yellowish at the base, number 120 to 600 per head.

Habitat

This species typically grows on barren cinder cones and young 'a'a lava flows in dry alpine areas at an elevation of 7,200 to 9,800 feet. The precipitation is only 30 to 50 inches annually. The community is subjected to frequent frosts and arid extremes, limiting vegetation (grasses, mosses, and alpine-adapted shrubs) to near the lower boundary of the community on bare gravel, debris, and cinders. Associated shrubs include 'ohi'a, na'ena'e, and pukiawe.

For a continued habitat description of Maui, see "Habitat Conditions on the Island of Maui, Hawaii," page 1955.

Historic Range

This species' present range is believed to be the same as its past distribution on Haleakala National Park within Haleakala Crater.

Current Distribution

There are presently 7 extant populations of this subspecies comprised of about 50,000 individuals. Currently restricted range is the biggest factor inhibiting the Haleakala silversword population success.

Conservation and Recovery

Currently, the greatest threat to this species is its restricted range. One destructive event could extirpate a significant portion of the population. The predation of the plant's pollinators by Argentine ants and yellow jackets threatens its reproductive capability.

The recovery of this and most other Hawaiian species depends on how well management practices can be implemented. The habitat of this and other Hawaiian species has undergone extreme alteration because of past and present land management practices, including deliberately introducing alien animals and plants, and agricultural and recreational development. To understand the recovery problems facing this species, it is necessary to understand the long-term causes of habitat destruction.

For a continued discussion of the threats to Hawaiian plants, see page 1831.

Bibliography

U.S. Fish and Wildlife Service. "Endangered and Threatened Wildlife and Plants; Determination of Endangered or Threatened Status for 15 Plants from the Island of Maui, Hawaii." *Federal Register*. Vol. 57, No. 95, May 15, 1992: 20772-20787.

Contacts

Pacific Islands Ecological Services
Field Office
Room 6307, 300 Ala Moana Blvd.
Honolulu, HI 96850
Phone: 808-541-2749
FAX: 808-541-2756

Adapted from data compiled by the Threatened and Endangered Species Information Institute (13950 W. 20th Ave., Golden, CO 80401) for *Beacham's International Threatened, Endangered, and Extinct Species* published on CD ROM, available from Beacham Publishing.

Ko'oko'olau

Bidens micrantha ssp. *kalealaha*

Arthur Medeiros

Status	Endangered
Listed	May 15, 1992
Family	Asteraceae (Aster)
Description	Erect perennial herb with narrow, tapering leaves and yellow flowers clustered at the top.
Habitat	Open canopy dry montane forests to dry shrublands, on sheer rock walls.
Threats	Habitat destruction by feral animals; alien plant species; low numbers.
Range	Hawaii (Maui)

Description

Ko'oko'olau, *Bidens micrantha* ssp. *kalealaha*, is an erect perennial herb. This aster is slightly woody at the base and 1.6 to 4.9 feet tall. The leaves are 2.4 to 7.5 inches long and usually with three to seven and sometimes nine lanceolate leaflets. The flower heads are arranged at the top of the plant and on side branches in open clusters of 15 to 50. Each flower head is 1 to 1.8 inches in diameter and comprises 5 sterile, yellow ray florets 0.6 to 1.1 inches long and 0.2 to 0.3 inches wide.

Habitat

Bidens micrantha ssp. *kalealaha* is found in open canopy dry montane forests to dry shrublands extending from 1,600 to 9,800 feet

in elevation. Annual precipitation ranges from 10 to 50 inches in seasonally dry montane forests, to about 60 inches in subalpine shrublands. The substrate is comprised mostly of blocky lava flows with little or no soil development. It typically grows on sheer rock walls at an elevation of 5,200 to 7,600 feet. Associated vegetation includes pilo, 'a'ali'i, and na'ena'e.

For a continued habitat description of Maui, see "Habitat Conditions on the Island of Maui, Hawaii," page 1955.

Historic Range and Current Distribution

Historically, this species was known from Lanai and East Maui, and from one collection on West Maui. This taxon presently only occurs on East Maui in Kahua, Manawainui to Wailaulau and in Haleakala National Park on state and federal land. The four known populations, which extend over a distance of about 9.5 by 2 miles, number no more than 2,000 individuals.

Conservation and Recovery

This species is vulnerable to habitat degradation and/or predation by feral goats and cattle; competition for space, light, water, and nutrients by naturalized, exotic species, especially kikuyu grass; and habitat loss due to fires.

The recovery of this and most other Hawaiian species depends on how well management practices can be implemented. The habitat of this and other Hawaiian species has undergone extreme alteration because of past and present land management practices, including deliberately introducing alien animals and plants, and agricultural and recreational development. To understand the recovery problems facing this species, it is necessary to understand the long-term causes of habitat destruction.

For a continued discussion of the threats to Hawaiian plants, see page 1831.

Bibliography

U.S. Fish and Wildlife Service. "Endangered and Threatened Wildlife and Plants; Determination of Endangered or Threatened Status for 15 Plants from the Island of Maui, Hawaii." *Federal Register.* Vol. 57, No. 95, May 15, 1992: 20772-20787.

Contacts

U.S. Fish and Wildlife Service
Regional Office
Eastside Federal Complex
911 N.S. 11th Avenue
Portland, OR 97232-4181
Phone: 503-231-6118

Pacific Islands Ecological Services
Field Office
Room 6307, 300 Ala Moana Blvd.
Honolulu, HI 96850
Phone: 808-541-2749
FAX: 808-541-2756

Adapted from data compiled by the Threatened and Endangered Species Information Institute (13950 W. 20th Ave., Golden, CO 80401) for *Beacham's International Threatened, Endangered, and Extinct Species* published on CD ROM, available from Beacham Publishing.

'Oha'wai

Clermontia oblongifolia ssp. *mauiensis*

Derral Herbst   *Color Plate C-3*

Status	Endangered
Listed	May 15, 1992
Family	Campanulaceae (Bellflower)
Description	Shrub or tree whose leaves are oblong with thickened, rounded teeth and 2-3 flowers that bunch together on a short stalk; the flowers are greenish white or purplish and the fruits are orange.
Habitat	Sides of ridges in 'ohi'a-dominated wet forests.
Threats	Habitat destruction by feral animals; competing plant species.
Range	Hawaii (Maui)

Description

The 'Oha'wai, *Clermontia oblongifolia* ssp *mauiensis*, is a shrub or tree that grows to heights of 6.6 to 23 feet. The leaves are located on petioles and are 1 to 4.5 inches long. These leaves are oblong or elliptic; have thickened, rounded teeth; and reach a length of 3 to 7.5 inches. This plant produces two, or sometimes three, flowers, bunched together on a 0.2 to 1.8 inches long stalk. The flower itself is 2.4 to 3.1 inches long. The calyx and corolla are similar in size and appearance in that each forms an arched tube which is greenish white or purplish on the outside and white or cream-colored on the inside. The orange-colored fruit is a spherical berry. This subspecies is distinguished from other *C. oblongifolia* by its leaf shape; the lengths of its leaves, the leaf stalk, and flower stalk; the shapes of the leaf tip and the flower bud; and the purple or magenta color of the fused stamens.

Habitat

Clermontia oblongifolia ssp. *mauiensis* typically grows on the sides of ridges in 'ohi'a-dominated wet forests at an elevation of 2,800 to 3,000 feet. The montane wet communities occur on the windward slopes, characterized by bogs with thick peat overlaying an impervious clay substrate with hummocks of sedges and grasses, stunted trees, and shrubs, at elevations between 3,900 and 7,200 feet, mainly on steep windward valley walls. The vegetation type is characterized by rich soil development, high rainfall of 100 inches annually, high diversity, and a rich understory.

Historic Range

Historically, this 'Oha'wai was known from Mahana and Kaiholena valleys on Lanai and from Honomanu Valley on Haleakala on East Maui.

Current Distribution

The only known individual of this 'Oha'-wai persists along a trail to Puu Kukui in the Honokowai section of the West Maui Natural Area Reserve on State land.

Conservation and Recovery

Because only a single individual of this species is known to exist, the lack of a genetic pool is likely to result in reduced reproductive vigor, and any collecting will seriously impair its survival. The rooting activities of feral pigs also pose a serious threat.

The plant fauna of Maui and Hawaii has currently fallen vulnerable to habitat degradation and/or predation by wild, feral, or domestic animals (goats, pigs, sheep, and cattle); competition for space, light, water, and nutrients by naturalized, exotic species; habitat loss due to fires; human recreational activities; and military exercises.

The recovery of this and most other Hawaiian species depends on how well management practices can be implemented. The habitat of this and other Hawaiian species has undergone extreme alteration because of past and present land management practices, including deliberately introducing alien animals and plants, and agricultural and recreational development. To understand the recovery problems facing this species, it is necessary to understand the long-term causes of habitat destruction.

For a continued discussion of the threats to Hawaiian plants, see page 1831.

Bibliography

U.S. Fish and Wildlife Service. "Endangered and Threatened Wildlife and Plants; Determination of Endangered or Threatened Status for 15 Plants from the Island of Maui, Hawaii." *Federal Register*. Vol. 57, No. 95, May 15, 1992: 20772-20787.

Contacts

Pacific Islands Ecological Services Field Office
Room 6307, 300 Ala Moana Blvd.
Honolulu, HI 96850
Phone: 808-541-2749
FAX: 808-541-2756

Adapted from data compiled by the Threatened and Endangered Species Information Institute (13950 W. 20th Ave., Golden, CO 80401) for *Beacham's International Threatened, Endangered, and Extinct Species* published on CD ROM, available from Beacham Publishing.

Haha
Cyanea lobata

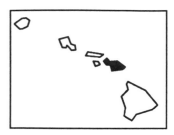

Type Specimen in Cornell Herbarium Joseph E. Rock

Status	Endangered
Listed	May 15, 1992
Family	Campanulaceae (Bellflower)
Description	Sparsely branched shrub with irregularly lobed leaves and a cluster of flowers having greenish white or purplish petals fused into a curved tube.
Habitat	Steep stream banks in mesic lowland forests.
Threats	Habitat destruction by feral animals; competing plant species.
Range	Hawaii (Maui)

Description

This haha, *Cyanea lobata*, grows to 4.3 to 7.5 feet. This shrub has few branches and may be smooth or occasionally rough due to small projections on the stems and lower leaf surfaces. The leaves are 12 to 20 inches long and 4 to 6 inches wide, with 12 to 25 irregular lobes on each side of the leaf. The flowers of *C. lobata* cluster in groups of 5 to 12. These flowers have greenish white or purplish petals fused into a curved tube 2.4 to 2.8 inches long and 0.2 to 0.4 inch wide. The yellow berries are spherical.

Habitat

This species typically grows on steep stream banks in mesic lowland forests at an elevation of 1,800 to 3,000 feet. The lowland mesic shrubland and forest habitats on West Maui and other Hawaiian islands occurs mainly at elevations between 100 and 5,300 feet in areas topographically unsuitable for agriculture. Annual precipitation ranges from less than 40 to 150 inches. The substrate is diverse: shallow rocky soils on steep slopes to deep soils in gulches and erosional plains.

For a continued habitat description of Maui, see "Habitat Conditions on the Island of Maui, Hawaii," page 1955.

Historic Range

C. lobata was historically known from Lanai and scattered locations throughout West Maui from Honokohau to Wailuku Valley.

Current Distribution

A known population of one to four individuals was destroyed in 1990 by a landslide following heavy rains in Waikapu Valley on West Maui. However, because of its wide historic range and its inacessibilty to survey, the plant is still believed extant, although, no report has been made of this species.

Conservation and Recovery

The plant fauna of Maui has currently fallen vulnerable to habitat degradation and/or predation by wild, feral, or domestic animals (goats, pigs, sheep, and cattle); competition for space, light, water, and nutrients by naturalized, exotic species; habitat loss due to fires; human recreational activities; and military exercises.

The recovery of this and most other Hawaiian species depends on how well management practices can be implemented. The habitat of this and other Hawaiian species has undergone extreme alteration because of past and present land management practices, including deliberately introducing alien animals and plants, and agricultural and recreational development. To understand the recovery problems facing this species, it is necessary to understand the long-term causes of habitat destruction.

For a continued discussion of the threats to Hawaiian plants, see page 1831.

Bibliography

U.S. Fish and Wildlife Service. "Endangered and Threatened Wildlife and Plants; Determination of Endangered or Threatened Status for 15 Plants from the Island of Maui, Hawaii." *Federal Register*. Vol. 57, No. 95, May 15, 1992: 20772-20787.

Contacts

Pacific Islands Ecological Services
Field Office
Room 6307, 300 Ala Moana Blvd.
Honolulu, HI 96850
Phone: 808-541-2749
FAX: 808-541-2756

Adapted from data compiled by the Threatened and Endangered Species Information Institute (13950 W. 20th Ave., Golden, CO 80401) for *Beacham's International Threatened, Endangered, and Extinct Species* published on CD ROM, available from Beacham Publishing.

Haha
Cyanea mceldowneyi

Robert J. Gustafson

Status	Endangered
Listed	May 15, 1992
Family	Campanulaceae (Bellflower)
Description	Unbranched shrub with prickly, hardened teeth leaves and a cluster of flowers whose petals are white with purple stripes.
Habitat	Wet montane forests.
Threats	Habitat destruction by feral animals; competing plant species.
Range	Hawaii (Maui)

Description

This haha, *Cyanea mceldowneyi*, is an unbranched shrub, with leaves 8 to 14 inches long. These leaves have wedge-shaped bases, hardened teeth, and occasionally a few short prickles on the upper surface. Immature leaves are distinguished by their shorter length, rounded bases, hardened marginal teeth, and a greater number of prickles. The flowers of *C. mceldowneyi* are a 5 to 7 member cluster with a 0.6 to 1.2 inch stalk. Each flower is on a 0.4 to 0.6 inch long stalk. The petals are white with purple stripes, fused into a curved tube, 1.6 inch long, 0.3 inch wide, and have small prickles on the lobes. Berries have not been observed.

Habitat

This species typically grows in wet montane forests at an elevation of 3,000 to 4,200 feet. Associated plant species include alani, manono, and 'ohi'a. The windward slopes contain the *montane wet communities*, which include bogs characterized by thick peat overlaying an impervious clay substrate with hummocks of sedges and grasses, stunted trees, and shrubs. Montane wet forests occur mainly on steep windward valley walls. The vegetation type is characterized by rich soil development, high rainfall of 100 inches annually, high diversity, and a rich understory.

For a continued habitat description of Maui, see "Habitat Conditions on the Island of Maui, Hawaii," page 1955.

Historic Range

Historically, *C. mceldowneyi* was known from Honomanu on East Maui. This plant remains in Waikamoi on privately owned land.

Current Distribution

There are two known populations of this species about 0.5 miles apart, comprised of a total of less than 30 individuals.

The limited population numbers and restricted range of this species implies a serious potential for extinction from stochastic events. Limited gene pool may depress reproductive vigor, or a single man-caused or natural environmental disturbance could destroy a significant percentage of extant individuals.

Conservation and Recovery

The plant fauna of Maui has currently fallen vulnerable to habitat degradation and/or predation by wild, feral, or domestic animals (goats, pigs, sheep, and cattle); competition for space, light, water, and nutrients by naturalized, exotic species; habitat loss due to fires; human recreational activities; and military exercises.

The recovery of this and most other Hawaiian species depends on how well management practices can be implemented. The habitat of this and other Hawaiian species has undergone extreme alteration because of past and present land management practices, including deliberately introducing alien animals and plants, and agricultural and recreational development. To understand the recovery problems facing this species, it is necessary to understand the long-term causes of habitat destruction.

For a continued discussion of the threats to Hawaiian plants, see page 1831.

Bibliography

U.S. Fish and Wildlife Service. "Endangered and Threatened Wildlife and Plants; Determination of Endangered or Threatened Status for 15 Plants from the Island of Maui, Hawaii." *Federal Register.* Vol. 57, No. 95, May 15, 1992: 20772-20787.

Contacts

Pacific Islands Ecological Services Field Office
Room 6307, 300 Ala Moana Blvd.
Honolulu, HI 96850
Phone: 808-541-2749
FAX: 808-541-2756

Adapted from data compiled by the Threatened and Endangered Species Information Institute (13950 W. 20th Ave., Golden, CO 80401) for *Beacham's International Threatened, Endangered, and Extinct Species* published on CD ROM, available from Beacham Publishing.

Ha'iwale
Cyrtandra munroi

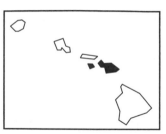

Steve Perlman, National Tropical Botanical Garden

Status	Endangered
Listed	May 15, 1992
Family	Gesneriaceae (Gesneria)
Description	Shrub with elliptic hairy leaves above and velvety, rust-colored hairs underneath; flowers cluster in three, with white petals fused into a tube; white berries are covered with fine hair.
Habitat	Rich, moist talus slopes in wet lowland forests.
Threats	Habitat destruction by feral animals; competing plant species.
Range	Hawaii (Maui, Lanai)

Description

Gesneriaceae are typically herbs and often grow on other plants. The leaves are usually opposite, simple, and exstipulate. The flowers of Gesneriaceae are bisexual, symmetrical, and grow either as solitary inflorescences or in clusters. The fruit is a capsule or berry.

The Ha'iwale, *Cyrtandra munroi*, is a shrub (rare in Gesneriaceae) with typical opposite, elliptic leaves. The leaves are 9.5 to 21 centimeters long and are mostly smooth to moderately hairy on the upper surface and covered with velvety, rust-colored hairs underneath. The flowers are usually arranged in clusters of three on stalks emerging from the leaf axils. The white petals are fused into a tube, 15 to 20 millimeters long. The white berries, covered with fine hair, are somewhat egg-shaped and 1.8 to 2.3 centimeters long.

Habitat

This species typically grows on rich, moist talus (accumulation of debris) slopes in wet lowland forests at an elevation of 1,000 to 3,000 feet. Associated plants species include kukui, lama, 'oha wai, 'ohi'a, and au.

The *lowland wet forest* habitat is composed primarily of native vegetation with canopies from 10 to 130 feet high in sheltered, well-drained, leeward slopes at elevations between 300 and 3,900 feet. Annual rainfall ranges from 60 to 200 inches. The substrate ranges from clay or organic muck over 'a'a lava to volcanic ash beds or young lava flows.

For a continued habitat description of Maui, see "Habitat Conditions on the Island of Maui, Hawaii," page 1955.

Historic Range

Historically, *C. munroi* was known from scattered collections from Lanaihale on Lanai and Makamakaole on West Maui. The species was considered common in the Maka-makaole area in 1971, but has not been sighted there since.

Current Distribution

The only known existing plant on West Maui was discovered in 1989 in Honolua Valley. Located about 5 miles from the Maka-makaole population, the discovery suggests that the historical distribution of the species was more widespread than previously thought. In 1991 two new populations were discovered on Lanai. One population of about 20 individuals was found in the Waiapaa and Kapohaku drainages, and a single plant was seen in the Maunalei drainage in a gulch.

Conservation and Recovery

The major threat to this species is the small number of existing individuals. On Lanai, strawberry guava is competing with both populations, while the population of 20 individuals on Maui is being impacted by deer.

The recovery of this and most other Hawaiian species depends on how well management practices can be implemented. The habitat of this and other Hawaiian species has undergone extreme alteration because of past and present land management practices, including deliberately introducing alien animals and plants, and agricultural and recreational development. To understand the recovery problems facing this species, it is necessary to understand the long-term causes of habitat destruction.

For a continued discussion of the threats to Hawaiian plants, see page 1831.

Bibliography

Culliney, J. *Islands in a Far Sea: Nature and Man in Hawaii*. San Francisco: Sierra Club Books, 1988. 410 pp.

U.S. Fish and Wildlife Service. "Endangered and Threatened Wildlife and Plants; Determination of Endangered or Threatened Status for 15 Plants from the Island of Maui, Hawaii." *Federal Register*. Vol. 57, No. 95, May 15, 1992: 20772-20787.

Contacts

Pacific Islands Ecological Services
  Field Office
Room 6307, 300 Ala Moana Blvd.
Honolulu, HI 96850
Phone: 808-541-2749
FAX: 808-541-2756

Adapted from data compiled by the Threatened and Endangered Species Information Institute (13950 W. 20th Ave., Golden, CO 80401) for *Beacham's International Threatened, Endangered, and Extinct Species* published on CD ROM, available from Beacham Publishing.

Hawaiian Red-Flowered Geranium
Geranium arboreum

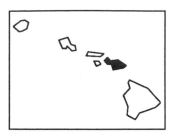

Robert Hobdy

Status	Endangered
Listed	May 13, 1992
Family	Geraniaceae (Geranium)
Description	Tall, many-branched shrub with veined leaves and curved, red flowers.
Habitat	Steep, narrow, damp canyon gulches.
Threats	Habitat destruction by feral pigs and cattle; competing plant species.
Range	Hawaii (Maui)

Description

The Hawaiian red-flowered geranium is a much branched, spreading wood shrub 6 to 12 feet tall. The leaves are thin, bright green, broad and rounded at the base, tapering toward the end, and 1 to 1.5 inches long. Each leaf has 5 to 9 main veins, and has edges notched with tooth-like projections. The flower petals are red, about 1 to 1.5 inches long; the upper three petals are erect, the lower two reflexed, causing the flower to appear curved. Due to the flower shape, this species is the only one in the genus that appears to be adapted to bird pollination.

Habitat

The Hawaiian red-flowered geranium grows in steep, narrow canyons on the north and west outer slopes of Haleakala between 5,000 and 7,000 feet in elevation, in an area that is roughly 9 miles in length and 0.15 mile in width. The environment of these gulches is damp, shaded part of the day, and protected, contrasting with the generally drier climate of the surrounding area. The moist habitat apparently is due to fog drip and run-off. The plants appear to obtain a significant amount of their water requirements by "combing" moisture out of their drifting fog. Vegetation in the ravines is often quite dense, and consists of mostly medium-sized woody shrubs, introduced grasses and weeds, and mixed ferns. The Hawaiian red-flowered geranium occurs in small isolated populations in the gulches and is a minor component of the vegetation. The habitat of the nearby and surrounding areas is subalpine dry forest or mesic scrub land; a few individuals grow near areas that have been converted to agricultural uses such as pasture land or experimental tree plots.

For a continued habitat description of Maui, see "Habitat Conditions on the Island of Maui, Hawaii," page 1955.

Historic Range

The original range and abundance of the species is unknown. However, late 19th and early 20th century collections indicate that it once grew on the southern slopes of Haleakaia, and that its distribution on the northern slopes extended beyond its presently known range.

Current Distribution

In 1992 there were 300 known individuals, found chiefly in the Polipoli Springs and Hosmer Grove—Puu Nianiau areas on the western and northwestern slopes of Haleakala on East Maui. About 250 plants occur on state-owned land within the Xula Forest Reserve; the remainder are mostly in Haleakala National Park, The Nature Conservancy's Waikamoni Preserve, or on Haleakala, Kaonoula, or Erehwon ranches.

Conservation and Recovery

The greatest immediate threats to this species are habitat disturbance by feral pigs, and competition from naturalized exotic vegetation, chiefly grasses and trees. Soil disturbance caused by trampling of cattle and rooting of pigs destroy plants and facilitate the encroachment of competing species. Other less important threats include browsing by cattle; fires; and in the Polipoli Springs area, pollen from exotic pine trees. At certain times of the year, pine pollen completely covers the stigmas of the geranium, precluding any fertilization by its own species. The small number of individual plants increases the potential for extinction from stochastic events, and the limited gene pool may depress reproductive vigor.

The recovery of this and most other Hawaiian species depends on how well management practices can be implemented. The habitat of this and other Hawaiian species has undergone extreme alteration because of past and present land management practices, including deliberately introducing alien animals and plants, and agricultural and recreational development. To understand the recovery problems facing this species, it is necessary to understand the long-term causes of habitat destruction.

For a continued discussion of the threats to Hawaiian plants, see page 1831.

Bibliography

U.S. Fish and Wildlife Service. "Endangered and Threatened Wildlife and Plants; Determination of Endangered Status for Geranium Arboreum (Hawaiian Red-Flowered Geranium)." *Federal Register.* Vol. 57, No. 93, May 13, 1992: 20589-20592.

Contacts

Pacific Islands Ecological Services
Room 6307, 300 Ala Moana Blvd.
Honolulu, HI 96850
Phone: 808-541-2749
FAX: 808-541-2756

Adapted from data compiled by Beacham Publishing for *Beacham's International Threatened, Endangered, and Extinct Species* published on CD ROM.

Nohoanu
Geranium multiflorum

Status	Endangered
Listed	May 15, 1992
Family	Geraniaceae (Geranium)
Description	Tall, many-branched shrub with veined leaves having grayish silky hairs on the lower surface, and clusters of flowers with white petals.
Habitat	Diverse vegetation types, from montane grasslands to wet forests and swamps, extending into the subalpine zone.
Threats	Habitat destruction by feral pigs; competing plant species.
Range	Hawaii (Maui)

Steve Perlman, National Tropical Botanical Garden

Description

The Geranium family is represented by herbs, subshrubs and occasionally tree-like plants. The leaves are alternate or opposite; palmately or pinnately lobed, dissected or compound. Venation of the leaves is often times palmate, stipulate. The flowers are bisexual, actinomorphic or slightly zygomorphic, cymose or in umbels. The fruit is described as a schizocarp and the one to several seeded mericarps split away from the fruit and roll or spiral up on to a central beak.

Nohoanu, *Geranium multiflorum* is a 1 to 3 meters tall, many-branched shrub. The veined leaves are oval, 4.5 to 7 centimeters long, and have grayish silky hairs observed generally on the lower surface. The clustered flowers of 25 to 50 have white petals 10 to 15 millimeters long with purple veins or bases. The single seed, contained in each carpel body (the seed-containing section of the fruit), is reddish brown. The carpel body is 3 millimeters long and topped with an elongated style 14 to 20 millimeters long, which twists to aid dispersal. This species is distinguished from others of the genus by its whitish, regularly symmetrical flowers and by the shape and pattern of teeth on its leaf margins.

Habitat

Geranium multiflorum spans diverse vegetation types, from montane grasslands to wet forests and swamps, extending into the subalpine zone (1,600 to 8,800 feet) with an annual range of precipitation from as low as 15 inches to over 100 inches. Occurring on the windward side of East Maui, this species is found mostly within wet forests, and typically grows in montane grasslands, open sedge swamps, fog-swept lava flows, and occassionally in subalpine shrublands dominated by mamane. Associated species in wet montane forests include 'ohelo, 'ohi'a, pilo, pukiawe, and 'ama'u. Substrates range from lava flows to rich soils.

For a continued habitat description of Maui, see "Habitat Conditions on the Island of Maui, Hawaii," page 1955.

Historic Range

Historically, Nohoanu was known from Ukulele, Waieleele, and Waianapanapa on East Maui.

Current Distribution

This species is known from Haleakala National Park, Hanawi Natural Area Reserve, Koolau Forest Reserve and Waikamoi Preserve. There are currently 11 known populations of Nohoanu extending over a distance of 6.5 by 3.5 miles. There are probably no more than 3,000 total individuals.

Conservation and Recovery

The major threats to this species are habitat destruction by feral pigs and goats, and competition with the encroaching alien plant, prickly Florida blackberry.

The recovery of this and most other Hawaiian species depends on how well management practices can be implemented. The habitat of this and other Hawaiian species has undergone extreme alteration because of past and present land management practices, including deliberately introducing alien animals and plants, and agricultural and recreational development. To understand the recovery problems facing this species, it is necessary to understand the long-term causes of habitat destruction.

For a continued discussion of the threats to Hawaiian plants, see page 1831.

Bibliography

U.S. Fish and Wildlife Service. "Endangered and Threatened Wildlife and Plants; Determination of Endangered or Threatened Status for 15 Plants from the Island of Maui, Hawaii." *Federal Register*. Vol. 57, No. 95, May 15, 1992: 20772-20787.

Culliney, J. *Islands in a Far Sea: Nature and Man in Hawaii*. San Francisco: Sierra Club Books, 1988. 410 pp.

Contacts

Pacific Islands Ecological Services
    Field Office
Room 6307, 300 Ala Moana Blvd.
Honolulu, HI 96850
Phone: 808-541-2749
FAX: 808-541-2756

Adapted from data compiled by the Threatened and Endangered Species Information Institute (13950 W. 20th Ave., Golden, CO 80401) for *Beacham's International Threatened, Endangered, and Extinct Species* published on CD ROM, available from Beacham Publishing.

Kio'ele
Hedyotis coriacea

Steve Perlman, National Tropical Botanical Garden

Status	Endangered
Listed	May 15, 1992
Family	Rubiaceae (Coffee)
Description	Small branched shrub with leathery leaves and flowers that cluster at the end of branches.
Habitat	Steep, rocky slopes in dry to mesic 'a'ali'i-dominated shrublands or forests.
Threats	Limited numbers, extirpation by fire.
Range	Hawaii (Maui, Hawaii)

Description

Kio'ele, *Hedyotis coriacea*, is a small shrub with leathery leaves which are generally elliptic to oblong in shape, 3 to 8 centimeters long. The clustered flowers are located at the ends of the branches, consisting of a few flowers per cluster. The petals are fleshy and fused into a 5 to 10 millimeter long tube. The capsules, which split open to release several dark brown seeds, are cup-to top-shaped.

Habitat

This species is found on steep, rocky slopes in dry to mesic 'a'ali'i-dominated shrublands or forests at an elevation of 1,560 to 7,500 feet. Associated plants species include 'ohi'a, pukiawe, maile, ko'oko'olau, and *Gouania*. Growing on steep windward valley walls, the vegetation type is characterized by rich soil development, high rainfall of 100 inches annually, high diversity, and a rich understory.

For a continued habitat description of Maui, see "Habitat Conditions on the Island of Maui," page 1955; and "Habitat Conditions on the Island of Hawaii," page 1834.

Historic Range

Historically, this species was known from the Waianae and Koolau Mountains on Oahu and Pohakuloa Training Area on the island of Hawaii. This species has not been located on the Oahu location.

Current Distribution

Considered extinct in recent years, this species was rediscovered in 1990 in the West

Maui Natural Area Reserve. In 1991 two individuals were rediscovered in the 1859 lava flow in the Pohakuloa Training Area. By 1992 only a single individual was known from West Maui and two from Hawaii (the Big Island).

Conservation and Recovery

The particular threats to this species are the small number of remaining individuals, and fire, which could extirpate the population. A dump located near the Lihau section of the West Maui National Area Reserve regularly burns and sets wildfires, immediately threatening the only known *H. coraccea* plant.

The recovery of this and most other Hawaiian species depends on how well management practices can be implemented. The habitat of this and other Hawaiian species has undergone extreme alteration because of past and present land management practices, including deliberately introducing alien animals and plants, and agricultural and recreational development. To understand the recovery problems facing this species, it is necessary to understand the long-term causes of habitat destruction.

For a continued discussion of the threats to Hawaiian plants, see page 1831.

Bibliography

U.S. Fish and Wildlife Service."Endangered and Threatened Wildlife and Plants; Determination of Endangered or Threatened Status for 15 Plants from the Island of Maui, Hawaii." *Federal Register*. Vol. 57, No. 95. May 15, 1992: 20772-20787.

Soil Conservation Service. *Land Resource Regions and Major Land Resource Areas of The United States*. Soil Conservation Service, 1981. 156 pp.

Soil Conservation Service. *Soil Survey of Island of Kauai, Oahu, Maui, Molokai, and Lanai, State of Hawaii*. Soil Conservation Service, 1972. 232 pp.

Culliney, J. *Islands in a Far Sea: Nature and Man in Hawaii*. San Francisco: Sierra Club Books, 1988. 410 pp.

Contacts

Pacific Islands Ecological Services
  Field Office
Room 6307, 300 Ala Moana Blvd.
Honolulu, HI 96850
Phone: 808-541-2749
FAX: 808-541-2756
Phone: 503-231-6118

Adapted from data compiled by the Threatened and Endangered Species Information Institute (13950 W. 20th Ave., Golden, CO 80401) for *Beacham's International Threatened, Endangered, and Extinct Species* published on CD ROM, available from Beacham Publishing.

Wawa'iole

Huperzia mannii

Steve Perlman, National Tropical Botanical Garden

Status	Endangered
Listed	May 15, 1992
Family	Lycopodiaceae (Clubmoss)
Description	Clustered red stems with leaves arranged in three rows, and bracted fruit bearing spikes; grows with another plant for support.
Habitat	Grows on plants such as 'ohi'a or Acacia koa in mesic to wet montane 'ohi'a/koa forests.
Threats	Habitat destruction by feral pigs; competing plant species.
Range	Hawaii (Maui, Hawaii, Kauai)

Description

Wawa'iole, *Huperzia mannii*, is a pendent epiphyte (growing on another plant) with clustered red stems, 4 to 10 centimeters long and less than 1 millimeter thick. The leaves are arranged in three rows on the stem and are pointed, flat and lanceolate. Fruiting spikes branch 4 to 6 times and are 12 to 20 centimeters long and 1 to 2 centimeters wide. The spikes possess bracts arranged in 2 to 4 ranks, measuring 1 millimeter long and function to conceal spore capsules.

Habitat

H. mannii typically grows on plants such as 'ohi'a or Acacia koa in mesic to wet montane 'ohi'a/koa forests on Maui and the island of Hawaii. Associated plant species include pilo, 'olapa, kawa'u, and kolea. Additional associates on the island of Hawaii are mamane and kaluaha.

The windward slopes contain the *montane wet communities*, which includes bogs characterized by thick peat overlaying an impervious clay substrate with hummocks of sedges and grasses, stunted trees, and shrubs. Montane wet forests occur mainly on steep windward valley walls. The vegetation type is characterized by rich soil development, high rainfall of 100 inches annually, high diversity, and a rich understory.

For a continued habitat description of Maui, see "Habitat Conditions on the Island of Maui," page 1955; and "Habitat Conditions on the Island of Hawaii," page 1834.

Historic Range

Historically, this species was known from Haelaau and Hanaula on West Maui, Captain Cook-Kona on the island of Hawaii, and Waiakoali on Kauai.

Current Distribution

This species is currently distributed on Kipahulu and Manawainui on East Maui, Lihau and Puu Kukui on West Maui, and Laupahoehoe Natural Area Reserve on the island of Hawaii on State and private land. Thirty-five individuals from 6 populations are known to exist. Stochastic events or extreme climatic changes could adversely affect the four populations of *H. mannii* due to the limited number of extant individuals and its restricted distribution.

Conservation and Recovery

The major threats to this species are habitat degradation and/or predation by pigs and cattle; competition for space, light, water, and nutrients by naturalized, exotic species, especially prickly Florida blackberry, and the small number of remaining individuals.

In 1991, the Manawainui population was fenced to protect it from feral animals. The recovery of this and most other Hawaiian species depends on how well management practices can be implemented. The habitat of this and other Hawaiian species has undergone extreme alteration because of past and present land management practices, including deliberately introducing alien animals and plants, and agricultural and recreational development. To understand the recovery problems facing this species, it is necessary to understand the long-term causes of habitat destruction.

For a continued discussion of the threats to Hawaiian plants, see page 1831.

Bibliography

U.S. Fish and Wildlife Service. "Endangered and Threatened Wildlife and Plants; Determination of Endangered or Threatened Status for 15 Plants from the Island of Maui, Hawaii." *Federal Register* Vol. 57, No. 95, May 15, 1992: 20772-20787.

Contacts

Pacific Islands Ecological Services
    Field Office
Room 6307, 300 Ala Moana Blvd.
Honolulu, HI 96850
Phone: 808-541-2749
FAX: 808-541-2756

Adapted from data compiled by the Threatened and Endangered Species Information Institute (13950 W. 20th Ave., Golden, CO 80401) for *Beacham's International Threatened, Endangered, and Extinct Species* published on CD ROM, available from Beacham Publishing.

Nehe

Lipochaeta kamolensis

Steve Perlman, National Tropical Botanical Garden

Status	Endangered
Listed	May 15, 1992
Family	Asteraceae (Aster)
Description	Trailing or climbing aster with yellow flower heads arranged singly or in pairs and bearing grayish-brown fruits.
Habitat	Bottom of rock ledges in dry scrub or in dry lowland forests.
Threats	Habitat destruction by cattle and feral pigs; competing plant species.
Range	Hawaii (Maui)

Description

This Nehe, *Lipochaeta kamolensis,* is a trailing or climbing aster with a woody base reaching 0.3 to 3 meters in length. The leaves are variable, ranging from long and narrow to triangular, 3 to 5.6 centimeters long. The upper and lower surfaces of the leaves are covered with small flat hairs, and the leaf margins are lobed or deeply curved. The flower heads are arranged singly or in pairs and are 2 to 2.5 centimeters in diameter. Each flower head comprises 6 yellow, ray florets about 8.5 to 9 millimeters long, and about 15 disk florets. The fruits are grayish-brown, wing-less achenes.

Habitat

This species typically grows along the bottom of rock ledges in dry to mesic scrub or dry lowland forests at an elevation of about 820 feet. Associated vegetation includes 'a'ali'i, grasses, and latana.

The *lowland dry vegetation* type occurs on the leeward side of the main Hawaiian Islands at an elevation of 15 to 2,000 feet. The climate of this vegetation is distinctly seasonal, with hot, dry summers and winter rainfall, usually less than 40 inches but sometimes ranging up to 80 inches annually.

For a continued habitat description of Maui, see "Habitat Conditions on the Island of Maui, Hawaii," page 1955.

Historic Range

Historically, *L. kamolensis* was known from Kamole Gulch, west of Kepuni Gulch, and southeast of Ulupalakua Ranch. This species still occurs in the same area on State-owned land.

Current Distribution

There is currently one known population of *L. kamolensis* consisting of several hundred individuals. Any stochastic events or extreme climatic changes could adversely affect this species because of the depauperate number of extant individuals.

Conservation and Recovery

This species is vulnerable to habitat degradation and/or predation by cattle and goats; fire, and the small number of populations subject to extinction by stocjastic events.

The recovery of this and most other Hawaiian species depends on how well management practices can be implemented. The habitat of this and other Hawaiian species has undergone extreme alteration because of past and present land management practices, including deliberately introducing alien animals and plants, and agricultural and recreational development. To understand the recovery problems facing this species, it is necessary to understand the long-term causes of habitat destruction.

For a continued discussion of the threats to Hawaiian plants, see page 1831.

Bibliography

U.S. Fish and Wildlife Service. "Endangered and Threatened Wildlife and Plants; Determination of Endangered or Threatened Status for 15 Plants from the Island of Maui, Hawaii." *Federal Register*. Vol. 57, No. 95, May 15, 1992: 20772-20787.

Contacts

U.S. Fish and Wildlife Service
Regional Office
Eastside Federal Complex
911 N.S. 11th Avenue
Portland, OR 97232-4181
Phone: 503-231-6118

Pacific Islands Ecological Services
  Field Office
Room 6307, 300 Ala Moana Blvd.
Honolulu, HI 96850
Phone: 808-541-2749
FAX: 808-541-2756

Adapted from data compiled by the Threatened and Endangered Species Information Institute (13950 W. 20th Ave., Golden, CO 80401) for *Beacham's International Threatened, Endangered, and Extinct Species* published on CD ROM, available from Beacham Publishing.

Lysimachia lydgatei
No Common Name

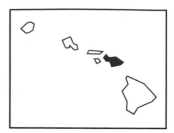

Robert Hobdy

Status	Endangered
Listed	May 15, 1992
Family	Primulaceae (Primrose)
Description	Sprawing, branched shrub with smooth stems and a single flower in the leaf axil.
Habitat	Sides of steep ridges in 'ohi'a-dominated lowland mesic shrubland.
Threats	Habitat destruction by feral animals; competing plant species.
Range	Hawaii (Maui)

Description

Lysimachia lydgatei is a branched, sprawling shrub with stems from 3 to 4 feet long. Immature and young stems have a dense covering of rust-colored hairs while older stems are glabrous. The leathery, elliptic leaves, 1.9 to 2.8 inches long, are densely covered with rust-colored hairs. The flowers are arranged singly in the leaf axils, but entire flowers have not been seen. Fruits are capsules about 0.2 inches long. This species is distinguished from others in the genus by the dense hairs on both the upper and lower surfaces of mature leaves.

Habitat

This species typically grows on the sides of steep ridges in 'ohi'a-dominated lowland mesic shrubland at an elevation of about 3,600 feet. Associated vegetation includes 'a'ali'i, 'ohelo, pukiawe, and mat ferns.

The *lowland mesic shrubland* and forest habitats on West Maui and other Hawaiian islands occurs mainly at elevations between 100 and 5,300 feet in areas topographically unsuitable for agriculture. Annual precipitation ranges from less than 40 to 150 inches. The substrate is diverse: shallow rocky soils on steep slopes to deep soils in gulches and erosional plains.

For a continued habitat description of Maui, see "Habitat Conditions on the Island of Maui, Hawaii," page 1955.

Historic Range and Current Distribution

L. lydgatei has and is only known from

West Maui. This plant is located on West Maui Natural Area Reserve on State-owned land. There are only a few individuals of *L. lydgatei* remaining, making it especially susceptible to any stochastic event or extreme climatic change.

Conservation and Recovery

The plant fauna of Maui has currently fallen vulnerable to habitat degradation and/or predation by wild, feral, or domestic animals (goats, pigs, sheep, and cattle); competition for space, light, water, and nutrients by alien species, especially prickly Florida blackberry; and habitat loss due to fires.

The recovery of this and most other Hawaiian species depends on how well management practices can be implemented. The habitat of this and other Hawaiian species has undergone extreme alteration because of past and present land management practices, including deliberately introducing alien animals and plants, and agricultural and recreational development. To understand the recovery problems facing this species, it is necessary to understand the long-term causes of habitat destruction.

For a continued discussion of the threats to Hawaiian plants, see page 1831.

Bibliography

U.S. Fish and Wildlife Service. "Endangered and Threatened Wildlife and Plants; Determination of Endangered or Threatened Status for 15 Plants from the Island of Maui, Hawaii." *Federal Register.* Vol. 57, No. 95, May 15, 1992: 20772-20787.

Contacts

Pacific Islands Ecological Services Field Office
Room 6307, 300 Ala Moana Blvd.
Honolulu, HI 96850
Phone: 808-541-2749
FAX: 808-541-2756

Adapted from data compiled by the Threatened and Endangered Species Information Institute. (13950 W. 20th Ave., Golden, CO 80401) for *Beacham's International Threatened, Endangered, and Extinct Species* published on CD ROM, available from Beacham Publishing.

Alani
Melicope mucronulata

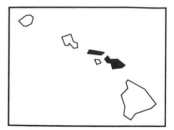

Status	Endangered
Listed	May 15, 1992
Family	Rutaceae (Citrus)
Description	Small tree with oval leaves, flower clusters of 3-9 flowers, and a seed bearing fruit.
Habitat	Steep, west- or north-facing, dry to mesic, forested lowland slopes.
Threats	Habitat destruction by cattle and feral animals; competition from plant species.
Range	Hawaii (Maui, Molokai)

No Photo Available for This Species

Description

This Alani, *Melicope mucronulata*, is a small tree with oval to elliptic-oval leaves, 8 to 15 centimeters long. This tree reaches heights of up to 4 meters. The flower clusters composed of 3 to 9 flowers are arranged in the leaf axils. The fruit is 2.4 to 2.8 centimeters wide and is made of separate section, each containing 1 to 2 seeds. This species is distinguished from others in the genus by the growth habit, the number of flowers in each flower cluster, the size and shape of the fruit, and the degree of hariness of the leaves and fruit walls.

Habitat

This species typically grows on steep, west- or north-facing, dry to mesic, forested lowland slopes at an elevation of 2,200 to 2,850 feet. Associated plants species include 'a'ali'i, 'ohi'a pukiawe, and na'ena'e.

The *lowland dry vegetation* type occurs on the leeward side of the main Hawaiian Islands at an elevation of 15 to 2,000 feet. The climate of this vegetation is distinctly seasonal, with hot, dry summers and winter rainfall, usually less than 40 inches but sometimes ranging up to 80 inches annually.

The *lowland mesic shrubland* and forest habitats on West Maui and other Hawaiian islands occurs mainly at elevations between 100 and 5,300 feet in areas topographically unsuitable for agriculture. Annual precipitation ranges from less than 40 to 150 inches. The substrate is diverse: shallow rocky soils on steep slopes to deep soils in gulches and erosional plains.

For a continued habitat description of Maui, see "Habitat Conditions on the Island of Maui," page 1955; and "Habitat Conditions on the Island of Molokai," page 1993.

Historic Range and Current Distribution

This species was known only from Kanaio in East Maui until 1983. Populations now exist on state-owned land on Maui and Kamakou Preserve on East Molokai. The two populations, which together extend over an area of 950 acres, contain a total of only five plants.

Conservation and Recovery

The plant fauna of Maui and Molokai has currently fallen vulnerable to habitat degradation and/or predation by wild, feral, or domestic animals (goats, pigs, sheep, and cattle); competition for space, light, water, and nutrients by naturalized, exotic species, particularly molasses grass; and habitat loss due to fires.

The recovery of this and most other Hawaiian species depends on how well management practices can be implemented. The habitat of this and other Hawaiian species has undergone extreme alteration because of past and present land management practices, including deliberately introducing alien animals and plants, and agricultural and recreational development. To understand the recovery problems facing this species, it is necessary to understand the long-term causes of habitat destruction.

For a continued discussion of the threats to Hawaiian plants, see page 1831.

Bibliography

U.S. Fish and Wildlife Service. "Endangered and Threatened Wildlife and Plants; Determination of Endangered or Threatened Status for 15 Plants from the Island of Maui, Hawaii." *Federal Register*. Vol. 57, No. 95, May 15, 1992: 20772-20787.

Contacts

Pacific Islands Ecological Services
   Field Office
Room 6307, 300 Ala Moana Blvd.
Honolulu, HI 96850
Phone: 808-541-2749
FAX: 808-541-2756

Adapted from data compiled by the Threatened and Endangered Species Information Institute (13950 W. 20th Ave., Golden, CO 80401) for *Beacham's International Threatened, Endangered, and Extinct Species* published on CD ROM, available from Beacham Publishing.

Schiedea haleakalensis
No Common Name

Robert J. Gustafson

Status	Endangered
Listed	May 15, 1992
Family	Caryophyllaceae (Pink)
Description	Shrub with fleshy, narrow leaves and a single vein, and green flowers clustered at the ends of branches.
Habitat	Sheer, arid subalpine cliffs.
Threats	Habitat destruction by feral animals; competing species.
Range	Hawaii (Maui)

Description

Schiedea haleakalensis is a glabrous (smooth with no hairs) shrub 30 to 60 centimeters tall with slightly fleshy, narrow leaves and a single vein. The clustered flowers are 3 to 5 centimeters long located at the ends of the branches. The flower has 5 green, oval sepals, which are 3 millimeters long; no petal; 5 nectaries; and 10 stamens. The capsules contain grayish to reddish brown seeds. This species differs from others in the genus on East Maui by its crowded, hairless inflorescence composed of bisexual flowers.

Habitat

This species typically grows on sheer, arid subalpine cliffs at an elevation of 6,000 to 7,000 feet. Associated vegetation includes 'ahinahina, ko'oko'olau, na'ena'e, and pamakani.

The *subalpine dry vegetation* type occurs on East Maui (and the Big Island) between 5,600 and 9,800 feet. The substrate is of cinder or weathered volcanic ash or bare lava with little or no soil development, partly due to the low annual precipitation of 15 to 40 inches. Periodic frost and occasional snow cover occur on the upper limits.

For a continued habitat description of Maui, see "Habitat Conditions on the Island of Maui, Hawaii," page 1955.

Historic Range and Current Distribution

The historical range of this species is unknown. *S. haleakalensis* is currently known only from Haleakala National Park on East

Maui. Currently there are two populations containing only 100 to 200 individuals. Stochastic events or extreme climatic changes could adversely affect this species due to the limited number of extant individuals and its restricted distribution.

Conservation and Recovery

The plant fauna of Maui has currently fallen vulnerable to habitat degradation and/or predation by wild, feral, or domestic animals (goats, pigs, sheep, and cattle); competition for space, light, water, and nutrients by naturalized, exotic ˜species; habitat loss due to fires; human recreational activities; and military exercises.

The recovery of this and most other Hawaiian species depends on how well management practices can be implemented. The habitat of this and other Hawaiian species has undergone extreme alteration because of past and present land management practices, including deliberately introducing alien animals and plants, and agricultural and recreational development. To understand the recovery problems facing this species, it is necessary to understand the long-term causes of habitat destruction.

For a continued discussion of the threats to Hawaiian plants, see page 1831.

Bibliography

U.S. Fish and Wildlife Service. "Endangered and Threatened Wildlife and Plants; Determination of Endangered or Threatened Status for 15 Plants from the Island of Maui, Hawaii." *Federal Register*. Vol. 57, No. 95, May 15, 1992: 20772-20787.

Contacts

Pacific Islands Ecological Services
    Field Office
Room 6307, 300 Ala Moana Blvd.
Honolulu, HI 96850
Phone: 808-541-2749
FAX: 808-541-2756

Adapted from data compiled by the Threatened and Endangered Species Information Institute (13950 W. 20th Ave., Golden, CO 80401) for *Beacham's International Threatened, Endangered, and Extinct Species* published on CD ROM, available from Beacham Publishing.

Peucedanum sandwicense   *(p. 1927)*   ▲

Clermontia lindseyana   *(p. 1839)*   ▼

▲   **Pigeon Wings**   *(p. 1783)*

▼   **Clover Lupine**   *(p. 1723)*

▲   Clay Reed-Mustard   *(p. 1738)*

Ben Lomond Spineflower   *(p. 1666)*   ▼

Star Cactus   *(p. 1692)*   ▲

▼   *Vernonia proctorii*   *(p. 1826)*

Kodachrome Bladderpod   *(p. 1719)*   ▼

▲   *Clermontia oblongifolia*   *(p. 1966)*

▲   **Avon Park Harebells**   *(p. 1775)*

Munroidendron racemosum   *(p. 1923)*   ▼

▲   *Clermontia peleana*   *(p. 1841)*

Haleakala Silversword   *(p. 1962)*   ▼

C-3

Pima Pineapple Cactus   *(p. 1684)* ▲

▼   White Birds-in-a-Nest   *(p. 1726)*

▲   *Brighamia insignis*   *(p. 1885)*

Rollandia crispa   *(p. 2035)* ▼

Clay's Hibiscus   *(p. 1905)* ▼

▲   Coastal California Gnatcatcher   *(p. 2086)*

Western Snowy Plover   *(p. 2082)*   ▲

▼   Spectacled Eider   *(p. 2089)*

▲   Delhi Sands Flower-Loving Fly   *(p. 2217)*

▲   St. Francis' Satyr Butterfly   *(p. 2214)*

Myrtle's Silverspot Butterfly   *(p. 2220)*   ▼

Karner Blue Butterfly *(p. 2210)* ▼

Royal Snail   *(p. 2181)*   ▲

Anthony's Riversnail   *(p. 2174)*   ▲

▼   Cave Crayfish   *(p. 2194)*

▼   Orange-Nacre Mucket   *(p. 2147)*

45710

Banbury Springs Lanx   *(p. 2176)*   ▲

▼   Bluemask Darter   *(p. 2106)*

▲ **Tidewater Goby** *(p. 2112)*

Relict Darter *(p. 2108)* ▼

Snake River Fall Chinook Salmon *(p. 2123)* ▼

California Spotted Owl (close relative of Mexican Spotted Owl)   *(p. 2092)*   ▲

▼   **American Black Bear**   *(p. 2073)*

Louisiana Black Bear   *(p. 2075)*   ▼

▼   **Giant Garter Snake**   *(p. 2099)*

HAWAIIAN PLANTS: MOLOKAI

Habitat Conditions on
the Island of Molokai, Hawaii

On October 8, 1992, the U.S. Fish and Wildlife Service listed as endangered or threatened sixteen plants from the island of Molokai, Hawaii. Habitat conditions on Molokai
are described here rather than being repeated in each of the species accounts.

Cyanea procera
Bidens wiebkei
Brighamia rockii
Canavalia molokaiensis
Cyanea mannii
Hedyotis mannii
Hibiscus arnottianus
   ssp. immaculatus
Clemontia oblongifolia
   ssp. brevipes
Melicope reflexa
Phyllostegia mannii
Pritchardi munroi
Schiedea lydgatei
Silene lanceolata
Silene alexandri
Tetramolopium rockii
Stenogyne bifida

The islands of Hawaii are of volcanic
origins and consist of coastal plains, upland
slopes and mountain ranges and summits.
Molokai, the fifth largest island in the State,
is 38 miles long and 10 miles wide. The
growing season is throughout the year except on the mountain summits. The principal
land uses on the island of Molokai are:
cropland, urban developments, military
installations, native and introduced forests,
watersheds, wildlife habitat, and pasture.
Molokai is divided into three main sections—West Molokai, East Molokai, and
Central Molokai.

These sections are characterized by four
distinct resource areas. The semiarid and
subhumid low mountain slopes covering the
east central portion of the island consists of
broad and nearly level slopes bisected by
rocky gulches; average annual precipitation
of 300 to 1,525 millimeters; and deep, well
drained, fine textured soils with an isohyperthermic temperature regime, an ustic or
aridic moisture regime and kaolinitic mineralogy; this area supports grass-shrub vegetation.

The southern reach of the island is composed of stony/rocky land. This area generally ranges from sea level to 900 meters
elevation; the landscape is sloping to steep
and is bisected by many drainageways;
average annual precipitation is 250 to 1,525
millimeters with the most precipitous season
falling between October and May; there are
no perennial streams or natural water storage facilities; the soils are very shallow and
stony; the primary land types are stony,
rock, rock outcrop, and rough mountainous
land; where a soil mantle occurs forest or
grass-shrub vegetation is associated including: buffelgrass, lantana, piligrass, klu bush,
Natal redtop, Kiawe, guava, aalii, ohia,
hehua, and pukiawe.

The western region, accounting for nearly
one-third of the island is characterized by
rough mountainous lands. This region's
elevation ranges from sea level to 1,500
meters. Many steep-sided gulches bisect this
steep to precipitous area; the average annual
precipitation is generally 1,900 to 6,350
millimeters; there are many perennial and

intermittent streams in this area; the soils are poorly drained on gently sloping to hills; land types of most of this area are rough broken land, rough mountainous land, and rock outcrop land; this area supports forest and shrub vegetation; ohia, hehua, falsestaghorn, koa, treefern, hilograss, lapalapa, Javaplum, and sedges grow in precipitous areas while kiawe, koa-haole, and fingergrass grow on the drier sites.

A small central section reaching north bordered by rough mountainous lands and low mountain slopes, is appropriately named the subhumid intermediate mountain slope. This area's average rainfall is from 750 to 1,900 millimeters, most of which occurs from October to May; the elevation is 200 to 1,300 meters; this area is steep to very steep, broken by numerous drainageways; there are no perennial streams in this area; the soils are deep to moderately deep and well drained. The vegetation supported by this region consists of lantana, Natal redtop, Bermudagrass, fingergrass, kiawe, koa-haole, guava, molassesgrass, aalii, joee, yellow foxtail, ohia, lehua, koa, silver oak, pukiawe, ricegrass, and Bostonfern forest vegetation.

Ko'oko'olau

Bidens wiebkei

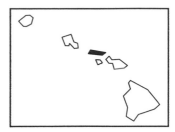

Steve Perlman, National Tropical Botanical Garden

Status	Endangered
Listed	October 8, 1992
Family	Asteraceae (Aster)
Description	Perennial herb with flower heads on side branches.
Habitat	Steep, exposed slopes in mesic shrublands and forests.
Threats	Habitat disturbance, predation by wild, feral, or domestic animals.
Range	Hawaii (Molokai)

Description

Ko'oko'olau, *Bidens wiebkei*, is a perennial herb that is woody at the base and grows from 0.5 to 1 meter tall. The opposite, pinnately compound leaves are 7 to 13 centimeters long and each has three to seven leaflets, 2.5 to 8 centimeters long and 1 to 2.5 centimeters wide. The flower heads are arranged on side branches in clusters of usually 10 to 30. Each flower head is 1.6 to 2.5 centimeters in diameter and is comprised of 4 to 6 sterile yellow ray florets, each about 10 to 12 millimeters long and 2 to 5 millimeters wide. The flower heads possess 9 to 18 bisexual yellow disk florets. The fruit of this plant is a brownish-black achene. This achene is curved or twisted and winged. This one-seed fruit is about 6 to 9 millimeters long and 0.9 to 2 millimeters wide. It is distinguished from other members of Bidens by its erect habit and the curved or twisted, winged achenes.

Habitat

The five known populations of this species are scattered along steep, exposed slopes in mesic shrublands and forests at 250 to 1,050 meters in elevation. Other associated plant species include *Antidesma* (hame), *Nestegis sandwicensis* (olopua), *Pisonia* (papala kepau), and *Scaevola gaudichaudii* (naupaka kuahiwi).

For a continued habitat description of Molokai, see "Habitat Conditions on the Island of Molokai, Hawaii," page 1993.

Historic Range and Current Distribution

Historically, this species was known from

Pelekunu and the easternmost section of Molokai at Halawa. It is still found near Halawa and was recently found on Puu Kolekole, just south of its historical range.

Conservation and Recovery

The plant fauna of Molokai has currently fallen vulnerable to habitat degradation and predation by wild, feral, or domestic animals (axis deer, goats, pigs, sheep, and cattle); competition for space, light, water, and nutrients by naturalized, exotic species; habitat loss due to fires; predation by rats; human recreational activities; and military exercises.

Cattle ranching on Molokai has played a significant role over most of the past 150 years in reducing areas of native vegetation to vast pastures of alien grasses. In 1960 about 61% of Molokai's lands were devoted to grazing, primarily in West and central Molokai. Cattle degrade the habitat by trampling and feeding on vegetation, eventually exposing the ground cover, increasing soil vulnerability to erosion. Red erosional scars resulting from decades of cattle disturbance, exacerbated by other feral ungulate activities, are still evident on West Molokai and the upper elevations of East Molokai. Cattle facilitate the spread of alien grasses and other plants.

Alteration of vegetation limits natural areas. It was here on the upper elevation mesic to wet forests of East Molokai, which the State designated a single protected area: the Molokai Forest Reserve. This reserve accounts for 30% of Molokai land area. Cattle ranching was succeeded in the 1920s by pineapple cultivation. Most of the land used for this agricultural activity had already been altered through the decades of cattle ranching. However, pineapple cultivation contributed to a high degree of erosion until its decline in the 1970s.

For a continued description of the threats to Hawaiian plants, see page 1831.

Bibliography

U.S. Fish and Wildlife Service. "Endangered and Threatened Wildlife and Plants; Determination of Endangered or Threatened Status for 16 Plants from the Island of Molokai, Hawaii." *Federal Register* Vol. 57, No. 196, October 8, 1992: 46325-45339.

Contacts

Pacific Islands Ecological Services
  Field Office
Room 6307, 300 Ala Moana Blvd.
Honolulu, HI 96850
Phone: 808-541-2749
FAX: 808-541-2756

Adapted from data compiled by the Threatened and Endangered Species Information Institute (13950 W. 20th Ave., Golden, CO 80401) for *Beacham's International Threatened, Endangered, and Extinct Species* published on CD ROM, available from Beacham Publishing.

Pua'ala

Brighamia rockii

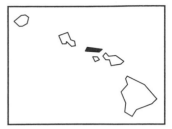

Warren Wagner

Status	Endangered
Listed	October 8, 1992
Family	Campanulaceae (Bellflower)
Description	Bellflower with oval leaves, fragrant flowers clustered in groups of 3 to 8.
Habitat	Rock crevices on inaccessible steep sea cliffs.
Threats	Habitat disturbance, predation by wild, feral, or domestic animals.
Range	Hawaii (Molokai)

Description

Pua'ala, *Brighamia rockii*, is a bellflower that grows as an unbranched plant 1 to 5 meters tall with a thickened succulent stem which tapers from the base. The fleshy, oval leaves are widest at their tips and are arranged in a rosette at the top of the plant. The leaves measure 6 to 22 centimeters long and 5 to 15 centimeters wide. The fragrant flowers are clustered in groups of three to eight on the leaf axils. Each flower cluster is on a stalk 3.5 to 7.5 centimeters long, and individual flowers connect to a stalk 6 to 12 millimeters long. The hypanthium has 10 ribs and is topped by 5 calyx lobes 2.5 to 8 millimeters long. The petals are fused into a green to yellowish-green tube which flares into five white, elliptic lobes. The fruit is a capsule 13 to 20 millimeters long, which contains numerous seeds. This species is an endemic Hawaiian genus which differs from other *Brighamia* species by the color of its petals, the longer calyx lobes, and the shorter flower stalks.

Habitat

This species grows in rock crevices on inaccessible steep sea cliffs along East Molokai's northern coastline in coastal dry to mesic forests or shrublands at an elevation of sea level to 1,540 feet. Associated species include *Canthium odoratum* (alahe'e), *Osteomeles anthyllidifolia* ('ulei), and *Scaevola* (nanpaka).

For a continued habitat description of Molokai, see "Habitat Conditions on the Island of Molokai, Hawaii," page 1993.

Historic Range

B. rockii once ranged along the northern coast of East Molokai from Kalaupapa to Halawa and may possibly have grown on Lanai and Maui.

Current Distribution

This species' range has decreased to fragmented populations along the northern coastline of East Molokai from Anapuhi Beach to Wailau Valley. A few individuals occur on state-owned sea stack of Huelo.

Conservation and Recovery

Damage by ungulates and competition with the exotic species Christmas berry are the primary threats to this species. The plant fauna of Molokai has currently fallen vulnerable to habitat degradation and/or predation by wild, feral, or domestic animals (axis deer, goats, pigs, sheep, and cattle); competition for space, light, water, and nutrients by naturalized, exotic species; habitat loss due to fires; predation by rats; human recreational activities; and military exercises.

Cattle ranching on Molokai has played a significant role over most of the past 150 years in reducing areas of native vegetation to vast pastures of alien grasses. In 1960 about 61% of Molokai's lands were devoted to grazing, primarily in West and central Molokai. Cattle degrade the habitat by trampling and feeding on vegetation, eventually exposing the ground cover, increasing soil vulnerability to erosion. Red erosional scars resulting from decades of cattle disturbance, exacerbated by other feral ungulate activities, are still evident on West Molokai and the upper elevations of East Molokai. Cattle facilitate the spread of alien grasses and other plants.

Alteration of vegetation limits natural areas. It was here on the upper elevation mesic to wet forests of East Molokai, which the State designated a single protected area: the Molokai Forest Reserve. This reserve accounts for 30% of Molokai land area. Cattle ranching was succeeded in the 1920s by pineapple cultivation. Most of the land used for this agricultural activity had already been altered through the decades of cattle ranching. However, pineapple cultivation contributed to a high degree of erosion until its decline in the 1970s.

For a continued discussion of the threats to Hawaiian plants, see page 1831.

Bibliography

U.S. Fish and Wildlife Service. "Endangered and Threatened Wildlife and Plants; Determination of Endangered or Threatened Status for 16 Plants from the Island of Molokai, Hawaii." *Federal Register* Vol. 57, No. 196, October 8, 1992: 46325-45339.

Contacts

Pacific Islands Ecological Services
    Field Office
Room 6307, 300 Ala Moana Blvd.
Honolulu, HI 96850
Phone: 808-541-2749
FAX: 808-541-2756

Adapted from data compiled by the Threatened and Endangered Species Information Institute (13950 W. 20th Ave., Golden, CO 80401) for *Beacham's International Threatened, Endangered, and Extinct Species* published on CD ROM, available from Beacham Publishing.

'Awikiwiki

Canavalia molokaiensis

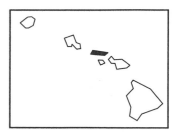

Steve Perlman, National Tropical Botanical Garden

Status	Endangered
Listed	October 8, 1992
Family	Fabaceae (Pea)
Description	Perennial climbing herb with twining branches and oval leaves.
Habitat	Exposed dry sites on steep slopes in mesic shrublands and forests.
Threats	Habitat disturbance, predation by wild, feral, or domestic animals.
Range	Hawaii (Molokai)

Description

'Awikiwiki, *Canavalia molokaiensis*, is a perennial climbing herb with twining branches. Each leaf is made up of three lanceolate or sometimes oval leaflets. Four to 15 flowers are arranged along the stalk which are 3 to 9 centimeters long. The calyx comprises a larger upper lip with two lobes and a smaller lower lip with three lobes. The five purple petals vary from 36 to 47 millimeters in length. The flattened pods are 12 to 16 centimeters long and enclose the flattened, dark reddish-brown, oblongelliptic seeds.

Habitat

'Awikiwiki typically grows in exposed dry sites on steep slopes in mesic shrublands and forests at 2,790 to 3,050 feet in elevation. Associated plant species are 'ohi'a, *Chamaesy-*

ce, Dodonaea viscosa, Styphelia tameiameiae and *Wikstroemia.*

For a continued habitat description of Molokai, see "Habitat Conditions on the Island of Molokai, Hawaii," page 1993.

Historic Range and Current Distribution

Historically, 'Awikiwiki was known from East Molokai, at Kalaupapa, Pelekunu, and Kahuaawi Gulch. This species' distribution is more restricted and its range is only from Kalaupapa to Waialeia, Kaunakakai, and Kamakou. It occurs on Kalaupapa National Historical Park and on private lands.

Conservation and Recovery

The plant fauna of Molokai has currently fallen vulnerable to habitat degradation and or predation by wild, feral, or domestic animals (axis deer, goats, pigs, sheep, and cattle); competition for space, light, water, and nutrients by naturalized, exotic species; habitat loss due to fires; predation by rats; human recreational activities; and military exercises.

Cattle ranching on Molokai has played a significant role over most of the past 150 years in reducing areas of native vegetation to vast pastures of alien grasses. In 1960 about 61% of Molokai's lands were devoted to grazing, primarily in West and central Molokai. Cattle degrade the habitat by trampling and feeding on vegetation, eventually exposing the ground cover, increasing soil vulnerability to erosion. Red erosional scars resulting from decades of cattle disturbance, exacerbated by other feral ungulate activities, are still evident on West Molokai and the upper elevations of East Molokai. Cattle facilitate the spread of alien grasses and other plants.

Alteration of vegetation limits natural areas. It was here on the upper elevation mesic to wet forests of East Molokai, where the State designated a single protected area: the Molokai Forest Reserve. This reserve accounts for 30% of Molokai land area. Cattle ranching was succeeded in the 1920s by pineapple cultivation. Most of the land used for this agricultural activity had already been altered through the decades of cattle ranching. However, pineapple cultivation contributed to a high degree of erosion until its decline in the 1970s.

For a continued discussion of the threats to Hawaiian plants, see page 1831.

Bibliography

U.S. Fish and Wildlife Service. "Endangered and Threatened Wildlife and Plants; Determination of Endangered or Threatened Status for 16 Plants from the Island of Molokai, Hawaii." *Federal Register* Vol. 57, No. 196, October 8, 1992: 46325-45339.

Contacts

Pacific Islands Ecological Services
Field Office
Room 6307, 300 Ala Moana Blvd.
Honolulu, HI 96850
Phone: 808-541-2749
FAX: 808-541-2756

Adapted from data compiled by the Threatened and Endangered Species Information Institute (13950 W. 20th Ave., Golden, CO 80401) for *Beacham's International Threatened, Endangered, and Extinct Species* published on CD ROM, available from Beacham Publishing.

'Oha'wai

Clemontia oblongifolia ssp. *brevipes*

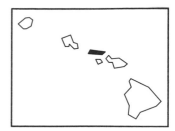

Derral Herbst   *Color Plate C-3*

Status	Endangered
Listed	October 8, 1992
Family	Campanulaceae (Bellflower)
Description	Terrestrial shrub or tree with short leaves, leaf stalks,and flower stalks.
Habitat	Volcanic soils of coastal plains, upland slopes, mountain ranges and summits.
Threats	Habitat disturbance, and predation by wild, feral, or domestic animals.
Range	Hawaii (Molokai)

Description

'Oha'wai, *Clemontia oblongifolia* ssp. *brevipes* is a terrestrial shrub or tree which reaches heights of up to 2 to 7 meters. This species' scientific name reflects upon its short leaves, leaf stalks, and flower stalks. The leaves of *C. o.* ssp. *brevipes* are on petioles 1.8 to 3 centimeters long. These leaves are lanceolate; have thickened, rounded teeth; and reach a length to 7 to 11 centimeters and a width of 2 to 5 cm. The flowers are grouped in two's or sometimes three's on the 5 to 10 millimeter stalk. The flower is 6 to 7.8 centimeters long; the calyx and corolla are similar in size and appearance, and each forms an arched tube which is greenish-white or purplish on the outside while the inside is white or cream colored. The fruit is an orange, spherical berry, 17 to 30 millimeters long.

Habitat

This species typically grows in volcanic soils of coastal plains, upland slopes, mountain ranges and summits on East Molokai.

For a continued habitat description of Molokai, see "Habitat Conditions on the Island of Molokai, Hawaii," page 1993.

Historic Range

A population located in the Kamakou area has not been seen for over 40 years and is believed to be extirpated.

Current Distribution

This species is known from a single population on the Kamakou Preserve owned by The Nature Conservancy. There has been no report of the species since 1982 in this location.

Conservation and Recovery

The plant fauna of Molokai has currently fallen vulnerable to habitat degradation and or predation by wild, feral, or domestic animals (axis deer, goats, pigs, sheep, and cattle); competition for space, light, water, and nutrients by naturalized, exotic species; habitat loss due to fires; predation by rats; human recreational activities; and military exercises.

Overgrazing by axis deer, and goats has irreparably damaged much native vegetation of Molokai and Hawaii.

Cattle ranching on Molokai has played a significant role over most of the past 150 years in reducing areas of native vegetation to vast pastures of alien grasses. In 1960 about 61% of Molokai's lands were devoted to grazing, primarily in West and central Molokai. Cattle degrade the habitat by trampling and feeding on vegetation, eventually exposing the ground cover, increasing soil vulnerability to erosion. Red erosional scars resulting from decades of cattle disturbance, exacerbated by other feral ungulate activities, are still evident on West Molokai and the upper elevations of East Molokai. Cattle facilitate the spread of alien grasses and other plants.

Alteration of vegetation limits natural areas. It was here on the upper elevation mesic to wet forests of East Molokai, which the State designated a single protected area: the Molokai Forest Reserve. This reserve accounts for 30% of Molokai land area. Cattle ranching was succeeded in the 1920s by pineapple cultivation. Most of the land used for this agricultural activity had already been altered through the decades of cattle ranching. However, pineapple cultivation contributed to a high degree of erosion until its decline in the 1970s.

For a continued discussion of the threats to Hawaiian plants, see page 1831.

Bibliography

U.S. Fish and Wildlife Service. "Endangered and Threatened Wildlife and Plants; Determination of Endangered or Threatened Status for 16 Plants from the Island of Molokai, Hawaii." *Federal Register* Vol. 57, No. 196, October 8, 1992: 46325-45339.

Contacts

Pacific Islands Ecological Services
 Field Office
Room 6307, 300 Ala Moana Blvd.
Honolulu, HI 96850
Phone: 808-541-2749
FAX: 808-541-2756

Regional Office
Eastside Federal Complex
911 N.S. 11th Avenue
Portland, OR 97232-4181
Phone: 503-231-6118

Adapted from data compiled by the Threatened and Endangered Species Information Institute (13950 W. 20th Ave., Golden, CO 80401) for *Beacham's International Threatened, Endangered, and Extinct Species* published on CD ROM, available from Beacham Publishing.

Haha

Cyanea mannii

Specimen, Berlin Herbarium

Status	Endangered
Listed	October 8, 1992
Family	Campanualaceae (Bellflower)
Description	Branched shrub with narrow leaves, smooth green flowers.
Habitat	Sides of deep gulches in 'ohi'a-dominated mesic to wet forests.
Threats	Habitat disturbance, predation by wild, feral, or domestic animals.
Range	Hawaii (Molokai)

Description

Cyanea mannii is a branched shrub 1.5 to 3 meters tall. The leaves are narrowly elliptic or lance-shaped and have hardened teeth along the leaf margins. Each flower cluster arises from the axil of a leaf on a stalk; these clusters comprise 6 to 12 flowers, each on a stalk 8 to 12 millimeters long. Each flower has a smooth, green hypanthium that is topped by triangular calyx lobes. The purplish corolla forms a nearly upright tube that ends in five spreading lobes. Berries have not been observed on this haha.

Habitat

This species typically grows on the sides of deep gulches in 'ohi'a-dominated mesic to wet forests at elevations of 3,000 to 4,000 feet on East Molokai.

For a continued habitat description of Molokai, see "Habitat Conditions on the Island of Molokai, Hawaii," page 1993.

Historic Range

Historically, *C. mannii* was known only from Kalae on East Molokai. Five populations have since been discovered in the east and west forks of Kawela Gulch on Kamakou Preserve owned by the Nature Conservancy on East Molokai.

Current Distribution

There are six populations of *C. mannii* consisting of about 40 individuals. Stochastic events or extreme climatic changes could prove catastrophic to this species because of the limited number of extant individuals and its restricted distribution.

Conservation and Recovery

The plant fauna of Molokai has currently fallen vulnerable to habitat degradation and or predation by wild, feral, or domestic animals (axis deer, goats, pigs, sheep, and cattle); competition for space, light, water, and nutrients by naturalized, exotic species; habitat loss due to fires; predation by rats; human recreational activities; and military exercises.

Overgrazing by axis deer, and goats has irreparably damaged much native vegetation of Molokai and Hawaii.

Cattle ranching on Molokai has played a significant role over most of the past 150 years in reducing areas of native vegetation to vast pastures of alien grasses. In 1960 about 61% of Molokai's lands were devoted to grazing, primarily in West and central Molokai. Cattle degrade the habitat by trampling and feeding on vegetation, eventually exposing the ground cover, increasing soil vulnerability to erosion. Red erosional scars resulting from decades of cattle disturbance, exacerbated by other feral ungulate activities, are still evident on West Molokai and the upper elevations of East Molokai. Cattle facilitate the spread of alien grasses and other plants.

Alteration of vegetation limits natural areas. It was here on the upper elevation mesic to wet forests of East Molokai, which the State designated a single protected area: the Molokai Forest Reserve. This reserve accounts for 30% of Molokai land area. Cattle ranching was succeeded in the 1920s by pineapple cultivation. Most of the land used for this agricultural activity had already been altered through the decades of cattle ranching. However, pineapple cultivation contributed to a high degree of erosion until its decline in the 1970s.

For a continued discussion of the threats to Hawaiian plants, see page 1831.

Bibliography

U.S. Fish and Wildlife Service. "Endangered and Threatened Wildlife and Plants; Determination of Endangered or Threatened Status for 16 Plants from the Island of Molokai, Hawaii." *Federal Register* Vol. 57, No. 196, October 8, 1992: 46325-45339.

Contacts

Pacific Islands Ecological Services
   Field Office
Room 6307, 300 Ala Moana Blvd.
Honolulu, HI 96850
Phone: 808-541-2749
FAX: 808-541-2756

Regional Office
Eastside Federal Complex
911 N.S. 11th Avenue
Portland, OR 97232-4181
Phone: 503-231-6118

Adapted from data compiled by the Threatened and Endangered Species Information Institute (13950 W. 20th Ave., Golden, CO 80401) for *Beacham's International Threatened, Endangered, and Extinct Species* published on CD ROM, available from Beacham Publishing.

Pilo

Hedyotis mannii

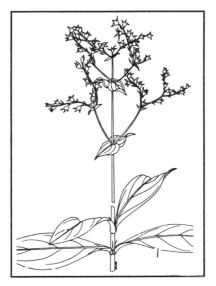

Yevonn Wilson-Ramsey

Status	Endangered
Listed	October 8, 1992
Family	Rubiaceae (Coffee)
Description	Small perennial plant with smooth, long stems and greenish-white fleshy trumpet-shaped petals.
Habitat	Dark, narrow, rocky gulch walls in mesic to wet forests.
Threats	Habitat disturbance, predation by wild, feral or domestic animals.
Range	Hawaii (Molokai, Lanai)

Description

Pilo is a perennial plant with smooth, usually 30 to 60 centimeters long, stems. The stem is woody at the base and four-angled. The leaves are opposite, thin in texture, elliptic to sometimes lanceolate, and are usually 8 to 18 centimeters long. Stipules are attached to the slightly winged leaf stalks where they join and clasp the stem. The stipules are triangular and have a point 4 to 11 millimeters long. The flowers of Pilo are arranged in loose clusters up to 30 centimeters long at the ends of the stems and are either bisexual or female. The green hypanthium is top-shaped with sepals at the top. The greenish-white, fleshy petals are fused into a trumpet shaped tube; the capsules are top-shaped.

Habitat

This species typically grows on dark, narrow, rocky gulch walls in mesic to wet forests at elevations of 490 to 3,450 feet. Associated plant species include mamaki, hapu'u, *Cyanea* (haha), and kopiko.

For a continued habitat description of Molokai, see "Habitat Conditions on the Island of Molokai, Hawaii," page 1993.

Historic Range

Historically Pilo was located on Lanai, Maui and Molokai. After not being seen for 50 years, the species was relocated in 1987 on East Molokai. In 1991 a new population was located on Lanai.

Current Distribution

Eleven individuals of Pilo are presently in existence on the Islands of Molokai and Lanai. Any stochastic events or extreme climatic changes could adversely affect this species (perhaps even extirpate) because of the limited number of extant individuals.

Conservation and Recovery

The plant fauna of the islands has currently fallen vulnerable to habitat degradation andor predation by wild, feral, or domestic animals (goats, pigs, sheep, and cattle); competition for space, light, water, and nutrients by naturalized, exotic species; habitat loss due to fires; human recreational activities; and military exercises.

Cattle ranching on Molokai has played a significant role over most of the past 150 years in reducing areas of native vegetation to vast pastures of alien grasses. In 1960 about 61% of Molokai's lands were devoted to grazing, primarily in West and central Molokai. Cattle degrade the habitat by trampling and feeding on vegetation, eventually exposing the ground cover, increasing soil vulnerability to erosion. Red erosional scars resulting from decades of cattle disturbance, exacerbated by other feral ungulate activities, are still evident on West Molokai and the upper elevations of East Molokai. Cattle facilitate the spread of alien grasses and other plants.

Alteration of vegetation limits natural areas. It was here on the upper elevation mesic to wet forests of East Molokai, which the State designated a single protected area: the Molokai Forest Reserve. This reserve accounts for 30% of Molokai land area. Cattle ranching was succeeded in the 1920s by pineapple cultivation. Most of the land used for this agricultural activity had already been altered through the decades of cattle ranching. However, pineapple cultivation contributed to a high degree of erosion until its decline in the 1970s.

For a continued discussion of the threats to Hawaiian plants, see page 1831.

Bibliography

U.S. Fish and Wildlife Service. "Endangered and Threatened Wildlife and Plants; Determination of Endangered or Threatened Status for 16 Plants from the Island of Molokai, Hawaii." *Federal Register* Vol. 57, No. 196, October 8, 1992: 46325-45339.

Contacts

Pacific Islands Ecological Services
   Field Office
Room 6307, 300 Ala Moana Blvd.
Honolulu, HI 96850
Phone: 808-541-2749
FAX: 808-541-2756

Regional Office
Eastside Federal Complex
911 N.S. 11th Avenue
Portland, OR 97232-4181
Phone: 503-231-6118

Adapted from data compiled by the Threatened and Endangered Species Information Institute (13950 W. 20th Ave., Golden, CO 80401) for *Beacham's International Threatened, Endangered, and Extinct Species* published on CD ROM, available from Beacham Publishing.

Koki'o Ke'oke'o

Hibiscus arnottianus ssp. *immaculatus*

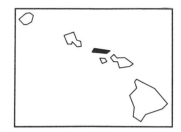

Derral Herbst

Status	Endangered
Listed	October 8, 1992
Family	Malvaceae (Mallow)
Description	Pure white flowering tree.
Habitat	Steep sea cliffs in mesic forests.
Threats	Habitat degradation, predation by wild, feral, or domestic animals.
Range	Hawaii (Molokai)

Description

Koki'o Ke'oke'o is a tree that reaches heights of up to 3 meters. It has alternate, oval, toothed leaves measuring 5 to 7 centimeters long. Six lance-shaped bracts are found under each of the faintly fragrant flowers, which are arranged singly near the ends of the branches. The calyx is 2.5 to 3 centimeters long and cleft into five teeth with long, narrow points. The flaring petals are pure white. Anthers on the spreading filament tips are 1 to 2 centimeters long, and are arranged singly near the ends of the branches. The capsules are enclosed by the sepals and contain long seeds, which are covered with yellowish-brown cilia.

Habitat

This species typically grows along steep sea cliffs in mesic forests between 50 and 1,600 feet in elevation on the northern coast of East Molokai.

For a continued habitat description of Molokai, see "Habitat Conditions on the Island of Molokai, Hawaii," page 1993.

Historic Range

H. a. ssp. *immaculatus* once ranged from Waihanau Valley east to Papalaua Valley on East Molokai.

Current Distribution

This species is now confined to a stretch

of the northern coast of East Molokai on private and State lands. The four populations of *H. a.* ssp. *immaculatus* numbering no more than 50 individuals indicate that stochastic events or extreme climatic changes could obliterate this species' well-being due to the depauperate number of extant individuals and its restricted distribution.

Conservation and Recovery

The plant fauna of Molokai has currently fallen vulnerable to habitat degradation andor predation by wild, feral, or domestic animals (goats, pigs, sheep, and cattle); competition for space, light, water, and nutrients by naturalized, exotic species; habitat loss due to fires; human recreational activities; and military exercises.

Cattle ranching on Molokai has played a significant role over most of the past 150 years in reducing areas of native vegetation to vast pastures of alien grasses. In 1960 about 61% of Molokai's lands were devoted to grazing, primarily in West and central Molokai. Cattle degrade the habitat by trampling and feeding on vegetation, eventually exposing the ground cover, increasing soil vulnerability to erosion. Red erosional scars resulting from decades of cattle disturbance, exacerbated by other feral ungulate activities, are still evident on West Molokai and the upper elevations of East Molokai. Cattle facilitate the spread of alien grasses and other plants.

Alteration of vegetation limits natural areas. It was here on the upper elevation mesic to wet forests of East Molokai, which the State designated a single protected area: the Molokai Forest Reserve. This reserve accounts for 30% of Molokai land area. Cattle ranching was succeeded in the 1920s by pineapple cultivation. Most of the land used for this agricultural activity had already been altered through the decades of cattle ranching. However, pineapple cultivation contributed to a high degree of erosion until its decline in the 1970s.

For a continued discussion of the threats to Hawaiian plants, see page 1831.

Bibliography

U.S. Fish and Wildlife Service. "Endangered and Threatened Wildlife and Plants; Determination of Endangered or Threatened Status for 16 Plants from the Island of Molokai, Hawaii." *Federal Register* Vol. 57, No. 196, October 8, 1992: 46325-45339.

Contacts

Pacific Islands Ecological Services
    Field Office
Room 6307, 300 Ala Moana Blvd.
Honolulu, HI 96850
Phone: 808-541-2749
FAX: 808-541-2756

Regional Office
Eastside Federal Complex
911 N.S. 11th Avenue
Portland, OR 97232-4181
Phone: 503-231-6118

Adapted from data compiled by the Threatened and Endangered Species Information Institute (13950 W. 20th Ave., Golden, CO 80401) for *Beacham's International Threatened, Endangered, and Extinct Species* published on CD ROM, available from Beacham Publishing.

Alani
Melicope reflexa

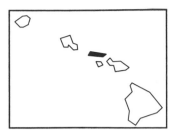

Status	Endangered
Listed	October 8, 1992
Family	Rutaceae (Citrus)
Description	Short, yellowish-brown shrub of the citrus family.
Habitat	Wet 'ohi'a-dominated forests.
Threats	Habitat disturbance, predation by wild, feral, or domestic animals.
Range	Hawaii (Molokai)

No Photo Available for This Spcies

Description

This Alani, *Melicope reflexa*, is a sprawling member of the citrus family. This shrub is 1 to 3 meters tall with short, yellowish-brown, short-lived cilia on new growth. The elliptical leathery leaves are opposite and thin measuring 8 to 14 centimeters long and 4 to 7 centimeters wide. The flowers are observed singly or in clusters of two or three from the leaf axil. The flower cluster has a stalk measuring 3 to 15 millimeters long, and each flower is on a 15 to 20 millimeter long stalk. Male flowers have not been observed, but the female flowers are made up of four overlapping sepals; four petals; an eight-lobed nectary disk; eight reduced, nonfunctional stamens; and a style about 4 millimeters long. The capsules are 20 to 33 millimeters wide with four sections which are fused to each other along about one-fourth of their length. One or two glossy black seeds are found in each section of the capsule.

Habitat

This species typically growns in wet 'ohi'a-dominated forests with native trees such as 'olapa at elevations between 2,490 and 3,900 feet.

For a continued habitat description of Molokai, see "Habitat Conditions on the Island of Molokai, Hawaii," page 1993.

Historic Range

Historically, this Alani occurred from a ridge between Hanalilolilo and Pepeopae in Kamakou Preserve to as far east as Halawa on East Molokai.

Current Distribution

The four remaining populations of fewer than a total of 1,000 individuals are on private land at the headwall of the Waikolu Valley, Wailau-Mapulehu summit and Kuku-inui Ridge, and at Honomuni, and are distributed over a distance of about 7.5 miles.

Conservation and Recovery

The plant fauna of Molokai has currently fallen vulnerable to habitat degradation andor predation by wild, feral, or domestic animals (axis deer, goats, pigs, sheep, and cattle); competition for space, light, water, and nutrients by naturalized, exotic species; habitat loss due to fires; predation by rats; human recreational activities; and military exercises. Overgrazing by axis deer, and goats has irreparably damaged much native vegetation of Molokai and Hawaii. These feral animals overgraze and expose the soil to erosion. Eight Axis deer were introduced to Molokai in 1868 and flourished to thousands by 1960. Goats were also introduced to the island in the 1800s, and despite the goatskin trade, these goats invaded the high elevation dry forests and are now invading the wetter regions along the northern coast of East Molokai. Feral pigs inhabit the wetter forested regions of Molokai in the Molokai Forest Reserve. These pigs root, trample and degrade native vegetation and habitat.

Cattle ranching on Molokai has played a significant role over most of the past 150 years in reducing areas of native vegetation to vast pastures of alien grasses. In 1960 about 61% of Molokai's lands were devoted to grazing, primarily in West and central Molokai. Cattle degrade the habitat by trampling and feeding on vegetation, eventually exposing the ground cover, increasing soil vulnerability to erosion. Red erosional scars resulting from decades of cattle disturbance, exacerbated by other feral ungulate activities, are still evident on West Molokai and the upper elevations of East Molokai. Cattle facilitate the spread of alien grasses and other plants.

Alteration of vegetation limits natural areas. It was here on the upper elevation

mesic to wet forests of East Molokai, which the State designated a single protected area: the Molokai Forest Reserve. This reserve accounts for 30% of Molokai land area. Cattle ranching was succeeded in the 1920s by pineapple cultivation. Most of the land used for this agricultural activity had already been altered through the decades of cattle ranching. However, pineapple cultivation contributed to a high degree of erosion until its decline in the 1970s.

For a continued discussion of the threats to Hawaiian plants, see page 1831.

Bibliography

U.S. Fish and Wildlife Service. "Endangered and Threatened Wildlife and Plants; Determination of Endangered or Threatened Status for 16 Plants from the Island of Molokai, Hawaii." *Federal Register* Vol. 57, No. 196, October 8, 1992: 46325-45339.

Contacts

Pacific Islands Ecological Services Field Office
Room 6307, 300 Ala Moana Blvd.
Honolulu, HI 96850
Phone: 808-541-2749

Adapted from data compiled by the Threatened and Endangered Species Information Institute (13950 W. 20th Ave., Golden, CO 80401) for *Beacham's International Threatened, Endangered, and Extinct Species* published on CD ROM, available from Beacham Publishing.

Phyllostegia mannii

No Common Name

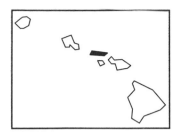

Ken Wood, National Tropical Botanical Garden

Status	Endangered
Listed	October 8, 1992
Family	Lamiaceae (Mint)
Description	Nonaromatic climbing vine with many-branched four-sided, hairy stems.
Habitat	Shaded sites in sometimes foggy and windswept, wet, open, 'ohi'a-dominated forests.
Threats	Habitat disturbance, predation by wild, feral, or domestic animals.
Range	Hawaii (Molokai)

Description

Phyllostegia mannii is a nonaromatic climbing vine with many-branched four-sided, hairy stems. The narrow triangular shaped or triangular-oval shaped leaves are opposite and ciliated and are 2 to 5.5 centimeters long. These leaves have coarsely toothed margins. The clusters of four to six flowers are arranged in each of several false whorls along an unbranched flowering stem 4 to 15 centimeters long. The calyx is a bell-shaped, lobed structure. The slightly curved, two-lipped corolla tube is about 7 to 8 millimeters long and is thought to be white. The plants bears fleshy, dark-green to black nutlets.

Habitat

This species grows in shaded sites in sometimes foggy and windswept, wet, open, 'ohi'a-dominated forests with a native shrub and tree fern (hapu'u) understory at elevations of 3,300 to 5,000 feet. Associated plant species include 'olapa, a few native ferns, and manono on East Molokai.

For a continued habitat description of Molokai, see "Habitat Conditions on the Island of Molokai, Hawaii," page 1993.

Historic Range

Historically, *P. mannii* was found from Hanalilolilo to Ohialele on East Molokai and at Ukulele on East Maui. This plant is believed to be extinct from Maui, as it has not been seen in over 70 years.

Current Distribution

This species is currently only known to be

located within the Nature Conservancy's Kamakou Preserve. Stochastic events or extreme climatic changes could dramatically affect the four remaining individuals of *P. mannii*.

Conservation and Recovery

The plant fauna of Molokai has currently fallen vulnerable to habitat degradation and/or predation by wild, feral, or domestic animals (axis deer, goats, pigs, sheep, and cattle); competition for space, light, water, and nutrients by naturalized, exotic species; habitat loss due to fires; predation by rats; human recreational activities; and military exercises.

Overgrazing by axis deer, and goats has irreparably damaged much native vegetation of Molokai and Hawaii. These feral animals overgraze and expose the soil to erosion. Eight Axis deer were introduced to Molokai in 1868 and flourished to thousands by 1960. Goats were also introduced to the island in the 1800s and despite the goatskin trade these goats invaded the high elevation dry forests and are now invading the wetter regions along the northern coast of East Molokai. Feral pigs inhabit the wetter forested regions of Molokai in the Molokai Forest Reserve and threaten habitat supporting *P. mannii*. These pigs root, trample and degrade native vegetation and habitat.

Cattle ranching on Molokai has played a significant role over most of the past 150 years in reducing areas of native vegetation to vast pastures of alien grasses. In 1960 about 61% of Molokai's lands were devoted to grazing, primarily in West and central Molokai. Cattle degrade the habitat by trampling and feeding on vegetation, eventually exposing the ground cover, increasing soil vulnerability to erosion. Red erosional scars resulting from decades of cattle disturbance, exacerbated by other feral ungulate activities,

are still evident on West Molokai and the upper elevations of East Molokai. Cattle facilitate the spread of alien grasses and other plants.

Alteration of vegetation limits natural areas. It was here on the upper elevation mesic to wet forests of East Molokai, which the State designated a single protected area: the Molokai Forest Reserve. This reserve accounts for 30% of Molokai land area. Cattle ranching was succeeded in the 1920s by pineapple cultivation. Most of the land used for this agricultural activity had already been altered through the decades of cattle ranching. However, pineapple cultivation contributed to a high degree of erosion until its decline in the 1970s.

For a continued discussion of the threats to Hawaiian plants, see page 1831.

Bibliography

U.S. Fish and Wildlife Service. "Endangered and Threatened Wildlife and Plants; Determination of Endangered or Threatened Status for 16 Plants from the Island of Molokai, Hawaii." *Federal Register* Vol. 57, No. 196, October 8, 1992: 46325-45339.

Contacts

Pacific Islands Ecological Services
   Field Office
Room 6307, 300 Ala Moana Blvd.
Honolulu, HI 96850
Phone: 808-541-2749
FAX: 808-541-2756

Adapted from data compiled by the Threatened and Endangered Species Information Institute (13950 W. 20th Ave., Golden, CO 80401) for *Beacham's International Threatened, Endangered, and Extinct Species* published on CD ROM, available from Beacham Publishing.

Haha

Cyanea procera

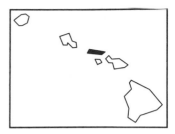

Ken Wood, National Tropical Botanical Garden

Status	Endangered
Listed	October 8, 1992
Family	Campanulaceae (Bellflower)
Description	Palmlike stalkless flowering tree with berries.
Habitat	Steep rock walls with thin soil on the southwest slope of a narrow gulch.
Threats	Habitat destruction, predation by wild, feral, or domestic animals.
Range	Hawaii (Molokai)

Description

Cyanea procera is a palmlike tree that reaches heights of up to 3 to 9 meters and has stalkless, lanceolate leaves with tiny hardened teeth along the margins. Each flower cluster has a stalk 25 to 40 millimeters long. Each individual flower has a hypanthium that is topped by shallow triangular calyx lobes. The purplish corolla forms a nearly upright or slightly curved tube that ends in five downwardly curving lobes which make the flower appear one-lipped. The berries are ellipse-shaped.

Habitat

The two known individuals of *C. procera* grow within 2 meters of each other on steep rock walls with thin soil on the southwest slope of a narrow gulch on Molokai, Hawaii. Associated plant species are *Asplenium* sp., *Coprosma ochracea* (pilo), *Pipturus albidus* and *Touchardia latifolia*.

For a continued habitat description of Molokai, see "Habitat Conditions on the Island of Molokai, Hawaii," page 1993.

Historic Range

Historically, *C. procera* was known from a site in the Kamalo region of East Molokai. In 1987 it was discovered at Puu O Kaeha on private land.

Current Distribution

Currently there are only 4 individuals of *C. procera* making it especially susceptible to any stochastic event or extreme climatic change. A event of such proportion could possibly extirpate this species because of the depauperate number of extant individuals..

Conservation and Recovery

The plant fauna of Molokai has currently fallen vulnerable to habitat degradation andor predation by wild, feral, or domestic animals (axis deer, goats, pigs, sheep, and cattle); competition for space, light, water, and nutrients by naturalized, exotic species; habitat loss due to fires; predation by rats; human recreational activities; and military exercises. Overgrazing by axis deer, and goats has irreparably damaged much native vegetation of Molokai and Hawaii.

Cattle ranching on Molokai has played a significant role over most of the past 150 years in reducing areas of native vegetation to vast pastures of alien grasses. In 1960 about 61% of Molokai's lands were devoted to grazing, primarily in West and central Molokai. Cattle degrade the habitat by trampling and feeding on vegetation, eventually exposing the ground cover, increasing soil vulnerability to erosion. Red erosional scars resulting from decades of cattle disturbance, exacerbated by other feral ungulate activities, are still evident on West Molokai and the upper elevations of East Molokai. Cattle facilitate the spread of alien grasses and other plants.

Alteration of vegetation limits natural areas. It was here on the upper elevation mesic to wet forests of East Molokai, which the State designated a single protected area: the Molokai Forest Reserve. This reserve accounts for 30% of Molokai land area. Cattle ranching was succeeded in the 1920s by pineapple cultivation. Most of the land used for this agricultural activity had already been altered through the decades of cattle ranching. However, pineapple cultivation contrib-uted to a high degree of erosion until its decline in the 1970s.

For a continued description of the threats to Hawaiian plants, see page 1831.

Bibliography

U.S. Fish and Wildlife Service. "Endangered and Threatened Wildlife and Plants; Determination of Endangered or Threatened Status for 16 Plants from the Island of Molokai, Hawaii." *Federal Register* Vol. 57, No. 196, October 8, 1992: 46325-45339.

Contacts

Pacific Islands Ecological Services
Field Office
Room 6307, 300 Ala Moana Blvd.
Honolulu, HI 96850
Phone: 808-541-2749
FAX: 808-541-2756

Adapted from data compiled by the Threatened and Endangered Species Information Institute (13950 W. 20th Ave., Golden, CO 80401) for *Beacham's International Threatened, Endangered, and Extinct Species* published on CD ROM, available from Beacham Publishing.

Loulu

Pritchardi munroi

Steve Perlman, National Tropical Botanical Garden

Status	Endangered
Listed	October 8, 1992
Family	Arecaceae (Palm)
Description	Palm with deeply segmented leaves and long drooping tips with spherical black, shiny fruit.
Habitat	Remnant dry to mesic forest.
Threats	Habitat disturbance, and predation by wild, feral, or domestic animals.
Range	Hawaii (Molokai)

Description

This Loulu, *Pritchardi munroi*, is a palm about 4 to 5 meters tall with a trunk up to about 30 centimeters in diameter. The leaf blade is about 88 centimeters long and has a petiole about 85 centimeters long. Both the ciliated leaves and ciliated petioles have scattered, mostly deciduous scales. The leaves are deeply segmented and have long, drooping tips. Numerous bisexual or functionally male flowers are arranged in clusters on hairy, branching stalks about 52 centimeters long which originate at the leaf bases. The flower consists of a cup-shaped, three-lobed calyx; three petals; six stamens; and three-lobed stigma. The mature nearly spherical fruit is shiny, black and about 2 to 2.2 centimeters in diameter.

Habitat

The only known population grows near the base of a small ravine in remnant dry to mesic forest at an elevation of about 2,000 feet on East Molokai. Associated plant species include 'a'ali'i, 'ohi'a, pukiawe, and hala pepe.

For a continued habitat description of Molokai, see "Habitat Conditions on the Island of Molokai, Hawaii," page 1993.

Historic Range

Historically, *P. munroi* was found in East Molokai. The last known wild specimen grows on privately owned land on Molokai.

Current Distribution

Historically, *P. munroi* was found in East Molokai. The last known wild specimen grows on privately owned land on Molokai.

Conservation and Recovery

The plant fauna of Molokai has currently fallen vulnerable to habitat degradation and/or predation by wild, feral, or domestic animals (axis deer, goats, pigs, sheep, and cattle); competition for space, light, water, and nutrients by naturalized, exotic species; habitat loss due to fires; predation by rats; human recreational activities; and military exercises.

Overgrazing by axis deer, and goats has irreparably damaged much native vegetation of Molokai and Hawaii. These feral animals overgraze and expose the soil to erosion. Eight Axis deer were introduced to Molokai in 1868 and flourished to thousands by 1960. Goats were also introduced to the island in the 1800s and despite the goatskin trade these goats invaded the high elevation dry forests and are now invading the wetter regions along the northern coast of East Molokai. Feral pigs inhabit the wetter forested regions of Molokai and threaten the habitat by rooting, trampling and degrading native vegetation.

Cattle ranching on Molokai has played a significant role over most of the past 150 years in reducing areas of native vegetation to vast pastures of alien grasses. In 1960 about 61% of Molokai's lands were devoted to grazing, primarily in West and central Molokai. Cattle degrade the habitat by trampling and feeding on vegetation, eventually exposing the ground cover, increasing soil vulnerability to erosion. Red erosional scars resulting from decades of cattle disturbance, exacerbated by other feral ungulate activities, are still evident on West Molokai and the upper elevations of East Molokai. Cattle facilitate the spread of alien grasses and other plants.

Alteration of vegetation limits natural areas. It was here on the upper elevation mesic to wet forests of East Molokai, which the State designated a single protected area: the Molokai Forest Reserve. This reserve accounts for 30% of Molokai land area. Cattle ranching was succeeded in the 1920s by pineapple cultivation. Most of the land used for this agricultural activity had already been altered through the decades of cattle ranching. However, pineapple cultivation contributed to a high degree of erosion until its decline in the 1970s.

For a continued discussion of the threats to Hawaiian plants, see page 1831.

Bibliography

U.S. Fish and Wildlife Service. "Endangered and Threatened Wildlife and Plants; Determination of Endangered or Threatened Status for 16 Plants from the Island of Molokai, Hawaii." *Federal Register* Vol. 57, No. 196, October 8, 1992: 46325-45339.

Contacts

Pacific Islands Ecological Services
    Field Office
Room 6307, 300 Ala Moana Blvd.
Honolulu, HI 96850
Phone: 808-541-2749
FAX: 808-541-2756

Adapted from data compiled by the Threatened and Endangered Species Information Institute (13950 W. 20th Ave., Golden, CO 80401) for *Beacham's International Threatened, Endangered, and Extinct Species* published on CD ROM, available from Beacham Publishing.

Schiedea lydgatei

No Common Name

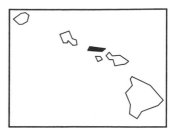

Steve Perlman, National Tropical Botanical Garden

Status	Endangered
Listed	October 8, 1992
Family	Caryophyllaceae (Pink)
Description	Low growing perennial with branched stems and woody at the base.
Habitat	Ridges and cattle trails in dry to mesic grasslands, shrublands, and forests with scattered native and alien trees.
Threats	Habitat disturbance, and predation by wild, feral, or domestic animals.
Range	Hawaii (Molokai)

Description

Schiedea lydgatei is a low growing, glabrous perennial that grows to 10 to 40 centimeters long. The stems are branched and woody at the base. The opposite, three-veined leaves are elliptic, 2 to 4.5 centimeters long. Bisexual flowers are arranged in loosely spreading clusters 10 to 17 centimeters long. The flowers comprise usually 5 distinct narrowly oval, green sepals; 5 nectaries; 10 stamens; and usually 3 styles. Petals are lacking. The capsules open when mature to reveal dark rufous seeds.

Habitat

This species is found along ridges and on cattle trails in dry to mesic grasslands, shrublands, and forests with scattered native and alien trees, at elevations of 2,000 to 2,100 feet on East Molokai. Associated plant species include 'a'ali'i, 'ohi'a, pukiawe, and uluhe.

For a continued habitat description of Molokai, see "Habitat Conditions on the Island of Molokai, Hawaii," page 1993.

Historic Range

Historically, *S. lydgatei* was found in Kalae, Poholua, Makolelau, and Ohia Gulch on East Molokai.

Current Distribution

This species is now known from Makakupai, Kawela and Makolelau. The five extant populations consisting of no more than 1,000 individuals are most pressured by a pervasive fire threat.

Conservation and Recovery

The plant fauna of Molokai has currently fallen vulnerable to habitat degradation and or predation by wild, feral, or domestic animals (axis deer, goats, pigs, sheep, and cattle); competition for space, light, water, and nutrients by naturalized, exotic species; habitat loss due to fires; predation by rats; human recreational activities; and military exercises.

Overgrazing by axis deer, and goats has irreparably damaged much native vegetation of Molokai and Hawaii. These feral animals overgraze and expose the soil to erosion. Eight Axis deer were introduced to Molokai in 1868 and flourished to thousands by 1960. Goats were also introduced to the island in the 1800s and despite the goatskin trade these goats invaded the high elevation dry forests and are now invading the wetter regions along the northern coast of East Molokai. Feral pigs inhabit the wetter forested regions of Molokai and threaten the habitat by rooting, trampling and degrading native vegetation.

Cattle ranching on Molokai has played a significant role over most of the past 150 years in reducing areas of native vegetation to vast pastures of alien grasses. In 1960 about 61% of Molokai's lands were devoted to grazing, primarily in West and central Molokai. Cattle degrade the habitat by trampling and feeding on vegetation, eventually exposing the ground cover, increasing soil vulnerability to erosion. Red erosional scars resulting from decades of cattle disturbance, exacerbated by other feral ungulate activities, are still evident on West Molokai and the upper elevations of East Molokai. Cattle facilitate the spread of alien grasses and other plants.

Alteration of vegetation limits natural areas. It was here on the upper elevation mesic to wet forests of East Molokai, which the State designated a single protected area: the Molokai Forest Reserve. This reserve accounts for 30% of Molokai land area. Cattle ranching was succeeded in the 1920s by pineapple cultivation. Most of the land used for this agricultural activity had already been altered through the decades of cattle ranching. However, pineapple cultivation contributed to a high degree of erosion until its decline in the 1970s.

For a continued discussion of the threats to Hawaiian plants, see page 1831.

Bibliography

U.S. Fish and Wildlife Service. "Endangered and Threatened Wildlife and Plants; Determination of Endangered or Threatened Status for 16 Plants from the Island of Molokai, Hawaii." *Federal Register* Vol. 57, No. 196, October 8, 1992: 46325-45339.

Contacts

Pacific Islands Ecological Services
    Field Office
Room 6307, 300 Ala Moana Blvd.
Honolulu, HI 96850
Phone: 808-541-2749
FAX: 808-541-2756

Adapted from data compiled by the Threatened and Endangered Species Information Institute (13950 W. 20th Ave., Golden, CO 80401) for *Beacham's International Threatened, Endangered, and Extinct Species* published on CD ROM, available from Beacham Publishing.

Silene alexandri

No Common Name

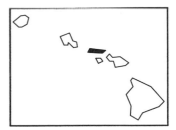

Ken Wood, National Tropical Botanical Garden

Status	Endangered
Listed	October 8, 1992
Family	Caryophyllaceae (Pink)
Description	Terrestrial shrub or tree with short leaves, leaf stalks,and flower stalks.
Habitat	Remnant dry forest and shrubland at an elevation between 2,000 and 2,500 feet.
Threats	Habitat disturbance, and predation by wild, feral, or domestic animals.
Range	Hawaii (Molokai)

Description

This member of the pink family is an erect perennial herb. *Silene alexandri* reaches height of up to 30 to 60 centimeters. The stem is woody at the base. The narrow, elliptic glabrous leaves are 30 to 65 millimeters long and 6 to 14 millimeters wide, and have a ciliated fringe along the margins. The flowers are arranged in open clusters with stalks 10 to 19 millimeters long. The 5-lobed, 10-veined, tubular calyx is 19 to 25 millimeters long and the 5 white, deeply-lobed, clawed petals extend about 4 to 6 millimeters beyond the calyx. The capsule is 14 to 16 millimeters long, but seeds have never been observed.

Habitat

The only known population, comprising fewer than 10 individuals, is found on a cattle trail in remnant dry forest and shrubland at an elevation between 2,000 and 2,500 feet. Associated plant species include 'a'ali'i, 'ohi'a, pukiawe, and uluhe.

For a continued habitat description of Molokai, see "Habitat Conditions on the Island of Molokai, Hawaii," page 1993.

Historic Range and Current Distribution

Historically, *S. alexandri* was known from Makolelau and Kamalo on East Molokai, but now it occurs only at Kamalo. Stochastic events or extreme climatic changes could adversely affect the 10 extant individuals of *S. alexandri* currently threatened by predation and fire.

Conservation and Recovery

The plant fauna of Molokai has currently fallen vulnerable to habitat degradation and or predation by wild, feral, or domestic animals (axis deer, goats, pigs, sheep, and cattle); competition for space, light, water, and nutrients by naturalized, exotic species; habitat loss due to fires; predation by rats; human recreational activities; and military exercises.

Overgrazing by axis deer, and goats has irreparably damaged much native vegetation of Molokai and Hawaii. These feral animals overgraze and expose the soil to erosion. Eight Axis deer were introduced to Molokai in 1868 and flourished to thousands by 1960. Goats were also introduced to the island in the 1800s and despite the goatskin trade these goats invaded the high elevation dry forests and are now invading the wetter regions along the northern coast of East Molokai. Feral pigs inhabit the wetter forested regions of Molokai and threaten the habitat by rooting, trampling and degrading native vegetation.

Cattle ranching on Molokai has played a significant role over most of the past 150 years in reducing areas of native vegetation to vast pastures of alien grasses. In 1960 about 61% of Molokai's lands were devoted to grazing, primarily in West and central Molokai. Cattle degrade the habitat by trampling and feeding on vegetation, eventually exposing the ground cover, increasing soil vulnerability to erosion. Red erosional scars resulting from decades of cattle disturbance, exacerbated by other feral ungulate activities, are still evident on West Molokai and the upper elevations of East Molokai. Cattle fa-cilitate the spread of alien grasses and other plants.

Alteration of vegetation limits natural areas. It was here on the upper elevation mesic to wet forests of East Molokai, which the State designated a single protected area: the Molokai Forest Reserve. This reserve accounts for 30% of Molokai land area. Cattle ranching was succeeded in the 1920s by pineapple cultivation. Most of the land used for this agricultural activity had already been altered through the decades of cattle ranching. However, pineapple cultivation contributed to a high degree of erosion until its decline in the 1970s.

For a continued discussion of the threats to Hawaiian plants, see page 1831.

Bibliography

U.S. Fish and Wildlife Service. "Endangered and Threatened Wildlife and Plants; Determination of Endangered or Threatened Status for 16 Plants from the Island of Molokai, Hawaii." *Federal Register* Vol. 57, No. 196, October 8, 1992: 46325-45339.

Contacts

Pacific Islands Ecological Services
Field Office
Room 6307, 300 Ala Moana Blvd.
Honolulu, HI 96850
Phone: 808-541-2749
FAX: 808-541-2756

Adapted from data compiled by the Threatened and Endangered Species Information Institute (13950 W. 20th Ave., Golden, CO 80401) for *Beacham's International Threatened, Endangered, and Extinct Species* published on CD ROM, available from Beacham Publishing.

Silene lanceolata
No Common Name

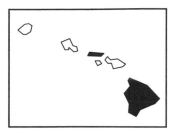

Robert B. Shaw

Status	Endangered
Listed	October 8, 1992
Family	Caryophyllaceae (Pink)
Description	Upright perennial plant with narrow leaves and white deeply-lobed, clawed petals.
Habitat	Cliff faces and ledges of gullies in dry to mesic shrubland.
Threats	Habitat disturbance, and predation by wild, feral, or domestic animals.
Range	Hawaii (Molokai, Hawaii)

Description

Silene lanceolata is an upright perennial plant with stems 15 to 20 centimeters long, which are woody at the base. The narrow leaves are 25 to 80 millimeters long, 2 to 11 millimeters wide, and glabrous except for a fringe of hairs near the base. The flowers are arranged in open clusters with stalks 8 to 23 millimeters long. The 5-toothed, 10 to veined calyx is about 7 to 9 millimeters long. The 5 white deeply-lobed, clawed petals are 6 millimeters long. The capsule is about 8 to 9 millimeters in length and opens at the top to release rufous colored seeds which are about 1 millimeter in diameter.

Habitat

The populations on the island of Hawaii grow in two dry habitat types: (1) shrubland dominated by dense naio, mamane, and pukiawe, and (2) a forest converted into a fountain grass grassland with 'a'ali'i, mamane, naio, and 'aheahea. On Molokai, this species grows on cliff faces and ledges of gullies in dry to mesic shrubland at an elevation of about 2,600 feet.

For a continued habitat description of Molokai, see "Habitat Conditions on the Island of Molokai, Hawaii," page 1993.

Historic Range

Historically, *S. lanceolata* inhabited the islands of Kauai, Molokai, Lanai and Hawaii.

Current Distribution

Currently this species is only found on East Molokai and Hawaii, although the Hawaiian population has not been observed since 1949. The two populations are located on federally owned Pohakuloa Training Area, Hawaii. The three known populations consist of a known 95 to 125 individuals are highly susceptible to ungulate and human activities, wildfires, military maneuvers, and invasion by the alien plant fountain grass. Extreme climatic changes could also irreparably affect *S. lanceolata* species due to its limited number of extant individuals and restricted distribution.

Conservation and Recovery

The plant fauna of Molokai has currently fallen vulnerable to habitat degradation and or predation by wild, feral, or domestic animals (axis deer, goats, pigs, sheep, and cattle); competition for space, light, water, and nutrients by naturalized, exotic species; habitat loss due to fires; predation by rats; human recreational activities; and military exercises.

Overgrazing by axis deer, and goats has irreparably damaged much native vegetation of Molokai and Hawaii. These feral animals overgraze and expose the soil to erosion. Eight Axis deer were introduced to Molokai in 1868 and flourished to thousands by 1960. Goats were also introduced to the island in the 1800s and despite the goatskin trade these goats invaded the high elevation dry forests and are now invading the wetter regions along the northern coast of East Molokai. Feral pigs inhabit the wetter forested regions of Molokai and threaten the habitat by rooting, trampling and degrading native vegetation.

Cattle ranching on Molokai has played a significant role over most of the past 150 years in reducing areas of native vegetation to vast pastures of alien grasses. In 1960 about 61% of Molokai's lands were devoted to grazing, primarily in West and central Molokai. Cattle degrade the habitat by tram-

pling and feeding on vegetation, eventually exposing the ground cover, increasing soil vulnerability to erosion. Red erosional scars resulting from decades of cattle disturbance, exacerbated by other feral ungulate activities, are still evident on West Molokai and the upper elevations of East Molokai. Cattle facilitate the spread of alien grasses and other plants.

Alteration of vegetation limits natural areas. It was here on the upper elevation mesic to wet forests of East Molokai, which the State designated a single protected area: the Molokai Forest Reserve. This reserve accounts for 30% of Molokai land area. Cattle ranching was succeeded in the 1920s by pineapple cultivation. Most of the land used for this agricultural activity had already been altered through the decades of cattle ranching. However, pineapple cultivation contributed to a high degree of erosion until its decline in the 1970s.

For a continued discussion of the threats to Hawaiian plants, see page 1831.

Bibliography

U.S. Fish and Wildlife Service. "Endangered and Threatened Wildlife and Plants; Determination of Endangered or Threatened Status for 16 Plants from the Island of Molokai, Hawaii." *Federal Register* Vol. 57, No. 196, October 8, 1992: 46325-45339.

Contacts

Pacific Islands Ecological Services
Room 6307, 300 Ala Moana Blvd.
Honolulu, HI 96850
Phone: 808-541-2749

Adapted from data compiled by the Threatened and Endangered Species Information Institute (13950 W. 20th Ave., Golden, CO 80401) for *Beacham's International Threatened, Endangered, and Extinct Species* published on CD ROM.

Stenogyne bifida
No Common Name

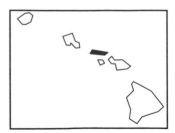

Steve Perlman, National Tropical Botanical Garden

Status	Endangered
Listed	October 8, 1992
Family	Lamiaceae (Mint)
Description	Climbing perennial mint with oval shaped leaves bearing black nutlet fleshy fruit.
Habitat	Steep ridges in 'ohi'a-dominated montane mesic to wet forests.
Threats	Habitat disturbance, and predation by wild, feral, or domestic animals.
Range	Hawaii (Molokai)

Description

Stenogyne bifida is a perennial herb, climbing, with glabrous to slightly ciliated four-angled stems. The opposite, membranous toothed leaves of this mint are oval or elliptical in shape, measuring 4.2 to 10 centimeters long. The leaves are glabrous with the exception of the midribs. The flowers of *S. bifida* are usually arranged in groups ranging from 2 to 6 in each of several whorls acute at the stems. The sepals are fused into a toothed calyx which is mostly glabrous, radially symmetrical, and narrowly bell-shaped. The petals are fused into a nearly straight, yellow tube 10 to 16 millimeters long. The fleshy fruit is a black nutlet.

Habitat

This species typically grows on steep ridges in 'ohi'a-dominated montane mesic to wet forests at elevations between 1,450 and 4,000 feet on East Molokai. Associated plant species include hapu'u, manono, 'olapa, kanawao, and 'ala'a.

For a continued habitat description of Molokai, see "Habitat Conditions on the Island of Molokai, Hawaii," page 1993.

Historic Range

The historical distribution of *S. bifida* was from Waianui to Pukoo Ridge, Molokai.

Current Distribution

Although this species' range has severely decreased, it is still located in portions of Molokai along a private/State land boundary. Ungulates are pervasive threats to *S. bifida* and may even eat this species when

available. This species is limited to three populations and any stochastic event or extreme climatic change could adversely affect this species because of the limited number of extant individuals and its restricted distribution.

Conservation and Recovery

The plant fauna of Molokai has currently fallen vulnerable to habitat degradation and or predation by wild, feral, or domestic animals (axis deer, goats, pigs, sheep, and cattle); competition for space, light, water, and nutrients by naturalized, exotic species; habitat loss due to fires; predation by rats; human recreational activities; and military exercises.

Overgrazing by axis deer, and goats has irreparably damaged much native vegetation of Molokai and Hawaii. These feral animals overgraze and expose the soil to erosion. Eight Axis deer were introduced to Molokai in 1868 and flourished to thousands by 1960. Goats were also introduced to the island in the 1800s and despite the goatskin trade these goats invaded the high elevation dry forests and are now invading the wetter regions along the northern coast of East Molokai. Feral pigs inhabit the wetter forested regions of Molokai and threaten the habitat by rooting, trampling and degrading native vegetation.

Cattle ranching on Molokai has played a significant role over most of the past 150 years in reducing areas of native vegetation to vast pastures of alien grasses. In 1960 about 61% of Molokai's lands were devoted to grazing, primarily in West and central Molokai. Cattle degrade the habitat by trampling and feeding on vegetation, eventually exposing the ground cover, increasing soil vulnerability to erosion. Red erosional scars resulting from decades of cattle disturbance, exacerbated by other feral ungulate activities,

are still evident on West Molokai and the upper elevations of East Molokai. Cattle facilitate the spread of alien grasses and other plants.

Alteration of vegetation limits natural areas. It was here on the upper elevation mesic to wet forests of East Molokai, which the State designated a single protected area: the Molokai Forest Reserve. This reserve accounts for 30% of Molokai land area. Cattle ranching was succeeded in the 1920s by pineapple cultivation. Most of the land used for this agricultural activity had already been altered through the decades of cattle ranching. However, pineapple cultivation contributed to a high degree of erosion until its decline in the 1970s.

For a continued discussion of the threats to Hawaiian plants, see page 1831.

Bibliography

U.S. Fish and Wildlife Service. "Endangered and Threatened Wildlife and Plants; Determination of Endangered or Threatened Status for 16 Plants from the Island of Molokai, Hawaii." *Federal Register* Vol. 57, No. 196, October 8, 1992: 46325-45339.

Contacts

Pacific Islands Ecological Services
Field Office
Room 6307, 300 Ala Moana Blvd.
Honolulu, HI 96850
Phone: 808-541-2749
FAX: 808-541-2756

Adapted from data compiled by the Threatened and Endangered Species Information Institute (13950 W. 20th Ave., Golden, CO 80401) for *Beacham's International Threatened, Endangered, and Extinct Species* published on CD ROM, available from Beacham Publishing.

Tetramolopium rockii
No Common Name

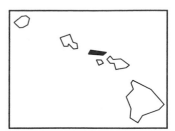

Warren Wagner

Status	Threatened
Listed	October 8, 1992
Family	Asteraceae (Aster)
Description	Shrub with short spatula-shaped leaves with long silky hairs on surface.
Habitat	Hardened calcareous sand dunes or ash-covered basalt in the coastal spray zone or coastal dry shrublands and grasslands.
Threats	Habitat disturbance, and predation by wild, feral, or domestic animals.
Range	Hawaii (Molokai)

Description

Tetramolopium rockii is a glandular, ciliated prostrate shrub which forms complexly branching mats 5 to 10 centimeters tall and 8 to 40 centimeters in diameter. Leaves of a variety of *Tetramolopium* are 2 to 3 centimeters long, and have slightly inrolled edges. The long silky hairs on the leaf surface indicate a white appearance. The leaves are spatula-shaped with glands and smooth margins. The flower heads are arranged singly at the ends of the flowering stalks that have a hemispherical involucre. There are approximately 50 to 100 white ray florets, surrounding 30 to 55 functionally male, yellow, funnel-shaped disk florets. The fruit is achene and is topped with white bristles. This species distinguishes itself from other *Tetramolopium* species by its growth habit; ciliated glandular surface; spatulate leaf shape, and yellow disk florets.

Habitat

This species is restricted to hardened calcareous sand dunes or ash-covered basalt in the coastal spray zone or coastal dry shrublands and grasslands between 30 and 650 feet on West Molokai. Associated plants species include *Frimbristylis cymosa*, hinahina, nehe, 'ilima, and 'aki'aki.

For a continued habitat description of Molokai, see "Habitat Conditions on the Island of Molokai, Hawaii," page 1993.

Historic Range

This species was first discovered at Moomomi on the Island of Molokai, Hawaii and is still extant in this area.

Current Distribution

This species occurs in areas of western Molokai including Kapalauao to Kahinaakalani and from Manalo Gulch to Kalani. The land that supports *T. rockii* is owned by the State of Hawaii (Hawaiian Home Lands), Kalaupapa National Historical Park and private entities. *T. rockii* populations are estimated to support 174,000 individuals. Stochastic events or extreme climatic changes could adversely affect this species because of its restricted distribution. Although *T. rockii* is threatened to some degree by competition, habitat destruction and predation by feral animals, fire, andor human activities, the relatively large number of existing individuals of *T. rockii* reduces the likelihood that this species will become extinct in the near future. Because the threats facing the species are limited at present, this species is not now in immediate danger of extinction throughout all or a significant portion of its range.

Conservation and Recovery

The plant fauna of Molokai has currently fallen vulnerable to habitat degradation and or predation by wild, feral, or domestic animals (axis deer, goats, pigs, sheep, and cattle); competition for space, light, water, and nutrients by naturalized, exotic species; habitat loss due to fires; predation by rats; human recreational activities; and military exercises.

Overgrazing by axis deer, and goats has irreparably damaged much native vegetation of Molokai and Hawaii. These feral animals overgraze and expose the soil to erosion. Eight Axis deer were introduced to Molokai in 1868 and flourished to thousands by 1960. Goats were also introduced to the island in the 1800s and despite the goatskin trade these goats invaded the high elevation dry forests and are now invading the wetter regions along the northern coast of East Molokai. Feral pigs inhabit the wetter forested regions of Molokai and threaten the habitat by rooting, trampling and degrading native vegetation.

Cattle ranching on Molokai has played a significant role over most of the past 150 years in reducing areas of native vegetation to vast pastures of alien grasses. In 1960 about 61% of Molokai's lands were devoted to grazing, primarily in West and central Molokai. Cattle degrade the habitat by trampling and feeding on vegetation, eventually exposing the ground cover, increasing soil vulnerability to erosion. Red erosional scars resulting from decades of cattle disturbance, exacerbated by other feral ungulate activities, are still evident on West Molokai and the upper elevations of East Molokai. Cattle facilitate the spread of alien grasses and other plants.

Alteration of vegetation limits natural areas. It was here on the upper elevation mesic to wet forests of East Molokai, which the State designated a single protected area: the Molokai Forest Reserve. This reserve accounts for 30% of Molokai land area. Cattle ranching was succeeded in the 1920s by pineapple cultivation. Most of the land used for this agricultural activity had already been altered through the decades of cattle ranching. However, pineapple cultivation contributed to a high degree of erosion until its decline in the 1970s.

For a continued discussion of the threats to Hawaiian plants, see page 1831.

Bibliography

U.S. Fish and Wildlife Service. "Endangered and Threatened Wildlife and Plants; Determination of Endangered or Threatened Status for 16 Plants from the Island of

Molokai, Hawaii." *Federal Register* Vol. 57,
No. 196, October 8, 1992: 46325-45339.

Contacts

Pacific Islands Ecological Services
   Field Office
Room 6307, 300 Ala Moana Blvd.
Honolulu, HI 96850
Phone: 808-541-2749
FAX: 808-541-2756

Regional Office
Eastside Federal Complex
911 N.S. 11th Avenue
Portland, OR 97232-4181
Phone: 503-231-6118

Adapted from data compiled by the Threatened
and Endangered Species Information Institute
(13950 W. 20th Ave., Golden, CO 80401) for *Beacham's International Threatened, Endangered, and Extinct Species* published on CD ROM, available
from Beacham Publishing.

HAWAIIAN PLANTS: OAHU

Habitat Conditions on the Island of Oahu, Hawaii

On March 28, 1994, the U.S. Fish and Wildlife Service listed as endangered or threatened eleven plants from the Koolau Mountain Range on the island of Oahu, Hawaii. On June 27, 1994 three more plants were listed from the Waianae Mountains; two other plants from the Waianae Mountains had been listed earlier. Habitat conditions on Oahu are described here rather than being repeated in each of the species accounts.

Koolau Mountain Range
Chamaesyce deppeana
Cyanea truncata
Cyrtandra crenata
Cyrtandra polyantha
Eugenia koolauensis
Hesperomannia arborescens
Lobelia oahuensis
Lycopodium nutans
Melicope (=Pelea) lydgatei
Rollandia crispa
Tetraplasandra gymnocarpa

Waianae Mountains
Cyanea grimesiana ssp. *obatae*
Gouania vitifolia
Diellia unisora
Marsilea villosa
Stenogyne kanehoana

The islands of Hawaii are of volcanic origin and consist of coastal plains, upland slopes and mountain ranges and summits. Oahu, the third largest island in the State, is 44 miles long and 30 miles wide. The land area is 386,560 acres. The island is formed from the remnants of two large shield volcanoes, the older Waianae Volcano on the west and the younger Koolau Volcano on the east. Their original shield volcano shape has been lost as a result of extensive erosion, and today these volcanoes are called "mountains" or "ranges." The island is divided into four main areas-the Waianae Range, the Koolau Range, the Schofield Plateau, and the coastal plains.

Waianae Range

The Waianae Mountains were built by eruptions along three rift zones. The two principal rift zones run in a northwestward and south-southeastward direction from the summit, and a lesser zone runs to the northeast. The range is approximately 40 miles long, and the caldera lies between the north side of Makaha Valley and the head of Nanakuli Valley. The Waianae Mountains are in the rain shadow of the parallel Koolau Mountains and except for Mt. Kaala, the highest point on Oahu (4,020 feet), receive much less rainfall. The median annual rainfall for the Waianae Mountains varies from 20 to 75 inches, with only the small summit area receiving the highest amount.

Because of its windward position, the Koolau Range traps precipitation, resulting in numerous streams and waterfalls. The range's most characteristic feature is a separated precipice rising abruptly on the eastern side from 500 to 2,500 feet. The highest point is Konahuanui, comprising two peaks 3,100 feet in elevation.

Western lava flows created the Schofield plateau, a saddle 14 miles long and 5 miles wide between the Koolau Range and the Waianae Range.

The *'ilima shrubland community* of the

coastal dry shrublands vegetation type occurs on sand dunes and poorly consolidated volcanic soils near shore environments, and is exposed to salt-laden winds. Coastal dry shrublands occur on all of the northwestern Hawaiian islands and along the coastlines of all the main islands, extending to about 1,000 feet in elevation. Because of the effects of the rain shadows, these communities are most extensively developed on the leeward sides of the higher islands. Annual rainfall is less than 45 inches and occurs primarily during the winter months of October to April. Much of the vegetation dies back during a prolonged drought that lasts most of the rest of the year.

The *lowland dry vegetation* comprises several plant comunities that occur at an elevation of 15 to 2,000 feet on the leeward side of all the main Hawaiian islands. The climate of this vegetation is distinctly seasonal, with hot, dry summers and winter rainfall, usually less than 40 inches but sometimes ranging up to 80 inches annually. The soils range from weathered silty loam to stony clay; rocky ledges with very shallow soil and recent, little-weathered lava are present.

The *diverse lowland mesic shrubland* and *forest habitats* on all the main Hawaiian islands occur mainly at elevations between 100 and 5,300 feet in areas topographically unsuitable for agriculture. Annual precipitation ranges from less than 40 to 150 inches, falling mostly in the winter months. This community occurs on diverse, well-weathered and well-drained substrates, ranging from rocky, shallow, organic muck soils to steep, rocky talus slopes, shallow rocky soils on steep slopes, to deep soil over soft weathered rock and gravelly alluvium in gulches and erosional plains. In the Waianae Mountains, this vegetation community is found in sheltered areas and comprises a rich diversity of native plants with no clearly dominant species.

Most of the area is steep to very steep and is broken by numerous drainageways. There are no perennial streams and the area consists primarily of rough broken land and deep to moderately deep soils that are well drained. The soils are gently sloping to very steep, and fine textured to moderately fine textured. Tropohumults are formed in deposits of basic igneous rock with an oxidic mineralogy and occur on the narrow ridges at the upper elevations. They have a surface layer and subsoil of reddish-brown silty clay and are underlain by soft weathered rock. Dystrandepts occur in concave positions on the steep side slopes and were derived primarily from volcanic ash mixed with colluvium. They are dark colored and have a surface layer of silt loam or silty clay loam.

'Akoko

Chamaesyce deppeana

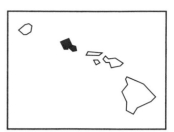

Robert J. Gustafson

Status	Endangered
Listed	March 28, 1994
Family	Euphorbiaceae (Spurge)
Description	Erect shrub up to 4 feet tall with fuzzy branches and hairless leaves, generally oval-shaped and often notched at their tips.
Habitat	Steep, exposed windswept slope growing with grasses and shrubs.
Threats	Competition from alien plants; habitat destruction by people; fire; limited numbers.
Range	Hawaii (Oahu)

Description

This 'akoko is an erect shrub up to 4 feet tall with fuzzy branches. The hairless leaves, generally oval-shaped and often notched at their tips, are between 0.2 and 0.8 inches long and 0.2 and 0.5 inches wide. They are arranged in two opposite rows along the stem. The leaf margins are usually toothed and rarely toothless. The small, petalless flower clusters (cyathia), 0.06 to 0.1 inches wide, are borne singly in the leaf axils and produce small capsules about 0.1 inch long. Seeds have not been observed. This species is distinguished from others in the genus by the following combination of characters: leaves arranged in two rows on opposite sides of the branches; glabrous leaves; notched leaf apexes; toothed leaf margin; and cyathia width.

Habitat

The only known population is scattered on a steep, exposed windswept slope growing with grasses and shrubs at an elevation of approximately 1,000 feet.

For a continued habitat description of Oahu, see "Habitat Conditions on the Island of Oahu, Hawaii," page 2031.

Historic Range and Current Distribution

Historically, 'akoko was known only from southern Oahu. Because of the few collections that were made were collected prior to the twentieth century, it was thought to be extinct. In 1986 Joel Lau and Sam Gon of The Nature Conservancy of Hawaii rediscovered the species on state land and in the southern Koolau Mountains of Oahu in Nuuanu Pali

Wayside State Park near the Pali Lookout.

Conservation and Recovery

The recovery of this and most other Hawaiian species depends on how well management practices can be implemented. The habitat of this and other Hawaiian species has undergone extreme alteration because of past and present land management practices, including deliberately introducing alien animals and plants, and agricultural and recreational development. To understand the recovery problems facing this species, it is necessary to understand the long-term causes of habitat destruction.

For a continued discussion of the threats to Hawaiian plants, see page 1831.

Bibliography

U.S. Fish and Wildlife Service. "Endangered and Threatened Wildlife and Plants: Endangered Status for 11 Plant Species from the Koolau Mountain Range, Island of Oahu, HI." *Federal Register*. March 28, 1994: 14482-14492.

Contacts

U.S. Fish and Wildlife Service
Regional Office
Eastside Federal Complex
911 N.S. 11th Avenue
Portland, OR 97232-4181
Phone: 503-231-6118

The Nature Conservancy of Hawaii
Suite 201, 1116 Smith Street
Honolulu, HI 96817
Phone: 808-537-4508
FAX: 808-545-2019

Pacific Islands Ecological Services
    Field Office
Room 6307, 300 Ala Moana Blvd.
Honolulu, HI 96850
Phone: 808-541-2749
FAX: 808-541-2756

Adapted from data compiled by Beacham Publishing for *Beacham's International Threatened, Endangered, and Extinct Species* published on CD ROM.

Rollandia crispa
No Common Name

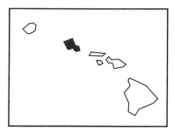

Loyal A. Mehrhoff   *Color Plate C-4*

Status	Endangered
Listed	March 28, 1994
Family	Campanulaceae (Bellflower)
Description	Unbranched shrub with broad, oval, toothed leaves, and clusters of 3 to 8 fuzzy, pale magenta flowers.
Habitat	Steep, open mesic forests to gentle slopes or moist gullies of closed wet forests.
Threats	Competition from alien plants; habitat destruction by feral pigs; limited numbers.
Range	Hawaii (Oahu)

Description

Rollandia crispa is an unbranched shrub with leaves clustered at the ends of succulent stems. The broad, oval leaves, 12 to 30 inches long and 3.5 to 6.3 inches wide, have undulating, smooth or toothed leaf margins. Each leaf is on a stalk 0.3 to 1.6 inches long. Clusters of 3 to 8 fuzzy flowers grow on stalks 0.8 to 1.2 inches long, with each flower borne on a stalk 0.4 to 0.8 inches long. The calyx lobes are oval or oblong, 0.2 to 0.5 inches long, and often overlapping at their base. The fused petals, 1.6 to 2.4 inches long, are fuzzy and pale magenta, with darker longitudinal stripes. The fruits are spherical berries 0.4 inch in diameter, that contain many minute, dark seeds.

R. crispa is distinguished from other species of this endemic Hawaiian genus by its leaf shape, distinct calyx lobes, and the length of the flowers and stalks of the flower clusters.

Habitat

This species is found in habitats ranging from steep, open mesic forests to gentle slopes or moist gullies of closed wet forests, at elevations between 600 and 2,400 feet. Associated plants include Ke'oka'o, haha, common Cyrtandra species, olona, and the introduced strawberry guava.

For a continued habitat description of Oahu, see "Habitat Conditions on the Island of Oahu, Hawaii," page 2031.

Historic Range

Historically, *R. crispa* was known from

scattered locations throughout the upper elevations of the Koolau Mountains of Oahu from Kaipapau Valley to the north Waialae Iki Ridge to the southeast.

Current Distribution

The species is now known from state and private lands in "Hidden Valley" (26 plants); Palolo Valley (1 plant); Kapakahi Gulch (1 plant); and Pia Valley (1 plant). The four populations are scattered over a distance of about 19 miles. Three of the populations contain a single, mature, flowering individual. The Hidden Valley population contains seven mature, flowering plants and 19 juvenile plants, giving a total of fewer than 30 individuals.

Conservation and Recovery

The major threats to *Rollandia crispa* are habitat alteration by feral pigs; competition with noxious alien plants, especially Koster's curse and strawberry guava; and stochastic extinction and reduced reproductive vigor due to the small number of remaining individuals, their limited gene pool, and restricted distribution.

The recovery of this and most other Hawaiian species depends on how well management practices can be implemented. The habitat of this and other Hawaiian species has undergone extreme alteration because of past and present land management practices, including deliberately introducing alien animals and plants, and agricultural and recreational development. To understand the recovery problems facing this species, it is necessary to understand the long-term causes of habitat destruction.

For a continued discussion of the threats to Hawaiian plants, see page 1831.

Bibliography

U.S. Fish and Wildlife Service. "Endangered and Threatened Wildlife and Plants: Endangered Status for 11 Plant Species from the Koolau Mountain Range, Island of Oahu, HI." *Federal Register*. March 28, 1994: 14482-14492.

Contacts

U.S. Fish and Wildlife Service
    Regional Office
Eastside Federal Complex
911 N.S. 11th Avenue
Portland, OR 97232-4181
Phone: 503-231-6118

Pacific Islands Ecological Services
    Field Office
Room 6307, 300 Ala Moana Blvd.
Honolulu, HI 96850
Phone: 808-541-2749
FAX: 808-541-2756

Adapted from data compiled by Beacham Publishing for *Beacham's International Threatened, Endangered, and Extinct Species* published on CD ROM.

Haha

Cyanea grimesiana ssp. *obatae*

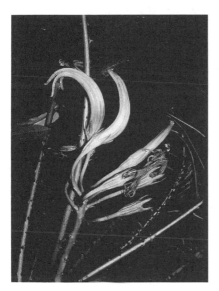

Robert J. Gustafson

Status	Endangered
Listed	June 27, 1994
Family	Campanulaceae (Bellflower)
Description	Unbranched shrub with small pickles with petals that are purplish or greenish and often striped with magenta.
Habitat	Steep, moist, shaded slopes in diverse mesic to wet forests.
Threats	Competition from alien plants; habitat destruction by feral pigs; limited numbers.
Range	Hawaii (Oahu)

Description

Cyanea grimesiana ssp. *obatae* is a shrub, usually unbranched, growing 3.3 to 10.5 feet tall. Its leaves are 10.5 to 23 inches long by 5.5 to 12.5 inches wide, and are deeply cut into 9 to 12 lobes per side. The plant usually has small pickles on its stem and leaves. Clusters of 6 to 12 stalked flowers arise from the leaf axils. Sepals are fused to the ovary, forming a cup 0.3 to 0.6 inches long with small, narrow, triangular lobes at the tips. The petals are purplish or greenish to yellow-white, often washed or striped with magenta, and are about 2 to 3 inches long by 0.2 to 0.4 inches wide. Fruits are elliptical orange berries 0.7 to 1.2 inches long. This species is distinguished from the other two subspecies by its short, narrow calyx lobes which are not fused or overlapping.

Habitat

Cyanea grimesiana ssp. *obatae* typically grows on steep, moist, shaded slopes in diverse mesic to wet forests at an elevation of 1,800 to 2,200 feet. Associated plants include mamaki, papala kepau, kukui, and various ferns.

For a continued habitat description of Oahu, see "Habitat Conditions on the Island of Oahu, Hawaii," page 2031.

Historic Range

Historically, this species is known from the southern Waianae Mountains from Puu Hapapa to Kaaikukai, a distance of about four miles.

Current Distribution

This taxon is known to be extant in Kaluaa Gulch, but may also still exist in Ekahanui and North Palawai Gulches. All populations are on privately owned land. Five plants are known from the Kaluaa population and as many as 13 plants may be found in the other two populations, although these populations have not been see in the last 10 years.

Conservation and Recovery

The major threats to this species are competition from alien plants such as Christmas berry and Koster's curse; predation of seed or fruits by introduced slugs; stochastic extinction and reduced reproductive vigor due to the small numbers of individuals; and habitat degradation by feral pigs.

The recovery of this and most other Hawaiian species depends on how well management practices can be implemented. The habitat of this and other Hawaiian species has undergone extreme alteration because of past and present land management practices, including deliberately introducing alien animals and plants, and agricultural and recreational development. To understand the recovery problems facing this species, it is necessary to understand the long-term causes of habitat destruction.

For a continued discussion of the threats to Hawaiian plants, see page 1831.

Bibliography

U.S. Fish and Wildlife Service. "Endangered and Threatened Wildlife and Plants: Endangered Status for Three Plants from the Waianae Mountains, Island of Oahu, HI." *Federal Register.* June 27, 1994: 32933-32939.

Contacts

U.S. Fish and Wildlife Service
   Regional Office
Eastside Federal Complex
911 N.S. 11th Avenue
Portland, OR 97232-4181
Phone: 503-231-6118

Pacific Islands Ecological Services
   Field Office
Room 6307, 300 Ala Moana Blvd.
Honolulu, HI 96850
Phone: 808-541-2749
FAX: 808-541-2756

Adapted from data compiled by Beacham Publishing for *Beacham's International Threatened, Endangered, and Extinct Species* published on CD ROM.

Haha

Cyanea truncata

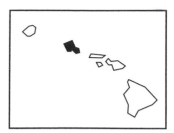

Dan Palmer

Status	Endangered
Listed	March 28, 1994
Family	Campanulaceae (Bellflower)
Description	Unbranched or sparsely branched shrub, with small sharp prickles, oval leaves, and clusters of 8 to 40 white flowers with magenta stripes.
Habitat	Windward slopes in mesic to wet forests.
Threats	Competition from alien plants; habitat destruction by feral pigs; limited numbers.
Range	Hawaii (Oahu)

Description

This haha, *Cyanea truncata*, is an unbranched or sparsely branched shrub covered with small sharp prickles. The oval leaves, which are widest above the middle area, are 8 to 24 inches long and 4 to 10 inches wide. The leaves are lined with hardened teeth along the margins. The upper surface of the leaf is hairless; the lower surface is hairy, has sparse projections, and is pale green. Clusters of 8 to 40 white flowers with magenta stripes are produced on horizontal or hanging stalks between 2 and 12 inches long. Each slightly curved flower is 1.3 to 1.7 inches long and about 0.3 inches wide, and has spreading corolla lobes that are one-fourth to one-half as long as the flower. The fruits are round orange berries about 0.4 inches long that contain many tiny seeds. *C. truncata* is distinguished from other members of this genus by the length of the flower cluster stalk and the size of the flowers and flower lobes.

Habitat

This haha typically grows on windward slopes in mesic to wet forests at elevations between 800 and 1,300 feet. Associated plants include koki'o ke'oke'o, lama, 'ohi'a, kukui, ha'iwale, ma'aloa, papala kepau, and 'awa.

For a continued habitat description of Oahu, see "Habitat Conditions on the Island of Oahu, Hawaii," page 2031.

Historic Range

Historically, *C. truncata* was known from

Punaluu, Waikane, and Waiahole in the norther Koolau Mountains of Oahu. These sites have not been recently surveyed because of their inaccessibility, but it is known that suitable habitat is present. One population of at least two individuals was known to exist in "Hidden Valley," a drainage northwest of Kaaawa Valley that terminates at Kaaawa Point in the Koolau Range; however, that population was destroyed by feral pigs.

Current Distribution

In 1991 John Obata discovered 20 immature lobeloids growing on private land along a gully floor further upstream from the site of the destroyed population. This was thought to be the only known population of this species. An individual from this sterile population was salvaged from pig-damaged areas in 1991, and this individual flowered in June 1993. This individual turned out to be *Rollandia crispa*, not *C. truncata*. A site visit in July 1993 determined that all the plants thought to be *C. truncata* were actually *R. crispa*. No individuals of *C. truncata* were located, though it is possible that juvenile plants could be found in the valley floor. At present, no confirmed population exists, although the species is not considered extinct.

Conservation and Recovery

The major threats to this haha are habitat degradation and predation by feral pigs; competition with alien plants, particularly Koster's curse and strawberry guava; and stochastic extinction and reduced reproductive vigor due to the small numbers of remaining individuals.

The recovery of this and most other Hawaiian species depends on how well management practices can be implemented.

The habitat of this and other Hawaiian species has undergone extreme alteration because of past and present land management practices, including deliberately introducing alien animals and plants, and agricultural and recreational development. To understand the recovery problems facing this species, it is necessary to understand the long-term causes of habitat destruction.

For a continued discussion of the threats to Hawaiian plants, see page 1831.

Bibliography

U.S. Fish and Wildlife Service. "Endangered and Threatened Wildlife and Plants: Endangered Status for 11 Plant Species from the Koolau Mountain Range, Island of Oahu, HI." *Federal Register*. March 28, 1994: 14482-14492.

Contacts

Pacific Islands Ecological Services
    Field Office
Room 6307, 300 Ala Moana Blvd.
Honolulu, HI 96850
Phone: 808-541-2749
FAX: 808-541-2756

Adapted from data compiled by Beacham Publishing for *Beacham's International Threatened, Endangered, and Extinct Species* published on CD ROM.

Ha'iwale

Cyrtandra crenata

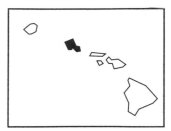

Status	Endangered
Listed	March 28, 1994
Family	Gesneriaceae (African Violet)
Description	Shrub with few branches; tufted lance-shaped, toothed, hairless, wrinkled leaves; and dense clusters of three to seven white flowers covered with thick brown hair.
Habitat	Ravines or gulches in mesic to wet forests.
Threats	Extinction due to the limited number of individuals.
Range	Hawaii (Oahu)

No Photo Available for This Species

Description

This ha'iwale, *Cyrtandra crenata*, is a shrub 3 to 7 feet tall with few branches. The leaves are arranged in whorls of three, tufted at the ends of the branches. The leaves are generally elliptic or lance-shaped, 4.7 to 11 inches long and 1.6 to 3.1 inches wide, and have toothed margins. The upper leaf surface is generally hairless and has a wrinkled texture; the lower surface has only sparse hairs. Dense clusters of three to seven white flowers, covered with thick brown hair, arise from the leaf axils. The calyx is bilaterally symmetrical, with the three upper lobes somewhat longer than the two lower lobes. The curved, funnel-shaped flowers, about 0.9 inches long and 0.2 inches wide, develop into fleshy, ellipsoid berries about 0.7 inches long that contain numerous tiny seeds. The berries, as well as various other plant parts, are covered with short-stalked, brownish, hemispherical glands. *C. crenata* is distinguished from other species in the genus by the combinations of its three-leaf arrangement, bilaterally symmetrical calyx, and brownish, hemispherical glands.

Habitat

Ha'iwale typically grows in ravines or gulches in mesic to wet forests between elevations of 1,250 and 2,400 feet. Associated plants include 'ohi'a, uluhe, and 'uki.

For a continued habitat description of Oahu, see "Habitat Conditions on the Island of Oahu, Hawaii," page 2031.

Historic Range

Historically, *C. crenata* was known from Waikane Valley along the Waikane-Schofield Trail in the Koolau Mountains.

Current Distribution

The species now remains below that trail about 0.5 miles from its historical location, at the boundary of private and state lands. The only known population has not been observed since 1947, and although the number of individuals is not known, it is thought to be very low.

Conservation and Recovery

The primary threat to this Ha'iwale is stochastic extinction and reduced reproductive vigor due to the species' restricted range and the small number of individuals thought to exist.

The recovery of this and most other Hawaiian species depends on how well management practices can be implemented. The habitat of this and other Hawaiian species has undergone extreme alteration because of past and present land management practices, including deliberately introducing alien animals and plants, and agricultural and recreational development. To understand the recovery problems facing this species, it is necessary to understand the long-term causes of habitat destruction.

For a continued discussion of the threats to Hawaiian plants, see page 1831.

Bibliography

U.S. Fish and Wildlife Service. "Endangered and Threatened Wildlife and Plants: Endangered Status for 11 Plant Species from the Koolau Mountain Range, Island of Oahu, HI." *Federal Register*. March 28, 1994: 14482-14492.

Contacts

Pacific Islands Ecological Services
  Field Office
Room 6307, 300 Ala Moana Blvd.
Honolulu, HI 96850
Phone: 808-541-2749
FAX: 808-541-2756

Adapted from data compiled by Beacham Publishing for *Beacham's International Threatened, Endangered, and Extinct Species* published on CD ROM.

Ha'iwale

Cyrtandra polyantha

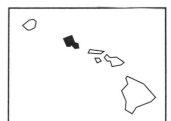

Yevonn Wilson-Ramsey

Status	Endangered
Listed	March 28, 1994
Family	Gesneriaceae (African Violet)
Description	Shrub with leathery, elliptic, unequal leaves attached oppositely along the stems, and 7 to 12 white flowers.
Habitat	Ridges of disturbed mesic valleys in the 'ohi'a forests.
Threats	Stochastic extinction and reduced reproductive vigor due to the small number of individuals.
Range	Hawaii (Oahu)

Description

This ha'iwale, *Cyrtandra polyantha*, is an unbranched or few-branched shrub 3 to 10 feet in height. Its leathery, elliptic, unequal leaves are 2 to 6.3 inches long and 0.7 to 2 inches wide, and attached oppositely along the stems. The upper surface of the leaves is conspicuously wrinkled and usually hairless, with the lower surface moderately to densely covered with pale brown hairs. Seven to 12 flowers are grouped in branched clusters in the leaf axils. The white petals, fused to form a cylindrical tube about 0.5 inches long, emerge from a radially symmetrical calyx 0.2 inches long, that is cleft from one-half to two-thirds its length. Each calyx lobe, narrowly triangular in shape, is sparsely hairy on the outside and hairless within. The fruits are white oval berries about 0.6 inches long that contain many seeds about 0.02 inches long. *C. polyantha* is distinguished from other species in the genus by the texture and hairiness of the leaf surfaces, and the length, shape, and degree of cleft of the calyx. This species differs from *C. crenata* by the lack of short-stalked glands and by its leathery leaves, opposite leaf arrangement, and radially symmetrical calyx.

Habitat

This species is believed to remain on ridges of disturbed mesic valleys in the 'ohi'a forests at elevations between 1,600 and 2,000 feet. Associated plants would include 'uki, uluhe, kanawao, pilo, and kopiko.

For a continued habitat description of

Oahu, see "Habitat Conditions on the Island of Oahu, Hawaii," page 2031.

Historic Range

Historically, *C. polyantha* was known from the Kalihi region and from Kuleplamoa Ridge above the Nui Valley on the leeward (southwest) side of the southern Koolau Mountains.

Current Distribution

Two populations located on the Kuliouou summit ridge and at the northwest head of the Hahaione Valley are approximately one mile apart on private and state land. One of the populations has not been visited within the past 50 years, and it is not known how many individuals remain. The most recently observed population, last seen in 1953, consists of one individual. The total number of extant individuals is not known, although only a few are believed to remain on ridges of disturbed mesic valleys in the 'ohi'a forests at elevations between 1,600 and 2,000 feet.

Conservation and Recovery

The primary threat to this Ha'iwale is stochastic extinction and reduced reproductive vigor due to the small number of individuals and their restricted distribution.

The recovery of this and most other Hawaiian species depends on how well management practices can be implemented. The habitat of this and other Hawaiian species has undergone extreme alteration because of past and present land management practices, including deliberately introducing alien animals and plants, and agricultural and recreational development. To understand the recovery problems facing this species, it is necessary to understand the long-term causes of habitat destruction.

For a continued discussion of the threats to Hawaiian plants, see page 1831.

Bibliography

U.S. Fish and Wildlife Service. "Endangered and Threatened Wildlife and Plants: Endangered Status for 11 Plant Species from the Koolau Mountain Range, Island of Oahu, HI." *Federal Register*. March 28, 1994: 14482-14492.

Contacts

U.S. Fish and Wildlife Service
    Regional Office
Eastside Federal Complex
911 N.S. 11th Avenue
Portland, OR 97232-4181
Phone: 503-231-6118

Pacific Islands Ecological Services
    Field Office
Room 6307, 300 Ala Moana Blvd.
Honolulu, HI 96850
Phone: 808-541-2749
FAX: 808-541-2756

Adapted from data compiled by Beacham Publishing for *Beacham's International Threatened, Endangered, and Extinct Species* published on CD ROM.

Diellia unisora

No Common Name

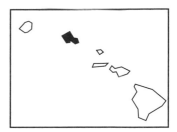

John Obata

Status	Endangered
Listed	June 27, 1994
Family	Polypodiaceae (Fern)
Description	Earth-growing fern with black, shiny frond stalks.
Habitat	Deep shade or open understory in dryland forest.
Threats	Competition from alien plants; habitat destruction by people; fire; limited numbers.
Range	Hawaii (Oahu)

Description

Diellia unisora grows from a slender erect rhizome (underground stem) 0.2 to 1.2 inches tall, which is covered with the bases of the leaf stalks and a few small black scales. Stalks of the fronds are black and shiny, and are 0.8 to 2 inches long. The fronds are linear, 3 to 12 inches tall by 0.2 to 1.2 inches wide, with 20 to 35 pinnae (leaflets) per side, and gradually narrowing towards the apex. The pinnae are usually strongly asymmetrical, unequally triangular, with mostly entire (smooth) margins. There usually is a single marginal sorus (the spore-producing body) running along the upper margin of the underside of the pinna.

This species is distinguished from others in the genus by a rhizome completely covered by the persisting bases of the leaf stalks, and few, very small scales, by sori mostly confined to the upper pinna margins, and by

delicate fonds gradually and symmetrically narrowing toward the apex.

Habitat

Diellia unisora is a terrestrial fern that typically grows in deep shade or open understory in dryland forest at an elevation of 1,750 to 2,500 feet. Associated plant species include strawberry guava, Christmas berry, 'ohi'a, and a mixture of alien and native grasses, forbs, and shrubs.

For a continued habitat description of Oahu, see "Habitat Conditions on the Island of Oahu, Hawaii," page 2031.

Historic Range and Current Distribution

Historically, this species was known from steep, grassy, rocky slopes on the western side of the Waianae Mountains. It is now known to occur in three areas of the southern Waianae Mountains: South Ekahanui Gulch, Palawai Gulch, and the Pualii-Napepeiauolelo Ridge. The three known populations that are on Lualualei Naval Reservation and on privately owned land, are scattered over a distance of about two miles, and contain 705 to 755 individuals.

Conservation and Recovery

The major threat to this species is competition from alien plant taxa Christmas berry, huehue haole, molasses grass, and strawberry guava. Habitat degradation by feral pigs is a potential threat.

The recovery of this and most other Hawaiian species depends on how well management practices can be implemented. The habitat of this and other Hawaiian species has undergone extreme alteration because of past and present land management practices, including deliberately introducing alien animals and plants, and agricultural and recreational development. To understand the recovery problems facing this species, it is necessary to understand the long-term causes of habitat destruction.

For a continued discussion of the threats to Hawaiian plants, see page 1831.

Bibliography

U.S. Fish and Wildlife Service. "Endangered and Threatened Wildlife and Plants: Endangered Status for Three Plants from the Waianae Mountains, Island of Oahu, HI." *Federal Register.* June 27, 1994: 32933-32939.

Contacts

Pacific Islands Ecological Services
    Field Office
Room 6307, 300 Ala Moana Blvd.
Honolulu, HI 96850
Phone: 808-541-2749
FAX: 808-541-2756

Adapted from data compiled by Beacham Publishing for *Beacham's International Threatened, Endangered, and Extinct Species* published on CD ROM.

Nioi

Eugenia koolauensis

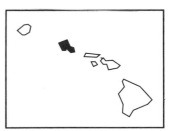

John Obata

Status	Endangered
Listed	March 28, 1994
Family	Myrtaceae (Myrtle)
Description	Small tree with branch tips covered with dense brown hair; leathery, oval or elliptic leaves; and one or two white flowers.
Habitat	Dry gulches and ridges in mesic forests dominated by 'ohi'a and lama.
Threats	Competition from alien plants; habitat destruction by feral pigs; limited numbers.
Range	Hawaii (Oahu)

Description

Nioi, *Eugenia koolauensis*, is a small tree between 7 and 23 feet tall, with branch tips covered with dense brown hair. The leathery, oval or elliptic leaves, 0.8 to 2 inches long and 0.4 to 1.3 inches wide, are densely hairy on the lower surface and have margins that curve under the leaves. One or two flowers grow from the leaf axils on stalks 0.04 to 0.3 inches long. The hypanthium (basal portion of the flower) is cone-shaped, about 0.1 inches long, and hairy. The four sepals of unequal length that comprise the hypanthium are attached to a circular nectary dish (fleshy, nectar-producing structure). The four white petals, which are oval or elliptic and 0.2 to 0.3 inches long, enclose numerous white stamens and are also attached to the nectary dish. The fruits are fleshy, yellow to red oval berries, 0.3 to 0.8 inches long, that usually contain one round seed. *E. koolauensis* is one of two species of the genus that are native to Hawaii, and is distinguished from the other species in having leaves that are densely hairy on the lower surface, and in having leaf margins that curve under the leaves.

Habitat

The five populations exist in dry gulches and ridges in mesic forests dominated by 'ohi'a and lama at elevations of 350 to 1,000 feet. Other associated vegetation includes kolea, olopua, hala pepe and alahe'e.

For a continued habitat description of Oahu, see "Habitat Conditions on the Island of Oahu, Hawaii," page 2031.

Historic Range

Historically, *E. koolauensis* was known from Maunaloa on western Molokai and from Kaipapau Valley, Hanaimoa and Kahawainui gulches, and a gully southeast of Kahuku on Oahu. This species is no longer believed to be extant on Molokai because the region where the first two individuals were found has been converted to pineapple fields.

Current Distribution

On Oahu, five populations now remain on state and private land in Papali Gulch, the north fork of Kamananui Stream, in the regions of Pupukea and Paumalu in the northern Koolau Mountains, and at Hawaiiloa, which is a disjunctive population in the southeastern Koolau Mountains. A total of fewer than 60 individuals remain in five populations.

Conservation and Recovery

The major threats to Nioi are habitat degradation by feral pigs, and competition with alien plants, especially Koster's curse, Christmas berry, strawberry guava and lantana. The limited numbers make it vulnerable to stochastic extinction and reduced reproductive vigor.

The recovery of this and most other Hawaiian species depends on how well management practices can be implemented. The habitat of this and other Hawaiian species has undergone extreme alteration because of past and present land management practices, including deliberately introducing alien animals and plants, and agricultural and recreational development. To understand the recovery problems facing this species, it is necessary to understand the long-term causes of habitat destruction.

For a continued discussion of the threats to Hawaiian plants, see page 1831.

Bibliography

U.S. Fish and Wildlife Service. "Endangered and Threatened Wildlife and Plants: Endangered Status for 11 Plant Species from the Koolau Mountain Range, Island of Oahu, HI." *Federal Register*. March 28, 1994: 14482-14492.

Contacts

Pacific Islands Ecological Services
   Field Office
Room 6307, 300 Ala Moana Blvd.
Honolulu, HI 96850
Phone: 808-541-2749
FAX: 808-541-2756

Adapted from data compiled by Beacham Publishing for *Beacham's International Threatened, Endangered, and Extinct Species* published on CD ROM.

Gouania vitifolia
No Common Name

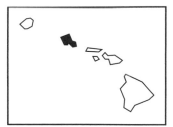

Robert J. Gustafson

Status	Endangered
Listed	June 27, 1994
Family	Rhamnaceae (Buckthorn)
Description	Climbing shrub or woody vine with tendrils, with small, papery, white petals and leaves.
Habitat	Dry, rocky ridges and slopes in dry shrubland or dry to mesic forests.
Threats	Competition from alien plants; habitat destruction by feral pigs; limited numbers.
Range	Hawaii (Oahu)

Description

Gouania vitifolia is a climbing shrub or woody vine with tendrils. Leaves are papery in texture with a moderate to dense covering of soft, short hairs on both surfaces. The leaves are elliptic to broadly oval in outline with toothed or lobed margins and 1.2 to 3.2 inches long by 0.8 to 1.0 inches wide. Flowers are arranged in axillary spikes 0.3 to 2.8 inches long. The flowers are small with sepals and petals ranging from 0.03 to 0.04 inches in length. Both the sepals and petals are white. The 2- or 3-winged fruit are about 0.4 inches long. Seeds are oval, glossary, dark brown, and about 0.1 to 0.2 inches long. This species is the only Hawaiian member of the genus with tendrils and toothed leaf margins.

Habitat

Although there is not much information, data from herbarium labels indicate that *G. vitifolia* prefers dry, rocky ridges and slopes in dry shrubland or dry to mesic forests at an elevation of about 2,000 feet. Associated plant species include Christmas berry, strawberry guava, kukui, huehue haole, and mamaki.

For a continued habitat description of Oahu, see "Habitat Conditions on the Island of Oahu, Hawaii," page 2031.

Historic Range

Historically, *G. vitifolia* was known from West Maui, the Kau District of the island of Hawaii, and the northwestern portion of the

Waianae Mountains in Makaleha, Keaau, and Waianae Kai valleys.

Current Distribution

A single population of five individuals was discovered in 1990 on the slopes of Waianae Kai Ridge on state-owned land. The five plants are close to one another, growing in a single patch in a forest of mostly naturalized, non-native species, and may represent clones of a single individual. A second smaller patch was discovered near the first, and probably represents a second clone.

Conservation and Recovery

The major threats to this species are competition from alien plants such as strawberry guava and Christmas berry; habitat destruction by feral pigs; and stochastic extinction and reduced reproductive vigor due to the small number of individuals.

The recovery of this and most other Hawaiian species depends on how well management practices can be implemented. The habitat of this and other Hawaiian species has undergone extreme alteration because of past and present land management practices, including deliberately introducing alien animals and plants, and agricultural and recreational development. To understand the recovery problems facing this species, it is necessary to understand the long-term causes of habitat destruction.

For a continued discussion of the threats to Hawaiian plants, see page 1831.

Bibliography

U.S. Fish and Wildlife Service. "Endangered and Threatened Wildlife and Plants: Endangered Status for Three Plants from the Waianae Mountains, Island of Oahu, HI." *Federal Register*. June 27, 1994: 32933-32939.

Contacts

U.S. Fish and Wildlife Service
  Regional Office
Eastside Federal Complex
911 N.S. 11th Avenue
Portland, OR 97232-4181
Phone: 503-231-6118

Pacific Islands Ecological Services
  Field Office
Room 6307, 300 Ala Moana Blvd.
Honolulu, HI 96850
Phone: 808-541-2749
FAX: 808-541-2756

Adapted from data compiled by Beacham Publishing for *Beacham's International Threatened, Endangered, and Extinct Species* published on CD ROM.

Hesperomannia arborescens
No Common Name

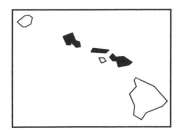

Status	Endangered
Listed	March 28, 1994
Family	Asteraceae (Aster)
Description	Small shrubby tree with lance-shaped, hairless leaves, and 2-10 yellowish flowers.
Habitat	Slopes or ridges in lowland wet forests and occasionally in scrub vegetation.
Threats	Competition from alien plants; habitat destruction by feral goats and pigs; fire; human impact; limited numbers.
Range	Hawaii (Oahu, Molokai, Maui)

John Obata

Description

Hesperomannia arborescens is a small shrubby tree that usually stands 5 to 16 feet tall. Its typically hairless leaves, 4 to 8 inches long and 1 to 3 inches wide, range from oval to lance-shaped and are about two to four times as long as they are wide. The flower heads, which are about 2.4 inches long, are either erect or ascending, and grow singly or in clusters of 2 to 10. They grow on thick, fuzzy stalks 0.2 to 0.6 inches long and about 0.1 inches in diameter. The involucre that surrounds each flower head is between 0.8 and 1.4 inches high, with the longest individual bracts growing to 1.1 inches. The yellow to yellowish brown florets that comprise each head are about 0.9 to 1.2 inches long and develop into 0.5 inch long achenes (dry, one-fruited fruits) topped with yellowish brown or purple-tinged bristles. This member of an endemic Hawaiian genus differs from other *Hesperomannia* species in having the following combination of characteristics: erect to ascending flower heads; thick flower stalks; and usually hairless and relatively narrow leaves.

Habitat

This species typically grows on slopes or ridges in lowland wet forests and occasionally in scrub vegetation at elevations between 1,200 and 2,500 feet. Associated vegetation includes 'ohi'a, olopua, uluhe, hame, kopiko, and common *Melicope* species. The Molokai population grows in lama and/or 'ohi'a-dominated lowland mesic forests with the same elevation.

For a continued habitat description, see "Habitat Conditions on the Island of Oahu," page 2031.; "Habitat Conditions on the

Island of Maui," page 1955; and "Habitat Conditions on the Island of Molokai," page 1993.

Historic Range

H. arborescens was formerly known from locations on three islands: Kaiholena and Kukui on Lanai; Pelekunu Trail on Molokai; and scattered populations throughout the Koolau Mountains, from Koolauloa and Pupukea at its northern extreme to Konahuanui at the southern end.

Current populations include the upslope of Kahuku, Laie and Malaekahane; along Poamoho Trail; above Poamoho Stream; along Waikane-Schofield Trail near the ridge summit; at Kipapa Gulch; on Halawa Ridge; and the upper Palolo Valley to Niu Valley. The Waikane-Schofield population occurs on the boundary of state (Ewa Forest Reserve) and Federal (Schofield Barracks Military Reservation) land.

On Molokai, one population of three individuals was found on state land in Olokui Natural Area Reserve.

A discovery in 1989 extends the species' range to the island of Maui, where two colonies totaling three individuals were discovered about 0.3 miles apart on state land in West Maui Natural Area Reserve between Lanilili and Keahikauo.

Current Distribution

This species is now known from 18 populations totaling fewer than 70 plants on the islands of Oahu, Molokai, and Maui. On Oahu, 15 populations, which total 50 to 60 individuals, have been observed since 1958 on private, city, state and Federal land at a few disjunctive locations over a distance of about 27 miles.

Conservation and Recovery

The major threats to *Hesperomannia arborescens* are habitat degradation by feral pigs and goats; competition with alien plants, especially Hilo grass, Koster's curse, strawberry guava; fire; impact by humans; stochastic extinction; and reduced reproductive vigor due to the species' limited numbers.

The recovery of this and most other Hawaiian species depends on how well management practices can be implemented. The habitat of this and other Hawaiian species has undergone extreme alteration because of past and present land management practices, including deliberately introducing alien animals and plants, and agricultural and recreational development. To understand the recovery problems facing this species, it is necessary to understand the long-term causes of habitat destruction.

For a continued discussion of the threats to Hawaiian plants, see page 1831.

Bibliography

U.S. Fish and Wildlife Service. "Endangered and Threatened Wildlife and Plants: Endangered Status for 11 Plant Species from the Koolau Mountain Range, Island of Oahu, HI." *Federal Register*. March 28, 1994: 14482-14492.

Contacts

Pacific Islands Ecological Services
  Field Office
Room 6307, 300 Ala Moana Blvd.
Honolulu, HI 96850
Phone: 808-541-2749
FAX: 808-541-2756

Adapted from data compiled by Beacham Publishing for *Beacham's International Threatened, Endangered, and Extinct Species* published on CD ROM.

Lobelia oahuensis

No Common Name

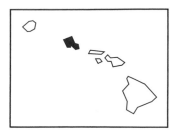

John Obata

Status	Endangered
Listed	March 28, 1994
Family	Campanulaceae (Bellflower)
Description	Stout, erect, unbranched shrub, with elliptic leaves and 50 to 200 flowers.
Habitat	Steep slopes along Koolau Mountain ridgetops; on summit cliffs in cloud-swept wet forests frequently exposed to heavy wind and rain.
Threats	Competition from alien plants.
Range	Hawaii (Oahu)

Description

Lobelia oahuensis is a stout, erect, unbranched shrub 3 to 10 feet tall. The elliptic leaves, which are 16 to 24 inches long and 1.6 to 2.4 inches wide, are typically stalkless and form a very dense rosette at the end of the stem. The upper surface of the leaves is hairless and the lower surface is covered with rather coarse, grayish or greenish hairs. The inflorescence is branched 3 to 5 times from its base, with each erect spike 3 to 5 feet tall and comprised of 50 to 200 flowers. Each flower measures 1.7 to 1.8 inches long and about 0.2 inches wide, with a 1.2 inch long bract just below it. The linear calyx lobes are about 0.6 long and 0.1 inch wide. The fruits are hairy, oval capsules 0.4 to 0.7 inches long and about 0.4 inches wide, that contain numerous brownish seeds.

Lobelia oahuensis differs from other members of the genus in having the following combination of characteristics: erect stems 3 to 10 feet long; dense rosettes of leaves at the end of stems; lower leaf surfaces covered with coarse grayish or greenish hairs; and flowers 1.7 to 1.8 inches long.

Habitat

This species grows on tree trunks, usually on open ridges and slopes in 'ohi'a-dominated wet forests and occasionally mesic forests at elevations between 2,000 and 3,500 feet. The vegetation in those areas usually includes kanawao, uluhe, 'uki, hame, and kopiko.

For a continued habitat description of

Oahu, see "Habitat Conditions on the Island of Oahu, Hawaii," page 2031.

Historic Range

Historically, this species was known from Kahana Ridge, Kipapa Gulch, and the southeastern Koolau Mountains of Oahu. The species grows on steep slopes along Koolau Mountain ridgetops from Waikane and Halawa to Mount Olympus and the summit ridges above Kuliouou and Wainmanalo, a distance of about 17 miles. A single mature individual was recently discovered on the boundary between state land and Schofield Barracks, extending the distribution of this species to the Waianae Mountain Range of Oahu.

Current Distribution

Nine populations totaling between 100 and 200 individuals are located on private and state land, or on the boundary of private, state and Federal land.

Conservation and Recovery

The primary threat to this species is the noxious alien plant Koster's curse because it effectively competes for water, space, light and nutrients.

The recovery of this and most other Hawaiian species depends on how well management practices can be implemented. The habitat of this and other Hawaiian species has undergone extreme alteration because of past and present land management practices, including deliberately introducing alien animals and plants, and agricultural and recreational development. To understand the recovery problems facing this species, it is necessary to understand the long-term causes of habitat destruction.

For a continued discussion of the threats to Hawaiian plants, see page 1831.

Bibliography

U.S. Fish and Wildlife Service. "Endangered and Threatened Wildlife and Plants: Endangered Status for 11 Plant Species from the Koolau Mountain Range, Island of Oahu, HI." *Federal Register*. March 28, 1994: 14482-14492.

Contacts

Pacific Islands Ecological Services
  Field Office
Room 6307, 300 Ala Moana Blvd.
Honolulu, HI 96850
Phone: 808-541-2749
FAX: 808-541-2756

Adapted from data compiled by Beacham Publishing for *Beacham's International Threatened, Endangered, and Extinct Species* published on CD ROM.

Wawae'iole

Lycopodium nutans

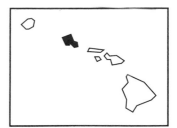

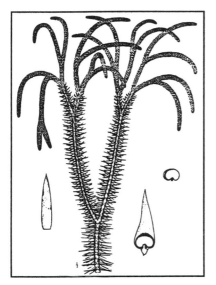

From *New Illustrated Flora of the Hawaiian Islands*

Status	Endangered
Listed	March 28, 1994
Family	Lycopodiaceae (Clubmoss)
Description	Erect or pendulous plant with stiff, flat, leathery leaves, and branches that end in thick, fruiting spikes.
Habitat	Tree trunks, usually on open ridges and slopes in 'ohi'a-dominated wet forests and occasionally mesic forests.
Threats	Competition from alien plants; stochastic extinction due to limited numbers.
Range	Hawaii (Oahu)

Description

Wawae'iole *Lycopodium nutans*, is an erect or pendulous herbaceous epiphyte (plant growing above ground on other plants). Its stiff, light green branches, 10 to 16 inches long and about 0.2 inches thick, are covered with stiff, flat, leathery leaves 0.5 to 0.6 inches long and about 0.1 inches wide, which overlap at acute angles. The leaves are arranged in six rows and arise directly from the branches. The branches end in thick, 2.8 to 5.1 inch long fruiting spikes that are unbranched or branched once or twice, and taper toward a downward-curving tip. Bracts on the fruiting spikes between 0.1 and 0.2 inches long, are densely layered and conceal the spore capsules.

This species is distinguished from others of the genus in Hawaii by its epiphytic habit, simple or forking fruit spikes, and larger, stiffer leaves.

Habitat

Wawae'iole grows on tree trunks, usually on open ridges and slopes in 'ohi'a-dominated wet forests and occasionally mesic forests at elevations between 2,000 and 3,500 feet. The vegetation in those areas usually includes kanawao, uluhe, 'uki, hame, and kopiko.

For a continued habitat description of Oahu, see "Habitat Conditions on the Island of Oahu, Hawaii," page 2031.

Historic Range

Historically, *L. nutans* was known from the island of Kauai and from scattered locations in the Koolau Mountains of Oahu bounded by Kaluanui Valley to the north, Paalaa to the west, and Mount Tantalus to the south. This species is now known from only two sites within its historic range: Kaluanui Valley and along Waikane-Schofield Trail on Oahu.

Current Distribution

One population, located on state land, was described as "scarce" when last observed in 1965. The other population, located about five miles away on the boundary of the Ewa Forest reserve and Schofield Military Barracks Reserve, grew in "several places" according to its collector in 1961. Two individuals of this population were observed in 1993 by Joel Lau. The entire species totals fewer than 50 known individuals.

Conservation and Recovery

The primary threat to Wawae'iole is stochastic extinction and reduced reproductive vigor due to the small number of remaining individuals and limited distribution. An additional threat is competition from noxious alien plants, especially Koster's curse and strawberry guava.

For a continued discussion of the threats to Hawaiian plants, see page 1831.

Bibliography

U.S. Fish and Wildlife Service. "Endangered and Threatened Wildlife and Plants: Endangered Status for 11 Plant Species from the Koolau Mountain Range, Island of Oahu, HI." *Federal Register*. March 28, 1994: 14482-14492.

Contacts

Pacific Islands Ecological Services
   Field Office
Room 6307, 300 Ala Moana Blvd.
Honolulu, HI 96850
Phone: 808-541-2749
FAX: 808-541-2756

Adapted from data compiled by Beacham Publishing for *Beacham's International Threatened, Endangered, and Extinct Species* published on CD ROM.

'Ihi'Ihi

Marsilea villosa

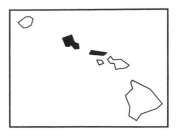

Robert J. Gustafson

Status	Endangered
Listed	June 22, 1992
Family	Marsileaceae (Pepperwort)
Description	Semiaquatic to aquatic fern similar to a four-leaved clover.
Habitat	Ponds and areas which will support its semiaquatic/aquatic habit.
Threats	Habitat degradation and/or predation by wild, feral, or domestic animals.
Range	Hawaii (Oahu, Molokai)

Description

'Ihi'Ihi, *Marsilea villosa*, is an semiaquatic to aquatic fern. This fern is similar to a four-leaved clover, is 5 to 25 centimeters tall with four leaflets at the tip of the stem. The leaves are in pairs and bear a small, hard spore case on a short stalk at its base when fertile. All parts of this plant may be covered with a rust-colored pubescence.

Habitat

M. villosa is an aquatic to semiaquatic fern that grows in small shallow depressions on level or gently sloping terrain. It requires periodic flooding to complete its life cycle. The spore cases normally are produced as the habitat begins to dry up and do not ripen unless the plant is drought stressed. When sufficient water is present, the plant reproduces vegetatively with young plants being produced on creeping rhizomes. The fern's habitat is dynamic, and may shrink or swell from year to year depending upon rainfall and other factors.

For a complete habitat description of Oahu, see "Habitat Conditions on the Island of Oahu," page 2031.; and "Habitat Conditions on the Island of Molokai," page 1993.

Historic Range and Current Distribution

This species was first collected in the Nuuanu Valley, Oahu and later at Mokio and Moomomi on Molokai. The three remaining populations are at Koko Head and the Lualualei Naval Reservation on Oahu and near Laau on Molokai. The largest site is in the Lualualei Valley, where clumps of this plant are scattered among kiawe trees in an area of approximately six acres. The Koko Head population covers about 0.5 acres, but comprises the largest number of individual plants. The population on Molokai measures roughly 7 feet by 25 feet.

Conservation and Recovery

Like all of the Islands of Hawaii, the plant fauna of Oahu and Molokai has currently fallen vulnerable to habitat degradation and/or predation by wild, feral, or domestic animals (goats, pigs, and cattle); competition for space, light, water, and nutrients by naturalized, exotic species; habitat loss due to fires; human recreational activities; and military exercises.

The most immediate threats to this species are competition from exotic vegetation, habitat degradation by off-road vehicles and cattle.

Off-road vehicles not only damage or destroy plants, but also disturb the soil promoting the invasion of competing exotic plant species.

A population of Koko Head has been partially fenced through a management agreement between the City and County and The Nature Conservancy of Hawaii to prevent damage and habitat degradation by off-road vehicles.

For a continued discussion of the threats to Hawaiian plants, see page 1831.

Bibliography

U.S. Fish and Wildlife Service. "Endangered and Threatened Wildlife and Plants; Determination of Endangered for *Marisilea villosa* ('Ihi'Ihi)." *Federal Register* Vol. 57, No. 120. June 22, 1992: 27863-27867.

Contacts

U.S. Fish and Wildlife Service
Regional Office
Eastside Federal Complex
911 N.S. 11th Avenue
Portland, OR 97232-4181
Phone: 503-231-6118

Pacific Islands Ecological Services
Field Office
Room 6307, 300 Ala Moana Blvd.
Honolulu, HI 96850
Phone: 808-541-2749
FAX: 808-541-2756

Adapted from data compiled by the Threatened and Endangered Species Information Institute (13950 W. 20th Ave., Golden, CO 80401) for *Beacham's International Threatened, Endangered, and Extinct Species* published on CD ROM, available from Beacham Publishing.

Alani

Melicope (=Pelea) lydgatei

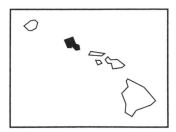

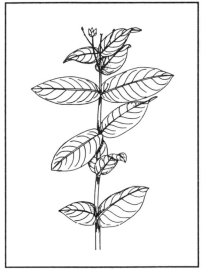

Yevonn Wilson-Ramsey

Status	Endangered
Listed	March 28, 1994
Family	Rutaceae (Citrus)
Description	Small shrub with glossy, papery, lance-shaped leaves, and aromatic greenish white flowers in clusters of two or three.
Habitat	Open ridges in mesic forests and occasionally in wet forests at elevations between 1,350 and 1,800 feet.
Threats	Stochastic extinction due to limited numbers.
Range	Hawaii (Oahu)

Description

This alani, *Melicope lydgatei*, is a small shrub with leaves arranged oppositely or in threes. The glossy, papery leaves, which are 1.6 to 5.1 inches long and 0.6 to 2.6 inches wide, vary from lance-shaped to oblong. Flowers are usually functionally unisexual, with both unisexual and bisexual flowers growing on the same plant. Its aromatic, greenish white flowers are about 0.2 to 0.3 inches long and arise singly or in clusters of two or three. The four-lobed capsules, which have sections fused for one-fourth to one-third their length, are between 0.6 and 0.9 inches wide, and contain one or two glossy black seeds about 0.2 inches long in each

section. Both the exocarp and endocarp (outermost and innermost layers of the fruit wall) are hairless. The species' leaf arrangement (opposite or in groups of three), the amount of fusion of the fruit sections, and the hairless exocarp and endocarp, distinguish it from others in the genus.

Habitat

This species typically grows in association with koa, 'ohi'a, uluhe, kopiko, and 'akakea lau nui, on open ridges in mesic forests and occasionally in wet forests at elevations between 1,350 and 1,800 feet.

For a continued habitat description of Oahu, see "Habitat Conditions on the Island of Oahu, Hawaii," page 2031.

Historic Range

This species was historically known throughout the Koolau Mountains of Oahu from Hauula to Kahana, Kipapa Gulch to Waimano, and Kalihi Valley to Wailupe Valley.

Current Distribution

Three populations presently exist: along Poamoho Trail near the boundary of Ewa Forest reserve; along Manana Trail in Ewa Forest Reserve; and along Peahinaia Trail on private land.

Conservation and Recovery

The recovery of this and most other Hawaiian species depends on how well management practices can be implemented. The habitat of this and other Hawaiian species has undergone extreme alteration because of past and present land management practices, including deliberately introducing alien animals and plants, and agricultural and recreational development. To understand the recovery problems facing this species, it is necessary to understand the long-term causes of habitat destruction.

For a continued discussion of the threats to Hawaiian plants, see page 1831.

Bibliography

U.S. Fish and Wildlife Service. "Endangered and Threatened Wildlife and Plants: Endangered Status for 11 Plant Species from the Koolau Mountain Range, Island of Oahu, HI." *Federal Register*. March 28, 1994: 14482-14492.

Contacts

Pacific Islands Ecological Services
Field Office
Room 6307, 300 Ala Moana Blvd.
Honolulu, HI 96850
Phone: 808-541-2749
FAX: 808-541-2756

Adapted from data compiled by Beacham Publishing for *Beacham's International Threatened, Endangered, and Extinct Species* published on CD ROM.

Stenogyne kanehoana
No Common Name

John Obata

Status	Endangered
Listed	May 13, 1992
Family	Lamiaceae (Mint)
Description	Vine with flowers in clusters of 3-6 per leaf axil, petals fused into strongly curved tube with white or pale yellow corolla lobes and fruit of fleshy black nutlets.
Habitat	Coastal plains, upland slopes and mountain ranges and summits of the Waianae Range, Oahu.
Threats	Predation by wild, feral, or domestic animals; fires, human recreational activities.
Range	Hawaii (Oahu)

Description

Stenogyne kanehoana is a climbing vine in the mint family with stems weakly 4 to angled, pubescent and 1 to 2 meters long. The leaves are oppositely arranged and are narrowly ovate to oblong to ovate, thin but densely pubescent. The flowers are in clusters of 3 to 6 per leaf axil; the petals are fused into a strongly curved tube about 2.7 to 4.2 centimeters long, white or pale yellow with short pink corolla lobes. The fruit consists of 4 fleshy black nutlets.

Habitat

S. kanehoana occurs under a canopy of mesic forest trees on a ridge leading to the summit of Puu Kanehoa in the Waianae Range. The Waianae Mountains were built by eruptions along three rift zones. The two principal rift zones run in a northwestward and south-southeastward direction from the summit, and a lesser zone runs to the northeast.

For a continued habitat description of Oahu, see "Habitat Conditions on the Island of Oahu, Hawaii," page 2031.

Historic Range

S. kanehoana is known from Puu Kanehoa, Puu Hapapa and Puu Kaua in the Waianae Mountains, Oahu, Hawaii.

Current Distribution

Very limited populations occur within a

canopy of mesic forest trees on a ridge leading to the summit of Puu Kanehoa in the Waianae Range.

Conservation and Recovery

Like all of the islands of Hawaii, the plant fauna of Oahu has currently fallen vulnerable to habitat degradation and/or predation by wild, feral, or domestic animals (goats, pigs, and cattle); competition for space, light, water, and nutrients by naturalized, exotic species; habitat loss due to fires; human recreational activities; and military exercises.

The recovery of this and most other Hawaiian species depends on how well management practices can be implemented. The habitat of this and other Hawaiian species has undergone extreme alteration because of past and present land management practices, including deliberately introducing alien animals and plants, and agricultural and recreational development. To understand the recovery problems facing this species, it is necessary to understand the long-term causes of habitat destruction.

For a continued discussion of the threats to Hawaiian plants, see page 1831.

Bibliography

U.S. Fish and Wildlife Service. "Endangered and Threatened Wildlife and Plants; Determination of Endangered Status for *Stenogyne kanehoana* (No Common Name), a Hawaiian Plant." May 13, 1992. *Federal Register* Vol. 57 No. 93, May 13, 1992: 20592-20595.

Contacts

Pacific Islands Ecological Services
Room 6307, 300 Ala Moana Blvd.
Honolulu, HI 96850
Phone: 808-541-2749
FAX: 808-541-2756

Regional Office
Eastside Federal Complex
911 N.S. 11th Avenue
Portland, OR 97232-4181
Phone: 503-231-6118

Adapted from data compiled by the Threatened and Endangered Species Information Institute (13950 W. 20th Ave., Golden, CO 80401) for *Beacham's International Threatened, Endangered, and Extinct Species* published on CD ROM, available from Beacham Publishing.

'Ohe'ohe

Tetraplasandra gymnocarpa

John Obata

Status	Endangered
Listed	March 28, 1994
Family	Araliaceae (Ginseng)
Description	Tree with hairless or with fuzzy, short-lived hairs and flowers clustered in threes in an umbrella-shaped arrangement.
Habitat	Windswept summit ridges or in gullies in wet or sometimes mesic forests.
Threats	Competition from alien plants; habitat destruction by feral pigs; limited numbers.
Range	Hawaii (Oahu)

Description

'Ohe'ohe, *Tetraplasandra gymnocarpa*, is a tree 8 to 33 feet tall, either hairless or with fuzzy, short-lived hairs on the young leaves and flower clusters. The leaves are 12 to 22 inches long with 7 to 21 leathery, oval to elliptic leaflets per leaf. Each leaflet is 2.8 to 7.1 inches long and 1.2 to 3.1 inches wide, and is folded upward along the midveins. The flowers are usually arranged in threes or in an umbrella-shaped arrangement. Petals are 0.2 to 0.3 inches long and usually number 5 or 6 per flower, with an equal number of stamens. The ovary, which usually has 3 or 4 sections, is atop the receptacle (base of the flower) in a superior position, due to the expansion of the ovary disk (outgrowth of the receptacle) and the reduction of the hypanthium (basal portion of the flower).

Fruits are purplish, oval or top-shaded drupes, 0.2 to 0.5 inches long, that enclose a papery endocarp and single seed.

T. gymnocarpa is distinguished from all other species in the genus in that its ovary appears fully superior.

Habitat

This species is typically found on windswept summit ridges or in gullies in wet or sometimes mesic forests between elevations of 820 and 2,790 feet. Associated plants include 'ohi'a, olapa, uluhe, kopiko, kamakahala and kolea.

For a continued habitat description of Oahu, see "Habitat Conditions on the Island of Oahu, Hawaii," page 2031.

Historic Range

T. gymnocarpa was historically known from Punahuu, Waikakalaua Gulch, Mount Olympus, and the region between Niu and Wailupe, all in the Koolau Mountains of Oahu.

Current Distribution

Fifteen populations are now scattered along summit ridges of the Koolau Mountains over a distance of 28 miles from the region of Paumalu at the northern extreme, to Kuliouou and Waimanalo at the southeasternmost point. One population in the Waianae Mountains, located on Palikea Ridge on the border of Federal and private land, was last visited in 1954, and it is not known if it still exists. Most populations contain between one and six individuals, giving a total of fewer than 40 individuals for the entire species. However, because *T. gymnocarpa* is difficult to distinguish from other species when infertile, the total number of individuals may be as high as a few hundred.

Conservation and Recovery

The primary threats to *T. gymnocarpa* are competition with the noxious alien plant, Koster's curse; habitat destruction by feral pigs; and reduced reproductive vigor due to the limited gene pool.

The recovery of this and most other Hawaiian species depends on how well management practices can be implemented. The habitat of this and other Hawaiian species has undergone extreme alteration because of past and present land management practices, including deliberately introducing alien animals and plants, and agricultural and recreational development. To understand the recovery problems facing this species, it is necessary to understand the long-term causes of habitat destruction.

For a continued discussion of the threats to Hawaiian plants, see page 1831.

Bibliography

U.S. Fish and Wildlife Service. "Endangered and Threatened Wildlife and Plants: Endangered Status for 11 Plant Species from the Koolau Mountain Range, Island of Oahu, HI." *Federal Register*. March 28, 1994: 14482-14492.

Contacts

Pacific Islands Ecological Services
    Field Office
Room 6307, 300 Ala Moana Blvd.
Honolulu, HI 96850
Phone: 808-541-2749
FAX: 808-541-2756

Adapted from data compiled by Beacham Publishing for *Beacham's International Threatened, Endangered, and Extinct Species* published on CD ROM.

MAMMALS AND BIRDS

Point Arena Mountain Beaver

Aplodontia rufa nigra

Dale T. Steele   (This beaver is a close relative)

Status	Endangered
Listed	December 12, 1991
Family	Aplodontidae (Beaver)
Description	Stout, compact, cylindrical beaver with broad head, flat puper surface, small eyes and ears.
Habitat	Cool, moist environments receiving heavy rainfall along the Pacific coast.
Food	Deciduous tree bark and leaves.
Reproduction	2 to 3 young per year.
Threats	Habitat loss or alteration due to development and grazing.
Range	California

Description

The Point Arena mountain beaver is similar in appearance to a tailless muskrat. The general body configuration is stout, compact and cylindrical. An average adult weighs about 2 to 2.5 kilograms, and measures about 32.8 centimeters in length. The head is broad, massive, laterally compressed, and notable for its flat upper surface and lack of postorbital processes. Long, stiff vibrissae are present. The eyes and rounded ears are quite small. It has short limbs of about equal length, the forelimbs have functionally opposed thumbs. All digits have long curved claws. A distinctive feature of this species is the cylindrical stump of a tail.

The Point Arena mountain beaver is a strikingly marked subspecies. The black coloration of adults is present as early as July.

Behavior

This species has a low reproductive rate compared to other rodent species. It is monestrous and usually does not give birth before its second year. All females in a population ovulate at about the same time, during a period of 5-7 weeks in mid or late winter, causing the breeding season to be quite limited. Gestation period is estimated at 28 to 30 days. Some parturition differences between subspecies have been noted. In general, the coastal subspecies are found to have earlier parturition dates, late February and March, than the inland or mountain subspecies, April and May.

The single litter usually contains 2 to 3 young. At birth the young are naked, blind and helpless. Vibrissae are present at birth. Lactation probably occurs for the first 2 months after parturition.

It was once thought that the Point Arena mountain beaver had some sort of social organization due to the extensive congregations in some localities. It now appears that some home ranges overlap, but populations consist of separate individuals independently utilizing available resources. The Point Arena mountain beaver vigorously defends its nests and burrows, and is considered non-migratory.

The Point Arena mountain beaver utilizes most, if not all, of the understory plants in its habitat as food. It prefers succulent herbaceous vegetation and deciduous tree bark and leaves. The main species eaten by the Point Arena mountain beaver include sword fern, cow-parsnip, salal, and nettle. This species appears to forage mainly during the night.

Habitat

The known range of the Point Arena mountain beaver is limited to a small area receiving heavy rainfall along the Pacific Coast, extending from British Columbia to central California. Within this area the species is limited to cool, moist environments. Inland subspecies appear dependent upon an insulating snow pack which moderates surface and burrow temperatures.

The climate in the area where the Point Arena mountain beaver is found is characterized as mild with little daily or annual temperature variation. Average annual temperature ranges from about 11 degrees Celsius (C) near the coast, to 15.5 degrees C in southern inland areas. This area has a short frost season, the average date of the first frost is December 15. The area has one of the longest growing seasons in California, over 300 days annually.

All known populations of the Point Arena mountain beaver have been found in either a sheltered gulch or on a steep, north-facing slope. Burrow systems are under dense stands of perennial vegetation where soil conditions allow for easy excavation. An abundant supply of food plants and moderately deep and firm soil with good drainage are found in this species' habitat.

The Point Arena mountain beaver is found in habitats with four main types of vegetation: coastal scrub, such as cow-parsnip, coyote brush, California blackberry, and poison-oak; coniferous forest, such as Douglas-fir, grand fir, and bishop pine; riparian, such as thimbleberry, nettle, elderberry, giant horsetail, and willows; and stabilized dunes.

The Point Arena mountain beaver lives in an extensive system of tunnels usually constructed about a foot from the surface. In coastal strands this species burrows under the shrubby vegetation.

Historic Range

No information on the historic range of the Point Arena mountain beaver is available. The subspecies is currently known from approximately 24 acres of land in Mendocino County, California.

Current Distribution

At the present time, only 10 populations are known, total number of individuals estimated at 100, the largest population containing 20 individuals.

The Point Arena mountain beaver is somewhat limited in maintaining its water balance and in thermoregulating. Anatomical and physiological data indicate that the species is incapable of producing a concentrated urine and, therefore, requires substantial daily amounts of water. This characteristic is believed to be responsible for its localized distribution in cool, moist areas. The Point Arena mountain beaver can thermoregulate adequately only over a relatively narrow band of ambient temperatures, 6 to 16 degrees C, the normal temperature range within the burrows. When surface temperatures are too warm, the subspecies will either seek refuge in its burrow or orient its body to maximize its ability to lose body heat passively.

The low reproductive rate is also a limiting factor for the subspecies. Decreased genetic variability due to the small number of remaining individuals is another problem.

Conservation and Recovery

The Point Arena mountain beaver appears to have suffered most from habitat alteration or loss. Development, cattle and sheep grazing, and farming have greatly reduced coastal scrub in the species' habitat. Habitat has also been opened somewhat by livestock trails. Private and county road construction have also encroached on the Point Arena mountain beaver habitat and caused higher mortality through vehicular traffic.

A proposed microwave tower within habitat occupied by the largest known population is the largest threat at this time. Construction of the tower would destroy habitat used by 10 of the 20 animals at this site.

The species' reputation as a burrower and forager in gardens, croplands and forests has caused decreases in its numbers through poisoning and trapping. However, none of the subspecies endemic to California are known to cause substantial damage to crops, nor are they generally found in intensively managed forest lands.

Predation by domestic and feral dogs as well as cats is a mortality factor for the species. Due to the small numbers of individuals, even one predator can seriously impact the population.

Potential recovery action for the Point Arena mountain beaver includes establishing a buffer around each population site and excluding further urban or other development within this zone of about 100 acres of total habitat or within adjacent potential habitat; installing protective fencing; implementing cooperative agreements to manage the species; and restricting pesticide application. Other recovery actions include minimizing human and domestic animal impact; increased protection, land acquisition or conservation easement; and development of Federal or State recovery programs.

Bibliography

Steele, Dale T. "A Review of the Population Status of the Point Arena Mountain Beaver (*Aplodontia rufa nigra*)." U.S. Fish and Wildlife Service. Sacramento, CA, 1986: 72 pp.

Smurthwaite, Donald. "Mountain Beaver: The Rodent that Gets No Respect." *American Forests* (May 1986).

Contacts

USFWS Regional Office
911 N.S. 11th Avenue
Portland, OR 97232-4181
Phone: 503-231-6118

Sacramento Ecological Services Field Office
2800 Cottage Way
Sacramento, CA 98525
Phone: 916-978-4866
FAX: 916-978-4613

Adapted from data compiled by the Threatened and Endangered Species Information Institute (13950 W. 20th Ave., Golden, CO 80401) for *Beacham's International Threatened, Endangered, and Extinct Species* published on CD ROM, available from Beacham Publishing.

Pacific Pocket Mouse

Perognathus longimembris pacificus

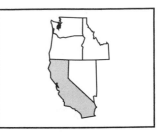

B. "Moose" Peterson

Status	Endangered
Listed	February 3, 1994 Emergency Rule
Family	Heteromyidae (Mice and Kangaroo Rats)
Description	Smallest of the pocket mice.
Habitat	Fine-grain, sandy substrates near coastal strand.
Food	Seeds of grasses and forbs.
Reproduction	Two litters a year ranging from 3 to 7 young.
Threats	Loss of habitat; feral/domestic cats; non-native red foxes.
Range	California

Description

The Pacific pocket mouse is the smallest subspecies of the little pocket mouse, ranging from about 4.3 to 4.9 inches long from nose to tip of tail. The tail, hind foot, and skull lengths and the size of skull structures are also the smallest of all little pocket mouse subspecies.

Behavior

Little pocket mice live up to 7.5 years in captivity and three to five years in the wild. Pregnant and lactating females have been found from April through June, and immatures have been reported form June through September. The little pocket mouse produces one or two litters ranging in size from three to seven young in a year.

Pacific pocket mice primarily eat the seeds of grasses and forbs, but occasionally eat leafy material and soil-dwelling insects.

The Pacific pocket mouse has a high metabolic rate, continually needs food supplies while active, and loses heat rapidly. Virtually all members of this family are nocturnal. It has limited capacity to store food. Little pocket mice may stay in their burrows continuously for up to 5 months in winter, alternating between periods of dormancy and feeding on stored seeds or hibernation in winter under adverse conditions.

The Pacific pocket mouse is likely adapted for burrowing or digging, relatively sedentary, and able to become dormant or hibernate in response to adverse environmental conditions.

While active above ground, little pocket mice have ranged up to 1,000 feet from their burrows in a 24-hour period. Little pocket mouse home ranges vary in size from 0.30 to 1.4 acres, and populations range in density from 0.4 to 2.2 individuals per acre.

Habitat

The Pacific pocket mouse occurs on fine-grain, sandy substrates in the immediate vicinity of the Pacific Ocean. The Pacific pocket mouse inhabits coastal strand, coastal dunes, river alluvium, and coastal sage scrub growing on marine terraces.

Historic Range

The Pacific pocket mouse is historically known from eight populations. Approximately 80 percent of all Pacific pocket mouse records are from 1931 or 1932. The species historically was detected in three areas of Los Angeles County: Marina del Rey/El Segundo, Wilmington, and Clifton. No records of the species exist in Los Angeles County since 1938.

The Pacific pocket mouse was found on "Spyglass Hill" in the San Joaquin Hills of Orange County from 1968 to 1971. G. G. Cantwell previously collected ten specimens at the Dana Point Headlands in 1932.

Current Distribution

The Pacific pocket mouse has been detected at three general locales in San Diego County: the San Onofre area, Santa Margarita River Estuary, and the lower Tijuana River Valley. Another report of a single Pacific pocket mouse in suitable habitat from Lux Canyon, Encinitas, in June 1989 is now considered probable by the observer.

The only known extant population of the Pacific pocket mouse was rediscovered in July 1993 on the Dana Point Headlands in Orange County, California. Between 25 to 39 individuals were detected during trapping surveys conducted into August 1993. This was the first time the species had been collected at this site since 1971. Numerous small-mammal survey and trapping efforts within its historical range have failed to locate any additional populations.

Conservation and Recovery

In Los Angeles County, two of the three historic locales for the Pacific pocket mouse have been developed, and the third (Marina del Rey/El Segundo has been substantially altered since the species was last detected there. The Hyperion area, which formerly contained relatively large expanses of coastal strand and wetland habitats, has been extensively developed.

In Orange County, the development of the Spyglass Hill area began in 1972. This development resulted in the destruction of the formerly occupied habitat at that site.

Although portions of the San Onofre area and the Santa Margarita River mouth in San Diego County remain relatively undisturbed, recent survey and small mammal trapping efforts at these locations failed to detect the presence of the Pacific pocket mouse. During the 1930s, Camp Pendleton Marine Corps Base did not exist and the city of Oceanside was immediately adjacent to the Santa Margarita River estuary. Much of the southern half of this estuary was destroyed in the early 1940s during the establishment of Camp Pendleton and the related construction of a boat basin and harbor facilities. In addition, the Oceanside area has been extensively developed since the Pacific pocket mouse was last recorded there in 1931, and little, if any, suitable habitat remains at that location.

Within the remaining undeveloped range of the Pacific pocket mouse, areas that contain suitable habitat for the species represent less than 10 percent of the remaining habitat.

The proliferation of non-native populations of the red fox in coastal southern California is well documented. Erickson (1993) has speculated that the red fox "may have hastened the demise of the Pacific pocket mouse in the El Segundo area," where the species apparently was well-represented historically.

Feral and/or domestic cats are threatening the only known population of the Pacific pocket mouse. A resident living immediately adjacent to the known population has reported that domestic cats had recently and repeatedly brought home a number of "tiny gray mice." Of all rodent captures at Dana Point Headlands reported by Brylski (1993), 81 percent were Pacific pocket mice.

Bibliography

U.S. Fish and Wildlife Service. "Endangered and Threatened Wildlife and Plants; Emergency Rule to List the Pacific Pocket Mouse as Endangered." *Federal Register* Vol. 59, No. 23, February 3, 1994: 5306-5311.

Contacts

USFWS Regional Office
Eastside Federal Complex
911 N.S. 11th Avenue
Portland, OR 97232-4181
Phone: 503-231-6118

Carlsbad Ecological Services Field Office
2730 Loker Avenue, West
Carlsbad, CA 92008
Phone: 619-431-9440
FAX: 619-431-9624

Adapted from data compiled by Beacham Publishing for *Beacham's International Threatened, Endangered, and Extinct Species* published on CD ROM.

American Black Bear
Ursus americanus

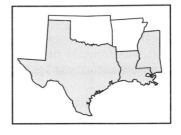

Leonard Lee Rue, III   *Color Plate C-8*

Status	Threatened
Listed	January 7, 1992
Family	Ursidae (Bear)
Description	Huge, bulky bear with long black hair, brownish or cinnamon color phases, short, bushy tail.
Habitat	Forests, swamps, and mountains.
Food	Omnivorous; plant shots, grasses, berries, ground squirrels, and fish.
Reproduction	Small cubs are born in January weighing 0.5 pound.
Threats	Fragmentation of habitat, multi-lane highways.
Range	Louisiana, Mississippi, Texas

Description

The American black bear is a huge, bulky mammal with long black hair, brownish or cinnamon color phases, and a short, bushy tail. The facial profile is blunt. Its eyes are small, nose pad broad, and nostrils large. The muzzle is yellowish brown with a white patch present on the lower throat and chest of some individuals. There are 5 toes on the front and hind feet with short curved claws. Large males may weigh more than 600 pounds although weight varies considerably throughout their range. Its head and body length extend from 4.5 to 5 feet with a shoulder height of from 2 to 3 feet.

Behavior

The American black bear is omnivorous and will eat almost anything. They feed on plant shoots, grasses, berries, lily bulbs, grubs, ants, ground squirrels, and fish. They will even eat garbage and carrion.

In the fall, the species gains weight in preparation for its annual sleep. They will find a den which will protect them from the outside world and hibernate while living off of stored body fat. They will sleep for several months. Yet, they are not true hibernators. Body temperature does not drop significantly and often they will wake and walk off from their dens. At the end of January, females give birth to small cubs which weigh only an average of 0.5 pounds. Birth occurs while still in the den during the winter hibernation.

Habitat

This species lives in the forests, swamps, and mountains of southern Mississippi, Louisiana, and east Texas. They require open clearings and areas in which they can hibernate in the winter. These areas include fallen trees, caves, or other such protected areas.

Historic Range and Current Distribution

The subspecies once occurred throughout southern Mississippi, all of Louisiana, and eastern Texas. Presently, the subspecies occurs only in Louisiana within the Tensas and Atchafalaya River Basins. These lands are owned both privately and publicly.

Conservation and Recovery

The habitat of the American black bear has suffered extensive modification with suitable habitat having been reduced by more than 80% as of 1980. The remaining habitat has been reduced in quality by fragmentation due to intrusion of humans and their structures (e.g., proximity to human disturbing activities, multi-lane highways, etc.), thereby stressing the remaining populations. The original 25,000,000 acres of bottomland forests of the lower Mississippi River Valley had been reduced to 5,000,000 acres, and through the early 1980's another 165,000 acres were being cleared annually. Some of the Mississippi River Delta counties in the lower Yazoo River Basin may have as little as 5% of the original bottomland hardwoods. Other habitat locations in the Tensas and Atchafalaya River Basins have been equally disrupted.

The subspecies, like other members of the species *U. americanus,* is not an old growth species; nor can it survive in open cropland conditions. An abundance of foods were produced following fairly severe timber harvests, and the subspecies utilized these cutover areas for escape cover, and in some cases, actually used treetops remaining from logging operations as winter denning sites for birthing of cubs. This leads USFWS to believe that maintaining occupied habitat in some form of timerland condition may be the single most critical factor in conserving this species, and that the principal threat to it is not normal forest management but conversion of these timbered habitats to croplands and other agricultural uses. For this reason, USFWS believes that the exemption provided in the special rule will not contribute to loss of habitat, but will provide for habitat diversity for the subspecies through continued forest management.

Bibliography

U.S. Fish and Wildlife Service. "Endangered and Threatened Wildlife and Plants; Threatened Status for the American black bear and Related Rules." *Federal Register.* Vol. 57, No. 4. January 7, 1992: 588-594.

Contacts

U.S. Fish and Wildlife
Ecological Services Field Office
Suite 102, Brandywine II
825 Kaliste Saloom Road
Lafayette, LA 70508
Phone: 318-262-6630
FAX: 318-262-6663

Adapted from data compiled by the Threatened and Endangered Species Information Institute (13950 W. 20th Ave., Golden, CO 80401) for *Beacham's International Threatened, Endangered, and Extinct Species* published on CD ROM, available from Beacham Publishing.

Louisiana Black Bear

Ursus americanus luteolus

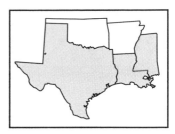

Louisiana Dept. of Wildlife and Fish   *Color Plate C-8*

Status	Endangered
Listed	January 7, 1992
Family	Ursidae (Bear)
Description	Large bear with long black hair, brownish or cinnamon color phases, short tail, small eyes and broad nose pad with large nostrils.
Habitat	Bottomland hardwood areas with dense underbrush.
Food	Omnivorous.
Reproduction	Litter of 1 to 2 cubs per season, every other year.
Threats	Loss of habitat due to agriculture, illegal trapping and killing.
Range	Louisiana, Mississippi, Texas

Description

The Louisiana black bear is a huge, bulky mammal with large males weighing more than 600 pounds. The species has long black hair, with brownish or cinnamon color phases often found in western parts of its range. The tail is short and well haired. The facial profile is rather blunt, the eyes small and the nose pad broad with large nostrils. The muzzle is yellowish brown and a white patch is sometimes present on the lower throat and chest. There are five toes on the front and hind feet with short curved claws.

Behavior

Infants are born in the mother's den sometime from December to February. The newborns weigh only about a half a pound, have little or no hair, and their eyes are closed. When the fur begins growing it is brown, but within a month or so it is quite black. Sharp teeth are well developed within a couple weeks. The cubs grow rapidly and leave the den in April or May, weighing about five pounds. Cubs begin climbing early, usually within three or four months. Parental care is given exclusively by the female, and usually lasts one and a half years. Nursing continues for approximately seven months after birth, but during this time the cub is eating a variety of other foods. The second winter, the female and her cubs den together. By the following spring the cubs could weigh 40 to over 100 pounds and be as big as the female. Late in the spring or summer the unit splits up, each going its separate way.

Females go into estrus sometime in June or July. Males follow scent trails laid down by the estrous females, mate, usually only staying together for one or two days. This species shows delayed implantation. In most other mammals, an egg fertilized by male sperm attaches itself to the wall of the female's uterus soon after mating. There it grows steadily until birth. In this species, the fertilized egg, having developed into a tiny ball, simply floats in the fluid within the uterus. Only when the mother is hibernating in her den does the fetus attach itself to the wall of the uterus and begin again to grow. The total time for growth is only 42-46 days, though pregnancy lasts about seven months. A normal litter consists of one to three cubs. Females normally give birth every other year, due to the long lactation period.

This species exists in ranges throughout its territory. Ranges do not usually overlap with other individuals, but may if there is a large amount of food in that territory. The species does not migrate, but does move freely throughout its range. There have also been examples of a homing instinct in this species. Individuals have traveled up to 140 miles to return to its range.

Louisiana black bear, like other members of *Ursidae*, are omnivorous, eating both animal and vegetable foods. Most of the species' diet is made up of vegetable matter. In the spring and fall, about half the species' diet is vegetation, rising to 80 percent in the summer. Much of the noninsect animal matter that the species eats is carrion, the bodies of animals that have died of starvation or other causes. Studies in the Great Smoky Mountains National Park and nearby areas show that grasses, herbs, berries and nuts make up 81 percent of the species' food; animal matter, most of it bees and beetles, is 11 percent; and garbage and other artificial foods are 8 percent.

Food habits show seasonal differentiation. When the species first comes out of its den in the spring, it depends mostly on grasses and weeds, along with the carrion of animals. Throughout the summer, berries and insects make up most of the species' diet. In early fall, some berries are still eaten along with the late-ripening species such as the gallberry. Late fall brings a rich diet of nuts to give the species extra energy as denning draws near.

The Louisiana black bear hibernates over the winter months. The length of hibernation depends primarily on the climate in the habitat. The species in Alaska hibernates up to seven months, in North Carolina it hibernates about five months, and in Florida's Apalachicola National Forest the species may not hibernate at all. Another factor that affects hibernation is food supply. If supplies are plentiful, hibernating may come later in the season. Hibernating individuals usually lower their heart rates from a normal resting rate of 40 beats per minute to 10 beats per minute over a period of two to four weeks. The species does not eat, drink, urinate or defecate during the hibernation period. It can be aroused quickly, returning to a normal heart rate in about half an hour. It is not certain how long the Louisiana black bear hibernates.

Habitat

The Louisiana black bear is found in a wide range of habitat. It is found most often in bottomland hardwood areas, such as oak, maple and beech of the Tensas and Atchafalaya River Basins. It may also use marshes along the lower rim of the Atchafalaya Basin and agricultural lands such as sugar cane and soybeans in other areas. As a rule the species can use many different habitats, but does require large areas of relatively undisturbed forest. Other characteristics the species' habitats have in common are dense underbrush for food and cover, and trees suitable for climbing.

Historic Range

This species once occurred throughout southern Mississippi, all of Louisiana, and eastern Texas. The historic range included all Texas counties east of and including Cass, Marion, Harrison, Upshur, Rusk, Cherokee, Anderson, Leon, Robertson, Burleson, Washington, Lavaca, Victoria, Refugio, and Aransas; all of Louisiana, and the southern Mississippi counties south of and including Washington, Humphreys, Holmes, Attala, Neshoba, and Lauderdale.

Current Distribution

Presently occupied habitat in Louisiana consists of two core areas, the Tensas and Atchafalaya River Basins. The total habitat area within these two areas is 200,000 to 228,000 acres, of which half is privately owned. Counties of past known populations in Louisiana include: Mary, Carroll, Madison, Tensas, Concordia, Point Coupee, St. Martin, Iberia, and Iberville. In Mississippi the species occurs in small numbers in the Mississippi Delta and in the loess bluffs bordering the Mississippi River floodplain. This species is known to occur on the Chettimanchi Reservation, the Fort Polk Army base, the Barksdale Air Force Base, and an Army ammunitions plant. Other Federally owned lands on which the species occur include: the Ozark National Forest, Jean Lafitte National Park, Atchafalaya National Wildlife Refuge, and the Great Smoky Mountains National Park.

Conservation and Recovery

The major cause of the Louisiana black bear's decline is loss of habitat, mainly due to agriculture. Suitable habitat for the species has been reduced by more than 80 percent as of 1980. The remaining habitat has been reduced in quality by fragmentation due to the intrusion of man and his structures (i.e. highways), thereby stressing the remaining population of individuals. The original 25,000,000 acres of bottomland forest of the lower Mississippi River Valley has been reduced to 5,000,000 acres, and through the early 1980s another 165,000 acres were being cleared annually. Some of the Mississippi River Delta counties in the lower Yazoo River Basin may have as little as five percent of the original bottomland hardwoods.

Of the habitat presently occupied by the Louisiana black bear in the Tensas River Basin, only 15 percent (about 100,000 acres) of the original bottomland forest remains; in Atchafalaya River Basin, only about 100,000 to 128,000 acres of forested lands remain. Nearly one half of the occupied habitat in the Atchafalaya River Basin is privately owned and under no plans for protection through conservation easements or acquisition.

Illegal trapping and killing of this species has been another limiting factor for the species. The appearance of an abnormally low density of this species in the Atchafalaya River may be an indicator of considerable illegal killing on private and public lands and needs to be studied further.

Studies are ongoing on the Tensas National Wildlife Refuge, in the lower Atchafalay River Basin and in Mississippi to delineate areas used by the species and assess management needs, and maps are in preparation that will show occupied habitat, areas of occasional sightings, potential habitat and possible corridors. Development of a restoration plan has already been initiated by the Black Bear Conservation Committee. The Service will make a critical habitat determination and assess whether designation of critical habitat is prudent.

Maintaining occupied habitat in some form of timberland condition may be the single most critical factor in conserving this species. Like other members of its species, the Louisiana black bear is not an old growth species; nor can it survive in open cropland conditions. It has been found that an abundance of the species' foods were produced following timber harvests, and that individuals also utilized these cutover areas for escape cover, and in some cases, actually used treetops remaining from logging operations as winter denning sites for birthing of cubs. This has led the Service to believe that normal forest management will provide habitat diversity for the species. Candidate den trees, such as bald cypress and tupelo gum with visible cavities occurring near rivers, lakes, streams, bayous, sloughs, or other water bodies, in occupied habitat are to be maintained. Stricter control of the illegal taking of the species needs to be enforced.

Bibliography

Ford, B. *Black Bear Spirit of the Wilderness.* Boston: Houghton Mifflin, 1981. 182 pp.

U.S. Fish and Wildlife Service."Endangered and Threatened Wildlife and Plants; Threatened Status for the Louisiana Black Bear and Related Rules." *Federal Register.* Vol. 57. January 7, 1992: 588-594.

U.S. Fish and Wildlife Service. Listing Proposals—June 1990. *Endangered Species Technical Bulletin.* 1990. Vol. XV, No. 7: 4.

U.S. Department of Defense. *Threatened and Endangered Wildlife Species on U.S. Army Installations,* 1991. p. 154.

Contacts

U.S. Fish and Wildlife Service
    Regional Office
Suite 200, 1875 Century Blvd.
Atlanta, GA 30345
Phone: 404-679-4000

Texas Parks and Wildlife Department
Endangered Resources Branch
Suite 100, 3000 IH-35 South
Austin, TX 78704
Phone: 512-448-4311
FAX: 512-440-8887

Austin Ecological Services Field Office
Suite 449, 611 East Sixth Street
Austin, TX 78701
Phone: 512-482-5436
FAX: 512-482-5442

Ecological Services Field Office
Suite A, 6578 Dogwood View Parkway
Jackson, MS 39213
Phone: 601-965-4900
FAX: 601-965-4340

Adapted from data compiled by the Threatened and Endangered Species Information Institute (13950 W. 20th Ave., Golden, CO 80401) for *Beacham's International Threatened, Endangered, and Extinct Species* published on CD ROM, available from Beacham Publishing.

Marbled Murrelet

Brachyramphus marmoratus marmoratus

B. "Moose" Peterson

Status	Threatened
Listed	October 1, 1992
Family	Alcidae (Auks, Puffins, Murres)
Description	Small bird with dark plumage above and heavily mottled below.
Habitat	Marine environment during majority of year; inland during breeding season.
Food	Fish and invertebrates.
Reproduction	Clutch size of 1 egg.
Threats	Habitat loss due to harvesting of old-growth forests.
Range	Alaska, California, Oregon, Washington

Description

The marbled murrelet is a small (9.75 inches) bird whose adult breeding plumage is dark above and heavily mottled below. Wintering adults have a mostly white chest and belly and a lighter colored back. This subspecies is not sexually dimorphic. Juveniles resemble wintering adults but have some mottling on the chest and belly. The bill and tail are dark brown to black.

Behavior

Sexual maturity is reached in two years. All adults do not breed every year; this may be in response to prey availability. When they do, as with most alcids, they only lay one egg in each clutch. Nesting occurs from mid-April through late September. The eggs are incubated for about 27 to 30 days and

the chicks fledge in about 27 to 28 days. Both males and females incubate the eggs in alternating 24-hour shifts. The chicks are altricial to semi-precocial and are generally fed once a day. Adults only carry one fish back from each feeding trip. Feeding flights most often occur at dawn and dusk.

Habitat

The marbled murrelet spends the majority of the year in the marine environment. They are primarily found inland only during the breeding season but can be observed inland during any month of the year.

This species appears to prefer older forest stands for nesting near the coastline. These sites are characterized by large trees (32 inches diameter at breast height), multi-storied stands, and a moderate to high canopy closure. The dominant tree species are

Douglas-fir in Oregon and Washington, and redwoods in California. In some areas, mature stands with old growth components are used. The areas must have trees with large branches or deformities to provide platforms for nests. Nests are generally placed in the oldest trees in the stand. The 16 nests found in California, Oregon, and Washington were all located in old-growth trees with a diameter at breast height of 35 to 210 inches. Nests are placed high in the tree in areas with good overhead protection.

Stand size is also an important factor. This species was most often found in stands over 500 acres in California.

Concentrations of murrelets at off-shore sites are almost always adjacent to older forests on the coast.

This species feeds by diving primarily in near-shore marine waters, usually in water 100 feet deep and within 500 feet of shore for fish and invertebrates. Some birds have been observed feeding along rivers and on inland lakes.

Adults are probably diurnal for the most part and appear to make feeding flights at dawn and dusk. The chicks may be sensitive to warm temperatures; their activity levels may drop as the temperature increases.

Historic Range

Historic records indicate this murrelet was common to plentiful along the California coast south to Monterey County and around the mouth of the Columbia River.

Current Distribution

This North American subspecies ranges from the Aleutian Archipelago in Alaska, eastward to Cook Inlet, Kodiak Island, Kenai Peninsula, and Prince William Sound, southward coastally throughout the Alexander Archipelago of Alaska, and through British Columbia, Washington, Oregon, to central California. Some birds may winter offshore in southern California as far south as San Diego. In California, this species is restricted to old-growth redwood forests in Del Norte, Humboldt, San Mateo, and Santa Cruz Counties. The marbled murrelet has been found up to 50 miles inland in Washington, 35 miles inland in Oregon, 22 miles inland in northern California, and 11 miles inland in central California. Over 90% of all observations were within 37 miles of the coast in the northern Washington Cascades, and most birds in Oregon were with 12 miles of the coast.

Most murrelet habitat in California is found on U.S. Forest Service or National Park Service lands. This species is found on Forest Service and Bureau of Land Management lands in Oregon and Washington. The National Audubon Society purchased a section of land in Oregon that supports the largest concentration of this species found in Oregon.

Conservation and Recovery

The primary reason for the decline of this species is habitat loss due to harvesting of old-growth forests along the Pacific Northwest coast; up to 85% of this forest type in western Oregon and Washington and 85% to 96% in California has been lost since logging began. Harvesting has been concentrated along the coasts in prime murrelet habitat.

Fire and windthrow have also been responsible for the loss of some areas of old-growth forest.

This species and all alcids are susceptible to mortality related to oil spills and fish harvesting using gill nets (the birds get caught in the nets and drown). These factors are minor compared to habitat loss related declines.

Active nests are hard to locate because of

their location high in the tree, low light conditions, and the infrequency of adult bird movements to and from the nest. People conducting nesting surveys should look for egg shell fragments, young found on the forest floor, birds flying through the forest beneath the canopy, birds observed landing in trees, and birds heard calling from a stationary perch. Intensive surveys should be conducted to locate active nests and to determine the species' life history and ecological requirements.

A system of Habitat Conservation Areas (HCA's) was developed as a part of the conservation strategy for the northern spotted owl. These areas have been recommended as "no harvest" areas and the Forest Service and Bureau of Land Management are not currently planning on harvesting in these areas. Some sections protected as HCA's include known murrelet habitat but these areas are not believed to provide adequate protection for the species.

Marbled murrelets have a high susceptibility to oil spills because they spend most of their time on the sea surface and feeding in local concentrations close to shore. During the *Exxon Valdez* spill in 1989, the number of murrelet carcasses recovered was from 612 to 642, which comprised nearly 12 percent of all carcasses recovered.

Marbled murrelets are found both during the nesting season and during winter in areas affected by oil shipping in Washington, Oregon, and California. Oiled murrelets have been reported in several Washington spills and California.

Bibliography

Ehrlich, P. R., D. S. Dobkin, and D. Wheye. *Birds in Jeopardy—the Imperiled and Extinct Birds of the United States and Canada, Including Hawaii and Puerto Rico.* Stanford: Stanford University Press, 1992. 259 pp.

Robbins, C. S., B. Bruun, and H. Zim. *Birds of North America—a Guide to Field Identification.* New York: Golden Press, 1983. 360 pp.

U.S. Fish and Wildlife Service. "Endangered and Threatened Wildlife and Plants; Determination of Threatened Status for the Washington, Oregon, and California Population of the Marbled Murrelet." *Federal Register* Vol. 57, No. 191. October 1, 1992: 45328-45337.

Contacts

U.S. Fish and Wildlife Service
Regional Office
Eastside Federal Complex
911 N.S. 11th Avenue
Portland, OR 97232-4181
Phone: 503-231-6118

Olympia Ecological Services Field Office
Suite 102, 3704 Griffin Lane, SE
Olympia, WA 98501-2192
Phone: 206-753-9440
FAX: 206-753-9008

Portland Ecological Services Field Office
2600 SE 98th Avenue
Portland, OR 97266
Phone: 503-231-6179
FAX: 503-231-6195

Adapted from data compiled by the Threatened and Endangered Species Information Institute (13950 W. 20th Ave., Golden, CO 80401) for *Beacham's International Threatened, Endangered, and Extinct Species* published on CD ROM, available from Beacham Publishing.

Western Snowy Plover
Charadrius alexandrinus nivosus

B. "Moose" Peterson   *Color Plate C-5*

Status	Threatened
Listed	March 5, 1993
Family	Charadiidae (Plover)
Description	Small, pale colored shorebird with dark patches on upper breast.
Habitat	Coastal beaches, salt ponds, and sand spits.
Food	Invertebrates in wet sand and kelp.
Reproduction	Average cluth size is 3 eggs.
Threats	Alien plants, urban development, sand mining.
Range	Arizona, California, Colorado, Kansas, Oklahoma, Oregon, Texas, Washington

Description

The snowy plover is a small, pale colored shorebird that is light above with a dark patch on the crown, sides of the head, and either side of its upper breast. Its underparts and portions of the head are white.

Behavior

The breeding season of coastal populations extends from mid-March through mid-September. Nest initiation and egg laying occurs from mid-March through mid-July. The usual clutch size is three eggs. Both sexes incubate the eggs.

Chicks are precocious, leaving the nest within hours after hatching to search for food. Fledgling (reaching flying age) requires an average of 31 days. Broods rarely remain in the nesting territory until fledgling occurs. The species will nest again after loss of a clutch or brood. Double brooding and polygamy (i.e. the female successfully hatches more than one brood in a nesting season with different mates) have been observed in coastal California and may also occur in Oregon. After loss of a clutch or brood or successful hatching of a nest, the species may nest again in the same colony site or move, sometimes up to several hundred miles, to colony sites to nest.

Nest success (percentage of nests hatching at least one egg) ranges from 0 to 80% for coastal species. Instances of low nest success have been attributed to a variety of factors, including predation, human disturbance, and inclement weather conditions. Reproductive success ranges from 0.05 to 2.40 young fledged per female, pair, or nest. In 1986, Wilson estimated that the species must fledge 0.8 young per females to maintain a stable population. Reproductive success falls far short of this threshold at many nesting sites.

The species breeds in loose colonies with the number of adults at coastal breeding sites ranging from two to 318. The coastal population consists of both resident and migratory birds. Some birds winter in the same areas used for breeding. Others migrate either north or south to wintering areas.

The species forages on invertebrates in the wet sand and among surf-cast kelp within the intertidal zone; in dry, sandy areas above the high tide; on salt pans; spoils sites; and along the edges of salt marshes and salt ponds.

The species is most active during the early morning when it is cool. Afternoons and evenings are spent resting or roosting when it is hot.

Habitat

The Pacific coast populations of the species breeds primarily on coastal beaches from southern Washington to southern Baja California, Mexico. Nesting habitat is unstable and ephemeral as a result of unconsolidated soul characteristics influenced by high winds, storms, wave action, and colonization by plants. Other less common nesting habitat includes salt pans, coastal dredged spoil disposal sites, dry salt ponds, and salt pond levees. Sand spits, dune-backed beaches, non-vegetated beach strands, open areas around estuaries, and beaches at river mouths are the preferred coastal habitats for nesting. The species winters primarily in coastal California and Mexico.

Nest sites occur in flat, open areas with sandy or saline substrates; vegetation and driftwood are usually sparse or absent. The majority of individuals are site-faithful returning to the same breeding site in subsequent breeding seasons.

Historic Range and Current Distribution

Historic records indicate that nesting individuals were once more widely distributed in coastal California, Oregon, and Washington than they are currently. In coastal California, the species bred at 53 locations prior to 1970. Since that time, no evidence of breeding birds has been found at 33 of these 53 sites, representing a 62% decline in breeding sites. The greatest losses of breeding habitat were in southern California, within the central portion of the coastal breeding range. In Oregon, the species historically nested at 29 locations on the coast. In 1990, only six nesting colonies remained, representing a 79% decline in active breeding sites. In Washington, the species formerly nested in at least five sites on the coast. Today, only two colony sites remain active, representing, at minimum, a 60% decline of breeding sites.

In addition to loss of nesting sites, the breeding population in California, Oregon, and Washington has declined 17% between 1977 and 1989. Declines in the breeding population have been specifically documented in Oregon and California. Breeding season surveys of the Oregon coast from 1978 to 1992 show that the number of adults have declined significantly at an average annual rate of about 5%. The number of adults has declined from a high of 139 in 1981 to a low of 30 in 1992. If the current trend continues, breeding individuals could disappear from coastal Oregon by 1999. In 1981, the coastal California breeding population was estimated to be 1,565 adults, an 11% decline.

Although there are no historic data for Washington, it is doubtful that the species' breeding population was ever very large in this state. However, loss of nesting sites probably has resulted in a reduction in overall population size. In recent years, fewer than 30 birds have nested on the southern coast of Washington. In 1991, there was only one successful brood detected in the state. Survey data also indicate a decline in wintering individuals, particularly in southern California. The number of individuals observed during Christmas Bird Counts from 1962 to 1984 significantly decreased in southern California despite an increase in observer participation in the counts. This observed decline was not accompanied by a significant loss of wintering habitat over the same time period.

This species is currently distributed along the Pacific coast from southern Washington to southern Baja California, Mexico, Colorado, Kansas, Oklahoma, and north-central Texas, as well as coastal areas of extreme southern Texas, and possibly extreme northeastern Mexico. Although previously observed only as a migrant in Arizona, small numbers have bred there in recent years. The species occurs on federal, state, and privately-owned land throughout its range. The species occupied a similar, more extensive range in the past over the same general areas.

Conservation and Recovery

The most important form of habitat loss to coastal breeding individuals has been encroachment of European beachgrass (*Ammophila arenaria*). This non-native plant was introduced to the west coast around 1898 to stabilize dunes. Since then, it has spread up and down the coast and now is found from British Columbia to southern California (Ventura County). European beachgrass is currently a major dune plant occurring at about 50% of California breeding sites and all of those in Oregon and Washington. Stabilizing sand dunes with European beachgrass has reduced the amount of non-vegetated area above the tideline, decreased the width of the beach, and increased its slope. These changes have reduced the amount of potential nesting habitat for the species on many beaches and may hamper brood movements. The beachgrass community also provides habitat for predators of the species which historically would have been largely precluded by the lack of cover in the dune community. In addition, the presence of beachgrass may adversely affect food supplies. The abundance and diversity of sand dune arthropods are markedly depressed in areas dominated by European beachgrass.

Urban development also has contributed significantly to the loss of breeding sites. The construction of residential and industrial developments, and recreational facilities, including placement of access roads, parking lots, summer homes, and supportive services, have permanently eliminated valuable nesting habitat on beaches in southern Washington, Oregon, and California. Species' use of human-made habitat, such as salt evaporators and dredged spoil sites, apparently has not compensated for loss or degradation of habitat in other areas.

Sand mining operations at numerous locations in California also may be eliminating potential habitat by interrupting buildup of the sand profile. Stabilization efforts also may interrupt this process, resulting in beach erosion and loss of nesting habitat.

In the habitat remaining for nesting, human activity (e.g., walking, jogging, running pets, horseback riding, off-road vehicle use, and beach raking) is a key factor in the ongoing decline in this species' breeding sites and the breeding populations in California, Oregon, and Washington.

In all of Los Angeles County and parts of Orange County, California, entire beaches are raked on a daily to weekly basis to remove trash and tidal debris. Even if human activity was low on these beaches, grooming activities completely preclude the possibility of successful nesting attempts. Food availability on raked beaches also may be depressed for both breeding and wintering populations, because surf-cast kelp and associated invertebrates are removed and the upper centimeter of sand substrate is disturbed.

Eggs, chicks, and adults of this species are taken by a variety of avian and mammalian predators. These losses, particularly to avian predators, are exacerbated by human disturbances. Of the many predators, American crows, ravens, and red fox have had a significantly adverse effect on reproductive success at several colony sites. Because crows and ravens, in particular, thrive in urban/agricultural areas, present day coastal populations of this species are probably greater than historic populations. Accumulations of trash at beaches attracts these as well as other predators, including striped skunks, gulls, and raccoons. At nesting sites on the Oregon coast, nest losses of up to 68% have been attributed to crows and ravens.

On most Federal land containing active breeding sites, few measures have been implemented specifically to this species. Most nesting areas on Federal land, with the exception of military bases, have unrestricted human access all year. In Oregon, the Corps of Engineers is proposing two projects to create or improve nesting habitat using dredged spoils. Access improvements for recreational purposes are ongoing at several beaches on Federal land.

Bibliography

U.S. Fish and Wildlife Service."Endangered and Threatened Wildlife and Plants; Determination of Threatened Status for the Pacific Coast Population of the Western Snowy Plover." *Federal Register* Vol. 58, No. 42. March 5, 1993: 12864-12874.

Contacts

U.S. Fish and Wildlife Service
Regional Office
P. O. Box 25486
Denver, CO 80225
Phone: 303-236-7920

U.S. Fish and Wildlife Service
Regional Office
P. O. Box 1306
Albuquerque, NM 87103
Phone: 505-766-2321
FAX: 505-766-8063

Adapted from data compiled by the Threatened and Endangered Species Information Institute (13950 W. 20th Ave., Golden, CO 80401) for *Beacham's International Threatened, Endangered, and Extinct Species* published on CD ROM, available from Beacham Publishing.

Coastal California Gnatcatcher
Polioptila californica californica

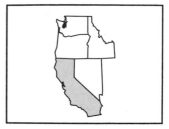

B. "Moose" Peterson   *Color Plate C-5*

Status	Threatened
Listed	March 30, 1993
Family	Muscicapidae (Thrush)
Description	Small, long-tailed bird dark blue-gray above and grayish-white below.
Habitat	Coastal sage scrub plant areas.
Food	Insects and spiders.
Reproduction	Clutch sizes average 4 eggs.
Threats	Urban and agricultural development.
Range	California

Description

The coastal California gnatcatcher, *Poliop-tila californica californica,* is one of three subspecies of the California gnatcatcher. It is is a small, long-tailed bird that is dark blue-gray above and grayish-white below. The tail is mostly black above and below. The male has a distinctive black cap that is absent during the winter. Both sexes have a distinctive white eye-ring. Vocalizations of this species include a call consisting of a rising and falling series of three, kitten-like mew notes.

Behavior

Breeding occurs from mid-March through mid-May. Nests are composed of grasses, bark strips, small leaves, spider webs, down, and other materials, and are often placed in coastal sagebrush about three feet above the ground. Clutch sizes average 4 eggs. Both males and females participate in all phases of the nesting cycle. Multiple broods in one season can occur but it is generally uncommon. Incubation lasts about 14 days and the chicks fledge in about 16 days. Juveniles are dependent upon or remain closely associated with their parents for up to several months following fledging. This subspecies is non-migratory.

Habitat

This species is found almost exclusively in the coastal sage scrub plant community with occasional occurrences in chaparral. The southern limit of its range coincides with the distributional boundary of this distinctive vegetation type. Coastal sage scrub vegetation is composed of relatively low-growing, summer (dry season) deciduous, and succulent plants. Dominant plant species include coastal sagebrush (*Artemisia californica*), various species of sage (*Salvia* spp.), California buckwheat (*Eriogonum fasciculatum*), lemonadeberry (*Rhus integrifolia*), California encelia (*Encelia californica*), prickly pear and cholla cactus (*Opuntia* spp.), and various species of Haplopappus. Within this plant community this bird can often be found in gullies, canyons, washes, and the lower parts of slopes.

Historic Range and Current Distribution

The coastal California gnatcatcher is restricted to coastal southern California and northwestern Baja California, Mexico from Los Angeles County south to El Rosario, Mexico including the California counties of Los Angeles, Orange, Riverside, and San Diego. It was formerly found north to Ventura and San Bernardino Counties.

Most of the gnatcatcher populations occur on private lands. About 21% (81,992 of 393,655 acres) of coastal sage scrub in southern California south of metro Los Angeles is publicly owned. About 64% or 52,500 acres are on military reservations including Camp Pendleton Marine Corps Base, El Toro Marine Corps Air Station, Fallbrook Naval Annex, and Miramar Naval Air Station. Other publicly held lands are administered by the California Department of Parks and Recreation, the Cities of San Diego and Lake Elsinore, the Southern California Metropolitan Water District and the counties of Orange, Riverside, and San Diego.

Conservation and Recovery

The coastal California gnatcatcher has been extirpated from the California counties of Ventura and San Bernardino and is close to extinction in Los Angeles County. This bird has been eliminated from 42 sites occupied prior to 1960. These losses are the result of development (primarily for urban and agricultural uses) of the coastal sage scrub community this bird is dependent upon. Estimated losses in this habitat type are from 65% to 90% of the original range. The human population in southern California has increased dramatically in the last 20 years. Most of these people now live in areas along the coast that formerly supported the coastal sage scrub community.

The loss of coastal sage scrub vegetation has been associated with an increasing degree of habitat fragmentation, which reduces habitat quality and promotes increased levels of nest predation and brood parasitism, and ultimately, increased rates of local extinction. Fragmentation also isolates many populations threatening the genetic integrity of this species.

The U.S. Fish and Wildlife Service is currently participating in a study of gnatcatcher ecology in western Riverside County that was initiated in the spring of 1992. This study involves intensive monitoring of three color-banded gnatcatcher subpopulations occupying three different landscape settings. Preliminary results of nest monitoring activities in 1992 indicate that the birds that occupy small, fragmented patches experienced high levels of nest parasitism by cowbirds and only one of 15 nests fledged a total of two young. Gnatcatcher nests on the grazed patch were also heavily parasitized and only 2 of 25 nests fledged a total of 4 young. The gnatcatchers in the more natural setting had only one case of cowbird parasitism (1 of 26 nests) and good reproductive success (11 of 26 nests fledged a total of 40 young). These findings strongly suggest that the adverse edge effects noted in fragmented forest habitats occur in shrubland communities as well.

Bibliography

U.S. Fish and Wildlife Service."Endangered
and Threatened Wildlife and Plants; Determination of Threatened Status for the
Coastal California Gnatcatcher." *Federal
Register* Vol. 58, No. 59. March 30, 1993:
16742-16757.

Contacts

U.S. Fish and Wildlife Service
Regional Office
Eastside Federal Complex
911 N.S. 11th Avenue
Portland, OR 97232-4181
Phone: 503-231-6118

Adapted from data compiled by the Threatened
and Endangered Species Information Institute
(13950 W. 20th Ave., Golden, CO 80401) for
*Beacham's International Threatened, Endangered, and
Extinct Species* published on CD ROM, available
from Beacham Publishing.

Spectacled Eider
Somateria [=arctonetta,=lampronetta] fischeri

Bev Grafel   *Color Plate C-5*

Status	Threatened
Listed	May 10, 1993
Family	Anathidae (Ducks and Geese)
Description	Large-bodied marine diving duck; male has a green head with a long, sloping forehead, large, distinctive white eye patches, a black chest and a white back.
Habitat	Arctic coasts.
Food	Benthic mollusks and crustaceans.
Threats	Fishing, oil exploration.
Range	Alaska, Russia

Description

The spectacled eider is a large-bodied marine diving duck and one of three eiders in the genus *Somateria*. The adult male has a green head with a long, sloping forehead, large, distinctive white eye patches, a black chest and a white back. Juveniles and adult females are brown with less distinct spectacle eye patches.

Behavior

The species is believed to feed mainly on benthic mollusks and crustaceans in shallow waters less than 98.3 feet deep. They may also forage on pelagic amphipods that are concentrated along the sea water-pack ice interface. On their coastal breeding grounds, they feed on aquatic crustaceans, aquatic insects, and plant materials.

Typical of most sea birds, the species is not active during one specific time of day over the other. Rather, its activity depends upon the sometimes unpredictable weather which occurs across its range. On winter evenings, it often loafs in rafts (a large number of birds congregate together on the open expanses of water). These are large areas of the sea formed by large numbers of floating birds.

Habitat

The species breeds discontinuously along the coast of Alaska. They also nest on St. Lawrence Island and along the Arctic coast of Russia. Their primary winter range is in the central and northwestern Bering Sea. Migrant flocks stage offshore from St. Lawrence Island, where they are seen regularly in the spring and fall. Only a few have been documented during the winter in nearshore waters of Alaska and British Columbia. Their nests are built on shorelines, islands, and meadows in coastal tundra, predominantly within 15 kilometers of the coast.

Historic Range and Current Distribution

The historic range of this species is thought to be the same as that of present. It is distributed along the coast of Alaska from the Nushagak Peninsula north to Barrow and east nearly to the Yukon border. The species also occurs in Russia.

Conservation and Recovery

The species has traditionally been harvested during migration, and birds and eggs have been taken on some nesting grounds for subsistence use by Alaskan and Siberian Native Americans. Historically, skins and feathers were used for clothing and bones were used for household purposes. Feathers have been applied to ceremonial fans and masks that are sold to tourists. Spring harvest of the species has provided an important traditional source of meat to coastal communities, however, the individuals taken for this use constitute a small portion of the total amount taken.

In recent years, the species has apparently been taken in low numbers for subsistence and minimally for sport use, but rangewide and local effects of this harvest are not documented.

The destruction of habitat is not known to be a factor in the decline of this species. Breeding habitat encompasses vast expanses of coastal tundra and ponds that remain predominantly unaltered and uninhabited. No development or other substantial threats to the species' principal breeding habitat on the Yukon Delta National Wildlife Refuge are foreseen.

Nesting habitat on the central coast of Alaska's North Slope, a small portion of the species' breeding range, has been altered by oil and gas development. Potential threats from this development include contamination from accidental spills, off road vehicle use, wetland filling, and indirect effects of human presence. While the extent of nesting habitat impacted by oil and gas development is presently small, industrial development could expand in the future.

Marine habitat requirements of the species are poorly understood. Past and present threats to suspected marine habitats could include toxic contaminants transported from Russian or North American sites, indirect impacts of shifting populations of species with overlapping food habits, and secondary effects of commercial fish and invertebrate harvests in the Bering Sea. The Service has not found evidence that these generalized threats have actually occurred, although minimal information is available on long-term changes in the Bering Sea ecosystem.

Future offshore oil and gas development could also pose a threat to the species. In outer continental shelf waters, proposed lease sales could result in active exploration and development within wintering, migration, and molting habitat. State-controlled, nearshore marine waters may also be leased and developed. Planned satellite telemetry research will help the Service delineate more precisely the marine habitats used by the species and permit a thorough assessment of these possible threats.

Eggs, young, and occasionally adults are preyed upon by mammalian and avian predators, particularly arctic fox, glaucous gulls, and parasitic jaegers. Rangewide or long-term effects of predation on the species' population have not been documented.

USFWS recently received reports of birds, including this species, accidentally striking commercial fishing vessels operating near the pack ice in the northern Bering Sea. Since these crab fishing boats are operating in potential wintering range for the species, accidental collisions may be a threat to the species. Hazardous materials are spilled regularly into the Bering Sea from shipwrecks and bilge discharges and some of these materials may enter benthic or pelagic food chains.

Bibliography

U.S. Fish and Wildlife Service."Endangered and Threatened Wildlife and Plants; Final Rule to List Spectacled Eider as Threatened." *Federal Register* Vol. 58, No. 88. May 10, 1993: 27474-27480.

Contacts

U.S. Fish and Wildlife Service
    Regional Office
1011 E. Tudor Road
Anchorage, AK 99503
Phone: 907-786-3542
FAX: 907-786-3635

Adapted from data compiled by the Threatened and Endangered Species Information Institute (13950 W. 20th Ave., Golden, CO 80401) for *Beacham's International Threatened, Endangered, and Extinct Species* published on CD ROM, available from Beacham Publishing.

Mexican Spotted Owl
Strix occidentalis lucida

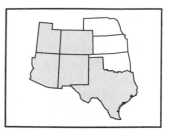

California Spotted Owl (close relative)
B. "Moose" Peterson

Color Plate C-8

Status	Threatened
Listed	March 16, 1993
Family	Strigidae (Owl)
Description	Dark brown owl with numerous large white plumage spots.
Habitat	Forested mountain and canyon areas.
Food	Mammals, birds, reptiles, and insects.
Reproduction	Nests in early March through early June; clutch of 1 to 4 eggs.
Threats	Destruction and modification of habitat caused by timber harvest and fires, increased predation.
Range	Arizona, Colorado, New Mexico, Texas, Utah

Description

The Mexican spotted owl is one of three spotted owl subspecies recognized by the American Ornithologists' Union. It is distinguished from the California (*S. o. occidentalis*) and northern (*S. o. caurina*) spotted owl subspecies chiefly by geographic distribution and plumage. In general, the background coloration of the Mexican spotted owl is a darker brown than the *S. o. occidentalis* and *S. o. caurina* subspecies. The plumage spots are larger, more numerous and whiter, giving it a lighter appearance overall.

Behavior

There is limited information available on the reproductive biology of this species, but it does nest in early March through early June. Owls most commonly lay eggs in April, but eggs have been found as early as March 2. Clutch size varies from one to 4 eggs, with most broods containing one or three owlets. The incubation period is approximately 30 days and most eggs hatch by the end of May. Incubation is carried out solely by the female. Males provide food for the female and young until the owlets are about two weeks old. The female then assists in capturing food for the young.

The female roosts at the nest until three to six days before the young fledge. Most owlets fledge in June, 34 to 36 days after hatching. They are unable to fly when they first leave the nest, but they become increasingly proficient at flight throughout the summer, and are "semi-independent" by late August or early September, although juvenile begging calls have been heard as late as September 30. Young are fully independent by early October.

Habitat

This species occupies a variety of vegetative habitats but these usually contain certain common characteristics. These characteristics include forested mountain and canyon areas containing a high stand density, and a high multistoried closed canopy resulting from and uneven-aged stand. Other characteristics include downed logs, snags, and mistletoe infection that are indicative of an old growth forest (usually more than 200 years old), and absence of active management. Much of the habitat is characterized by steep slopes and canyons with rocky cliffs.

This owl occupies vegetative communities that consist primarily of warm-temperate and cold-temperate forests, and to a lesser extent, woodlands and riparian deciduous forest. The mixed-conifer community appears to be most frequently used. Mixed-conifer forests contain several species of overstory trees. The understory of these forests provides roosting sites for the Mexican spotted owl.

The vegetative communities used by this species vary across its range. In southeastern Arizona, habitat use is almost equally split between mixed-conifer and Madrean Evergreen Forest and Woodland. Within these vegetative zones, particularly at lower elevations, the species is usually found in steep, forested canyons with rocky cliffs. At the northern edge of their range in northeastern Arizona, southwestern Colorado, and Utah, this species may occur year-round at 4,400 to 6,800 feet within the pinon-juniper zone, below mixed-conifer forests. These habitats often include narrow shady, cool canyons in sandstone slickrock. Owls roost in the riparian vegetation of canyon bottoms, on ledges, or cavities in the slickrock canyon walls.

Results of the first seasons of an ongoing telemetry study in canyon habitats in southern Utah and Colorado showed that during the fall and winter months, 46 percent of owl locations occurred on mesa-tops, benches and warm slopes above the canyons. Movement out of the canyons indicates a shift during winter from summer-use areas inside the canyons and on cool slopes, to warmer areas.

Habitats suitable for nesting appear to be more restricted than those required for foraging or roosting. Areas with high canopy closure and at least a few old-growth trees are usually selected for nesting. One study showed that witches'-broom and tree stick platforms were the most frequently used nesting substrates; tree cavities and ledges were the next most commonly used. Most nest trees occurred at an elevation of 5,500 to 9,000 feet, on northwest or east facing slopes, indicating a preference for the cooler portion of the habitat. Most nest trees were on a slope less than 40 percent.

The diet of the Mexican spotted owl consists of a variety of mammals, birds, reptiles, and insects with mammals, mainly woodrats, making up the bulk of the diet throughout the owls' range.

This species appears to winter in the home range associated with their breeding area.

Historic Range

The distribution of this species ranges from the southern Rocky Mountains in Colorado and the Colorado Plateau in southern Utah, southward through Arizona and New Mexico and, discontinuously, through Texas and the Sierra Madre Occidental and Oriental to the mountains at the southern end of the Mexican Plateau. It is most abundant in forests in New Mexico and Arizona.

The historic range of this species is thought to be similar to its present distribution, with the inclusion of some low elevation sites.

Current Distribution

Today, the most significant population of the species is in Utah: six pairs and three single birds occur in Zion National Park. The total number of birds in Utah is estimated at 26 pairs and 19 single birds, in San Juan County. In Colorado, current Mexican spotted owl records total two pairs and 10 single birds, from the San Juan Mountains, and from the Front Range as far north as the vicinity of Denver, mainly in Montezuma County. In Texas, all of the species' records are from the Guadalupe Mountains near the New Mexico border. Today there is only one pair of birds.

In Arizona, the species is known from the Colorado Plateau in the north, the basin and range mountains of the southeastern part of the state, and the rugged transition zone between these provinces in central and east central Arizona in the Counties of Cochise and Graham. The largest concentration of this species occurs in the central and east central forests along the Mogollon Rim, in the White Mountains, and on the volcanic peaks near Flagstaff. This region takes in all or part of five national forests and two Indian reservations. The number of owls reported by various agencies at the end of 1990 from this area totaled 124 pairs and 77 single birds. Current total records for Arizona amount to 153 pairs and 108 single birds.

In New Mexico, the species has been reported from most of the major mountain ranges including the Sangre de Cristo, Jemez, Manzano, Sacramento, Mogollon, Tularosa, San Francisco, San Mateo, and Black Range Mountains. Current numbers total 129 pairs and 85 single birds.

In Mexico, occurrence information on the species is limited, but most of the site records have been concentrated near the U.S. border in northeastern Sonora and northwestern Chihuauha, with large gaps in the known distribution and very few records south and east of there. Available evidence suggests that this species has never been common in Mexico. Today, there are approximately two pairs and 4 single birds in this country.

This owl occurs on land administered by the U.S. Forest Service, Bureau of Land Management, Bureau of Indian Affairs, National Park Service, and some private land. In 1992, the Forest Service reported 620 single and paired owls on its lands in Arizona and New Mexico, with a total of 4,698, 807 acres (67%) of suitable owl habitat on their lands. In 1990, a total of five pairs and 22 single owls were known to occur on Indian reservations, with 878,000 acres (13%) of suitable owl habitat on these lands. In 1992, a total of one pair and five single birds were reported on Bureau of Land Management lands in Colorado, Utah, Arizona, and New Mexico, with 711,000 acres of suitable habitat. In 1990, a total of eight pairs and 16 single birds were known from National Park Service lands, covering approximately 23 parks and monuments, with 238,100 to 437,600 acres (5%) of suitable habitat. There are no population numbers for birds on State-owned lands, but the State of New Mexico owns 177,400 to 202,400 acres (3%) of suitable habitat. An estimated 5,000 acres of suitable owl habitat on private land is much less than 1% of the total. The total acreage of suitable habitat (6,815,557 acres) on these lands is probably overestimated.

Conservation and Recovery

The main threats facing this species include destruction and modification of habitat caused by timber harvest and fires, increased predation associated with habitat fragmentation, and lack of adequate protective regulations.

On New Mexico and Arizona Forest Service lands, an estimated 1,037,000 acres of suitable habitat has been converted to unsuitable habitat due to man-caused and natural events. Of this, 816,000 acres (78.7%) was lost due to human activities, primarily timber harvest, and 221,000 acres (21.3%) was lost due to natural causes, primarily fire. Forty percent of this loss has occurred since 1980, which represents a rate of habitat loss of approximately 10% in the last decade, on Arizona and New Mexico national forests. Of the estimated suitable owl habitat on Arizona and New Mexico national forest land, 59 percent (1,987,000 acres) is available for timber harvest.

Forest plans for five of the 11 New Mexico and Arizona national forests now contain provisions to allow cable or skyline logging on slopes greater than 40 percent. Steep slopes typically provide superior habitat by virtue of the owl's preference for the topography, rock outcrops and/or cliffs, and the generally cooler microclimates often supporting multilayered mixed-conifer forest. Entering steeper slopes will result in a larger proportion of harvest in mixed-conifer forests, the primary owl habitat. Thus, harvest of steep slopes could impact habitat that is very limited and critical to maintaining this species in an area.

The habitat fragmentation that occurs with current timber harvest practices also poses a threat to this species. This owl is an interior forest bird that is largely dependent on uneven-aged forests. By modifying and fragmenting uneven-aged forests as is done in the Southwest, habitat suitability for supporting self-sustaining and well distributed populations of this bird will be decreased. At a large scale, fragmentation may isolate larger contiguous populations into increasingly smaller and more isolated clusters of breeding pairs by reducing the overall quality of available suitable nesting, roosting, and foraging habitat. In addition to reducing total owl numbers, this isolation may create genetic problems that result from inbreeding as well as dispersal problems. Small-scale fragmentation will erode the quality of home range habitat for individual owls. Fragmentation on a cutting-unit level can degrade habitat for this species by affecting prey availability, interfering with the owl's primary hunting technique, and destroying the crucial microclimate attributes of the nest/roost sites. Simultaneously, this level of fragmentation will likely enhance habitat quality for owl predators such as great horned owls and red-tailed hawks. Increased predation may combine with decreased nesting success (due to habitat degradation and reduced prey availability) to severely impact this species.

A variety of steps must be taken to preserve and help recover this species. The key to protecting this bird is habitat management and maintenance, which means maintaining or improving the condition of a stand. A variety of uneven-aged silvicultural treatments can be used to maintain or improve appropriate habitat. Some of these treatments include single tree selection, thinning from below, free thinning, small group selection, and intermediate cuts including improvement, salvage, sanitation, thinning, etc.

The entire habitat range of this species must be studied in order to identify the habitat conditions and management direction necessary to maintain reproductive pairs of this bird. It is necessary to standardize procedures used by different governmental agencies to inventory and monitor this species' habitat and populations. Procedures must be identified to establish core areas and Management Territories based on inventory monitoring and other data. More information on the habitat use, demographics, diet, dispersal, ecological interactions, and response to silviculture treatments must be obtained in order to achieve the recovery goals. Five years of intensive data collection and studies have begun in order to determine the best ways to save this bird.

The following home range characteristics of the Mexican spotted owl come from a telemetry study conducted in northern Arizona using eight radio-tagged owls. Home range size for single owls varied from 702 to 2,386 acres, with an average size 1,601 acres. The combined home ranges occupied by pairs averaged 2,092 acres. An average of 66% of a pair's home range was used by both owls. The areas of overlap were the nest area, the primary roost, and the foraging area. Within the home range, owls appear to have core areas that are consistently used. Core areas of individuals averaged 336 acres, and core areas for pairs averaged 398 acres. These high use areas tended to correspond to steep slopes. Although seasonal movements varied between owls, most remained within their summer home ranges throughout the year.

It has been observed that this species mainly hunts by moving from tree to tree, spending from a few seconds to several hours watching and listening for prey. The perches are approximately 20 feet above the ground. Because owls launch their attack at relatively short distances from their prey, a multistoried forest with many potential perches is advantageous to owls seeking food.

This species has plumage that is similar to boreal-zone owls, apparently as an adaptation for periods of winter temperatures. They are inefficient at dissipating body heat. To compensate for this inefficiency, they roost and nest in areas of mature forest with a dense multilayered canopy, often on a north

slope, near water, or in a canyon that receives cold air drainage. Such sites are one to six degrees Celsius cooler than other nearby habitat.

Hawks and great horned owls prey on the Mexican spotted owl. Young owls also suffer from avian predation.

Bibliography

U.S. Fish and Wildlife Service."Endangered and Threatened Wildlife and Plants; Final Rule to List the Mexican Spotted Owl As a Threatened Species." *Federal Register.* Vol. 58, No. 49. March 16, 1993: 14248-14271.

Contacts

U.S. Fish and Wildlife Service
   Regional Office
P. O. Box 1306
Albuquerque, NM 87103
Phone: 505-766-2321
FAX: 505-766-8063

U.S. Fish and Wildlife Service
Regional Office
P. O. Box 25486
Denver, CO 80225
Phone: 303-236-7920

Adapted from data compiled by the Threatened and Endangered Species Information Institute (13950 W. 20th Ave., Golden, CO 80401) for *Beacham's International Threatened, Endangered, and Extinct Species* published on CD ROM, available from Beacham Publishing.

REPTILES
AND
FISHES

Giant Garter Snake
Thamnophis gigas

George Hansen   *Color Plate C-8*

Status	Threatened
Listed	October 20, 1993
Family	Colubridae (Water Snake)
Description	Large brownish snake with black spots, separated by a yellow dorsal stripe.
Habitat	Marshes, sloughs, ponds, small lakes, low gradient streams, drainage canals and rice fields.
Food	Small fishes, tadpoles, and frogs.
Reproduction	Brood of 10 to 46 young.
Threats	Urbanization, flooding, contaminants, agricultural and maintenance activities, and introduced predators.
Range	California

Description

The giant garter snake reaches a total length of a least 162 centimeters. Females are slightly longer and heavier than males. Viewed dorsally, the background coloration varies from brown to olivaceous with a checkered pattern of black spots, separated by a yellow dorsal stripe and two light colored lateral stripes. Individuals in the northern Sacramento Valley tend to be darker with more pronounced mid-dorsal and lateral stripes. The ventral surface is cream to olivaceous or brownish and is sometimes infused with orange, especially in northern populations.

Behavior

Upon emergence of the burrow after the dormancy period, males immediately search for a mate. The breeding season extends through March and April, and females give birth to live young from late July through early September. Brood size is variable, ranging from 10 to 46 young. At birth, young average about 20.6 centimeters snout-vent length and 305 grams. Young immediately scatter into dense cover and absorb their old sacs, after which they begin feeding on their own. Although growth rates are variable, young typically more than double in size by one year. Sexual maturity occurs about three years in males and five years in females.

The giant garter snake feeds on small fishes, tadpoles, and frogs.

This species is active in the early-spring through mid-fall; in the winter the giant garter snake experiences dormancy.

Habitat

Endemic to valley floor wetlands in the Sacramento and San Joaquin Valleys of California, the giant garter snake inhabits marshes, sloughs, ponds, small lakes, low gradient streams, and other waterways and agricultural wetlands, such as irrigation and drainage canals and rice fields.

Habitat requirements consist of:

1) Adequate water during the snake's active season.
2) Emergent, herbaceous wetland vegetation, such as cattails and bulrushes, for escape cover and foraging habitat during the active season.
3) Grassy banks and openings in water side vegetation for basking.
4) Higher elevation uplands for cover and refuge from flood waters during the snake's dormant season in the winter.

Throughout its winter dormancy period, the giant garter snake inhabits small mammal burrows and other crevices above flood elevations. This species is known to select burrows with sunny aspects along south and west facing slopes.

Historic Range

Historically, this species extended from Sacramento and Contra Costa Counties southward to Buena Vista Lake, near Bakersfield in Kern County. Prior to 1970, the giant garter snake was known from 17 locations. Five of the localities were around Los Banos, Merced County. This snake has been extirpated from Buena Vista Lake and Kern Lake in Kern County, and from Tulare Lake and other riparian areas in Kings and Tulare Counties.

In 1970, the range of the giant garter snake extended from Fresno County northward to Butte County. There have been no sightings of the species from Fresno County northward to San Joaquin County after 1980.

Current Distribution

Giant garter snake populations currently range from rice production zones in Sacramento, Sutter, Butte, Colusa, and Glenn Counties; along the western border of the Yolo Bypass in Yolo County; and along the eastern fringes of the Sacramento-San Joaquin River delta from the Laguna Creek-Elk Grove region of central Sacramento County southward to the Stockton area of San Joaquin County. Thirteen populations have been identified using locality records collected since the mid-1970s.

Conservation and Recovery

The giant garter snake is currently threatened by habitat loss and effects from urbanization, flooding, contaminants, agricultural and maintenance activities, and introduced predators.

A number of land use practices and other human activities currently threaten the survival of the giant garter snake throughout its remaining range. Although some populations have persisted at low population levels in artificial wetlands associated with agricultural and flood control activities, many of these altered wetlands are now threatened with urban development. Examples of these activities include: a new city proposed in San Joaquin County which would threaten known or potential habitat for the Badger and Willow Creek population; the Sacramento Metropolitan Area Investigation, a 400-year flood protection project proposed by the Corps of Engineers and local governments for over 3,240 hectares of agricultural lands and open space threaten an estimated 45 kilometers of small water way habitat potentially inhabited by portions of the Yolo Basin/Willow Slough population of the giant garter snake; in the Laguna Creek-Elk Grove region of Sacramento County, 11 proposed residential developments and associated stream channelization projects would threaten portions of the Sacramento Basin population.

By the 1940s and 1950s, reclamation of wetlands for agriculture and other purposes completely extirpated the species from the southern one-third of its range.

Certain agricultural practices can destroy habitat that supports the giant garter snake. Activities such as intensive vegetation control activities and livestock grazing threatens this species by fragmenting and isolating available habitat. Livestock grazing along the edges of water sources degrades habitat quality by reducing vegetative cover. Overall, grazing has contributed to the elimination and reduction of the quality of available habitat at four known locations.

Collection and harassment associated with recreational activities apparently cause a substantial impact in certain areas. Recreational activity disturbs basking snakes; this in turn disturbs the snake's thermoregulatory processes.

The California Fish and Game Department stopped mark and recapture studies after noting that the snakes were slow to recuperate from injuries sustained during the process.

Unidentified parasitic worms have been found in the American Basin population of the giant garter snake. Snakes infected with the worms seemed to display reduced appetites and growth rates. All infected snakes eventually died after lingering malaise; some reached 12 to 14 months of age before perishing. The worms taken after death of the snake were 5 to 8 centimeters, about 1/4

millimeter thick, and colored with alternating narrow rings of red and beige; the worms emerged from noticeable lumps at any location along the ventral or dorsal skin surfaces.

Predation levels on the giant garter snake have increased due to a number of factors. A number of native mammals and birds are likely known predators of the giant garter snake including raccoons, skunks, opossums, foxes, hawks, egrets, and herons. The abundance and diversity of predators and diminishing escape cover in remaining habitat suggest that predation pressure on this species is probably severe. The high fecundity and extremely wary behavior of the giant garter snake provide additional evidence that the species has developed physiological and behavioral adaptations to help withstand predatory pressure. In 1986 Hansen observed that nearly all the snakes captured and examined possessed scars or recent injuries presumably acquired during attacks by predators.

Domestic cats prey upon the giant garter snake. In addition, introduced aquatic species such as largemouth bass and catfish are opportunistic predators of many species, including the giant garter snake. Introduction of the bullfrog, *Rana catesbeianna,* further escalates the threat of predation to this snake.

The giant garter snake inhabits water management facilities adjacent to rice fields. The seasonal flooding and draining of rice ponds may provide an adequate forage base and may prevent establishment of populations of large predatory fish. Intensive control of vegetation along water delivery and drainage facilities eliminates remaining habitat and prevents reestablishment of former habitat. Such activities may kill or prove harmful to the giant garter snake.

This snake is vulnerable to changes in water management, due to its dependance on the availability of wetlands. Contaminants, such as fertilizers and pesticides, could adversely affect the giant garter snake populations by degrading water quality and reducing prey populations. Selenium contamination of agricultural drainwater appears to pose a severe threat to any population that inhabits the grasslands region of Merced County.

Conservation measures provided to species listed as endangered or threatened pursuant to the Endangered Species Act include recognition, recovery actions, requirements for Federal protection, and prohibitions against certain practices. Recognition through listing encourages conservation measures by Federal, international, and private agencies, groups, and individuals.

This species is listed as threatened under the California Endangered Species Act. This Act and the California Environmental Quality Act are the only environmental legislation at the state level which benefit this species. Some city and county governments have adopted protective measures and ordinances which may also dictate protection for the giant garter snake.

Populations inhabiting wetlands on private and public lands fall under regulatory jurisdiction of the Corps of Engineers pursuant to the Clean Water and the Rivers and Harbors Acts.

Bibliography

U.S. Fish and Wildlife Service. 1992. *Endangered and Threatened Wildlife and Plants*. 50 CFR 17.11 & 17.12. U.S. Fish and Wildlife Service, 1992. 38 pp.

Contacts

USFWS Regional Office
Eastside Federal Complex
911 N.S. 11th Avenue
Portland, OR 97232-4181
Phone: 503-231-6118

Sacramento Ecological Services Field Office
Room E-1803/1823
2800 Cottage Way
Sacramento, CA 98525
Phone: 916-978-4866
FAX: 916-978-4613

Adapted from data compiled by the Threatened and Endangered Species Information Institute (13950 W. 20th Ave., Golden, CO 80401) for *Beacham's International Threatened, Endangered, and Extinct Species* published on CD ROM, available from Beacham Publishing.

Blue Shiner

Cyprinella [=Notropis] caerulea

J. Malcolm Pierson

Status	Endangered
Listed	April 22, 1992
Family	Cyprinidae (Minnow)
Description	Medium-sized dusky blue minnow with pale yellow fins.
Habitat	Clear, cool water over sand and gravel substrate among cobble.
Food	Insects.
Reproduction	Spawns from early May to late August.
Threats	Degradation fo water quality due to sewage pollution, strip-mining activity, urbanization.
Range	Alabama, Georgia, Tennessee

Description

The blue shiner, *Cyprinella (=Notropis) caerulea*, is a medium-sized minnow attaining a length of about 4 inches. Coloration is dusky blue with pale yellow fins. The species has a distinct lateral line and diamond-shaped scales outlined with melanophores.

Behavior

Isolation and fragmentation characterize present populations of the blue shiner. This species spawns from early May to late August.

Habitat

The blue shiner occurs in the east and central farming and forest region. The aver-age annual precipitation is 1,025 to 1,275 millimeters and the average annual temperature is 9 to 17 degrees Celsius. The topography of nearly one-half of this region consists of steeply sloping, mainly forest land, used for both recreation and timber production. Udults and Udalfs are the most extensive soils. Fluvents occur along streams and are cropped intensively throughout the region, but do not occur extensively.

Small farms are characteristic of this region and primarily grow corn, soybeans, small grains, and hay.

Specifically, the blue shiner occurs in clear, cool water over sand and gravel substrate among cobble.

Historic Range

This species is historically known from

the Cahaba and Coosa River systems. It is likely that the species once occupied most of the upper Coosa and Alabama Rivers. In 1971, the minnow was last collected from the Cahaba River system.

Current Distribution

Currently, the species is found in Alabama in Weogulka and Choccolocco Creeks and the lower reaches of Little River. Also found in Tennessee, the species ranges in the Conasuaga River and the tributary, Minnewauga Creek. In Georgia, the blue shiner is found in the Conasuaga and Coosawattee Rivers, including various tributaries. The species no longer exists in Big Wills Creek, a tributary of the upper Coosa River.

Conservation and Recovery

The reason for the decline of the blue shiner is likely a result of water quality degradation due to urbanization, sewage pollution, and strip-mining activity in the upper Cahaba River basin.

Increases in blue-green algae and losses of vascular plants are indicators of the degradation of the water quality in the Cahaba River. Low oxygen levels coupled with high levels of total inorganic nitrogen and total phosphorous have also been documented on the river. These modifications in habitat have had adverse effects on the species.

Other factors that have reduced the species' range are reservoirs for flood control, hydropower, and impoundment. Such human alterations of the environment have caused the isolation of the blue shiner populations. Fragmented populations may be more vulnerable to environmental changes. Furthermore, genetic diversity might be lowered as fewer mating pairs form.

A formal recovery plan has not yet been designated for the blue shiner but is pending. Because the species is listed under the Endangered Species Act, recovery actions, requirements for Federal protection, recognition of status, and prohibition against certain practices are provided as conservation measures for the species. The Endangered Species Act allocates responsibility to Federal agencies for evaluating actions with respect to the species. This includes, but is not limited to, the monitoring of activities that may impact the species, enforcing regulations, and protecting critical habitat once it has been designated.

The Corps of Engineers, the Environmental Protection Agency, the Federal Highway Administration, and the Federal Regulatory Commission will consider the species when planning their respective activities.

The species is not nearly as pervasive as it once was. Rather, the species occurs in the Coosawattee River, the Turniptown Creek, and at seven sites on the Conasuaga River, including three of its tributaries. Several of these populations do not come in contact with other populations, and it is speculated that distance, topography, and sites with poor water quality acting as barriers may separate one population from another.

Such isolation makes the species more vulnerable to environmental changes and may lower genetic diversity.

Bibliography

U.S. Fish and Wildlife Service. "Endangered and Threatened Wildlife and Plants; Threatened Status for Two Fish, the Goldline Darter (*Percina aurolineata*) and the Blue Shiner (*Cyprinella (=Notropis)caerulea*)." *Federal Register.* Vol. 57, No. 78, April 22, 1992: 14786-14789.

Contacts

U.S. Fish and Wildlife Service
Regional Office
Suite 200, 1875 Century Blvd.
Atlanta, GA 30345
Phone: 404-679-4000

Adapted from data compiled by the Threatened
and Endangered Species Information Institute
(13950 W. 20th Ave., Golden, CO 80401) for
*Beacham's International Threatened, Endangered, and
Extinct Species* published on CD ROM, available
from Beacham Publishing.

Bluemask Darter
Etheostoma (doration) sp.

Steven R. Layman   *Color Plate C-6*

Status	Endangered
Listed	December 27, 1993
Family	Cyprinidae (Minnow)
Description	Small bright to dullish blue darter.
Habitat	Slow to moderate waters flowing over sand and fine gravel substrates.
Threats	Siltation and pollutants from coal mining, gravel mining, poor land use practices and waste discharges.
Range	Tennessee

Description

The bluemask darter is a small darter, reaching a length of only about 1.75 inches. Spawning males are covered with bright blue. Females and nonbreeding males are bluish in color but not nearly as brightly colored.

Behavior

The bluemask darter occupies areas with slow to moderate flow over sand and fine gravel substrates. This type of habitat is seemingly limited within the Caney Fork River system of central Tennessee.

Habitat

The bluemask darter is thought to be endemic to the Caney Fork River system, Cumberland River basin, in central Tennessee.

Historic Range

Historically this species was known from five rivers in the Caney Fork River system.

Current Distribution

Presently this darter is known from only four rivers in Van Buren, Warren, Grundy and White Counties.

Conservation and Recovery

The bluemask darter's distribution has been reduced by such factors as impoundments, water withdrawal, and the general deterioration of water quality resulting from siltation and pollutants contributed by coal mining, gravel mining, poor land use practices and waste discharges.

Bibliography

U.S. Fish and Wildlife Service. "Endangered and Threatened Wildlife and Plants; Determination of Endangered Status for the Relict Darter and Bluemask (=Jewel) Darter." *Federal Register* Vol. 58, No. 246, December 27, 1993: 68480-68486.

Contacts

Ecological Services Field Office
446 Neal Street
Cookeville, TN 38501
Phone: 615-528-6481
FAX: 615-528-7075

Adapted from data compiled by the Threatened and Endangered Species Information Institute (13950 W. 20th Ave.; Golden, CO 80401) for *Beacham's International Threatened, Endangered, and Extinct Species* published on CD ROM, available from Beacham Publishing.

Relict Darter

Etheostoma chienense

Ronald R. Cicerello   *Color Plate C-7*

Status	Endangered
Listed	December 27, 1993
Family	Cyprinidae (Minnow)
Description	Small darter with light colored backs and sides, with brown mottling and six to eight dark brown saddles.
Habitat	Headwater areas in slow-flowing pools, usually associated with gravel sand and leaf litter substrates.
Threats	Channelization and deterioration of water quality.
Range	Kentucky

Description

The relict darter is a small fish, measuring only 2.5 inches standard length. Females and nonbreeding males have light colored backs and sides, with brown mottling and six to eight dark brown saddles. This species has white unmarked undersides. Spawning males display gray to dark brown both laterally and dorsally; on the undersides, light tan can be observed.

Behavior

The food habits of this species are unknown. This fish only inhabits limited areas and is known to spawn in only one location.

Habitat

The relict darter is endemic to the Bayou du Chien system. Adults are concentrated in headwater areas in slow-flowing pools, usually associated with gravel sand and leaf litter substrates near fallen tree branches, undercut bands, or overhanging stream-bank vegetation.

Historic Range and Current Distribution

This species has only been recorded from nine locations in Graves and Hickman Counties, Kentucky.

Conservation and Recovery

This species' distribution has been reduced due to channelization and deterioration of water quality (a direct result of siltation and pollutants contributed by poor land use parctices and by waste discharge).

During a 1991 status survey it was recognized that much of the Bayou du Cheien system of which this darter is endemic, was channelized and sinuosity had been reduced or was eliminated, undercut banks were lost, stream-bank vegetation and instream cover were removed and smaller streams had only intermittant flow. Additionally the area has been utilized for agricultural purposes, and the watershed has been deforested.

Conservation measures provided to species listed as endangered or threatened pursuant to the Act include recognition, recovery actions, requirements for Federal protection, and prohibitions against certain practices. Recognition through listing encourages conservation measures by Federal, international, and private agencies, groups, and individuals.

In the State of Kentucky, collection of fish and wildlife for scientific purposes is prohibited without a State collecting permit.

Bibliography

U.S. Fish and Wildlife Service. "Endangered and Threatened Wildlife and Plants; Determination of Endangered Status for the Relict Darter and Bluemask (Jewel) Darter." *Federal Register* Vol. 58, No. 246. December 27, 1993: 68480-68586.

Contacts

U.S. Fish and Wildlife Service
    Regional Office
Suite 200, 1875 Century Blvd.
Atlanta, GA 30345
Phone: 404-679-4000

Adapted from data compiled by the Threatened and Endangered Species Information Institute (13950 W. 20th Ave., Golden, CO 80401) for *Beacham's International Threatened, Endangered, and Extinct Species* published on CD ROM, available from Beacham Publishing.

Duskytail Darter
Etheostoma (=Catonotus) sp.

Richard Biggins

Status	Endangered
Listed	April 27, 1993
Family	Percidae (Perch)
Description	Darter 2 inches in length and straw to olive colored.
Habitat	Gently flowing shallow pools and eddy areas of large creeks and moderately large rivers .
Food	Insects and vegetation.
Threats	Siltation and other pollution from poor land use practices and coal mining.
Range	Tennessee, Virginia

Description

The duskytail darter is 2 inches long and is straw to olivaceous in color. Species of the same genus have a naked dorsal region from the middle of the first dorsal fin forward. The body depth is less than 7 times the body length. The body is slender.

Behavior

The specific food habits of this species are not adequately understood; members of *Percidae* generally feed on insects and vegetation.

Habitat

The duskytail darter inhabits gently flowing shallow pools and eddy areas of large creeks and moderately large rivers in the Tennessee and Cumberland River systems.

This species' distribution overlaps the Oak-Hickory Ecosystem and Nashville Basin. The elevation is about 200 meters. Most of the outer part of the Basin is deeply dissected and consists of steep slopes between narrow rolling ridgetops and narrow valleys. The inner part of the Basin is predominantly undulating and rolling. The average annual precipitation is about 35 to 45 inches. The soils of this ecosystem are varied, have a thermic temperature regime, an udic moisture regime and a clay subsoil.

Historic Range

Historically, this species has been collected from seven stream reaches; the duskytail darter is believed extirpated from Abrams Creek, Blount County, Tennessee and South Fork Holston River, Sullivan County, Tennessee.

Current Distribution

The duskytail darter is known from five reaches of the Tennessee and Cumberland River systems. The Little River population inhabits about nine river miles. This population is potentially threatened by water withdrawal and increasing residential and commercial development in the watershed. In the Citico Creek this species is affected by stream-side habitat destruction.

This darter inhabits about 17 river miles of Copper Creek and may comprise the largest population. This population is currently threatened by siltation, riparian erosion, and agricultural pollution.

The duskytail darter has been taken from one site on the Big South Fork of the Cumberland River. This particular population is faced with the threat of runoff as a result of coal mine activities in the upper watershed above Big South Fork National Recreational Area.

Conservation and Recovery

Generally this species of *Etheostoma* is threatened by water quality degradation as a result of siltation and other pollution from poor land use practices, coal mining and waste discharge.

The Tennessee and Cumberland Rivers are renowned as two of the most severely altered riverine systems due to many anthropogenic activities. Most of the main stem of both rivers and many tributaries are impounded. In addition, there has been a loss of the riverine habitat and impoundments usually alter downstream aquatic habitats.

Siltation and toxic runoff have been the result of coal mining activities which unavoidably have adversely affected many reaches. Runoff from urban areas has also degraded water and substrate quality. The aquatic faunal diversity has declined due to this habitat destruction.

Due to the limited distribution of this species, a stochastic event such as an accidental toxic chemical spill could cause extirpation. As the populations are separated by impoundments, natural recolonization of an extirpated population would be virtually impossible.

The duskytail darter is not generally protected from threats other than take without a State permit, and future activities which could impact this species are the issuance of permits for hydroelectric facility construction and operation, coal mining, reservoir construction, stream alterations, wastewater facility development, pesticide registration and road and bridge construction.

Bibliography

U.S. Fish and Wildlife Service. "Endangered and Threatened Wildlife and Plants; Determination of Endangered Status for the Duskytail Darter, Palezone Shiner and Pygmy Madtom." *Federal Register* Vol. 58, No. 79, April 27, 1993: 25758-25763.

Contacts

USFWS Regional Office
Suite 200, 1875 Century Blvd.
Atlanta, GA 30345
Phone: 404-679-4000

Adapted from data compiled by the Threatened and Endangered Species Information Institute (13950 W. 20th Ave., Golden, CO 80401) for *Beacham's International Threatened, Endangered, and Extinct Species* published on CD ROM, available from Beacham Publishing.

Tidewater Goby

Eucyclobius newberryi

B. "Moose" Peterson

Color Plate C-7

Status	Endangered
Listed	February 4, 1994
Family	Gobiidae (Goby)
Description	Small fish with large pectoral fins and a ventral sucker-like disk formed by the complete fusion of the pelvic fins.
Habitat	California lagoons with low salinity.
Food	Carnivorous small aquatic invertebrates.
Reproduction	Nesting activities commence in late April through early May.
Threats	Habitat alteration.
Range	California

Description

The tidewater goby is a small fish, rarely exceeding 2 inches in length. It has large pectoral fins and a ventral sucker-like disk formed by the complete fusion of the pelvic fins.

Behavior

Peak nesting activities commence in late April through early May, when male gobies dig a vertical nesting burrow 4 to 8 inches deep in clean, coarse sand. Suitable water temperatures for nesting are 75.6° to 79.6°F with salinities of five to 10 parts per thousand. Male gobies remain in the burrows to guard the eggs, which are hung from the ceiling and walls of the burrow until hatch-

ing. Larval gobies are found midwater around vegetation until they become benthic.

Habitat

The tidewater goby is almost unique among fishes along the Pacific coast of the United States in its restriction to waters with low salinities. All populations are generally found at the upper end of lagoons in salinities less than 10 parts per thousand, although gobies have been collected and reared in slightly higher salinities.

The tidewater goby occurs in loose aggregations of a few to several hundred individuals on the substrate in shallow water less than three feet deep, although they have been observed in depths up to 7.6 feet.

Historic Range

Historically, the tidewater goby occurred in at least 87 of California's coastal lagoons. Since 1900 it has disappeared from approximately 50 percent of formerly occupied lagoons.

Current Distribution

The tidewater goby is discontinuously distributed throughout California, ranging from Tillas Slough (mouth of the Smith River) in Del Norte County south to Agua Hedionda Lagoon in San Diego County. Areas of precipitous coastlines that preclude the formation of lagoons at stream mouths have created three gaps in the distribution of the goby. Gobies are apparently absent from the Humboldt Bay and Ten Mile River; Point Arena and Salmon Creek; and Monterey Bay and Arroyo del Oso.

Conservation and Recovery

The major factor adversely affecting the tidewater goby is coastal development projects that have caused a loss of coastal saltmarsh habitat. Coastal marsh habitats have been drained and reclaimed for residential and industrial developments. Waterways have been dredged for navigation and harbors, resulting in permanent and direct loss of wetland habitats, as well as indirect losses due to changes in salinity. Coastal road construction projects have severed the connection between marshes and the ocean, resulting in unnatural temperature and salinity profiles that the tidewater goby cannot tolerate.

Furthermore, upstream water diversions adversely affect the tidewater goby by altering downstream flows, thereby diminishing the extent of marsh habitats that occurred historically at the mouths of most rivers and creeks in California. Alterations of flows upstream of coastal lagoons have already changed the distribution of downstream salinity regimes. Since the tidewater goby has relatively narrow salinity tolerances, changes in salinity distribution due to upstream water diversions may adversely affect both the size and distribution of goby populations.

No critical habitat or recovery plan have been designated. The Santa Ynez estuary is owned by the U.S. Air Force, which is subject to the conservation mandate and prohibitions against jeopardy.

Roughly ten percent of the coastal lagoons presently containing tidewater goby are under Federal ownership. Over 40 percent are entirely or partly owned and managed by the State of California. The remainder are privately owned.

Bibliography

U.S. Fish and Wildlife Service. "Endangered and Threatened Wildlife and Plants; Determination of Endangered Status for the Tidewater Goby." *Federal Register* Vol. 59, No. 24, February 4, 1994: 5494-5498.

Contacts

U.S. Fish and Wildlife Service
Ventura Field Office
2140 Eastman Avenue, Suite 100
Ventura, CA 93003
805-644-1766

Adapted from data compiled by Beacham Publishing for *Beacham's International Threatened, Endangered, and Extinct Species* published on CD ROM.

Delta Smelt
Hypomesus transpacificus

B. "Moose" Peterson

Status	Endangered
Listed	March 5, 1993
Family	Osmeridae (Smelt)
Description	Slender-bodied translucent fish with steely-blue sheen.
Habitat	Fresh and brackish shallow water with low salinity.
Food	Copepods, amphipods and opossum shrimp.
Reproduction	1200 to 2600 eggs between February and June.
Threats	Drought, chemicals.
Range	California

Description

The delta smelt is a slender-bodied fish typically 2.36 to 2.76 inches long. Some individuals may reach a standard length of 4.73 inches. Live specimens are nearly translucent and have a steely-blue sheen to their sides. Occasionally there may be one chromatophore between the mandibles, but usually none are present. Its mouth is small, with a maxilla that does not extend past the mid-point of the eye. The eyes are relatively large; the orbit width is contained about 3.5 to 4 times in the head length. Small, pointed teeth are present in the upper and lower jaws. The first gill arch has 27 to 33 gill rakers and there are seven branchiostegal rays. There are 9 to 10 dorsal fin rays, 8 pelvic fin rays, 10 to 12 pectoral fin rays, and 15 to 17 anal fin rays. The lateral line is incomplete and has 53 to 60 scales along it.

There are 4 to five pyloric caeca.

Behavior

Analysis of length-frequency data has led scientists to determine that the delta smelt has an annual life span. Juveniles grow from 1.58 to 1.97 inches by early August. They become sexually mature adults from 2.17 to 2.76 inches. The largest individual on record is 4.96 inches, but normally the species rarely grows larger than 3.15 inches. By June, individuals longer than 1.97 inches are rare throughout their range, indicating that adults die after spawning.

Delta smelts have a low fecundity, producing from 1,247 to 2,590 eggs per female, when compared to two other species of *Osmeridae* occurring in California that exhibit fecundities from 5,000 to 25,000 eggs per female. The species spawns in freshwater at temperatures from about seven to 15 degrees Celsius (C) between February and June. Most spawning occurs in the dead-end sloughs and shallow edge-waters of channels. The adhesive demersal eggs attach to hard substrates such as rocks, gravel, tree roots, and submerged branches. Based on data from a closely related species, *H. transpacificus* eggs probably hatch in 12 to 14 days. The planktonic larvae are transported downstream to the mixing zone between salt water and freshwater. The species migrates from spawning freshwater areas to mixing zones.

The primary foods for all life stages of the delta smelt are nauplius, copepodite, copepodid, and adult stages of the euryhaline copepod *Eurytemora affinis*. Pelagic larvae are zooplanktivores and feed on copepods, cladocerans, and amphipods. Adults consume *E. affinis* during all times of the year. The opossum shrimp is secondarily important as food for adults, and cladocerans are consumed seasonally.

Habitat

H. transpacificus is the only smelt endemic to California and the only true native estuarine species found in the Sacramento-San Joaquin estuary, known as the Delta. It is a euryhaline species, a species adapted to living in fresh and brackish water, that occupies estuarine areas with salinities below 2 grams per liter. It rarely occurs in estuarine waters with more than 10 to 12 ppt salinity, about one-third sea water.

Delta smelt is adapted for life in the mixing zone of the Sacramento-San Joaquin estuary. The estuary is an ecosystem where the mixing zone and salinity levels are determined by the interaction of river outflow and tidal action. Individuals appear to be most abundant in shallow, low salinity water associated with the mixing zone, except when they spawn.

The larvae require the high microzooplankton densities produced by the mixing zone environment. The best survival and growth of larvae occurs when the mixing zone occupies a large geographic area, including extensive shoal regions that provide suitable spawning substrates within the euphotic zone (depths less than 4 meters).

During periods of drought and increased water diversions, the mixing zone and associated delta smelt populations are shifted farther upstream in the Delta. The mixing zone is now primarily located in river channels during the entire year because of increased water exports and diversions. When located upstream, the mixing zone becomes confined to the deep river channels, becomes smaller in total surface area, contains very few shoal areas of suitable spawning substrates, may have swifter, more turbulent water currents, and lacks high zooplankton productivity. Reproduction of the species is very likely adversely affected now that the mixing zone is located in the main channels of the Delta.

Historic Range

The delta smelt is endemic to California and the only true native estuarine species found in the Delta. Historically, the fish occurred from Suisun Bay upstream into the Sacramento and San Joaquin Rivers. The species historically congregated in upper Suisun Bay and Motezuma Slough when the Sacramento and San Joaquin river flows were high. During very high river outflows, some individuals would be washed into San Pablo Bay.

The species is now rare in Suisun Bay, and virtually absent from Suisun Marsh where it was once seasonally common. The center of the species abundance has shifted to the Sacramento River channel in the Delta.

Current Distribution

Delta smelt populations have decreased by nearly 90 percent in the past 20 years. The species is highly vulnerable to extinction because of its short life span, present small population size, and restricted distribution. The limited gene pool may result in depressed reproductive vigor and loss of genetic variation.

Studies into the population biology of the delta smelt have shed some light into the requirements of the species. Freshwater flows seem to set an upper limit to the species' stock recruitment within a year. Although other environmental factors, both physical and biological, may further depress the population, the proportion of time when water flows are reversed in the lower San Joaquin River during the egg and larval stages probably is the major source of density-independent mortality to the species. Larger adult populations are associated with higher freshwater outflows because these flows produced higher plant and animal life.

Conservation and Recovery

The delta smelt occurs only in Suisun Bay and the Sacramento-San Joaquin estuary near San Francisco Bay in California. The species has declined nearly 90 percent over the last 20 years, and is primarily threatened by large freshwater exports from the Sacramento River and San Joaquin River diversions for agriculture and urban use. Prolonged drought, introduced nonindigenous aquatic species, reduction in abundance of key food organisms, and agricultural and industrial chemicals also threaten this species.

The decline in the species' population was concurrent with increased human changes to seasonal Delta hydrology, freshwater exports, and the accompanying changes in the temporal, spatial, and relative ratios of water diversions. Delta water diversions and exports presently total up to about nine million acre-feet per year. State and Federal projects presently export about six million acre-feet per year when there is sufficient water available, and in-Delta agricultural uses result in diversion of about three million additional acre-feet per year. The Fish & Wildlife Service is currently aware of another 21 major Central Valley Project, State Water Project, or private organizations' proposals that will result in increased water exports from the Delta. This will reduce water inflow to the Delta, changing the timing and volume of Delta inflow, or increasing heavy metal contamination into the Delta.

Since 1983, the proportion of water exported from the Delta during October through March has been higher than in earlier years. The timing of these proportionally higher exports have coincided with the species' spawning season. During periods of high export pumping and low to moderate river outflows, reaches of the San Joaquin River reverse direction and flow to the pumping plants located in the southern Delta. During this reversal flow, out-migrating larval and juvenile fish of many species become disoriented. Large mortalities occur as a result of entrainment and predation by striped bass at the various pumping plants and other water diversion sites. Net positive riverine flows and estuarine outflows of sufficient magnitude are required for *H. transpacificus* larvae to be carried downstream into the upper end of the mixing zone of the estuary rather than upstream to the pumping plants.

During periods of drought and increased water diversions, the mixing zone and associated delta smelt populations are shifted farther upstream in the Delta. When located upstream, the mixing zone becomes confined to the deep river channels, becomes smaller in total surface area, contains very few shoal areas of suitable spawning substrates, may have swifter, more turbulent water currents, and lacks high zooplankton productivity.

Harvesting of the species is not known to be a major limiting factor, though some individuals are harvested as a non-target by-catch in commercial bait fisheries for other baitfish species. Predation by striped bass, as mentioned above, has become a limiting factor coupled with the reversal of flow in riverine habitats.

Poor water quality may also be limiting factor of *H. transpacificus*. All major rivers in the species' range are exposed to large volumes of agricultural and industrial chemicals that are applied in the California Central Valley watersheds. Agricultural chemicals and their residues, and chemicals originating in urban runoff, find their way into the rivers and estuaries. In the Colusa Basin Drainage Canal, significant toxicity has been documented in striped bass embryos and larvae, medaka larvae, the major food organism of the striped bass larvae and juveniles, and the opposum shrimp (*Neomysis mercedis*). Some heavy metal contaminants have been released into the Delta from industrial and mining enterprises. These compounds could adversely affect the species' survival.

Nonindigenous aquatic species have been introduced into the Delta by untreated discharges of ship ballast water. Several introduced species adversely affect the delta smelt. An Asian clam (*Potamocorbula amurensis*), introduced as larvae at the beginning of the present drought, was first discovered in the Suisun Bay in October of 1986. By June of 1987, the Asian clam was nearly everywhere in Suisun, San Pablo, and San Francisco Bays irrespective of salinity, water depth, and sediment type at densities greater than 10,000 individuals per square meter. This clam could potentially play an impor-

tant role in affecting the phytoplankton dynamics in the estuary. It may have an affect on the fish by decreasing phytoplankton and by directly consuming the smelt's primary food. Weakened larvae due to reduced food availability or feeding efficiency causing decreased food ingestion rates makes the species more vulnerable to starvation or predation.

Water diversions throughout the species' range has been the major cause of the species decline. Future diversions must be carefully considered so as not to further jeopardize the species. Stricter regulation on chemical runoff into the Delta region needs to be established. Discharges of ship ballast water must be properly treated to inhibit further introduction of nonindigenous species into the habitat. Stocking of the area with striped bass should be discontinued due to the increase predation threat caused by this species. Reintroduction of *E. affinis*, the species' main food source, should be instigated to lessen the chance of the smelt's starvation. Captive breeding programs for the species should be implemented to increase the genetic variance and increase the species' chance for survival.

The public must be educated to the importance of this species to allow these recovery actions to be implemented. Lobbyists for dam construction and agricultural forces attempt to demean the importance of this and other species that stand in the way of their intended financial success.

Bibliography

U.S. Fish and Wildlife Service. 1993. "Endangered and Threatened Wildlife and Plants; Determination of Threatened Status for the Delta Smelt." *Federal Register* Vol. 58, March 5, 1993: 12854-12863.

Contacts

USFWS Regional Office
Eastside Federal Complex
911 N.S. 11th Avenue
Portland, OR 97232-4181
Phone: 503-231-6118

Sacramento Ecological Services Field Office
Room E-1803/1823
2800 Cottage Way
Sacramento, CA 98525
Phone: 916-978-4866
FAX: 916-978-4613

Ventura Ecological Services Field Office
Suite 100, 2140 Eastman Avenue
Ventura, CA 93003
Phone: 805-644-1766
FAX: 818-904-6288

Carlsbad Ecological Services Field Office
2730 Loker Avenue, West
Carlsbad, CA 92008
Phone: 619-431-9440
FAX: 619-431-9624

Adapted from data compiled by the Threatened
and Endangered Species Information Institute
(13950 W. 20th Ave., Golden, CO 80401) for
*Beacham's International Threatened, Endangered, and
Extinct Species* published on CD ROM, available
from Beacham Publishing.

Palezone Shiner

Notropis sp. cf. *procne*

Ron Cicerello

Status	Endangered
Listed	April 27, 1993
Family	Cyprinidae (Minnow)
Description	Small slender translucent and straw-colored minnow with a dark midlateral stripe.
Habitat	Large creeks and small rivers in the Tennessee and Cumberland River systems.
Threats	Siltation and other pollution from poor land use practices, coal mining and waste discharge.
Range	Tennessee

Description

The Palezone shiner is a small slender minnow with a translucent and straw-colored with a dark midlateral stripe. Information pertaining to specific biological functions will be more available with formal description of the species.

Behavior

The food habits of this species are not specifically known.

Habitat

This *Notropis* species inhabits large creeks and small rivers in the Tennessee and Cumberland River systems and inhabits flowing pools and runs with sand, gravel, and bedrock substrates.

This Palezone shiner's distribution overlaps the Oak-Hickory Ecosystem and Nashville Basin. The elevation is about 200 meters. Most of the outer part of the Basin is deeply dissected and consists of steep slopes between narrow rolling ridgetops and narrow valleys. The inner part of the Basin is predominantly undulating and rolling. The average annual precipitation is about 35 to 45 inches. The soils of this ecosystem are varied, have a thermic temperature regime, an udic moisture regime and a clay subsoil.

Historic Range and Current Distribution

This *Notropis* species has only been collected from four rivers, despite extensive collection efforts in the Tennessee and Cumberland River Systems. These rivers are the

Paint Rock River, Jackson County, Alabama; the Little South Fork Cumberland River, Wayne and McCreary Counties, Kentucky; Marrowbone Creek, Cumberland County, Kentucky; and Cove Creek, Clinch River drainage, Campbell County, Tennessee.

Conservation and Recovery

Generally the Palezone shiner is threatened by water quality degradation as a result of siltation and other pollution from poor land use practices, coal mining and waste discharge.

The Tennessee and Cumberland Rivers are renowned as two of the most severely altered riverine systems due to many anthropogenic activities. Most of the main stem of both rivers and many tributaries are impounded. In addition, there has been a loss of the riverine habitat and impoundments usually alter downstream aquatic habitats.

Siltation and toxic runoff have been the result of coal mining activities which unavoidably have adversely affected many reaches. Runoff from urban areas has also degraded water and substrate quality. The aquatic faunal diversity has declined due to this habitat destruction.

Due to the limited distribution of this species a stochastic event such as an accidental toxic chemical spill could cause extirpation. As the populations are separated by impoundments natural recolonization of an extirpated population would be virtually impossible.

Future activities which could impact this species are the issuance of permits for hydroelectric facility construction and operation, coal mining, reservoir construction, stream alterations, wastewater facility development, pesticide registration and road and bridge construction.

The Tennessee Valley Authority has indicated that the Point Rock River population is in the timber-sourcing area for three proposed wood-chip mills. Any large-scale timber harvesting could lead to population-level effects. Three wood-processing companies have applied to the Nashville District, U.S. Army Corps of Engineers for permits under section 10 of the Rivers and Harbors Act and section 404 of the Clean Water Act and to the Tennessee Valley Authority for shoreline leases and section 26-A permits to construct and operate wood-chip mills located between Bridgeport, Alabama and New Hope, Tennessee.

Bibliography

U.S. Fish and Wildlife Service. "Endangered and Threatened Wildlife and Plants; Determination of Endangered Status for the Duskytail Darter, Palezone Shiner and Pygmy Madtom." *Federal Register* Vol. 58, No. 79. April 27, 1993: 25758-25763.

Contacts

U.S. Fish and Wildlife Service
Regional Office
Suite 200, 1875 Century Blvd.
Atlanta, GA 30345
Phone: 404-679-4000

Ecological Services Field Office
446 Neal Street
Cookeville, TN 38501
Phone: 615-528-6481
FAX: 615-528-7075

Adapted from data compiled by the Threatened and Endangered Species Information Institute (13950 W. 20th Ave., Golden, CO 80401) for *Beacham's International Threatened, Endangered, and Extinct Species* published on CD ROM, available from Beacham Publishing.

Pygmy Madtom
Noturus stanauli

J. R. Shute

Status	Endangered
Listed	April 25, 1993
Family	Ictaluridae (Catfish)
Description	Smallest member of the catfish family; an unusually long adipose fin.
Habitat	Moderate to large rivers on shallow pea-size gravel shoals with moderate to strong current.
Threats	Siltation and other pollution from poor land use practices, coal mining and waste discharge.
Range	Tennessee

Description

The madtoms are the smallest members of the catfish family. Madtoms can be distinguished by their small size and an unusually long adipose fin and round tail fin.

The pygmy madtom is the smallest of the known madtoms, reaching a maximum length of 1.5 inches. The pigmentation of this species is very dark above the body midline and light below.

Behavior

These fish possess a dangerous venomous pectoral spine with which they will not hesitate to inflict a wound in self-defense.

Habitat

This species is found in moderate to large rivers on shallow pea-size gravel shoals with moderate to strong current.

This species' distribution overlaps the Oak-Hickory Ecosystem and Nashville Basin. The elevation is about 200 meters. Most of the outer part of the Basin is deeply dissected and consists of steep slopes between narrow rolling ridgetops and narrow valleys. The inner part of the Basin is predominantly undulating and rolling. The average annual precipitation is about 35 to 45 inches. The soils of this ecosystem are varied, have a thermic temperature regime, an udic moisture regime and a clay subsoil.

Historic Range and Current Distribution

This species has only been collected from the Duck River, Humphreys County, Tennessee, and from the Clinch River, Hancock County, Tennessee, despite the efforts of an extensive survey of the Tennessee River Valley.

Conservation and Recovery

Generally this species of the pygmy madtom is threatened by water quality degradation as a result of siltation and other pollution from poor land use practices, coal mining and waste discharge.

The Tennessee and Cumberland Rivers are renowned as two of the most severely altered riverine systems due to many anthropogenic activities. Most of the main stem of both rivers and many tributaries are impounded. In addition, there has been a loss of the riverine habitat and impoundments usually alter downstream aquatic habitats.

Siltation and toxic runoff have been the result of coal mining activities which unavoidably have adversely affected many reaches. Runoff from urban areas has also degraded water and substrate quality. The aquatic faunal diversity has declined due to this habitat destruction.

Due to the limited distribution of this species, a stochastic event such as an accidental toxic chemical spill could cause extirpation. As the populations are separated by impoundments natural recolonization of an extirpated population would be virtually impossible.

The pygmy madtom is not generally protected from threats other than take without a State permit.

Future activities which could impact this species are the issuance of permits for hydroelectric facility construction and operation, coal mining, reservoir construction, stream alterations, wastewater facility development, pesticide registration and road and bridge construction.

Conservation measures provided to species listed as endangered or threatened pursuant to the Endangered Species Act include recognition, recovery actions, requirements for Federal protection, and prohibitions against certain practices. Recognition through listing encourages conservation measures by Federal, international, and private agencies, groups, and individuals.

Bibliography

U.S. Fish and Wildlife Service. "Endangered and Threatened Wildlife and Plants; Determination of Endangered Status for the Duskytail Darter, Palezone Shiner and Pygmy Madtom." *Federal Register* Vol. 58, No. 79. April 25, 1993: 25758-25763.

Contacts

U.S. Fish and Wildlife Service
    Regional Office
Suite 200, 1875 Century Blvd.
Atlanta, GA 30345
Phone: 404-679-4000

Ecological Services Field Office
446 Neal Street
Cookeville, TN 38501
Phone: 615-528-6481
FAX: 615-528-7075

Adapted from data compiled by the Threatened and Endangered Species Information Institute (13950 W. 20th Ave., Golden, CO 80401) for *Beacham's International Threatened, Endangered, and Extinct Species* published on CD ROM, available from Beacham Publishing.

Snake River
Fall Chinook Salmon
Oncorhynchus tshawytscha

Status	Endangered
Listed	April 22, 1992
Family	Salmondiae (Trout)
Description	Unspotted, silvery salmon; in spawning season fish develop reddish orange coloration.
Habitat	Spawns on gravel near shore of alpine lake, migrates to ocean.
Food	Plankton, aquatic invertebrates, insects, smaller fish.
Reproduction	Clutch of about 2,000 eggs.
Threats	Hydroelectric dams, water diversions.
Range	Idaho, Oregon, Washington

B. "Moose" Peterson   *Color Plate C-7*

Description

Trapping studies conducted in 1954 and 1955 showed that juvenile Snake River fall Chinook salmon moving through the lower Snake River in March and April were less than 50 millimeters in length, whereas those migrating in May and June were 60 to 80 millimeters.

The mean length of female fish collected from the upper Columbia River ranged from 86 to 88.6 centimeters, compared to a range of 75.2 to 83.8 centimeters in collections from the Snake River. Juveniles from the Columbia River also averaged a bit larger in length than those from the Snake River. These size differences may reflect environmental differences between the upper Columbia and Snake Rivers and/or genetic differences

between the two populations.

Behavior

The Snake River fall Chinook salmon is distinguished from other chinook salmon species according to the time adults enter fresh water to begin the spawning migration. In the Columbia River basin, adults migrate upstream past the Bonneville Dam from August to October. This species can be divided into two physiologically distinct types: "tules" and "upriver brights." Tules, which are confined to the lower river tributaries, are sexually mature when they enter fresh water as adults, as indicated by their dark coloration. In contrast, fall-run fish destined to spawn in upriver areas are known as "brights" because they mature more slowly (having greater distance to travel upriver before spawning) and therefore retain their silvery oceanic coloration well into their freshwater migration. Bright runs are found in the upper Columbia and Snake Rivers and in the Deschutes River in Oregon.

Juvenile behavior also distinguishes the Snake River fall Chinook salmon from other chinook salmon. Other salmon migrate swiftly to sea as yearling smolts, whereas this species moves seaward slowly as subyearlings.

Adults enter the Columbia River in July and August and reach the mouth of the Snake River from the middle of August through October. Spawning occurs in the main stem and in the lower reaches of large tributaries in October and November. Based on what is known about this species, juveniles in the Snake River presumably emerge from the gravel in March and April, and downstream migration usually begins within several weeks of emergence. The young reportedly tend to linger in the lower Columbia River and may spend a considerable portion of their first year in the estuary. Adults return to the Snake River at ages two to five, with age four the most common age at spawning.

Members of the subfamily Salmoninae (trout, salmon, charr) are primarily carnivorous. They consume a wide variety of small animals; as the fishes grow to larger sizes they generally become piscivorous.

Habitat

This species has been the most common in the Snake River Basin. This is due to the unique ecological features of the area, such as characteristic freshwater habitats, and contrasting ocean distribution patterns.

There have been substantial water quality differences documented from the Columbia and Snake Rivers. The mean monthly summer water temperature in the Snake River was recorded at 6 to 8 degrees Celsius higher than at Rock Island Dam in the upper Columbia River. It has also been found that monthly means for pH and total alkalinity differ between the rivers. Monthly means for pH and alkalinity of 8.2 and 99 ppm, respectively, have been found at the mouth of the Snake River, and means of 7.8 and 64 ppm have been found in the Columbia River at Pasco, Washington. In addition, the Snake River is typically much more turbid than the Columbia River.

The preferred temperature range for chinook salmon has been described as somewhere in the range of 50-60 degrees Fahrenheit.

This species spawns and rears in mainstem areas or the lower parts of major tributaries.

Historic Range

Historically, this species was widely distributed throughout the Snake River and many of its major tributaries from its confluence with the Columbia River near Pasco, Washington, upstream 615 miles to Shoshone Falls, Idaho. The Snake River is the largest tributary of the Columbia River. The most important spawning grounds for this species in the Snake River were between Huntington, Idaho, and Auger Falls, Idaho.

Current Distribution

Today, this species has natural populations in the main-stem Snake River from the upper limit of the Lower Granite Dam reservoir to Hells Canyon Dam (approximately 165 km), and the lower reaches of the Tucannon, Grande Ronde, Imnaha, Salmon, and Clearwater Rivers. These bodies of water occur in: Washington, in the counties of

Asotin, Whitman, Garfield, Columbia, Adams, Walla Walla, Franklin, Benton, Klickitat, Clark, Cowlitz, Wahkiakum, Pacific, and Skamania; Idaho, in the counties of Nes Perce, Adams, and Idaho; and in Oregon.

There is no direct information available regarding the ocean distribution of this species.

Conservation and Recovery

This species is threatened by hydropower development, water withdrawal and diversions, water storage, irrigation diversions, siltation and pollution from sewage, harvest, competition, drought, livestock grazing, logging, road building, mining, and inadequate regulatory mechanisms.

Hydropower development has resulted in: blockage and inundation of habitat; turbine-related mortality of juvenile fish; increased delay of juvenile migration through the Snake and Columbia Rivers; increased predation on juvenile salmon in reservoirs; and increased delays in the movement of adults to their spawning grounds.

Drought is the principal natural condition that may have contributed to reduce the Snake River fall Chinook salmon production. Annual mean stream flows for the 1977 water year were generally the lowest on record for many streams since the late nineteenth century. The 1990 water year became the fourth consecutive year of drought conditions in the Snake River Basin. Drought conditions also prevailed for the 1991 water year.

This species was historically capable of sustaining high harvest rates, but following the degradation of the Snake and Columbia River ecosystems, harvest rates may have contributed to the further decline of the population. Today, current harvest rates of 69 percent are probably higher than the population can sustain.

There are a number of recovery measures that can be undertaken in order to increase and stabilize the population. These measures include: alternative harvest management; modifications to the juvenile fish transportation program; shifting flood control responsibilities to provide water for downstream migrants; Snake River reservoir drawdown; irrigation screening; tagging of hatchery fish; and various research activities to conserve the species.

The Lyons Ferry Hatchery initiated the artificial propagation of the Snake River fall Chinook salmon following the substantial decline of the species, in order to offset impacts resulting from the construction of hydroelectric facilities on the Lower Snake River (Lower Granite, Little Goose, Lower Monumental and Ice Harbor Dams). This facility is intended to preserve the integrity of this species.

Bibliography

U.S. Fish and Wildlife Service. "Endangered and Threatened Species; Threatened Status for Snake River Spring/Summer Chinook Salmon; Threatened Status for Snake River Fall Chinook Salmon." *Federal Register*. Vol. 57, April 22, 1992.

Contacts

Boise Ecological Services Field Office
4696 Overland Road, Room 576
Boise, ID 83705
Phone: 208-334-1931
FAX: 208-334-9493

Adapted from data compiled by the Threatened and Endangered Species Information Institute (13950 W. 20th Ave., Golden, CO 80401) for *Beacham's International Threatened, Endangered, and Extinct Species* published on CD ROM, available from Beacham Publishing.

Spring/Summer Run Chinook Salmon

Oncorhynchus tshawytscha

Status	Threatened
Listed	April 22, 1992
Family	Salmonidae (Trout)
Description	Streamlined body, pointed snout, triangular body fins, and a slightly forked tail fin.
Habitat	Fresh water lakes, then migrates to the Pacific Ocean.
Food	Plankton, invertebrates, insects, and smaller fish.
Reproduction	Sexually mature when they return to fresh water as adults.
Threats	Hydropower development, irrigation diversions, siltation and pollution.
Range	Idaho, Oregon, Washington

USFWS

Description

The Snake River spring/summer run chinook salmon is distinguished from other chinook salmon species according to the time adults enter fresh water to begin the spawning migration. This "run-time" may also constitute different life histories as well as physical characteristics.

The spring/summer run chinook are known as tules and are confined to the lower river tributaries. They are sexually mature when they enter fresh water as adults and are dark colored. Chinooks have a streamlined body, pointed snout, triangular body fins, and a slightly forked tail fin. In the ocean, this species is observed to be steel blue and gray over its entire body, with green dorsally and laterally. Silver blue to white color can be seen on the lower sides and belly. During the spawning season, the body color changes to a dark green across the head, back and sides. The snout of the male becomes hooked and the jaw teeth are exposed. All of the reproductive adults die after spawning.

The spring/summer race migrates swiftly to sea as yearling smolts. In its oceanic habitat, this species is colored silver over its entire length.

Behavior

During migration, smolts require clear

passages through freshwater rivers to the Pacific Ocean and a water flow strong enough to take them to the Pacific before the physiological changes producing the ability to survive in salt water have been completely developed.

During the first one or two years of their lives, the Snake River population feeds on freshwater plankton found in inland lakes. After migrating to the Pacific Ocean, these salmon feed on plankton, aquatic invertebrates, insects, and smaller fish. When migrating back inland to spawn, adults do not feed but live off their own body flesh. The species is diurnal.

Habitat

The Snake River spring/summer salmon lives in both salt and fresh water during different stages of its life history (anadromous). During the first one or two years of their lives, this species lives in fresh water lakes which provide loose gravel for nest construction and plankton for the feeding needs of fry. Inland the topography is one of rolling plateaus and gently sloping basins at an elevation of 600 to 1,700 meters. This area is part of the Snake River Plains/Sagebrush ecosystem. This broad ecosystem occupies plains and plateaus derived from lava flows, ancient lake beds and broad basins of alluvium. Forage production of the land is low, and annual grasses have invaded much of the rangeland. The plains bordering the Snake River and its tributaries are irrigated. The sloping lava plains of this area have a thin to moderately thick cover of loess. In places the river is quite deep giving way to steep-walled canyons. The average annual precipitation for this area is 175 to 325 millimeters. There is little or no precipitation in the summer, attributing to seasonal droughts. The dominant soils associated are Orthids, Argids, and Orthents. They have a mesic temperature regime. Moderately coarse textured Torriorthents, Camborthids, Calciorthids, and Calcixerolls are also extensive in this area. This area supports shrubgrass vegetation. Big sagebrush, winterfat, shadscale, Indian rice grass, needle and thread, Thurber needle grass, and Sandberg blue grass grow on the lower Snake River Plains.

Historic Range and Current Distribution

Spring/summer chinook salmon are known from the mainstream Snake River, Tucannon River, Grande Ronde River, Imnaha River and Salmon River.

Snake River spring/summer chinook salmon spawning and rearing is now sparsely distributed throughout the Grande Ronde, Imnaha, Salmon and Tucannon subbasins, and Asotin, Granite, and Sheep Creeks.

In December of 1992 critical habitat was designated for the spring/summer chinook salmon. This habitat is the Grande Ronde, Imnaha, Salmon, and Tucannon subbasins; Asotin, Granite, and Sheep Creeks; the Snake River from its confluence with Sheep Creek to its confluence with the Columbia River; the Columbia River from its confluence with the Snake River to the Pacific Ocean.

Conservation and Recovery

This species was once greatly valued as a food source, however, low escapements and protective efforts have curtailed harvest levels.

Hydropower development has resulted in a number of factors affecting the spring/summer chinook salmon. These effects include: blockage and inundation of habitat; turbine-related mortality for juveniles; increased delay of juvenile migration; increased predation on juvenile salmon; and increased delay of adults to spawning areas. This species is further affected by water withdrawal and storage, irrigation diversions, siltation and pollution from sewage, farming, grazing, logging and mining.

Spring/summer chinooks are subject to harvest in the Columbia River net fisheries and in some recreational fisheries. Although these fisheries are directed toward other species the chinooks may be incidentally taken or killed.

Hatchery programs have also contributed to the demise of the spring/summer chinook salmon. These hatcheries are taking fish for broodstocks; behavioral and genetic interactions are taking place. These hatchery fish also compete with spring/summer chinooks as well as prey on them and spread disease.

Due to the extreme impact of hydroelectric development, artificial propagation programs were initiated. The objective of this effort was to offset juvenile salmon and adult passage mortality resulting from hydroelectric development. These efforts have thus far been fruitless and spring/summer chinook numbers continue to fall.

Critical habitat has been proposed for the spring/summer chinook. Designation is anticipated and would contribute to species conservation by identifying important areas and describing the features within these areas. This in turn alerts public and private entities to the area's ecological importance.

Bibliography

Groves, C. and R. Moseley. "Rare, Threatened and Endangered Plants and Animals of Idaho." Idaho Department of Fish and Game: Conservation Data Center, Nongame and Endangered Wildlife Program, 1992. 38 pp.

National Marine Fisheries Service. "Endangered and Threatened Species; Threatened Status for Snake River Spring/ Summer Chinook Salmon, Threatened Status for Snake River Fall Chinook Salmon." *Federal Register*. Vol. 57, No. 78. April 22, 1992: 14653-14663.

Waples, R., R. P. Jones, Jr., B. R. Beckman, and G. A. Swan. NOAA Technical Memorandum NMFS F/NWC-201. Status Review for Snake River Fall Chinook Salmon. National Marine Fisheries Service, 1991. 73 pp.

Contacts

Idaho Department of Fish and Game
600 S. Walnut Street, Box 25
Boise, ID 83707
Phone: 208-334-3402
Fax: 208-334-2114

U.S. Fish and Wildlife Service
Regional Office
Eastside Federal Complex
911 N.S. 11th Avenue
Portland, OR 97232-4181
Phone: 503-231-6118

Boise Ecological Services Field Office
4696 Overland Road, Room 576
Boise, ID 83705
Phone: 208-334-1931
FAX: 208-334-9493

Adapted from data compiled by the Threatened and Endangered Species Information Institute (13950 W. 20th Ave., Golden, CO 80401) for *Beacham's International Threatened, Endangered, and Extinct Species* published on CD ROM, available from Beacham Publishing.

Oregon Chub

Oregonichthys crameri

Dale Skeesick

Status	Endangered
Listed	October 18, 1993
Family	Cyprinidae (Minnow)
Description	Small brownish-yellow minnow.
Habitat	Low velocity water flow with depositional substrates.
Food	Copepods, cladocerans, larvae.
Reproduction	Spawng occurs April-August, producing 147 to 671 eggs.
Threats	Elimination of its backwater habitats; creation of flood control structures; chemical spills; competition.
Range	Oregon

Description

The Oregon chub is a small minnow measuring up to 35 millimeter. The scales on the lower body are brownish-yellow, while the upper scales are brown to white. The fins are almost clear and almost transparent.

Behavior

Males that measure over 35 millimeters standard length defend territories in or near aquatic vegetation. The number of eggs produced per female range from 147 to 671. Spawning occurs from the end of April through early August when water temperatures range from 16 degrees Celsius to 28 degrees Celsius.

Adults feed primarily on copepods, cladocerans, and chironomid larvae.

Habitat

The Oregon chub was once distributed through sloughs and overflow ponds. Population sites are typically low-or zero-velocity water flow conditions, depositional substrates, and abundant aquatic, or overhanging riparian, vegetation.

Historic Range and Current Distribution

The Oregon chub was formerly distributed throughout the lower elevation backwaters of the Willamette River drainage. Populations of the chub are now restricted to the Middle Fork Willamette River near Dexter and Lookout Point Reservoirs in Lone County, Oregon. Small numbers of the chub have also been observed in recent years on the lower North Santiam River, which forms the boundary between Linn and Marion Counties and in Gray Creek within the Finley National Wildlife Refuge in Benton County. In 1992 an additional population was discovered in a tributary to Lake Creek in Linn County.

Conservation and Recovery

It is believed the Oregon chub has been adversely affected by changes in and elimination of its backwater habitats. The mainstem of the Willamette River was formerly a braided channel with numerous secondary channels, meanders, oxbows, and overflow ponds that may have provided habitat for the chub. However, the construction of flood control projects and revetments have altered historical flooding patterns and eliminated much of the river's braided channel pattern. The period of construction of flood control structures directly coincides with the period of decline of this species.

This species is threatened by chemical spills, competition, and loss of habitat. Direct mortality is a potential threat from chemical spills from overturned truck or tail tankers, runoff or accidental spills of brush control and agricultural chemicals and overflow from chemical toilets in campgrounds. Competition for resources and predation may be a result of intentional or accidental introductions of nonindigenous fishes. Habitat loss has resulted from siltation of shallow habitats from logging and construction activities, unauthorized fill activities, and changes in water level or flow conditions from construction, diversions, or natural desiccation.

Conservation measures provided to species listed as endangered or threatened pursuant to the Act include recognition, recovery actions, requirements for Federal protection, and prohibitions against certain practices. Recognition through listing encourages conservation measures by Federal, international, and private agencies, groups, and individuals.

Bibliography

U.S. Fish and Wildlife Service. "Endangered and Threatened Wildlife and Plants; Determination of Endangered Status for the Oregon Chub." *Federal Register* Vol. 58, No. 199. October 18, 1993: 53800-53804.

Contacts

U.S. Fish and Wildlife Service
    Regional Office
Eastside Federal Complex
911 N.S. 11th Avenue
Portland, OR 97232-4181
Phone: 503-231-6118

Portland Ecological Services Field Office
2600 SE 98th Avenue
Portland, OR 97266
Phone: 503-231-6179
FAX: 503-231-6195

Adapted from data compiled by the Threatened and Endangered Species Information Institute (13950 W. 20th Ave., Golden, CO 80401) for *Beacham's International Threatened, Endangered, and Extinct Species* published on CD ROM, available from Beacham Publishing.

Goldline Darter

Percina aurolineata

J. Malcolm Pierson

Status	Threatened
Listed	April 22, 1992
Family	Percidae (Perch)
Description	Brownish-red darter with amber stripes and white belly.
Habitat	Gravel or sand substrate interspersed among cobble and small boulders.
Threats	Reservoir construction, water pollution.
Range	Alabama, Georgia

Description

The goldline darter is a slender fish that reaches about three inches in length. It is brownish-red with amber stripes along its pale to dusky upper back. It has a white belly with a series of square lateral and dorsal blotches that are separated by a pale or gold-colored longitudinal stripe.

Behavior

The fragmented populations the goldline darter in the upper Coosa and Cahaba Rivers appear to be reproducing. Any population that is stressed by a factor such as eutrophication, is more likely to succumb to disease and predation even if they are natural occurrences.

Habitat

The goldline darter can be found over a gravel or sand substrate that is interspersed among cobble and small boulders. It prefers a moderate to swift current, and water depths greater than two feet.

Historic Range

Historically, the goldline darter occurred in 49 miles of the Cahaba River, and seven miles of the Little Cahaba River in Alabama. It has also been collected from the upper Coosa River drainage in the Coosawattee, Ellijay and Cartecay Rivers and tributaries, and in the Alabama River.

Current Distribution

Presently, the goldline darter survives on fragmented populations in the upper Coosa River system in the Coosawattee River, Georgia, in seven miles of the Little Cahaba River, and in 27 miles of the Cahaba River system in Alabama.

Conservation and Recovery

The range of this fish has declined due to water pollution and the construction of reservoirs. Water pollution is responsible for the decline of the goldline darter in the Cahaba River system. There are ten municipal wastewater treatment plants in this basin, 35 mining areas, one coalbed methane and 67 other permitted discharges. During low flows, almost all of the water in some stretches of this river are treated sewage effluent. Nutrients in the sewage are contributing to eutrophication of the river, which removes oxygen from the water, and adversely affects the fish. Eutrophication is also responsible for the decline of vascular plants in the river, which also adversely affects this species. Increased siltation resulting from surface mining, the operation of limestone quarries and cement plants, road construction, and site preparation for gas drilling operations all contribute to the degradation of water quality in this river. In the future, methane gas extraction in the basin could also affect the water quality.

In the Alabama and upper Coosa River, impoundments for hydropower, navigation, and flood control have probably wiped out all goldline darter populations in this area. These reservoirs have also fragmented and isolated the populations of this species in the Cahaba River system from those in the upper Coosa River tributary. Isolated populations are susceptible to environmental changes. This isolation threatens genetic variability as well as inhibits reproductive success.

Conservation measures that are provided to species listed as threatened or endangered include recognition, recovery actions, requirements for Federal protection, and prohibitions against certain practices.

Although some of the wastewater treatment facilities along the Cahaba river have recently been upgraded, this has not completely stopped the problem of enrichment.

Bibliography

U.S. Fish and Wildlife Service. "Endangered and Threatened Wildlife and Plants; Threatened Status for Two Fish, the Goldline Darter (*Percina aurolineata*) and Blue Shiner (*Cyprinella caerulea*)." *Federal Register* Vol. 57, April 22, 1992: 14786-14790.

Contacts

USFWS Regional Office
Suite 200, 1875 Century Blvd.
Atlanta, GA 30345
Phone: 404-679-4000

Ecological Services Field Office
Suite 310, 6620 Southpoint Drive, South
Jacksonville, FL 32216-0912
Phone: 904-232-2580
FAX: 904-232-2404

Adapted from data compiled by the Threatened and Endangered Species Information Institute (13950 W. 20th Ave., Golden, CO 80401) for *Beacham's International Threatened, Endangered, and Extinct Species* published on CD ROM, available from Beacham Publishing.

MUSSELS

Freshwater Mussels
from the Mobile River Basin

On March 17, 1993, the U.S. Fish and Wild-life Service listed as endangered or threat-ened eleven freshwater mussels in the Mo-bile River drainage. Because all of these species are found in the Mobile River basin, their habitat is impacted by similar threats and they exhibit similar behavior patterns, which are described here rather than being repeated in each of the species accounts.

Alabama Moccasinshell
Coosa Moccasinshell
Dark Pigtoe
Fine-Lined Pocketbook
Orange-Nacre Mucket
Ovate Clubshell
Southern Pigtoe
Southern Clubshell
Southern Acornshell
Triangular Kidneyshell
Upland Combshell

Life Cycle and Reproduction

The life of mussels is complex, and repro-duction often depends upon a stable habi-tat—unaltered stream conditions, clean water, and an undisturbed stream bottom. The cycle also depends upon the abundance of suitable fish hosts to complete the mus-sel's larval development.

To reproduce, males discharge sperm, which are dispersed by stream currents. In the process of feeding, females nearby or downstream, take in sperm, which fertilizes eggs stored in the female's gills. The gills are modified as brood pouches (marsupia) where the glochidia (larvae) hatch and begin to develop. After a time, these glochidia are released into the stream. A few mussels have inner parts that resemble a tiny min-now and can be manipulated to lure host fish. When a fish gets close to the shell, the mussel expels its glochidia.

Glochidia have tiny bean- or spoon-shaped valves that attach to the gill fila-ments of host fish. Glochidia can only prog-ress to the juvenile stage while attached to the fish's gills. Those that do not fortuitously encounter a host fish do not survive when released by the female mussel. They sink to the bottom and die.

When the juvenile has developed a shell and is large enough to survive on its own, it detaches from the host fish and falls to the stream bottom, beginning a long association with a single stretch of stream. Maturing mussels bury themselves in riffles and shoals with only the shell margins and feeding siphons exposed to the water. Some mussels live as long as 50 years or more.

The family Unionidae, which includes all of the freshwater mussels in the U.S., is separated into two groups based on the length of time the glochidia remain in the female's marsupia. The eggs of the short-term (tachytictic) breeders are fertilized in spring and glochidia are released by late summer of the same year. Long-term (brady-tictic) breeders hold developing glochidia in the brood pouch over winter and release them in spring.

Feeding

Freshwater mussels feed by siphoning phytoplankton and other plant matter from the water. Undigestible particles are expelled from the shell by reverse siphoning. Silt in the water can kill mussels by clogging their feeding siphons.

There are no known interspecific differences in feeding among freshwater mussels. The glochidia are obligate parasites on the gills or fins of fish. Adult mussels are filter-feeders and consume particulate matter in the water column. Identifiable stomach contents almost invariably include desmids, diatoms, algae, protozoa, and zooplankters.

Most freshwater mussel species display seasonal variations in activity associated with water temperature and reproduction. Metabolic rate is, in part, positively correlated with temperature. Many ectothermic species have the capacity to adjust their metabolic rates in response to long-term changes in temperature. Thus, metabolic rates do not continue to rise as temperatures rise in the summer and they do not continue to fall during the winter as temperatures decline.

Some freshwater mussels also show diurnal changes in metabolic rates that indicate a tendency toward nocturnal activity patterns. Mussels may move to the surface to feed at night and move deeper into the substrate during the day—one way to avoid predators that hunt by visual contact.

These species are non-migratory.

Mobile River Basin Habitat

The Mobile River basin drains about 43,700 square miles and is the largest Gulf Coast drainage east of the Mississippi River. The basin is composed of seven major river systems: The Mobile Delta (Mobile and Tensaw Rivers); Tombigbee; Black Warrior; Alabama; Cahaba; Coosa; and Tallapoosa Rivers and their tributaries. These rivers drain a variety of physiographic provinces, including the Appalachian Plateau, Alabama Valley and Ridge, Piedmont upland, and East Gulf Coastal Plain. The basin's size, diversity of habitat, and geographical isolation have resulted in a high degree of variation and endemism in the unionid mussel fauna.

Conservation and Recovery

Habitat modification, sedimentation, and water quality degradation represent the major threats to this species. These freshwater mussels do not tolerate impoundments. More than 1,000 miles of large and small river habitat in the Mobile River drainage has been impounded for navigation, flood control, water supply, and/or hydroelectric production purposes. Impoundments adversely affect riverine mussels by: killing them during construction and dredging; suffocation by accumulating sediments; lowered food and oxygen availability by the reduction of water flow; and the local extirpation of host fish. Other forms of habitat modification such as channelization, channel clearing and de-snagging, and gravel mining result in stream bed scour and erosion, increased turbidity, reduction of groundwater levels, sedimentation, and changes in the aquatic community structure. Sedimentation may cause direct mortality by deposition and suffocation and eliminate or reduce recruitment of juvenile mussels. Suspended sediments can also interfere with feeding. Activities that historically caused sedimentation of streams and rivers in the drainages where this mussel occurs include: channel modification; agriculture; forestry; mining; and industrial and residential development.

Other types of water quality degradation from both point and non-point sources affect this species. Stream discharge from these sources may result in decreased dissolved oxygen concentration, increased acidity and conductivity, and other changes in water chemistry which may impact the mussels and/or their fish hosts. Pint sources of water quality degradation include municipal and industrial effluents, and coalbed methane produced water discharge. Non-point sources include runoff from cultivated fields, pastures, private wastewater effluents, agricultural feedlots and poultry houses, active and abandoned coal mine sites, and highway and road drainages.

About 230 river miles of the Coosa River have been impounded for hydropower by a series of six dams. Water quality degradation caused by textile and carpet mill wastes led to the loss of several known mussel communities in several streams in this river system.

Water quality degradation is a major problem in the Cahaba River system. There are ten municipal wastewater treatment plants, 35 surface mining areas, one coalbed methane operation and 67 other permitted discharges in this river system. Siltation from surface mining, road construction, and oil and gas development is also a problem.

More than 1,000 miles of large and small river habitat in the Mobile River drainage have been impounded for navigation, flood control, water supply, and/or hydroelectric production purposes. Impoundments adversely affect riverine mussels by: killing them during construction and dredging; suffocation by accumulating sediments; lowered food and oxygen availability by the reduction of water flow; and the local extirpation of host fish. Other forms of habitat modification such as channelization, channel clearing and de-snagging, and gravel mining result in stream bed scour and erosion, increased turbidity, reduction of groundwater levels, sedimentation, and changes in the aquatic community structure. Sedimentation may cause direct mortality by deposition and suffocation and eliminate or reduce recruitment of juvenile mussels. Suspended sediments can also interfere with feeding. Activities that historically caused sedimentation of streams and rivers in the drainages

where this mussel occurs include: channel modification; agriculture; forestry; mining; and industrial and residential development.

Actions needed for the recovery of these mussel include:

(1) Conduct population and habitat surveys to determine the status and range of the species.
(2) Determine specific threats to the species and minimize or eliminate these threats.
(3) Identify essential habitat areas in need of protection. Make use of land agreements, mussel sanctuaries, Scenic River status and land acquisition.
(4) It is unlikely that the species will recover unless new populations are established by introducing individuals back into the historic range. Methods to accomplish this might include introduction of adult/juvenile mussels, glochidia infected host fish, and artificially cultured individuals.
(5) Control the incidental or illegal take of mussels by commercial and non-commercial collecting.

Upland Combshell

Epioblasma metastriata

A. E. Spreitzer

Status	Endangered
Listed	March 17, 1993
Family	Unionidae (Freshwater Mussel)
Description	Small to medium mussel with a yellowish-brown or tawny shell, sometimes containing small green dots or broken green rays.
Habitat	Gravel riffles in streams.
Threats	Impoundments, gravel and mining, water pollution.
Range	Alabama, Georgia, Tennessee

Description

The upland combshell is a mussel that rarely exceeds 2.4 inches in length. The shell is rhomboidal to quadrate in shape; the species is dimorphic. Males are moderately inflated with a broadly curved posterior ridge. Females are considerably inflated, with a sharply elevated posterior ridge that swells broadly post-ventrally forming a well-developed sulcus (the groove anterior to the posterior ridge). The periostracum (epidermis) color varies from yellowish-brown to tawny, and may or may not have broken green rays, or small green spots. Hinge teeth are well-developed and heavy.

Behavior

See "Freshwater Mussels from the Mobile River Basin," page 2135.

Habitat

The upland combshell has been collected from the Mobile drainage within the past 20 years and is believed to currently exist in the drainage.

The upland combshell inhabits high quality lotic habitats with stable gravel and sandy-gravel substrates. Little else is known about the habitat requirements of this species.

The habitat of the glochidia is initially in the gills of the female then in the water column, and finally attached to a suitable host fish. Habitat associations or requirements for the juvenile stage are unknown.

Historic Range

The upland combshell has historically been found in the following river systems in

Alabama, Georgia, and Tennessee: the Black Warrior River and tributaries (Mulberry Fork and Valley Creek); Cahaba River and tributaries (Little Cahaba River, Buck Creek); and the Coosa River and tributaries (Choccolocco Creek, Etowah, Conasauga, and Chatooga Rivers).

Current Distribution

This species' population size is extremely small. The most recent record from the Coosa River drainage is a Conasauga River collection of a single specimen in 1988. The upland combshell was last recorded in the Cahaba River system in 1973 at which time the population size was said to be greatly reduced. And, finally, the last record for the Black Warrior River system was in the early 1900s. The species was not found in a 1990 survey of all three river systems.

The upland combshell is limited by an extremely low population size/low gene pool, population isolation, and possibly by competition from exotic species, primarily the Asiatic clam (*Corbicula fluminea*). Other limiting factors for this species are unknown as are specific estimates of populations.

Conservation and Recovery

See "Freshwater Mussels from the Mobile River Basin," page 2135.

Bibliography

U.S. Fish and Wildlife Service. "Endangered and Threatened Wildlife and Plants; Endangered Status for Eight Freshwater Mussels and Threatened Status for Three Freshwater Mussels in the Mobile River Drainage." *Federal Register* Vol. 58, No. 50, March 17, 1993: 14330-14340.

Contacts

USFWS Regional Office
Suite 200, 1875 Century Blvd.
Atlanta, GA 30345
Phone: 404-679-4000

Ecological Services Field Office
P. O. Drawer 1190
Daphne, AL 36526
Phone: 205-441-5181
FAX: 205-441-6222

Ecological Services Field Office
446 Neal Street
Cookeville, TN 38501
Phone: 615-528-6481
FAX: 615-528-7075

Adapted from data compiled by the Threatened and Endangered Species Information Institute (13950 W. 20th Ave., Golden, CO 80401) for *Beacham's International Threatened, Endangered, and Extinct Species* published on CD ROM, available from Beacham Publishing.

Southern Acornshell
Epioblasma othcaloogensis

A. E. Spreitzer

Status	Endangered
Listed	March 17, 1993
Family	Unionidae (Freshwater Mussel)
Description	Small mussel with a round to oval shiny yellow shell.
Habitat	Gravel riffles in streams.
Threats	Impoundments, water pollution.
Range	Alabama, Georgia, Tennessee

Description

The southern acornshell is a small mussel about 1.2 inches in length with a round to ovate shell. The species is sexually dimorphic, with a swollen posterior ridge in females. The periostracum is smooth, shiny, and yellow in color.

Behavior

See "Freshwater Mussels from the Mobile River Basin," page 2135.

Habitat

The southern acornshell inhabits high quality lotic habitats with stable gravel and sandy-gravel substrates. Little else is known about the habitat requirements of this species.

The habitat of the glochidia is initially in the gills of the female, then in the water column, and finally attached to a suitable host fish. Habitat associations or requirements for the juvenile stage are unknown.

Historic Range

The southern acornshell was historically found in the upper Coosa River system, including the Conasauga River, Cowan's Creek, and Othcalooga Creek; and the Cahaba River above the fall line. The southern acornshell was last collected in the Cahaba River drainage in 1938. Surveys in 1973 and 1991 failed to locate the species there.

Current Distribution

This species is now restricted to streams in the Coosa River drainage in Alabama and

Georgia. Recent records for the southern acornshell in the Coosa River drainage were from the Conasauga River above Dalton, Georgia. Specimens were last collected in this drainage from 1966 to 1968. Surveys in 1990 and 1991 failed to locate the species there.

Conservation and Recovery

See "Freshwater Mussels from the Mobile River Basin," page 2135.

Bibliography

U.S. Fish and Wildlife Service. "Endangered and Threatened Wildlife and Plants; Endangered Status for Eight Freshwater Mussels and Threatened Status for Three Freshwater Mussels in the Mobile River Drainage." *Federal Register* Vol. 58, No. 50, March 17, 1993: 14330-14340.

Contacts

USFWS Regional Office
Suite 200, 1875 Century Blvd.
Atlanta, GA 30345
Phone: 404-679-4000

Ecological Services Field Office
P. O. Drawer 1190
Daphne, AL 36526
Phone: 205-441-5181
FAX: 205-441-6222

Ecological Services Field Office
446 Neal Street
Cookeville, TN 38501
Phone: 615-528-6481
FAX: 615-528-7075

Adapted from data compiled by the Threatened and Endangered Species Information Institute (13950 W. 20th Ave., Golden, CO 80401) for *Beacham's International Threatened, Endangered, and Extinct Species* published on CD ROM, available from Beacham Publishing.

Northern Riffleshell Mussel

Epioblasma torulosa rangiana

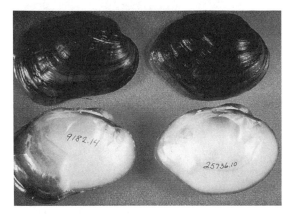

Tom Watters

Status	Endangered
Listed	January 22, 1993
Family	Unionidae (Freshwater Mussel)
Description	Small to medium-sized mussel with a brownish-yellow outer shell and white inner shell.
Habitat	Large and small streams with firmly packed sand and fine to coarse gravel.
Threats	Loss of habitat and degrated water quality.
Range	Kentucky, Michigan, Ohio, Pennsylvania

Description

The Northern riffleshell mussel is a small to medium size mussel, up to three inches long. The species expresses sexual dimorphism. The male is irregular ovate in outline, with a wide shallow sulcus just anterior to the posterior ridge. The female is obovate in outline, greatly expanded postventrally. This post-ventral expansion is very broadly rounded. The shell exterior is brownish yellow to yellowish green with fine green rays. The inside of the shell is normally white, rarely pink.

Behavior

The species' complicated reproductive cycle includes one or more species of fish where a larval form of the species, known as a glochidium, attaches to the gills, fins, or skin of the fish and is nourished for a short time period. This relationship is generally species-specific. Many aspects of the life history of the species are not known.

Like other freshwater mussels, this species feeds and respires by filtering macroscopic food particles and oxygen from the water column. The periodicity of this species is not currently known.

Habitat

The species occurs in a wide variety of streams, large and small, preferring runs with a bottom composed of firmly packed sand and fine to coarse gravel.

Historic Range

In the past, the species was known to occur in Illinois, Indiana, Kentucky, Michigan, Ohio, Pennsylvania, and West Virginia. It also extended north into Ontario. It was widespread in the Ohio River basin in rivers such as the Ohio, Allegheny, Scioto, Kanawha, Little Kanawha, Licking, Kentucky, Wabash, White, Vermillion, Mississinewa, Tippecanoe, Tennessee, Green, and Salt Rivers. It was also located in the Maumee River basin and tributaries of western Lake Erie such as the Huron River and the River Raison. Also, it occurred in southern Michigan and western Ontario in streams such as the St. Clair, Black, Ausable, and Sydenham Rivers.

Current Distribution

Today, it is found in the Green River in Edmonson and Hart Counties, Kentucky. In Pennsylvania, it occurs in French Creek of Crawford, Venango, and Mercer Counties; LeBoeuf Creek, Erie County, and the Allegheny River, Warren and Forest Counties. It is also found in the upper two miles of the Detroit River from Lake St. Clair to Belle Isle, Wayne County, Michigan and in Big Darby Creek, Pickaway County, Ohio.

Conservation and Recovery

This species was once widespread through the Ohio River watershed with the highest concentrations occurring in the northern portion of the basin and western Lake Erie drainage. It has undergone a greater than 95% range reduction.

Since the species is sedentary, it is extremely susceptible to environmental degradation. The range reductions are attributed to physical loss of habitat and degraded water quality related primarily to water impoundments, channelization, streamback clearing, and agriculture. Impacts associated with run-off from human waste, chemical outfalls, and coal mining have also affected

many tributaries. Increased turbidity and suspended sediments can result in increased water temperature, decreased oxygen levels, and siltation. Smothering from siltation, in turn, decreases or eliminates the species' ability to breathe, feed, and reproduce. Impacts to the fish species' composition can also affect reproduction since a fish host is an integral component of the species' reproductive cycle. These factors continue to threaten the remaining habitats and populations of this species.

The species has been extirpated from Illinois, Indiana, West Virginia, and Ontario. Most recent population losses include the Black River, Sanilac County, Michigan, as a result of channelization and draining for agriculture, which occurred in 1989. In 1991, the USFWS became aware that the Sydenham River population had been extirpated because of siltation, most likely a result of intense farming. Loss, probably due to siltation, of a population in Fish Creek of the St. Josephs River was also documented in 1991. Surveys conducted during 1991 failed to find the species in its former locations in the Elk River, West Virginia, and the Tippecanoe River, Indiana.

Predation on mussels is a natural occurrence. Predators, such as freshwater drum, river otter, and muskrats, are known to feed on the species. In a time when the species was widespread and abundant, the impact of this predation was insignificant. However, at the present time, their greatly reduced distribution and populations have made them susceptible to predators, especially muskrats. During a 1988 survey of the French Creek Pennsylvania population, at least 200 of this species had been harvested by muskrats.

The exotic, prolific zebra mussel, (*Dreissena polymarpha*), accidentally introduced to North America in the mid-1980s, poses a severe threat to all native mussel fauna through the competition for space, food, and survival of glochidia. Presently, the zebra mussel, which was conveyed to the area through ship ballast water from interior European ports, is abundant in the lower Great Lakes. During the fall of 1992, biologists determined that zebra mussel infestation posed a severe threat to native species of mussels.

The high potential of a toxic chemical spill from a ship or factory in the Detroit and St. Clair Rivers threaten this species. A number of toxic spills have occurred in the "Chemical Valley" near Sarnia, Ontario.

Conservation measures provided to species listed as endangered or threatened under the Endangered Species Act include recognition, recovery actions, requirements, for Federal protection, and prohibitions against certain practices. Recognition through listing encourages and results in conservation actions by Federal, State, and private agencies, groups, and individuals. The Endangered Species Act provides for possible land acquisition and cooperation with the States and requires that recovery actions be carried out for all listed species.

Bibliography

U.S. Fish and Wildlife Service. "Clubshell (*Pleurobema clava*) and Northern Riffleshell (*Epioblasma torulosa rangiana*) Recovery Plan." Technical/Agency Draft. Hadley, Massachusetts. 1993. 55 pp.

Contacts

U.S. Fish and Wildlife Service
    Regional Office
Suite 200, 1875 Century Blvd.
Atlanta, GA 30345
Phone: 404-679-4000

U.S. Fish and Wildlife Service
    Regional Office
Federal Building
Fort Snelling
Twin Cities, MN 55111
Phone: 612-725-3500
FAX: 612-725-3526

U.S. Fish and Wildlife Service
300 Westgate Center Drive
Hadley, MA 01035
Phone: 413-253-8659

Adapted from data compiled by the Threatened and Endangered Species Information Institute (13950 W. 20th Ave., Golden, CO 80401) for *Beacham's International Threatened, Endangered, and Extinct Species* published on CD ROM, available from Beacham Publishing.

Fine-Lined Pocketbook

Lampsilis altilis

A. E. Spreitzer

Status	Threatened
Listed	March 17, 1993
Family	Unionidae (Freshwater Mussel)
Description	Medium-size mussel with a yellow-brown to blackish shell with fine rays.
Habitat	Gravel riffles in streams
Threats	Impoundments, gravel and mining, water pollution.
Range	Alabama, Georgia

Description

The fine-lined pocketbook is a medium-sized mussel seldom over four inches in length. The shell is subovate. The ventral margin of the shell is angled posteriorly in females, resulting in a pointed posterior margin. The periostracum is yellow-brown to blackish and has fine rays on the posterior half. The nacre is white, becoming iridescent posteriorly.

Behavior

See "Freshwater Mussels from the Mobile River Basin," page 2135.

Habitat

The fine-lined pocketbook inhabits high quality lotic habitats with stable gravel and sandy-gravel substrates. This species is generally found in small river and creek habitats. Little else is known about the habitat requirements of this species.

The habitat of the glochidia is initially in the gills of the female, then in the water column, and finally attached to a suitable host fish. Habitat associations or requirements for the juvenile stage are unknown.

Historic Range

This species' historic range included the Tombigbee River (Sipsey and Buttahatchee Rivers); Black Warrior River and tributaries (Sipsey Fork, Brushy and Capsey Creeks); Cahaba River and tributaries (Little Cahaba and Buck Creeks); Alabama River and a tributary, Tatum Creek; Tallapoosa River drainage (Chewacla and Opintlocco Creeks); and the Coosa River and tributaries (Choccolocco and Talladega Creeks).

Current Distribution

The fine-lined pocketbook is currently limited to the headwaters of the Sipsey Fork of the Black Warrior River drainage; Alabama River drainage (Tatum Creek); Cahaba River drainage (Little Cahaba River); Coosa River drainage (Conasauga River); and the Tallapoosa River drainage (Chewacla and Opintlocco Creeks). The fine-lined pocketbook was last collected from the Tombigbee River drainage in the early 1900s. Specimens were collected in the Black Warrior River tributaries in 1985; no specimens were located in a 1990 survey but localized populations were found in Sipsey Fork tributaries and the North River in 1992. The fine-lined pocketbook was listed as abundant in the Cahaba River drainage in 1973; a specimen was collected in 1979 and two live specimens were collected in 1986 but a 1991 survey failed to locate this mussel. Collections from the Alabama River drainage were last recorded in 1981. Specimens from the Coosa and Tallapoosa River drainages were last taken in 1991. This species may have been eliminated from most river habitats (except the Coosa and Conasauga Rivers) throughout its range.

Conservation and Recovery

See "Freshwater Mussels from the Mobile River Basin," page 2135.

Bibliography

U.S. Fish and Wildlife Service. "Endangered and Threatened Wildlife and Plants; Endangered Status for Eight Freshwater Mussels and Threatened Status for Three Freshwater Mussels in the Mobile River Drainage." *Federal Register* Vol. 58, No. 50, March 17, 1993: 14330-14340.

Contacts

USFWS Regional Office
Suite 200, 1875 Century Blvd.
Atlanta, GA 30345
Phone: 404-679-4000

Ecological Services Field Office
P. O. Drawer 1190
Daphne, AL 36526
Phone: 205-441-5181
FAX: 205-441-6222

Ecological Services Field Office
446 Neal Street
Cookeville, TN 38501
Phone: 615-528-6481
FAX: 615-528-7075

Adapted from data compiled by the Threatened and Endangered Species Information Institute (13950 W. 20th Ave., Golden, CO 80401) for *Beacham's International Threatened, Endangered, and Extinct Species* published on CD ROM, available from Beacham Publishing.

Orange-Nacre Mucket
Lampsilis perovalis

A. E. Spreitzer

Color Plate C-6

Status	Threatened
Listed	March 17, 1993
Family	Unionidae (Freshwater Mussel)
Description	Medium-size mussel with an oval, moderately thick, inflated, yellow to dark reddish shell that may or may not have green rays.
Habitat	Gravel riffles in streams.
Threats	Impoundments, gravel and mining, water pollution.
Range	Alabama, Georgia, Mississippi, Tennessee

Description

The orange-nacre mucket is a medium-sized mussel two to 3.6 inches in length. The shell is ovate, moderately thick, and inflated. The posterior margin of the shell of mature females is obliquely truncate. The nacre is usually rose colored, pink, or occasionally white. The periostracum varies from yellow to dark reddish brown, and may or may not have green rays.

Behavior

See "Freshwater Mussels from the Mobile River Basin," page 2135.

Habitat

The orange-nacre mucket inhabits high quality lotic habitats with stable gravel and sandy-gravel substrates. Little else is known about the habitat requirements of this species.

The habitat of the glochidia is initially in the gills of the female, then in the water column, and finally attached to a suitable host fish. Habitat associations or requirements for the juvenile stage are unknown.

Historic Range

This species was historically found in the Tombigbee River drainage (Lubbub Creek, Buttahatchee, Sipsey and East Fork Tombigbee Rivers); Black Warrior River drainage (Brushy Creek, Mulberry and Sipsey Forks); Alabama River; and the Cahaba River drainage (Little Cahaba River).

Current Distribution

The orange-nacre mucket is currently limited to the Buttahatchee River and a short reach of the East Fork Tombigbee River; headwaters of the Sipsey Fork; and the Sipsey and Little Cahaba Rivers. Specimens have not been collected in the Alabama River since 1834. This mussel may have been eliminated from the Mulberry Fork of the Black Warrior River.

Conservation and Recovery

See "Freshwater Mussels from the Mobile River Basin," page 2135.

Bibliography

U.S. Fish and Wildlife Service. "Endangered and Threatened Wildlife and Plants; Endangered Status for Eight Freshwater Mussels and Threatened Status for Three Freshwater Mussels in the Mobile River Drainage." *Federal Register* Vol. 58, No. 50, March 17, 1993: 14330-14340.

Contacts

USFWS Regional Office
Suite 200, 1875 Century Blvd.
Atlanta, GA 30345
Phone: 404-679-4000

Ecological Services Field Office
P. O. Drawer 1190
Daphne, AL 36526
Phone: 205-441-5181
FAX: 205-441-6222

Ecological Services Field Office
446 Neal Street
Cookeville, TN 38501
Phone: 615-528-6481
FAX: 615-528-7075

Ecological Services Field Office
Suite A, 6578 Dogwood View Parkway
Jackson, MS 39213
Phone: 601-965-4900
FAX: 601-965-4340

Adapted from data compiled by the Threatened and Endangered Species Information Institute (13950 W. 20th Ave., Golden, CO 80401) for *Beacham's International Threatened, Endangered, and Extinct Species* published on CD ROM, available from Beacham Publishing.

Carolina Heelsplitter

Lasmigona decorata

126709

USFWS

Status	Endangered
Listed	June 30, 1993
Family	Unionidae (Freshwater Mussel)
Description	Ovate, trapezoid-shaped, unsculptured greenish-brown to dark brown shell.
Habitat	Mud, muddy sand, or muddy gravel substrates along stable, well-shaped stream banks.
Threats	Habitat degradation.
Range	North Carolina

Description

The Carolina heelsplitter has an ovate, trapezoid-shaped, unsculptured shell. The shell of the largest specimen ever collected measured 118 millimeters in length, 40 millimeters in width, and 63.5 millimeters in height. The shell's outer surface varies from greenish-brown to dark brown in color, and shells from younger specimens have faint greenish-brown or black rays. The nacre (inside surface) is often pearly-white to bluish white, grading to orange in the area of the umbo (knob at the hinge). However, in older specimens the entire nacre may be a mottled pale orange.

Behavior

Reproductive characteristics for this spe-cies are probably similar to other freshwater mussels. Males release sperm into the water column. Females then take in the sperm through their siphons during feeding and respiration. The fertilized eggs are retained in the gills until the larvae fully develop. Gravid females have been observed during mid-May. Glochidia attach themselves to the gills or fins of their fish hosts following their release from the gills. Fish host species are unknown.

Habitat

The Carolina heelsplitter has been re-corded from small to large streams and rivers, as well as ponds. The ponds referred to in historic records are believed to have been mill ponds on some of the smaller streams. The species is now known to occur in only three small streams and one small river and is usually found in mud, muddy sand, or muddy gravel substrates along stable, well-shaped stream banks. The stability of the streambanks appears to be very important to this species.

Historic Range

The historical distribution of this species included the Catawba River, Mecklenburg County, North Carolina; several streams and "ponds" in the Catawba River system around the Charlotte areas of Mecklenburg County, North Carolina; one small stream in the Pee Dee River system in Cabarrus County, North Carolina; and an area in South Carolina referred to as the "Abbeville District" (possibly the Saluda River system). An additional record in the Oconee River in Georgia is believed to be a misidentification.

Current Distribution

Between 1987 and 1990, surveys funded by the U.S. Fish and Wildlife Service were conducted. A total of 687 sites in 356 different streams, rivers, and impoundments within the historic range and potential habitat of the Carolina Heelsplitter were surveyed including the Saluda River, Catawba River, Pee Dee River, Broad River, Rocky River, and Lynches River systems. Only three populations were located: one in a Catawba River tributary in Union County, North Carolina; the second in a tributary of the Rocky River (Pee Dee River system), Union County, North Carolina; and the third in the Lynches River drainage (Pee Dee River system) in Chesterfield, Lancaster, and Kershaw Counties, South Carolina (this was the largest population).

Conservation and Recovery

Habitat loss/degradation and increases in water pollution caused by impoundments, stream channelization, dredging, sand mining, sewage effluents, and poorly implemented agricultural, forestry, and commercial/residential development practices are believed to be the primary factors leading to the decline and extirpation of this species from large sections of its historic range.

All three known populations are bordered by private lands except for small sections of road rights-of-ways and a State bridge.

The Lynches River sites receive heavy nutrient and pollutant loads from wastewater treatment plants and other point and nonpoint sources.

In some areas, vegetation has been cleared right up to the stream banks which increases the siltation of the streams, eliminates shading, and destabilizes the streambanks (a key habitat component for this species).

Actions needed to protect the Carolina Heelsplitter include:

(1) Pursuing legal protection for the species and its habitat.
(2) Conducting population and habitat surveys to determine the status and range of the species, if feasible.
(3) Testing the potential for reintroducing the species into its historic range.
(4) Determining life history and ecological requirements for *L. decorata*.

Population sizes may be too low to allow intensive research and population manipulation.

Bibliography

Thorp, J. H., and A. P. Covich. *Ecology and Classification of North American Freshwater Invertebrates*. San Diego: Academic Press, 1991. 911 pp.

U.S. Fish and Wildlife Service. "Endangered and Threatened Wildlife and Plants; *Lasmigona decorata* (Carolina Heelsplitter) Determined to be Endangered." *Federal Register*. Vol. 58, No. 124: 34926-34931.

Contacts

U.S. Fish and Wildlife Service
Regional Office
Suite 200, 1875 Century Blvd.
Atlanta, GA 30345
Phone: 404-679-4000

Ecological Services Field Office
330 Ridgefield Court
Asheville, NC 28806
Phone: 704-665-1195
FAX: 704-665-2782

Adapted from data compiled by the Threatened and Endangered Species Information Institute (13950 W. 20th Ave., Golden, CO 80401) for *Beacham's International Threatened, Endangered, and Extinct Species* published on CD ROM, available from Beacham Publishing.

Alabama Moccasinshell

Medionidus acutissimus

A. E. Spreitzer

Status	Threatened
Listed	March 17, 1993
Family	Unionidae (Freshwater Mussel)
Description	Small, delicate mussel with a narrow, elliptical yellow to brown shell.
Habitat	Gravel riffles in streams.
Threats	Impoundments, water pollution.
Range	Alabama, Georgia, Mississippi

Description

The Alabama moccasinshell is a small, delicate mussel growing to 1.2 inches in length. The shell is narrowly elliptical, thin, with a well-developed, acute, posterior ridge terminating in an acute point on the posterior ventral margin. The posterior slope is finely corrugated. The periostracum is yellow to brownish yellow, with broken green rays across the entire surface of the shell. The thin nacre is translucent along the margins and salmon-colored in the umbos (beak cavity).

Behavior

See "Freshwater Mussels from the Mobile River Basin," page 2135.

Habitat

The Alabama moccasinshell inhabits high quality lotic habitats with stable gravel and sandy-gravel substrates. Little else is known about the habitat requirements of this species.

The habitat of the glochidia is initially in the gills of the female, then in the water column, and finally attached to a suitable host fish. Habitat associations or requirements for the juvenile stage are unknown.

Historic Range

This species' historic range included the Alabama River; Tombigbee River and tributaries (Luxapalila Creek, Buttahatchee and Sipsey Rivers); Black Warrior River and tributaries (Mulberry Fork, Brushy Creek); Cahaba River; and Coosa River and tributaries (Talladega, Choccolocco Creeks, Chatooga River).

Current Distribution

The Alabama moccasinshell is currently found in Luxapalila Creek, Buttahatchee and

Sipsey Rivers in the Tombigbee River drainage; headwaters of the Sipsey Fork of the Black Warrior River drainage; and the Conasauga River. This species was last collected in the Cahaba River drainage in 1973. A 1990 survey discovered one specimen in the Conasauga River and a 1991 survey did not find the species in the Coosa River drainage.

Conservation and Recovery

See "Freshwater Mussels from the Mobile River Basin," page 2135.

Bibliography

U.S. Fish and Wildlife Service. "Endangered and Threatened Wildlife and Plants; Endangered Status for Eight Freshwater Mussels and Threatened Status for Three Freshwater Mussels in the Mobile River Drainage." *Federal Register* Vol. 58, No. 50, March 17, 1993: 14330-14340.

Contacts

USFWS Regional Office
Suite 200, 1875 Century Blvd.
Atlanta, GA 30345
Phone: 404-679-4000

Ecological Services Field Office
P. O. Drawer 1190
Daphne, AL 36526
Phone: 205-441-5181
FAX: 205-441-6222

Ecological Services Field Office
446 Neal Street
Cookeville, TN 38501
Phone: 615-528-6481
FAX: 615-528-7075

Adapted from data compiled by the Threatened and Endangered Species Information Institute (13950 W. 20th Ave., Golden, CO 80401) for *Beacham's International Threatened, Endangered, and Extinct Species* published on CD ROM, available from Beacham Publishing.

Coosa Moccasinshell

Medionidus parvulus

Status	Endangered
Listed	March 17, 1993
Family	Unionidae (Freshwater Mussel)
Description	Small to medium mussel with yellow to dark brown shell with fine green rays.
Habitat	Gravel riffles in streams.
Threats	Impoundments, gravel and mining, water pollution.
Range	Alabama, Georgia, Tennessee

Description

The Coosa moccasinshell, *Medionidus parvulus*, is a small mussel which rarely exceeds 1.6 inches in shell length. The shell is thin and fragile, elongate and elliptical to rhomboidal in shape. The posterior ridge is inflated, smoothly rounded, terminating in a broadly rounded point; the posterior slope is finely corrugated. The periostracum is yellow-brown to dark brown and has fine green rays. The nacre is blue, occasionally with salmon-colored spots.

Behavior

See "Freshwater Mussels from the Mobile River Basin," page 2121.

Habitat

Coosa moccasinshell inhabits high quality lotic habitats with stable gravel and sandy-gravel substrates. Little else is known about the habitat requirements of this species.

The habitat of the glochidia is initially in the gills of the female, then in the water column, and finally attached to a suitable host fish. Habitat associations or requirements for the juvenile stage are unknown.

Historic Range and Current Distribution

Coosa moccasinshell has been found in the following river systems: the Cahaba River; the Black Warrior River and it's tributaries (Sipsey Fork); and the Coosa River and it's tributaries (Choccolocco Creek, Chatooga, Conasauga and Little Rivers).

Recent surveys have found this species in the Sipsey Fork of the Black Warrior River system, and the Little and Conasauga Rivers of the Coosa River system. Surveys of the Cahaba River system in 1938, 1973 and 1991 failed to locate the species.

Conservation and Recovery

See "Freshwater Mussels from the Mobile River Basin," page 2121.

Bibliography

Thorp, J. H., and A. P. Covich. *Ecology and classification of North American freshwater invertebrates*. San Diego, CA: Academic Press, Inc., 1991.

U.S. Fish and Wildlife Service. "Endangered and Threatened Wildlife and Plants; Endangered Status for Eight Freshwater Mussels and Threatened Status for Three Freshwater Mussels in the Mobile River Drainage." *Federal Register* Vol. 58, No. 50, March 17, 1993: 14330-14340.

Contacts

USFWS Regional Office
Suite 200, 1875 Century Blvd.
Atlanta, GA 30345
Phone: 404-679-4000

Ecological Services Field Office
P. O. Drawer 1190
Daphne, AL 36526
Phone: 205-441-5181
FAX: 205-441-6222

Ecological Services Field Office
446 Neal Street
Cookeville, TN 38501
Phone: 615-528-6481
FAX: 615-528-7075

Adapted from data compiled by the Threatened and Endangered Species Information Institute (13950 W. 20th Ave., Golden, CO 80401) for *Beacham's International Threatened, Endangered, and Extinct Species* published on CD ROM, available from Beacham Publishing.

Clubshell Mussel

Pleurobema clava

Craig W. Stihler

Status	Endangered
Listed	January 22, 1993
Family	Unionidae (Freshwater Mussel)
Description	Small to medium sized mussel with bright yellow to brown outer shell and white inside.
Habitat	Clean swept sand and gravel in medium to small rivers and streams.
Threats	Predation by muskrats.
Range	Kentucky, Michigan, Ohio, Pennsylvania, West Virginia

Description

The clubshell mussel is small to medium in size, and up to three inches long. The outline of the shell is wedge-shaped and solid. The exterior of the shell is bright yellow to brown with bright green blotchy rays; the inside of the shell is white.

Behavior

The species possesses a complicated reproductive cycle that includes one or more species of fish. A larval form of the species, known as a glochidium, attaches to the gills, fins, or skin of the fish and is nourished for a short time period. This relationship is generally species-specific.

Habitat

The species occurs in clean swept sand and gravel in medium to small rivers and streams. It has been found buried in clean loose sand to a depth of two to four inches.

Historic Range and Current Distribution

Presently, the species occurs in portions of 12 streams in six states. It is found in the Green River in Edmonson and Hart Counties, Kentucky. In Pennsylvania, it occurs in French Creek in Crawford, Venango, and Mercer Counties; in LeBoeuf Creek in Erie County; and in the Allegheny River in Warren and Forest Counties. In Indiana, the species is found in the Tippecanoe River in Kosciusko, Fulton, Pulaskia, and Tippecanoe

Counties. In Ohio, it is found in Fish Creek of the St. Josephs River in Williams County. In Michigan, it is found in the West Branch of the St. Josephs River across Hillsdale County. In West Virginia, it is found in the Elk River of Braxtion and Clay Counties.

Conservation and Recovery

The species has been extirpated from Alabama, Illinois, and Tennessee, and is no longer found in many streams elsewhere in its former range. Domestic and industrial waste and navigation developments have eliminated or reduced populations of the species on the upper Ohio and Wabash River watersheds. The newly rediscovered Elk River populations of this species in West Virginia could be affected by plans for deep coal mining in the watershed, which might create sedimentation, heavy metal leaching, and acidification of the water.

Predation on mussels is a natural occurrence. Predators, such as freshwater drum, river otter, and muskrats, are known to feed on the species. In a time when the species was widespread and abundant, the impact of this predation was insignificant. However, at the present time, their greatly reduced distribution and populations have made them susceptible to predators, especially muskrats. During a 1988 survey of the French Creek, Pennsylvania population, at least 200 northern riffleshell mussels (*Epioblasma torulosa rangiana*) had been harvested by muskrats. It was also noted that *P. clava* is less susceptible to mammalian predators because of its burying behavior.

Although extensive, unexplained, die-offs have occurred in the past in the Mississippi River drainage, these were for the most part restricted to large rivers. This species prefers medium to small rivers and streams. Disease has not been documented as a factor affecting its population dynamics.

The exotic, prolific zebra mussel, (*Dreissena polymarpha*), accidentally introduced to North America in the mid-1980s, poses a severe threat to all native mussel fauna through the competition for space, food, and survival of glochidia. Presently, the zebra mussel, which was conveyed to the area through ship ballast water from interior European ports, is abundant in the lower Great Lakes. During the fall of 1992, biologists determined that zebra mussel infestation posed a severe threat to native species of mussels.

Conservation measures provided to species listed as endangered or threatened under the Endangered Species Act include recognition, recovery actions, requirements, for Federal protection, and prohibitions against certain practices. Recognition through listing encourages and results in conservation actions by Federal, State, and private agencies, groups, and individuals. The Endangered Species Act provides for possible land acquisition and cooperation with the States and requires that recovery actions be carried out for all listed species.

Because of the species' sedentary nature and susceptibility to a wide variety of changes in water quality, the species is highly vulnerable to vandalism. Due to the low number of reproducing populations of this species, even a single such incident could be catastrophic. The publication of critical habitat maps could increase this risk.

USFWS also finds that designation of critical habitat for this species is not presently determinable. Most existing populations are located in widely scattered streams of declining suitability. The number and location of stream habitats required to provide for the long-term survival of existing populations have not been identified.

Bibliography

U.S. Fish and Wildlife Service. "Endangered and Threatened Wildlife and Plants; Determination of Endangered Status for the Northern Riffleshell Mussel (*Eploblasma Torulosa Ranglana*) and the Clubshell Mussel (*Pleurobema Clava*)." *Federal Register* Vol. 58, No. 13. January 22, 1993: 5638-5642.

Contacts

U.S. Fish and Wildlife Service
Regional Office
Suite 200, 1875 Century Blvd.
Atlanta, GA 30345
Phone: 404-679-4000

U.S. Fish and Wildlife Service
Regional Office
Federal Building
Fort Snelling
Twin Cities, MN 55111
Phone: 612-725-3500
FAX: 612-725-3526

U.S. Fish and Wildlife Service
Regional Office
300 Westgate Center Drive
Hadley, MA 01035
Phone: 413-253-8659

Adapted from data compiled by the Threatened and Endangered Species Information Institute (13950 W. 20th Ave., Golden, CO 80401) for *Beacham's International Threatened, Endangered, and Extinct Species* published on CD ROM, available from Beacham Publishing.

Southern Clubshell

Pleurobema decisum

A. E. Spreitzer

Status	Endangered
Listed	March 17, 1993
Family	Unionidae (Freshwater Mussel)
Description	Medium-size mussel with a thick shell and a heavy hinge plate.
Habitat	Gravel riffles in streams.
Threats	Impoundments, gravel and mining, water pollution.
Range	Alabama, Georgia, Mississippi, Tennessee

Description

The Southern clubshell is a medium-sized mussel about 2.8 inches in length with a thick shell and a heavy hinge plate and teeth. The shell outline is roughly rectangular, produced posteriorly with the umbos terminal with the anterior margin, or nearly so. The posterior ridge is moderately inflated and ends abruptly with little development of the posterior slope at the dorsum of the shell. The periostracum is yellow to yellow-brown with occasional green rays or spots on the umbo in young specimens. The Southern clubshell is distinguished from a closely related species, the black clubshell (also called Curtis' pearly mussel) by it's elongate shape, lighter color, and the presence of a well-defined sulcus in the latter species.

Behavior

See "Freshwater Mussels from the Mobile River Basin," page 2135.

Habitat

The Southern clubshell inhabits high quality lotic habitats with stable gravel and sandy-gravel substrates. Little else is known about the habitat requirements.

The habitat of the glochidia is initially in the gills of the female, then in the water column, and finally attached to a suitable host fish. Habitat associations or requirements for the juvenile stage are unknown.

Historic Range

The Southern clubshell was historically known from every major stream system in the Mobile River basin including the Alabama River (Bogue Chitto Creek), Tombigbee River (Buttahatchee, East Fork Tombigbee, and Sipsey Rivers and Bull Mountain, Luxapalila, and Lubbub Creeks), Black Warrior River, Cahaba and Little Cahaba Rivers, Tallapossa River (Uphapee and Chewacla Creeks), and the Coosa River (Oostanaula, Conasauga, Etowah, Chatooga, and Coosawattee Rivers and Kelly, Talladega and Shoal Creeks).

Current Distribution

This species' current distribution is limited to the Alabama River (Bogue Chitto Creek); the Tombigbee River (Buttahatchee, East Fork Tombigbee, and Sipsey Rivers); and the Tallapossa River (Chewacla Creek).

Conservation and Recovery

See "Freshwater Mussels from the Mobile River Basin," page 2135.

Bibliography

U.S. Fish and Wildlife Service. "Endangered and Threatened Wildlife and Plants; Endangered Status for Eight Freshwater Mussels and Threatened Status for Three Freshwater Mussels in the Mobile River Drainage." *Federal Register* Vol. 58, No. 50, March 17, 1993: 14330-14340.

Contacts

USFWS Regional Office
Suite 200, 1875 Century Blvd.
Atlanta, GA 30345
Phone: 404-679-4000

Ecological Services Field Office
P. O. Drawer 1190
Daphne, AL 36526
Phone: 205-441-5181
FAX: 205-441-6222

Ecological Services Field Office
446 Neal Street
Cookeville, TN 38501
Phone: 615-528-6481
FAX: 615-528-7075

Adapted from data compiled by the Threatened and Endangered Species Information Institute (13950 W. 20th Ave., Golden, CO 80401) for *Beacham's International Threatened, Endangered, and Extinct Species* published on CD ROM, available from Beacham Publishing.

Dark Pigtoe
Pleurobema furvum

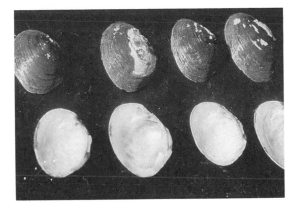

A. E. Spreitzer

Status	Endangered
Listed	March 17, 1993
Family	Unionidae (Freshwater Mussel)
Description	Small to medium mussel with an oval, moderately inflated dark reddish brown shell with closely spaced, dark growth lines.
Habitat	Gravel riffles in streams
Threats	Impoundments, gravel and mining, water pollution.
Range	Alabama

Description

The dark pigtoe is a small to medium sized mussel, growing to lengths of 2.4 inches. The shell is oval and moderately inflated. Beaks are located in the anterior portion of the shell. The posterior ridge is abruptly rounded and terminates in a broadly rounded, subcentral, posterior point. The periostracum is dark reddish brown with numerous and closely spaced, dark growth lines. The hinge plate is wide and the teeth are heavy and large, especially in older specimens. The nacre approaches white in the umbos, and is highly iridescent on the posterior margin.

Behavior

See "Freshwater Mussels from the Mobile River Basin," page 2135.

Habitat

The dark pigtoe inhabits high quality lotic habitats with stable gravel and sandy-gravel substrates. Little else is known about the habitat requirements of this species.

The habitat of the glochidia is initially in the gills of the female, then in the water column, and finally attached to a suitable host fish. Habitat associations or requirements for the juvenile stage are unknown.

Historic Range and Current Distribution

The historic distribution of this species was probably limited to the Black Warrior River system, Alabama, above the fall line.

Specimens were found in tributaries of the Black Warrior (Sipsey Fork, North River) in 1986, 1991, and 1992.

Conservation and Recovery

See "Freshwater Mussels from the Mobile River Basin," page 2135.

Bibliography

U.S. Fish and Wildlife Service. "Endangered and Threatened Wildlife and Plants; Endangered Status for Eight Freshwater Mussels and Threatened Status for Three Freshwater Mussels in the Mobile River Drainage." *Federal Register* Vol. 58, No. 50, March 17, 1993: 14330-14340.

Thorp, J. H., and A. P. Covich. *Ecology and classification of North American freshwater invertebrates.* San Diego, CA: Academic Press, 1991.

Contacts

Ecological Services Field Office
P. O. Drawer 1190
Daphne, AL 36526
Phone: 205-441-5181
FAX: 205-441-6222

Adapted from data compiled by the Threatened and Endangered Species Information Institute (13950 W. 20th Ave., Golden, CO 80401) for *Beacham's International Threatened, Endangered, and Extinct Species* published on CD ROM, available from Beacham Publishing.

Southern Pigtoe
Pleurobema georgianum

Status	Endangered
Listed	March 17, 1993
Family	Unionidae (Freshwater Mussel)
Description	Small to medium mussel with a somewhat compressed yellow to yellow brown shell, and numerous dark brown growth lines.
Habitat	Gravel riffles in streams.
Threats	Impoundments, gravel and mining, water pollution.
Range	Alabama, Georgia, Tennessee

No Photo Available for This Species

Description

The southern pigtoe is a small to medium sized mussel that is generally under 2.4 inches in length. The shell is elliptical to ovate and somewhat compressed. The posterior slope is smoothly rounded. The pseudocardinal teeth are small but well-developed, and the nacre is white. The periostracum is yellow to yellow-brown. Growth lines are numerous and may be dark brown. Small specimens may have green spots at the growth lines along the posterior ridge and near the umbo.

Behavior

See "Freshwater Mussels from the Mobile River Basin," page 2135.

Habitat

The southern pigtoe inhabits high quality lotic habitats with stable gravel and sandy-gravel substrates. Little else is known about the habitat requirements of this species.

The habitat of the glochidia is initially in the gills of the female, then in the water column, and finally attached to a suitable host fish. Habitat associations or requirements for the juvenile stage are unknown.

Historic Range

The southern pigtoe's historic range apparently was restricted to the Coosa River system. Museum specimens of this species were collected from Coosa River, Shoal Creek, and the Chatooga and Conasauga Rivers.

Current Distribution

Live specimens were collected from this river system in 1974, 1987, and 1990. One fresh dead specimen was collected from the

Conasauga River in 1991. A 1991 survey did not find any live specimen in the Coosa River drainage.

Conservation and Recovery

See "Freshwater Mussels from the Mobile River Basin," page 2135.

Bibliography

U.S. Fish and Wildlife Service. "Endangered and Threatened Wildlife and Plants; Endangered Status for Eight Freshwater Mussels and Threatened Status for Three Freshwater Mussels in the Mobile River Drainage." *Federal Register* Vol. 58, No. 50, March 17, 1993: 14330-14340.

Contacts

USFWS Regional Office
Suite 200, 1875 Century Blvd.
Atlanta, GA 30345
Phone: 404-679-4000

Ecological Services Field Office
P. O. Drawer 1190
Daphne, AL 36526
Phone: 205-441-5181
FAX: 205-441-6222

Ecological Services Field Office
446 Neal Street
Cookeville, TN 38501
Phone: 615-528-6481
FAX: 615-528-7075

Adapted from data compiled by the Threatened and Endangered Species Information Institute (13950 W. 20th Ave., Golden, CO 80401) for *Beacham's International Threatened, Endangered, and Extinct Species* published on CD ROM, available from Beacham Publishing.

Ovate Clubshell

Pleurobema perovatum

A. E. Spreitzer

Status	Endangered
Listed	March 17, 1993
Family	Unionidae (Freshwater Mussel)
Description	Small to medium mussel with an oval to elliptical yellow to dark brown shell, and a well developed, broadly rounded, often concave posterior ridge.
Habitat	Gravel riffles in streams.
Threats	Impoundments, gravel and mining, water pollution.
Range	Alabama, Georgia, Mississippi, Tennessee

Description

The ovate clubshell is a small to medium sized mussel that rarely exceeds 2.0 inches in length. The shell is ovate to elliptical and has nearly terminal, inflated umbos. The posterior ridge is well-developed, broadly rounded, and often concave. The posterior slope is produced well beyond the posterior ridge. Periostracum color varies from yellow to dark brown, and occasionally has broad green rays that may cover most of the umbo and posterior ridge. The nacre is white. Due to the nearly terminal umbos in some specimens, *P. perovatum* may be mistaken for young southern clubshells (*P. decisum*). They may be distinguished from the latter by their thinner shells, and a gently sloping, well developed posterior slope.

Behavior

See "Freshwater Mussels from the Mobile River Basin," page 2135.

Habitat

The ovate clubshell inhabits high quality lotic habitats with stable gravel and sandy-gravel substrates. Little else is known about the habitat requirements of this species.

The habitat of the glochidia is initially in the gills of the female, then in the water column, and finally attached to a suitable host fish. Habitat associations or requirements for the juvenile stage are unknown.

Historic Range

This species' historic distribution included the Tombigbee River and tributaries (Buttahatchee and Sipsey Rivers; Luxapalila, Coal-fire and Lubbub Creeks); Black Warrior River and tributaries (Locust Fork; Village, Prairie, Big Prairie, Brushy and Blackwater Creeks); Alabama River; Cahaba River and the tributary Buck Creek; Chewacla, Upha-pee and Opintlocco Creeks in the Tallapoosa drainage; and the Coosa River and tributaries (Conasauga and Etowah Rivers, and Holy Creek).

Current Distribution

The ovate clubshell is now limited to the Buttahatchee and Sipsey Rivers in the Tombigbee River drainage, Blackwater Creek and Locust Fork in the Black Warrior drainage, and Chewacla Creek in the Tallapoosa drainage. Specimens were last collected in the Coosa drainage in 1974 and in the Cahaba River in 1978. The species was not found in the Coosa River or Cahaba River drainages in a 1991 survey.

Conservation and Recovery

See "Freshwater Mussels from the Mobile River Basin," page 2135.

Bibliography

U.S. Fish and Wildlife Service. "Endangered and Threatened Wildlife and Plants; Endangered Status for Eight Freshwater Mussels and Threatened Status for Three Freshwater Mussels in the Mobile River Drainage" *Federal Register* Vol. 58, No. 50, March 17, 1993: 14330-14340.

Contacts

USFWS Regional Office
Suite 200, 1875 Century Blvd.
Atlanta, GA 30345
Phone: 404-679-4000

Ecological Services Field Office
P. O. Drawer 1190
Daphne, AL 36526
Phone: 205-441-5181
FAX: 205-441-6222

Ecological Services Field Office
446 Neal Street
Cookeville, TN 38501
Phone: 615-528-6481
FAX: 615-528-7075

Adapted from data compiled by the Threatened and Endangered Species Information Institute (13950 W. 20th Ave., Golden, CO 80401) for *Beacham's International Threatened, Endangered, and Extinct Species* published on CD ROM, available from Beacham Publishing.

Triangular Kidneyshell
Ptychobranchus greeni

A. E. Spreitzer

Status	Endangered
Listed	March 17, 1993
Family	Unionidae (Freshwater Mussel)
Description	Medium to large mussel with an oval to elliptical yellow-brown shell, and fine and wavy, or wide and broken, green rays.
Habitat	Gravel riffles in streams.
Threats	Impoundments, gravel and mining, water pollution.
Range	Alabama, Georgia, Tennessee

Description

The triangular kidneyshell is a medium to large mussel growing up to 4.0 inches in length. The shell is ovate to elliptical, strongly compressed, and may be flattened ventral to the umbos. The posterior ridge is broadly rounded and terminates in a broad round point post-ventrally. The pseudocardinal teeth are heavy, and the laterals are heavy, gently curved and short. The periostracum is straw-yellow in young mussels, but becomes yellow-brown with age. It may have fine and wavy, or wide and broken, green rays anterior to the posterior ridge.

Behavior

See "Freshwater Mussels from the Mobile River Basin," page 2135.

Habitat

The triangular kidneyshell inhabits high quality lotic habitats with stable gravel and sandy-gravel substrates. Little else is known about the habitat requirements of this species.

The habitat of the glochidia is initially in the gills of the female, then in the water column, and finally attached to a suitable host fish. Habitat associations or requirements for the juvenile stage are unknown.

Historic Range

This species' historic range included the Black Warrior River and tributaries (Mulberry Fork, Locust Fork, North and Little Warrior Rivers, Brushy Creek, Sipsey Fork); Cahaba River; and the Coosa River and tributaries (Choccolocco Creek; Chatooga, Conasauga, and Etowah Rivers).

Current Distribution

The triangular kidneyshell is currently limited to the headwaters of the Sipsey Fork and Little Warrior River in the Black Warrior River drainage; and the Conasauga River in the Coosa drainage. Specimens were lasted collected in the Cahaba River in 1979. Surveys in 1991 failed to find other historically known populations.

Conservation and Recovery

See "Freshwater Mussels from the Mobile River Basin," page 2135.

Bibliography

U.S. Fish and Wildlife Service. "Endangered and Threatened Wildlife and Plants; Endangered Status for Eight Freshwater Mussels and Threatened Status for Three Freshwater Mussels in the Mobile River Drainage." *Federal Register* Vol. 58, No. 50, March 17, 1993: 14330-14340.

Contacts

USFWS Regional Office
Suite 200, 1875 Century Blvd.
Atlanta, GA 30345
Phone: 404-679-4000

Ecological Services Field Office
P. O. Drawer 1190
Daphne, AL 36526
Phone: 205-441-5181
FAX: 205-441-6222

Ecological Services Field Office
446 Neal Street
Cookeville, TN 38501
Phone: 615-528-6481
FAX: 615-528-7075

Adapted from data compiled by the Threatened and Endangered Species Information Institute (13950 W. 20th Ave., Golden, CO 80401) for *Beacham's International Threatened, Endangered, and Extinct Species* published on CD ROM, available from Beacham Publishing.

SNAILS AND CRUSTACEANS

Aquatic Snails
In South Central Idaho

On December 14, 1992, the U.S. Fish and Wildlife Service listed five aquatic snails in south central Idaho as threatened or endangered. Because all of these species are found in the Snake River Plains/Sagebrush ecosystem, their habitat is impacted by similar threats and they are characterized by similar descriptions, which are explained here rather than being repeated in each of the species accounts.

Banbury Springs Lanx
Bliss River Rapids Snail
Idaho Springsnail
Snake River Physa Snail
Utah Valvata Snail

Description

The shell of springsnails ranges in length from six to ten millimeters in height; its shape is ovate to conical or pointed, with two to eight whorls. The calcareous portion of the shell lacks a color pattern while the periostracus (protective outer layer) may or may not have a pattern. The aperture (orifice) is a minute opening without notches, canals, siphonal grooves, or teeth. The sculpture (pattern of ridges) is usually smooth but is sometimes observed as reticulate (marked with veins), spines or cords. The shell cover is horny, without an internal appendage. The foot is strong, mobile, shortened at the front, and retractable. The foot bares a mucous groove across the front edge; it is rounded and has a rear pedal gland; pedal tentacles, lobes or feelers are absent. Movement of *Hydrobiids* is generally by gliding. The head bears threadlike tentacles; the eyes are usu-

ally on the side at the outer bases of the tentacles. Body coloration is usually grayish-black. The mantle cavity does not have tentacles, although a single tentacle may sometimes be observed. The tongue is long and slender, and the central tooth is usually angular. The stomach has a crystalline style (appendage). The fecal pellets are elliptical, circular, or ovoid. The central nervous system is not highly concentrated.

Habitat

This species occupies the Snake River Plains/Sagebrush ecosystem. This ecosystem occurs primarily on the Columbia Plateaus, in the Northwestern states and the central portion of the Great Basin including Utah, Nevada, southern Idaho, parts of Wyoming and Colorado. This broad ecosystem occupies plains and plateaus derived from lava flows, ancient lake beds, and broad basins of alluvium. In Idaho nearly half of this area is federally owned; the remainder is in farms and ranches. Most of the federally owned land is rangeland. Forage production is low, and annual grasses have invaded much of the rangeland. The plains bordering the Snake River and its tributaries are irrigated. Potatoes, grain, sugar beets, beans, and alfalfa hay are the principal crops. The elevation in this area ranges from 600 to 1,700 meters. These nearly level to steeply sloping lava plains have a thin to moderately thick cover of loess. In places, the river is quite deep giving way to steep-walled canyons. Alluvial fans, terraces, and bottom land are gently sloping to moderately sloping. The average annual precipitation for this area is 175 to 325 millimeters. There is little or no precipitation in the summer, attributing to seasonal droughts. This area supports shrub-grass vegetation. Big sagebrush, winterfat, shadscale, Indian ricegrass, needleandthread, Thurber needle grass, and Sandberg blue grass grow on the lower Snake River Plains.

The Snake River and its tributaries provide essential habitat to the springsnail and other sensitive native species such as the Shortface lanx or giant Columbia River limpet, the Shoshone sculpin, the Bliss Rapids snail, the Snake River physa snail, the Banbury Spring lanx, and the Utah valvata snail. These areas contain some of the last mainstem Snake River habitats with the full range of native molluscan species present, and represent a unique aquatic community.

Conservation and Recovery

The free-flowing, cool water environments required by this species have been impacted by and are vulnerable to continued adverse habitat modification and deteriorating water quality from hydroelectric development, peak-loading effects from existing hydroelectric project operations, water withdrawal and diversions, water pollution, and inadequate regulatory mechanisms. With the exception of segments of land owned by The Nature Conservancy (Thousand Springs) the aquatic habitats occupied by the Idaho springsnail are virtually unprotected from the aforementioned threats.

The lotic fauna of the middle Snake River have been declining for several years due to fragmentation of remaining free-flowing habitats and deteriorating water quality. Hydroelectric development throughout the Snake River has directly impacted the species through inundation of lotic habitats, isolating segmented populations, and impacting suitable shallow water shoreline habitat from project-caused flow fluctuations. Water quality degradation continues from

increased water use and withdrawal, aggravated by recent drought induced low flows. The 121 mile stretch of the Snake River is impacted by agricultural return flows; runoff from between 500 and 600 dairies and feedlots; effluent from over 140 private, state, and Federal fish culture facilities; and point source (e.g. municipal sewage) discharge. The ultimate impact of these factors are increased nutrient loads and concentrations which adversely affect the lotic fauna. Nutrient loading contributes to dense blooms of free-living and attached filamentous algae, which the species cannot utilize. This algae will often cover rock surfaces, effectively displacing suitable snail habitats and food resources. Stream sediments will also become anoxic as high biochemical oxygen demand during the aquatic growing season and seasonal algae dieoffs occur.

Currently, the Idaho Power Company has received a preliminary permit to evaluate the development of the A. J. Wiley hydropower project on the lower Salmon Falls Dam tailwater. The reservoir created would inundate and destroy mainstem riverine habitats for existing populations of the Idaho springsnail. Another project currently under evaluation at the Bliss Dam tailwaters would also inundate the species' habitat.

A more recent threat is the discovery of the New Zealand mudsnail in the middle Snake River. The eurytopic mudsnail is experiencing explosive growth in the river and shows a wide range of tolerance for water fluctuations, velocity, temperature and turbidity. The mudsnail species seems to prefer warmer, polluted waters over pristine cold spring environments. This species has already been observed to form dark mats of individuals in habitat formerly preferred by the Idaho springsnail. Potamopygus has been observed at densities of nearly 400 individuals per square inch. This species is parthenogenic (capable of reproducing without copulation) and ovoviparous (producing eggs that hatch outside the body), which contributes to the ability to build large populations rapidly and recover from population crashes. *Potamopyrgus* competes directly for habitats of the Idaho springsnail in the mainstem Snake River.

The Idaho department of Water Resources regulates water development in the Snake River basin. At present, there is no specific allocation of water on the mainstem middle Snake River for fish and wildlife, although maintenance flows for fish and wildlife on several tributary streams to the Snake River have been established.

Conservation measures provided to species listed as endangered or threatened pursuant to the Endangered Species Act include recognition, recovery actions, requirements for Federal protection, and prohibitions against certain practices. Recognition through listing encourages conservation measures by Federal, international, and private agencies, groups, and individuals.

Changes in the use of stored water in the Snake River basin to assist recovery efforts for other threatened and endangered species may also impact this species and its habitat. The Bonneville Power Administration, State of Idaho, and Idaho Power Company are exploring alternatives to assist outmigrating endangered Snake River Sockeye salmon and threatened Spring and Summer Chinook from utilizing water from the upper Snake River Basin. The Idaho Department of Health and Welfare, Division of Environmental Quality, under authority of the State Nutrient Management Act, is coordinating efforts to identify and implement preventative actions which will reduce nutrient loading to the middle Snake River. These efforts will address pollution control strategies.

Listing of the springsnails as Endangered or Threatened species will result in increased protection of remaining free-flowing riverine habitat required by this species and other sensitive native species such as the shortface lanx or giant columbia River limpet, the Shoshone sculpin, the Banbury Springs lanx, the Idaho springsnail, the Snake River Physa snail, and the Utah Valvata snail.

The U.S. Army Corps of Engineers is also involved in the permitting of projects on the Snake River through their authority under the Clean Water Act. Listing of the species as Endangered entails that the Corps will be required to initiate formal consultation on any project that may affect this species.

Anthony's Riversnail
Athearnia anthonyi

Richard Biggins   *Color Plate C-6*

Status	Endangered
Listed	April 15, 1994
Family	Hydrobidae (Freshwater snail)
Description	Relatively large freshwater snail that is ovate and olive green to yellowish brown in color.
Habitat	Shoal areas of tributaries of big rivers.
Food	Diatoms and plant debris.
Reproduction	Annual life cycle.
Threats	Siltation contributed by coal mining, poor land use practices, and waste discharges.
Range	Tennessee, Alabama

Description

This relatively large freshwater snail, which grows to about one inch in length, is ovate and olive green to yellowish brown in color.

Behavior

This species eats diatoms and plant debris, which it grazes along mud surfaces, rocky surfaces and macrophytes. Anthony's riversnail has an annual life cycle.

Habitat

Anthony's riversnail is a big-river species that was historically associated with the shoal areas in the main stem of the Tennessee River and the lower reaches of some of its tributaries. Presently, only two small populations are known to survive—one in the Sequatchie River, Marion County, Tennessee; and one in Limestone Creek, Limestone County, Alabama.

Historic Range

Anthony's riversnail is a big-river species that was historically associated with the shoal areas in the main stem of the Tennessee River and the lower reaches of some of its tributaries. There are historical records of the species from the following rivers in Tennessee: lower French Broad, Nolichucky, Clinch, Beaver Creek, Little Tennessee, Tellico, Sequatchie, Little Sequatchie, Battle Creek; in Georgia from South Chickamauga and Tiger Creeks; and in Alabama from Limestone Creek.

Current Distribution

Presently, only two small populations are known to survive—one in the Sequatchie River, Marion County, Tennessee; and one in Limestone Creek, Limestone County, Alabama.

Because this species has an annual life cycle, the number of individuals varies from year to year, and the precise number of individuals is unknown. The Anthony's riversnail has an extremely limited distribution and low numbers.

Conservation and Recovery

Many populations were lost when much of the Tennessee River and the lower reaches of its tributaries were impounded. The general water quality deterioration that has resulted from siltation and other pollutants contributed by coal mining, poor land use practices, and waste discharges was likely responsible for the species' further decline. These factors continue to impact the Sequatchie River and Limestone Creek populations. Further, timber harvesting for wood chip mills proposed for southeastern Tennessee and northeastern Alabama could impact this species.

Both existing populations inhabit short river reaches; thus, they are very vulnerable to extirpation from accidental toxic chemical spills. As the Sequatchie River and Limestone Creek are isolated by impoundments from other Tennessee tributaries, recolonization of any extirpated populations would be unlikely without human intervention. Additionally, because these populations are isolated, their long-term genetic viability is questionable.

Because this species is very rare, with populations restricted to extremely short stream reaches, unregulated taking for any purpose could threaten its continued existence. Therefore, FWS decided not to designate critical habitat since the publication of precise population locations would increase the collection threat. FWS also determined that there was little advantage to the snail to designate critical habitat.

FWS notified Federal agencies that could have a program affecting this species. No specific proposed Federal actions were identified that would likely affect the species. Federal activities that could occur and impact the species include, but are not limited to, the carrying out or the issuance of permits for reservoir construction, stream alteration, wastewater facility development, pesticide registration, and road and bridge construction.

Bibliography

U.S. Fish and Wildlife Service. "Endangered and Threatened Wildlife and Plants: Determination of Endangered Status for the Royal Snail and Anthony's Riversnail." *Federal Register*, April 15, 1994: 17994-17998.

Contacts

Ecological Services Field Office
446 Neal Street
Cookeville, TN 38501
Phone: 615-528-6481
FAX: 615-528-7075

Ecological Services Field Office
P. O. Drawer 1190
Daphne, AL 36526
Phone: 205-441-5181
FAX: 205-441-6222

Adapted from data compiled by Beacham Publishing for *Beacham's International Threatened, Endangered, and Extinct Species* published on CD ROM.

Banbury Springs Lanx
Lanx (undescribed species)

Status	Endangered
Listed	December 14, 1992
Family	Lancidae (Lanx)
Description	Shell with a uniform, red cinnamon color whose body length and height exceed its width.
Habitat	Free-flowing cool spring alcoves.
Food	Plant debris or diatoms.
Reproduction	Copulation after a courtship ritual during late winter or early spring.
Range	Idaho

William H. Mullins, USFWS   *Color Plate C-6*

Description

The Banbury Springs lanx is distinguished with a shell of uniform red cinnamon color, a subcentral apex. This pulmonate snail's length and height exceed its width. Lancids lack either lungs or gills and respire through unusually heavy vascularized mantles, making them highly susceptible to water quality degradation.

Behavior

After reproduction during the late winter-early spring season, older adults will most likely expire. The hermaphroditic reproduction of this species involves the exchange of spermatophores. Courtship entails investigation using tentacles and mouths. Slowly edging closer the snails rear up at right angles to the ground with the bases of their feet in full contact. Supported by the tip of their shells and the hind part of the feet, the male and female open their orifices while caressing each other with their tentacles.

The detritivorous characteristics of this species restricts it to a diet of diatoms and plant debris. The Banbury Springs lanx grazes along mud surfaces, rocky surfaces and macrophytes.

Habitat

The Banbury Springs lanx occupies the Snake River Plains/Sagebrush ecosystem. It is restricted to a few isolated free-flowing reaches or spring alcove habitats of the Snake River. This aquatic system is characterized by cold, well-oxygenated, unpolluted water. The Banbury Springs lanx occurs on stable, cobble-boulder substratum only in flowing waters in the Snake River and also in a few spring alcove habitats in the Hagerman Valley. The species does not burrow in sediments and normally avoids surfaces with attached plants. Known river colonies of the Banbury Springs lanx occur only in areas associated with spring influences or rapids edge environments and tend to flank shorelines. Generally, the species requires cold (15 to 18 degrees Celsius) clean, well-oxygenated swift flowing waters on boulder or cobble substratum. The Banbury Springs lanx is found most often on smooth basalt and avoids surfaces with large aquatic macrophytes of filamentous green algae. This species has been collected at depths from 30 to 75 centimeters. In a 1992 report the species was found in water as shallow as five cm but this species is most commonly found in depths of 15 cm.

For a continued discussion, see "Aquatic Snails In South Central Idaho," page 2171.

Historic Range

This limpet was first discovered in 1988 at Banbury Springs with a second population found in nearby Box Canyon Springs in 1989. During 1991, a mollusc survey at the Thousand Springs Preserve revealed a third population in Minnie Miller Springs.

Current Distribution

This species is currently known from Banbury Springs, Box Canyon Springs and Thousand Springs.

Population density for this species was in the range of 4 to 48 per square meter on the Thousand Springs Preserve. The total adult population at the Preserve was estimated at between 600 to 1,200 individuals. These surveys were conducted in the spring alcoves in which the species was originally located. This snail occurs in the least disturbed spring habitats at Banbury Springs, Box Canyon Springs and Thousand Springs.

Conservation and Recovery

The primary limiting factors attributing to the demise of this species are water diversion and water pollution. A more recent threat stems from competition with an exotic species, *Potamopyrgus antipodarum*, although the impact of competition is thought to be rather limited for the Banbury Springs lanx. This snail experiences a die-off of older adults during the late winter-early spring season following reproduction.

The free-flowing, cool water environments required by this species have been impacted by and are vulnerable to continued adverse habitat modification and deteriorating water quality from hydroelectric development, peak-loading effects from existing hydroelectric project operations, water withdrawal and diversions, water pollution, and inadequate regulatory mechanisms.

Water quality degradation continues from increased water use and withdrawal, aggravated by recent drought induced low flows. The 121 mile stretch of the Snake River is impacted by agricultural return flows; runoff from between 500 and 600 dairies and feedlots; effluent from over 140 private, state, and Federal fish culture facilities; and point source (e.g. municipal sewage) discharge. The ultimate impact of these factors are increased nutrient loads and concentrations which adversely affect the lotic fauna. Nutrient loading contributes to dense blooms of free-living and attached filamentous algae, which the species cannot utilize. This algae will often cover rock surfaces, effectively displacing suitable snail habitats and food resources. Stream sediments will also become anoxic as high biochemical oxygen demand during the aquatic growing season and seasonal algae dieoffs occur.

A more recent threat is the discovery of

the New Zealand mudsnail in the middle Snake River. The eurytopic mudsnail is experiencing explosive growth in the river and shows a wide range of tolerance for water fluctuations, velocity, temperature and turbidity. The mudsnail species seems to prefer warmer, polluted waters over pristine cold spring environments.

For a continued discussion, see "Aquatic Snails In South Central Idaho," page 2171.

Bibliography

Bickel, D. 1977. *Utah-Colorado Survey*. U.S. Fish and Wildlife Service. 59 pp.

U.S. Fish and Wildlife Service. "Endangered and Threatened Wildlife and Plants; Determination of Endangered or Threatened Status for Five Aquatic Snails in South Central Idaho." *Federal Register.* Vol. 57, No. 240. December 14, 1992: 59244-59257.

U.S. Fish and Wildlife Service. *Endangered Species Technical Bulletin*. 1993. Vol. XVIII, No. 01: 15.

Contacts

U.S. Fish and Wildlife Service
Regional Office
Eastside Federal Complex
911 N.S. 11th Avenue
Portland, OR 97232-4181
Phone: 503-231-6118

Boise Ecological Services Field Office
4696 Overland Road, Room 576
Boise, ID 83705
Phone: 208-334-1931
FAX: 208-334-9493

Adapted from data compiled by the Threatened and Endangered Species Information Institute (13950 W. 20th Ave., Golden, CO 80401) for *Beacham's International Threatened, Endangered, and Extinct Species* published on CD ROM, available from Beacham Publishing.

Snake River Physa Snail

Physa natricina

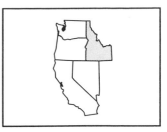

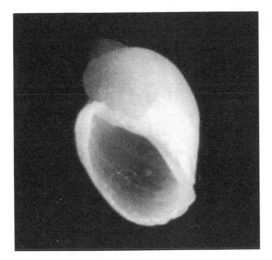

William H. Mullins

Status	Endangered
Listed	December 14, 1992
Family	Physidae (Physa)
Description	Amber to brown color snails with a thin, oval-shaped shell that spirals to the left.
Habitat	Free-flowing cool spring alcoves.
Food	Plant debris or diatoms.
Reproduction	Copulation after a courtship ritual during late winter or early spring.
Range	Idaho

Description

The Snake River physa snail, *Physa natricina*, is a "living fossil" in that it is a relict from ancient lakes from Pleistocene-Holocene and rivers from southeastern Idaho and northern Utah. This species possesses a five to seven millimeter long shell with three to 3.5 whorls. Fresh shells are amber to brown in color. *Physids* (Bladder snails) have lungs and are quite similar to the *Lancids*. This family possesses a sinitral thin oval-shaped shell that spirals to the left and the body openings are on the left side. The final whorl contributes to about four-fifths of shell bulk. These snails have a broad tantaculate and the mantle margin covers the shell.

Behavior

Physids possess a lung-like mantle cavity, feed on algae, and delineate trails with mucus. The hermaphroditic reproduction of this species involves the exchange of spermatophores. Courtship entails investigation using tentacles and mouths. Slowly edging closer the snails rear up at right angles to the ground with the bases of their feet in full contact. Supported by the tip of their shells and the hind part of the feet, the male and female open their orifices while caressing each other with their tentacles.

The detritivorous characteristics of this species restricts it to a diet of diatoms and plant debris. This snail grazes along mud surfaces, rocky surfaces and macrophytes.

Habitat

This snail occurs on the undersides of gravel to boulder substratum in swift current in the mainstem Snake River. Specimens have been recorded from boulders in the deepest accessible part of the river at the margins of rapids.

For a continued discussion, see "Aquatic Snails In South Central Idaho," page 2171.

Historic Range and Current Distribution

Fossil records of the snail occur in deposits from Pleistocene-Holocene lakes and rivers from southeastern Idaho and northern Utah.

This species' current range is believed to be from Grandview upstream through the Hagerman Reach in Gooding, Idowyhee, and Elmore Counties, Idaho.

The native bottom fauna has been virtually eliminated in the type locality (Gooding County), however, and the species is believed to be extirpated from this region.

Conservation and Recovery

The free-flowing, cool water environments required by this species have been impacted by and are vulnerable to continued adverse habitat modification and deteriorating water quality from hydroelectric development, peak-loading effects from existing hydroelectric project operations, water withdrawal and diversions, water pollution, and inadequate regulatory mechanisms.

Water quality degradation continues from increased water use and withdrawal, aggravated by recent drought induced low flows. The 121 mile stretch of the Snake River is impacted by agricultural return flows; runoff from between 500 and 600 dairies and feedlots; effluent from over 140 private, state, and Federal fish culture facilities; and point source (e.g. municipal sewage) discharge. The ultimate impact of these factors are increased nutrient loads and concentrations which adversely affect the lotic fauna. Nutri-

ent loading contributes to dense blooms of free-living and attached filamentous algae, which the species cannot utilize. This algae will often cover rock surfaces, effectively displacing suitable snail habitats and food resources. Stream sediments will also become anoxic as high biochemical oxygen demand during the aquatic growing season and seasonal algae dieoffs occur.

A more recent threat is the discovery of the New Zealand mudsnail in the middle Snake River. The eurytopic mudsnail is experiencing explosive growth in the river and shows a wide range of tolerance for water fluctuations, velocity, temperature and turbidity. The mudsnail species seems to prefer warmer, polluted waters over pristine cold spring environments.

For a continued discussion, see "Aquatic Snails In South Central Idaho," page 2171.

Bibliography

U.S. Fish and Wildlife Service. "Endangered and Threatened Wildlife and Plants; Determination of Endangered or Threatened Status for Five Aquatic Snails in South Central Idaho." *Federal Register.* Vol. 57, No. 240. December 14, 1992: 59244-59257.

Contacts

Boise Ecological Services Field Office
4696 Overland Road, Room 576
Boise, ID 83705
Phone: 208-334-1931
FAX: 208-334-9493

Adapted from data compiled by the Threatened and Endangered Species Information Institute (13950 W. 20th Ave., Golden, CO 80401) for *Beacham's International Threatened, Endangered, and Extinct Species* published on CD ROM, available from Beacham Publishing.

Royal Snail

Pyrgulopsis (=Marstonia) ogmorhaphe

Richard Biggins   *Color Plate C-6*

Status	Endangered
Listed	April 15, 1994
Family	Hydrobidae (Freshwater Snail)
Description	Small annual snail with a thin, conical-shaped shell.
Habitat	Leaves and twigs in the quieter pools downstream from the spring source.
Food	Diatoms and plant debris.
Reproduction	Annual life cycle.
Threats	Siltation contributed by coal mining, poor land use practices, and waste discharges.
Range	Tennessee

Description

The royal snail is a small (usually less than .25 inches in length) annual species distinguished from other closely related species by its relatively large size; its large number of whorls (5.2 to 5.8); its deeply incised, suture-producing, strongly shouldered whorls which are almost flat above; its complete aperture, which is broadly ovate in shape with a rounded posterior corner; its outer lip, which is slightly arched forward in lateral profile; its thin shell; its conical terete shape; and its enlarged bursa copulatrix with a completely exposed duct.

Behavior

This species eats diatoms and plant debris and has an annual life cycle.

Habitat

Royal snails are generally found in the diatomaceous "ooze" and on leaves and twigs in the quieter pools downstream from the spring source.

Historic Range

The royal snail is known only from two spring runs in the Sequatchie River system in Marion County, Tennessee.

Current Distribution

Because this species has an annual life cycle, the number of individuals varies from year to year, and the precise number of individuals is unknown. The royal snail has an extremely limited distribution and low numbers.

Conservation and Recovery

While no populations are known to have been lost, the general deterioration of the water quality that has resulted from siltation and other pollutants contributed by coal mining, poor land use practices, and waste discharges likely are impacting the species. This could result in serious, irreversible decline of the species. Additionally, both existing populations inhabit extremely limited areas, and they are very vulnerable to extirpation from accidental toxic chemical spills or vandalism. Other threats include road construction; agricultural, municipal, industrial, and mining runoff, both direct and from sub surface flows; cattle grazing; vandalism; and pollution from trash thrown into the spring. Further, timber harvesting for wood chip mills proposed for southeastern Tennessee and northeastern Alabama could impact this species.

Because this species is very rare, with populations restricted to extremely short stream reaches, unregulated taking for any purpose could threaten its continued existence. Therefore, FWS decided not to designate critical habitat since the publication of precise population locations would increase the collection threat. FWS also determined that there was little advantage to the snail to designate critical habitat.

FWS notified Federal agencies that could have a program affecting this species. No specific proposed Federal actions were identified that would likely affect the species. Federal activities that could occur and impact the species include, but are not limited to, the carrying out or the issuance of permits for reservoir construction, stream alteration, wastewater facility development, pesticide registration, and road and bridge construction.

Bibliography

U.S. Fish and Wildlife Service. "Endangered and Threatened Wildlife and Plants: Determination of Endangered Status for the Royal Snail and Anthony's Riversnail." *Federal Register*, April 15, 1994: 17994-17998.

Contacts

Ecological Services Field Office
446 Neal Street
Cookeville, TN 38501
Phone: 615-528-6481
FAX: 615-528-7075

Adapted from data compiled by Beacham Publishing for *Beacham's International Threatened, Endangered, and Extinct Species* published on CD ROM.

Idaho Springsnail
Fontelicella idahoensis

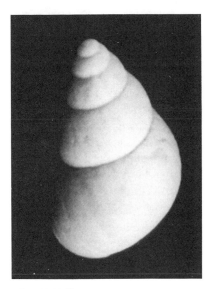

William H. Mullins

Status	Endangered
Listed	December 14, 1992
Family	Hydrobidae (Springsnail)
Description	A living fossil with a narrowly elongate shell with 5.5 to 6 whorls.
Habitat	Free-flowing cool spring alcoves.
Food	Plant debris or diatoms.
Range	Idaho

Description

The Idaho springsnail is a relict of the Pleistocene Lake Idaho and is considered and "living fossil." It has a narrowly elongate shell reaching a length of five to seven millimeters. This species is observed to have up to 5.5 to six whorls. The calcareous portion of the shell lacks a color pattern while the periostracus may or may not have a pattern. The aperture is holostomatous, without notches, canals, siphonal grooves, or denticulations. The foot is strong, mobile, truncate anteriorly and retractile. It bares lateral auriculate lobes and a mucous groove across the anterior edge; it is rounded and has a posterior pedal gland. The snail moves generally by gliding. The head bears filiform tentacles; the eyes are usually lateral at the outer bases of the tentacles. Body coloration is usually grayish-black.

Behavior

This species is restricted to a diet of diatoms and plant debris which grazes along mud surfaces, rocky surfaces and macrophytes.

Habitat

The Idaho springsnail is found only in permanent, flowing waters of the mainstem Snake River. This snail is not found in any of the Snake River tributaries or marginal springs. It occurs on mud or sand associated with gravel to boulder size substratum. This species often attaches itself to vegetation such as common associate *Potamogeton*, in riffles.

The Snake River and its tributaries provide essential habitat to the springsnail and other sensitive native species such as the

Shortface lanx or giant Columbia River limpet, the Shoshone sculpin, the Bliss Rapids snail, the Snake River physa snail, the Banbury Spring lanx (Lanx no sp.), and the Utah Valvata snail. These areas contain some of the last mainstem Snake River habitats with the full range of native molluscan species present, and represent a unique aquatic community.

For a continued discussion, see "Aquatic Snails In South Central Idaho," page 2171.

Historic Range and Current Distribution

Fossil records of the Idaho springsnail indicate this species to have been distributed throughout much of southern Idaho. This species is currently distributed discontinuously in the mainstem Snake River from sites from C. J. Strike Reservoir and upstream to Bancroft Springs in Owyhee and Elmore Counties, Idaho.

Conservation and Recovery

The free-flowing, cool water environments required by this species have been impacted by and are vulnerable to continued adverse habitat modification and deteriorating water quality from hydroelectric development, peak-loading effects from existing hydroelectric project operations, water withdrawal and diversions, water pollution, and inadequate regulatory mechanisms.

Water quality degradation continues from increased water use and withdrawal, aggravated by recent drought induced low flows. The 121 mile stretch of the Snake River is impacted by agricultural return flows; runoff from between 500 and 600 dairies and feedlots; effluent from over 140 private, state, and Federal fish culture facilities; and point source (e.g. municipal sewage) discharge. The ultimate impact of these factors are increased nutrient loads and concentrations which adversely affect the lotic fauna. Nutrient loading contributes to dense blooms of free-living and attached filamentous algae, which the species cannot utilize. This algae will often cover rock surfaces, effectively displacing suitable snail habitats and food resources. Stream sediments will also become anoxic as high biochemical oxygen demand during the aquatic growing season and seasonal algae dieoffs occur.

A more recent threat is the discovery of the New Zealand mudsnail in the middle Snake River. The eurytopic mudsnail is experiencing explosive growth in the river and shows a wide range of tolerance for water fluctuations, velocity, temperature and turbidity. The mudsnail species seems to prefer warmer, polluted waters over pristine cold spring environments.

For a continued discussion, see "Aquatic Snails In South Central Idaho," page 2171.

Bibliography

U.S. Fish and Wildlife Service. "Endangered and Threatened Wildlife and Plants; Determination of Endangered or Threatened Status for Five Aquatic Snails in South Central Idaho." *Federal Register*. Vol. 57, No. 240. December 14, 1992: 59244-59257.

Contacts

Boise Ecological Services Field Office
4696 Overland Road, Room 576
Boise, ID 83705
Phone: 208-334-1931
FAX: 208-334-9493

Adapted from data compiled by the Threatened and Endangered Species Information Institute (13950 W. 20th Ave., Golden, CO 80401) for *Beacham's International Threatened, Endangered, and Extinct Species* published on CD ROM.

Bruneau Hot Springsnail

Pyrgulopsis bruneauensis

Pat Olmstead

Status	Endangered
Listed	January 25, 1993
Family	Hydrobiidae (Springsnail)
Description	Thin, transparent, white-clear shell with a black appearance.
Habitat	Plains and plateaus of the Snake River.
Food	Aquatic insects, diatoms.
Reproduction	Lays single round to oval eggs on hard surfaces throughout the year.
Threats	Drought, mining of aquifer system, cattle grazing.
Range	Idaho

Description

The Bruneau Hot springsnail, *Pyrgulopsis bruneauensis*, has a small, globose to low-conic shell as an adult. The shell is 5.5 millimeters with 3.75 to 4.25 whorls. Fresh shells are thin, transparent, white-clear, with a black appearance attributed to pigmentation. Other distinguishing features include a verge with a small lobe bearing a single distal glandular ridge and elongate, muscular filament.

Behavior

The hermaphroditic reproduction of this species involves the exchange of spermatophores. Courtship entails investigation using tentacles and mouths. Slowly edging closer the snails rear up at right angles to the ground with the bases of their feet in full contact. Supported by the tip of their shells and the hind part of the feet, the male and female open their orifices while caressing each other with their tentacles. This species lays single round to oval eggs on hard surfaces such as rock. They may deposit eggs on other snails' shells when other hard surfaces are unavailable. Sexual maturity can occur at two months. Reproduction occurs throughout the year except when inhibited by high or low temperatures.

Habitat

Bruneau Hot springsnail occupies the Snake River Plains/Sagebrush ecosystem. This ecosystem occurs primarily on the Columbia Plateaus in the northwestern states and the central portion of the Great Basin, including Utah, Nevada, southern Idaho, parts of Wyoming and Colorado. This broad ecosystem occupies plains and plateaus derived from lava flows, ancient lake beds, and broad basins of alluvium. In Idaho nearly half of this area is federally owned; the remainder is in farms and ranches. Most of the federally owned land is rangeland. Forage production is low, and annual grasses have invaded much of the rangeland. The plains bordering the Snake River and its tributaries, are irrigated. Potatoes, grain, sugar beets, beans, and alfalfa hay are the principal crops. The elevation in this area ranges from 600 to 1,700 meters. These nearly level to steeply sloping lava plains have a thin to moderately thick cover of silt. In places, the river is quite deep giving way to steep-walled canyons. Alluvial fans, terraces, and bottom land are gently sloping to moderately sloping. The average annual precipitation for this area is 175 to 325 millimeters. There is little or no precipitation in the summer, attributing to seasonal droughts. The dominant soils associated are Orthids, Argids, and Orthents. They have a mesic temperature regime. This area supports shrub-grass vegetation. Big sagebrush, winterfat, shadscale, Indian ricegrass, needle-and-thread, Thurber needle grass, and Sandberg blue grass grow on the lower Snake River Plains.

Also associated to this species' distribution is the Owyhee High Plateau. This region is characterized by rolling plateaus in gently sloping basins ranging in elevation from 1,400 to 2,300 meters. Alluvial deposits are found along the Bruneau River. The soils are Xeroll. They are deep to shallow, medium textured to fine textured soils and have a mesic, frigid, or cryic temperature regime. This area supports shrub-grass vegetation characterized by big sagebrush or low sagebrush.

Most of the springs and seeps containing Bruneau Hot springsnail are small (0.15 square meters to 37 square meters) in area. These sites are located above the high-water mark of the Bruneau River and are separated by distances of less than one meter. The species is found in flowing thermal springs and seeps with temperature regimes of 15.7 to 35.7 degrees Celsius. The highest density per square meter of snails was at a locality with temperatures ranging from 24.8 to 35.7 degrees Celsius. This species attaches itself to exposed surfaces of various substrates, including rocks, gravel, sand, mud, and algal film. During the winter, however, the springsnail is most often located on the underside of outflow substrates, habitats least exposed to cold temperatures. In madicolous habitats the species has been found in water depths less than one centimeter. Bruneau Hot springsnail has been found in 100 percent of the current velocity regimes.

Historic Range and Current Distribution

The Bruneau Hot springsnail is only found in the springflows of Hot Creek and small, slowing thermal springs and seeps along 8.5 kilometers of the Bruneau River. The type locality (Indian Bathtub in Hot Creek) and most of the springs along the Bruneau River upstream of Hot Creek are on lands administered by the Bureau of Land Management. Lands downstream of the Indian Bathtub and Hot Creek are on private land.

Conservation and Recovery

The major threat to Bruneau Hot springsnail is the reduction or reduced water levels in thermal spring habitats from ground water withdrawal/mining of the regional geothermal aquifer system. Within the past 25 years, flows from the Indian Bathtub springs has decreased. This has in effect restricted this species' habitat area and has, therefore, reduced its numbers. Studies indicate that recharge prior to ground water development in the Bruneau-Grandview area equalled approximately 23,000 acre feet per year, while ground water development pumpage in the area during 1991 was approximately 34,700 acre feet. This indicates that withdrawals exceeded the estimate rate of recharge by nearly 12,000 acre feet during 1991. Studies also indicate that by 1991 *P. bruneauensis* has declined by approximately 50 percent from 1982 estimates. Additionally, ongoing drought conditions since the mid-1980s have resulted in increased use of ground water for irrigation in the Bruneau basin. This has caused the extent of seepage at several of this species' spring sources to be reduced. Habitat has also been lost as a result of sedimentation from flash flooding. This occurs quite often in the Indian Bathtub spring area; heavy sedimentations of gravel, sand, and silt were reported in 1992 to cover over and eliminate the species' remaining habitat in the Indian Bathtub and upper Hot Creek.

Cattle grazing also impacts habitats, especially those along Hot Creek. Cattle trample instream substrates and habitats causing direct mortalities and displacement. Cattle also browse and remove riparian vegetation that shades Hot Creek, allowing temperatures to rise, and this in turn affects reproduction and could be lethal. Lastly, livestock grazing in an adjacent watershed in combination with the ongoing drought has resulted in a denuding of soils and vegetation to such an extent that flash floods dump sediment into Hot Creek that has covered over and totally eliminated much seep and spring habitats.

Recreational activities may also affect this species. Bathers create temporary dams to form thermal pools and improved conditions for bathing. These pools modify habitat and remove essential substrates. These pools also alter and destroy the madicolous algal habitats preferred by Bruneau Hot springsnail.

Conservation measures provided to species listed as endangered or threatened pursuant to the Act include recognition, recovery actions, requirements for Federal protection, and prohibitions against certain practices. Recognition through listing encourages conservation measures by Federal, international, and private agencies, groups, and individuals.

The Bureau of Land Management will most likely be subject to consultation prior to issuance of livestock grazing permits and granting authorizations that would lead to drilling of new wells or increased ground water use.

Bibliography

U.S. Fish and Wildlife Service. 1993. "Endangered and Threatened Wildlife and Plants; Determination of Endangered Status for the Bruneau Hot springsnail in Southwestern Idaho." *Federal Register* Vol. 58, No. 14: 5938-5946.

Contacts

Boise Ecological Services Field Office
4696 Overland Road, Room 576
Boise, ID 83705
Phone: 208-334-1931
FAX: 208-334-9493

Adapted from data compiled by the Threatened and Endangered Species Information Institute (13950 W. 20th Ave., Golden, CO 80401) for *Beacham's International Threatened, Endangered, and Extinct Species* published on CD ROM, available from Beacham Publishing.

Bliss Rapids Snail
Undescribed

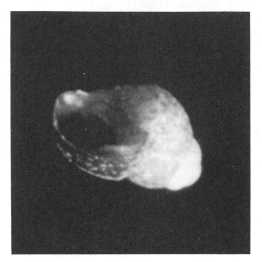

Status	Threatened
Listed	December 14, 1992
Family	Hydrobiidae (Springsnail)
Description	Colorless or orange-red snail with smaller rounded whorls.
Habitat	Free-flowing cool spring alcoves.
Food	Plant debris or diatoms.
Reproduction	Egg laying occurs with 2 months of reproduction.
Threats	Deteriorating water quality from hydroelectric development, competition with other snails.
Range	Idaho

Description

The Bliss Rapids snail, an undescribed member of the Hydrobiidae family, is a "living fossil." This is due to the fact that it is a relict from ancient lakes. The Bliss Rapids snail is a survivor of the late Pliocene (Blancan) Lake Idaho.

This snail is 0.8 to 0.10 inches long with three whorls and is roughly ovoid in shape. There are two color variants or morphs of the Bliss Rapids snail. One is the colorless or "pale form" and the other is the orange-red or "orange form." The pale morph is slightly smaller with rounded whorls with more melanin pigment on the body.

Behavior

Reproduction in the Bliss Rapids snail varies according to habitat; occurring Octo-ber to February in mainstem Snake River colonies and February to May in large-spring colonies. Egg laying occurs within two months of reproduction and eggs appear to hatch within one month. Adult snails exhibit a strong seasonal die off after reproduction. This species is known to migrate only to food sources.

Habitat

The Bliss Rapids snail is restricted to a few isolated free-flowing reaches or spring alcove habitats of the Snake River. This aquatic system is characterized by cold, well-oxygenated, unpolluted water. The Bliss Rapids snail occurs on stable, cobble-boulder substratum only in flowing waters in the Snake River and also in a few spring alcove habitats in the Hagerman Valley. The species does not burrow in sediments and normally avoids surfaces with attached plants. Known river colonies of the Bliss Rapids snail occur only in areas associated with spring influences or rapids edge environments and tend to flank shorelines. Generally, the species requires cold, clean, well-oxygenated flowing water of low turbidity. The species is found at varying depths if dissolved oxygen and temperature requirements persist and is found in shallow, less than .4 inch, permanent cold springs. This snail is thought to be somewhat photophobic and resides on the lateral sides and undersides of rocks during daylight. The species will migrate to graze on perilithon on the uppermost surfaces of rocks nocturnally. The Bliss Rapids snail can be locally quite abundant, and is especially abundant on smooth rock surfaces with common encrusting red algae.

For a continued discussion, see "Aquatic Snails In South Central Idaho," page 2171.

Historic Range

Prior to 1987, the Bliss Rapids snail was known primarily from the mainstem Snake River boulder bars above King Hill and upstream in Box Canyon Springs. Prior to dam construction there was probably a single population throughout the historic range and possibly upstream as well.

Current Distribution

Based on live collections, the species currently exists as fragmented populations primarily concentrated in the Hagerman reach in tailwaters of Bliss and Lower Salmon Dams and Thousand Springs, Minnie Miller Springs, Banbury Springs, Niagara Springs, and Box Canyon Springs. This species occurs on Federally owned lands (Shoshone Bannock Tribal Reservation and lands owned by the Bureau of Land Management). The Bliss Rapids snail is also protected through its occurrence on the Thousand Springs Preserve owned by the Nature Conservancy.

Conservation and Recovery

The free-flowing, cool water environments required by this species have been impacted by and are vulnerable to continued adverse habitat modification and deteriorating water quality from hydroelectric development, peak-loading effects from existing hydroelectric project operations, water withdrawal and diversions, water pollution, and inadequate regulatory mechanisms. The Bliss Rapids snail may also be adversely affected by competition with an exotic snail (*Potamopyrgus antipodarum*). With the exception of segments of land owned by The Nature Conservancy (Thousand Springs), the aquatic habitats occupied by this species are virtually unprotected from the aforementioned threats.

The lotic fauna of the middle Snake River has been declining for several years due to fragmentation of remaining free-flowing habitats and deteriorating water quality. Hydroelectric development throughout the Snake River has directly impacted species through inundation of lotic habitats, isolating segmented populations, and impacting suitable shallow water shoreline habitat from project-caused flow fluctuations. Water quality degradation continues from increased water use and withdrawal, aggravated by recent drought induced low flows. The ultimate impact of these factors are increased nutrient loads and concentrations which adversely affect the lotic fauna. Nutrient loading contributes to dense blooms of free-living and attached filamentous algae, which the species cannot utilize. This algae will often cover rock surfaces, effectively displacing suitable snail habitats and food resources. Stream sediments will also become anoxic as high biochemical oxygen demand during the aquatic growing season and seasonal algae die-offs occur.

A more recent threat is the discovery of the New Zealand mudsnail in the middle Snake River. The eurytopic mudsnail is experiencing explosive growth in the river and shows a wide range of tolerance for water fluctuations, velocity, temperature and turbidity. The mudsnail species seems to prefer warmer, polluted waters over pristine cold spring environments. This species has already been observed to form dark mats of individuals in habitat formerly preferred by the Bliss Rapids snail. Potamopygus has been observed at densities of nearly 400 individuals per square inch. This species is parthenogenic and ovoviparous, which contributes to the ability to build large populations rapidly and recover from population crashes. The species is eurytopic and shows very little preference for substrate type or size.

Ground water mining or withdrawal may also impact spring stream habitats of the Bliss Rapids snail population above American Falls Reservoir. Biologists of the Shoshone Bannock Tribal Reservation have observed water fluctuations and seasonal declines in spring flows along this stretch of the Snake River concurrent with the irrigation season. Winter cattle grazing and recreational access may also be impacting spring habitats of the Bliss Rapids snail on the Shoshone Bannock Reservation. Although access is controlled, waterfowl hunters, and to some extent fishermen, utilize these spring areas throughout the fall and early winter.

Changes in the use of stored water in the Snake River basin to assist recovery efforts for other threatened and endangered species may also impact this species and its habitat. The Bonneville Power Administration, State of Idaho, and Idaho Power Company are exploring alternatives to assist outmigrating endangered Snake River Sockeye salmon and threatened Spring and Summer Chinook from utilizing water from the upper Snake River Basin. The Idaho Department of Health and Welfare, Division of Environmental Quality, under authority of the State Nutrient Management Act, is coordinating efforts to identify and implement preventative actions which will reduce nutrient loading to the middle Snake River. These efforts will address pollution control strategies.

For a continued discussion, see "Aquatic Snails In South Central Idaho," page 2171.

Bibliography

U.S. Fish and Wildlife Service. "Endangered and Threatened Wildlife and Plants; Determination of Endangered or Threatened Status for Five Aquatic Snails in South Central Idaho." *Federal Register.* Vol. 57, No. 240. December 14, 1992: 59244-59257.

Contacts

U.S. Fish and Wildlife Service
Eastside Federal Complex
911 N.S. 11th Avenue
Portland, OR 97232-4181
Phone: 503-231-6118

Boise Ecological Services Field Office
4696 Overland Road, Room 576
Boise, ID 83705
Phone: 208-334-1931
FAX: 208-334-9493

Adapted from data compiled by the Threatened and Endangered Species Information Institute (13950 W. 20th Ave., Golden, CO 80401) for *Beacham's International Threatened, Endangered, and Extinct Species* published on CD ROM, available from Beacham Publishing.

Utah Valvata Snail

Valvata utahensis

Status	Endangered
Listed	December 14, 1992
Family	Valvatidae (Valvata)
Description	Small four-whorled snail with a dull to glossy shell.
Habitat	Free-flowing cool spring alcoves of the Snake River.
Food	Plant debris or diatoms.
Reproduction	Eggs hatch outside the body.
Threats	Deteriorating water quality from hydroelectric development, competition with other snails.
Range	Idaho

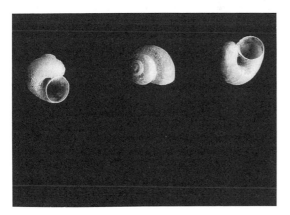

Stephen D. Duke

Description

The Utah valvata snail, like other members of the Valvatidae family, is distinguished by a conically spiraled shell that is wider than high with up to four whorls. This snail is 4.5 millimeters long. The luster of the shell is dull to glossy, and the aperture is mostly rounded. The umbilicus (depression) is usually clearly defined and is smooth or has fine spiral striae.

The tonguelike organ is short; a central tooth is widened basally and bears a triangular medial cusp and marginal serrations; the lateral tooth is fairly long, lacks lateral expansion and is multicuspid; the marginal teeth are also denticulate, usually with a distinct central cusp. Valvata possess a single pair of salivary glands, which are long and irregularly cylindrical.

Behavior

Valvatidae are hermaphroditic (both sexes), but probably rarely use self-fertilization. Valvata produce eggs that hatch outside the body; the egg capsules occur in gelatinous masses, and the free larval stage is suppressed.

This species is restricted to a diet of diatoms and plant debris which it grazes along mud surfaces, rocky surfaces and macrophytes.

Habitat

The Utah valvata snail is restricted to a few isolated free-flowing reaches or spring alcove habitats of the Snake River. This aquatic system is characterized by cold, well-oxygenated, unpolluted water. This species lives in deep pools adjacent to rapids or in perennial flowing waters associated with large spring complexes. It avoids areas with heavy currents or rapids. The snail prefers well-oxygenated areas of non-reducing calcareous mud or mud-sand substrate among beds of submergent aquatic vegetation. The species is absent from pure gravel boulder bottoms. A common associate is Chara, which concentrates both calcium carbonate and silicon oxide.

For a continued discussion, see "Aquatic Snails In South Central Idaho," page 2171.

Historic Range

This species historically occupied the Snake River from Grandview to just above Thousand Springs with a disjunct population in the American Falls Dam tailwater near Eagle Rock damsite. This taxa was also known from northern Utah.

Current Distribution

This species is believed to be extirpated from Utah. Parts of the species' habitat are owned by the State of Idaho and the Bureau of Land Management. This species also inhabits privately owned lands, including Thousand Springs Preserve. The Utah valvata snail is restricted to the Snake River from C. J. Strike Reservoir upstream to Milner Dam in Cassia and Twin Falls Counties, Idaho.

Conservation and Recovery

The free-flowing, cool water environments required by this species have been impacted by and are vulnerable to continued adverse habitat modification and deteriorating water quality from hydroelectric development, peak-loading effects from existing hydroelectric project operations, water withdrawal and diversions, water pollution, and inadequate regulatory mechanisms.

Water quality degradation continues from increased water use and withdrawal, aggravated by recent drought induced low flows. The 121 mile stretch of the Snake River is impacted by agricultural return flows; runoff from between 500 and 600 dairies and feedlots; effluent from over 140 private, state, and Federal fish culture facilities; and point source (e.g. municipal sewage) discharge. The ultimate impact of these factors are increased nutrient loads and concentrations which adversely affect the lotic fauna. Nutrient loading contributes to dense blooms of free-living and attached filamentous algae, which the species cannot utilize. This algae will often cover rock surfaces, effectively displacing suitable snail habitats and food resources. Stream sediments will also become anoxic as high biochemical oxygen demand during the aquatic growing season and seasonal algae die-offs occur.

A more recent threat is the discovery of the New Zealand mudsnail in the middle Snake River. The eurytopic mudsnail is experiencing explosive growth in the river and shows a wide range of tolerance for water fluctuations, velocity, temperature and turbidity. The mudsnail species seems to prefer warmer, polluted waters over pristine cold spring environments.

For a continued discussion, see "Aquatic Snails In South Central Idaho," page 2171.

Bibliography

U.S. Fish and Wildlife Service. "Endangered and Threatened Wildlife and Plants; Determination of Endangered or Threatened Status for Five Aquatic Snails in South Central Idaho." *Federal Register.* Vol. 57, No. 240. December 14, 1992: 59244-59257.

Contacts

Boise Ecological Services Field Office
4696 Overland Road, Room 576
Boise, ID 83705
Phone: 208-334-1931
FAX: 208-334-9493

Adapted from data compiled by the Threatened and Endangered Species Information Institute (13950 W. 20th Ave., Golden, CO 80401) for *Beacham's International Threatened, Endangered, and Extinct Species* published on CD ROM, available from Beacham Publishing.

Cave Crayfish

Cambarus aculabrum

Kristine A. Herbert   *Color Plate C-6*

Status	Endangered
Listed	April 27, 1993
Family	Cambaridae (Crayfish)
Description	Small, white obligate cave-dwelling crayfish with no pigment and reduced eyes.
Habitat	Along walls or edges of cave pools.
Food	Unknown, but probably roots, stems, and leaf fragments.
Reproduction	Egg laying likely occurs in late winter and early spring.
Threats	Depletion of oxygenated water.
Range	Arkansas

Description

The cave crayfish is a small, white obligate cave-dwelling crayfish. The body length of this species has been measured to reach up to 48 millimeters. This species has no pigment and has reduced eyes. It also has an acute or subacute apex of the antermomedian lobe of the epistome.

First form males are distinguished by a fully formed and hardened first pleopod. These males can be further distinguished from closely related *C. setosus* and *C. tartarus* by the absence of a transverse groove separating the proximolateral love from the shaft on the first pleopod. It differs from *C. zophanaster* in that it possesses a longer central projection of the first pleopod that also has a shallow subapical notch.

Behavior

The reproductive habits of this species, as well and other sociobiological information, is not known at this time. This species, however, displays similar reproductive characteristics of other decopods. The males probably begin molting into the reproductive state in late summer with copulation occurring in late summer and fall. Egg laying likely occurs in late winter and early spring. Most males molt back to the nonreproductive form during April.

Habitat

The cave crayfish inhabits an Ozarkain solution channel located in the Mississippian cherty-limestone Boone Formation. A stream runs through the entire length of this 2,000 meter cave. This cave also contains a lake that was formed by the collapse of the cave roof. Water exits the cave approximately 300 meters from the lake. This species also occurs in another solution tunnel containing a small stream.

The cave crayfish is most commonly found along the walls of the pool, or along stream edges.

Historic Range and Current Distribution

The type locality of this species is Logan Cave as well as its associated stream and lake. The cave crayfish is also known from nearby Bear Hollow Cave and its associated stream. Both of these areas are located in Benton County, Arkansas.

As life history information pertaining to this particular species is limited, accurate population numbers are still unknown. In a 1990 survey of Logan Cave, lake, and stream, three individuals were seen, one already dead. In this same survey a single crayfish was identified in the Bear Hollow Cave stream. No survey has resulted in sightings of more then nineteen and many yield no sighting.

In an observation of other cave crayfish and troglobitic species, small population sizes have been a result of reduced food sources. As an adaptation to this it has also been observed that these species display a lower metabolic rate, increased longevity, delayed maturity and reproduction and decreased fecundity. The otherwise adaptive characteristic could make the cave crayfish highly vulnerable to environmental pollution and limit this species' ability to recover.

Conservation and Recovery

Conservation measures provided to species listed as endangered or threatened pursuant to the Act include recognition, recovery actions, requirements for Federal protection, and prohibitions against certain practices. Recognition through listing encourages conservation measures by Federal, international, and private agencies, groups, and individuals.

In 1989 the U.S. Fish and Wildlife Service purchased 123.9 acres at Logan Cave (the cave crayfish's original locality). This attempt will facilitate preservation activities initiated by USFWS. The rest of the area, however, is privately owned.

A collecting permit is required for collecting for any species, except for fish bait under State regulations. Troglobites are protected from possession and sale by Arkansas State law.

Potential conservation measures and federal involvement are expected to include:

(1) Environmental Protection Agency: Clean Water Act's provisions for pesticide registration and waste management actions.
(2) Corps of Engineers: Inclusion of the cave crayfish in project planning and operation and during permit review.
(3) Federal Highway Administration : Consideration of the cave crayfish in bridge and road construction in known areas of occupance.
(4) Farmers Home Administration: Consideration of impacts of the cave crayfish in loan processes.
(5) Soil Conservation Service: Inclusion of the cave crayfish in farmer's assistance programs.

Bibliography

U.S. Fish and Wildlife Service. 1993. "Endangered and Threatened Wildlife and Plants; Determination of Endangered

Status Determined for the Cave Crayfish (*Cambarus aculabrum*)." *Federal Register* Vol. 58, No. 79. April 27, 1993: 25742-25746.

Contacts

U.S. Fish and Wildlife Service
Regional Office
Suite 200, 1875 Century Blvd.
Atlanta, GA 30345
Phone: 404-679-4000

Adapted from data compiled by the Threatened and Endangered Species Information Institute (13950 W. 20th Ave., Golden, CO 80401) for *Beacham's International Threatened, Endangered, and Extinct Species* published on CD ROM, available from Beacham Publishing.

Riverside Fairy Shrimp

Streptocephalus woottoni

Status	Endangered
Listed	August 3, 1993
Family	Streptocephalidae (Freshwater crustacean)
Description	Small freshwater crustacean with a red color on the ninth and eighth abdominal.
Habitat	Vernal pools in areas with Mediterranean climates.
Food	Plankton, algae, small crustaceans.
Reproduction	Eggs are hatched into larvae.
Threats	Habitat loss.
Range	California

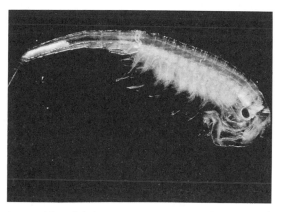

S. texanus (close relative)   Bruce Farnsworth

Description

The Riverside fairy shrimp is a small freshwater crustacean. Both males and females have a red color covering all of the ninth and 30 to 40 percent of the eighth abdominal segments. Mature males are between 0.56 inches and 0.92 inches in length. The frontal appendage is cylindrical, double-lobed at the tip, and extends only part way to the distal end of the basal segment of the antenna. The spur of the thumb is a simple blade-like process. The finger has two teeth; the proximal tooth is shorter than the distal tooth. The distal tooth has a lateral shoulder that is equal to about half the tooth's total length measured along the proximal edge. The brood pouch extends to abdominal segments 7, 8, or 9. The cercopods are as in the male.

Behavior

The species begins life from resting eggs from which they are hatched into a larvae stage after which there are dozens of molts before an individual reaches maturity. Even as adults, they continue to molt throughout their lives.

The species is for the most part a filter-feeder. They feed on plankton and algae. Yet, they also may eat particles ranging in size from algae to small crustaceans. Thus, the species is omnivorous.

This species most likely shows seasonal variations in activity related to reproduction and changes in temperature regime.

Habitat

The species occurs in vernal pools which form in areas with Mediterranean climates where slight depressions become seasonally wet or inundated following fall and winter rains. Water remains in these pools for a few months at a time, due to an impervious layer such as hard pan, clay, or basalt beneath the soil surface. Gradual drying occurs during the spring. The pools form on mesa tops or valley floors and are interspersed among very low hills usually referred to as mima mounds.

A number of studies were conducted on vernal pools in San Diego County, California. For mapping and description purposes, a standardized system was developed for the designation of these vernal pools. A series letter is used to denote vernal pools in a general region, and numbers are used to designate several pool groups within the series. This species is known to occur within two pool series in San Diego.

For a continued discussion of the shrimp's habitat, see "Vernal Pool Habitats in San Diego County, California," page 1761.

Historic Range and Current Distribution

The species is known from four vernal pools in a 37 square mile area in southwestern Riverside County, California, and from one population in Orange County, California. In San Diego County in the fall of 1989, the species was discovered within vernal pools on Miramar Naval Air Station and Otay Mesa. However, since the 1989 discovery of the species in San Diego County, numerous vernal pool complexes in the county have been surveyed without additional populations being found. The species was also found at two locations in Baja, California, Mexico in the past.

Conservation and Recovery

The habitat and range of this species has been greatly reduced. Vernal pools, existing as slight depressions on flat mesas, are found in locations that are especially vulnerable to one or more of the following habitat disturbances: urban and agricultural development, off-road vehicle use, cattle trampling, human trampling, road development, military activities, and water management activities. Many pool groups were entirely eliminated and replaced with urban or agricultural developments.

The vernal pool habitat upon which this species depends is also vulnerable to destruction due to alteration of the watershed. In some cases, an increase in pool water volume due to urban run-off has led to more prolonged periods of inundation, and at the other extreme, some pools have been drained or blocked from their source of water.

Pools have also been degraded due to the use of off-road vehicles, which have impacted the habitats of this species. These vehicles compact soils, crush plants when water is in the pools, cause turbidity, and leave deep ruts. The damage may alter the microhydrology of the pools. Dirt roads that go through or adjacent to pools are widened as motorists try to avoid the inevitable mud puddles. Thus, pools are gradually destroyed by vehicles traveling on dirt roads. Vehicle access and damage has occurred on virtually all remaining vernal pool complexes.

Preliminary designs by the California Department of Transportation for a state route running near this species' habitat include alignments that sever the existing natural connection between two of the largest remaining vernal pool complexes on Otay Mesa. The construction of this new major highway access route into Otay Mesa would further facilitate its development.

An existing local airport is presently being evaluated as a potential site for an international airport servicing San Diego. This proposal includes alternative runway alignments that would destroy portions of one of the two largest remaining vernal pool complexes. A binational airport is also being considered for Otay Mesa, although these plans are too preliminary to allow assessment of potential impacts to vernal pools. An increase in the number of vehicle trips in this area would occur as a result of the airport, and this increased traffic would likely lead to a demand for more roads, which could directly impact the pools.

Habitat trampling, and in some cases trampling of the species itself, due to livestock grazing occurs on Otay Mesa in areas where several vernal pool complexes collectively contain all four of the proposed species. Organisms within the pools may be trampled and killed by livestock prior to reproduction. Soil may become compacted or eroded, and water may be impacted with sediment.

Otay Mesa is a common area for travel from Mexico to the United States; hence, habitat and plants are threatened with trampling by humans. Also, the Immigration and Naturalization Service has proposed several projects at the international border, including border lighting, that could result in direct adverse impacts to vernal pools on Otay Mesa, due to construction activities.

The species has very narrow habitat requirements. It is only found in deep lowland pools that retain water through the warmer weather of late spring. It will not hatch in pools that receive cool waters from early winter rains, such as those pools on the Santa Rosa Plateau, nor will they hatch in shallow pools.

It is vulnerable to land use changes affecting the small number of pools that meet the species' strict habitat requirements. Of the four remaining pools supporting the species in Riverside County, only one is greater than one acre in size. This pool is within a planned development. Other sites supporting the species may lack some of the topical vegetation of vernal pools, but that condition probably reflects impacts from past agricultural activities. One pool is located within an approved tract for a housing development.

A third pool is on a parcel that is currently proposed for a housing development, adjacent to a golf course. This pool is in an agricultural field and was disced. The Environmental Impact Report prepared by a consultant for the developer of this project failed to acknowledge the existence of the species on the site. Representatives of the landowner expressed a willingness to offer some protection for this site. However, as discussed above, a currently proposed road project would impact the pool.

A fourth pool that contains this species is located partially on private land and partially on an Indian reservation. The portion on private land was cultivated during 1990. The region's drought conditions over the last two to three years may have rendered the pool dry enough to be plowed. A fifth pool was recently converted into a gravel pit. Only one documented population occurs in Orange County.

Other factors have greatly impacted the existence of this species, including introduction of non-native plant species, competition with invading species, trash dumping, fire, fire suppression activities, and drought. The low numbers of vernal pool habitats remaining and their scattered distributions make this species vulnerable to extinction due to future events that are unpredictable, human, or naturally caused.

Many vernal pools on Otay Mesa are dominated by non-native plants such as the common grass *Lolinm perenne*. This species is tolerant of inundation and crowds out the native vernal pool species. Ranchers introduced non-native species into some areas to increase the amount of forage available to livestock. Excessive cover of weedy non-native grasses was noted in six of the pool groups and partially explained two extirpations of *P. nudruscula.*

Trash dumping also degrades vernal pools. Chunks of concrete, tires, refrigerators, sofas, and other pieces of garbage or debris were found in pools containing this species. This trash crushes, or shades vernal pool plants, disrupts the hydrologic functions of the pool, and in some cases may release toxic substances.

Bibliography

Thorp, James H., and Alan P. Covich, eds. *Ecology and Classification of North American Freshwater Invertebrates.* New York: Academic Press, 1991: 765-769.

U.S. Fish and Wildlife Service. "Endangered and Threatened Wildlife and Plants; Endangered Status the Riverside Fairy Shrimp." *Federal Register* Vol. 58, No. 147. August 3, 1993: 41384-41391.

Contacts

U.S. Fish and Wildlife Service
Regional Office
Eastside Federal Complex
911 N.S. 11th Avenue
Portland, OR 97232-4181
Phone: 503-231-6118

Ecological Services Field Office
Room E-1803/1823
2800 Cottage Way
Sacramento, CA 98525
Phone: 916-978-4866

Adapted from data compiled by the Threatened and Endangered Species Information Institute (13950 W. 20th Ave., Golden, CO 80401) for *Beacham's International Threatened, Endangered, and Extinct Species* published on CD ROM, available from Beacham Publishing.

Lee County Cave Isopod
Lirceus usdagalun

Lynda Richardson

Status	Endangered
Listed	November 20, 1992
Family	Cirolanidae (Cave Isopod)
Description	Eyeless, unpigmented crustacean-like isopod.
Habitat	Subterranean freshwater pools.
Food	Detritus.
Threats	Habitat disturbance, pollution.
Range	Virginia

Description

The Lee County cave isopod is an eyeless, unpigmented crustacean-like species measuring 0.2 to 0.3 inches in length. The body is about 64 percent longer than wide, and the head is about one-third as long as wide, with deep incisions on its lateral margins.

Behavior

Unlike most other members of its genus, the Lee County cave isopod has adapted to a totally subterranean aquatic existence.

This isopod is undoubtedly a food item in the diet of certain natural predators, including cave salamanders and possibly cave crayfish.

Specific food items eaten by this isopod are unknown. However, it is believed that this species feeds on decaying organic matter consisting of deciduous leaf litter, twigs and other wood particles. Parts from dead insects, presumably from decomposition of epigean insects that wash into the aquifer, are also eaten. It is also likely that this species feeds on bacteria, fungi and other microorganisms associated with the organic matter.

Habitat

The area the Lee County cave isopod inhabits is riddled with caves, sinks and ravines in a water-soluble limestone substrate (karst). Such areas are particularly susceptible to contamination of groundwater from surface contaminants leaching through the porous substrate.

Historic Range

This isopod was known historically from two cave systems, located approximately six miles apart, in Lee County, Virginia.

Current Distribution

The Lee County cave isopod is known to occur in only one cave in Lee County, Virginia. Since the discovery of *L. usdagalun* in 1971, biologists have conducted intensive searches of caves in Lee and surrounding counties with the specific goal of finding any additional populations of this species. Although these searches have revealed no additional populations of *L. usdagalun*, other isopod species of the genus *Lirceus* have been located in some other caves. When other species fill *L. usdagalum's* ecological niche in a closed cave ecosystem, there is virtually no chance of finding *L. usdagalum*.

Conservation and Recovery

This isopod was extirpated by groundwater pollution from one of the two cave systems it originally occupied. This pollution resulted when large quantities of sawdust, the by-product of a sawmill operation, were piled on the ground surface over the cave. Rainwater leached tannins and other toxins from the sawdust and transferred these through the porous substrate into the underlying groundwater, stripping oxygen from the water. Prior to its extirpation, a study comparing the populations in the two caves discovered that the populations differed in many ways. The unique characteristics of the extirpated population have been lost to the species forever.

The Lee County cave isopod could be adversely affected by an increase in human foot traffic through the cave, which could increase siltation in the streams it occupies. Presently, the location of the cave is not widely known, which led USFWS to determine not to designate critical habitat.

Bibliography

Holsinger, J. R. 1979. *Freshwater and terrestrial arthropods freshwater and terrestrial isopod crustaceans (order Isopoda). Proc. of symp. on endangered and threatened plants and animals in Virginia.* Virginia Polytechnic Institute & State University, Blacksburg.

Contacts

U.S. Fish and Wildlife Service
Annapolis Field Office
1825 Virginia Street
Annapolis, MD 21401
410-269-5448

Adapted from data compiled by Beacham Publishing for *Beacham's International Threatened, Endangered, and Extinct Species* published on CD ROM.

INSECTS AND ARACHNIDS

Coffin Cave Mold Beetle

Batrisodes texanus

Alan Eaton

Status	Endangered
Listed	August 18, 1993
Family	Psfor sphidae (Mold Beetle)
Description	Small, long-legged eyeless beetle with no metathoracic wings and a smooth, curved flat head.
Habitat	Limestone caves, sinkholes, and other subterranean voids.
Food	Eggs, feces, nymphs and dead body parts.
Threats	Land development, pollution, and fire ants.
Range	Texas

Description

The Coffin Cave mold beetle is a small, long-legged eyeless beetle with short elytra leaving five abdominal tergites which are exposed. It has no metathoracic wings. The body length of this species is measured at 2.60 to 2.88 millimeters. The males possess a vague groove across the head anterior to the antennal bases. The lateral sides of the head are smooth, curved and flat. A few granules are observed where one might think the eyes should be.

Behavior

Sexual dimorphism is observed in that the female lacks the transverse impression anterior to the antennal bases. The tenth antennal segment is somewhat wider and longer than the ninth. In males the tenth antennal seg-

ment is twice as wide as the ninth.

The Coffin Cave mold beetle is a troglobite. A troglobite is a species which spends its entire life in openings underground usually with small or absent eyes, attenuated appendages, and other adaptations to its subsurface dwelling.

Habitat

This species spends its entire life underground. It is endemic to the karst (limestone) formations. These formations include caves, sinkholes, and other subterranean voids. It is dependent on outside moisture and nutrient inputs generated from the subsurface. This species inhabits areas of the cave where temperature and humidity are constant.

The surface vegetation ranges from pasture land to mature oak-juniper woodland.

Karst is formed by the slow dissolution of

calcium carbonate from limestone bedrock by mildly acidic ground water. This process results in subterranean voids resembling a honeycomb. The water enters the subsurface through cracks, crevices, and other openings, dissolving soluble beds of rock.

Nutrients to this ecosystem are provided from the outside surface washed in. These nutritional sources include plant material, feces, eggs and carrion. Cave crickets are believed to provide an important component to the nutritional balance of this cave ecosystem. These crickets introduce nutrients through eggs, feces, nymphs and dead body parts on which many invertebrates are known to feed.

Historic Range and Current Distribution

As this species was not described until 1992, its past distribution is not known. This species occurs in two caves in the North Williamson County karst fauna region and three caves in the Georgetown karst fauna region in Williamson County, Texas.

Conservation and Recovery

The primary threat to the Coffin Cave mold beetle is habitat loss due to urban development activities. Continued urban expansion such as residential subdivisions, schools, golf courses, roads, commercial and industrial facilities, etc. poses a threat in the form of cave filling or collapse, water diversion, vegetation/fauna alteration, and increased pollution.

Some caves have already been filled as a result of road construction and building site preparation. Development directly above caves could result in the collapse of cave ceilings.

Ranchers may have also filled some caves. Justification is placed in reducing hiding places for predators of cattle and goats as well as preventing these animals from falling into the formations.

Troglobites rely upon and in fact require a controlled environment of high humidity and constant temperature. If water drainage paths are altered, this balance is no longer on an even keel. Water diversion away from the caves could lead to the direct mortality of this species. Increased water infiltration could lead to flooding and loss of air space.

As the karst ecosystem relies on the infiltration of nutrients from the surface, a fluctuation in the vegetation or fauna would alter nutrient supplies. During development, native vegetation may be replaced with non-native species, as well as cause the introduction of exotic animal species, such as fire ants. An overall nutrient depletion would result. The removal of vegetation could also lead to temperature fluctuations, a change in moisture regime and potential for contamination and increased sedimentation from soil erosion.

Bibliography

U.S. Fish and Wildlife Service. "Endangered and Threatened Wildlife and Plants; Coffin Cave Mold Beetle (*Batrisodes texanus*) and the Bone Cave Harvestman (*Texella reyesi*) Determined to Be Endangered." *Federal Register* Vol. 58, No. 158: 43818-43819.

Contacts

U.S. Fish and Wildlife Service
Regional Office
P. O. Box 1306
Albuquerque, NM 87103
Phone: 505-766-2321
FAX: 505-766-8063

Hungerford's Crawling Water Beetle

Brychius hungerfordi

USFWS

Status	Endangered
Listed	March 7, 1994
Family	Haliplidae (Water Beetle)
Description	Small, distinctive, yellowish brown beetle.
Habitat	Cool riffles of clean streams with an inorganic substrate.
Food	Herbivorous.
Reproduction	Larvae probably go through three instar phases and pupate in the moist soil above the water line.
Threats	Modification of habitat due to human activity; over-collecting; limited numbers.
Range	Michigan

Description

Hungerford's crawling water beetle is a small (4.2 millimeter), distinctive, yellowish brown beetle with irregular dark markings and longitudinal stripes over the elytra, each of which is comprised of a series of fine, closely spaced and darkly pigmented punctures. Males tend to be smaller than females.

In Spangler's (1954) original study, specimens ranged from 3.7 millimeters in length and 1.9 millimeters in width (a male) to 4.35 millimeters in length and 2.25 millimeters in width (a female). Males are characterized by thickened tarsal segments of the front legs with small tufts of hair on the first three segments. This species can be differentiated from all other *Haliplidae* in Michigan by the shape of its pronotum (dorsal plate of the thorax), the sides of which are nearly parallel for the basal two-thirds and are widened mid-laterally.

Behavior

Hungerford's crawling water beetle is thought to live longer than one year and to overwinter as larvae in the dense aquatic vegetation at the stream's edge. As with other Haliplidae, larvae probably go through three instar phases and pupate in the moist soil above the water line. Adults and larvae are seldom captured together, and they appear to inhabit different microhabitats in the stream. Adults are more apt to be found in stronger currents, foraging for algae on gravel and stone.

Compared to other *Haliplidae*, the adults are strong swimmers, and they obtain oxygen by swimming to the surface or crawling to the water line at the edge of the stream. Larvae obtain oxygen directly from the water and are found in association with dense mats of vegetation which offer protection and foraging. The growth form of this vegetative cover may be more important than the plant composition. Both adults and larvae are herbivorous but little is known about their specific dietary requirements or feeding adaptations. However, it is likely that they scrape food material from rocks by grasping with their tarsal claws and scraping with their distally flattened and singled notched mandibles which are slightly medially cupped. This speculation is based on observations of the beetles crawling from rock to rock stopping occasionally to grip a rock for varying lengths of time.

There is no evidence that this species has a dispersal flight. No adults have been found at blacklight stations, and the adults seem unusually reluctant to fly. It is possible that if this species disperses by flying, it is during a very brief period of time in the spring. The primary mode of dispersal appears to be movement within the stream.

Habitat

The east branch of the Maple River, which is the site of the largest population of Hungerford's crawling water beetle, is a small stream surrounded by forest with a partially open canopy so sunlight reaches the water. The stream is cool (15 to 20 degrees Celcius) with a relatively fast-flowing current and a substrate of limestone gravel and rock. The forest is intact, the beaver populations are healthy, and their dams function to stabilize water levels so the riffles below the dams remain predictable from year to year.

Historic Range

Although streams in the Great Lakes states, especially Michigan, Wisconsin and Minnesota, have been extensively surveyed during the past 30 years, no additional populations of Hungerford's crawling water beetle have been discovered. The survey resulted in the discovery of the only known population in Canada.

Current Distribution

Although streams in the Great Lakes states, especially Michigan, Wisconsin and Minnesota, have been extensively surveyed during the past 30 years, no additional populations of Hungerford's crawling water beetle have been discovered. The survey resulted in the discovery of the only known population in Canada.

The largest population presently occurs in the East Branch of the Maple River in a pristine portion of stream on the boundary of the University of Michigan Biological Station. Two smaller populations are known from the East Branch of the Black River, Montmorency County, Michigan; and the North Saugeen River at Scone, Bruce County, Ontario.

Conservation and Recovery

Because adult beetles must swim to the surface for air, they are vulnerable to predation by fish, tadpoles and other aquatic insects. The warmer summer water temperatures force the trout population to deeper waters in Lake Kathleen, giving the beetles an opportunity to repopulate.

It appears that human activity in or near the habitat may be speeding up the loss of the species. The removal of existing beaver dams upstream poses a significant threat to the beetle: the downstream side of the beaver dams serve as a riffle and aeration site because they retain sediments and organic material, raise water temperature, and modify nutrient cycling, decomposition dynamics, and riparian zone structure and composition.

Potential threats that may result in modification of the species' habitat include certain fish management activities, such as removal or introduction of fish; stream-side logging and heavy siltation resulting from logging, impoundment, bank stabilization with structures that create an artificial shoreline; stream pollution; and general stream degradation. In Michigan, one site has already been impounded by a dam, and the Ontario site has been impounded upstream.

Given the rate of recreational development and the demands for fish, wildlife, and forest management in northern Michigan, unknown populations of Hungerford's crawling water beetle could be easily extirpated before they are discovered, increasing the need to protect existing populations. Because only three populations of this species are known to exist, loss of even a few individuals could severely affect the continued existence of the species.

Although current scientific research has mostly involved capture and release rather than collecting, the species will continue to draw scientific interest and collection should be regulated. Because of the species' rarity, there is the possibility that amateur scientific collections could occur.

Because all three known populations occur immediately downstream from a roadway, accidental events such as a chemical spill, or the cumulative effects of road salt runoff, pose a threat.

Because of its limited numbers, the beetle faces reduced reproductive vigor and the possibility of stochastic extinction.

At the present time recovery efforts related to these problems are restricted to legal instruments already in force. The Endangered Species Act requires Federal agencies to evaluate their actions with respect to any listed species. The act also prohibits any imports or exports of listed species, or to offer them for sale. Laws also prohibit any malicious damage or removal of species from their habitat. In the case of this species, the Fish and Wildlife Service has not recommended designating Critical Habitat because of the potential of increased pressure put on the species by vandals or hikers.

The most important regulatory control for protecting this species is the issuance of permits that would modify the beetle's habitat.

Bibliography

U. S. Fish and Wildlife Service. "Endangered and Threatened Wildlife and Plants; Determination of Endangered Status for Hungerford's Crawling Water Beetle." *Federal Register* Vol. 59, No. 44. March 7, 1994: 10580-10584.

Contacts

Ecological Services Field Office
U.S. Fish and Wildlife Service
302 Manly Miles Building
1405 South Harrison Road
East Lansing, MI 48823
Phone: 517-337-6650
FAX: 517-337-6899

Adapted from data compiled by Beacham Publishing for *Beacham's International Threatened, Endangered, and Extinct Species* published on CD ROM.

Karner Blue Butterfly

Lycaeides melissa samuelis

Ann B. Swengel

Color Plate C-5

Status	Endangered
Listed	December 14, 1992
Family	Lycaenidae (Gossamer-Winged Butterfly)
Description	Small, silvery-blue (males) or grayish brown and orange (females) butterfly.
Habitat	Sandplains with grassy openings within dry pine/scrub oak barrens.
Host	Wild lupine.
Reproduction	Usually has two broods each year.
Threats	Silviculture, urbanization.
Range	Illinois, Indiana, Michigan, Minnesota, New Hampshire, New York, Wisconsin

Description

The Karner Blue Butterfly has a wingspan of 0.87 to 1.26 inches. The dorsal side of the male is silvery blue or dark blue with narrow black margins. The females are grayish brown dorsally, with irregular bands of orange inside the narrow black border on the upper wings. Both sexes are slate grey on the ventral side with the orange bands showing more regularity, and black spots circled with white.

Behavior

This butterfly usually has two broods each year. Eggs that have overwintered from the previous year hatch in April. The larvae feed on wild lupine leaves and mature rapidly. Near the end of May, they pupate and adult butterflies emerge very late in May in most years. The adults are typically in flight for the first 10 to 15 days of June, when the wild lupine is in bloom. Females lay eggs on or near the wild lupine plants. The eggs hatch in about one week and the larvae feed for about three weeks. Then they pupate, and the second brood adults appear in the second or third week of July. This time, the eggs are laid among plant litter or on grass blades at the base of the lupines, or on lupine pods or stems. By early August, no adults remain, and these eggs do not hatch until the following spring.

The Karner blue butterfly frequently occurs with other rare butterfly species such as the Persius Duskywing (*Erynnis persius*) and the Frosted Elfin (*Incisalia irus*).

The presence of wild lupine is essential to

the occurrence and survival of this species. Unaltered by humans, a pine barren ecosystem is likely to be a mosaic of interspersed woody vegetation, such as pitch pine and scrub oak and more open areas characterized by wild lupine, grasses, and other plants such as spreading dogbane (*Apocynum androsaemifolium*) and New Jersey tea (*Ceanothus americanus*) which serve as nectar for adult butterflies.

Habitat

The habitat of the Karner blue butterfly is characterized by the presence of wild lupine, a member of the pea family. Wild lupine is the only known larval food plant for this butterfly and is, therefore, closely tied to the butterfly's ecology and distribution. In eastern New York and New Hampshire, the habitat typically includes sandplain communities, and grassy openings within very dry, sandy pitch pine/scrub oak barrens. In the Midwest, the habitat is also dry and sandy, including oak savanna and jack pine areas, and dune/sandplain communities. It is believed that this species originally occurred as shifting clusters of populations, or metapopulations, across a vast fire-swept landscape covering thousands of acres. While the fires resulted in localized extirpation, post-fire vegetational succession promoted colonization and rapid population buildups. Periodic disturbance is necessary to maintain openings in the canopy for wild lupine to thrive. A variety of other understory plants associated with the habitat serve as nectar sources for the adult butterflies.

Historic Range

The distribution of this species is very discontinuous, and generally follows the northern limits of wild lupine. Eight major population clusters of the butterfly were known historically from portions of Wisconsin, Michigan, Minnesota, Indiana, Illinois, Ohio, Massachusetts, New Hampshire, Pennsylvania, New York, and Ontario. Over the past 100 years, this species' numbers have apparently declined rangewide by 99 percent or more. Over 90 percent of the decline occurred in the last 10 to 15 years. It is now extirpated from Massachusetts, Pennsylvania, and Ohio.

Current Distribution

The New York Natural Heritage Program maintains a state list of approximately 50 individual Karner blue butterfly sites, comprising about ten site-clusters, all found in the area known as the Albany Pine Bush and at scattered locations extending about 40 miles to the north. Once the site of a massive Karner blue butterfly population, Albany Pine Bush is the locality from which the butterfly was first described. There are also unverified records of this species in Manhattan and Brooklyn from the mid 1800s. A decline of 85 to 98 percent in the Albany Pine Bush over the past decade has been noted, exclusive of one site that has remained stable. The decline in population has been described as dropping from numbers of around 80,000 in 1979, to around 1,000 in 1987, to 100 to 200 in 1990. North of the Albany Pine Bush, one disturbed site located at an airport has persisted with numbers estimated around 14,000 in 1990. This population is several times larger than all the other New York sites combined. The majority of extant Karner blue butterfly sites in New York are in municipal and private ownership. Other landowners include a State Park, The Nature Conservancy, and Saratoga County.

In New Hampshire, the Concord Pine Barrens along the Merrimack River support the only remaining occurrence of this species in New England. The sole population is extremely low in numbers and occurs on a privately owned, two to three acre site within a power line right-of-way bordering an industrial park, and on the grounds of a nearby airport. The results of 1990 surveys reported by The Nature Conservancy showed a decline in the population size from an estimated 2,000 to 3,000 individuals in 1983 to an estimated 250 to 400 individuals in 1990. During that survey, the species was not found at two other sites in the Concord Pine Barrens where it had been documented in 1983.

In Wisconsin, 33 of 36 historical occurrence sites were surveyed during 1990. Survey results revealed that the species was found at only 11 of the 33 historical sites visited. Although 23 previously unknown populations were discovered, the numbers of Karner blue butterfly observed were very small at most sites. Only three sites had 50 or more individuals observed, with none greater than 100. At least half of Wisconsin's populations are small, isolated, and cannot be considered secure or viable in the long term. However, a very good number of quite sizeable populations occur on publicly owned properties offering good opportunities for long-term protection and management. Over three fourths of the Wisconsin sites are on publicly administered lands, including Necedah National Wildlife Refuge, Department of Defense, Wisconsin Department of Natural Resources, and County Forest.

The Karner blue butterfly has declined throughout its range in Michigan. It still occurs in six of seven counties from which it was known historically, but the existing populations are greatly reduced and have become highly fragmented within expanses of suitable habitat.

Surveys in Indiana in 1990 yielded the following results: this species was recon-

firmed at one known site, and was rediscovered on three of seven historical sites. Searches at 27 sites identified as potentially suitable for the species yielded six new locations for the species. However, all extant sites in Indiana are in two population clusters within two counties. Six sites are located on Indiana Dunes National Lakeshore, and other landowners include a county park and recreational department, a school district, and The Nature Conservancy.

During the 1990 surveys of 50 potentially suitable sites in Minnesota, the Karner blue butterfly was located in two areas. Both sites are on a State Wildlife Management Area, in the vicinity of one of the historical locations. Studies conducted in 1991 revealed three new sites within one half to three miles of the sites surveyed in 1990. Low numbers of individuals were observed at all five sites, with none greater than 14.

This species was presumed extirpated from Illinois until the species was relocated there in August 1992. A total of seven butterflies, including five males and two females, were reported from a lupine site in the northern part of the state.

Conservation and Recovery

Throughout its range, changes in the habitat occupied by this species resulting from silviculture, urbanization, and the declining frequency of wildfires are largely the reasons for its decline. Modification and fragmentation of remaining areas are continuing threats to the survival of this butterfly. In addition to direct destruction of suitable habitat, urbanization has led to fire suppression on interspersed habitat; in the absence of fire, vegetational succession has made this habitat unsuitable.

Although in the past there have been large scientific collections of the Karner blue butterfly, they are not believed to be a significant factor in the decline of this species. However, any future take could potentially damage recovery efforts.

Disease and predation have not been documented as factors in the decline of this species.

As the continued survival of this species is dependent on the presence of wild lupine, any actions or lack thereof, that affect populations of wild lupine will affect Karner blue butterfly populations.

With small, isolated, and declining populations, this butterfly is particularly vulnerable to extinction. Extreme isolation will prevent the influx of new genetic material, leading to highly inbred populations that have low viability and/or fecundity.

Vegetation control measures implemented in the fall of 1990 at the Concord site opened habitat for the butterfly's obligate food source, wild lupine, and seeds collected have been planted in several test plots. If these plantings are successful, the butterfly population should increase.

In March of 1991 the Service and conservation groups persuaded the New Hampshire Department of Environmental Services to deny the City of Concord's application to spread municipal sludge over 200 acres of remnant pine barren habitat at the city airport.

USFWS's New England Field Office, the State, and The Nature Conservancy continue to work with the City of Concord to set aside pine barren preserves for the butterfly and other rare species.

Bibliography

Schweitzer, D. F., 1989. "Fact sheet for the Karner Blue Butterfly with special reference to New York." The Nature Conservancy, internal document, 7 pp.

U.S. Fish and Wildlife Service. *Federal Register*. Rules and regulations. Vol. 57, No. 240. December 14, 1992: 59236-59243.

Contacts

U.S. Fish and Wildlife Service
    Regional Office
Federal Building, Fort Snelling
Twin Cities, MN 55111
Phone: 612-725-3500
FAX: 612-725-3526

Ecological Services Field Office
22 Bridge Street
Concord, NH 03301-4901
Phone: 603-225-1411
FAX: 603-225-1467

Massachusetts Natural Heritage and
    Endangered Species Program
Division of Fisheries and Wildlife
100 Cambridge Street
Boston, MA 02202
Phone: 617-727-9194
FAX: 617-727-7288

Adapted from data compiled by the Threatened and Endangered Species Information Institute (13950 W. 20th Ave., Golden, CO 80401) for *Beacham's International Threatened, Endangered, and Extinct Species* published on CD ROM, available from Beacham Publishing.

Saint Francis' Satyr

Neonympha mitchellii francisci

Steve Hall   *Color Plate C-5*

Status	Endangered
Listed	Emergency Rule April 18, 1994
Family	Nymphalidae (Satyrs, Wood Nymphs)
Description	Fairly small, dark brown butterfly with conspicuous dark maroon "eyespots" on the the wings.
Habitat	Wide, wet meadows dominated by sedges.
Food	Graminoids (seeds, grasses, grains)
Reproduction	Two adult flights or generations per year.
Threats	Overcollecting
Range	North Carolina

Description

Saint Francis' satyr is a fairly small, dark brown butterfly with a wingspan of 33 to 44 millimeters. Saint Francis' satyr and Mitchell's satyr (*N. m. mitchellii*), the northern subspecies, which was classified as endangered on May 20, 1992, are nearly identical in size and show only a slight degree of sexual size dimorphism. Like most species in the wood nymph group, Saint Francis' satyr has conspicuous "eyespots" on the lower surfaces of the wings. These eyespots are dark maroon brown in the center, reflecting a silver cast in certain lights. The border of these dark eyespots is straw yellow in color, with an outermost border of dark brown. The eyespots are usually round to slightly oval and are well developed on the fore wings as well as on the hind wing. The spots are accented by two bright orange bands

along the posterior wing edges and two darker brown bands across the central portion of each wing. Saint Francis' satyr, like its subspecies, can be distinguished from its North American congener, *N. areolata*, by the latter's well-marked eyespots on the upper wing surfaces and brighter orange bands on the hind wing, as well as by its lighter coloration and stronger flight.

Behavior

The annual life cycle of Saint Francis' satyr, unlike Mitchell's satyr, is bivoltine, having two adult flights or generations per year. Larval host plants are believed to be graminoids associated with grasses, sedges, and rushes. Little else is known about the life history of this butterfly.

Habitat

The habitat occupied by this satyr consists primarily of wide, wet meadows dominated by sedges and other wetland graminoids. In North Carolina sandhills, such meadows are often relics of beaver activity. Unlike the habitat of Mitchell's satyr, the North Carolina species' habitat cannot be properly called a fen because the waters of this sandhills region are extremely poor in organic nutrients. The boggy areas of the sandhills are quite acidic as well as ephemeral, succeeding either to procosin or swamp forest if not kept open by frequent beaver activity. Under the natural regime of frequent forest fires ignited by summer thunderstorms, the sandhills were once covered with a much more open type of woodland, dominated by longleaf pine, wiregrass, and other fire tolerant species. The type of forest that currently exists along the creek inhabited by Saint Francis' satyr can grow up only under a long period of fire suppression. The dominance on this site of loblolly pine is due primarily to past forestry management practices and not any form of natural succession.

Historic Range

Saint Francis' satyr is extremely restricted geographically, and Mitchell's satyr has been eliminated from approximately half of its range in North Carolina. Extensive searches have been made of suitable habitat in North and South Carolina, but no other populations have been found. The current narrow distribution could be the result of the enormous environmental changes that have occurred in the southern coastal plains within the last 100 years. Only the discovery of additional populations or fossil remains can clarify this situation. Steve Hall (1993) states that "in order for *francisci* to have survived over the past 10,000 years, there must surely have been more populations and greater numbers of individuals than apparently now exist." Reductions in *francisci*'s range would have accompanied the extensive loss of wetland habitats in the coastal plain.

Current Distribution

Saint Francis's satyr is now known to exist in only a single population fragmented into less than six small colonies that occupy a total area no larger than a few square miles. In 1989 Parshall and Kral estimated that the single known population produced less than 100 individuals a year, but by 1991 the species appeared to be extinct.

Conservation and Recovery

The enormous changes in the southern coastal plain during the past 100 years have severely altered the butterfly's habitat. The boggy areas of the sandhills are quite acidic as well as ephemeral, succeeding cither to procosin or swamp forest if not kept open by frequent beaver activity. Beavers had been virtually eliminated from North Carolina by the turn of the century, and although beaver reintroduction began in 1939, it took several decades before they again became an agent for creation of the sage meadow habitats favored by Saint Francis' satyr.

In Steve Hall's 1993 study, he states that "As the landscape mosaic of open woodlands and wetlands of the coastal plain declined through the past two centuries, the range of *francisci* must have become increasingly fragmented. Although the isolated populations may have persisted as long as suitable habitat remained, the structure of their meta populations would have been destroyed" and they would have had less access to new habitats because the absence of forest fires would have allowed the forest to become denser.

Saint Francis' satyr is highly prized by collectors, including commercial collectors who often systematically collect every individual available. Several populations are known to have been obliterated by collectors, and others are known to be extremely vulnerable to this threat. The single known population was so hard hit by collectors in the three years following its initial discovery that it was believed to have been collected to extinction. Collectors reportedly visited the known site every day throughout the flight periods, taking every adult they saw. North Carolina law does not protect insects from collection, and the Department of Defense has no regulations restricting collection of military land.

Because the range and numbers of Saint Francis' satyr are so small, the species is threatened by catastrophic climatic events, inbreeding, disease and parasitism. Part of the occupied area is adjacent to regularly traveled roads, where there is the threat of toxic spills onto the species' wetland habitat.

Other potential threats include pest control programs for mosquitoes and gypsy moths, and beaver control.

Current military use of the species' habitat is favorable; the frequent fires caused by shelling are undoubtedly a reason why the species survives on military lands and not on surrounding private lands. Department of Defense personnel are aware of the species' plight and have been cooperative in protection efforts. Troop movements have been directed away from areas where the satyr occurs.

FWS determined that to designate critical habitat would further expose the butterfly to collectors. Because the current habitat is on military land, no further protection is needed beyond that stipulated by the Endangered Species Act.

Bibliography

U.S. Fish and Wildlife Service. "Endangered and Threatened Wildlife and Plant; Emergency Rule to List the Saint Francis Satyr as Endangered." *Federal Register* Vol. 59, No. 74. April 18, 1994: 18324-18327.

Contacts

Ecological Services Field Office
330 Ridgefield Court
Asheville, NC 28806
Phone: 704-665-1195
FAX: 704-665-2782

USFWS Regional Office
Suite 200, 1875 Century Blvd.
Atlanta, GA 30345
Phone: 404-679-4000

Adapted from data compiled by Beacham Publishing for *Beacham's International Threatened, Endangered, and Extinct Species* published on CD ROM.

Delhi Sands Flower-Loving Fly

Rhaphiomidas terminatus abdominalis

Greg Ballmer   *Color Plate C-5*

Status	Endangered
Listed	September 23, 1993
Family	Apioceridae (Orthorrhaphous Dipteran Insect)
Description	Fly with an orange-brown elongated body and dark brown oval spots on its ventral surface.
Habitat	Sandy, fine soils within or adjacent to consolidated dunes.
Food	Flower nectar.
Reproduction	Eggs are deposited in sand and metamorphosis takes a year.
Threats	Conversion of habitat to agricultural use and commercial sites.
Range	California

Description

The Delhi Sands flower-loving fly has an elongated body with a long tubular proboscis, which is used to extract nectar from flowers. This fly is about one inch long, orange-brown in color, and has dark brown oval spots on the upper surface of the abdomen.

Behavior

The life history of this fly is not well known, but is probably similar to that of other members of this genus. These flies inhabit arid or semi-arid regions, and may occur in sparsely vegetated sand dune habitats. Adults take nectar from flowers by means of an elongate proboscis. The prefer-

ence of the species for sparsely vegetated areas may be related to the insect's behavior of flying low, usually less than three feet above the ground. The vegetation may aid in the selection of egg-laying sites.

Mating behavior has not been observed in the wild, although it is known that eggs are deposited in sand. In captivity a female produced over 50 eggs within a ten day period. Larval development takes place in the sand and metamorphosis probably takes a full year.

This species is a strong flier and, like a hummingbird, is capable of stationary, hovering flight. The Delhi Sands flower-loving fly probably makes a single annual flight period during August and September. A skewed ratio of males to females (about 2:1) suggests that, as with many other insects, males are more active, spending much of their time flying and investigating vegetation or the sand surface for resting females. The single annual flight suggests that development to metamorphosis takes a full year. Pupas work their way to the surface prior to emergence as adults.

Habitat

The habitat of this fly is sandy, fine soils within or adjacent to consolidated dunes. These soil types are generally called "Delhi" fine sand. Delhi soils cover about 40 square miles in several irregular patches, extending from the cities of Colton to Ontario and Chino in northwestern Riverside and southwestern San Bernardino Counties. Much of the area of Delhi soils has been used for agriculture, chiefly grapes and citrus, since the 1800s. More recently, this area has been used for dairies, housing tracts, and industrial sites. Dominant vegetation includes wild buckwheat, croton, and telegraph weed.

Historic Range

Based on this species' present distribution, it is thought that it once occurred throughout much of the entire area (40 square miles) of the Delhi fine sand soil.

This fly occurs in San Bernardino and Riverside Counties, California. Documented distribution of this insect extends from the eastern margin of the Delhi fine sand formation in Colton to near its western limit in Mira Loma.

Current Distribution

The Delhi Sands flower-loving fly currently occurs at five locations in southern California: four in southwestern San Bernardino County, and one in Riverside County, just south of the San Bernardino County line.

All known colonies occur on privately owned land within an eight mile radius circle.

Conservation and Recovery

The major threats to the Delhi Sands flower-loving fly are habitat loss and degradation. Historic and recent agricultural, residential, and commercial development have significantly reduced suitable habitat. Most of the former habitat was destroyed by agricultural development in the 1800s, and the remaining suitable habitat continues to be destroyed by the construction of homes and businesses, and their associated roads and infrastructure. Soil disturbances are being caused by grading, plowing, discing to remove vegetation for fire control, and off-road vehicle use. The use of off-road vehicles may also contribute to the loss of native vegetation and subsequent invasion of weedy, non-native species. Illegal dumping of abandoned automobiles and other trash has also contributed to habitat degradation.

The Delhi Sands flower-loving fly will not return to previously farmed areas. Agricultural fields may return or be restored to suitable habitat over time; however, the potential of this species to recolonize degraded sites is unknown, although this behavior may be pivotal to its recovery.

The use of pesticides in agricultural areas and their persistence in the soil may have harmful effects on this species. Furthermore, the level of disturbance at a given site may favor exotic over native vegetation, which may preclude use by the fly.

Although flies in general are not especially popular with collectors, the Delhi Sands flower-loving fly is prized because of its unusual size, coloration, and rarity. A dedicated collector could readily eliminate this species, given its small isolated populations. Even scientific collecting, or repeated handling and marking, particularly of the females, could eliminate populations through loss of genetic variability. Collection of females dispersing from a colony could also reduce the probability that new colonies will be established.

Bibliography

U.S. Fish and Wildlife Service. "Endangered and Threatened Wildlife and Plants; Determination of Endangered Status for the Delhi Sands Flower-loving Fly." *Federal Register* Vol. 58, No. 183. September 23, 1993: 49881-49887.

Contacts

U.S. Fish and Wildlife Service
  Regional Office
Eastside Federal Complex
911 N.S. 11th Avenue
Portland, OR 97232-4181
Phone: 503-231-6118

Adapted from data compiled by the Threatened and Endangered Species Information Institute (13950 W. 20th Ave., Golden, CO 80401) for *Beacham's International Threatened, Endangered, and Extinct Species* published on CD ROM, available from Beacham Publishing.

Myrtle's Silverspot Butterfly
Speyeria zerene myrtleae

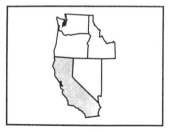

Gary M. Fellers   *Color Plate C-5*

Status	Endangered
Listed	June 22, 1992
Family	Nymphalidae (Brush-Footed Butterfly)
Description	Medium-sized butterfly with golden brown upper wings with black spots and lines.
Habitat	Coastal foredunes and coastal dune scrub communities.
Reproduction	Eggs are laid in the debris and dried stems of the larval food plant.
Threats	Alien plants, sand mining, military operations
Range	California

Description

Myrtle's silverspot is a medium-sized butterfly with a wingspan of about 55 millimeters. The upper surfaces of the wings are golden brown and possess many black spots and lines. The undersides are brown to orange-brown matriculated with tan and black lines and conspicuous silver and black spots. The basal areas of the wings and body are densely pubescent.

Behavior

After hatching the caterpillars wander a short distance and spin a silk pad on which they spend the winter. The larvae are dark-colored with several dorsal branching spines. After diapause the larvae find the larval foodplant (*Viola* sp.). After about seven to ten weeks the larvae form pupa within a chamber of leaves. Adults emerge about two weeks later and live for about three weeks.

Habitat

Myrtle's silverspot butterfly is associated with the California Coastal Redwood Belt, Siskiyou-Trinity Area, Central California Coastal Valleys, and Central California Coast Range. Broadly, these regions have an elevation from sea level to 900 meters; average annual precipitation of 300 to 850 millimeters distributed throughout the year; perennial streams and lakes are distributed throughout the regions and glacial and alluvial deposits in the valley also yield large quantities of water. The erosion hazard is high in this area and is stabilized only by plant cover. Much of this land is federally owned and the remaining is used for lumbering, grazing, wildlife habitat and recreation.

This species is restricted to the coastal foredunes and coastal dune scrub communities and associated habitats occupied by coastal scrub or coastal terrace prairie. In the dune systems north of Monterey Bay, sand-stabilizing rhizomatous grasses, *Ammophila arenaria* and *Elymus mollis* generally dominate the vegetation of the foredunes. *Ammophila arenaria*, European beach grass or marram grass, is an alien species that has largely replaced the native Elymus-dominated foredune community. Beach grass is believed to be a powerful geomorphic agent due to its ability to build continuous wall-like foredunes, which were not previously in this region. Although the Elymus-dominated foredune community exists around Monterey Bay, these foredunes typically consist of low hillocks and mounds that are sparsely populated with generally succulent, tap-rooted perennial herbs. *Abronia latifolia, Ambrosia chamissonis, Calystegia solandella, Camissonia* spp., *Carpobrotus aequilaterus, C. edulis* and *Fragaria chiloensis* are common associates. The stabilization of the dunes by *Ammophila arenaria* has permitted the colonization of formerly active backdune areas with a mixture of native and alien plants. These backdune areas consist of a soft, woody, dense plant community of short shrubs and sub-shrubs, and herbaceous plants.

Eggs are laid in the debris and dried stems of *Viola* sp. (the larval food plant).

Historic Range

This species historically was distributed from San Mateo County north to the mouth of the Russian River in Sonoma County.

Current Distribution

Currently this species is known from populations in Marin and Sonoma Counties. Two populations are located within Sonoma State Beach and on the peninsula west of Bodega Harbor. One population also occurs in Point Reyes National Seashore.

Conservation and Recovery

This butterfly is threatened by a number of factors including: invasion of alien plants (displacing this species' larval food plant), proposed commercial and residential development, military operational uses, and off-road vehicle damage. Potential threats include sand mining, disposal of dredged material from adjacent bays and waterways and stochastic extinction due to depauperate numbers.

The introduction and invasion of California's ecosystems by alien plants have adversely affected this species by replacing its larval food plant. The invasion of *Ammophila arenaria* has resulted in the development of wall-like foredunes and colonization of native and alien plants. Other alien species include sea-rocket (*Cakile* spp.), ice plant or sea-fig (*Carpobrotus* spp.), and several annual grasses and forbs generally restricted to wetland habitats within the dunes. In many cases, these aliens outcompete and largely supplant the native dune vegetation.

This species has limited historical distributions and likely has been eliminated from all but a small fraction of its historical dune or associated habitats. Today, this species generally persists as small "island" populations surrounded by urban areas, roads, trails, agricultural lands, competing alien plants, and other lands made unsuitable.

Conservation measures provided to species listed as endangered or threatened pursuant to the Act include recognition, recovery actions, requirements for Federal protection, and prohibitions against certain practices. Recognition through listing encourages conservation measures by Federal, international, and private agencies, groups, and individuals.

Bibliography

U.S. Fish and Wildlife Service. "Endangered and Threatened Wildlife and Plants; Six Plants and Myrtle's Silverspot Butterfly From Coastal Dunes in Northern and Central California Determined to Be Endangered." *Federal Register* Vol. 57, No. 120. June 22, 1992: 27848-27858.

Contacts

U.S. Fish and Wildlife Service
  Regional Office
Eastside Federal Complex
911 N.S. 11th Avenue
Portland, OR 97232-4181
Phone: 503-231-6118

Ecological Services Field Office
Room E-1803/1823
2800 Cottage Way
Sacramento, CA 98525
Phone: 916-978-4866
FAX: 916-978-4613

Adapted from data compiled by the Threatened and Endangered Species Information Institute (13950 W. 20th Ave., Golden, CO 80401) for *Beacham's International Threatened, Endangered, and Extinct Species* published on CD ROM, available from Beacham Publishing.

Bone Cave Harvestman

Texella reyesi

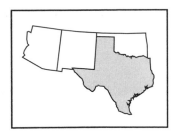

Wyman Meinzer, USFWS

Status	Endangered
Listed	August 18, 1993
Family	Phalangodidae (Harvestman)
Description	Long-legged, blind, pale orange harvestman.
Habitat	Limestone caves, sinkholes, and other subterranean voids.
Food	Eggs, feces, nymphs and dead body parts.
Threats	Land development, pollution, vandalism and fire ants.
Range	Texas

Description

The Bone Cave harvestman is a troglobite, which is a species which spends its entire life in openings underground usually with small or absent eyes, attenuated appendages, and other adaptations to its subsurface dwelling.

This species is a long-legged, blind, pale orange harvestman. It measures 1.41 to 2.67 millimeters in body length. Scute length is 1.26 to 1.69 millimeters. The leg II length is 6.10 to 11.79 millimeters. The leg II to scute length is 4.30 to 8.68 millimeters. The exoskeleton is rough. A few small tubercles can be observed on the eye mound, which is broadly conical; the retina is absent; the cornea variable. The penis possesses a ventral plate prong and is round apically. There are two dorsal, 17 lateral and four ventral setae. The apical spine of this species is bent and apically pointed; its length is 0.05 millimeters. The glans have a basal knob which appears narrow and conical in shape. The middle lobe is long and the parastylar lobes are claw-shaped. The stylus of the Bone Cave harvestman is long, curved and ventrally carinate; apically spatulate. The basal fold is well developed.

Juveniles are white to yellow in color, while adults are pale orange. This species displays geographical polymorphism. Northern populations have longer legs, a smoother exoskeleton, and reduced or absent corneas.

Behavior

This species spends its entire life underground. It is endemic to the karst (limestone) formations. These formations include caves, sinkholes, and other subterranean voids.

The Bone Cave harvestman is sensitive to

less-than-saturated humidities. Most individuals are found only under large rocks, but are occasionally seen walking on moist floors. In Temples of Thor Cave, individuals are typically found on a rough slope about 30 meters from the entrance in absolute darkness. In this particular area humidity is high.

Habitat

This species is dependent on outside moisture and nutrient inputs generated from the subsurface. This species inhabits areas of the cave where temperature and humidity are constant. The surface vegetation ranges from pasture land to mature oak-juniper woodland.

Karst is formed by the slow dissolution of calcium carbonate from limestone bedrock by mildly acidic ground water. This process results in subterranean voids resembling a honeycomb. The water enters the subsurface through cracks, crevices, and other openings, dissolving soluble beds of rock.

Nutrients to this ecosystem are provided from the outside surface washed in. These nutritional sources include plant material, feces, eggs and carrion. Cave crickets are believed to provide an important component to the nutritional balance of this cave ecosystem. These crickets introduce nutrients through eggs, feces, nymphs and dead body parts on which many invertebrates are known to feed.

Racoon feces provide a rich medium for fungi growth which, in turn, is a haven for collembolans (small insects).

Historic Range and Current Distribution

The Bone Cave harvestman was originally discovered in 1989 in Bone Cave, Williamson County, Texas.

As this species has only been distinguished as a separate species of *Texella* recently, past distribution is difficult to ascertain. This species currently inhabits 54 caves, 46 known occurrences and eight possible locations from northern Travis to northern Williamson Counties, Texas.

Conservation and Recovery

This species and seven other invertebrates of the karst (limestone) formations are threatened by land development, pollution, vandalism and/or fire ants.

The primary threat to Bone Cave harvestman is habitat loss due to urban development activities. Continued urban expansion such as residential subdivisions, schools, golf courses, roads, commercial and industrial facilities, etc. poses a threat in the form of cave filling or collapse, water diversion, vegetation/fauna alteration, and increased pollution.

Some caves have already been filled as a result of road construction and building site preparation. Development directly above caves could result in the collapse of cave ceilings.

Ranchers may have also filled some caves. Justification is placed in reducing hiding places for predators of cattle and goats as well as preventing these animals from falling into the formations.

Troglobites rely upon and in fact require a controlled environment of high humidity and constant temperature. If water drainage paths are altered, this balance is no longer on an even keel. Water diversion away from the caves could lead to the direct mortality of this species. Increased water infiltration could lead to flooding and loss of air space.

As the karst ecosystem relies on the infiltration of nutrients from the surface, a fluctuation in the vegetation or fauna would alter nutrient supplies. During development, native vegetation may be replaced with non-native species, as well as cause the introduction of exotic animal species, such as fire ants. An overall nutrient depletion would result. The removal of vegetation could also lead to temperature fluctuations, a change in moisture regime and potential for contamination and increased sedimentation from soil erosion.

Bibliography

U.S. Fish and Wildlife Service. "Endangered and Threatened Wildlife and Plants; Coffin Cave Mold Beetle (*Batrisodes texanus*) and the Bone Cave Harvestman (*Texella reyesi*) Determined to Be Endangered." *Federal Register* Vol. 58, No. 158: 43818-43819.

Contacts

U.S. Fish and Wildlife Service
Regional Office
P. O. Box 1306
Albuquerque, NM 87103
Phone: 505-766-2321
FAX: 505-766-8063

Adapted from data compiled by the Threatened and Endangered Species Information Institute (13950 W. 20th Ave., Golden, CO 80401) for *Beacham's International Threatened, Endangered, and Extinct Species* published on CD ROM, available from Beacham Publishing.

CONVERTING FROM THE METRIC SYSTEM TO THE IMPERIAL SYSTEM

TO CONVERT **MILLIMETERS** TO **INCHES**, MULTIPLY BY .039
Sample conversions rounded off

MM	1	2	3	4	5	6	7	8	9	10
IN	.04	.08	.12	.16	.2	.23	.27	.31	.35	.39
MM	15	20	30	40	50	60	70	80	90	100
IN	.59	.78	1.2	1.6	2	2.3	2.7	3.1	3.5	3.9

TO CONVERT **CENTIMETERS** TO **INCHES**, MULTIPLY BY .394
Sample conversions rounded off

CM	1	2	3	4	5	6	7	8	9	10
IN	.4	.8	1.2	1.6	2	2.4	2.8	3.2	3.5	3.9
CM	15	20	30	40	50	60	70	80	90	100
IN	5.9	7.9	11.8	15.8	19.7	23.6	27.6	31.5	35.5	39.4

TO CONVERT **DECIMETERS** TO **FEET**, MULTIPLY BY .328
Sample conversions rounded off

DM	1	2	3	4	5	6	7	8	9	10
FT	.3	.5	.7	.8	1.6	2	2.3	2.6	3	3.3

TO CONVERT **METERS** TO **FEET**, MULTIPLY BY 3.281
Sample conversions rounded off

M	1	1.5	2	2.5	3	3.5	4	4.5	5	5.5
FT	3.3	4.9	6.5	8.2	9.8	11.5	13.1	14.8	16.4	18
M	6	6.5	7	7.5	8	8.5	9	9.5	10	20
FT	19.7	21.3	22.9	24.6	26.2	27.9	29.5	31.2	32.8	65.6

TO CONVERT **KILOMETERS** TO **MILES**, MULTIPLY BY 0.621
Sample conversions rounded off

KM	10	20	30	40	50	60	70	80	90	100
MI	6.2	12.4	18.6	24.8	31	37.2	43.5	49.7	55.9	62.1

TO CONVERT **HECTARES** TO **SQUARE MILES**, MULTIPLY BY 0.004
Sample conversions rounded off

HA	100	200	300	400	500	600	700	800	900	1000
SM	.4	.8	1.2	1.6	2	2.4	2.8	3.2	3.6	4

TO CONVERT **GRAMS** TO **OUNCES**, MULTIPLY BY 0.035
Sample conversions rounded off

G	1	2	3	4	5	6	7	8	9	10
O	.04	.07	.11	.14	.18	.21	.25	.28	.32	.35
G	15	20	30	40	50	60	70	80	90	100
O	.53	.7	1.1	1.4	1.8	2.1	2.5	2.8	3.2	3.5

TO CONVERT **KILOGRAMS** TO **POUNDS**, MULTIPLY BY 2.205
Sample conversions rounded off

KG	1	1.5	2	2.5	3	3.5	4	4.5	5	5.5
LB	2.2	3.3	4.4	5.5	6.6	7.7	8.8	9.9	11	12.1
KG	6	6.5	7	7.5	8	8.5	9	9.5	10	20
LB	13.2	14.3	15.4	16.5	17.6	18.7	19.8	20.9	22	44.1

Common to Scientific Name Index — Volume 4

NOTE: This index lists only common names of species in this volume. Since most Hawaiian and Puerto Rican plant species do not have common names, refer to the Cumulative Index for listing by scientific name.)

PLANTS

Hilo Ischaemum	*Ischaemum byrone*	1859
Holy Ghost Ipomopsis	*Ipomopsis sancti-spiritus*	1708
Howell's Spineflower	*Chorizanthe howellii*	1661
Ka'u Silversword	*Argyroxiphium kauense*	1836
Kauila	*Colubrina oppositifolia*	1845
Kodachrome Bladderpod	*Lesquerella tumulosa*	1719
Laukahi Kuahiwi	*Plantago hawaiensis*	1869
Leedy's Roseroot	*Sedum intergrifolium* ssp. *leedyi*	1746
Lewton's Polygala	*Polygala lewtonii*	1785
Louisiana Quillwort	*Isoetes louisianensis*	1711
Marsh Sandwort	*Arenaria paludicola*	1656
Menzies' Wallflower	*Erysimum menziesii*	1696
Monterey Gilia	*Gilia tenuiflora* ssp. *arenaria*	1705
Monterey Spineflower	*Chorizanthe pungens* var. *pungens*	1664
Morefield's Leather Flower	*Clematis morefieldii*	1674
Nelson's Checker-Mallow	*Sidalcea nelsoniana*	1749
Okeechobee Gourd	*Cucurbita okeechobeensis* ssp. *okeechobeensis*	1686
Otay Mesa Mint	*Pogogyne nudiuscula*	1766
Palo Colorado	*Ternstroemia luquillensis*	1816
Palo de Jazmin	*Styrax portoricensis*	1812
Penland Alpine Fen Mustard	*Eutrema penlandii*	1702
Pigeon Wings	*Clitoria fragrans*	1783
Pima Pineapple Cactus	*Coryphantha scheeri* var. *robustispina*	1684
Robust Spineflower	*Chorizanthe robusta* var. *robusta* var. *hartwegii*	1668
San Diego Button-Celery	*Eryngium aristulatum* var. *parishii*	1768
Sandlace	*Polygonella myriophylla*	1787
Scrub Buckwheat	*Eriogonum longifolium* var. *gnaphalifolium*	1777
Seabeach Amaranth	*Amaranthus pumilus*	1653
Sensitive Joint-Vetch	*Aeschynomene virginica*	1649
Short-Leaved Rosemary	*Conradina brevifolia*	1677
Smooth Coneflower	*Echinacea laevigata*	1689
Sonoma Spineflower	*Chorizanthe valida*	1671
Star or Sea Urchin Cactus	*Astrophytum asterias*	1692

Telephus Spurge	*Euphorbia telephioides*	1699
Ute Ladies' Tresses	*Spiranthes diluvialis*	1753
Wahine Noho Kula	*Isodendrion pyrifolium*	1861
White Birds-in-a-Nest	*Macbridea alba*	1726

MAMMALS

American Black Bear	*Ursus americanus*	2073
Louisiana Black Bear	*Ursus americanus luteolus*	2075
Pacific Pocket Mouse	*Perognathus longimembris pacificus*	2070
Point Arena Mountain Beaver	*Aplodontia rufa nigra*	2067

BIRDS

Coastal California Gnatcatcher	*Polioptila californica californica*	2086
Marbled Murrelet	*Brachyramphus marmoratus marmoratus*	2079
Mexican Spotted Owl	*Strix occidentalis lucida*	2092
Spectacled Eider	*Somateria fischeri*	2089
Western Snowy Plover	*Charadrius alexandrinus nivosus*	2082

REPTILES

| Giant Garter Snake | *Thamnophis gigas* | 2099 |

FISHES

Blue Shiner	*Cyprinella (=Notropis) caerulea*	2103
Bluemask Darter	*Etheostoma (doration) sp.*	2106
Delta Smelt	*Hypomesus transpacificus*	2114
Duskytail Darter	*Etheostoma (=catonotus) sp.*	2110
Goldline Darter	*Percina aurolineata*	2131
Oregon Chub	*Oregonichthys crameri*	2129
Palezone shiner	*Notropis sp. cf. procne*	2119
Pygmy madtom	*Noturus stanauli*	2121
Relict Darter	*Etheostoma chienense*	2108
Snake River Fall Chinook Salmon	*Oncorhynchus tshawytscha*	2123
Spring/Summer Run Chinook Salmon	*Oncorhynchus tshawytscha*	2126

| Tidewater Goby | *Eucyclobius newberryi* | 2112 |

MUSSELS

Alabama Moccasinshell	*Medionidus acutissimus*	2152
Carolina Heelsplitter	*Lasmigona decorata*	2149
Clubshell Mussel	*Pleurobema clava*	2156
Coosa Moccasinshell	*Medionidus parvulus*	2154
Dark Pigtoe	*Pleurobema furvum*	2161
Fine-Lined Pocketbook	*Lampsilis altilis*	2145
Northern Riffleshell	*Epioblasma torulosa rangiana*	2142
Orange-Nacre Mucket	*Lampsilis perovalis*	2147
Ovate Clubshell	*Pleurobema perovatum*	2165
Southern Acornshell Mussel	*Epioblasma othcaloogensis*	2140
Southern Clubshell	*Pleurobema decisum*	2159
Southern Pigtoe	*Pleurobema georgianum*	2163
Triangular Kidneyshell	*Ptychobranchus greeni*	2167
Upland Combshell Mussel	*Epioblasma metastriata*	2138

SNAILS

Anthony's Riversnail	*Athearnia anthonyi*	2174
Banbury Springs Lanx	*Lanx (undescribed species)*	2176
Bliss Rapids Snail	*Undescribed species*	2188
Bruneau Hot Springsnail	*Pyrgulopsis bruneauensis*	2185
Idaho Springsnail	*Fontelicella idahoensis*	2183
Royal Snail	*Pyrgulopsis (=Marstonia) ogmorhaphe*	2181
Snake River Physa Snail	*Physa natricina*	2179
Utah Valvata Snail	*Valvata utahensis*	2191

CRUSTACEANS

Cave Crayfish	*Cambarus aculabrum*	2194
Lee County Cave Isopod	*Lirceus usdagalun*	2201
Riverside Fairy Shrimp	*Streptocephalus woottoni*	2197

INSECTS AND ARACHNIDS

State by State Occurrence — Volume 4

ALABAMA

Alabama Moccasinshell	*Medionidus acutissimus*
Alabama Streak-sorus Fern	*Thelypteris pilosa* var. *alabamensis*
American Chaffseed	*Scwalbea americana*
Anthony's Riversnail	*Athearnia anthonyi*
Blue Shiner	*Cyprinella (=Notropis) caerulea*
Coosa Moccasinshell	*Medionidus parvulus*
Dark Pigtoe	*Pleurobema furvum*
Fine-Lined Pocketbook	*Lampsilis altilis*
Goldline Darter	*Percina aurolineata*
Morefield's Leather Flower	*Clematis morefieldii*
Orange-Nacre Mucket	*Lampsilis perovalis*
Ovate Clubshell	*Pleurobema perovatum*
Southern Acornshell	*Epioblasma othcaloogensis*
Southern Clubshell	*Pleurobema decisum*
Southern Pigtoe	*Pleurobema georgianum*
Triangular Kidneyshell	*Ptychobranchus greeni*
Upland Combshell	*Epioblasma metastriata*

ALASKA

Spectacled Eider	*Somateria fischeri*

ARIZONA

Mexican Spotted Owl	*Strix occidentalis lucida*
Pima Pineapple Cactus	*Coryphantha scheeri* var. *robustispina*

ARKANSAS

Cave Crayfish	*Cambarus aculabrum*

CALIFORNIA

Beach Layia	*Layia carnosa*
Ben Lomond Spineflower	*Chorizanthe pungens* var. *hartwegiana*
Ben Lomond Wallflower	*Erysimum teretifolium*
Butte County Meadowfoam	*Limnanthes floccosa* ssp. *californica*

California Orcutt Grass	*Orcuttia californica*
Clover Lupine	*Lupinus tidestromii*
Coastal California Gnatcatcher	*Polioptila californica californica*
Delhi Sands Flower-Loving Fly	*Rhaphiomidas terminatus abdominalis*
Delta Smelt	*Hypomesus transpacificus*
Gambel's Watercress	*Rorippa gambellii*
Giant Garter Snake	*Thamnophis gigas*
Howell's Spineflower	*Chorizanthe howellii*
Marbled Murrelet	*Brachyramphus marmoratus marmoratus*
Marsh Sandwort	*Arenaria paludicola*
Menzies' Wallflower	*Erysimum menziesii*
Monterey Gilia	*Gilia tenuiflora* ssp. *arenaria*
Monterey Spineflower	*Chorizanthe pungens* var. *pungens*
Myrtle's Silverspot Butterfly	*Speyeria zerene myrtleae*
Otay Mesa Mint	*Pogogyne nudiuscula*
Pacific Pocket Mouse	*Perognathus longimembris pacificus*
Point Arena Mountain Beaver	*Aplodontia rufa nigra*
Riverside Fairy Shrimp	*Streptocephalus woottoni*
Robust Spineflower	*Chorizanthe robusta* var. *robusta* var. *hartwegii*
San Diego Button-Celery	*Eryngium aristulatum* var. *parishii*
Sonoma Spineflower	*Chorizanthe valida*
Tidewater Goby	*Eucyclobius newberryi*
Western Snowy Plover	*Charadruis alexandrinus nivosus*

COLORADO

Mexican Spotted Owl	*Strix occidentalis lucida*
Penland Alpine Fen Mustard	*Eutrema penlandii*
Ute Ladies' Tresses	*Spiranthes diluvialis*
Western Snowy Plover	*Charadruis alexandrinus nivosus*

CONNECTICUT

| American Chaffseed | *Scwalbea americana* |

DELAWARE

| American Chaffseed | *Scwalbea americana* |

FLORIDA

| American Chaffseed | *Scwalbea americana* |
| Apalachicola Rosemary | *Conradina glabra* |

Avon Park Harebells	*Crotalaria avonensis*
Beach Jacquemontia	*Jacquemontia reclinata*
Britton's Beargrass	*Nolina brittoniana*
Cladonia perforata	*Florida perforate cladonia*
Etonia Rosemary	*Conradina etonia*
Florida Skullcap	*Scutellaria floridana*
Godfrey's Butterwort	*Pinguicula ionantha*
Lewton's Polygala	*Polygala lewtonii*
Okeechobee Gourd	*Cucurbita okeechobeensis* ssp. *okeechobeensis*
Pigeon Wings	*Clitoria fragrans*
Sandlace	*Polygonella myriophylla*
Scrub Buckwheat	*Eriogonum longifolium* var. *gnaphalifolium*
Short-Leaved Rosemary	*Conradina brevifolia*
Telephus Spurge	*Euphorbia telephioides*
White Birds-in-a-Nest	*Macbridea alba*

GEORGIA

Alabama Moccasinshell	*Medionidus acutissimus*
American Chaffseed	*Scwalbea americana*
Blue Shiner	*Cyprinella (=Notropis) caerulea*
Coosa Moccasinshell	*Medionidus parvulus*
Fine-Lined Pocketbook	*Lampsilis altilis*
Goldline Darter	*Percina aurolineata*
Orange-Nacre Mucket	*Lampsilis perovalis*
Ovate Clubshell	*Pleurobema perovatum*
Smooth Coneflower	*Echinacea laevigata*
Southern Acornshell	*Epioblasma othcaloogensis*
Southern Clubshell	*Pleurobema decisum*
Southern Pigtoe	*Pleurobema georgianum*
Triangular Kidneyshell	*Ptychobranchus greeni*
Upland Combshell	*Epioblasma metastriata*

HAWAII

Alani	*Abutilon sandwicense*
Liliwai	*Acaena exigua*
Mahoe	*Alectryon macrococcus*
Ka'u Silversword	*Argyroxiphium kauense*
'Ahinahina (=Haleakala silversword)	*Argyroxiphium sandwicense* ssp. *macrocephalum*
Ko'oko'olau	*Bidens micrantha* ssp. *kalealaha*
Ko'oko'olau	*Bidens wiebkei*

'Olulu	*Brighamia insignis*
Pua'ala	*Brighamia rockii*
'Awikiwiki	*Canavalia molokaiensis*
'Akoko	*Chamaesyce deppeana*
No Common Name	*Chamaesyce halemanui*
'Oha wai	*Clermontia lindseyana*
'Oha'wai	*Clermontia oblongifolia* ssp. *brevipes*
'Oha'wai	*Clermontia oblongifolia* ssp. *mauiensis*
'Oha wai	*Clermontia peleana*
'Oha wai	*Clermontia pyrularia*
Kauila	*Colubrina oppositifolia*
Haha	*Cyanea asarifolia*
Haha	*Cyanea copelandii* ssp. *copelandii*
Haha	*Cyanea grimesiana* ssp. *obatae*
Haha	*Cyanea hamatiflora* ssp. *carlsonii*
Haha	*Cyanea lobata*
Haha	*Cyanea mannii*
Haha	*Cyanea mceldowneyi*
Haha	*Cyanea pinnatifida*
Haha	*Cyanea procera*
Haha	*Cyanea shipmanii*
Haha	*Cyanea stictophylla*
Haha	*Cyanea truncata*
Ha'iwala	*Cyrtandra crenata*
Ha'iwale	*Cyrtandra giffardii*
Ha'iwale	*Cyrtandra limahuliensis*
Ha'iwale	*Cyrtandra munroi*
Ha'iwala	*Cyrtandra polyantha*
Ha'iwale	*Cyrtandra tintinnabula*
No Common Name	*Delissea rhytidosperma*
No Common Name	*Diellia pallida*
No Common Name	*Diellia unisora*
No Common Name	*Dubautia latifolia*
Nioi	*Eugenia koolauensis*
Heau	*Exocarpos luteolus*
Hawaiian Red-Flowered Geranium	*Geranium arboreum*
Nohoanu	*Geranium multiflorum*
No Common Name	*Gouania vitifolia*
'Awiwi	*Hedyotis cookiana*
Kio'ele	*Hedyotis coriacea*
Pilo	*Hedyotis mannii*
No Common Name	*Hesperomannia arborescens*
Koki'o Ke'oke'o	*Hibiscus arnottianus ssp. immaculatus*
Clay's Hibiscus	*Hibiscus clayi*

Wawa'iole	*Huperzia mannii*
Hilo Ischaemum	*Ischaemum byrone*
Wahine Noho Kula	*Isodendrion pyrifolium*
Nehe	*Lipochaeta fauriei*
Nehe	*Lipochaeta kamolensis*
Nehe	*Lipochaeta micrantha*
Nehe	*Lipochaeta waimeaensis*
No Common Name	*Lobelia oahuensis*
Wawae'iol	*Lycopodium nutans*
No Common Name	*Lysimachia lydgatei*
'Ihi'Ihi	*Mariscus fauriei*
No Common Name	*Marsilea villosa*
No Common Name	*Melicope (=Pelea) lydgatei*
Alani	*Melicope haupuensis*
Alani	*Melicope knudsenii*
Alani	*Melicope mucronulata*
Alani	*Melicope pallida*
Alani	*Melicope quadrangularis*
Alani	*Melicope reflexa*
No Common Name	*Munroidendron racemosum*
'Aiea	*Nothocestrum breviflorum*
'Aiea	*Nothocestrum peltatum*
Hoiei	*Ochrosia kilaueaensis*
Makou	*Peucedanum sandwicense*
No Common Name	*Phyllostegia mannii*
No Common Name	*Phyllostegia waimeae*
Laukahi kuahiwi	*Plantago hawaiensis*
Hawaiian Bluegrass	*Poa sandvicensis*
No Common Name	*Poa siphonoglossa*
Po'e	*Portulaca sclerocarpa*
Loulu	*Pritchardia munroi*
Loulu	*Pritchardia affinis*
Kaulu	*Pteralyxia kauaiensis*
No Common Name	*Rollandia crispa*
No Common Name	*Schiedea haleakalensis*
No Common Name	*Schiedea lydgatei*
No Common Name	*Schiedea spergulina* var. *leiopoda*
No Common Name	*Schiedea spergulina* var. *spergulina*
No Common Name	*Silene alexandri*
No Common Name	*Silene hawaiiensis*
No Common Name	*Silene lanceolata*
Popolo 'aiakeakua	*Solanum sandwicense*
No Common Name	*Stenogyne bifida*
No Common Name	*Stenogyne campanulata*

No Common Name	*Stenogyne kanehoana*
No Common Name	*Tetramolopium arenarium*
No Common Name	*Tetramolopium rockii*
'Ohe'oh	*Tetraplasandra gymnocarpa*
Dwarf Iliau	*Wilkesia hobdyi*
No Common Name	*Xylosma crenatum*
A'e	*Zanthoxylum hawaiiense*

IDAHO

Banbury Springs Lanx	*Lanx (undescribed species)*
Bliss Rapids Snail	*Undescribed*
Bruneau Hot Springsnail	*Pyrgulopsis bruneauensis*
Idaho Springsnail	*Fontelicella idahoensis*
Snake River Physa Snail	*Physa natricina*
Snake River Fall Chinook Salmon	*Oncorhynchus tshawytscha*
Spring/Summer Run Chinook Salmon	*Oncorhynchus tshawytscha*
Utah Valvata Snail	*Valvata utahensis*

ILLINOIS

| Karner Blue Butterfly | *Lycaeides melissa samuelis* |

INDIANA

| Karner Blue Butterfly | *Lycaeides melissa samuelis* |

KANSAS

| Western Snowy Plover | *Charadrius alexandrinus nivosus* |

KENTUCKY

American Chaffseed	*Scwalbea americana*
Clubshell Mussel	*Pleurobema clava*
Northern Riffleshell Mussel	*Epioblasma torulosa rangiana*
Relict Darter	*Etheostoma chienense*

LOUISIANA

| American Black Bear | *Ursus americanus* |

| Louisiana Black Bear | *Ursus americanus luteolus* |
| Louisiana Quillwort | *Isoetes louisianensis* |

MARYLAND

| American Chaffseed | *Scwalbea americana* |
| Sensitive Joint-vetch | *Aeschynomene virginica* |

MASSACHUSETTS

| American Chaffseed | *Scwalbea americana* |

MICHIGAN

Clubshell Mussel	*Pleurobema clava*
Hungerford's Crawling Water Beetle	*Brychius hungerfordi*
Karner Blue Butterfly	*Lycaeides melissa samuelis*
Northern Riffleshell Mussel	*Epioblasma torulosa rangiana*

MINNESOTA

| Karner Blue Butterfly | *Lycaeides melissa samuelis* |
| Leedy's Roseroot | *Sedum intergrifolium* spp. *leedyi* |

MISSISSIPPI

Alabama Moccasinshell	*Medionidus acutissimus*
American Black Bear	*Ursus americanus*
American Chaffseed	*Scwalbea americana*
Louisiana Black Bear	*Ursus americanus luteolus*
Orange-Nacre Mucket	*Lampsilis perovalis*
Ovate Clubshell	*Pleurobema perovatum*
Southern Clubshell	*Pleurobema decisum*

NEVADA

| Ute Ladies' Tresses | *Spiranthes diluvialis* |
| Western Snowy Plover | *Charadrius alexandrinus nivosus* |

NEW HAMPSHIRE

| Karner Blue Butterfly | *Lycaeides melissa samuelis* |

NEW JERSEY

American Chaffseed   *Scwalbea americana*
Sensitive Joint-vetch   *Aeschynomene virginica*

NEW MEXICO

Holy Ghost Ipomopsis   *Ipomopsis sancti-spiritus*
Mexican Spotted Owl   *Strix occidentalis lucida*
Western Snowy Plover   *Charadrius alexandrinus nivosus*

NEW YORK

American Chaffseed   *Scwalbea americana*
Karner Blue Butterfly   *Lycaeides melissa samuelis*
Leedy's Roseroot   *Sedum intergrifolium* ssp. *Leedyi*
Seabeach Amaranth   *Amaranthus pumilus*

NORTH CAROLINA

American Chaffseed   *Scwalbea americana*
Carolina Heelsplitter   *Lasmigona decorata*
Saint Francis' Satyr   *Neonympha mitchellii francisci*
Seabeach Amaranth   *Amaranthus pumilus*
Sensitive Joint-vetch   *Aeschynomene virginica*
Smooth Coneflower   *Echinacea laevigata*

OHIO

Clubshell Mussel   *Pleurobema clava*
Northern Rifleshell Mussel   *Epioblasma torulosa rangiana*

OKLAHOMA

Western Snowy Plover   *Charadrius alexandrinus nivosus*

OREGON

Applegate's Milk-vetch   *Astragalus applegatei*
Marbled Murrelet   *Brachyramphus marmoratus marmoratus*
Nelson's Checker-Mallow   *Sidalcea nelsoniana*
Oregon Chub   *Oregonichthys crameri*

Snake River Fall Chinook Salmon   *Oncorhynchus tshawytscha*
Spring/Summer Run Chinook Salmon   *Oncorhynchus tshawytscha*
Western Snowy Plover   *Charadrius alexandrinus nivosus*

PENNSYLVANIA

Clubshell Mussel   *Pleurobema clava*
Northern Rifleshell Mussel   *Epioblasma torulosa rangiana*

SOUTH CAROLINA

American Chaffseed   *Scwalbea americana*
Seabeach Amaranth   *Amaranthus pumilus*
Smooth Coneflower   *Echinacea laevigata*

TENNESSEE

Palezone Shiner   *Notropis sp. cf. procne*
American Chaffseed   *Scwalbea americana*
Anthony's Riversnail   *Athearnia anthonyi*
Blue Shiner   *Cyprinella (=Notropis) caerulea*
Bluemask Darter   *Etheostoma (doration) sp.*
Coosa Moccasinshell   *Medionidus parvulus*
Duskytail Darter   *Etheostoma catonotus sp.*
Orange-Nacre Mucket   *Lampsilis perovalis*
Ovate Clubshell   *Pleurobema perovatum*
Pygmy Madtom   *Noturus stanauli*
Royal Snail   *Pyrgulopsis (=Marstonia) ogmorhaphe*
Southern Acornshell   *Epioblasma othcaloogensis*
Southern Clubshell   *Pleurobema decisum*
Southern Pigtoe   *Pleurobema georgianum*
Triangular Kidneyshell   *Ptychobranchus greeni*
Upland Combshell   *Epioblasma metastriata*

TEXAS

American Black Bear   *Ursus americanus*
Bone Cave Harvestman   *Texella reyesi*
Coffin Cave Mold Beetle   *Batrisodes texanus*
Louisiana Black Bear   *Ursus americanus luteolus*
Mexican Spotted Owl   *Strix occidentalis lucida*
Star or Sea Urchin Cactus   *Astrophytum asterias*

| Western Snowy Plover | *Charadrius alexandrinus nivosus* |

UTAH

Barneby Reed Mustard	*Schoenocrambe barnebyi*
Clay Reed-Mustard	*Schoenocrambe argillacea*
Kodachrome Bladderpod	*Lesquerella tumulosa*
Mexican Spotted Owl	*Strix occidentalis lucida*
Ute Ladies' Tresses	*Spiranthes diluvialis*
Western Snowy Plover	*Charadrius alexandrinus nivosus*

VIRGINIA

Duskytail Darter	*Etheostoma sp.*
American Chaffseed	*Scwalbea americana*
Lee County Cave Isopod	*Lirceus usdagalun*
Sensitive Joint-vetch	*Aeschynomene virginica*
Smooth Coneflower	*Echinacea laevigata*

WASHINGTON

Marbled Murrelet	*Brachyramphus marmoratus marmoratus*
Nelson's Checker-Mallow	*Sidalcea nelsoniana*
Snake River Fall Chinook Salmon	*Oncorhynchus tshawytscha*
Spring/Summer Run Chinook Salmon	*Oncorhynchus tshawytscha*

WEST VIRGINIA

| Clubshell Mussel | *Pleurobema clava* |

WISCONSIN

| Karner Blue Butterfly | *Lycaeides melissa samuelis* |

PUERTO RICO

No Common Name	*Adiantum vivesii*
No Common Name	*Aristida chaseae*
No Common Name	*Auerodendron pauciflorum*
Capa Rosa	*Callicarpa ampla*
No Common Name	*Calyptranthes thomasiana*

No Common Name	*Elaphoglossum serpens*
No Common Name	*Leptocereus grantianus*
No Common Name	*Lyonia truncata* var. *proctorii*
No Common Name	*Myrcia paganii*
No Common Name	*Polystichum calderonense*
Palo de Jazmin	*Styrax portoricensis*
No Common Name	*Tectaria estremerana*
Palo Colorado	*Ternstroemia luquillensis*
No Common Name	*Thelypteris Inabonensis*
No Common Name	*Thelypteris verecunda*
No Common Name	*Thelypteris yaucoensis*
No Common Name	*Vernonia proctorii*

Glossary

Acaulescent: stemless or nearly stemless.

Achene: a small, thin drywalled one-seeded fruit, such as that of a buttercup or dandelions, that does not split when ripe.

Acicular: pointed or needle-shaped.

Actinomorphic: having radial symmetry; divided into two or more planes with similar halves.

Acuminate: tapering to a sharp point.

Acute lobe: a rounded projection ending on a short point.

Adaptation: the features of an animal that enable it to survive in its environment.

Adaxially: relating to or being positioned on the side toward a plant's stem.

Adipose: related to animal fat.

Adnate: joined to or fused with another part, as parts not normally united.

Adult: sexually mature individual.

Adventitious: appearing in an unusual place or in an irregular or sporadic manner.

Aerial: activities in birds and insects that occur in flight.

Agamospermy: a phenomenon found in plants in which the asexual development of diploid (having genetically similar chromosomes) cells is incomplete due to the abnormal development of the pollen and the embryo sac.

Aggregrate: crowded in a dense cluster.

Agonistic: combative.

Albumin: any of several simple, water soluble proteins that are coagulated by heat and are found in egg white, blood serum, milk, animal tissues, and many plant juices.

Algae: microscopic, single-celled plants.

Alkali: soluble mineral salts found in natural water and arid soils.

Alkaline: contains soluble mineral salts; opposite of acidic.

Allochthonous: originating elsewhere, or living in a different habitat.

Alluvial deposits: sediment deposited by flowing water.

Alluvion: flow of water against a shore or bank.

Alluvium: sediment deposited by a flowing river.

Alpine: a region that occurs above the tree-line and below the snow-line on temperate and tropical mountains.

Alternate: leaves that do not grow opposite one another on the stem.

Altricial: young birds that are helpless and naked when hatched.

Alveolar: pertaining to the jaw section containing the tooth sockets.

Amblyopsids: The cave fishes; ray fishes distinguished by the structure of the paired fins, supported by the dermal rays.

Amphibian: animal capable of living in both water and land habitats.

Amphipod: a small crustacean of the order Amphipoda, including sand fleas.

Anadromous: migrating from salt water to fresh water to spawn.

Andepts: soils with a low bulk density and therefore are light and fluffy; most are acidic.

Androecium: the stamens of a flower considered collectively.

Anestrus: an interval of sexual dormancy between two periods of estrus (period of sexual activity).

Angiosperm: includes the whole range of flowering plants, the most abundant and conspicuous present-day plants, about 250,000 species worldwide.

Angulation: the formation of angles.

Animal: a generically used term to designate all species other than plants.

Antennae: head appendages in invertebrates.

Anterior: to the front.

Anterior margin: in zoology, toward the forward or ventral end; in botany, inferior or lower; facing away from the axis.

Anthesis: the blooming of a flower or the time the flower is in full bloom.

Aperture: orifice; hole or opening.

Apex: the tip.

Apical: pertaining to or located at the apex (tip).

Apiculate: ending with a sharp, abrupt tip.

Apomixis: a rare reproductive process in which a new individual is produced from a female cell other than an egg cell.

Aquatic: living in water.

Arachnid: a class of species that includes spiders, scorpions, mites and ticks.

Arboreal: living in trees.

Arboricide: chemicals used to defoliate or kill trees, usually in clearing land for agriculture.

Areoles: the small space between veins in a leaf or insect wings.

Argiustoll: a soil that is darkly colored with an accumulation of silicate clay layers with an average temperature between 5 and 8 degrees Celsius.

Arthropod: invertebrate organism with a horny, segmented external covering and jointed limbs; includes insects, crustaceans, arachnids (such as spiders), and myriapods (such as centipedes).

Association: group of species that are dependent on one another.

Assurgent: slanting or curving upward.

Attenuate: gradually tapering to a point.

Auricular: the feathers covering the opening of a bird's ear; pertaining to hearing.

Awed: having bristles.

Awn: a slender, bristlelike tip, such as those found on spikelets in many grasses.

Axil: the angle between the upper surface of a stalk and its stem or between a branch and its trunk.

Baleen: plates located in the upper jaws of whales that filter plankton from sea water.

Banana poka: woody vine that poses a serious problem to mesic forests on Kauai and Hawaii by covering trees, reducing the amount of light that reaches trees and understory, and causes damage and death to trees by the weight of the vine.

Barbel: a slender, whisker-like sensory organ on the head of a fish or other aquatic animal.

Barred: white or light colored lines; generally refers to barring on the dorsal side of a fish or the breast/belly of a bird.

Basal: located at or pertaining to the base.

Bask: behavior in animals of absorbing sunlight for extended periods.

Basketgrass: perennial grass that is naturalized in shaded mesic valleys and forests, and sometimes in wet forests on most of the main Hawaiian islands.

Beak cavities: a hollow portion in the tip of the umbo of a bivalve mollusk shell.

Beak: the appendage birds use to gather food; the cone-shaped structure in mussels.

Benthic: pertaining to organisms living on the bottom of a lake or sea.

Bicuspid: having two points at the cusp; a tooth with two points.

Biennial-monocarpic: producing a single fruit every other year.

Bifid: divided into two equal parts or lobes.

Bifurcate penis: male sexual organ with two forks.

Bill: the appendage birds use to gather food.

Bipinnately: having leaflets, lobes or divisions in a feather-like arrangement on every other side of a common axis.

Bivalve: in mollusks, the protective shell composed of two hinged halves.

Bivalve mollusk: a mollusk, such as a clam, whose shell consists of two hinged parts.

Bivoltine: having two adult flights, or generations, per year.

Black twig borer: small beetle which burrows into branches, introduces a pathogenic fungus as food for its larvae, and lays its eggs.

Blowhole: the breathing hole located on the head of a whale.

Blubber: a thick layer of fat beneath the skin of a whale.

Boreal: a conifer-dominate forest occurring in the northern high latitudes, bounded on the north by tundra (treeless plain) and to the south by broad-leaved, deciduous forests.

Brachiation: moving through trees by swinging from limb to limb.

Bract: the lifelike part of a plant located below the flower, usually small and sometimes brightly colored; leaves that bracket the flower of a plant.

Branchia: a gill or similar breathing organ.

Breaching: leaping of a whale from the water.

Brood: offspring raised together.

Brood pouch: gill structure in freshwater mussels that is modified to store developing glochidia (larva that have hooks to attach to a host fish).

Brood parasitism: when a bird of one species lays eggs in the nest of a different species to the detriment of the host bird's own young.

Broomsedge: perennial, tufted, fire-adapted grass which is naturalized on Oahu and Hawaii along roadsides and in disturbed dry to mesic forest and shrubland.

Browsing: feeding by plant-eating animals.

Bud: a small protuberance (knob) on a stem or branch containing an undeveloped leaf or flower.

Bursa copulatrix: a saclike, bodily cavity used in copulation.

Bursa: a saclike bodily cavity.

Caducous: dropping off or shedding at an early stage of development, as the gills of amphibians or the leaves of plants.

Caespitose: growing in dense tufts or clumps; matted.

Calcareous: composed of calcium carbonate.

Caldera: a large crater formed by a volcanic explosion or by the collapse of a volcanic cone.

Calyx: the outer protective covering of a flower consisting of leaflike, usually green segments called sepals.

Campanulate: bell shaped.

Cannibalistic: the practice among some animals of eating the flesh of their own species.

Canthal: either of two angles formed by the junction of the eyelids.

Carapace: a hard structure covering all or part of the body, such as a turtle's shell.

Carina: a keel-shaped ridge, such as that on the breastbone of a bird or the petal of certain flowers.

Carpel: the central, ovule-bearing, female organ of a plant.

Caryopsis: a one-celled, one-seeded dry fruit, such as wheat, that has its outer covering fused to its surface.

Caudal: near the tail or hind parts.

Caudal fin: the tail fin of a fish.

Caudal peduncle: a narrowing of the body in front of the caudal fin.

Caudex: the woody trunk-like stem, such as that of a tree fern; the thickened base of the stem in some perennial plants.

Caudices: the woody trunk-like stems, such as those of a tree fern; the thickened base of the stem in some perennial plants.

Caulescent: having a stem showing above the ground.

Cauline: growing on a stem.

Cephalic: pertaining to the head or skull.

Cerambycid: a member of the longhorn beetle family, Cerambycidae.

Cere: a fleshy swelling at the base of the upper part of the beak in certain birds, such as parrots and falcons.

Cespitose: growing in dense tufts or clumps; matted.

Channel: the bed or deeper part of a stream, river or harbor.

Channelization: the process of deepening a river bed.

Chaparral: a dense thicket of shrubs and small trees.

Chasmogamous: showy insect-pollinated flowers.

Chela: a pincher-like claw of a crustacean, such as a crab or lobster.

Chelicerae: two pincher-like appendages near the mouth of an arachnid used for grasping.

Chelonian: belonging to the order of Chelonia, which includes turtles and tortoises.

Chemoreception: the reaction of a sense organ to a chemical stimulus.

Chinaberry: small tree widely cultivated and naturalized on most of the main Hawaiian Islands.

Chitin: a semitransparent horny substance forming the principal component of crustacean shells, insect exoskeletons, and the cell walls of certain fungi.

Chlorophylous leaves: producing chlorophyll (green pigment) during photosynthesis.

Chromatophore: a pigment producing cell, or a pigmented animal cell that can change the color of the skin, as in some lizards.

Ciliate: having microscopic, hairlike appendages extending from a cell and often capable of rhythmical motions.

Cilium: microscopic, hairlike appendage extending from a cell and often capable of rhythmical motions.

Circumscissile: splitting or opening along a transverse circular line.

Cirolanid facies: the characteristics or appearance of a population of isopod crustaceans.

Cirri: slender, flexible appendages, such as tentacles or feelers.

CITES: An international treaty, the purpose of which is to protect endangered species. This is accomplished through the illegalization of trade of these species across international boundaries.

Cladoceran: a small, aquatic crustacean, including water fleas, of the order of Cladocerana.

Class: a taxonomic classification of organisms belonging to related orders. This is the common category by which most animals are referred, such as birds, reptiles, insects, crustaceans, arachnids, amphibians, snails, and mammals; or plants, such as ferns, mosses, and mushrooms.

Clawed: having a narrow petiole-like base.

Cleft: in botany, having deeply divided lobes or divisions.

Cleistogamous: small flowers that lack petals and are self-pollinating; characterized by self-fertilization in an unopened, budlike state.

Cloaca: the cavity into which the intestinal, genital, and urinary tracts open in vertebrates, such as fish, reptiles and birds.

Cloud forest: high-altitude forest with a dense undergrowth of dwarf trees, ferns, mosses, and other plants that grow on the trunks of the trees.

Clump: a thick grouping of plants or trees.

Cluster: a group of similar elements, such as flowers on a plant, occurring closely together.

Clutch: the number of eggs laid in one breeding.

Cocoon: the tough protective covering wherein insect larvae pupate (take their adult form).

Coleopteran: an insect, such as beetles, characterized by fore wings modified to form tough protective covers for the hind wings.

Collembolans: small insects.

Colonial: forming colonies; an inhabitant of a colony.

Colonize: to establish a population in a new territory.

Colony: group of the same species living or growing together.

Commissure: in botany, a surface by which adhering carpels (female organ of a plant) are joined.

Community: a group of plant species that grow in stable association.

Competition: the interaction between different species vying for the same ecological niche, habitat or food supply.

Compound leaf: composed of separate, smaller leaflets.

Congener: a member of the same kind, class or group; an organisim belonging to the same genus as another.

Coniferous forest: comprised primarily of evergreens, usually located in cool, dry climates.

Convective: the transfer of heat or other atmospheric properties by massive motion, especially motion directed upward.

Copepods: small marine and freshwater crustaceans of the order Copepoda.

Copulation: the process by which sperm is transferred from the male to the female.

Coquis: associated with a marine clam of the genus Donax.

Coralline: pertaining to or resembling coral; also red algae covered with a calcareous substance and forming stony deposits.

Cordate: having a heart-shaped outline.

Coriaceous: coarse; leathery.

Corneous: horny, or composed or a hornlike substance.

Corolla: the inner portion of a flower.

Costa: a rib, such as the midrib of a leaf or a thickened anterior vein of an insect's wing.

Costae: ribs, such as the midrib of a leaf or a thickened anterior vein of an insect's wing.

Cotyledon: in botany, a leaf of a plant embryo, being the first or one of the first to appear from a sprouting seed; in anatomy, the lobule of the placenta.

Courtship: behavior in animals prior to mating.

Coverts: one of the feathers covering the longer main feathers of a bird's wing or tail.

Covey: group of birds, usually applied to game birds such as quail.

Crepuscular: becoming active at twilight or before sunrise.

Crest: a tuft or ridge on the head of a bird or other animal.

Cross-blotches: indistinct sequenced specks on a fish.

Crustaceans: invertebrates that include shrimps, crabs and other small marine species.

Ctenoid: having narrow segments or spines resembling the teeth of a comb; fish with ctenoid scales.

Culm: the jointed stem of a grass or sedge.

Cuneate: narrow wedge-shaped leaves that taper toward the base.

Cusp: the fold or flap of a heart valve; also, a pointed end.

Cutaneous: affecting the skin.

Cuticle: the layer of waxlike, water-repellent material covering the epidermis (outer layer) of plants.

Cyathia: small petalless flowers.

Cycle: a series of events that occurs repeatedly in the same sequence.

Cyme: a flat-topped flower cluster that blooms from the center toward the edges, and whose main axis is terminated by a flower.

Cymose: pertaining to a cyme (a flat-topped flower cluster that blooms from the center toward the edges, and whose main axis is terminated by a flower).

Cyprinid: small freshwater fish of the family Cyprinidae, which includes minnows, carps, and shiners.

Cyprinodont: small, soft-finned fish of the family Cyprinodontidae, which includes killifishes and topminnows.

DDT: a pesticide that causes eggshell thinning in birds.

Decapod: ten-legged arthropods.

Deciduous: shedding or losing foliage at the end of a growing season, such as trees losing leaves in the fall.

Decumbent: growing along the ground but erect at the apex (tip).

Decussate: arranged on a stem in opposite pairs at right angels to those above and below.

Deforestation: the process of clearing forests.

Dehiscent: opening at the pores or splitting to release seeds within a fruit or pollen from an anther.

Demersal: species that inhabit the bottom or near bottom of the sea.

Dentate: edged with tooth-like projections.

Denticulate: finely toothed.

Depressed: the body form of a reptile that is flattened laterally.

Dermal: pertaining to the skin.

Desert: habitat with low rainfall and sparse vegetation.

Desiccation: the process of drying out.

Desmid: green, unicellular freshwater algae of the family Desmidiaceae that often forms chain-like colonies.

Detritus: decomposing organisms that serve as a food supply to many species.

Dextral: pertaining to the right side; in zoology, pertaining to a gastropod shell that has its aperture (opening) to the right when facing the observer with the apex (top) upward.

Diapause: a period during which growth or development is suspended, as in insects.

Diatom: minute unicellular or colonial (living in colonies) algae having siliceous cell walls consisting of two overlapping symmetrical parts.

Dichasium: a flat-topped flower cluster having two lateral stems branching from the main axis.

Dichromatize: to become divided into parts or branches.

Digitate: originating from one point.

Digitigrade: walking so that only the toes touch the ground.

Dimorphic: having two distinct forms.

Dimorphism: the occurrence of two distinct forms of the same parts, such as leaves, flowers or stamens, in a single plant or in plants of the same kind; in zoology, differing characteristics between male and female.

Dioecious: having male and female flowers borne on separate plants.

Diploid: having a homologous (genetically the same) pair of chromosomes for each characteristic except sex.

Disk: the round center of a ray flower, such as a daisy, around which petals are arranged.

Dispersal: migration of individuals from their home range.

Display: a pattern of behavior that serves as communication between species, such as mating rituals.

Distal: anatomically located far from the origin or line of attachment.

Distal: located far from the origin of attachment.

Distichous: arranged in two vertical rows or ranks on opposite sides of an axis.

Disturbed area: habitat whose native vegetation has been altered.

Diurnal: plants that open during daylight and close at night; animals that are active during the day and sleep at night.

Diversity: the number of differing species in a habitat.

Division: in botany, a taxonomic grouping of organisms belonging to similar classes; the equivalent of phylum.

Dorsal: situated at the rear of an animal, such as the dorsal fin in a fish.

Dorsoventral: extending from a dorsal (rear) to a ventral (front) surface.

Dorsum: a part of an organ analogous to the back.

Drupe: fruit with a firm outer layer, a fleshy inner layer, and a stony inner layer surrounding a single seed.

Echolocation: the ability of an animal, such as a bat or dolphin, to orient itself by the reflection of sound it has produced.

Ecology: the study of the relationship of plants and animals to each other and to their habitats.

Ecosystem: a community of organisms that interact with each other and their environment.

Ectocone: an ecological community of mixed vegetation formed by the overlapping of adjoining communities.

Edaphic: pertaining to the soil as it affects living organisms.

Ellipsoid: an ellipse-shaped surface.

Elytral: the thickened, hard fore-wing of a beetle or a platelike respiratory structure on the dorsal surface of a scale worm.

Emarginate: having a notched tip.

Embryo: an organism in the early stages of development; unhatched.

Endangered Species Act of 1973: The purposes of the Act are to determine on the basis of scientific evidence alone whether any species is endangered or threatened and to "list" the ones that are; to prohibit anyone from harming a listed species; protect the species from illegal trade; and to prevent government programs from jeopardizing a listed species.

Endemic: species that are native to a specific region; non-endemic species are called "exotic"

Endocarp: innermost layers of the fruit wall.

Entire: a leaf whose margin is undivided.

Entisols: soils without natural genetic horizons or with weakly developed horizons.

Entomology: the study of insects.

Environment: all the conditions that affect the growth and sustenance of organisms.

Environmental stress: stress on a species caused by the dwindling of resources necessary to sustain an organism's survival.

Epipetalous: united on the petals.

Epiphyseal: part of the bone, often the end of a long bone, that develops separated from the main portion of the cartilage.

Epiphyte: a plant, such as certain orchids and ferns, that grows on another plant for mechanical support but not for nutrients; epiphytes are not considered parasites.

Epiphytic: pertaining to an epiphyte (a plant, such as certain orchids and ferns, that grows on another plant for mechanical support but not for nutrients); not rooted in the soil.

Epiphytically: not rooted in the soil.

Epithet: term used as a descriptive substitute for the name.

Ericoid habitat: occurring in association with an ericaceous (heath family) shrub layer.

Erose: irregularly notched, toothed, or indented.

Estivate: to pass the summer in dormancy.

Estrus: a regularly recurring period of ovulation and sexual excitement in mammals other than humans.

Euphotic zone: occurring in depths less than 4 meters.

Euryhaline: adapted to living in fresh or brackish water.

Eutrophic: pertaining to a body of water in which the increase of mineral and organic nutrients has reduced the dissolved oxygen, producing an environment that favors plant over animal life.

Eutrophication: in a body of water, the process in which the increase of mineral and organic nutrients has reduced the oxygen, producing an environment that favors plants over animal life.

Exocarp: outermost layers of the fruit wall.

Exotic: a plant or organism that is not endemic to a region; non-native, introduced.

Exstipulate: having no stipules.

Extinct: a species that has no surviving individuals.

Extirpate: to eliminate a population.

Faculatatively: adaptive to varying environments.

Falcate: curved and tapering to a point.

Family: a taxonomic category below Order and above Genus based on the grouping of related genera. For example, within the **Class** called birds, the families are grouped into categories such as falcons, sparrows, ducks, and parrots.

Fascicles: a bundlelike cluster of flowers, stems or leaves.

Fasciculate: clustering of flowers, stems or leaves.

Fauna: animal life.

Femoral: pertaining to the thigh.

Fen: low, flat, swampy land; a bog.

Fertilization: the union of a sperm and egg that stimulates growth of the embryo.

Filiform: threadlike.

Filter feeding: in marine life, the process of filtering food from water through a siphoning organ.

Fimbriate: fringed, as the edge of a petal or the opening of a duct.

Fin: that portion of a fish's body that propels it or assists in swimming.

Fish ladder: a device constructed by people that assists spawning fish to pass an obstruction, usually a dam.

Flagellum: whip-like extensions of unicellular organisms, usually used for locomotion.

Flank: the side or lateral part of the body.

Fledgling: stage of development in birds when flight feathers are developed.

Flora: plants of a region or period.

Floriferous: bearing flowers.

Foliaceous: having leaves or a leaflike structure.

Follicle: a single-chambered fruit that splits along only one seam to release its seeds.

Fontanelle: the soft membranous intervals between the incompletely ossified cranial bones of a fetus or infant.

Food chain: interdependence of feeding organisms that prey upon lower or more vulnerable species. Frequently, if one species in a food chain is eliminated, all species within the chain are affected. For example, when farmers exterminated prairie dogs in the midwest, a dramatic decline in the black footed ferret occurred.

Fossil: an impression or cast of a plant or animal preserved in rock.

Fossorial: adapted to burrowing or digging.

Fostering: when the young of one species are raised by parents of a related species.

Fountain grass: fire-adapted bunch grass that spead widely over bare lava flows and open areas on the island of Hawaii. It invades Hawaii's dry forests where it interferes with plant regeneration, carries fires into areas not usually prone to fires, and increases the likelihood of fire.

Frog: a smooth-skinned amphibian, usually aquatic or semi-aquatic.

Frontal shield: area covering the forehead of birds.

Fruit dispersal: release of seeds or pollen.

Fuscous: dusky; dark gray or grayish brown.

Fusiform: tapering at each end; spindle shaped.

Galea: a helmet-shaped part, as in the upper part of certain plants and insects.

Gallinaceous: characteristic of the order Galliformes, which includes common domestic fowl, pheasants, turkeys and grouse.

Gallinule: wading bird characteristically having dark, iridescent plummage.

Gamete: a mature sperm or egg capable of participating in fertilization.

Ganglia: in anatomy, a group of nerve cells located outside the brain or spinal cord in vertebrates; in pathology, a cystic lesion resembling a cyst-like tumor.

Gastropods: a mollusk of the class Gastropoda, including snails, slugs, and limpets, characteristically having a single, usually coiled shell and a ventral muscular mass serving as an organ of locomotion.

Genetic: pertaining to characteristics that are passed by chromosomes from one generation to the next.

Genus: principal subdivision of a family, such as rattlesnakes (**genus**) being a type of snake (**family**), which is a type of serpent (**order**), which is a type of reptile (**class**).

Geomorphologic agent: a force causing change in land forms.

Gestation period: amount of time the developing young are carried within the body of the mother.

Gill slits: the openings in the gill that permit water to enter.

Gills: the principal respiratory organ of a fish.

Glabrous: having no hairs; smooth.

Glaciate: to subject to glacial action; to cover with ice or a glacier.

Globose: spherical.

Glochidia: a parasitic larva, produced by freshwater mussels, that have hooks to attach to a host fish.

Glume: a chaffy basal bract on the spikelet of a grass.

Gonad: testicle or ovary; an organ that produces reproductive cells.

Gonopodium: a penetrating organ used in copulation.

Gonopore: a reproductive aperture or pore.

Graminivorous: feeding on grasses, seeds or grain.

Graminoids: the food of graminivorous species that includes grasses, seeds, and grain.

Granivorous: feeding on grain and seeds.

Grasslands: ground dominated by grasses and lacking in trees as a result of the amount of rainfall.

Gravid: pregnant.

Group: in the animal kingdom, the division of species into amphibians, arachnids, birds, crustaceans, fish, insects, mammals, mussels, reptiles, and snails.

Gular: pertaining to or located on the throat.

Gynaecandrous: staminate and pistallate flowers that are located on the same spike.

Gynoecium: the female reproductive organs of a flower; the pistil or pistils collectively.

Habit: characteristic appearance, form, or manner of growth of a plant.

Habitat: the locality and conditions which support the life of an organism.

Hacking: to release a captive-bred bird into the wild.

Haploid: having half the number of normal chromosomes.

Haplustolls: a well- to moderately well-drained darkly colored soil that is textured of loamy, very fine sand.

Hatchling: a young animal that has just emerged from its shell.

Head shields: easily identifiable structures which arch over the lip in some nematodes (threadlike worms).

Headpool: headwater pool.

Heads: Dense flower clusters.

Heliothermic: organisms that maintain a comparatively high body temperature by basking in the sun.

Helper: in birds, a bird without young of her own that assists in the nurturing of other young.

Henry's crabgrass: annual grass that forms thick mats, and has been naturalized for lawns and pastures.

Herbaceous: green and leaflike in appearance and texture.

Herbicide: a chemical used to kill plants.

Herbivore: species that feed mainly on plants.

Hermaphrodite: an organism, such as a worm, having male and female reproductive organs in the same individual.

Heteromorphic: possessing two sets of stamens (male reproductive organs in plants) of unequal length.

Heterostylous: a polymorphism of flowers which helps to prevent self-pollination by having various lengths of styles and stamens between individuals of a species.

Hexapod: six-legged arthropods.

Hibernacula: a case, covering or structure in which an organism remains dormant for the winter; the shelter of a hibernating animal.

Hilo grass: one of several grasses introduced for cattle fodder that have become noxious weeds. Hilo grass rapidly forms a dense ground cover in wet habitats. Its small, hairy seeds are easily transported on animals or carried by the wind through native forests.

Hispid: covered with stiff or rough hair, or bristles.

Holostomatous: a minute opening of a leaf or stem through which gases and water vapor pass.

Holotype: the specimen used as the basis of the original published description of a taxonomic species.

Home range: an area defined by the habitual movements of an animal.

Host fish: a fish on which mussel larvae reside until they are capable of surviving on their own.

Host: an organism that harbors and provides nourishment for a parasite.

Hummock: a low mound, ridge or knoll.

Humults: freely drained ultisols which have a high content of organic matter.

Hyaline: a glossy or transparent appearance.

Hybrid: an offspring produced by parents of different species; for example, a donkey and a horse produce a mule.

Hypanthium: the modified, often enlarged floral receptacle of various plants, having a cup-shaped or tubular form; the basal portion of the flower.

Hypogynous: having floral parts or organs that are below and not in contact with the ovary.

Hypothermic: abnormally low body temperature.

Immature: juvenile; in insects, the larval stage of development.

Imperforate: having no opening.

Impoundment: accumulation of water in a reservoir.

Incubation: keeping eggs warm until they hatch.

Indian tribal law: laws that extend to Native Americans certain exceptions to the protective measures of the Endangered Species Act, such as taking for sustenance limited quantities of endangered species.

Individual: a single member of a population.

Indusium: the covering of the sorus of a fern.

Inflated: in botany, hollow and enlarged.

Inflorescence: flower cluster.

Insectivore: an organism that feeds primarily on insects.

Instar: the stage between molts in insects; larval development stages.

Interbrood intervals: period between producing young.

Interneural: in between nerves.

Intersupraocular scales: scales above and between the eyes.

Introduced: a plant or animal that has been brought in from outside a region; also called "exotic" or "non-native."

Invasion: the migration of a species into a new area, usually to the detriment of organisms already living there.

Invertebrate: animals lacking a backbone, such as insects.

Involucre: a whorl of leaflike scales or bracts beneath or around a flower or flower cluster.

Ironwood: large, fast-growing tree that shades out other plants, consumes much of the available nutrients, and possibly releases a chemical agent that prevents other plants from growing beneath it.

Isohyperthermic: an equally high temperature regime of soils (above 25 degrees Celsius at 50 centimeters depth).

Isohypothermic: uniformly low body temperature.

Isolated: a portion of a breeding population that is cut off from the rest of the population.

Isopod: crustacean of the order Isopoda, which includes sow bugs and gribbles.

IUCN Red Data Book: the official listing document of threatened species worldwide by the Swiss organization, International Union for Conservation of Nature and Natural Resources, now known as the World Conservation Union.

Karst: limestone formations.

Keel: a prominent ridge on the back of an animal.

Keratin: a tough, fibrous protein substance that forms the outer layer of epidermal structures (protective covering) such as hair, nails, horns and hoofs.

Keratinized: two-edged tooth.

Kikuyu grass: aggressive, perennial grass introduced as a pasture grass, which chokes out other plants and prevents their seedlings from become established. Declared a noxious weed.

Kingdom: the highest taxonomic division into which organisms are classified, as either animals or plants. Some organisms not readily classified as plants or animals, such as amoebae and paramecium, are sometimes classified in a third kingdom called Protista.

Koa haole: a naturalized shrub which is sometimes the dominant species in low elevation, dry, disturbed areas on all the main Hawaiian islands.

Krill: small marine creatures that serve as an important food supply to fish, whales, and birds.

Kuchler system: An approximation of the potential natural vegetation of the U.S., established by A. W. Kuchler.

Lacustrine: living or growing in lakes.

Lamella: a thin scale, plate or layer, as found in the gills of a bivalve mollusk and the gills of a mushroom.

Lanceolate: narrow and tapering at each end.

Lantana: an aggressive, thicket-forming plant introduced to the Hawaiian islands as an ornamental plant; it grows on all the main islands in mesic forests, dry shrublands, and other dry, disturbed habitats.

Larva: a pre-adult form of a species that does not resemble the adult.

Lateral: pertaining to the side.

Leaf blade: the flat, extended part of the leaf.

Legume: a pod, such as a pea or bean, that splits into two valves with seeds attached to the lower edge of one of the valves.

Lemma: the outer, lower bract enclosing the flower in a grass spikelet.

Lenticels: small pores on the surface of stems of woody plants that allow the passage of gases to and from the interior tissue.

Lepidopterous: insects with four wings covered with small scales, including moths and butterflies.

Life cycle: the sequence of events in the progression of an organism from birth to death.

Limnetic: pertaining to the deeper, open waters or lakes or ponds.

Linear leaf: long, narrow leaf, characterized by parallel veins.

Lithic: pertaining to stone, or lithium-based.

Littoral: a shore or coastal region.

Live-bearing: giving birth to fully-developed young; ovoviviparous.

Lobed leaf: characterized by rounded projections.

Localized: found within a limited geographic area.

Loculicidal: a small cavity or compartment within an organ or part, such as a plant ovary.

Loess: a buff to gray, fine-grained silt or clay, thought to be a deposit from wind-blown dust.

Lore: the area between a bird's eye and the base of the bill; the area between the snout and eye of a snake or fish.

Lotic: pertaining to or living in moving water.

Lunular: crescent shaped.

Lycaenid: a member of the family Lycaenidae; a heteroneuran lepidopteran insect, including moths and butterflies.

Macrophytes: microscopic plants in an aquatic environment.

Maculation: the spotted markings on a plant or animal, such as the spots on a leopard.

Mamma: an organ of female mammals that contains milk-producing glands.

Mammal: vertebrates that are warm-blooded, usually possess hair, and nourish their young on the mother's milk.

Mandible: the lower jaw in vertebrates; either the upper or lower part of the beak in birds; any one of several mouth parts in insects.

Mandibular: pertaining to the jaw.

Mangabey: a monkey of equatorial Africa, having a long tail and relatively long muzzle.

Mangrove: a tropical tree with exposed roots forming an interlocking mass; often vital to stabilizing shore lines.

Mantle: the cerebral cortex; the wings, shoulder feathers, and back of a bird when colored differently from the rest of the body; in mollusks and brachipods, the membrane between the body and shell.

Manzanita: an evergreen shrub of Pacific North America bearing white or pink flowers in clusters.

Marcescent: withering but not falling off, as a blossom that persists on a twig after flowering.

Margin: the edge of a flower or insect's wing.

Marsupial: a mammal of the order Marsupialia, found mainly in Australia, that includes kangaroos, opossums and wombats; set apart by urogenital and skeletal differences.

Marsupium: an external abdominal pouch in female marsupials that contains mammary glands (breasts) and that shelters the young; also, a temporary egg pouch in animals.

Medial: situation in or extending toward the middle.

Melanistic: darkness of the skin, hair or eyes resulting from high pigmentation (coloration).

Melanophore: a chromatophore (pigment producing cell, or a pigmated animal cell that can change the color of the skin, as in some lizards) that contains melanin (a dark pigment).

Membrane: a thin, pliable layer of tissue covering surfaces or connecting regions, structures or organs of a plant or animal.

Membranous: pertaining to a membrane, a thin, pliable layer of tissue covering surfaces or connecting regions, structures or organs of a plant or animal.

Mesic distichlis meadows: well-drained grassy meadows.

Mesic: between dry and wet.

Mesocone: protrusion in gastropods.

Metabolism: chemical process within an organism to release energy.

Metamorphosis: development from one stage of maturity to the next, usually with marked change in appearance.

Metatarsus: a part of the hind foot in four-legged animals or in the foot of birds.

Microclimate: the conditions immediately surrounding an organism, often differing significantly from the environment as a whole.

Migration: the seasonal movement of animals from one territory to another.

Migratory Bird Treaty Act: This treaty of 1918 provides legal protection of migratory birds; it also paved the way for cooperation in avian management between the U.S. and bordering countries.

Mogotes: small outcrop.

Mollusk: animals that have a muscular foot and a dorsal shell, such as snails and mussels.

Molt: to shed the outer covering.

Monocarpic: producing a single fruit.

Monoclinous: having pistils and stamens in the same flower.

Monoecious: having male and female reproductive organs in separate flowers on the same plant.

Monogamous: having one mate for life.

Monophagous: eating only one kind of food.

Monophyletic: pertaining to a single phylum of plants or animals; derived from one source.

Monotypic: the only member of its genus.

Montane forest: forest located at the middle altitude of a mountain.

Montane: mountainous.

Morph: any individual of a polymorphic (the occurrence of different forms, stages, or color types in organisms of the same species) group.

Morphology: the biological study of the form and structure of living organisms.

Mosaic bones: bone tissue composed of somatic cells of genetically different types; this phenomenon is caused by gene or chromosome mutations.

Mucronate: a sharp tip of some plants and animal organs.

Mucronulate: having a sharp terminal point or spiny tip.

Mycelium: the vegetative part of a fungus consisting of a mass of branching, threadlike filaments called hyphae.

Mycorrhizae: the symbiotic (mutually beneficial) association of the mycelium (filaments) of a fungus with the roots of a plant.

Myriapod: an arthropod, such as a centipede, with segmented bodies and many legs.

Nacre: Mother-of-pearl.

Native: indigenous; original to the region; not introduced from another region; endemic.

Nectar: secretion from plants that attracts pollinators.

Nectary dish: fleshy, nectar-producing structure.

Nematode: a worm of the phylum Nematoda, having unsegmented, threadlike bodies, many of which are parasitic, as the hookworm.

Nester: a species that nests.

New World Monkey: monkeys inhabiting the tropical forests of the Western hemisphere, primarily South and Central America.

Niche: the adaptive position of a species within the ecosystem.

Nocturnal: active at night.

Non-native: alien to an area; sometimes called "exotic"; not endemic.

Nuchal: pertaining to the neck; in insects, the dorsal region of the thorax.

Nuehal hump: any hump on the nape of the neck.

Nutrient: food substance that promotes growth.

Oblanceolate: broader and rounded at the apex (tip) and tapering at the base.

Obligate lacustrine suckers: fish (suckers) that can survive only in lakes.

Obligate: a type of plant that almost always (greater than 99% of the time), under natural conditions, occurs in wetlands.

Ocellus: a small simple eye found in many invertebrates; a marking resembling an eye.

Ocreolae: sheafs composed of one or more stipules, enclosing the leafstalk.

Off-road vehicle: vehicles designed to travel over rough terrain and, incidentally, often destroy wildlife.

Oligotrophic: lacking in plant nutrients and having an abundance of dissolved oxygen throughout.

Olivaceous: olive green color.

Omnivore: a species that eats a large variety of foods.

Oostegites: plates on the thoracic limbs of certain crustaceans, forming a brood-pouch in which the young develop.

Operculum: a lid or flap covering an aperture, such as the gill cover in fish or the horny shell cover in snails.

Opportunistic: a species that adapts its feeding habits to the most available food source.

Order: a systematic grouping of organisms belonging to similar families. The order divides the class into animals that share many common characteristics. For example, the **Class** called "reptiles" is further divided into the **Order** of turtles and snakes.

Ossify: to change into bone.

Ostracods: minute, chiefly freshwater crustaceans of the order Ostracoda that have a bivalve carapace (a shell with two hinged parts).

Overgrazing: occurs when animals feed too long in one area, causing destruction of vegetation and erosion of soil.

Oviparous: producing eggs that hatch outside the body.

Oviposition: to lay eggs.

Ovoid: egg shaped.

Ovotestis: the reproductive gland of some hermaphroditic gastropods.

Ovoviparous: the condition in which eggs are hatched within the mother and born alive.

Ovum: the female reproductive cell (eggs) in animals.

Pair bond: a long-term relationship between a male and a female. Pair bond species mate for one or several breeding seasons while monogamous species mate for life.

Palea: small, chafflike bract enclosing the flower of a grass spikelet.

Pallial: pertaining to the mantle (membrane between the body and shell) of a mollusk.

Palmate: having leaflets or lobes radiating from one point; resembling a palm.

Palmate leaf: divided so as to radiate from one point-like a hand.

Panicle: a flower cluster that is loosely and irregularly branched; a complex, branched inflorescence.

Paniculate-cymose: irregularly branched flower cluster blooming from the center.

Papillae: a small, nipple-like projection.

Parasite: an organism that extracts nutrients from another host organism.

Parasitic stage: the period during the development of an organism in which it feeds on and is sheltered by a different organism (host).

Paratypes: A specimen other than the holotype which was collected before the original description but has been deemed one of the specimens upon which the original description was based.

Parietal: in anatomy, relating to either of the parietal bones, which are two large, irregularly quadrilateral bones that form, with the occipital bones, the sides and top of the skull; in botany, attached to the ovary wall.

Parthenogenic: reproduction without contact between the sexual organs.

Parturition: pertaining to childbirth or labor.

Passerines: birds of the order Passerineformes, which includes perching birds and song birds, such as jays, blackbirds, finches, warblers and sparrows.

Paucispiral: growth lines on a snail's operculum occurring as a few, rapidly expanding spirals.

Pectin: colloidal substances found in ripe fruits, such as apples; pectin is used commercially to jell foods, drugs and cosmetics.

Pectinase: a plant enzyme that catalyzes the hydrolysis of pectin.

Pectoral: in animals, pertaining to the chest muscle; in fish, the fin located nearest the head.

Pedicel: small stalks bearing a single flower.

Pedicellate: supported by a pedicel (small stalk).

Pedipalpi: appendages of an arachnid that are modified for sensory functions.

Peduncle: in botany, a stalk or stem bearing a solitary flower; in zoology, a starlike structure in invertebrate animals.

Pelage: the coat of a mammal consisting of hair, fur, wool or other soft covering as distinct from bare skin.

Pelagic: ocean-dwelling.

Pendent: hanging down, dangling or suspended.

Pendulous: hanging loosely so as to swing or sway.

Peraeonal: a segment of a snail's shell.

Percoid: pertaining to the suborder of fish including perches, sunfishes, groupers, and grunts.

Perfect: possessing both male and female flowers.

Perianth: the outer envelope of a flower.

Peridotite: igneous rocks having a granite-like texture.

Periodicity: recurring patterns of behavior.

Periostracum: A protective layer covering the outer portion of a mollusk shell.

Periphyton: stationery organisms that live attached to surfaces projecting from the bottom of a freshwater environment.

Peristone: in botany, a circular row of toothless appendages surrounding the mouth of a moss capsule; in zoology, the area around the mouth in certain invertebrates.

Peritoneum: abdominal cavity.

Petal: a segment of the corolla of a flower.

Petiole: in botany, the stalk by which a leaf is attached to the stem; in zoology, the slender stalk-like connection between the thorax and the abdomen in certain insects.

Petrel: seabirds of the order Procellariiformes, especially the storm petrel.

pH: a measure of the acidity or alkalinity of a solution, numerically equivalent to 7 for neutral solutions; the numerical scale increases with alkalinity and decreases with acidity.

Phacelia: Gastric filament; functions to kill or paralyze live prey taken into the stomach of the species.

Phalanger: a small, arboreal marsupial of Australia having a long tail and dense wooly fur.

Pharyngeal teeth: teeth developed on the pharyngeal bone in many fishes.

Phenology: the study of periodic biological occurrences and behavior, such as flowering, breeding, and migration.

Phenophases: leaf color change.

Phenotype: organisms exhibiting similar environmentally and genetically observable appearances.

Photoperiod: the number of hours of light in a given day.

Photosynthesis: the process by which plants convert light to chemical energy and synthesize organic compounds from inorganic compounds, such as carbon dioxide to oxygen.

Phreatic water: ground water.

Phyllite: a green, gray or red metamorphic rock similar to slate.

Phylum: after dividing organisms by their kingdoms–animals and plants–the phylum distinguishes organisms by their bodily structure; for example, sponges form one group within the phylum while mollusks and arthropods form two other groups. Vertebrates (animals with backbones) are grouped into a separate phylum, called a subphylum, which includes mammals and birds; the divisions of the animal kingdom, synonymous to the division of plants.

Phytoplankton: aquatic, microscopic plants.

Pilose: covered with fine hair or down.

Pinna: one of the leaflets in a featherlike leaf.

Pinnae: leaflets in a featherlike arrangement.

Pinnate leaf: compound leaf with leaflets arranged in pairs along a stem.

Pinnate: having leaflets, lobes or divisions in a feather-like arrangement on each side of a common axis, as in many compound leaves.

Pinnatifid: having pinnately (arranged on either side of a common axis) cleft lobes or divisions.

Piscivorous: feeding on fish.

Pistil: the seed-bearing organ of a flower.

Planispiral: having a shell coiled in one plane.

Plastron: the ventral (under) surface of the shell of a turtle or tortoise.

Plate loss: a phenomena experienced in which there is a loss of scutes, lamina or other than flat structure.

Plecopteran nymphs: The immature larval stage of a stonefly.

Pleistocene: belonging to the geologic period characterized by northern glaciation and the appearance of early forms of humans.

Pocosin: a swamp in an upland coastal region.

Poikilothermic: having a body temperature that varies with the external environment, sometimes called "cold blooded."

Pollination: the process by which pollen is transported to the female parts of a flower.

Pollution: the disruption of an ecosystem by contaminants.

Polyandry: having an indefinite number of stamens (male reproductive organs).

Polyembryonic: having multiple embryos.

Polygamy: having more than one mate at the same time. More specifically, the female hatches more than one brood in a nesting season with different mates.

Polymorphism: the occurrence of different forms, stages, or color types in organisms of the same species.

Population: a group of individuals within a defined area that is capable of interbreeding.

Postcleithrum: a membrane-bone between the cleithrum and the supracleithrum in the pectoral girdle of a bony fish. These three bones are of dermal origin and are superimposed upon the original cartilaginous pectoral girdle which consists of the scapulae and coracoids.

Posterior margin: toward the back end; used in reference to mussel/clam anatomy.

Posterior: the rear or tail region of an animal.

Postocular: behind the eyes.

Precambrian: the oldest and most expansive of geological periods characterized by the appearance of primitive life forms.

Precocial: pertaining to birds that are covered with down and capable of mobility when first hatched.

Predator: an animal that hunts other animals for food.

Premaxillae: bones located in front of and between the maxillary bones in the upper jaw of vertebrates.

Prey: animals that are hunted by predators.

Proandrous: condition in which the stamens (male organ) of a flower mature before the pistil (female organ) is receptive.

Proboscis: a long flexible snout or trunk, as of an elephant; the slender, tubular feeding and sucking structure of some insects.

Process: an appendage; a part extending or projecting from an organ or organism.

Progenitor: a direct ancestor or originator of the line of descent.

Proliferous: reproducing freely by means of buds and side branches; freely producing buds or offshoots, sometimes from unusual places.

Pronotum: plates covering the first segment of the thorax in insects.

Propagules: portion of an organism capable of producing a new individual.

Prosoma: the anterior (front) portion of the body of an invertebrate when primitive segmentation is not evident.

Prostrate: growing flat along the ground; similiar to decumbent except that with decumbent growth the plant becomes erect at the apex.

Protozoa: single-shelled, usually microscopic organisms of the phylum or sub kingdom Protozoa, which included the most primitive forms of animal life.

Protractile premaxillaries: bones located in the upper jaw of vertebrates that are capable of being extended.

Psyllid: any of various plant lice of the family Chermidae.

Puberulent: covered with minute hairs or very fine down.

Puberulous: covered with minute or fine hairs.

Pubescent: covered with short hairs or soft down; also, having reached puberty.

Pulmonate: having lungs or a lung-like structure.

Pulvinate: having a swelling at the base; used as a leafstalk; cushionlike.

Punctate: having tiny spots, points or depressions.

Pupa: the inactive stage in the metamorphosis (evolution) of many insects following the larval stage and preceding the adult form.

Pupal stage: the non-feeding period when larval tissues are reformed into adult structure inside a cocoon.

Pupation: to become a pupa (pre adult).

Pustule: a small swelling similar to a blister or pimple.

Quadrate: in zoology, a bone or cartilage of the skull joining the upper and lower jaws in birds, fish, reptiles and amphibians.

Quartzipsamment: sandy, quartz-based soil.

Raceme: the arrangement of flowers singly along a common main stalk, as in the lily of the valley.

Rachis: the main stem of an inflorescence (flower cluster); the stalk that bears the flowers.

Rack: the antlers of mammals in the family Cervidae, including deer and moose.

Radio tracking: using an affixed transmitter to follow the movements of an animal.

Radipose: a fleshy fin posterior to the dorsal.

Radula: in mollusks, a flexible tongue-like organ with rows of horny teeth on the surface.

Range: geographical area wherein a species resides.

Raptor: a bird of prey.

Rays: the flat blades that encircle a flower disk; in zoology, one of the bony spines supporting the membrane of a fish's fin; also, a description for the color pattern or ridges on a shell.

Receptacle: base of the flowers.

Redds: the eggs deposited in one spawning season in fish.

Refugia: multiple places of protection or shelter (refuges).

Refugial population: the plants or animals protected in a refuge.

Regolith: the layer of loose rock material resting on bedrock, and constituting the surface of most land.

Relict: a localized species or population that has survived from an earlier epoch.

Reproductive phenology: the study of breeding as related to weather.

Reticulate: marked with lines resembling a network, as in the veins of a leaf.

Retrices: stiff tail feathers used for maneuvering during flight.

Revolute: rolled back on the under surface from the tip, as in some leaves before they open.

Rhizomate: a root-like, usually horizontal stem growing under or along the ground that sends out roots from its lower surface and leaves from its upper surface.

Rhomboidal: shaped-like a parallelogram with unequal adjacent sides.

Riffle: a rocky shoal or sandbar lying just below the surface of a river.

Riparian: pertaining to the bank of a natural course of water.

Rosette: a circular cluster of leaves or other plant parts.

Rufous: strong yellowish pink to moderate orange or reddish-brown color.

Rugose: having a rough and ridged surface, as in prominently veined leaves.

Sagittal: relating to the structure that unites the two parietal bones of the skull.

Salamander: type of amphibian characterized by a tail.

Salverform: a phenomenon in which a flower has united petals in which the calyx and corolla (perianth) are the same size, shape and texture. The perianth extends from the center of the flower, and the corolla has an elongated slender tube and a flared flat limb.

Saprophyte: a plant that lives on or derives nourishment from dead or decaying organic matter.

Savanna (savannah): an extensive tropical vegetation dominated by grasses with varying mixtures of bushes and trees in open, wet land.

Scabrous: rough-surfaced, bearing short stiff hairs, scales or points.

Scandent: climbing.

Scapular: one of the feathers covering the shoulder of a bird.

Scarious: thin, membraneous and dry.

Scavenger: an animal that feeds on dead animals it did not kill.

Schizocarp: a dry fruit that breaks open at maturity. It is derived from two or more female stalks and matures as a single fruit.

Sclerophyllous forest: characterized by thick hard foliage.

Sclerotization: the process by which the cuticle of an insect is hardened.

Scorpiod: curved or curled-like the tail of a scorpion.

Scrape: a shallow depression that serves as a nest.

Scrub: a plant community characterized by scattered, low-growing trees and shrubs, interspersed with herbs, grasses, and patches of bare soil.

Sculpture: the ridges or outer markings on a shell.

Scute: a horny, chitinous or bony external plate or scale, such as the shell of a turtle.

Seepage water: water flowing toward stream channels after infiltration into the ground.

Sepal: usually green segments forming the calyx (outer covering) of a flower.

Sericeous: covered with silky hairs.

Serrate: having notched, toothlike projections.

Serrations: a series of teeth or notches.

Serrulate: having small, toothlike notches along the edge.

Sessile: in botany, stalkless and attached directly to the base; in zoology, permanently attached, not free-moving.

Sheath: a protective covering, such as the tubular base of a leaf surrounding a stem.

Shiner: small, often silvery North American fish of the family Cyprinidae.

Silicle: a short, flat pod that is divided by a membranous partition and splits at both seams.

Silique: a long pod that is divided by a membranous partition and splits at both seams, such as the fruit of the mustards.

Siltation: the process of depositing silt.

Sinistral: in zoology, pertaining to a gastropod shell that has its aperture (opening) to the left when facing the observer with the apex (top) up.

Sinuses: in botany, a notch or indentation between lobes of a leaf or corolla.

Siphon: a tubular organ, especially in aquatic invertebrates such as squids and clams, by which water is taken in or expelled.

Slackwater: the period at high or low tide when there is no visible flow of water; an area in a sea or river unaffected by currents.

Solifluction: freezing and thawing soil.

Solitary: individual that lives alone.

Sori: clusters of spore cases borne by ferns on the underside of the fronds; groups of spore-producing bodies.

Sorus: a cluster of spore cases borne by ferns on the underside of the fronds.

Spatulate: shaped like a spatula, having a broad, flat, flexible blade.

Spawning: laying and fertilizing of fish eggs, often involving migration to stream headwaters.

Specialization: evolution of a species so that it occupies a narrow place or niche in the community.

Species: a group of organisms with distinct characteristics that is capable of interbreeding and producing like offspring; the basic taxonomic category, such as the San Francisco Garter Snake being a distinct biological type of water snake.

Spike: a long flower cluster arranged along a stem.

Spikelets: subclusters of flowers.

Spikes: unbranched clusters of unstalked flowers.

Spine: in zoology, the spinal column of a vertebrate; in botany, a sharp-pointed, usually woody part extending from the stem of a plant.

Spinifex: any of a variety of Australian grasses growing in arid regions and having spiny leaves or seeds.

Spiracle: a secondary gill slit positioned in front of the primary gill slits.

Sporangium: a sac-like structure within which fungal spores are formed; spores are released when the sac ruptures.

Spurs: branches with much shortened internodes.

Squamation: an arrangement of scales, as on a fish.

Stamen: the pollen producing reproductive organ (male) of a flower, usually consisting of a filament and an anther.

Staminate: bearing stamens but lacking pistils.

Statoconia: one of the calcareous granules found in the statocyst of certain animals.

Statocysts: small organs of balance in many invertebrates, consisting of a fluid-filled sac containing statoliths that help to indicate position when the animal moves.

Statolith: a small, movable concentration of calcium carbonate.

Stellate: shaped like a star; radiating from a center.

Stipe: a stalk or stalk-like structure, such as the stem-like support of the cap of a mushroom or the main stem of a fern frond.

Stipitate: having a stipe or being supported by a stipe (stalk).

Stipules: one of the usually small paired leaf-like appendages at the base of a leaf or leafstalk.

Stochastic: chance or random events that could lead to the extinction or extirpation of a species.

Stoma: a minute opening of a leaf or stem through which gases and water vapor pass.

Strawberry guava: widely naturalized on all the main Hawaiian Islands, this plant is found in mesic and wet forests in the Koolau Mountains. Strawberry guava develops into dense stands in which few other plants can grow. Feral pigs eat the plant, and disburse its seeds throughout the forest.

Striae: many lines.

Style: a slender, tubular, or bristle-like appendage; in botany, the slender part of a pistal rising from the ovary.

Sub-rhomboidal: less than rhomboidal in shape (like a parallelogram with unequal adjacent sides).

Subalpine: a conifer-dominated forest which occurs in temperate latitudes; related to the boreal forest.

Subgenus: taxonomical category between a genus and a species, such as dogs (**genus**) being divided into spaniels and terriers.

Subphylum: subdivision of phylum composed of closely related groups of animals, such as vertebrates.

Subsessile: attached below the base.

Subspecies: a subgroup that may in outward appearance and behavior appear to be identical to other members of the species but which possess characteristics that are biologically different.

Substrate: composition of stream bed; the surface on which a plant grows or is attached.

Subterminal mouth: located nearly at the end.

Subtropical: regions bordering on the tropics.

Succession: progressive changes in the composition of a plant community.

Succulent: a plant having thick, fleshy leaves or stems that conserve moisture.

Sucker: in zoology, a chiefly North American fish having a thick-lipped mouth adapted for feeding by sucking; in botany, a secondary shoot arising from the base of a trunk.

Suffrutescent: having a woody stem or base.

Sulcus: narrow fissures separating cerebral convolutions (convex folds on the surface of the brain).

Superclass: taxonomic level between phylum and class; a combination of classes, such as fish.

Supralabials: above the lip.

Supraoculars: above the eye.

Sutures: in biology, a seam-like joint or line of articulation, such as the line of dehiscence (an opening that releases seeds) in a seed or fruit; in anatomy, the line of junction between two bones, especially the skull.

Sympatric: occupying the same geographic area without interbreeding.

Synchronous: in biology, the birth of all the young, usually hatching from eggs, at the same time.

Syndactyl: having two or more wholly fused digits (fingers or toes).

Synonyms: a taxonomic name that is equivalent to or replaced by another name.

Tadpole: the larva of a frog or toad.

Taenioglossate: a long narrow tongue-like structure or a ribbon with tooth-like structure.

Talus: a slope formed by the accumulation of debris; a sloping mass of debris at the base of a cliff.

Taproot: the main root of a plant, usually stouter than the lateral roots and growing straight downward from the stem.

Tarsus: the distal segmented structure on the leg of an insect or arachnid; in vertebrates, the section of the foot between the leg and metatarsus.

Tautonym: a taxonomic designation, such as *Gorilla gorilla,* commonly used in zoology in which the genus and species names are the same.

Taxon: a group of organisms with common characteristics constituting one of the categories in taxonomic classification, such as phylum, order or family.

Taxonomy: the science of classifying organisms.

Teeth: notched projects along the edge of a leaf, flower or wing.

Tendril: a long, slender, coiling root-like extension that attaches climbing plants to their surface.

Terete: cylindrical but usually slightly tapering at both ends, circular in cross section, and smooth-surfaced.

Terminal: in biology, appearing at the end of a stem, branch or stalk.

Terrapin: a type of freshwater turtle.

Terrestrial: living on land.

Territory: an area that an animal will defend against intruders.

Tertiary dichasia: the third flower cluster.

Tertiary: the short flight feathers nearest the body on the inner edge of a bird's wing.

Tetradynamous: having four long stamens and two short ones, as in the androecium of the Cruciferea.

Thoracic: situated near the thorax; the second or middle region in insects bearing the true legs and wings; in animals, the part of the body between the neck and the diaphragm.

Thrum: loose ends or fringe.

Tneuiflora: a specific name.

Toad: a warty-skinned, land frog.

Tolerance limit: physical extremities beyond which a species cannot survive.

Tomentum: covering of closely matted woolen hairs.

Tomial: cutting edge of a bird's bill.

Torpic: lethargic, dormant.

Torpor: a state of inactivity.

Tortoise: a land turtle.

Tribe: taxonomic category between family and genus.

Trichotomous: divided into three parts.

Tridentate: long, three-pronged fork.

Troglobite: a cave-dwelling species.

Troglobitic: cave-dwelling; in animals, a species that lives its completes its lifecyle in openings underground (like a cave), usually with small or absent eyes, attenuated appendages, and other adaptations to the subsurface environment.

Trophic: response to a specified stimulus.

Truncate: shortened.

Tubercle: in mussels a small raised area that limits water loss and prevents entry by microorganisms; a small knobby prominence on a plant or animal.

Tuberculation: having tubercles (small raised area in mussels that limits water loss).

Tundra: a treeless plain of the Arctic and Antarctic, characterized by a low, grassy sward, and dominated by sedges, rushes, lichens, and dwarf-woody species.

Turbid: muddy; having sediment or foreign particles stirred up.

Turtle: any shelled reptile.

Ultisol: a type of mineral soil with an accumulation of silicate clay layers with an average soil temperature of 8 degrees Celsius or higher.

Ultramafic: excessively rich in magnesium and iron.

Umbel: an umbrella-like flower cluster.

Umbilicus: a small opening or depression similar to a navel, such as the hollow base of the shell of a mollusk.

Umbo: knoblike proturbence, such as the prominence near the hinge of a mollusk.

Umbonate: knob-like protuberance.

Umbos: the beak cavity in mussels.

Undershell: plastron.

Undulate: moving in a smooth, wave-like motion.

Ungulate: having hoofs.

Unionids: fresh water mussels.

Uniserial: arranged in one row or in one sequence.

Univoltine: one flight season.

Uronites: part of an abdominal appendage of some crustaceans.

Uropods: one pair of rear abdominal appendages of certain crustaceans, including lobsters and shrimp.

Ustic: a soil temperature regime common to subhumid and semiarid regions; moisture is limited; temperatures range between 5 degrees Celsius and 8 degrees Celsius at 50 centimeters depth.

Utricle: a small, bladder-like, one-seeded fruit.

Valves: one of the paired hinged shells of mollusks; one of the sections into which a seed pod or fruit splits.

Vannal: veins.

Variety: a closer taxonomic relationship than subspecies.

Veliger: a larvae stage of a mollusk characterized by the presence of a hairlike swimming organ.

Venation: the distribution or arrangement of veins.

Vent: the anal opening of the body.

Venter: in anatomy, the abdomen or belly; in biology, a swollen structure or part similar to a belly.

Ventral: located at the lower side of a fish or bird.

Ventrum: anal region.

Vermiculation: worm-like marks; the condition of being worm eaten.

Vertebrate: an animal with a backbone.

Vestigial: a small, degenerate rudimentary organ that is a nonfunction remnant of an organ that was fully developed in earlier generations.

Vesture: a covering, especially cloth.

Vibrissa: feather near the beak of an insectivorous (insect eating) bird.

Villous: covered with fine, unmatted hair.

Viviparous: in zoology, giving birth to living offspring that develop within the mother's body; in botany, producing seeds that germinate before becoming detached from the parent plant.

Wetlands: marshes.

Whorl: three or more leaves radiating from a single point.

Wingbar: white or light colored lines or bars on a bird's wing near the shoulder.

Xeric: adaptable to an extremely dry habitat.

Xeromorphic: adaptable to drought conditions.

Xerophyte: a plant that can grow in very dry conditions and is able to withstand periods of drought.

Zero-plated: lacking scutes, lamina, or other than flat structures.

Zooplankters: floating, often microscopic aquatic animals.

Zygomorphic: organisms that are bilaterally symmetrical and capable of being divided along a single longitudinal plane.

Zygotes: the cell formed through sexual union.

Cumulative Index
Volumes 1-4

A

'Ahinahina (=Haleakala) Silversword, 1962
'Aiea, 1865, 1925
'Akoko, 2033
'Awikiwiki, 1999
'Awiwi, 1903
A'a, 645
A'e, 1879
A'o, 683
Abies fraseri, 381
Abortopetalum eremitopetalum, 1181
Abortopetalum sandwicense, 1183
Abronia macrocarpa, 1
Abutilon cryptopetalum, 1181
Abutilon eremitopetalum, 1181
Abutilon menziesii, 3
Abutilon sandwicense, 1183
Acaena exigua, 1957
Acanthaceae (Acanthus), 240
Acanthomintha obovata ssp. *duttonii*, 5
Acanthus Family, 240
Accipitriidae (Eagles and Hawks),
   584, 624, 694
Achatinellidae (Hawaiian Tree Snails), 1041
Achyranthes rotundata, 7
Acipenser brevirostrum, 801
Acipenser oxyrhynchus, 801
Acipenser oxyrhynchus desotoi, 1407
Acipenseridae (Sturgeon), 801, 1407, 1433
Aconitum noveboracense, 9, 1047
Acrocephalus familiaris familiaria, 561
Acrocephalus familiaris kingi, 561
Actinonaias ligamentina, 1449
Adiantaceae (Maidenhair Fern), 1792
Adiantum vivesii, 1792
Ae'o, 634
Aeschynomene virginica, 1649
African Violet, 1855, 1857, 1892, 2041, 2043
Agalinis acuta, 11
Agavaceae (Agave), 13
Agave arizonica, 13
Agave Family, 13
Agelaius phoenicus, 563

Agelaius xanthomus, 563
Agelaius xanthomus monensis, 563
Agelaius xanthomus xanthomus, 563
Ahinahina, 35
Akepa
   Hawaii, 640
   Maui, 640
Akialoa
   Kauai, 632
Akiapolaau, 630
Akohekohe, 662
Akoko
   Ewa Plains, 184
Alabama Beach Mouse, 518
Alabama Canebrake Pitcher Plant, 353
Alabama Cave Shrimp, 1031
Alabama Cavefish, 950
Alabama Lamp Pearly Mussel, 989
Alabama Leather Flower, 95, 273
Alabama Moccasinshell, 2152
Alabama Red-Bellied Turtle, 768
Alabama Streak-sorus Fern, 1756
Alae Ke'o Ke'o, 610
Alae'ula, 613
Alala, 599
Alamosa Springsnail, 1465
Alasmidonta heterodon, 1439
Alcidae (Auks, Puffins, Murres), 2079
Alectryon macrococcus, 1959
Aleutian Canada Goose, 581
Aleutian Shield Fern, 329
Alismataceae (Water-plantain), 347, 1340
Alligator
   American, 727
Alsinidendron obovatum, 1186
Alsinidendron trinerve, 1188
Alsophila dryopteroides, 120
Amaranth
   Seabeach, 1653
Amaranth Family, 7
Amaranthaceae (Amaranth), 7, 1305, 1653
Amaranthus pumilus , 1653
Amargosa Niterwort, 283, 933

Amargosa Pupfish
  Ash Meadows, 827, 933
Amargosa Vole, 494
Amazona agilis, 565
Amazona ventralis, 565
Amazona vittata, 565
Amber Darter, 915, 917
Amber Snail
  Chittenango ovate, 1056
Ambersnail
  Kanab, 1461
Amblema torulosa, 972
Amblyopsidae (Cavefish), 803, 950
Amblyopsis rosae, 803
Amblyopsis spelea, 803
Ambrysus amargosus, 238, 933, 1061
Ambystoma macrodactylum croceum, 783
Ambystomidae (Salamander), 783
American Black Bear, 2073
American Burying Beetle, 1093
American Chaffseed, 1744
American Crocodile, 727
American Hart's-Tongue Fern, 319
American Peregrine Falcon, 607
American Toad
  dwarf, 789
Ammodramus maritimus mirabilis, 568
Ammodramus savannarum floridanus, 570
Ammospiza maritimus mirabilis, 568
Amnicola neomexicana, 1463
Amorpha crenulata, 15
Amphianthus
  little, 17
Amphianthus pusillus, 17
Amphipod
  Hay's Spring, 1035
Amphispiza belli clementeae, 572
Amsinckia grandiflora, 19
Amsonia kearneyana, 21
Anacardiaceae (Cashew), 1334
Anas laysanensis, 574
Anas oustaleti, 576
Anas wyvilliana, 576
Anastasia Island Beach Mouse, 521
Anathidae (Ducks and Geese), 2089
Anatidae (Ducks and Geese), 574, 576, 656, 581
Ancistrocactus tobuschii, 23
Anguispira cumberlandiana, 1044
Anguispira picta, 1044

Annonaceae (Custard-Apple), 41, 126
Anole
  Culebra Island giant, 719
Anolis roosevelti, 719
Antelope
  Sonoran pronghorn, 427
Antelope Family, 427
Anthony's Riversnail, 2174
Antilocapra americana sonoriensis, 427
Antilocapridae (Antelope), 427
Antioch Dunes Evening-Primrose, 287
Antrolana lira, 1023
Apache Trout, 938
Apalachicola Rosemary, 1681
Aphelocoma coerulescens coerulescens, 579
Apiaceae (Parsley), 172, 174, 261, 289, 337, 1342, 1768, 1927
Apioceridae (Orthorrhaphous Dipteran Insect), 2217
Apios priceana, 1190
Aplodontia rufa nigra, 2067
Aplodontidae (Beaver), 2067
Aplomado Falcon
  northern, 604
Apocynaceae (Dogbane), 21, 122, 1867, 1937
Apodemia mormo langei, 176, 1063
Appalachian Monkeyface Pearly Mussel, 1014
Applegate's Milk-vetch, 1659
Aquifoliaceae (Holly), 226
Arabis macdonaldiana, 25
Arabis serotina, 27
Araliaceae (Ginseng), 1923, 2063
Arcidens wheeleri, 1441
Arctic Peregrine Falcon, 607
Arctocephalus townsendi, 429
Arctomecon humilis, 29
Arctostaphylos hookeri ssp. *ravenii*, 31
Arctostaphylos pungens var. *ravenii*, 31
Arecaceae (Palm), 1204, 1873, 2015
Arenaria paludicola, 1656
Arenia cumberlandensis, 33
Argemone pleiacantha ssp. *pinnatisecta*, 1193
Argyroxiphium kauense, 1836
Argyroxiphium sandwicense ssp. *sandwicense*, 35
Argyroxiphium sandwicense ssp. *macrocephalum* 35, 1962
Aristida chaseae, 1794
Aristida portoricensis, 1195
Aristolochiaceae (Birthwort), 212

B

Brychius hungerfordi, 2207
Buckthorn Family, 198, 425, 1253, 1796, 1845, 1974, 1976, 2049
Buckwheat
  clay-loving wild, 170
  gypsum wild, 166
  Scrub Buckwheat, 1777
  steamboat, 168
Buckwheat Family, 81, 168, 170, 327, 1661, 1664, 1666, 1668, 1671, 1777, 1787
Buffalo Clover
  running, 405
Bufo americanus charlesmithi, 789
Bufo hemiophrys baxteri, 787
Bufo hemiophrys hemiophrys, 787
Bufo houstonensis, 789
Bufonidae (Toad), 787, 789, 795
Bulimulidae (Tree Snail), 1052
Bulrush
  barbed bristle, 1351
  northeastern, 1351
Bunched Arrowhead, 347
Bunched Cory Cactus, 106
Burke's Goldfields, 1275
Burying Beetle
  American, 1093
Bush-Clover
  prairie, 246
Bush-Mallow
  San Clemente Island, 271
Buteo solitarius, 584
Butte County Meadowfoam, 1721
Buttercup
  autumn, 341
Buttercup, 1674
Buttercup Family, 9, 95, 128, 341, 393
Butterfly
  bay checkerspot, 1075
  El Segundo blue, 1071
  giant swallowtail, 1081
  Karner Blue, 2210
  Lange's metalmark, 176, 287, 1063
  lotis blue, 1089
  mission blue, 1085
  Mitchell's satyr, 1478
  Myrtle's Silverspot, 2220
  Oregon silverspot, 1097
  Palos Verdes blue, 1079
  Saint Francis' Satyr, 2214
  San Bruno elfin, 1065
  Schaus swallowtail, 509, 1081
  Smith's blue, 1073
  Uncompahgre fritillary, 1469
Buxaceae (Boxwood), 67
Buxus vahlii, 67
Buzzard
  king, 675
  Mexican, 675

C

Cackling Canada Goose, 581
Cactaceae (Cactus), 23, 83, 85, 104, 106, 108, 110, 112, 140, 142, 144, 146, 148, 150, 152, 154, 156, 281, 299, 301, 303, 305, 307, 361, 363, 365, 1255, 1308, 1684, 1692, 1804
Cactus
  Arizona hedgehog, 152
  Bakersfield, 1308
  black lace, 150
  Brady pincushion, 299, 301, 363
  bunched cory, 106
  Chisos Mountain hedgehog, 142
  Cochise pincushion, 108
  Davis' green pitaya, 156
  fragrant prickly-apple, 83
  Key tree, 85
  Knowlton, 301, 303
  Kuenzler hedgehog, 146
  Lee pincushion, 110
  Lloyd's hedgehog, 148
  Lloyd's mariposa, 281
  Mesa Verde, 363
  Nellie cory, 104
  Nichol's turk's head, 140
  Peebles Navajo, 301, 305
  pima pineapple, 1684
  purple-spined hedgehog, 144
  San Rafael, 301
  Siler pincushion, 299, 301, 307
  Sneed pincushion, 112
  spineless hedgehog, 154
  Tobusch fishhook, 23
  Uinta Basin hookless, 361
  Wright fishhook, 363, 365
Caesalpiniaceae (Cassia), 1208
Cahaba Shiner, 1414
California Brown Pelican, 666

California Clapper Rail, 687
California Condor, 621
California Freshwater Shrimp, 1037
California Gray Whale, 467
California Jewelflower, 1210
California Least Tern, 700
California Longhorn Beetle, 1067
California Orcutt Grass, 1764
California Vole, 494
Caliptrogyne occidentalis, 1204
Callicarpa ampla , 1798
Callirhoe scabriuscula, 69
Callophrys mossii bayensis, 1065
Calyptranthes thomasiana, 1800
Calyptronoma rivalis, 1204
Cambala speobia, 1091
Cambaridae (Crayfish), 1025, 1027, 1029, 2194
Cambarus aculabrum, 2194
Cambarus zophonastes, 1025
Camissonia benitensis, 71
Camissonia contorta, 71
Campanula floridana, 73
Campanula robinsiae, 73
Campanulaceae (Bellflower), 73, 1224, 1226, 1228,
    1230, 1296, 1839, 1841, 1843, 1847, 1849,
    1851,1853, 1863, 1890, 1894, 1966, 1968, 1970,
    1997, 2001, 2003, 2013, 2035, 2037, 2039, 2053
Campephilus principalis, 586
Campion
    Fringed, 1356
Canada Goose
    Aleutian, 581
    cackling, 581
Canadian Toad, 787
Canavalia molokaiensis, 1999
Canby's Dropwort, 289
Canine Family, 444, 448, 553, 556
Canis lupus, 444
Canis lupus baileyi, 444
Canis lupus hodophylax, 444
Canis lupus pallipes, 444
Canis rufus floridanus, 448
Canis rufus gregoryi, 448
Canis rufus rufus, 448
Canpanula robinsiae, 240
Cantheria collina, 999
Canthyria steinstansana, 960
Capa Rosa, 1798
Cape Fear Shiner, 905

Cape Sable Seaside Sparrow, 568
Caprimulgidae (Nightjar), 588
Caprimulgus noctitherus, 588
Caprimulgus vociferus, 588
Carabidae (Ground Beetle), 1069, 1095
Caracara
    Audubon's crested, 675
Caracara cheriway audubonii, 675
Caracara Eagle, 675
Cardamine micranthera, 1206
Caretta caretta, 721
Carex misera, 381
Carex specuicola, 75
Caribbean Monk Seal, 498
Caribou
    woodland, 533
Carolina Heelsplitter, 2149
Carolina Northern Flying Squirrel, 480
Carrion Beetle, 1093
Carter's Mustard, 417, 419, 425
Carter's Panicgrass, 293
Carunculina cylindrellus, 1018
Caryophyllaceae (Pink), 33, 192, 295, 359, 1186,
    1188, 1344, 1346, 1354, 1356, 1656, 1875, 2017,
    2019, 2021, 1988, 1939, 1941
Cashew Family, 1334
Cassia Family, 1208
Cassia mirabilis, 1208
Castelleja grisea, 77
Cat's Eye
    Barneby, 194
    Terlingua Creek, 1222
Catfish
    Yaqui, 889
Catfish Family, 889, 909, 911, 913, 1416, 2121
Cathartidae (New World Vulture), 621
Catostomidae (Sucker), 805, 807, 809, 811, 813,
    833, 1436
Catostomus microps, 805
Catostomus warnerensis, 807
Cats, 469, 472, 474, 476, 478
Caulanthus californicus, 1210
Cave Crayfish, 1025, 2194
Cave Isopods, 1023, 2201
Cave Shrimp
    Alabama, 1031
    Florida, 1459
    Kentucky, 1031, 1033
    Squirrel Chimney, 1459

Cougar
  eastern, 472
Cowania subintegra, 114
Coyote Thistle
  Loch Lomond, 172
Cracking Pearly Mussel, 1447
Crane
  Mississippi sandhill, 618
  sandhill, 615
  whooping, 615
Cranes, 615, 618
Crangonyctidae (Amphipod), 1035
Cranichis ricartii, 1220
Crassulaceae (Stonecrop), 136, 1746
Crayfish
  cave, 1025, 2194
  Nashville, 1027
  Shasta, 1029
Creeper
  Hawaii, 660
  Molokai, 664
Crenichthys baileyi, 817
Crenichthys baileyi baileyi, 815, 884
Crenichthys baileyi grandis, 815
Crenichthys nevadae, 817
Crenulate Lead-Plant, 15
Crescentia portoricensis, 116
Cress
  McDonald's rock, 25
  shale barren rock, 27
  toad-flax, 194
Crested Caracara
  Audubon's, 675
Crested Honeycreeper, 662
Crocodile
  American, 727
Crocodylus acutus, 727
Crotalaria avonensis, 1775
Crotalus willardi obscurus, 729
Crotaphytus silus, 747
Crotaphytus wislizenii silus, 747
Crow
  Hawaiian, 599
Crows and Jays, 579, 599
Crustacean, 2197
Cryptantha barnebyi, 194
Cryptantha crassipes, 1222
Cuban Plain Pigeon, 597
Cuban Snail Kite, 694

Cucubalus polypetalus, 1356
Cucurbita okeechobeensis ssp. *okeechobeensis*, 1686
Cucurbitaceae (Gourd), 413, 1686
Cui-ui, 811
Culebra Island Giant Anole, 719
Cumberland Bean Pearly Mussel, 1020
Cumberland Monkeyface Pearly Mussel, 1011
Cumberland Rosemary, 1218
Cumberland Sandwort, 33
Cuneate Bidens, 61
Cupressaceae (Cypress), 118
Cupressus abramsiana, 118
Cupressus goveniana, 118
Cupressus sargentii, 118
Curlew
  Eskimo, 658
Curtis' Pearly Mussel, 962
Curtus' Mussel, 1001
Custard-Apple Family, 41, 126
Cutthroat Trout
  greenback, 946
  Lahontan, 812, 942
  Paiute, 944
Cyanea asarifolia, 1890
Cyanea copelandii spp. *copelandii*, 1847
Cyanea gibsonii, 1224
Cyanea grimesiana ssp. *obatae*, 2037
Cyanea hamatiflora ssp. *carlsonii*, 1849
Cyanea lobata, 1968
Cyanea macrostegia var. *gibsonii*, 1224
Cyanea mannii, 2003
Cyanea mceldowneyi, 1970
Cyanea pinnatifida, 1226
Cyanea procera, 2013
Cyanea regina, 1228
Cyanea selachicauda, 1226
Cyanea shipmanii, 1851
Cyanea stictophylla, 1853
Cyanea superba, 1228
Cyanea truncata, 2039
Cyanea undulata, 1230
Cyathea dryopteroides, 120
Cyatheaceae (Fern), 120
Cycladenia
  Jones, 122
Cycladenia humilis var. *jonesii*, 122
Cyclura stegnegeri, 731
Cynomys leucurus, 451
Cynomys parvidens, 451

Hawaiian Bluegrass, 1931
Hawaiian Common Moorhen, 613
Hawaiian Coot, 610
Hawaiian Crow, 599
Hawaiian Duck, 576
Hawaiian Gardenia, 190
Hawaiian Goose, 656
Hawaiian Hawk, 584
Hawaiian Hoary Bat, 483
Hawaiian Honeycreeper, 628, 630, 632, 638, 640,
    643, 660, 662, 664, 677, 679
Hawaiian Monk Seal, 483, 498
Hawaiian Petrel, 681
Hawaiian Red-Flowered Geranium, 1974
Hawaiian Stilt, 634
Hawaiian Tree Snails, 1041
Hawaiian Vetch, 415
Hawaiian Wild Broad-Bean, 415
Hawk
    Hawaiian, 584
Hawks and Eagles, 584, 624, 694
Hawksbill Sea Turtle, 743
Hay's Spring Amphipod, 1035
Heartleaf
    dwarf-flowered, 212
Heath Family, 31, 343, 1806
Heather
    mountain golden, 218
Heau, 1901
Hedeoma apiculatum, 206
Hedeoma todsenii, 206, 208
Hedgehog Cactus
    Arizona, 152
    Chisos Mountain, 142
    Kuenzler, 146
    Lloyd's, 148
    purple-spined, 144
    spineless, 154
Hedyotis
    Na Pali Beach, 1263
Hedyotis cookiana, 1903
Hedyotis coriacea, 1978
Hedyotis degeneri, 1257
Hedyotis mannii, 2005
Hedyotis montana, 381
Hedyotis parvula, 1259
Hedyotis purpurea var. *montana*, 1261
Hedyotis st. johnii, 1263
Helianthus schweinitzii, 1265

Helicodiscidae (Mountain Snail), 1054
Heliotrope Milk-Vetch, 45
Heller's Blazing Star, 252, 381
Helonias bullata, 210
Hemignathus lucidus affinis, 628
Hemignathus lucidus hanapepe, 628
Hemignathus lucidus lucidus, 628
Hemignathus munroi, 630
Hemignathus procerus, 632
Hemignathus wilsoni, 630
Hemistena lata, 1447
Heraclides aristodemus ponceanus, 1081
Heraclides cresphontes cramer, 1081
Hesperia leonardus montana, 1083
Hesperiidae (Silver-Spotted Skipper), 1083
Hesperomannia arborescens, 2051
Hesperomannia arborescens var. *oahuensis*, 1267
Hesperomannia arbuscula, 1267
Hesperomannia arbuscula ssp. *oahuensis*, 1267
Hesperomannia arbuscula var. *pearsallii*, 1267
Hesperomannia lydgatei, 1269
Hesperomannia mauiensis, 1267
Hesperomannia oahuensis, 1267
Heteromyidae (Kangaroo Rat), 453, 455, 458,
    460, 462
Heteromyidae (Mice and Kangaroo Rats), 2070
Heterotheca floridana, 89
Heterotheca ruthii, 321
Hexastylis naniflora, 212
Heydotis
    mountain, 381
Hibiscadelphus distans, 214
Hibiscus arnottianus ssp. *immaculatus*, 2007
Hibiscus clayi, 1905
Higgins' Eye Pearly Mussel, 983
Highlands Scrub Hypericum, 224
Higo Chumbo, 1255
Higuero de Sierra, 116
Hiko White River Springfish, 815, 884
Hillebrand's Gouania, 198
Hilo Ischaemum, 1859
Himantopus mexicanus knudseni, 634
Hinckley Oak, 339
Hispanolian Parrot, 565
Hoary Bat
    Hawaiian, 483
Hoary Marmot, 489
Hoffmannseggia glauca, 216
Hoffmannseggia tenella, 216

Modoc Sucker, 805
Mohave Tui Chub, 865
Moho braccatus, 645
Mohr's Barbara's-Buttons, 273
Mold Beetle
  Kretschmarr Cave, 1095, 1099
Mold Beetle, 2205
Mole Skink
  blue-tailed, 745, 762
  peninsular, 745
Molokai Creeper, 664
Molokai Thrush, 647
Mona Boa, 739, 741
Mona Ground Iguana, 731
Monachus monachus, 498
Monachus schauinslandi, 483, 498
Monachus tropicalis, 498
Monito Gecko, 772
Monk Seal
  Caribbean, 498
  Hawaiian, 483, 498
  Mediterranean, 498
Monkey-Flower
  Michigan, 1300
Monkeyface Pearly Mussel
  Appalachian, 1014
  Cumberland, 1011
Monkshood
  northern wild, 9, 1047
Montane Skipper
  Pawnee, 1083
Monterey Gilia, 1705
Monterey Spineflower, 1664
Moorhen
  Hawaiian common, 613
Morefield's Leather Flower, 1674
Morning Glory Family, 65, 1714
Morro Bay Kangaroo Rat, 453
Mosquitofish, 861
Moth
  Kern primrose sphinx, 1077
Mount Graham Red Squirrel, 542
Mountain Golden Heather, 218
Mountain Hedyotis, 381
Mountain Lion, 472
Mountain Snail
  Virginia fringed, 1054
Mountain Sweet Pitcher Plant, 355
Mouse

Alabama beach, 518
Anastasia Island beach, 521
Choctawhatchee beach, 518
Key Largo cotton, 516
Pacific pocket, 2070
Perdido Key beach, 518
salt marsh harvest, 536
southeastern beach, 521
western harvest, 536
Mouse and Rat Family, 494, 496, 509, 516, 518,
  521, 536, 1387, 1389
Munroidendron racemosum, 1923
Muridae (Mice and Rats), 494, 496, 509, 516, 518,
  521, 536, 1387, 1389
Muscicapidae (Thrush), 2086
Muscicapidae; Subfamily Turdinae (Thrush), 561,
  647, 649, 651
Musk Turtle
  flattened, 774
Mussel
  Alabama lamp pearly, 989
  Appalachian monkeyface pearly, 1014
  Arkansas fatmucket, 1449
  birdwing pearly, 955
  cracking pearly, 1447
  Cumberland monkeyface pearly, 1011
  Cumberland bean pearly, 1020
  Curtis' pearly, 962
  Curtus, 1001
  dromedary pearly, 958
  dwarf wedge, 1439
  fanshell, 1443
  fat pocketbook pearly, 1009
  fine-rayed pigtoe pearly, 978
  golf stick pearly, 1451
  green-blossom pearly, 970, 972
  Higgins' eye pearly, 983
  inflated heelsplitter, 1455
  James River spiny, 960, 999
  Judge Tait's, 1007
  little-wing pearly, 993
  Louisiana pearlshell, 991
  Marshall's, 1003
  orange-footed pearly, 997
  Ouachita rock-pocketbook, 1441
  pale lilliput pearly, 1018
  penitent, 966
  pink mucket pearly, 985
  purple cat's paw pearly, 1445

Osterhout Milk-Vetch, 47, 311
Otariidae (Eared Seal), 429, 1384
Otay Mesa Mint, 1766
Otter
  southern sea, 464
Ottoschulzia rhodoxylon, 1310
Ou, 679
Ouachita Rock-Pocketbook, 1441
Ovate Clubshell Mussel, 2165
Owens Pupfish, 831
Owens Tui Chub, 865, 867
Owl
  northern spotted, 1397
Owl, 2092
  Mexican spotted, 2092
Owl Family, 1397
Owl's Clover, 1075
Oxyloma haydeni ssp. *kanabensis*, 1461
Oxypolis canbyi, 289
Oxytropis campestris var. *chartacea*, 291
Ozark Big-Eared Bat, 527
Ozark Cavefish, 803

P

Pacifastacus fortis, 1029
Pacific Pocket Mouse, 2070
Pahranagat Roundtail Chub, 883
Pahrump Killifish, 835
Paintbrush
  San Clemente Island Indian, 77
Painted Snake Coiled Forest Snail, 1044
Paiute Cutthroat Trout, 944
Palaemonetes cummingi, 1459
Palaemonias alabamae, 1031
Palaemonias ganteri, 1031, 1033
Palaemonidae, 1459
Pale Lilliput Pearly Mussel, 1018
Palezone Shiner, 2119
Palila, 638
Pallid Sturgeon, 1433
Palm Family, 1204, 1873, 2015
Palma de Manaca, 1204
Palmate-Bracted Bird's-Beak, 100
Palmeria dolei, 662
Palo Colorado, 1816
Palo de Jazmin, 1812
Palo de Nigua, 102
Palo de Ramon, 55

Palo de Rosa, 1310
Palos Verdes Blue Butterfly, 1079
Paludina magnifica, 1467
Panicgrass
  Carter's, 293
Panicum carteri, 293
Panther
  Florida, 469
Panther, 472
Papaveraceae (Poppy), 30, 1193
Papery Whitlow-Wort, 295, 425
Papilio aristodemus ponceanus, 510, 1081
Papilio ponceana, 1081
Papilionidae (Swallowtail Butterfly), 1081
Paronychia chartacea, 295, 425
Paroreomyza flammea, 664
Parrot
  Hispanolian, 565
  Jamaican black-billed, 565
  Puerto Rican, 565
  thick-billed, 692
Parrotbill
  Maui, 677
Parsley Family, 172, 174, 261, 289, 337,
  1342, 1768, 1927
Pawnee Montane Skipper, 1083
Pawpaw
  beautiful, 126
  four-petal, 41
  Rugel's, 126
Pea
  Bolander's sweet, 1089
Pea
  slender rush, 216
Pea Family, 15, 43, 45, 47, 49, 51, 53, 57, 188, 216,
  246, 263, 265, 277, 291, 405, 415, 1190, 1197,
  1199, 1232, 1364, 1649, 1659, 1723, 1783, 1775,
  1999
Pearlshell
  Louisiana, 991
Pearly Mussel
  Alabama lamp, 989
  Appalachian monkeyface, 1014
  birdwing, 955
  cracking, 1447
  Cumberland bean, 1020
  Cumberland monkeyface, 1011
  Curtis, 962
  dromedary, 958

Plethodontidae (Lungless Salamander), 785, 793, 797, 799, 1403, 1405
Pleurobema clava, 2156
Pleurobema collina, 999
Pleurobema curtum, 1001
Pleurobema decisum, 2159
Pleurobema furvum, 2161
Pleurobema georgianum, 2163
Pleurobema gibberum, 1453
Pleurobema marshalli, 1003
Pleurobema perovatum, 2165
Pleurobema plenum, 1005
Pleurobema taitianum, 1007
Plover
  piping, 590
  snowy, 590
  western snowy, 2082
Plum
  scrub, 335, 425
Plymouth Red-Bellied Turtle, 770
Po'e, 1871
Poa sandvicensis, 1931
Poa siphonoglossa, 1934
Poaceae (Grass), 293, 391, 411, 423, 1195, 1764, 1794, 1859, 1931, 1934
Poeciliidae (Livebearer), 855, 857, 859, 861, 928
Poeciliopsis occidentalis occidentalis, 928
Poeciliopsis occidentalis sonoriensis, 928
Pogogyne abramsii, 323
Pogogyne nudiuscula , 1766
Pogonia
  small whorled, 236
Point Arena Mountain Beaver , 2067
Polemoniaceae (Phlox), 160, 1247, 1312, 1705, 1708
Polioptila californica californica, 2086
Pollack Whale, 436
Polyborus cheriway audubonii, 675
Polyborus plancus audubonii, 675
Polyborus plancus cheriway, 675
Polyborus vulgaris, 675
Polygala
  tiny, 325
Polygala arenicola, 325
Polygala lewtonii , 1785
Polygala smallii, 325
Polygalaceae (Milkwort), 325, 1785
Polygonaceae (Buckwheat), 81, 166, 168, 170, 327, 1661, 1664, 1666, 1668, 1671, 1777, 1787
Polygonella basiramia, 295, 327

Polygonella ciliata, 327
Polygonella ciliata var. *basiramia*, 327
Polygonella myriophylla , 1787
Polygra platysayoides, 1058
Polygyridae (Land Snail), 1048, 1050, 1058
Polygyriscus virginianus, 1054
Polypodiaceae (Fern), 329, 1237, 2045
Polystichum aleuticum, 329
Polystichum calderonense, 1810
Pondberry, 256
Pondweed
  Little Aguja, 1326
Pondweed Family, 1326
Poo-uli, 643
Popolo 'aiakeakua, 1943
Poppy
  bearclaw, 29
  Colville bearclaw, 29
  dwarf bear, 29
  Sacramento prickly, 1193
Poppy Family, 29, 1193
Poppy-Mallow
  Texas, 69
Porpoise
  harbor, 523
Portulaca sclerocarpa, 1871
Portulacaceae (Purslane), 1871
Potamilus capax, 1009
Potamilus inflatus, 1455
Potamogeton clystocarpus, 1326
Potamogetonaceae (Pondweed), 1326
Potato-Bean
  Price's, 1190
Potentilla robbinsiana, 331
Prairie Bush-Clover, 246
Prairie Chicken
  Attwater's, 710
Prairie-Clover
  leafy, 1232
Prairie Dog
  Utah, 451
Prairie Pigeon, 658
Prairie Trout-Lily, 178
Presidio Manzanita, 31
Price's Potato-Bean, 1190
Prickly-Apple Cactus
  fragrant, 83
Prickly-Ash
  St. Thomas, 421

Caribbean monk, 498
eared, 429
Guadalupe fur, 429
Hawaiian monk, 483, 498
Mediterranean monk, 498
Seaside Sparrow
Cape Sable, 568
Sebastopol Meadowfoam, 1288
Sedge
Navajo, 75
Sedge Family, 1249, 1337, 1351
Sedum intergrifolium spp. *leedyi*, 1746
Sedum spathulifolium, 1065
Sei Whale, 436
Senecio franciscanus, 369
Sensitive Joint-Vetch, 1649
Sentry Milk-Vetch, 1199
Shagreen
Magazine Mountain, 1050
Shale Barren Rock-Cress, 27
Shasta Crayfish, 1029
Shearwater
Newell's manx, 683
Newell's Townsend's, 683
Shenandoah Salamander, 1405
Shield Fern
Aleutian, 329
Shijimiaeoides battoides allyni, 1071
Shijimiaeoides enoptes smithi, 1073
Shiner
beautiful, 879, 903
Cape Fear, 905
Pecos bluntnose, 907
red, 904
Rio Grande, 907
Shiner
Cahaba, 1414
Shiner
Blue , 2103
Palezone, 2119
Shiny Pigtoe Pearly Mussel, 981
Short-Leaved Rosemary, 1677
Short's Goldenrod, 379
Shortnose Sturgeon, 801
Shortnose Sucker, 809
Shrew
Dismal Swamp southeastern, 540
Shrike
San Clemente Island loggerhead, 636

Shrimp
Alabama cave, 1031
California freshwater, 1037
Florida cave, 1459
Kentucky cave, 1031, 1033
Squirrel Chimney Cave, 1459
Shrimp
Riverside fairy, 2197
Sidalcea nelsoniana, 1749
Sidalcea nelsoniana, 371
Sidalcea pedata, 371, 395
Silene alexandri, 2019
Silene baldwinii, 1356
Silene hawaiiensis, 1875
Silene lanceolata, 2021
Silene perlmanii, 1354
Silene polypetala, 1356
Siler Pincushion Cactus, 299, 301, 307
Silphidae (Carrion Beetle), 1093
Silver Rice Rat, 1389
Silver-Spotted Skipper, 1083
Silverside
Waccamaw, 899
Silverspot Butterfly
Oregon, 1097
Silversword
Mauna Kea, 35
Sisyrinchium dichotomum, 1366
Skink
blue-tailed mole, 745, 762
peninsular mole, 745
sand, 745, 762
Skipper
Pawnee montane, 1083
Skullcap
large-flowered, 367
Slackwater Darter, 839
Slender Chub, 885
Slender-Horned Spineflower, 81
Slender-Petaled Mustard, 371, 395
Slender Rush-Pea, 216
Slender Salamander
desert, 785
Small-Anthered Bittercress, 1206
Small Kauai Thrush, 651
Small Whorled Pogonia, 236
Small's Milkpea, 188
Smelts, 2114
Smith's Blue Butterfly, 1073

Styrax Family, 389, 1812
Styrax portoricensis, 1812
Styrax texana, 389
Succinea chittenangoensis, 1056
Succinea hawkinsi, 1461
Succineida (Land Snail), 1056, 1461
Sucker
  June, 813
  Lost River, 833
  Modoc, 805
  razorback, 1436
  shortnose, 809
  Warner, 807
Sucker Family, 805, 807, 809, 811, 813, 833, 1436
Sumac
  Michaux's, 1334
Sunflower
  Schweinitz's, 1265
Sunflower Family, 1243, 1269, 1372
Sunray
  Ash Meadows, 158, 275
Swallenia alexandrae, 285, 391
Swallowtail Butterfly
  giant, 1081
  Schaus, 509, 1081
Swamp Pink, 210
Swift Fox
  northern, 556
  southern, 556
Swift Fox, 553
Sylvilagus palustris hefneri, 1392
Syncaris pacifica, 1037

T

Tamiasciurus hudsonicus grahamensis, 542
Tan Riffle Shell, 976
Tar River Spinymussel, 960, 999
Tartarocreagris texana, 1091
Taxaceae (Yew), 399
Tea, 1816
Tectaria estremerana, 1814
Telephus Spurge, 1699
Telespyza cantans, 706
Telespyza ultima, 708
Tennessee Purple Coneflower, 138
Tennessee Yellow-Eyed Grass, 1382
Terlingua Creek Cat's Eye, 1222
Tern

California least, 700
  least, 697
  roseate, 703
Ternstroemia luquillensis, 1816
Ternstroemia subsessilis, 1818
Testudinidae (Tortoise), 750, 753
Tetramolopium arenarium, 1877
Tetramolopium chamissonis var. *luxurians,* 1370
Tetramolopium filiforme, 1368
Tetramolopium lepidotum ssp. *lepidotum,* 1370
Tetramolopium lepidotum var. *luxurians,* 1370
Tetramolopium remyi, 1372
Tetramolopium rockii, 2025
Tetraplasandra gymnocarpa, 2063
Texamaurops reddelli, 1095, 1099
Texas Bitterweed, 222
Texas Blind Salamander, 799
Texas Bobwhite, 594
Texas Poppy-Mallow, 69
Texas Snowbells, 389
Texas Trailing Phlox, 1312
Texas Wildrice, 423, 793, 841, 857
Texella reddelli, 1101
Texella reyesi, 2223
Thalictrum cooleyi, 393
Thamnophis gigas, 2099
Thamnophis sirtalis tetrataenia, 776
Theaceae (Tea), 1816
Thelypodium stenopetalum, 371, 395
Thelypteridaceae (Marsh Fern), 1756, 1822
Thelypteridaceae (Wood Fern), 1810, 1814,
  1820, 1824
Thelypteris inabonensis, 1820
Thelypteris pilosa var. *alabamensis,* 1756
Thelypteris verecunda, 1822
Thelypteris yaucoensis, 1824
Thermosphaeroma thermophilum, 1039
Thick-Billed Parrot, 692
Thistle
  Loch Lomond coyote, 172
  Pitcher's, 91, 377
  Sacramento Mountains, 93
Threats to Hawaiian plants, 1831
Thrush
  large Kauai, 649
  Molokai, 647
  small Kauai, 651
Thrushes, 561, 647, 649, 651, 2086
Thymelaeaceae (Mezereum), 124

hawksbill sea, 743
Kemp's Ridley sea, 757
leatherback sea, 733
loggerhead sea, 721
olive Ridley sea, 760
Plymouth red-bellied, 770
ringed sawback, 755
yellow-blotched map, 1401
Twinpod
Dudley Bluffs, 1318
Tympanuchus cupido attwateri, 710
Typhlichthys subterraneus, 803
Typhlomolge rathbuni, 799

U

Ua'u, 681
Uhiuhi, 277
Uinta Basin Hookless Cactus, 361
Uma inornata, 778
Unarmored Threespine Stickleback, 863
Uncompahgre Fritillary Butterfly, 1469
Unio curtus, 1001
Unio heterodon, 1439
Unio penitus, 966
Unio powelli, 1449
Unionidae (Freshwater Mussel), 955, 958, 960, 962,
964, 966, 968, 970, 972, 974, 976, 978, 981, 983,
985, 987, 989, 993, 995, 997, 999, 1001, 1003,
1005, 1007, 1009, 1011, 1014, 1016, 1018, 1020,
1439, 1441, 1443, 1445, 1447, 1449, 1451, 1457,
2138, 2140, 2142, 2149, 2156, 2138, 2140, 2145,
2147, 2152, 2154, 2159, 2161, 2163, 2165, 2167
Upland Combshell Mussel, 2138
Urera kaalae, 1374
Ursidae (Bear), 548, 2073, 2075
Ursus americanus, 2073
Ursus americanus luteolus, 2075
Ursus arctos horribilis, 548
Urticaceae (Nettle), 1302, 1374
Utah Prairie Dog, 451
Utah Valvata Snail, 2191
Utahia sileri, 307
Ute Ladies' Tresses, 1753

V

Vahl's Boxwood, 67
Valley Elderberry Longhorn Beetle, 1067
Valvata utahensis, 2191

Valvatidae (Valvata), 2191
Vancouver Island Marmot, 489
Vaquita, 523
Verbena
large-fruited sand, 1
Verbena, 1798
Verbenaceae (Verbena), 102, 1798
Vermivora bachmanii, 712
Vernonia proctorii, 1826
Vespertilionidae (Bat), 483, 503, 506, 527, 530
Vetch
Ash Meadows milk, 51, 275
Hawaiian, 415
heliotrope milk, 45
Jesup's milk, 53
Osterhout milk, 47, 311
Rydberg milk, 49
Vicia menziesii, 415
Villosa trabalis, 1020
Vine Fern, 1802
Viola adunca, 1097
Viola chamissoniana ssp. *chamissoniana*, 1376
Viola helenae, 1378
Viola helioscopia, 1376
Viola lanaiensis, 1380
Violaceae (Violet), 1271, 1376, 1378, 1380,
1711, 1861, 1948
Violet
western blue, 1097
Violet Family, 1271, 1376, 1378, 1380, 1711, 1861,
1948
Viperidae (Viper), 729
Vireo
black-capped, 714
least Bell's, 716
Vireo atricapillus, 714
Vireo belli arizonae, 716
Vireo belli pusillus, 716
Vireo bellii bellii, 716
Vireonidae (Vireo), 714, 716
Virgin River Chub, 1411
Virginia Big-Eared Bat, 530
Virginia Fringed Mountain Snail, 1054
Virginia Northern Flying Squirrel, 480
Virginia Round-Leaf Birch, 59
Virginia Spiraea, 1361
Vittadinia chamissonis, 1370
Vittadinia remyi, 1372
Viviparidae (Live-bearing Snail), 1467

Wolf
  gray, 444
  Indian, 444
  Japanese, 444
  Mexican, 444
  red, 448
  timber, 444
Wood Bison, 442
Wood Fern, 1810, 1814, 1820, 1824
Wood Stork, 653
Wood Warbler Family, 601, 1394
Woodland Caribou, 533
Woodpecker
  ivory-billed, 586
  red-cockaded, 670
Woodrat
  Key Largo, 509
Wooly-Star
  Hoover's, 1247
  Santa Ana River, 160
Wooly-Threads
  San Joaquin, 1278
Wort
  papery whitlow, 295, 425
Woundfin, 926
Wright Fishhook Cactus, 363, 365
Wyoming Toad, 787

X

Xantusia henshawi, 781
Xantusia riversiana, 781
Xantusia vigilis, 781
Xantusiidae (Lizard), 781
Xerobates agassizii, 750
Xylosma crenatum, 1950
Xyrauchen texanus, 1436
Xyridaceae (Yellow-eyed grass), 1382, 1702
Xyris tennesseensis, 1382

Y

Yaqui Catfish, 889
Yaqui Chub, 881
Yaqui Topminnow, 928
Yellow-Blossom Pearly Mussel, 964
Yellow-Blotched Map Turtle, 1401
Yellow Cheek Darter, 849
Yellow-Eyed Grass Family, 1382
Yellow-Eyed Grass

Tennessee, 1382
Yellow-Shouldered Blackbird, 563
Yellowfin Madtom, 911
Yew Family, 399
Yuma Clapper Rail, 690

Z

Zanthoxylum hawaiiense, 1879
Zanthoxylum thomassianum, 421
Zizania texana, 423, 794, 841, 857
Ziziphus
  Florida, 425
Ziziphus celata, 425
Zuni Fleabane, 164